2009 DOCUMENTS SUPPLEMENT FOR

INTERNATIONAL BUSINESS TRANSACTIONS: CONTRACTING ACROSS BORDERS

and

INTERNATIONAL BUSINESS TRANSACTIONS: FOREIGN INVESTMENT

First Editions

■ ■ ■

By

Ralph H. Folsom
Professor of Law
University of San Diego

Michael Wallace Gordon
John H. and Mary Lou Dasburg Professor of Law
University of Florida

John A. Spanogle, Jr.
William Wallace Kirkpatrick Professor of Law
The George Washington University

Peter L. Fitzgerald
Professor of Law
Stetson University College of Law

AMERICAN CASEBOOK SERIES®

WEST®

A Thomson Reuters business

Mat #40839393

610 Opperman Drive
St. Paul, MN 55123
1–800–313–9378

Printed in the United States of America

ISBN: 978-0-314-20616-9

TEXT IS PRINTED ON 10% POST CONSUMER RECYCLED PAPER

Preface

This Documents Supplement is designed to accompany the first editions of **International Business Transactions: Contracting Across Borders** and **International Business Transactions: Foreign Investment.** Nearly every Problem in these coursebooks in some way involves the application of documentary law. This Supplement provides primary legal authority indispensable to resolution of the many issues raised in each problem.

This Documents Supplement reflects the latest changes in law, including the UN Convention on E–Commerce, the Convention on Choice of Court Agreements, the Uniform Foreign-Country Money Judgments Act, the Foreign Investment and National Security Act of 2007 and the EU Regulation on Jurisdiction and Recognition and Enforcement of Judgments. We continue to include CISG, the New York Convention, conventions on stand-by letters of credit and bribery, the Rome and Brussels Conventions, the WTO TRIMS Agreement, as well as the UCC and other uniform acts and U.S. trade statutes. The materials are edited to provide those portions of each law which are introductory to understanding the nature of the organization or law, or which are applicable to resolving the problems.

Your suggestions as to what might be added to the next edition of this Supplement, as well as to the coursebooks, are most welcome.

RALPH H. FOLSOM
rfolsom@sandiego.edu
MICHAEL W. GORDON
gordon@law.ufl.edu
JOHN A. SPANOGLE
aspanogle@law.gwu.edu
PETER L. FITZGERALD
fitz@law.stetson.edu

May 2009

*

PREFACE

TABLE OF CONTENTS

INTERNATIONAL BUSINESS TRANSACTIONS: CONTRACTING ACROSS BORDERS

and

INTERNATIONAL BUSINESS TRANSACTIONS: FOREIGN INVESTMENT

First Editions

*

DOCUMENT 1

UNITED NATIONS CONVENTION ON CONTRACTS FOR THE INTERNATIONAL SALE OF GOODS (1980) (SELECTED PROVISIONS)

[This Convention (CISG) was prepared by the United Nations Commission on International Trade Law (UNCITRAL) and issued for signature through a United Nations Diplomatic Conference in Vienna in 1980. As its Final Clauses (Articles 89–101) indicate, CISG became effective as a multilateral treaty on January 1 twelve months after ten nations ratified it. On December 11, 1986, China, Italy and the United States became the ninth, tenth, and eleventh nations to ratify the Convention. Thus, CISG became effective within its scope of application (see Article 1) on January 1, 1988. It governs all international sales contracts within Article 1 concluded after that date, although the parties may expressly "opt out" of its coverage under Article 6.

As of February 1, 2009, the following 73 countries are Contracting States to CISG: Argentina, Armenia, Australia, Austria, Belarus, Belgium, Bosnia and Herzegovina, Bulgaria, Burundi, Canada, Chile, China, Colombia, Croatia, Cuba, Cyprus, Czech Republic, Denmark, Ecuador, Egypt, El Salvador, Estonia, Finland, France, Gabon, Georgia, Germany, Ghana, Greece, Guinea, Honduras, Hungary, Iceland, Iraq, Israel, Italy, Japan, Kyrgystan, Latvia, Lebanon, Lesotho, Liberia, Lithuania, Luxembourg, Macedonia, Mauritania, Mexico, Moldova, Mongolia, Montenegro, the Netherlands, New Zealand, Norway, Paraguay, Peru, Poland, Republic of Korea, Romania, Russian Federation, Saint Vincent and Grenadines, Serbia, Singapore, Slovakia, Slovenia, Spain, Sweden, Switzerland, Syria, Uganda, Ukraine, U.S.A., Uruguay, Uzbekistan, Venezuela, and Zambia.

In the United States, CISG is considered a self-executing treaty, so no domestic, federal legislation was enacted, or is necessary. Courts may apply the Convention directly to the issues raised by individual litigants who are parties to international sales contracts covered by Article 1.]

THE STATES PARTIES TO THIS CONVENTION

BEARING IN MIND the broad objectives in the resolutions adopted by the sixth special session of the General Assembly of the United Nations on the establishment of a New International Economic Order,

CONSIDERING that the development of international trade on the basis of equality and mutual benefit is an important element in promoting friendly relations among States,

BEING OF THE OPINION that the adoption of uniform rules which govern contracts for the international sale of goods and take into account the different social, economic and legal systems would contribute to the removal of legal barriers in international trade and promote the development of international trade,

HAVE AGREED as follows:

PART I. SPHERE OF APPLICATION AND GENERAL PROVISIONS

CHAPTER I. SPHERE OF APPLICATION

Article 1

(1) This Convention applies to contracts of sale of goods between parties whose places of business are in different States:

(a) when the States are Contracting States; or

(b) when the rules of private international law lead to the application of the law of a Contracting State.

(2) The fact that the parties have their places of business in different States is to be disregarded whenever this fact does not appear either from the contract or from any dealings between, or from information disclosed by, the parties at any time before or at the conclusion of the contract.

(3) Neither the nationality of the parties nor the civil or commercial character of the parties or of the contract is to be taken into consideration in determining the application of this Convention.

[The United States has declared a reservation under Article 95, and therefore is not bound by Article 1(1)(b).]

Article 2

This Convention does not apply to sales:

(a) of goods bought for personal, family or household use, unless the seller, at any time before or at the conclusion of the contract, neither knew nor ought to have known that the goods were bought for any such use;

(b) by auction;

(c) on execution or otherwise by authority of law;

(d) of stocks, shares, investment securities, negotiable instruments or money;

(e) of ships, vessels, hovercraft or aircraft;

(f) of electricity.

Article 3

(1) Contracts for the supply of goods to be manufactured or produced are to be considered sales unless the party who orders the goods undertakes to supply a substantial part of the materials necessary for such manufacture or production.

(2) This Convention does not apply to contracts in which the preponderant part of the obligations of the party who furnishes the goods consists in the supply of labour or other services.

Article 4

This Convention governs only the formation of the contract of sale and the rights and obligations of the seller and the buyer arising from such a contract. In particular, except as otherwise expressly provided in this Convention, it is not concerned with:

(a) the validity of the contract or of any of its provisions or of any usage;

(b) the effect which the contract may have on the property in the goods sold.

Article 5

This Convention does not apply to the liability of the seller for death or personal injury caused by the goods to any person.

Article 6

The parties may exclude the application of this Convention or, subject to article 12, derogate from or vary the effect of any of its provisions.

CHAPTER II. GENERAL PROVISIONS

Article 7

(1) In the interpretation of this Convention, regard is to be had to its international character and to the need to promote uniformity in its application and the observance of good faith in international trade.

(2) Questions concerning matters governed by this Convention which are not expressly settled in it are to be settled in conformity with the general principles on which it is based or, in the absence of such principles, in conformity with the law applicable by virtue of the rules of private international law.

Article 8

(1) For the purposes of this Convention statements made by and other conduct of a party are to be interpreted according to his intent where the other party knew or could not have been unaware what that intent was.

(2) If the preceding paragraph is not applicable, statements made by and other conduct of a party are to be interpreted according to the understanding that a reasonable person of the same kind as the other party would have had in the same circumstances.

(3) In determining the intent of a party or the understanding a reasonable person would have had, due consideration is to be given to all relevant circumstances of the case including the negotiations, any practices which the parties have established between themselves, usages and any subsequent conduct of the parties.

Article 9

(1) The parties are bound by any usage to which they have agreed and by any practices which they have established between themselves.

(2) The parties are considered, unless otherwise agreed, to have impliedly made applicable to their contract or its formation a usage of which the parties knew or ought to have known and which in international trade is widely known to, and regularly observed by, parties to contracts of the type involved in the particular trade concerned.

Article 10

For the purposes of this Convention:

(a) if a party has more than one place of business, the place of business is that which has the closest relationship to the contract and its performance, having regard to the circumstances known to or contemplated by the parties at any time before or at the conclusion of the contract;

(b) if a party does not have a place of business, reference is to be made to his habitual residence.

Article 11

A contract of sale need not be concluded in or evidenced by writing and is not subject to any other requirement as to form. It may be proved by any means, including witnesses.

Article 12

Any provision of article 11, article 29 or Part II of this Convention that allows a contract of sale or its modification or termination by agreement or any offer, acceptance or other indication of intention to be made in any form other than in writing does not apply where any party has his place of business in a Contracting State which has made a declaration under article 96 of this Convention. The parties may not derogate from or vary the effect of this article.

Article 13

For the purposes of this Convention "writing" includes telegram and telex.

PART II. FORMATION OF THE CONTRACT

Article 14

(1) A proposal for concluding a contract addressed to one or more specific persons constitutes an offer if it is sufficiently definite and indicates the intention of the offeror to be bound in case of acceptance. A proposal is sufficiently definite if it indicates the goods and expressly or implicitly fixes or makes provision for determining the quantity and the price.

(2) A proposal other than one addressed to one or more specific persons is to be considered merely as an invitation to make offers, unless the contrary is clearly indicated by the person making the proposal.

* * *

Article 17

An offer, even if it is irrevocable, is terminated when a rejection reaches the offeror.

Article 18

(1) A statement made by or other conduct of the offeree indicating assent to an offer is an acceptance. Silence or inactivity does not in itself amount to acceptance.

(2) An acceptance of an offer becomes effective at the moment the indication of assent reaches the offeror. An acceptance is not effective if the indication of assent does not reach the offeror within the time he has fixed or, if no time is fixed, within a reasonable time, due account being taken of the circumstances of the transaction, including the rapidity of the means of communication employed by the offeror. An oral offer must be accepted immediately unless the circumstances indicate otherwise.

(3) However, if, by virtue of the offer or as a result of practices which the parties have established between themselves or of usage, the offeree may indicate assent by performing an act, such as one relating to the dispatch of the goods or payment of the price, without notice to the offeror, the acceptance is effective at the moment the act is performed, provided that the act is performed within the period of time laid down in the preceding paragraph.

Article 19

(1) A reply to an offer which purports to be an acceptance but contains additions, limitations or other modifications is a rejection of the offer and constitutes a counter-offer.

(2) However, a reply to an offer which purports to be an acceptance but contains additional or different terms which do not materially alter

the terms of the offer constitutes an acceptance, unless the offeror, without undue delay, objects orally to the discrepancy or dispatches a notice to that effect. If he does not so object, the terms of the contract are the terms of the offer with the modifications contained in the acceptance.

(3) Additional or different terms relating, among other things, to the price, payment, quality and quantity of the goods, place and time of delivery, extent of one party's liability to the other or the settlement of disputes are considered to alter the terms of the offer materially.

* * *

PART III. SALE OF GOODS

CHAPTER I. GENERAL PROVISIONS

Article 25

A breach of contract committed by one of the parties is fundamental if it results in such detriment to the other party as substantially to deprive him of what he is entitled to expect under the contract, unless the party in breach did not foresee and a reasonable person of the same kind in the same circumstances would not have foreseen such a result.

Article 26

A declaration of avoidance of the contract is effective only if made by notice to the other party.

* * *

Article 28

If, in accordance with the provisions of this Convention, one party is entitled to require performance of any obligation by the other party, a court is not bound to enter a judgment for specific performance unless the court would do so under its own law in respect of similar contracts of sale not governed by this Convention.

Article 29

(1) A contract may be modified or terminated by the mere agreement of the parties.

(2) A contract in writing which contains a provision requiring any modification or termination by agreement to be in writing may not be otherwise modified or terminated by agreement. However, a party may be precluded by his conduct from asserting such a provision to the extent that the other party has relied on that conduct.

CHAPTER II. OBLIGATIONS OF THE SELLER

Article 30

The seller must deliver the goods, hand over any documents relating to them and transfer the property in the goods, as required by the contract and this Convention.

Section I.

Delivery of the Goods and Handing Over of Documents

Article 31

If the seller is not bound to deliver the goods at any other particular place, his obligation to deliver consists:

(a) if the contract of sale involves carriage of the goods—in handing the goods over to the first carrier for transmission to the buyer;

(b) if, in cases not within the preceding subparagraph, the contract relates to specific goods, or unidentified goods to be drawn from a specific stock or to be manufactured or produced, and at the time of the conclusion of the contract the parties knew that the goods were at, or were to be manufactured or produced at, a particular place—in placing the goods at the buyer's disposal at that place;

(c) in other cases—in placing the goods at the buyer's disposal at the place where the seller had his place of business at the time of the conclusion of the contract.

Article 32

(1) If the seller, in accordance with the contract or this Convention, hands the goods over to a carrier and if the goods are not clearly identified to the contract by markings on the goods, by shipping documents or otherwise, the seller must give the buyer notice of the consignment specifying the goods.

(2) If the seller is bound to arrange for carriage of the goods, he must make such contracts as are necessary for carriage to the place fixed by means of transportation appropriate in the circumstances and according to the usual terms for such transportation.

(3) If the seller is not bound to effect insurance in respect of the carriage of the goods, he must, at the buyer's request, provide him with all available information necessary to enable him to effect such insurance.

Article 33

The seller must deliver the goods:

(a) if a date is fixed by or determinable from the contract, on that date;

(b) if a period of time is fixed by or determinable from the contract, at any time within that period unless circumstances indicate that the buyer is to choose a date; or

(c) in any other case, within a reasonable time after the conclusion of the contract.

Article 34

If the seller is bound to hand over documents relating to the goods, he must hand them over at the time and place and in the form required by the contract. If the seller has handed over documents before that time, he may, up to that time, cure any lack of conformity in the documents, if the exercise of this right does not cause the buyer unreasonable inconvenience or unreasonable expense. However, the buyer retains any right to claim damages as provided for in this Convention.

Section II.

Conformity of the Goods and Third Party Claims

Article 35

(1) The seller must deliver goods which are of the quantity, quality and description required by the contract and which are contained or packaged in the manner required by the contract.

(2) Except where the parties have agreed otherwise, the goods do not conform with the contract unless they:

(a) are fit for the purposes for which goods of the same description would ordinarily be used;

(b) are fit for any particular purpose expressly or impliedly made known to the seller at the time of the conclusion of the contract, except where the circumstances show that the buyer did not rely, or that it was unreasonable for him to rely, on the seller's skill and judgement;

(c) possess the qualities of goods which the seller has held out to the buyer as a sample or model;

(d) are contained or packaged in the manner usual for such goods or, where there is no such manner, in a manner adequate to preserve and protect the goods.

(3) The seller is not liable under subparagraphs (a) to (d) of the preceding paragraph for any lack of conformity of the goods if at the time of the conclusion of the contract the buyer knew or could not have been unaware of such lack of conformity.

Article 36

(1) The seller is liable in accordance with the contract and this Convention for any lack of conformity which exists at the time when the risk passes to the buyer, even though the lack of conformity becomes apparent only after that time.

(2) The seller is also liable for any lack of conformity which occurs after the time indicated in the preceding paragraph and which is due to a breach of any of his obligations, including a breach of any guarantee that for a period of time the goods will remain fit for their ordinary purpose or

for some particular purpose or will retain specified qualities or characteristics.

Article 37

If the seller has delivered goods before the date for delivery, he may, up to that date, deliver any missing part or make up any deficiency in the quantity of the goods delivered, or deliver goods in replacement of any nonconforming goods delivered or remedy any lack of conformity in the goods delivered, provided that the exercise of this right does not cause the buyer unreasonable inconvenience or unreasonable expense. However, the buyer retains any right to claim damages as provided for in this Convention.

Article 38

(1) The buyer must examine the goods, or cause them to be examined, within as short a period as is practicable in the circumstances.

(2) If the contract involves carriage of the goods, examination may be deferred until after the goods have arrived at their destination.

(3) If the goods are redirected in transit or redispatched by the buyer without a reasonable opportunity for examination by him and at the time of the conclusion of the contract the seller knew or ought to have known of the possibility of such redirection or redispatch, examination may be deferred until after the goods have arrived at the new destination.

Article 39

(1) The buyer loses the right to rely on a lack of conformity of the goods if he does not give notice to the seller specifying the nature of the lack of conformity within a reasonable time after he has discovered it or ought to have discovered it.

(2) In any event, the buyer loses the right to rely on a lack of conformity of the goods if he does not give the seller notice thereof at the latest within a period of two years from the date on which the goods were actually handed over to the buyer, unless this time-limit is inconsistent with a contractual period of guarantee.

* * *

Article 42

(1) The seller must deliver goods which are free from any right or claim of a third party based on industrial property or other intellectual property, of which at the time of the conclusion of the contract the seller knew or could not have been unaware, provided that the right or claim is based on industrial property or other intellectual property:

(a) under the law of the State where the goods will be resold or otherwise used, if it was contemplated by the parties at the time of the conclusion of the contract that the goods would be resold or otherwise used in that State; or

(b) in any other case, under the law of the State where the buyer has his place of business.

(2) The obligation of the seller under the preceding paragraph does not extend to cases where:

(a) at the time of the conclusion of the contract the buyer knew or could not have been unaware of the right or claim; or

(b) the right or claim results from the seller's compliance with technical drawings, designs, formulae or other such specifications furnished by the buyer.

Article 43

(1) The buyer loses the right to rely on the provisions of article 41 or article 42 if he does not give notice to the seller specifying the nature of the right or claim of the third party within a reasonable time after he has become aware or ought to have become aware of the right or claim.

(2) The seller is not entitled to rely on the provisions of the preceding paragraph if he knew of the right or claim of the third party and the nature of it.

Article 44

Notwithstanding the provisions of paragraph (1) of article 39 and paragraph (1) of article 43, the buyer may reduce the price in accordance with article 50 or claim damages, except for loss of profit, if he has a reasonable excuse for his failure to give the required notice.

Section III.

Remedies for Breach of Contract by the Seller

Article 45

(1) If the seller fails to perform any of his obligations under the contract or this Convention, the buyer may:

(a) exercise the rights provided in articles 46 to 52;

(b) claim damages as provided in articles 74 to 77.

(2) The buyer is not deprived of any right he may have to claim damages by exercising his right to other remedies.

* * *

Article 46

(1) The buyer may require performance by the seller of his obligations unless the buyer has resorted to a remedy which is inconsistent with this requirement.

(2) If the goods do not conform with the contract, the buyer may require delivery of substitute goods only if the lack of conformity constitutes a fundamental breach of contract and a request for substitute goods is made either in conjunction with notice given under article 39 or within a reasonable time thereafter.

* * *

Article 47

(1) The buyer may fix an additional period of time of reasonable length for performance by the seller of his obligations.

(2) Unless the buyer has received notice from the seller that he will not perform within the period so fixed, the buyer may not, during that period, resort to any remedy for breach of contract. However, the buyer is not deprived thereby of any right he may have to claim damages for delay in performance.

Article 48

(1) Subject to article 49, the seller may, even after the date for delivery, remedy at his own expense any failure to perform his obligations, if he can do so without unreasonable delay and without causing the buyer unreasonable inconvenience or uncertainty of reimbursement by the seller of expenses advanced by the buyer. However, the buyer retains any right to claim damages as provided for in this Convention.

(2) If the seller requests the buyer to make known whether he will accept performance and the buyer does not comply with the request within a reasonable time, the seller may perform within the time indicated in his request. The buyer may not, during that period of time, resort to any remedy which is inconsistent with performance by the seller.

(3) A notice by the seller that he will perform within a specified period of time is assumed to include a request, under the preceding paragraph, that the buyer make known his decision.

(4) A request or notice by the seller under paragraph (2) or (3) of this article is not effective unless received by the buyer.

Article 49

(1) The buyer may declare the contract avoided:

(a) if the failure by the seller to perform any of his obligations under the contract or this Convention amounts to a fundamental breach of contract; or

(b) in case of non-delivery, if the seller does not deliver the goods within the additional period of time fixed by the buyer in accordance with paragraph (1) of article 47 or declares that he will not deliver within the period so fixed.

* * *

Article 50

If the goods do not conform with the contract and whether or not the price has already been paid, the buyer may reduce the price in the same proportion as the value that the goods actually delivered had at the time of the delivery bears to the value that conforming goods would have had at that time. However, if the seller remedies any failure to perform his obligations in accordance with article 37 or article 48 or if the buyer refuses to accept performance by the seller in accordance with those articles, the buyer may not reduce the price.

Article 51

(1) If the seller delivers only a part of the goods or if only a part of the goods delivered is in conformity with the contract, articles 46 to 50 apply in respect of the part which is missing or which does not conform.

(2) The buyer may declare the contract avoided in its entirety only if the failure to make delivery completely or in conformity with the contract amounts to a fundamental breach of the contract.

* * *

CHAPTER III. OBLIGATIONS OF THE BUYER

Article 53

The buyer must pay the price for the goods and take delivery of them as required by the contract and this Convention.

Section I.

Payment of the Price

Article 54

The buyer's obligation to pay the price includes taking such steps and complying with such formalities as may be required under the contract or any laws and regulations to enable payment to be made.

* * *

Article 57

(1) If the buyer is not bound to pay the price at any other particular place, he must pay it to the seller:

(a) at the seller's place of business; or

(b) if the payment is to be made against the handing over of the goods or of documents, at the place where the handing over takes place.

(2) The seller must bear any increase in the expenses incidental to payment which is caused by a change in his place of business subsequent to the conclusion of the contract.

Article 58

(1) If the buyer is not bound to pay the price at any other specific time, he must pay it when the seller places either the goods or documents controlling their disposition at the buyer's disposal in accordance with the contract and this Convention. The seller may make such payment a condition for handing over the goods or documents.

(2) If the contract involves carriage of the goods, the seller may dispatch the goods on terms whereby the goods, or documents controlling their disposition, will not be handed over to the buyer except against payment of the price.

(3) The buyer is not bound to pay the price until he has had an opportunity to examine the goods, unless the procedures for delivery or payment agreed upon by the parties are inconsistent with his having such an opportunity.

* * *

Section III.

Remedies for Breach of Contract by the Buyer

Article 61

(1) If the buyer fails to perform any of his obligations under the contract or this Convention, the seller may:

(a) exercise the rights provided in articles 62 to 65;

(b) claim damages as provided in articles 74 to 77.

(2) The seller is not deprived of any right he may have to claim damages by exercising his right to other remedies.

* * *

Article 62

The seller may require the buyer to pay the price, take delivery or perform his other obligations, unless the seller has resorted to a remedy which is inconsistent with this requirement.

Article 63

(1) The seller may fix an additional period of time of reasonable length for performance by the buyer of his obligations.

(2) Unless the seller has received notice from the buyer that he will not perform within the period so fixed, the seller may not, during that period, resort to any remedy for breach of contract. However, the seller is not deprived thereby of any right he may have to claim damages for delay in performance.

Article 64

(1) The seller may declare the contract avoided:

(a) if the failure by the buyer to perform any of his obligations under the contract or this Convention amounts to a fundamental breach of contract; or

(b) if the buyer does not, within the additional period of time fixed by the seller in accordance with paragraph (1) of article 63, perform his obligation to pay the price or take delivery of the goods, or if he declares that he will not do so within the period so fixed.

* * *

CHAPTER IV. PASSING OF RISK

Article 66

Loss of or damage to the goods after the risk has passed to the buyer does not discharge him from his obligation to pay the price, unless the loss or damage is due to an act or omission of the seller.

Article 67

(1) If the contract of sale involves carriage of the goods and the seller is not bound to hand them over at a particular place, the risk passes to the buyer when the goods are handed over to the first carrier for transmission to the buyer in accordance with the contract of sale. If the seller is bound to hand the goods over to a carrier at a particular place, the risk does not pass to the buyer until the goods are handed over to the carrier at that place. The fact that the seller is authorized to retain documents controlling the disposition of the goods does not affect the passage of the risk.

(2) Nevertheless, the risk does not pass to the buyer until the goods are clearly identified to the contract, whether by markings on the goods, by shipping documents, by notice given to the buyer or otherwise.

* * *

Article 70

If the seller had committed a fundamental breach of contract, articles 67, 68 and 69 do not impair the remedies available to the buyer on account of the breach.

CHAPTER V. PROVISIONS COMMON TO THE OBLIGATIONS OF THE SELLER AND OF THE BUYER

Section I.

Anticipatory Breach and Instalment Contracts

Article 71

(1) A party may suspend the performance of his obligations if, after the conclusion of the contract, it becomes apparent that the other party will not perform a substantial part of his obligations as a result of:

(a) a serious deficiency in his ability to perform or in his creditworthiness; or

(b) his conduct in preparing to perform or in performing the contract.

(2) If the seller has already dispatched the goods before the grounds described in the preceding paragraph become evident, he may prevent the handing over of the goods to the buyer even though the buyer holds a document which entitles him to obtain them. The present paragraph relates only to the rights in the goods as between the buyer and the seller.

(3) A party suspending performance, whether before or after dispatch of the goods, must immediately give notice of the suspension to the other party and must continue with performance if the other party provides adequate assurance of his performance.

Article 72

(1) If prior to the date for performance of the contract it is clear that one of the parties will commit a fundamental breach of contract, the other party may declare the contract avoided.

(2) If time allows, the party intending to declare the contract avoided must give reasonable notice to the other party in order to permit him to provide adequate assurance of his performance.

(3) The requirements of the preceding paragraph do not apply if the other party has declared that he will not perform his obligations.

Article 73

(1) In the case of a contract for delivery of goods by instalments, if the failure of one party to perform any of his obligations in respect of any instalment constitutes a fundamental breach of contract with respect to that instalment, the other party may declare the contract avoided with respect to that instalment.

(2) If one party's failure to perform any of his obligations in respect of any instalment gives the other party good grounds to conclude that a fundamental breach of contract will occur with respect to future instalments, he may declare the contract avoided for the future, provided that he does so within a reasonable time.

(3) A buyer who declares the contract avoided in respect of any delivery may, at the same time, declare it avoided in respect of deliveries already made or of future deliveries if, by reason of their interdependence, those deliveries could not be used for the purpose contemplated by the parties at the time of the conclusion of the contract.

Section II.

Damages

Article 74

Damages for breach of contract by one party consist of a sum equal to the loss, including loss of profit, suffered by the other party as a consequence of the breach. Such damages may not exceed the loss which the party in breach foresaw or ought to have foreseen at the time of the conclusion of the contract, in the light of the facts and matters of which he then knew or ought to have known, as a possible consequence of the breach of contract.

Article 75

If the contract is avoided and if, in a reasonable manner and within a reasonable time after avoidance, the buyer has bought goods in replacement or the seller has resold the goods, the party claiming damages may recover the difference between the contract price and the price in the substitute transaction as well as any further damages recoverable under article 74.

Article 76

(1) If the contract is avoided and there is a current price for the goods, the party claiming damages may, if he has not made a purchase or resale under article 75, recover the difference between the price fixed by the contract and the current price at the time of avoidance as well as any further damages recoverable under article 74. If, however, the party claiming damages has avoided the contract after taking over the goods, the current price at the time of such taking over shall be applied instead of the current price at the time of avoidance.

(2) For the purpose of the preceding paragraph, the current price is the price prevailing at the place where delivery of the goods should have been made or, if there is no current price at that place, the price at such other place as serves as a reasonable substitute, making due allowance for differences in the cost of transporting the goods.

Article 77

A party who relies on a breach of contract must take such measures as are reasonable in the circumstances to mitigate the loss, including loss of profit, resulting from the breach. If he fails to take such measures, the party in breach may claim a reduction in the damages in the amount by which the loss should have been mitigated.

* * *

Section IV.

Exemptions

Article 79

(1) A party is not liable for a failure to perform any of his obligations if he proves that the failure was due to an impediment beyond his control and that he could not reasonably be expected to have taken the impediment into account at the time of the conclusion of the contract or to have avoided or overcome it or its consequences.

(2) If the party's failure is due to the failure by a third person whom he has engaged to perform the whole or a part of the contract, that party is exempt from liability only if:

(a) he is exempt under the preceding paragraph; and

(b) the person whom he has so engaged would be so exempt if the provisions of that paragraph were applied to him.

(3) The exemption provided by this article has effect for the period during which the impediment exists.

(4) The party who fails to perform must give notice to the other party of the impediment and its effects on his ability to perform. If the notice is not received by the other party within a reasonable time after the party who fails to perform knew or ought to have known of the impediment, he is liable for damages resulting from such non-receipt.

(5) Nothing in this article prevents either party from exercising any right other than to claim damages under this Convention.

* * *

Section V.

Effects of Avoidance

Article 81

(1) Avoidance of the contract releases both parties from their obligations under it, subject to any damages which may be due. Avoidance does not affect any provision of the contract for the settlement of disputes or any other provision of the contract governing the rights and obligations of the parties consequent upon the avoidance of the contract.

(2) A party who has performed the contract either wholly or in part may claim restitution from the other party of whatever the first party has supplied or paid under the contract. If both parties are bound to make restitution, they must do so concurrently.

Article 82

(1) The buyer loses the right to declare the contract avoided or to require the seller to deliver substitute goods if it is impossible for him to make restitution of the goods substantially in the condition in which he received them.

(2) The preceding paragraph does not apply:

(a) if the impossibility of making restitution of the goods or of making restitution of the goods substantially in the condition in which the buyer received them is not due to his act or omission;

(b) if the goods or part of the goods have perished or deteriorated as a result of the examination provided for in article 38; or

(c) if the goods or part of the goods have been sold in the normal course of business or have been consumed or transformed by the buyer in the course of normal use before he discovered or ought to have discovered the lack of conformity.

* * *

PART IV. FINAL PROVISIONS

* * *

Article 92

(1) A Contracting State may declare at the time of signature, ratification, acceptance, approval or accession that it will not be bound by Part II of this Convention or that it will not be bound by Part III of this Convention.

(2) A Contracting State which makes a declaration in accordance with the preceding paragraph in respect of Part II or Part III of this Convention is not to be considered a Contracting State within paragraph (1) of article 1 of this Convention in respect of matters governed by the Part to which the declaration applies.

Article 93

(1) If a Contracting State has two or more territorial units in which, according to its constitution, different systems of law are applicable in relation to the matters dealt with in this Convention, it may, at the time of signature, ratification, acceptance, approval or accession, declare that this Convention is to extend to all its territorial units or only to one or more of them, and may amend its declaration by submitting another declaration at any time.

* * *

Article 94

(1) Two or more Contracting States which have the same or closely related legal rules on matters governed by this Convention may at any time declare that the Convention is not to apply to contracts of sale or to their formation where the parties have their places of business in those States. Such declarations may be made jointly or by reciprocal unilateral declarations.

(2) A Contracting State which has the same or closely related legal rules on matters governed by this Convention as one or more non-Contracting States may at any time declare that the Convention is not to apply to contracts of sale or to their formation where the parties have their places of business in those States.

* * *

Article 95

Any State may declare at the time of the deposit of its instrument of ratification, acceptance, approval or accession that it will not be bound by subparagraph (1)(b) of article 1 of this Convention.

[The United States has declared a reservation to CISG under Article 95].

Article 96

A Contracting State whose legislation requires contracts of sale to be concluded in or evidenced by writing may at any time make a declaration in accordance with article 12 that any provision of article 11, article 29, or Part II of this Convention, that allows a contract of sale or its modification or termination by agreement or any offer, acceptance, or other indication of intention to be made in any form other than in writing, does not apply where any party has his place of business in that State.

* * *

DOCUMENT 2

UNITED NATIONS CONVENTION ON THE RECOGNITION AND ENFORCEMENT OF FOREIGN ARBITRAL AWARDS (1958, ENACTED BY THE UNITED STATES 1970) (NEW YORK CONVENTION)

Public Law 91–368, Approved July 31, 1970, 9 U.S.C. §§ 201–208, 84 Stat. 692

§ 201. Enforcement of Convention

The Convention on the Recognition and Enforcement of Foreign Arbitral Awards of June 10, 1958, shall be enforced in United States courts in accordance with this chapter.

CONVENTION ON THE RECOGNITION AND ENFORCEMENT OF FOREIGN ARBITRAL AWARDS

Article I

1. This Convention shall apply to the recognition and enforcement of arbitral awards made in the territory of a State other than the State where the recognition and enforcement of such awards are sought, and arising out of differences between persons, whether physical or legal. It shall also apply to arbitral awards not considered as domestic awards in the State where their recognition and enforcement are sought.

2. The term "arbitral awards" shall include not only awards made by arbitrators appointed for each case but also those made by permanent arbitral bodies to which the parties have submitted.

3. When signing, ratifying or acceding to this Convention, or notifying extension under article X hereof, any State may on the basis of reciprocity declare that it will apply the Convention to the recognition and enforcement of awards made only in the territory of another Contracting State. It may also declare that it will apply the Convention only to differences arising out of legal relationships, whether contractual or not, which are considered as commercial under the national law of the State making such declaration.

Article II

1. Each Contracting State shall recognize an agreement in writing under which the parties undertake to submit to arbitration all or any differences which have arisen or which may arise between them in respect of a defined legal relationship, whether contractual or not, concerning a subject matter capable of settlement by arbitration.

2. The term "agreement in writing" shall include an arbitral clause in a contract or an arbitration agreement, signed by the parties or contained in an exchange of letters or telegrams.

3. The court of a Contracting State, when seized of an action in a matter in respect of which the parties have made an agreement within the meaning of this article, shall, at the request of one of the parties, refer the parties to arbitration, unless it finds that the said agreement is null and void, inoperative or incapable of being performed.

Article III

Each Contracting State shall recognize arbitral awards as binding and enforce them in accordance with the rules of procedure of the territory where the award is relied upon, under the conditions laid down in the following articles. There shall not be imposed substantially more onerous conditions or higher fees or charges on the recognition or enforcement of arbitral awards to which this Convention applies than are imposed on the recognition or enforcement of domestic arbitral awards.

Article IV

1. To obtain the recognition and enforcement mentioned in the preceding article, the party applying for recognition and enforcement shall, at the time of the application, supply:

(a) The duly authenticated original award or a duly certified copy thereof;

(b) The original agreement referred to in article II or a duly certified copy thereof.

2. If the said award or agreement is not made in an official language of the country in which the award is relied upon, the party applying for recognition and enforcement of the award shall produce a translation of these documents into such language. The translation shall be certified by an official or sworn translator or by a diplomatic or consular agent.

Article V

1. Recognition and enforcement of the award may be refused, at the request of the party against whom it is invoked, only if that party furnishes to the competent authority where the recognition and enforcement is sought, proof that:

(a) The parties to the agreement referred to in article II were, under the law applicable to them, under some incapacity, or the said agreement is not valid under the law to which the parties have subjected it or, failing any indication thereon, under the law of the country where the award was made; or

(b) The party against whom the award is invoked was not given proper notice of the appointment of the arbitrator or of the arbitration proceedings or was otherwise unable to present his case; or

(c) The award deals with a difference not contemplated by or not falling within the terms of the submission to arbitration, or it contains decisions on matters beyond the scope of the submission to arbitration, provided that, if the decisions on matters submitted to arbitration can be separated from those not so submitted, that part of the award which contain decisions on matters submitted to arbitration may be recognized and enforced; or

(d) The composition of the arbitral authority or the arbitral procedure was not in accordance with the agreement of the parties, or, failing such agreement, was not in accordance with the law of the country where the arbitration took place; or

(e) The award has not yet become binding on the parties, or has been set aside or suspended by a competent authority of the country in which, or under the law of which, that award was made.

2. Recognition and enforcement of an arbitral award may also be refused if the competent authority in the country where recognition and enforcement is sought finds that:

(a) The subject matter of the difference is not capable of settlement by arbitration under the law of that country; or

(b) The recognition or enforcement of the award would be contrary to the public policy of that country.

Article VI

If an application for the setting aside or suspension of the award has been made to a competent authority referred to in article V(1)(e), the authority before which the award is sought to be relied upon may, if it considers it proper, adjourn the decision on the enforcement of the award and may also, on the application of the party claiming enforcement of the award, order the other party to give suitable security.

* * *

Article XIV

A Contracting State shall not be entitled to avail itself of the present Convention against other Contracting States except to the extent that it is itself bound to apply the Convention.

* * *

Article XVI

1. This Convention, of which the Chinese, English, French, Russian and Spanish texts shall be equally authentic, shall be deposited in the archives of the United Nations.

2. The Secretary–General of the United Nations shall transmit a certified copy of this Convention to the States contemplated in article VIII.

Done at New York June 10, 1958: entered into force for the United States December 29, 1970, subject to declarations.*

Appendix

Federal Arbitration Act Provisions Enacting New York Convention 9 U.S.C. §§ 201–208

§ 202. Agreement or Award Falling Under the Convention

An arbitration agreement or arbitral award arising out of a legal relationship, whether contractual or not, which is considered as commercial, including a transaction, contract, or agreement described in section 2 of this title, falls under the Convention. An agreement or award arising out of such a relationship which is entirely between citizens of the United States shall be deemed not to fall under the Convention unless that relationship involves property located abroad, envisages performance or enforcement abroad, or has some other reasonable relation with one or more foreign states. For the purpose of this section a corporation is a citizen of the United States if it is incorporated or has its principal place of business in the United States.

§ 203. Jurisdiction; Amount in Controversy

An action or proceeding falling under the Convention shall be deemed to arise under the laws and treaties of the United States. The district courts of the United States (including the courts enumerated in section 460 of title 28) shall have original jurisdiction over such an action or proceeding, regardless of the amount in controversy.

§ 204. Venue

An action or proceeding over which the district courts have jurisdiction pursuant to section 203 of this title may be brought in any such court in which save for the arbitration agreement an action or proceeding with respect to the controversy between the parties could be brought, or in such court for the district and division which embraces the place designat-

* The United States of America will apply the Convention, on the basis of reciprocity, to the recognition and enforcement of only those awards made in the territory of another Contracting State.

The United States of America will apply the Convention only to differences arising out of legal relationships, whether contractual or not, which are considered as commercial under the national law of the United States.

The Convention applies to all of the territories for the international relations of which the United States of America is responsible.

ed in the agreement as the place of arbitration if such place is within the United States.

§ 205. Removal of Cases From State Courts

Where the subject matter of an action or proceeding pending in a State court relates to an arbitration agreement or award falling under the Convention, the defendant or the defendants may, at any time before the trial thereof, remove such action or proceeding to the district court of the United States for the district and division embracing the place where the action or proceeding is pending. The procedure for removal of causes otherwise provided by law shall apply, except that the ground for removal provided in this section need not appear on the face of the complaint but may be shown in the petition for removal. For the purposes of Chapter 1 of this title any action or proceeding removed under this section shall be deemed to have been brought in the district court to which it is removed.

§ 206. Order to Compel Arbitration; Appointment of Arbitrators

A court having jurisdiction under this chapter may direct that arbitration be held in accordance with the agreement at any place therein provided for, whether that place is within or without the United States. Such court may also appoint arbitrators in accordance with the provisions of the agreement.

§ 207. Award of Arbitrators; Confirmation; Jurisdiction; Proceeding

Within three years after an arbitral award falling under the Convention is made, any party to the arbitration may apply to any court having jurisdiction under this chapter for an order confirming the award as against any other party to the arbitration. The court shall confirm the award unless it finds one of the grounds for refusal or deferral of recognition or enforcement of the award specified in the said Convention.

§ 208. Chapter 1; Residual Application

Chapter 1 applies to actions and proceedings brought under this chapter to the extent that that chapter is not in conflict with this chapter or the Convention as ratified by the United States.

DOCUMENT 3

UNITED NATIONS CONVENTION ON INDEPENDENT GUARANTEES AND STAND-BY LETTERS OF CREDIT (1995) (SELECTED PROVISIONS)*

CHAPTER I. SCOPE OF APPLICATION

Article 1. Scope of application

(1) This Convention applies to an international undertaking referred to in article 2:

(a) If the place of business of the guarantor/issuer at which the undertaking is issued is in a Contracting State, or

(b) If the rules of private international law lead to the application of the law of a Contracting State, unless the undertaking excludes the application of the Convention.

(2) This Convention applies also to an international letter of credit not falling within article 2 if it expressly states that it is subject to this Convention.

(3) The provisions of articles 21 and 22 apply to international undertakings referred to in article 2 independently of paragraph (1) of this article.

Article 2. Undertaking

(1) For the purposes of this Convention, an undertaking is an independent commitment, known in international practice as an independent guarantee or as a stand-by letter of credit, given by a bank or other institution or person ("guarantor/issuer") to pay to the beneficiary a certain or determinable amount upon simple demand or upon demand accompanied by other documents, in conformity with the terms and any documentary conditions of the undertaking, indicating, or from which it is to be inferred, that payment is due because of a default in the performance of an obligation, or because of another contingency, or for money borrowed or advanced, or on account of any mature indebtedness undertaken by the principal/applicant or another person.

(2) The undertaking may be given:

* In force. There are eight Contracting States: Belarus, Ecuador, El Salvador, Gabon, Kuwait, Liberia, Panama and Tunisia.

(a) At the request or on the instruction of the customer ("principal/applicant") of the guarantor/issuer;

(b) On the instruction of another bank, institution or person ("instructing party") that acts at the request of the customer ("principal/applicant") of that instructing party; or

(c) On behalf of the guarantor/issuer itself.

* * *

Article 3. Independence of undertaking

For the purposes of this Convention, an undertaking is independent where the guarantor/issuer's obligation to the beneficiary is not:

(a) Dependent upon the existence or validity of any underlying transaction, or upon any other undertaking (including stand-by letters of credit or independent guarantees to which confirmations or counter-guarantees relate); or

(b) Subject to any term or condition not appearing in the undertaking, or to any future, uncertain act or event except presentation of documents or another such act or event within a guarantor/issuer's sphere of operations.

Article 4. Internationality of undertaking

(1) An undertaking is international if the places of business, as specified in the undertaking, of any two of the following persons are in different States: guarantor/issuer, beneficiary, principal/applicant, instructing party, confirmer.

(2) For the purposes of the preceding paragraph:

(a) If the undertaking lists more than one place of business for a given person, the relevant place of business is that which has the closest relationship to the undertaking;

(b) If the undertaking does not specify a place of business for a given person but specifies its habitual residence, that residence is relevant for determining the international character of the undertaking.

CHAPTER II. INTERPRETATION

Article 5. Principles of interpretation

In the interpretation of this Convention, regard is to be had to its international character and to the need to promote uniformity in its application and the observance of good faith in the international practice of independent guarantees and stand-by letters of credit.

Article 6. Definitions

For the purposes of this Convention and unless otherwise indicated in a provision of this Convention or required by the context:

(a) "Undertaking" includes "counter-guarantee" and "confirmation of an undertaking";

(b) "Guarantor/issuer" includes "counter-guarantor" and "confirmer";

(c) "Counter-guarantee" means an undertaking given to the guarantor/issuer of another undertaking by its instructing party and providing for payment upon simple demand or upon demand accompanied by other documents, in conformity with the terms and any documentary conditions of the undertaking, indicating, or from which it is to be inferred, that payment under that other undertaking has been demanded from, or made by, the person issuing that other undertaking;

(d) "Counter-guarantor" means the person issuing a counter-guarantee;

(e) "Confirmation" of an undertaking means an undertaking added to that of the guarantor/issuer, and authorized by the guarantor/issuer, providing the beneficiary with the option of demanding payment from the confirmer instead of from the guarantor/issuer, upon simple demand or upon demand accompanied by other documents, in conformity with the terms and any documentary conditions of the confirmed undertaking, without prejudice to the beneficiary's right to demand payment from the guarantor/issuer;

(f) "Confirmer" means the person adding a confirmation to an undertaking;

(g) "Document" means a communication made in a form that provides a complete record thereof.

CHAPTER III. FORM AND CONTENT OF UNDERTAKING

Article 7. Issuance, form and irrevocability of undertaking

(1) Issuance of an undertaking occurs when and where the undertaking leaves the sphere of control of the guarantor/issuer concerned.

(2) An undertaking may be issued in any form which preserves a complete record of the text of the undertaking and provides authentication of its source by generally accepted means or by a procedure agreed upon by the guarantor/issuer and the beneficiary.

(3) From the time of issuance of an undertaking, a demand for payment may be made in accordance with the terms and conditions of the undertaking, unless the undertaking stipulates a different time.

(4) An undertaking is irrevocable upon issuance, unless it stipulates that it is revocable.

* * *

Article 11. Cessation of right to demand payment

(1) The right of the beneficiary to demand payment under the undertaking ceases when:

(a) The guarantor/issuer has received a statement by the beneficiary of release from liability in a form referred to in paragraph (2) of article 7;

(b) The beneficiary and the guarantor/issuer have agreed on the termination of the undertaking in the form stipulated in the undertaking or, failing such stipulation, in a form referred to in paragraph (2) of article 7;

(c) The amount available under the undertaking has been paid, unless the undertaking provides for the automatic renewal or for an automatic increase of the amount available or otherwise provides for continuation of the undertaking;

(d) The validity period of the undertaking expires in accordance with the provisions of article 12.

(2) The undertaking may stipulate, or the guarantor/issuer and the beneficiary may agree elsewhere, that return of the document embodying the undertaking to the guarantor/issuer, or a procedure functionally equivalent to the return of the document in the case of the issuance of the undertaking in non-paper form, is required for the cessation of the right to demand payment, either alone or in conjunction with one of the events referred to in subparagraphs (a) and (b) of paragraph (1) of this article. However, in no case shall retention of any such document by the beneficiary after the right to demand payment ceases in accordance with subparagraph (c) or (d) of paragraph (1) of this article preserve any rights of the beneficiary under the undertaking.

Article 12. Expiry

The validity period of the undertaking expires:

(a) At the expiry date, which may be a specified calendar date or the last day of a fixed period of time stipulated in the undertaking, provided that, if the expiry date is not a business day at the place of business of the guarantor/issuer at which the undertaking is issued, or of another person or at another place stipulated in the undertaking for presentation of the demand for payment, expiry occurs on the first business day which follows;

(b) If expiry depends according to the undertaking on the occurrence of an act or event not within the guarantor/issuer's sphere of operations, when the guarantor/issuer is advised that the act or event has occurred by presentation of the document specified for that purpose in the undertaking or, if no such document is specified, of a certification by the beneficiary of the occurrence of the act or event;

(c) If the undertaking does not state an expiry date, or if the act or event on which expiry is stated to depend has not yet been established by presentation of the required document and an expiry date has not been stated in addition, when six years have elapsed from the date of issuance of the undertaking.

CHAPTER IV. RIGHTS, OBLIGATIONS AND DEFENCES

Article 13. Determination of rights and obligations

(1) The rights and obligations of the guarantor/issuer and the beneficiary arising from the undertaking are determined by the terms and conditions set forth in the undertaking, including any rules, general conditions or usages specifically referred to therein, and by the provisions of this Convention.

(2) In interpreting terms and conditions of the undertaking and in settling questions that are not addressed by the terms and conditions of the undertaking or by the provisions of this Convention, regard shall be had to generally accepted international rules and usages of independent guarantee or stand-by letter of credit practice.

Article 14. Standard of conduct and liability of guarantor/issuer

(1) In discharging its obligations under the undertaking and this Convention, the guarantor/issuer shall act in good faith and exercise reasonable care having due regard to generally accepted standards of international practice of independent guarantees or stand-by letters of credit.

(2) A guarantor/issuer may not be exempted from liability for its failure to act in good faith or for any grossly negligent conduct.

Article 15. Demand

(1) Any demand for payment under the undertaking shall be made in a form referred to in paragraph (2) of article 7 and in conformity with the terms and conditions of the undertaking.

(2) Unless otherwise stipulated in the undertaking, the demand and any certification or other document required by the undertaking shall be presented, within the time that a demand for payment may be made, to the guarantor/issuer at the place where the undertaking was issued.

(3) The beneficiary, when demanding payment, is deemed to certify that the demand is not in bad faith and that none of the elements referred to in subparagraphs (a), (b) and (c) of paragraph (1) of article 19 are present.

Article 16. Examination of demand and accompanying documents

(1) The guarantor/issuer shall examine the demand and any accompanying documents in accordance with the standard of conduct referred to in paragraph (1) of article 14. In determining whether documents are in facial conformity with the terms and conditions of the undertaking, and are consistent with one another, the guarantor/issuer shall have due regard to the applicable international standard of independent guarantee or stand-by letter of credit practice.

(2) Unless otherwise stipulated in the undertaking or elsewhere agreed by the guarantor/issuer and the beneficiary, the guarantor/issuer shall have reasonable time, but not more than seven business days following the day of receipt of the demand and any accompanying documents, in which to:

(a) Examine the demand and any accompanying documents;

(b) Decide whether or not to pay;

(c) If the decision is not to pay, issue notice thereof to the beneficiary.

The notice referred to in subparagraph (c) above shall, unless otherwise stipulated in the undertaking or elsewhere agreed by the guarantor/issuer and the beneficiary, be made by teletransmission or, if that is not possible, by other expeditious means and indicate the reason for the decision not to pay.

Article 17. Payment

(1) Subject to article 19, the guarantor/issuer shall pay against a demand made in accordance with the provisions of article 15. Following a determination that a demand for payment so conforms, payment shall be made promptly, unless the undertaking stipulates payment on a deferred basis, in which case payment shall be made at the stipulated time.

(2) Any payment against a demand that is not in accordance with the provisions of article 15 does not prejudice the rights of the principal/applicant.

* * *

Article 19. Exception to payment obligation

(1) If it is manifest and clear that:

(a) Any document is not genuine or has been falsified;

(b) No payment is due on the basis asserted in the demand and the supporting documents; or

(c) Judging by the type and purpose of the undertaking, the demand has no conceivable basis, the guarantor/issuer, acting in good faith, has a right, as against the beneficiary, to withhold payment.

(2) For the purposes of subparagraph (c) of paragraph (1) of this article, the following are types of situations in which a demand has no conceivable basis:

(a) The contingency or risk against which the undertaking was designed to secure the beneficiary has undoubtedly not materialized;

(b) The underlying obligation of the principal/applicant has been declared invalid by a court or arbitral tribunal, unless the undertaking indicates that such contingency falls within the risk to be covered by the undertaking;

(c) The underlying obligation has undoubtedly been fulfilled to the satisfaction of the beneficiary;

(d) Fulfilment of the underlying obligation has clearly been prevented by wilful misconduct of the beneficiary;

(e) In the case of a demand under a counter-guarantee, the beneficiary of the counter-guarantee has made payment in bad faith as guarantor/issuer of the undertaking to which the counter-guarantee relates.

(3) In the circumstances set out in subparagraphs (a), (b) and (c) of paragraph (1) of this article, the principal/applicant is entitled to provisional court measures in accordance with article 20.

CHAPTER V. PROVISIONAL COURT MEASURES

Article 20. Provisional court measures

(1) Where, on an application by the principal/applicant or the instructing party, it is shown that there is a high probability that, with regard to a demand made, or expected to be made, by the beneficiary, one of the circumstances referred to in subparagraphs (a), (b) and (c) of paragraph (1) of article 19 is present, the court, on the basis of immediately available strong evidence, may:

(a) Issue a provisional order to the effect that the beneficiary does not receive payment, including an order that the guarantor/issuer hold the amount of the undertaking, or

(b) Issue a provisional order to the effect that the proceeds of the undertaking paid to the beneficiary are blocked, taking into account whether in the absence of such an order the principal/applicant would be likely to suffer serious harm.

(2) The court, when issuing a provisional order referred to in paragraph (1) of this article, may require the person applying therefor to furnish such form of security as the court deems appropriate.

(3) The court may not issue a provisional order of the kind referred to in paragraph (1) of this article based on any objection to payment other than those referred to in subparagraphs (a), (b) and (c) of paragraph (1) of article 19, or use of the undertaking for a criminal purpose.

CHAPTER VI. CONFLICT OF LAWS

Article 21. Choice of applicable law

The undertaking is governed by the law the choice of which is:

(a) Stipulated in the undertaking or demonstrated by the terms and conditions of the undertaking; or

(b) Agreed elsewhere by the guarantor/issuer and the beneficiary.

Article 22. Determination of applicable law

Failing a choice of law in accordance with article 21, the undertaking is governed by the law of the State where the guarantor/issuer has that place of business at which the undertaking was issued.

CHAPTER VII. FINAL CLAUSES

Article 23. Depositary

The Secretary–General of the United Nations is the depositary of this Convention.

Article 24. Signature, ratification, acceptance, approval, accession

(1) This Convention is open for signature by all States at the Headquarters of the United Nations, New York, until 11 December 1997.

* * *

Article 25. Application to territorial units

(1) If a State has two or more territorial units in which different systems of law are applicable in relation to the matters dealt with in this Convention, it may, at the time of signature, ratification, acceptance, approval or accession, declare that this Convention is to extend to all its territorial units or only one or more of them, and may at any time substitute another declaration for its earlier declaration.

* * *

Article 27. Reservations

No reservations may be made to this Convention.

Article 28. Entry into force

(1) This Convention enters into force on the first day of the month following the expiration of one year from the date of the deposit of the fifth instrument of ratification, acceptance, approval or accession.

(2) For each State which becomes a Contracting State to this Convention after the date of the deposit of the fifth instrument of ratification, acceptance, approval or accession, this Convention enters into force on the first day of the month following the expiration of one year after the date of the deposit of the appropriate instrument on behalf of that State.

(3) This Convention applies only to undertakings issued on or after the date when the Convention enters into force in respect of the Contracting State referred to in subparagraph (a) or the Contracting State referred to in subparagraph (b) of paragraph (1) of article 1.

Article 29. Denunciation

(1) A Contracting State may denounce this Convention at any time by means of a notification in writing addressed to the depositary.

* * *

DOCUMENT 4

UNITED NATIONS CONVENTION ON THE USE OF ELECTRONIC COMMUNICATIONS IN INTERNATIONAL CONTRACTS (2005) (SELECTED PROVISIONS)

CHAPTER I. SPHERE OF APPLICATION

Article 1. Scope of Application

1. This Convention applies to the use of electronic communications in connection with the formation or performance of a contract between parties whose places of business are in different States.

2. The fact that the parties have their places of business in different States is to be disregarded whenever this fact does not appear either from the contract or from any dealings between the parties or from information disclosed by the parties at any time before or at the conclusion of the contract.

3. Neither the nationality of the parties nor the civil or commercial character of the parties or of the contract is to be taken into consideration in determining the application of this Convention.

Article 2. Exclusions

1. This Convention does not apply to electronic communications relating to any of the following:

(a) Contracts concluded for personal, family or household purposes;

(b) (i) Transactions on a regulated exchange; (ii) foreign exchange transactions; (iii) inter-bank payment systems, inter-bank payment agreements or clearance and settlement systems relating to securities or other financial assets or instruments; (iv) the transfer of security rights in sale, loan or holding of or agreement to repurchase securities or other financial assets or instruments held with an intermediary.

2. This Convention does not apply to bills of exchange, promissory notes, consignment notes, bills of lading, warehouse receipts or any transferable document or instrument that entitles the bearer or beneficiary to claim the delivery of goods or the payment of a sum of money.

Article 3. Party Autonomy

The parties may exclude the application of this Convention or derogate from or vary the effect of any of its provisions.

CHAPTER II. GENERAL PROVISIONS

Article 4. Definitions

For the purposes of this Convention:

(a) "Communication" means any statement, declaration, demand, notice or request, including an offer and the acceptance of an offer, that the parties are required to make or choose to make in connection with the formation or performance of a contract;

(b) "Electronic communication" means any communication that the parties make by means of data messages;

(c) "Data message" means information generated, sent, received or stored by electronic, magnetic, optical or similar means, including, but not limited to, electronic data interchange, electronic mail, telegram, telex or telecopy;

(d) "Originator" of an electronic communication means a party by whom, or on whose behalf, the electronic communication has been sent or generated prior to storage, if any, but it does not include a party acting as an intermediary with respect to that electronic communication;

(e) "Addressee" of an electronic communication means a party who is intended by the originator to receive the electronic communication, but does not include a party acting as an intermediary with respect to that electronic communication;

(f) "Information system" means a system for generating, sending, receiving, storing or otherwise processing data messages;

(g) "Automated message system" means a computer program or an electronic or other automated means used to initiate an action or respond to data messages or performances in whole or in part, without review or intervention by a natural person each time an action is initiated or a response is generated by the system;

(h) "Place of business" means any place where a party maintains a nontransitory establishment to pursue an economic activity other than the temporary provision of goods or services out of a specific location.

Article 5. Interpretation

1. In the interpretation of this Convention, regard is to be had to its international character and to the need to promote uniformity in its application and the observance of good faith in international trade.

2. Questions concerning matters governed by this Convention which are not expressly settled in it are to be settled in conformity with the general principles on which it is based or, in the absence of such principles, in conformity with the law applicable by virtue of the rules of private international law.

Article 6. Location of the Parties

1. For the purposes of this Convention, a party's place of business is presumed to be the location indicated by that party, unless another party demonstrates that the party making the indication does not have a place of business at that location.

2. If a party has not indicated a place of business and has more than one place of business, then the place of business for the purposes of this Convention is that which has the closest relationship to the relevant contract, having regard to the circumstances known to or contemplated by the parties at any time before or at the conclusion of the contract.

3. If a natural person does not have a place of business, reference is to be made to the person's habitual residence.

4. A location is not a place of business merely because that is: (a) where equipment and technology supporting an information system used by a party in connection with the formation of a contract are located; or (b) where the information system may be accessed by other parties.

5. The sole fact that a party makes use of a domain name or electronic mail address connected to a specific country does not create a presumption that its place of business is located in that country.

Article 7. Information Requirements

Nothing in this Convention affects the application of any rule of law that may require the parties to disclose their identities, places of business or other information, or relieves a party from the legal consequences of making inaccurate, incomplete or false statements in that regard.

CHAPTER III. USE OF ELECTRONIC COMMUNICATIONS IN INTERNATIONAL CONTRACTS

Article 8. Legal Recognition of Electronic Communications

1. A communication or a contract shall not be denied validity or enforceability on the sole ground that it is in the form of an electronic communication.

2. Nothing in this Convention requires a party to use or accept electronic communications, but a party's agreement to do so may be inferred from the party's conduct.

Article 9. Form Requirements

1. Nothing in this Convention requires a communication or a contract to be made or evidenced in any particular form.

2. Where the law requires that a communication or a contract should be in writing, or provides consequences for the absence of a writing, that requirement is met by an electronic communication if the information contained therein is accessible so as to be usable for subsequent reference.

3. Where the law requires that a communication or a contract should be signed by a party, or provides consequences for the absence of a signature, that requirement is met in relation to an electronic communication if:

(a) A method is used to identify the party and to indicate that party's intention in respect of the information contained in the electronic communication; and

(b) The method used is either:

(i) As reliable as appropriate for the purpose for which the electronic communication was generated or communicated, in the light of all the circumstances, including any relevant agreement; or

(ii) Proven in fact to have fulfilled the functions described in subparagraph (a) above, by itself or together with further evidence.

4. Where the law requires that a communication or a contract should be made available or retained in its original form, or provides consequences for the absence of an original, that requirement is met in relation to an electronic communication if:

(a) There exists a reliable assurance as to the integrity of the information it contains from the time when it was first generated in its final form, as an electronic communication or otherwise; and

(b) Where it is required that the information it contains be made available, that information is capable of being displayed to the person to whom it is to be made available.

5. For the purposes of paragraph 4 (a):

(a) The criteria for assessing integrity shall be whether the information has remained complete and unaltered, apart from the addition of any endorsement and any change that arises in the normal course of communication, storage and display; and

(b) The standard of reliability required shall be assessed in the light of the purpose for which the information was generated and in the light of all the relevant circumstances.

Article 10. Time and Place of Dispatch and Receipt of Electronic Communications

1. The time of dispatch of an electronic communication is the time when it leaves an information system under the control of the originator or of the party who sent it on behalf of the originator or, if the electronic communication has not left an information system under the control of the originator or of the party who sent it on behalf of the originator, the time when the electronic communication is received.

2. The time of receipt of an electronic communication is the time when it becomes capable of being retrieved by the addressee at an

electronic address designated by the addressee. The time of receipt of an electronic communication at another electronic address of the addressee is the time when it becomes capable of being retrieved by the addressee at that address and the addressee becomes aware that the electronic communication has been sent to that address. An electronic communication is presumed to be capable of being retrieved by the addressee when it reaches the addressee's electronic address.

3. An electronic communication is deemed to be dispatched at the place where the originator has its place of business and is deemed to be received at the place where the addressee has its place of business, as determined in accordance with article 6.

4. Paragraph 2 of this article applies notwithstanding that the place where the information system supporting an electronic address is located may be different from the place where the electronic communication is deemed to be received under paragraph 3 of this article.

Article 11. Invitations to Make Offers

A proposal to conclude a contract made through one or more electronic communications which is not addressed to one or more specific parties, but is generally accessible to parties making use of information systems, including proposals that make use of interactive applications for the placement of orders through such information systems, is to be considered as an invitation to make offers, unless it clearly indicates the intention of the party making the proposal to be bound in case of acceptance.

Article 12. Use of Automated Message Systems for Contract Formation

A contract formed by the interaction of an automated message system and a natural person, or by the interaction of automated message systems, shall not be denied validity or enforceability on the sole ground that no natural person reviewed or intervened in each of the individual actions carried out by the automated message systems or the resulting contract.

Article 13. Availability of Contract Terms

Nothing in this Convention affects the application of any rule of law that may require a party that negotiates some or all of the terms of a contract through the exchange of electronic communications to make available to the other party those electronic communications which contain the contractual terms in a particular manner, or relieves a party from the legal consequences of its failure to do so.

Article 14. Error in Electronic Communications

1. Where a natural person makes an input error in an electronic communication exchanged with the automated message system of another party and the automated message system does not provide the person with an opportunity to correct the error, that person, or the party on whose

behalf that person was acting, has the right to withdraw the portion of the electronic communication in which the input error was made if:

(a) The person, or the party on whose behalf that person was acting, notifies the other party of the error as soon as possible after having learned of the error and indicates that he or she made an error in the electronic communication; and

(b) The person, or the party on whose behalf that person was acting, has not used or received any material benefit or value from the goods or services, if any, received from the other party.

2. Nothing in this article affects the application of any rule of law that may govern the consequences of any error other than as provided for in paragraph 1.

CHAPTER IV. FINAL PROVISIONS

* * *

Article 16. Signature, Ratification, Acceptance or Approval

1. This Convention is open for signature by all States at United Nations Headquarters in New York from 16 January 2006 to 16 January 2008.

2. This Convention is subject to ratification, acceptance or approval by the signatory States.

3. This Convention is open for accession by all States that are not signatory States as from the date it is open for signature.

4. Instruments of ratification, acceptance, approval and accession are to be deposited with the Secretary–General of the United Nations.

Article 17. Participation by Regional Economic Integration Organizations

1. A regional economic integration organization that is constituted by sovereign States and has competence over certain matters governed by this Convention may similarly sign, ratify, accept, approve or accede to this Convention. The regional economic integration organization shall in that case have the rights and obligations of a Contracting State, to the extent that that organization has competence over matters governed by this Convention. Where the number of Contracting States is relevant in this Convention, the regional economic integration organization shall not count as a Contracting State in addition to its member States that are Contracting States.

* * *

4. This Convention shall not prevail over any conflicting rules of any regional economic integration organization as applicable to parties whose

respective places of business are located in States members of any such organization, as set out by declaration made in accordance with article 21.

* * *

Article 19. Declarations on the Scope of Application

1. Any Contracting State may declare, in accordance with article 21, that it will apply this Convention only:

(a) When the States referred to in article 1, paragraph 1, are Contracting States to this Convention; or

(b) When the parties have agreed that it applies.

2. Any Contracting State may exclude from the scope of application of this Convention the matters it specifies in a declaration made in accordance with article 21.

Article 20. Communications Exchanged Under Other International Conventions

1. The provisions of this Convention apply to the use of electronic communications in connection with the formation or performance of a contract to which any of the following international conventions, to which a Contracting State to this Convention is or may become a Contracting State, apply:

Convention on the Recognition and Enforcement of Foreign Arbitral Awards (New York, 10 June 1958);

Convention on the Limitation Period in the International Sale of Goods (New York, 14 June 1974) and Protocol thereto (Vienna, 11 April 1980);

United Nations Convention on Contracts for the International Sale of Goods (Vienna, 11 April 1980);

* * *

United Nations Convention on Independent Guarantees and Stand-by Letters of Credit (New York, 11 December 1995);

* * *

2. The provisions of this Convention apply further to electronic communications in connection with the formation or performance of a contract to which another international convention, treaty or agreement not specifically referred to in paragraph 1 of this article, and to which a Contracting State to this Convention is or may become a Contracting State, applies, unless the State has declared, in accordance with article 21, that it will not be bound by this paragraph.

3. A State that makes a declaration pursuant to paragraph 2 of this article may also declare that it will nevertheless apply the provisions of this Convention to the use of electronic communications in connection with the formation or performance of any contract to which a specified international convention, treaty or agreement applies to which the State is or may become a Contracting State.

4. Any State may declare that it will not apply the provisions of this Convention to the use of electronic communications in connection with the formation or performance of a contract to which any international convention, treaty or agreement specified in that State's declaration, to which the State is or may become a Contracting State, applies, including any of the conventions referred to in paragraph 1 of this article, even if such State has not excluded the application of paragraph 2 of this article by a declaration made in accordance with article 21.

Article 21. Procedure and Effects of Declarations

1. Declarations under article 17, paragraph 4, article 19, paragraphs 1 and 2, and article 20, paragraphs 2, 3 and 4, may be made at any time. Declarations made at the time of signature are subject to confirmation upon ratification, acceptance or approval.

* * *

3. A declaration takes effect simultaneously with the entry into force of this Convention in respect of the State concerned. However, a declaration of which the depositary receives formal notification after such entry into force takes effect on the first day of the month following the expiration of six months after the date of its receipt by the depositary.

4. Any State that makes a declaration under this Convention may modify or withdraw it at any time by a formal notification in writing addressed to the depositary. The modification or withdrawal is to take effect on the first day of the month following the expiration of six months after the date of the receipt of the notification by the depositary.

Article 22. Reservations

No reservations may be made under this Convention.

Article 23. Entry Into Force

1. This Convention enters into force on the first day of the month following the expiration of six months after the date of deposit of the third instrument of ratification, acceptance, approval or accession.

2. When a State ratifies, accepts, approves or accedes to this Convention after the deposit of the third instrument of ratification, acceptance, approval or accession, this Convention enters into force in respect of that State on the first day of the month following the expiration of six months after the date of the deposit of its instrument of ratification, acceptance, approval or accession.

Article 24. Time of Application

This Convention and any declaration apply only to electronic communications that are made after the date when the Convention or the declaration enters into force or takes effect in respect of each Contracting State.

* * *

DOCUMENT 5

CONVENTION ON THE SERVICE ABROAD OF JUDICIAL AND EXTRAJUDICIAL DOCUMENTS IN CIVIL OR COMMERCIAL MATTERS (1965)

20 U.S.T. 361, 1969 WL 97765 (U.S. Treaty), T.I.A.S. No. 6638

Article 1

The present Convention shall apply in all cases, in civil or commercial matters, where there is occasion to transmit a judicial or extrajudicial document for service abroad.

This Convention shall not apply where the address of the person to be served with the document is not known.

CHAPTER I—JUDICIAL DOCUMENTS

Article 2

Each contracting State shall designate a Central Authority which will undertake to receive requests for service coming from other contracting States and to proceed in conformity with the provisions of articles 3 to 6.

Each State shall organise the Central Authority in conformity with its own law.

Article 3

The authority or judicial officer competent under the law of the State in which the documents originate shall forward to the Central Authority of the State addressed a request conforming to the model annexed to the present Convention, without any requirement of legalisation or other equivalent formality.

The document to be served or a copy thereof shall be annexed to the request. The request and the document shall both be furnished in duplicate.

Article 4

If the Central Authority considers that the request does not comply with the provisions of the present Convention it shall promptly inform the applicant and specify its objections to the request.

Article 5

The Central Authority of the State addressed shall itself serve the document or shall arrange to have it served by an appropriate agency, either—

(a) by a method prescribed by its internal law for the service of documents in domestic actions upon persons who are within its territory, or

(b) by a particular method requested by the applicant, unless such a method is incompatible with the law of the State addressed.

Subject to sub-paragraph (b) of the first paragraph of this article, the document may always be served by delivery to an addressee who accepts it voluntarily.

If the document is to be served under the first paragraph above, the Central Authority may require the document to be written in, or translated into, the official language or one of the official languages of the State addressed.

That part of the request, in the form attached to the present Convention, which contains a summary of the document to be served, shall be served with the document.

Article 6

The Central Authority of the State addressed or any authority which it may have designated for that purpose, shall complete a certificate in the form of the model annexed to the present Convention.

The certificate shall state that the document has been served and shall include the method, the place and the date of service and the person to whom the document was delivered. If the document has not been served, the certificate shall set out the reasons which have prevented service.

The applicant may require that a certificate not completed by a Central Authority or by a judicial authority shall be countersigned by one of these authorities.

The certificate shall be forwarded directly to the applicant.

Article 7

The standard terms in the model annexed to the present Convention shall in all cases be written either in French or in English. They may also be written in the official language, or in one of the official languages, of the State in which the documents originate.

The corresponding blanks shall be completed either in the language of the State addressed or in French or in English.

Article 8

Each contracting State shall be free to effect service of judicial documents upon persons abroad, without application of any compulsion, directly through its diplomatic or consular agents.

Any State may declare that it is opposed to such service within its territory, unless the document is to be served upon a national of the State in which the documents originate.

Article 9

Each contracting State shall be free, in addition, to use consular channels to forward documents, for the purpose of service, to those authorities of another contracting State which are designated by the latter for this purpose.

Each contracting State may, if exceptional circumstances so require, use diplomatic channels for the same purpose.

Article 10

Provided the State of destination does not object, the present Convention shall not interfere with—

(a) the freedom to send judicial documents, by postal channels, directly to persons abroad,

(b) the freedom of judicial officers, officials or other competent persons of the State of origin to effect service of judicial documents directly through the judicial officers, officials or other competent persons of the State of destination,

(c) the freedom of any person interested in a judicial proceeding to effect service of judicial documents directly through the judicial officers, officials or other competent persons of the State of destination.

Article 11

The present Convention shall not prevent two or more contracting States from agreeing to permit, for the purpose of service of judicial documents, channels of transmission other than those provided for in the preceding articles and, in particular, direct communication between their respective authorities.

Article 12

The service of judicial documents coming from a contracting State shall not give rise to any payment or reimbursement of taxes or costs for the services rendered by the State addressed.

The applicant shall pay or reimburse the costs occasioned by—

(a) the employment of a judicial officer or of a person competent under the law of the State of destination,

(b) the use of a particular method of service.

Article 13

Where a request for service complies with the terms of the present Convention, the State addressed may refuse to comply therewith only if it deems that compliance would infringe its sovereignty or security.

It may not refuse to comply solely on the ground that, under its internal law, it claims exclusive jurisdiction over the subject-matter of the action or that its internal law would not permit the action upon which the application is based.

The Central Authority shall, in case of refusal, promptly inform the applicant and state the reasons for the refusal.

Article 14

Difficulties which may arise in connection with the transmission of judicial documents for service shall be settled through diplomatic channels.

Article 15

Where a writ of summons or an equivalent document had to be transmitted abroad for the purpose of service, under the provisions of the present Convention, and the defendant has not appeared, judgment shall not be given until it is established that—

(a) the document was served by a method prescribed by the internal law of the State addressed for the service of documents in domestic actions upon persons who are within its territory, or

(b) the document was actually delivered to the defendant or to his residence by another method provided for by this Convention,

and that in either of these cases the service or the delivery was effected in sufficient time to enable the defendant to defend.

Each contracting State shall be free to declare that the judge, notwithstanding the provisions of the first paragraph of this article, may give judgment even if no certificate of service or delivery has been received, if all the following conditions are fulfilled—

(a) the document was transmitted by one of the methods provided for in this Convention,

(b) a period of time of not less than six months, considered adequate by the judge in the particular case, has elapsed since the date of the transmission of the document,

(c) no certificate of any kind has been received, even though every reasonable effort has been made to obtain it through the competent authorities of the State addressed.

Notwithstanding the provisions of the preceding paragraphs the judge may order, in case of urgency, any provisional or protective measures.

Article 16

When a writ of summons or an equivalent document had to be transmitted abroad for the purpose of service, under the provisions of the present Convention, and a judgment has been entered against a defendant who has not appeared, the judge shall have the power to relieve the defendant from the effects of the expiration of the time for appeal from the judgment if the following conditions are fulfilled—

(a) the defendant, without any fault on his part, did not have knowledge of the document in sufficient time to defend, or knowledge of the judgment in sufficient time to appeal, and

(b) the defendant has disclosed a prima facie defence to the action on the merits.

An application for relief may be filed only within a reasonable time after the defendant has knowledge of the judgment.

Each contracting State may declare that the application will not be entertained if it is filed after the expiration of a time to be stated in the declaration, but which shall in no case be less than one year following the date of the judgment.

This article shall not apply to judgments concerning status or capacity of persons.

CHAPTER II—EXTRAJUDICIAL DOCUMENTS

Article 17

Extrajudicial documents emanating from authorities and judicial officers of a contracting State may be transmitted for the purpose of service in another contracting State by the methods and under the provisions of the present Convention.

CHAPTER III—GENERAL CLAUSES

Article 18

Each contracting State may designate other authorities in addition to the Central Authority and shall determine the extent of their competence.

The applicant shall, however, in all cases, have the right to address a request directly to the Central Authority.

Federal States shall be free to designate more than one Central Authority.

Article 19

To the extent that the internal law of a contracting State permits methods of transmission, other than those provided for in the preceding articles, of documents coming from abroad, for service within its territory, the present Convention shall not affect such provisions.

Article 20

The present Convention shall not prevent an agreement between any two or more contracting States to dispense with—

(a) the necessity for duplicate copies of transmitted documents as required by the second paragraph of article 3,

(b) the language requirements of the third paragraph of article 5 and article 7,

(c) the provisions of the fourth paragraph of article 5,

(d) the provisions of the second paragraph of article 12.

Article 21

Each contracting State shall, at the time of the deposit of its instrument of ratification or accession, or at a later date, inform the Ministry of Foreign Affairs of the Netherlands of the following—

(a) the designation of authorities, pursuant to articles 2 and 18,

(b) the designation of the authority competent to complete the certificate pursuant to article 6,

(c) the designation of the authority competent to receive documents transmitted by consular channels, pursuant to article 9.

Each contracting State shall similarly inform the Ministry, where appropriate, of—

(a) opposition to the use of methods of transmission pursuant to articles 8 and 10,

(b) declarations pursuant to the second paragraph of article 15 and the third paragraph of article 16,

(c) all modifications of the above designations, oppositions and declarations.

* * *

Designations and Declarations Made on the Part of the United States in Connection with the Deposit of the United States Ratification

1. In accordance with Article 2, the United States Department of State is designated as the Central Authority to receive requests for service from other Contracting States and to proceed in conformity with Articles 3 to 6.

FORMS (REQUEST AND CERTIFICATE)
SUMMARY OF THE DOCUMENT TO BE SERVED
(annexes provided for Articles 3, 5, 6 and 7)

ANNEX TO THE CONVENTION
Forms
REQUEST FOR SERVICE ABROAD OF JUDICIAL OR EXTRAJUDICIAL DOCUMENTS

Convention on the Service Abroad of Judicial and Extrajudicial Documents in Civil or Commercial Matters,
signed at The Hague, the 15th of November 1965.

Identity and address of the applicant	Address of receiving authority

The undersigned applicant has the honour to transmit - in duplicate - the documents listed below and, in conformity with Article 5 of the above-mentioned Convention, requests prompt service of one copy thereof on the addressee, *i.e,*

(identity and address) ....

a) in accordance with the provisions of sub-paragraph *(a)* of the first paragraph of Article 5 of the Convention*.

b) in accordance with the following particular method (sub-paragraph *(b)* of the first paragraph of Article 5)*: ....

c) by delivery to the addressee, if he accepts it voluntarily (second paragraph of Article 5)*.

The authority is requested to return or to have returned to the applicant a copy of the documents - and of the annexes* - with a certificate as provided on the reverse side.

List of documents

....

....

....

....

....

....

Done at . . . . , the . . . .

Signature and/or stamp.

* Delete if inappropriate.

Reverse of the request
CERTIFICATE

The undersigned authority has the honour to certify, in conformity with Article 6 of the Convention,

1) that the document has been served*

- the (date)

....

- at (place, street, number)

....

....

- in one of the following methods authorised by Article 5:

a) in accordance with the provisions of sub-paragraph *(a)* of the first paragraph of Article 5 of the Convention*.

b) in accordance with the following particular method*:

....

....

c) by delivery to the addressee, who accepted it voluntarily* .

The documents referred to in the request have been delivered to:

- (identity and description of person)
- ....

....

- relationship to the addressee (family, business or other):
- ....

....

....

2) that the document has not been served, by reason of the following facts*:

....

....

....

In conformity with the second paragraph of Article 12 of the Convention, the applicant is requested to pay or reimburse the expenses detailed in the attached statement*.

Annexes

Documents returned: ....

....

....

In appropriate cases, documents establishing the service:

....

....

Done at . . . . , the . . . .

Signature and/or stamp.

* Delete if inappropriate.

SUMMARY OF THE DOCUMENT TO BE SERVED
Convention on the Service Abroad of Judicial and Extrajudicial Documents in Civil or Commercial Matters,
signed at The Hague, the 15th of November 1965.
(Article 5, fourth paragraph)

Name and address of the requesting authority:

....

....

Particulars of the parties*:

....

....

JUDICIAL DOCUMENT**

Nature and purpose of the document:

....

....

Nature and purpose of the proceedings and, where appropriate, the amount in dispute:

....

....

Date and place for entering appearance**:

....

....

Court which has given judgment**:

....

....

Date of judgment**:

....

Time-limits stated in the document**:

....

....

EXTRAJUDICIAL DOCUMENT**

Nature and purpose of the document:

....

....

Time-limits stated in the document**:

....

....

* If appropriate, identity and address of the person interested in the transmission of the document.

** Delete if inappropriate.

DOCUMENT 6

CONVENTION ON THE TAKING OF EVIDENCE ABROAD IN CIVIL OR COMMERCIAL MATTERS (1968) (INCLUDING SELECTED ARTICLE 23 DECLARATIONS AND MODEL LETTERS OF REQUEST)

23 U.S.T. 2555, 1972 WL 122493 (U.S. Treaty), T.I.A.S. No. 7444

CHAPTER I—LETTERS OF REQUEST

Article 1

In civil or commercial matters a judicial authority of a Contracting State may, in accordance with the provisions of the law of that State, request the competent authority of another Contracting State, by means of a Letter of Request, to obtain evidence, or to perform some other judicial act.

A Letter shall not be used to obtain evidence which is not intended for use in judicial proceedings, commenced or contemplated.

The expression "other judicial act" does not cover the service of judicial documents or the issuance of any process by which judgments or orders are executed or enforced, or orders for provisional or protective measures.

Article 2

A Contracting State shall designate a Central Authority which will undertake to receive Letters of Request coming from a judicial authority of another Contracting State and to transmit them to the authority competent to execute them. Each State shall organize the Central Authority in accordance with its own law.

Letters shall be sent to the Central Authority of the State of execution without being transmitted through any other authority of that State.

Article 3

A Letter of Request shall specify—

(a) the authority requesting its execution and the authority requested to execute it, if known to the requesting authority;

(b) the names and addresses of the parties to the proceedings and their representatives, if any;

(c) the nature of the proceedings for which the evidence is required, giving all necessary information in regard thereto;

(d) the evidence to be obtained or other judicial act to be performed.

Where appropriate, the Letter shall specify, inter alia—

(e) the names and addresses of the persons to be examined;

(f) the questions to be put to the persons to be examined or a statement of the subject-matter about which they are to be examined;

(g) the documents or other property, real or personal, to be inspected;

(h) any requirement that the evidence is to be given on oath or affirmation, and any special form to be used;

(i) any special method or procedure to be followed under Article 9.

A Letter may also mention any information necessary for the application of Article 11.

No legalization or other like formality may be required.

Article 4

A Letter of Request shall be in the language of the authority requested to execute it or be accompanied by a translation into that language.

Nevertheless, a Contracting State shall accept a Letter in either English or French, or a translation into one of these languages, unless it has made the reservation authorized by Article 33.

A Contracting State which has more than one official language and cannot, for reasons of internal law, accept Letters in one of these languages for the whole of its territory, shall, by declaration, specify the language in which the Letter or translation thereof shall be expressed for execution in the specified parts of its territory. In case of failure to comply with this declaration, without justifiable excuse, the costs of translation into the required language shall be borne by the State of origin.

A Contracting State may, by declaration, specify the language or languages other than those referred to in the preceding paragraphs, in which a Letter may be sent to its Central Authority.

Any translation accompanying a Letter shall be certified as correct, either by a diplomatic officer or consular agent or by a sworn translator or by any other person so authorized in either State.

Article 5

If the Central Authority considers that the request does not comply with the provisions of the present Convention, it shall promptly inform the authority of the State of origin which transmitted the Letter of Request, specifying the objections to the Letter.

Article 6

If the authority to whom a Letter of Request has been transmitted is not competent to execute it, the Letter shall be sent forthwith to the authority in the same State which is competent to execute it in accordance with the provisions of its own law.

Article 7

The requesting authority shall, if it so desires, be informed of the time when, and the place where, the proceedings will take place, in order that the parties concerned, and their representatives, if any, may be present. This information shall be sent directly to the parties or their representatives when the authority of the State of origin so requests.

Article 8

A Contracting State may declare that members of the judicial personnel of the requesting authority of another Contracting State may be present at the execution of a Letter of Request. Prior authorization by the competent authority designated by the declaring State may be required.

Article 9

The judicial authority which executes a Letter of Request shall apply its own law as to the methods and procedures to be followed.

However, it will follow a request of the requesting authority that a special method or procedure be followed, unless this is incompatible with the internal law of the State of execution or is impossible of performance by reason of its internal practice and procedure or by reason of practical difficulties.

A Letter of Request shall be executed expeditiously.

Article 10

In executing a Letter of Request the requested authority shall apply the appropriate measures of compulsion in the instances and to the same extent as are provided by its internal law for the execution of orders issued by the authorities of its own country or of requests made by parties in internal proceedings.

Article 11

In the execution of a Letter of Request the person concerned may refuse to give evidence in so far as he has a privilege or duty to refuse to give the evidence—

(a) under the law of the State of execution; or

(b) under the law of the State of origin, and the privilege or duty has been specified in the Letter, or, at the instance of the requested authority, has been otherwise confirmed to that authority by the requesting authority.

A Contracting State may declare that, in addition, it will respect privileges and duties existing under the law of States other than the State of origin and the State of execution, to the extent specified in that declaration.

Article 12

The execution of a Letter of Request may be refused only to the extent that—

(a) in the State of execution the execution of the Letter does not fall within the functions of the judiciary; or

(b) the State addressed considers that its sovereignty or security would be prejudiced thereby.

Execution may not be refused solely on the ground that under its internal law the State of execution claims exclusive jurisdiction over the subject-matter of the action or that its internal law would not admit a right of action on it.

Article 13

The documents establishing the execution of the Letter of Request shall be sent by the requested authority to the requesting authority by the same channel which was used by the latter.

In every instance where the Letter is not executed in whole or in part, the requesting authority shall be informed immediately through the same channel and advised of the reasons.

Article 14

The execution of the Letter of Request shall not give rise to any reimbursement of taxes or costs of any nature.

Nevertheless, the State of execution has the right to require the State of origin to reimburse the fees paid to experts and interpreters and the costs occasioned by the use of a special procedure requested by the State of origin under Article 9, paragraph 2.

The requested authority whose law obliges the parties themselves to secure evidence, and which is not able itself to execute the Letter, may, after having obtained the consent of the requesting authority, appoint a suitable person to do so. When seeking this consent the requested authority shall indicate the approximate costs which would result from this procedure. If the requesting authority gives its consent it shall reimburse any costs incurred; without such consent the requesting authority shall not be liable for the costs.

CHAPTER II—TAKING OF EVIDENCE BY DIPLOMATIC OFFICERS, CONSULAR AGENTS AND COMMISSIONERS

Article 15

In a civil or commercial matter, a diplomatic officer or consular agent of a Contracting State may, in the territory of another Contracting State and within the area where he exercises his functions, take the evidence without compulsion of nationals of a State which he represents in aid of proceedings commenced in the courts of a State which he represents.

A Contracting State may declare that evidence may be taken by a diplomatic officer or consular agent only if permission to that effect is given upon application made by him or on his behalf to the appropriate authority designated by the declaring State.

Article 16

A diplomatic officer or consular agent of a Contracting State may, in the territory of another Contracting State and within the area where he exercises his functions, also take the evidence, without compulsion, of nationals of the State in which he exercises his functions or of a third State, in aid of proceedings commenced in the courts of a State which he represents, if-

(a) a competent authority designated by the State in which he exercises his functions has given its permission either generally or in the particular case, and

(b) he complies with the conditions which the competent authority has specified in the permission.

A Contracting State may declare that evidence may be taken under this Article without its prior permission.

Article 17

In a civil or commercial matter, a person duly appointed as a commissioner for the purpose may, without compulsion, take evidence in the territory of a Contracting State in aid of proceedings commenced in the courts of another Contracting State if—

(a) a competent authority designated by the State where the evidence is to be taken has given its permission either generally or in the particular case; and

(b) he complies with the conditions which the competent authority has specified in the permission.

A Contracting State may declare that evidence may be taken under this Article without its prior permission.

Article 18

A Contracting State may declare that a diplomatic officer, consular agent or commissioner authorized to take evidence under Articles 15, 16 or 17, may apply to the competent authority designated by the declaring State for appropriate assistance to obtain the evidence by compulsion. The declaration may contain such conditions as the declaring State may see fit to impose.

If the authority grants the application it shall apply any measures of compulsion which are appropriate and are prescribed by its law for use in internal proceedings.

Article 19

The competent authority, in giving the permission referred to in Articles 15, 16 or 17, or in granting the application referred to in Article 18, may lay down such conditions as it deems fit, inter alia, as to the time and place of the taking of the evidence. Similarly it may require that it be given reasonable advance notice of the time, date and place of the taking of the evidence; in such a case a representative of the authority shall be entitled to be present at the taking of the evidence.

Article 20

In the taking of evidence under any Article of this Chapter persons concerned may be legally represented.

Article 21

Where a diplomatic officer, consular agent or commissioner is authorized under Articles 15, 16 or 17 to take evidence—

(a) he may take all kinds of evidence which are not incompatible with the law of the State where the evidence is taken or contrary to any permission granted pursuant to the above Articles, and shall have power within such limits to administer an oath or take an affirmation;

(b) a request to a person to appear or to give evidence shall, unless the recipient is a national of the State where the action is pending, be drawn up in the language of the place where the evidence is taken or be accompanied by a translation into such language;

(c) the request shall inform the person that he may be legally represented and, in any State that has not filed a declaration under Article 18, shall also inform him that he is not compelled to appear or to give evidence;

(d) the evidence may be taken in the manner provided by the law applicable to the court in which the action is pending provided that such manner is not forbidden by the law of the State where the evidence is taken;

(e) a person requested to give evidence may invoke the privileges and duties to refuse to give the evidence contained in Article 11.

Article 22

The fact that an attempt to take evidence under the procedure laid down in this Chapter has failed, owing to the refusal of a person to give evidence, shall not prevent an application being subsequently made to take the evidence in accordance with Chapter I.

CHAPTER III—GENERAL CLAUSES

Article 23

A Contracting State may at the time of signature, ratification or accession, declare that it will not execute Letters of Request issued for the purpose of obtaining pre-trial discovery of documents as known in Common Law countries.

Article 24

A Contracting State may designate other authorities in addition to the Central Authority and shall determine the extent of their competence. However, Letters of Request may in all cases be sent to the Central Authority.

Federal States shall be free to designate more than one Central Authority.

Article 25

A Contracting State which has more than one legal system may designate the authorities of one of such systems, which shall have exclusive competence to execute Letters of Request pursuant to this Convention.

Article 26

A Contracting State, if required to do so because of constitutional limitations, may request the reimbursement by the State of origin of fees and costs, in connection with the execution of Letters of Request, for the service of process necessary to compel the appearance of a person to give evidence, the costs of attendance of such persons, and the cost of any transcript of the evidence.

Where a State has made a request pursuant to the above paragraph, any other Contracting State may request from that State the reimbursement of similar fees and costs.

Article 27

The provisions of the present Convention shall not prevent a Contracting State from—

(a) declaring that Letters of Request may be transmitted to its judicial authorities through channels other than those provided for in Article 2;

(b) permitting, by internal law or practice, any act provided for in this Convention to be performed upon less restrictive conditions;

(c) permitting, by internal law or practice, methods of taking evidence other than those provided for in this Convention.

Article 28

The present Convention shall not prevent an agreement between any two or more Contracting States to derogate from—

(a) the provisions of Article 2 with respect to methods of transmitting Letters of Request;

(b) the provisions of Article 4 with respect to the languages which may be used;

(c) the provisions of Article 8 with respect to the presence of judicial personnel at the execution of Letters;

(d) the provisions of Article 11 with respect to the privileges and duties of witnesses to refuse to give evidence;

(e) the provisions of Article 13 with respect to the methods of returning executed Letters to the requesting authority;

(f) the provisions of Article 14 with respect to fees and costs;

(g) the provisions of Chapter II.

* * *

Article 33

A State may, at the time of signature, ratification or accession exclude, in whole or in part, the application of the provisions of paragraph 2 of Article 4 and of Chapter II. No other reservation shall be permitted.

Each Contracting State may at any time withdraw a reservation it has made; the reservation shall cease to have effect on the sixtieth day after notification of the withdrawal.

When a State has made a reservation, any other State affected thereby may apply the same rule against the reserving State.

Article 34

A State may at any time withdraw or modify a declaration.

Article 35

A Contracting State shall, at the time of the deposit of its instrument of ratification or accession, or at a later date, inform the Ministry of Foreign Affairs of the Netherlands of the designation of authorities, pursuant to Articles 2, 8, 24 and 25.

A Contracting State shall likewise inform the Ministry, where appropriate, of the following—

(a) the designation of the authorities to whom notice must be given, whose permission may be required, and whose assistance may be invoked in the taking of evidence by diplomatic officers and consular agents, pursuant to Articles 15, 16 and 18 respectively;

(b) the designation of the authorities whose permission may be required in the taking of evidence by commissioners pursuant to Article 17 and of those who may grant the assistance provided for in Article 18;

(c) declarations pursuant to Articles 4, 8, 11, 15, 16, 17, 18, 23 and 27;

(d) any withdrawal or modification of the above designations and declarations;

(e) the withdrawal of any reservation.

Article 36

Any difficulties which may arise between Contracting States in connection with the operation of this Convention shall be settled through diplomatic channels.

* * *

HAGUE EVIDENCE CONVENTION

Declarations pursuant to Article 23

Standard Declaration (made by all states except the United States, Czechoslovakia, and Israel, and those states following the British example):

[The Federal Republic of Germany] declares in pursuance of Article 23 of the Convention that it will not, in its territory, execute Letters of Request issued for the purpose of obtaining pre-trial discovery of documents as known in Common Law countries.

British Declaration (made by the United Kingdom and Singapore):

In accordance with Article 23 Her Majesty's Government declare that the United Kingdom will not execute Letters of Request issued for the purpose of obtaining pre-trial discovery of documents. Her Majesty's Government further declare that Her Majesty's Government understand "Letters of Request issued for the purpose of obtaining pre-trial discovery of documents" for the purposes of the foregoing Declaration as including any Letter of Request which requires a person:—

a. to state what documents relevant to the proceedings to which the Letter of Request relates are, or have been, in his possession, custody, or power; or

b. to produce any documents other than particular documents specified in the Letter of Request as being documents appearing to the requesting court to be, or to be likely to be, in his possession, custody or power.

Letter from Ministry of Justice Federal Republic of Germany

(October 16, 1990)

... With reference to the issuance of an order concerning discovery of documents pursuant to Section 14(2) of the German Law for the Implementation of the Hague Evidence Convention of 1970, I hereby inform you that there is hardly any prospect for the issuance of such an order. It can only be suggested to counsel for German firms which are supposed to produce documents to apply to the American court for appointment of a commissioner, so that the document production in Germany may take place in accordance with the rules of the judicial administration of the respective states ...

MODEL FOR LETTERS OF REQUEST RECOMMENDED FOR USE IN APPLYING THE HAGUE CONVENTION OF 18 MARCH 1970 ON THE TAKING OF EVIDENCE ABROAD IN CIVIL OR COMMERCIAL MATTERS

Request for International Judicial Assistance Pursuant to the Hague Convention of 18 March 1970 on the Taking of Evidence in Civil or Commercial Matters

N.B. Under the first paragraph of article 4, the Letter of Request shall be in the language of the authority requested to execute it or be accompanied by a translation into that language. However, the provisions of the second and third paragraphs may permit use of other languages.

In order to avoid confusion, please spell out the name of the month in each date.

I. *(Items to be included in all Letters of Request.)*

1. Sender ____*(identity and address)*____
   ____
   ____

2. Central Authority of the Requested State ____*(identity and address)*____
   ____
   ____

3. Person to whom the executed request is to be returned ____*(identity and address)*____
   ____
   ____

II. *(Items to be included in all Letters of Request.)*

4. In conformity with article 3 of the Convention, the undersigned applicant has the honour to submit the following request:

   5. a. Requesting judicial authority (article 3, a) ____*(identity and address)*____
      ____
      ____

      b. To the competent authority of (article 3, a) ____*(the requested State)*____
      ____
      ____

6. Names and addresses of the parties and their representatives (article 3, b)
   a. Plaintiff ______________________
   b. Defendant ______________________
   c. Other parties ______________________

7. Nature and purpose of the proceedings and summary of the facts (article 3, c) ______________________

8. Evidence to be obtained or other judicial act to be performed (article 3, d) ______________________

III. *(Items to be completed where applicable.)*

9. Identity and address of any person to be examined (article 3, e) ______________________

10. Questions to be put to the persons to be examined or statement of the subject-matter about which they are to be examined (article 3, f) ______________________ *(or see attached list)* ______________________

11. Documents or other property to be inspected (article 3, g) ______________________ *(specify whether it is to be produced, copied, valued, etc.)* ______________________

12. Any requirement that the evidence be given on oath or affirmation and any special form to be used (article 3, h) ______________________ *(In the event that the evidence cannot be taken in the manner requested, specify whether it is to be taken in such manner as provided by local law for the formal taking of evidence.)* ______________________

13. Special methods or procedure to be followed (articles 3, i and 9) ______________________

14. Request for notification of the time and place for the execution of the Request and identity and address of any person to be notified (article 7) ______________________

15. Request for attendance or participation of judicial personnel of the requesting authority at the execution of the letter of Request ______________________
16. Specification of privilege or duty to refuse to give evidence under the law of the State of origin (article 11, b) ______________________
17. The fees and costs incurred which are reimbursable under the second paragraph of article 14 or under article 26 of the Convention will be borne by ____*(identity and address)*____

IV. *(Items to be included in all Letters of Request.)*

18. Date of request ______________________
19. Signature and seal of the requesting authority ______________________

Document 7

Convention on Choice of Court Agreements, Hague Conference on Private International Law, 30 June 2005

The States Parties to the present Convention,

Desiring to promote international trade and investment through enhanced judicial co-operation,

Believing that such co-operation can be enhanced by uniform rules on jurisdiction and on recognition and enforcement of foreign judgments in civil or commercial matters,

Believing that such enhanced co-operation requires in particular an international legal regime that provides certainty and ensures the effectiveness of exclusive choice of court agreements between parties to commercial transactions and that governs the recognition and enforcement of judgments resulting from proceedings based on such agreements,

Have resolved to conclude this Convention and have agreed upon the following provisions—

CHAPTER I — SCOPE AND DEFINITIONS

Article 1 Scope

1. This Convention shall apply in international cases to exclusive choice of court agreements concluded in civil or commercial matters.

2. For the purposes of Chapter II, a case is international unless the parties are resident in the same Contracting State and the relationship of the parties and all other elements relevant to the dispute, regardless of the location of the chosen court, are connected only with that State.

3. For the purposes of Chapter III, a case is international where recognition or enforcement of a foreign judgment is sought.

Article 2 Exclusions from scope

1. This Convention shall not apply to exclusive choice of court agreements—

a) to which a natural person acting primarily for personal, family or household purposes (a consumer) is a party;

b) relating to contracts of employment, including collective agreements.

2. This Convention shall not apply to the following matters—

a) the status and legal capacity of natural persons;

b) maintenance obligations;

c) other family law matters, including matrimonial property regimes and other rights or obligations arising out of marriage or similar relationships;

d) wills and succession;

e) insolvency, composition and analogous matters;

f) the carriage of passengers and goods;

g) marine pollution, limitation of liability for maritime claims, general average, and emergency towage and salvage;

h) anti-trust (competition) matters;

i) liability for nuclear damage;

j) claims for personal injury brought by or on behalf of natural persons;

k) tort or delict claims for damage to tangible property that do not arise from a contractual relationship;

l) rights *in rem* in immovable property, and tenancies of immovable property;

m) the validity, nullity, or dissolution of legal persons, and the validity of decisions of their organs;

n) the validity of intellectual property rights other than copyright and related rights;

o) infringement of intellectual property rights other than copyright and related rights, except where infringement proceedings are brought for breach of a contract between the parties relating to such rights, or could have been brought for breach of that contract;

p) the validity of entries in public registers.

3. Notwithstanding paragraph 2, proceedings are not excluded from the scope of this Convention where a matter excluded under that paragraph arises merely as a preliminary question and not as an object of the proceedings. In particular, the mere fact that a matter excluded under paragraph 2 arises by way of defence does not exclude proceedings from the Convention, if that matter is not an object of the proceedings.

4. This Convention shall not apply to arbitration and related proceedings.

5. Proceedings are not excluded from the scope of this Convention by the mere fact that a State, including a government, a governmental agency or any person acting for a State, is a party thereto.

6. Nothing in this Convention shall affect privileges and immunities of States or of international organisations, in respect of themselves and of their property.

Article 3 Exclusive choice of court agreements

For the purposes of this Convention—

a) "exclusive choice of court agreement" means an agreement concluded by two or more parties that meets the requirements of paragraph *c)* and designates, for the purpose of deciding disputes which have arisen or may arise in connection with a particular legal relationship, the courts of one Contracting State or one or more specific courts of one Contracting State to the exclusion of the jurisdiction of any other courts;

b) a choice of court agreement which designates the courts of one Contracting State or one or more specific courts of one Contracting State shall be deemed to be exclusive unless the parties have expressly provided otherwise;

c) an exclusive choice of court agreement must be concluded or documented—

i) in writing; or

ii) by any other means of communication which renders information accessible so as to be usable for subsequent reference;

d) an exclusive choice of court agreement that forms part of a contract shall be treated as an agreement independent of the other terms of the contract. The validity of the exclusive choice of court agreement cannot be contested solely on the ground that the contract is not valid.

Article 4 Other definitions

1. In this Convention, "judgment" means any decision on the merits given by a court, whatever it may be called, including a decree or order, and a determination of costs or expenses by the court (including an officer of the court), provided that the determination relates to a decision on the merits which may be recognised or enforced under this Convention. An interim measure of protection is not a judgment.

2. For the purposes of this Convention, an entity or person other than a natural person shall be considered to be resident in the State—

a) where it has its statutory seat;

b) under whose law it was incorporated or formed;

c) where it has its central administration; or

d) where it has its principal place of business.

CHAPTER II — JURISDICTION

Article 5 Jurisdiction of the chosen court

1. The court or courts of a Contracting State designated in an exclusive choice of court agreement shall have jurisdiction to decide a

dispute to which the agreement applies, unless the agreement is null and void under the law of that State.

2. A court that has jurisdiction under paragraph 1 shall not decline to exercise jurisdiction on the ground that the dispute should be decided in a court of another State.

3. The preceding paragraphs shall not affect rules—

a) on jurisdiction related to subject matter or to the value of the claim;

b) on the internal allocation of jurisdiction among the courts of a Contracting State. However, where the chosen court has discretion as to whether to transfer a case, due consideration should be given to the choice of the parties.

Article 6 Obligations of a court not chosen

A court of a Contracting State other than that of the chosen court shall suspend or dismiss proceedings to which an exclusive choice of court agreement applies unless—

a) the agreement is null and void under the law of the State of the chosen court;

b) a party lacked the capacity to conclude the agreement under the law of the State of the court seised;

c) giving effect to the agreement would lead to a manifest injustice or would be manifestly contrary to the public policy of the State of the court seised;

d) for exceptional reasons beyond the control of the parties, the agreement cannot reasonably be performed; or

e) the chosen court has decided not to hear the case.

Article 7 Interim measures of protection

Interim measures of protection are not governed by this Convention. This Convention neither requires nor precludes the grant, refusal or termination of interim measures of protection by a court of a Contracting State and does not affect whether or not a party may request or a court should grant, refuse or terminate such measures.

CHAPTER III — RECOGNITION AND ENFORCEMENT

Article 8 Recognition and enforcement

1. A judgment given by a court of a Contracting State designated in an exclusive choice of court agreement shall be recognised and enforced in other Contracting States in accordance with this Chapter. Recognition or enforcement may be refused only on the grounds specified in this Convention.

2. Without prejudice to such review as is necessary for the application of the provisions of this Chapter, there shall be no review of the

merits of the judgment given by the court of origin. The court addressed shall be bound by the findings of fact on which the court of origin based its jurisdiction, unless the judgment was given by default.

3. A judgment shall be recognised only if it has effect in the State of origin, and shall be enforced only if it is enforceable in the State of origin.

4. Recognition or enforcement may be postponed or refused if the judgment is the subject of review in the State of origin or if the time limit for seeking ordinary review has not expired. A refusal does not prevent a subsequent application for recognition or enforcement of the judgment.

5. This Article shall also apply to a judgment given by a court of a Contracting State pursuant to a transfer of the case from the chosen court in that Contracting State as permitted by Article 5, paragraph 3. However, where the chosen court had discretion as to whether to transfer the case to another court, recognition or enforcement of the judgment may be refused against a party who objected to the transfer in a timely manner in the State of origin.

Article 9 Refusal of recognition or enforcement

Recognition or enforcement may be refused if—

a) the agreement was null and void under the law of the State of the chosen court, unless the chosen court has determined that the agreement is valid;

b) a party lacked the capacity to conclude the agreement under the law of the requested State;

c) the document which instituted the proceedings or an equivalent document, including the essential elements of the claim,

i) was not notified to the defendant in sufficient time and in such a way as to enable him to arrange for his defence, unless the defendant entered an appearance and presented his case without contesting notification in the court of origin, provided that the law of the State of origin permitted notification to be contested; or

ii) was notified to the defendant in the requested State in a manner that is incompatible with fundamental principles of the requested State concerning service of documents;

d) the judgment was obtained by fraud in connection with a matter of procedure;

e) recognition or enforcement would be manifestly incompatible with the public policy of the requested State, including situations where the specific proceedings leading to the judgment were incompatible with fundamental principles of procedural fairness of that State;

f) the judgment is inconsistent with a judgment given in the requested State in a dispute between the same parties; or

g) the judgment is inconsistent with an earlier judgment given in another State between the same parties on the same cause of action, provided that the earlier judgment fulfils the conditions necessary for its recognition in the requested State.

Article 10 Preliminary questions

1. Where a matter excluded under Article 2, paragraph 2, or under Article 21, arose as a preliminary question, the ruling on that question shall not be recognised or enforced under this Convention.

2. Recognition or enforcement of a judgment may be refused if, and to the extent that, the judgment was based on a ruling on a matter excluded under Article 2, paragraph 2.

3. However, in the case of a ruling on the validity of an intellectual property right other than copyright or a related right, recognition or enforcement of a judgment may be refused or postponed under the preceding paragraph only where—

a) that ruling is inconsistent with a judgment or a decision of a competent authority on that matter given in the State under the law of which the intellectual property right arose; or

b) proceedings concerning the validity of the intellectual property right are pending in that State.

4. Recognition or enforcement of a judgment may be refused if, and to the extent that, the judgment was based on a ruling on a matter excluded pursuant to a declaration made by the requested State under Article 21.

Article 11 Damages

1. Recognition or enforcement of a judgment may be refused if, and to the extent that, the judgment awards damages, including exemplary or punitive damages, that do not compensate a party for actual loss or harm suffered.

2. The court addressed shall take into account whether and to what extent the damages awarded by the court of origin serve to cover costs and expenses relating to the proceedings.

Article 12 Judicial settlements (transactions judiciares)

Judicial settlements (*transactions judiciares*) which a court of a Contracting State designated in an exclusive choice of court agreement has approved, or which have been concluded before that court in the course of proceedings, and which are enforceable in the same manner as a judgment in the State of origin, shall be enforced under this Convention in the same manner as a judgment.

Article 13 Documents to be produced

1. The party seeking recognition or applying for enforcement shall produce—

a) a complete and certified copy of the judgment;

b) the exclusive choice of court agreement, a certified copy thereof, or other evidence of its existence;

c) if the judgment was given by default, the original or a certified copy of a document establishing that the document which instituted the proceedings or an equivalent document was notified to the defaulting party;

d) any documents necessary to establish that the judgment has effect or, where applicable, is enforceable in the State of origin;

e) in the case referred to in Article 12, a certificate of a court of the State of origin that the judicial settlement or a part of it is enforceable in the same manner as a judgment in the State of origin.

2. If the terms of the judgment do not permit the court addressed to verify whether the conditions of this Chapter have been complied with, that court may require any necessary documents.

3. An application for recognition or enforcement may be accompanied by a document, issued by a court (including an officer of the court) of the State of origin, in the form recommended and published by the Hague Conference on Private International Law.

4. If the documents referred to in this Article are not in an official language of the requested State, they shall be accompanied by a certified translation into an official language, unless the law of the requested State provides otherwise.

Article 14 Procedure

The procedure for recognition, declaration of enforceability or registration for enforcement, and the enforcement of the judgment, are governed by the law of the requested State unless this Convention provides otherwise. The court addressed shall act expeditiously.

Article 15 Severability

Recognition or enforcement of a severable part of a judgment shall be granted where recognition or enforcement of that part is applied for, or only part of the judgment is capable of being recognised or enforced under this Convention.

CHAPTER IV — GENERAL CLAUSES

Article 16 Transitional provisions

1. This Convention shall apply to exclusive choice of court agreements concluded after its entry into force for the State of the chosen court.

2. This Convention shall not apply to proceedings instituted before its entry into force for the State of the court seised.

Article 17 Contracts of insurance and reinsurance

1. Proceedings under a contract of insurance or reinsurance are not excluded from the scope of this Convention on the ground that the contract of insurance or reinsurance relates to a matter to which this Convention does not apply.

2. Recognition and enforcement of a judgment in respect of liability under the terms of a contract of insurance or reinsurance may not be limited or refused on the ground that the liability under that contract includes liability to indemnify the insured or reinsured in respect of—

a) a matter to which this Convention does not apply; or

b) an award of damages to which Article 11 might apply.

Article 18 No legalisation

All documents forwarded or delivered under this Convention shall be exempt from legalisation or any analogous formality, including an Apostille.

Article 19 Declarations limiting jurisdiction

A State may declare that its courts may refuse to determine disputes to which an exclusive choice of court agreement applies if, except for the location of the chosen court, there is no connection between that State and the parties or the dispute.

Article 20 Declarations limiting recognition and enforcement

A State may declare that its courts may refuse to recognise or enforce a judgment given by a court of another Contracting State if the parties were resident in the requested State, and the relationship of the parties and all other elements relevant to the dispute, other than the location of the chosen court, were connected only with the requested State.

Article 21 Declarations with respect to specific matters

1. Where a State has a strong interest in not applying this Convention to a specific matter, that State may declare that it will not apply the Convention to that matter. The State making such a declaration shall ensure that the declaration is no broader than necessary and that the specific matter excluded is clearly and precisely defined.

2. With regard to that matter, the Convention shall not apply—

a) in the Contracting State that made the declaration;

b) in other Contracting States, where an exclusive choice of court agreement designates the courts, or one or more specific courts, of the State that made the declaration.

Article 22 Reciprocal declarations on non-exclusive choice of court agreements

1. A Contracting State may declare that its courts will recognise and enforce judgments given by courts of other Contracting States designated

in a choice of court agreement concluded by two or more parties that meets the requirements of Article 3, paragraph *c)*, and designates, for the purpose of deciding disputes which have arisen or may arise in connection with a particular legal relationship, a court or courts of one or more Contracting States (a non-exclusive choice of court agreement).

2. Where recognition or enforcement of a judgment given in a Contracting State that has made such a declaration is sought in another Contracting State that has made such a declaration, the judgment shall be recognised and enforced under this Convention, if—

a) the court of origin was designated in a non-exclusive choice of court agreement;

b) there exists neither a judgment given by any other court before which proceedings could be brought in accordance with the non-exclusive choice of court agreement, nor a proceeding pending between the same parties in any other such court on the same cause of action; and

c) the court of origin was the court first seised.

Article 23 Uniform interpretation

In the interpretation of this Convention, regard shall be had to its international character and to the need to promote uniformity in its application.

Article 24 Review of operation of the Convention

The Secretary General of the Hague Conference on Private International Law shall at regular intervals make arrangements for—

a) review of the operation of this Convention, including any declarations; and

b) consideration of whether any amendments to this Convention are desirable.

Article 25 Non-unified legal systems

1. In relation to a Contracting State in which two or more systems of law apply in different territorial units with regard to any matter dealt with in this Convention—

a) any reference to the law or procedure of a State shall be construed as referring, where appropriate, to the law or procedure in force in the relevant territorial unit;

b) any reference to residence in a State shall be construed as referring, where appropriate, to residence in the relevant territorial unit;

c) any reference to the court or courts of a State shall be construed as referring, where appropriate, to the court or courts in the relevant territorial unit;

d) any reference to a connection with a State shall be construed as referring, where appropriate, to a connection with the relevant territorial unit.

2. Notwithstanding the preceding paragraph, a Contracting State with two or more territorial units in which different systems of law apply shall not be bound to apply this Convention to situations which involve solely such different territorial units.

3. A court in a territorial unit of a Contracting State with two or more territorial units in which different systems of law apply shall not be bound to recognise or enforce a judgment from another Contracting State solely because the judgment has been recognised or enforced in another territorial unit of the same Contracting State under this Convention.

4. This Article shall not apply to a Regional Economic Integration Organisation.

Article 26 Relationship with other international instruments

1. This Convention shall be interpreted so far as possible to be compatible with other treaties in force for Contracting States, whether concluded before or after this Convention.

2. This Convention shall not affect the application by a Contracting State of a treaty, whether concluded before or after this Convention, in cases where none of the parties is resident in a Contracting State that is not a Party to the treaty.

3. This Convention shall not affect the application by a Contracting State of a treaty that was concluded before this Convention entered into force for that Contracting State, if applying this Convention would be inconsistent with the obligations of that Contracting State to any non-Contracting State. This paragraph shall also apply to treaties that revise or replace a treaty concluded before this Convention entered into force for that Contracting State, except to the extent that the revision or replacement creates new inconsistencies with this Convention.

4. This Convention shall not affect the application by a Contracting State of a treaty, whether concluded before or after this Convention, for the purposes of obtaining recognition or enforcement of a judgment given by a court of a Contracting State that is also a Party to that treaty. However, the judgment shall not be recognised or enforced to a lesser extent than under this Convention.

5. This Convention shall not affect the application by a Contracting State of a treaty which, in relation to a specific matter, governs jurisdiction or the recognition or enforcement of judgments, even if concluded after this Convention and even if all States concerned are Parties to this Convention. This paragraph shall apply only if the Contracting State has made a declaration in respect of the treaty under this paragraph. In the case of such a declaration, other Contracting States shall not be obliged to apply this Convention to that specific matter to the extent of any inconsis-

tency, where an exclusive choice of court agreement designates the courts, or one or more specific courts, of the Contracting State that made the declaration.

6. This Convention shall not affect the application of the rules of a Regional Economic Integration Organisation that is a Party to this Convention, whether adopted before or after this Convention—

a) where none of the parties is resident in a Contracting State that is not a Member State of the Regional Economic Integration Organisation;

b) as concerns the recognition or enforcement of judgments as between Member States of the Regional Economic Integration Organisation.

CHAPTER V — FINAL CLAUSES

Article 27 Signature, ratification, acceptance, approval or accession

1. This Convention is open for signature by all States.

2. This Convention is subject to ratification, acceptance or approval by the signatory States.

3. This Convention is open for accession by all States.

4. Instruments of ratification, acceptance, approval or accession shall be deposited with the Ministry of Foreign Affairs of the Kingdom of the Netherlands, depositary of the Convention.

Article 28 Declarations with respect to non-unified legal systems

1. If a State has two or more territorial units in which different systems of law apply in relation to matters dealt with in this Convention, it may at the time of signature, ratification, acceptance, approval or accession declare that the Convention shall extend to all its territorial units or only to one or more of them and may modify this declaration by submitting another declaration at any time.

2. A declaration shall be notified to the depositary and shall state expressly the territorial units to which the Convention applies.

3. If a State makes no declaration under this Article, the Convention shall extend to all territorial units of that State.

4. This Article shall not apply to a Regional Economic Integration Organisation.

Article 29 Regional Economic Integration Organisations

1. A Regional Economic Integration Organisation which is constituted solely by sovereign States and has competence over some or all of the matters governed by this Convention may similarly sign, accept, approve or accede to this Convention. The Regional Economic Integration Organisation shall in that case have the rights and obligations of a Contracting State, to the extent that the Organisation has competence over matters governed by this Convention.

2. The Regional Economic Integration Organisation shall, at the time of signature, acceptance, approval or accession, notify the depositary in writing of the matters governed by this Convention in respect of which competence has been transferred to that Organisation by its Member States. The Organisation shall promptly notify the depositary in writing of any changes to its competence as specified in the most recent notice given under this paragraph.

3. For the purposes of the entry into force of this Convention, any instrument deposited by a Regional Economic Integration Organisation shall not be counted unless the Regional Economic Integration Organisation declares in accordance with Article 30 that its Member States will not be Parties to this Convention.

4. Any reference to a "Contracting State" or "State" in this Convention shall apply equally, where appropriate, to a Regional Economic Integration Organisation that is a Party to it.

Article 30 Accession by a Regional Economic Integration Organisation without its Member States

1. At the time of signature, acceptance, approval or accession, a Regional Economic Integration Organisation may declare that it exercises competence over all the matters governed by this Convention and that its Member States will not be Parties to this Convention but shall be bound by virtue of the signature, acceptance, approval or accession of the Organisation.

2. In the event that a declaration is made by a Regional Economic Integration Organisation in accordance with paragraph 1, any reference to a "Contracting State" or "State" in this Convention shall apply equally, where appropriate, to the Member States of the Organisation.

Article 31 Entry into force

1. This Convention shall enter into force on the first day of the month following the expiration of three months after the deposit of the second instrument of ratification, acceptance, approval or accession referred to in Article 27.

2. Thereafter this Convention shall enter into force—

a) for each State or Regional Economic Integration Organisation subsequently ratifying, accepting, approving or acceding to it, on the first day of the month following the expiration of three months after the deposit of its instrument of ratification, acceptance, approval or accession;

b) for a territorial unit to which this Convention has been extended in accordance with Article 28, paragraph 1, on the first day of the month following the expiration of three months after the notification of the declaration referred to in that Article.

Article 32 Declarations

1. Declarations referred to in Articles 19, 20, 21, 22 and 26 may be made upon signature, ratification, acceptance, approval or accession or at any time thereafter, and may be modified or withdrawn at any time.

2. Declarations, modifications and withdrawals shall be notified to the depositary.

3. A declaration made at the time of signature, ratification, acceptance, approval or accession shall take effect simultaneously with the entry into force of this Convention for the State concerned.

4. A declaration made at a subsequent time, and any modification or withdrawal of a declaration, shall take effect on the first day of the month following the expiration of three months after the date on which the notification is received by the depositary.

5. A declaration under Articles 19, 20, 21 and 26 shall not apply to exclusive choice of court agreements concluded before it takes effect.

Article 33 Denunciation

1. This Convention may be denounced by notification in writing to the depositary. The denunciation may be limited to certain territorial units of a non-unified legal system to which this Convention applies.

2. The denunciation shall take effect on the first day of the month following the expiration of twelve months after the date on which the notification is received by the depositary. Where a longer period for the denunciation to take effect is specified in the notification, the denunciation shall take effect upon the expiration of such longer period after the date on which the notification is received by the depositary.

Article 34 Notifications by the depositary

The depositary shall notify the Members of the Hague Conference on Private International Law, and other States and Regional Economic Integration Organisations which have signed, ratified, accepted, approved or acceded in accordance with Articles 27, 29 and 30 of the following—

a) the signatures, ratifications, acceptances, approvals and accessions referred to in Articles 27, 29 and 30;

b) the date on which this Convention enters into force in accordance with Article 31;

c) the notifications, declarations, modifications and withdrawals of declarations referred to in Articles 19, 20, 21, 22, 26, 28, 29 and 30;

d) the denunciations referred to in Article 33.

In witness whereof the undersigned, being duly authorised thereto, have signed this Convention.

Done at The Hague, on 30 June 2005, in the English and French languages, both texts being equally authentic, in a single copy which shall be deposited in the archives of the Government of the Kingdom of the

Netherlands, and of which a certified copy shall be sent, through diplomatic channels, to each of the Member States of the Hague Conference on Private International Law as of the date of its Twentieth Session and to each State which participated in that Session.

B. The following Recommendation relating to the Convention on Choice of Court Agreements—

The Twentieth Session

Recommends to the States Parties to the *Convention on Choice of Court Agreements* to use the following form confirming the issuance and content of a judgment given by the court of origin for the purposes of recognition and enforcement under the Convention—

RECOMMENDED FORM UNDER THE CONVENTION ON CHOICE OF COURT AGREEMENTS ("THE CONVENTION")

(Sample form confirming the issuance and content of a judgment given by the court of origin for the purposes of recognition and enforcement under the Convention)

1. (THE COURT OF ORIGIN) ....

ADDRESS ....

TEL. ....

FAX ....

E–MAIL ....

2. CASE/DOCKET NUMBER ....

3. .... (PLAINTIFF)

v.

.... (DEFENDANT)

4. (THE COURT OF ORIGIN) gave a judgment in the above-captioned matter on (DATE) in (CITY, STATE).

5. This court was designated in an exclusive choice of court agreement within the meaning of Article 3 of the Convention:

YES NO

UNABLE TO CONFIRM

6. If yes, the exclusive choice of court agreement was concluded or documented in the following manner:

7. This court awarded the following payment of money *(please indicate, where applicable, any relevant categories of damages included)*:

8. This court awarded interest as follows *(please specify the rate(s) of interest, the portion(s) of the award to which interest applies, the date from which interest is computed, and any further information regarding interest that would assist the court addressed)*:

9. This court included within the judgment the following costs and expenses relating to the proceedings *(please specify the amounts of any such awards, including, where applicable, any amount(s) within a monetary award intended to cover costs and expenses relating to the proceedings)*:

10. This court awarded the following non-monetary relief *(please describe the nature of such relief)*:

11. This judgment is enforceable in the State of origin:

YES NO

UNABLE TO CONFIRM

12. This judgment (or a part thereof) is currently the subject of review in the State of origin:

YES NO

UNABLE TO CONFIRM

If "yes" please specify the nature and status of such review:

13. Any other relevant information:

14. Attached to this form are the documents marked in the following list *(if available)*:

a complete and certified copy of the judgment;

the exclusive choice of court agreement, a certified copy thereof, or other evidence of its existence;

if the judgment was given by default, the original or a certified copy of a document establishing that the document which instituted the proceedings or an equivalent document was notified to the defaulting party;

any documents necessary to establish that the judgment has effect or, where applicable, is enforceable in the State of origin;

(list if applicable):

in the case referred to in Article 12 of the Convention, a certificate of a court of the State of origin that the judicial settlement or a part of it is enforceable in the same manner as a judgment in the State of origin;

other documents: . . . .

15. Dated this . . . . .day of . . . ., 20. . . at . . . .

16. Signature and / or stamp by the court or officer of the court:

CONTACT PERSON:

TEL.:

FAX:

E–MAIL:

Document 8

Agreement Establishing the World Trade Organization (Selected Provisions)

The *Parties* to this Agreement,

Recognizing that their relations in the field of trade and economic endeavour should be conducted with a view to raising standards of living, ensuring full employment and a large and steadily growing volume of real income and effective demand, and expanding the production of and trade in goods and services, while allowing for the optimal use of the world's resources in accordance with the objective of sustainable development, seeking both to protect and preserve the environment and to enhance the means for doing so in a manner consistent with their respective needs and concerns at different levels of economic development,

Recognizing further that there is need for positive efforts designed to ensure that developing countries, and especially the least developed among them, secure a share in the growth in international trade commensurate with the needs of their economic development,

Being desirous of contributing to these objectives by entering into reciprocal and mutually advantageous arrangements directed to the substantial reduction of tariffs and other barriers to trade and to the elimination of discriminatory treatment in international trade relations,

Resolved, therefore, to develop an integrated, more viable and durable multilateral trading system encompassing the General Agreement on Tariffs and Trade, the results of past trade liberalization efforts, and all of the results of the Uruguay Round of Multilateral Trade Negotiations,

Determined to preserve the basic principles and to further the objectives underlying this multilateral trading system,

Agree as follows:

Article I

Establishment of the Organization

The World Trade Organization (hereinafter referred to as "the WTO") is hereby established.

Article II

Scope of the WTO

1. The WTO shall provide the common institutional framework for the conduct of trade relations among its Members in matters related to

the agreements and associated legal instruments included in the Annexes to this Agreement.

2. The agreements and associated legal instruments included in Annexes 1, 2 and 3 (hereinafter referred to as "Multilateral Trade Agreements") are integral parts of this Agreement, binding on all Members.

3. The agreements and associated legal instruments included in Annex 4 (hereinafter referred to as "Plurilateral Trade Agreements") are also part of this Agreement for those Members that have accepted them, and are binding on those Members. The Plurilateral Trade Agreements do not create either obligations or rights for Members that have not accepted them.

4. The General Agreement on Tariffs and Trade 1994 as specified in Annex 1A (hereinafter referred to as "GATT 1994") is legally distinct from the General Agreement on Tariffs and Trade, dated 30 October 1947, annexed to the Final Act Adopted at the Conclusion of the Second Session of the Preparatory Committee of the United Nations Conference on Trade and Employment, as subsequently rectified, amended or modified (hereinafter referred to as "GATT 1947").

Article III

Functions of the WTO

1. The WTO shall facilitate the implementation, administration and operation, and further the objectives, of this Agreement and of the Multilateral Trade Agreements, and shall also provide the framework for the implementation, administration and operation of the Plurilateral Trade Agreements.

2. The WTO shall provide the forum for negotiations among its Members concerning their multilateral trade relations in matters dealt with under the agreements in the Annexes to this Agreement. The WTO may also provide a forum for further negotiations among its Members concerning their multilateral trade relations, and a framework for the implementation of the results of such negotiations, as may be decided by the Ministerial Conference.

3. The WTO shall administer the Understanding on Rules and Procedures Governing the Settlement of Disputes (hereinafter referred to as the "Dispute Settlement Understanding" or "DSU") in Annex 2 to this Agreement.

4. The WTO shall administer the Trade Policy Review Mechanism (hereinafter referred to as the "TPRM") provided for in Annex 3 to this Agreement.

5. With a view to achieving greater coherence in global economic policymaking, the WTO shall cooperate, as appropriate, with the International Monetary Fund and with the International Bank for Reconstruction and Development and its affiliated agencies.

Article IV

Structure of the WTO

1. There shall be a Ministerial Conference composed of representatives of all the Members, which shall meet at least once every two years. The Ministerial Conference shall carry out the functions of the WTO and take actions necessary to this effect. The Ministerial Conference shall have the authority to take decisions on all matters under any of the Multilateral Trade Agreements, if so requested by a Member, in accordance with the specific requirements for decision-making in this Agreement and in the relevant Multilateral Trade Agreement.

2. There shall be a General Council composed of representatives of all the Members, which shall meet as appropriate. In the intervals between meetings of the Ministerial Conference, its functions shall be conducted by the General Council. The General Council shall also carry out the functions assigned to it by this Agreement. The General Council shall establish its rules of procedure and approve the rules of procedure for the Committees provided for in paragraph 7.

3. The General Council shall convene as appropriate to discharge the responsibilities of the Dispute Settlement Body provided for in the Dispute Settlement Understanding. The Dispute Settlement Body may have its own chairman and shall establish such rules of procedure as it deems necessary for the fulfilment of those responsibilities.

4. The General Council shall convene as appropriate to discharge the responsibilities of the Trade Policy Review Body provided for in the TPRM. The Trade Policy Review Body may have its own chairman and shall establish such rules of procedure as it deems necessary for the fulfilment of those responsibilities.

5. There shall be a Council for Trade in Goods, a Council for Trade in Services and a Council for Trade–Related Aspects of Intellectual Property Rights (hereinafter referred to as the "Council for TRIPS"), which shall operate under the general guidance of the General Council. The Council for Trade in Goods shall oversee the functioning of the Multilateral Trade Agreements in Annex 1A. The Council for Trade in Services shall oversee the functioning of the General Agreement on Trade in Services (hereinafter referred to as "GATS"). The Council for TRIPS shall oversee the functioning of the Agreement on Trade–Related Aspects of Intellectual Property Rights (hereinafter referred to as the "Agreement on TRIPS"). These Councils shall carry out the functions assigned to them by their respective agreements and by the General Council. They shall establish their respective rules of procedure subject to the approval of the General Council. Membership in these Councils shall be open to representatives of all Members. These Councils shall meet as necessary to carry out their functions.

* * *

Article V

Relations With Other Organizations

* * *

Article VI

The Secretariat

* * *

Article VII

Budget and Contributions

* * *

Article VIII

Status of the WTO

* * *

Article IX

Decision–Making

1. The WTO shall continue the practice of decision-making by consensus followed under GATT 1947.[1] Except as otherwise provided, where a decision cannot be arrived at by consensus, the matter at issue shall be decided by voting. At meetings of the Ministerial Conference and the General Council, each Member of the WTO shall have one vote. Where the European Communities exercise their right to vote, they shall have a number of votes equal to the number of their member States [2] which are Members of the WTO. Decisions of the Ministerial Conference and the General Council shall be taken by a majority of the votes cast, unless otherwise provided in this Agreement or in the relevant Multilateral Trade Agreement.[3]

2. The Ministerial Conference and the General Council shall have the exclusive authority to adopt interpretations of this Agreement and of the Multilateral Trade Agreements. In the case of an interpretation of a Multilateral Trade Agreement in Annex 1, they shall exercise their authority on the basis of a recommendation by the Council overseeing the functioning of that Agreement. The decision to adopt an interpretation shall be taken by a three-fourths majority of the Members. This para-

1. The body concerned shall be deemed to have decided by consensus on a matter submitted for its consideration, if no Member, present at the meeting when the decision is taken, formally objects to the proposed decision.

2. The number of votes of the European Communities and their member States shall in no case exceed the number of the member States of the European Communities.

3. Decisions by the General Council when convened as the Dispute Settlement Body shall be taken only in accordance with the provisions of paragraph 4 of Article 2 of the Dispute Settlement Understanding.

graph shall not be used in a manner that would undermine the amendment provisions in Article X.

3. In exceptional circumstances, the Ministerial Conference may decide to waive an obligation imposed on a Member by this Agreement or any of the Multilateral Trade Agreements, provided that any such decision shall be taken by three fourths [4] of the Members unless otherwise provided for in this paragraph.

(a) A request for a waiver concerning this Agreement shall be submitted to the Ministerial Conference for consideration pursuant to the practice of decision-making by consensus. The Ministerial Conference shall establish a time-period, which shall not exceed 90 days, to consider the request. If consensus is not reached during the time-period, any decision to grant a waiver shall be taken by three fourths of the Members.

(b) A request for a waiver concerning the Multilateral Trade Agreements in Annexes 1A or 1B or 1C and their annexes shall be submitted initially to the Council for Trade in Goods, the Council for Trade in Services or the Council for TRIPS, respectively, for consideration during a time-period which shall not exceed 90 days. At the end of the time-period, the relevant Council shall submit a report to the Ministerial Conference.

4. A decision by the Ministerial Conference granting a waiver shall state the exceptional circumstances justifying the decision, the terms and conditions governing the application of the waiver, and the date on which the waiver shall terminate. Any waiver granted for a period of more than one year shall be reviewed by the Ministerial Conference not later than one year after it is granted, and thereafter annually until the waiver terminates. In each review, the Ministerial Conference shall examine whether the exceptional circumstances justifying the waiver still exist and whether the terms and conditions attached to the waiver have been met. The Ministerial Conference, on the basis of the annual review, may extend, modify or terminate the waiver.

5. Decisions under a Plurilateral Trade Agreement, including any decisions on interpretations and waivers, shall be governed by the provisions of that Agreement.

Article X

Amendment

1. Any Member of the WTO may initiate a proposal to amend the provisions of this Agreement or the Multilateral Trade Agreements in Annex 1 by submitting such proposal to the Ministerial Conference. The Councils listed in paragraph 5 of Article IV may also submit to the Ministerial Conference proposals to amend the provisions of the corre-

4. A decision to grant a waiver in respect of any obligation subject to a transition period or a period for staged implementation that the requesting Member has not performed by the end of the relevant period shall be taken only by consensus.

sponding Multilateral Trade Agreements in Annex 1 the functioning of which they oversee. Unless the Ministerial Conference decides on a longer period, for a period of 90 days after the proposal has been tabled formally at the Ministerial Conference any decision by the Ministerial Conference to submit the proposed amendment to the Members for acceptance shall be taken by consensus. Unless the provisions of paragraphs 2, 5 or 6 apply, that decision shall specify whether the provisions of paragraphs 3 or 4 shall apply. If consensus is reached, the Ministerial Conference shall forthwith submit the proposed amendment to the Members for acceptance. If consensus is not reached at a meeting of the Ministerial Conference within the established period, the Ministerial Conference shall decide by a two-thirds majority of the Members whether to submit the proposed amendment to the Members for acceptance. Except as provided in paragraphs 2, 5 and 6, the provisions of paragraph 3 shall apply to the proposed amendment, unless the Ministerial Conference decides by a three-fourths majority of the Members that the provisions of paragraph 4 shall apply.

2. Amendments to the provisions of this Article and to the provisions of the following Articles shall take effect only upon acceptance by all Members:

Article IX of this Agreement;

Articles I and II of GATT 1994;

Article II:1 of GATS;

Article 4 of the Agreement on TRIPS.

3. Amendments to provisions of this Agreement, or of the Multilateral Trade Agreements in Annexes 1A and 1C, other than those listed in paragraphs 2 and 6, of a nature that would alter the rights and obligations of the Members, shall take effect for the Members that have accepted them upon acceptance by two thirds of the Members and thereafter for each other Member upon acceptance by it. The Ministerial Conference may decide by a three-fourths majority of the Members that any amendment made effective under this paragraph is of such a nature that any Member which has not accepted it within a period specified by the Ministerial Conference in each case shall be free to withdraw from the WTO or to remain a Member with the consent of the Ministerial Conference.

4. Amendments to provisions of this Agreement or of the Multilateral Trade Agreements in Annexes 1A and 1C, other than those listed in paragraphs 2 and 6, of a nature that would not alter the rights and obligations of the Members, shall take effect for all Members upon acceptance by two thirds of the Members.

5. Except as provided in paragraph 2 above, amendments to Parts I, II and III of GATS and the respective annexes shall take effect for the Members that have accepted them upon acceptance by two thirds of the Members and thereafter for each Member upon acceptance by it. The

Ministerial Conference may decide by a three-fourths majority of the Members that any amendment made effective under the preceding provision is of such a nature that any Member which has not accepted it within a period specified by the Ministerial Conference in each case shall be free to withdraw from the WTO or to remain a Member with the consent of the Ministerial Conference. Amendments to Parts IV, V and VI of GATS and the respective annexes shall take effect for all Members upon acceptance by two thirds of the Members.

6. Notwithstanding the other provisions of this Article, amendments to the Agreement on TRIPS meeting the requirements of paragraph 2 of Article 71 thereof may be adopted by the Ministerial Conference without further formal acceptance process.

7. Any Member accepting an amendment to this Agreement or to a Multilateral Trade Agreement in Annex 1 shall deposit an instrument of acceptance with the Director–General of the WTO within the period of acceptance specified by the Ministerial Conference.

8. Any Member of the WTO may initiate a proposal to amend the provisions of the Multilateral Trade Agreements in Annexes 2 and 3 by submitting such proposal to the Ministerial Conference. The decision to approve amendments to the Multilateral Trade Agreement in Annex 2 shall be made by consensus and these amendments shall take effect for all Members upon approval by the Ministerial Conference. Decisions to approve amendments to the Multilateral Trade Agreement in Annex 3 shall take effect for all Members upon approval by the Ministerial Conference.

9. The Ministerial Conference, upon the request of the Members parties to a trade agreement, may decide exclusively by consensus to add that agreement to Annex 4. The Ministerial Conference, upon the request of the Members parties to a Plurilateral Trade Agreement, may decide to delete that Agreement from Annex 4.

10. Amendments to a Plurilateral Trade Agreement shall be governed by the provisions of that Agreement.

Article XI

Original Membership

1. The contracting parties to GATT 1947 as of the date of entry into force of this Agreement, and the European Communities, which accept this Agreement and the Multilateral Trade Agreements and for which Schedules of Concessions and Commitments are annexed to GATT 1994 and for which Schedules of Specific Commitments are annexed to GATS shall become original Members of the WTO.

2. The least-developed countries recognized as such by the United Nations will only be required to undertake commitments and concessions to the extent consistent with their individual development, financial and trade needs or their administrative and institutional capabilities.

Article XII

Accession

1. Any State or separate customs territory possessing full autonomy in the conduct of its external commercial relations and of the other matters provided for in this Agreement and the Multilateral Trade Agreements may accede to this Agreement, on terms to be agreed between it and the WTO. Such accession shall apply to this Agreement and the Multilateral Trade Agreements annexed thereto.

2. Decisions on accession shall be taken by the Ministerial Conference. The Ministerial Conference shall approve the agreement on the terms of accession by a two-thirds majority of the Members of the WTO.

3. Accession to a Plurilateral Trade Agreement shall be governed by the provisions of that Agreement.

Article XIII

Non–Application of Multilateral Trade Agreements Between Particular Members

1. This Agreement and the Multilateral Trade Agreements in Annexes 1 and 2 shall not apply as between any Member and any other Member if either of the Members, at the time either becomes a Member, does not consent to such application.

2. Paragraph 1 may be invoked between original Members of the WTO which were contracting parties to GATT 1947 only where Article XXXV of that Agreement had been invoked earlier and was effective as between those contracting parties at the time of entry into force for them of this Agreement.

3. Paragraph 1 shall apply between a Member and another Member which has acceded under Article XII only if the Member not consenting to the application has so notified the Ministerial Conference before the approval of the agreement on the terms of accession by the Ministerial Conference.

4. The Ministerial Conference may review the operation of this Article in particular cases at the request of any Member and make appropriate recommendations.

5. Non-application of a Plurilateral Trade Agreement between parties to that Agreement shall be governed by the provisions of that Agreement.

Article XIV

Acceptance, Entry into Force and Deposit

1. This Agreement shall be open for acceptance, by signature or otherwise, by contracting parties to GATT 1947, and the European Communities, which are eligible to become original Members of the WTO in accordance with Article XI of this Agreement. Such acceptance shall

apply to this Agreement and the Multilateral Trade Agreements annexed hereto. This Agreement and the Multilateral Trade Agreements annexed hereto shall enter into force on the date determined by Ministers in accordance with paragraph 3 of the Final Act Embodying the Results of the Uruguay Round of Multilateral Trade Negotiations and shall remain open for acceptance for a period of two years following that date unless the Ministers decide otherwise. An acceptance following the entry into force of this Agreement shall enter into force on the 30th day following the date of such acceptance.

2. A Member which accepts this Agreement after its entry into force shall implement those concessions and obligations in the Multilateral Trade Agreements that are to be implemented over a period of time starting with the entry into force of this Agreement as if it had accepted this Agreement on the date of its entry into force.

3. Until the entry into force of this Agreement, the text of this Agreement and the Multilateral Trade Agreements shall be deposited with the Director–General to the CONTRACTING PARTIES to GATT 1947. The Director–General shall promptly furnish a certified true copy of this Agreement and the Multilateral Trade Agreements, and a notification of each acceptance thereof, to each government and the European Communities having accepted this Agreement. This Agreement and the Multilateral Trade Agreements, and any amendments thereto, shall, upon the entry into force of this Agreement, be deposited with the Director–General of the WTO.

4. The acceptance and entry into force of a Plurilateral Trade Agreement shall be governed by the provisions of that Agreement. Such Agreements shall be deposited with the Director–General to the CONTRACTING PARTIES to GATT 1947. Upon the entry into force of this Agreement, such Agreements shall be deposited with the Director–General of the WTO.

Article XV

Withdrawal

1. Any Member may withdraw from this Agreement. Such withdrawal shall apply both to this Agreement and the Multilateral Trade Agreements and shall take effect upon the expiration of six months from the date on which written notice of withdrawal is received by the Director–General of the WTO.

2. Withdrawal from a Plurilateral Trade Agreement shall be governed by the provisions of that Agreement.

Article XVI

Miscellaneous Provisions

1. Except as otherwise provided under this Agreement or the Multilateral Trade Agreements, the WTO shall be guided by the decisions,

procedures and customary practices followed by the CONTRACTING PARTIES to GATT 1947 and the bodies established in the framework of GATT 1947.

2. To the extent practicable, the Secretariat of GATT 1947 shall become the Secretariat of the WTO, and the Director–General to the CONTRACTING PARTIES to GATT 1947, until such time as the Ministerial Conference has appointed a Director–General in accordance with paragraph 2 of Article VI of this Agreement, shall serve as Director–General of the WTO.

3. In the event of a conflict between a provision of this Agreement and a provision of any of the Multilateral Trade Agreements, the provision of this Agreement shall prevail to the extent of the conflict.

4. Each Member shall ensure the conformity of its laws, regulations and administrative procedures with its obligations as provided in the annexed Agreements.

5. No reservations may be made in respect of any provision of this Agreement. Reservations in respect of any of the provisions of the Multilateral Trade Agreements may only be made to the extent provided for in those Agreements. Reservations in respect of a provision of a Plurilateral Trade Agreement shall be governed by the provisions of that Agreement.

6. This Agreement shall be registered in accordance with the provisions of Article 102 of the Charter of the United Nations.

DONE at Marrakesh this fifteenth day of April one thousand nine hundred and ninety-four, in a single copy, in the English, French and Spanish languages, each text being authentic.

DONE at Marrakesh this fifteenth day of April one thousand nine hundred and ninety-four, in a single copy, in the English, French and Spanish languages, each text being authentic.

Explanatory Notes:

The terms "country" or "countries" as used in this Agreement and the Multilateral Trade Agreements are to be understood to include any separate customs territory Member of the WTO.

In the case of a separate customs territory Member of the WTO, where an expression in this Agreement and the Multilateral Trade Agreements is qualified by the term "national", such expression shall be read as pertaining to that customs territory, unless otherwise specified.

LIST OF ANNEXES

ANNEX 1

ANNEX 1A: Multilateral Agreements on Trade in Goods

General Agreement on Tariffs and Trade 1994

Agreement on Agriculture

Agreement on the Application of Sanitary and Phytosanitary Measures

Agreement on Textiles and Clothing

Agreement on Technical Barriers to Trade

Agreement on Trade–Related Investment Measures

Agreement on Implementation of Article VI of the General Agreement on Tariffs and Trade 1994

Agreement on Implementation of Article VII of the General Agreement on Tariffs and Trade 1994

Agreement on Preshipment Inspection

Agreement on Rules of Origin

Agreement on Import Licensing Procedures

Agreement on Subsidies and Countervailing Measures

Agreement on Safeguards

ANNEX 1B: General Agreement on Trade in Services and Annexes

ANNEX 1C: Agreement on Trade–Related Aspects of Intellectual Property Rights

ANNEX 2

Understanding on Rules and Procedures Governing the Settlement of Disputes

ANNEX 3

Trade Policy Review Mechanism

ANNEX 4

Plurilateral Trade Agreements

Agreement on Trade in Civil Aircraft

Agreement on Government Procurement

International Dairy Agreement

International Bovine Meat Agreement

ANNEX 1A

MULTILATERAL AGREEMENTS ON TRADE IN GOODS

General interpretative note to Annex 1A:

In the event of conflict between a provision of the General Agreement on Tariffs and Trade 1994 and a provision of another agreement in Annex 1A to the Agreement Establishing the World Trade Organization (referred to in the agreements in Annex 1A as the "WTO Agreement"), the provision of the other agreement shall prevail to the extent of the conflict.

DOCUMENT 9

WTO AGREEMENT ON TRADE–RELATED ASPECTS OF INTELLECTUAL PROPERTY RIGHTS (SELECTED PROVISIONS)

Table of Contents

AGREEMENT ON TRADE–RELATED ASPECTS OF INTELLECTUAL PROPERTY RIGHTS

Members,

Desiring to reduce distortions and impediments to international trade, and taking into account the need to promote effective and adequate protection of intellectual property rights, and to ensure that measures and procedures to enforce intellectual property rights do not themselves become barriers to legitimate trade;

Recognizing, to this end, the need for new rules and disciplines concerning:

(a) the applicability of the basic principles of GATT 1994 and of relevant international intellectual property agreements or conventions;

(b) the provision of adequate standards and principles concerning the availability, scope and use of trade-related intellectual property rights;

(c) the provision of effective and appropriate means for the enforcement of trade-related intellectual property rights, taking into account differences in national legal systems;

(d) the provision of effective and expeditious procedures for the multilateral prevention and settlement of disputes between governments; and

(e) transitional arrangements aiming at the fullest participation in the results of the negotiations;

Recognizing the need for a multilateral framework of principles, rules and disciplines dealing with international trade in counterfeit goods;

Recognizing that intellectual property rights are private rights;

Recognizing the underlying public policy objectives of national systems for the protection of intellectual property, including developmental and technological objectives;

Recognizing also the special needs of the least-developed country Members in respect of maximum flexibility in the domestic implementation of laws and regulations in order to enable them to create a sound and viable technological base;

Emphasizing the importance of reducing tensions by reaching strengthened commitments to resolve disputes on trade-related intellectual property issues through multilateral procedures;

Desiring to establish a mutually supportive relationship between the WTO and the World Intellectual Property Organization (referred to in this Agreement as "WIPO") as well as other relevant international organizations;

Hereby agree as follows:

PART I

GENERAL PROVISIONS AND BASIC PRINCIPLES

Article 1

Nature and Scope of Obligations

1. Members shall give effect to the provisions of this Agreement. Members may, but shall not be obliged to, implement in their law more extensive protection than is required by this Agreement, provided that such protection does not contravene the provisions of this Agreement. Members shall be free to determine the appropriate method of implementing the provisions of this Agreement within their own legal system and practice.

2. For the purposes of this Agreement, the term "intellectual property" refers to all categories of intellectual property that are the subject of Sections 1 through 7 of Part II.

3. Members shall accord the treatment provided for in this Agreement to the nationals of other Members.[1] In respect of the relevant intellectual property right, the nationals of other Members shall be understood as those natural or legal persons that would meet the criteria for eligibility for protection provided for in the Paris Convention (1967), the Berne Convention (1971), the Rome Convention and the Treaty on Intellectual Property in Respect of Integrated Circuits, were all Members of the WTO members of those conventions.[2] Any Member availing itself of the possibilities provided in paragraph 3 of Article 5 or paragraph 2 of Article 6 of the Rome Convention shall make a notification as foreseen in those provisions to the Council for Trade–Related Aspects of Intellectual Property Rights (the "Council for TRIPS").

Article 2

Intellectual Property Conventions

1. In respect of Parts II, III and IV of this Agreement, Members shall comply with Articles 1 through 12, and Article 19, of the Paris Convention (1967).

2. Nothing in Parts I to IV of this Agreement shall derogate from existing obligations that Members may have to each other under the Paris

1. When "nationals" are referred to in this Agreement, they shall be deemed, in the case of a separate customs territory Member of the WTO, to mean persons, natural or legal, who are domiciled or who have a real and effective industrial or commercial establishment in that customs territory.

2. In this Agreement, "Paris Convention" refers to the Paris Convention for the Protection of Industrial Property; "Paris Convention (1967)" refers to the Stockholm Act of this Convention of 14 July 1967. "Berne Convention" refers to the Berne Convention for the Protection of Literary and Artistic Works; "Berne Convention (1971)" refers to the Paris Act of this Convention of 24 July 1971. "Rome Convention" refers to the International Convention for the Protection of Performers, Producers of Phonograms and Broadcasting Organizations, adopted at Rome on 26 October 1961. "Treaty on Intellectual Property in Respect of Integrated Circuits" (IPIC Treaty) refers to the Treaty on Intellectual Property in Respect of Integrated Circuits, adopted at Washington on 26 May 1989. "WTO Agreement" refers to the Agreement Establishing the WTO.

Convention, the Berne Convention, the Rome Convention and the Treaty on Intellectual Property in Respect of Integrated Circuits.

Article 3

National Treatment

1. Each Member shall accord to the nationals of other Members treatment no less favourable than that it accords to its own nationals with regard to the protection[3] of intellectual property, subject to the exceptions already provided in, respectively, the Paris Convention (1967), the Berne Convention (1971), the Rome Convention or the Treaty on Intellectual Property in Respect of Integrated Circuits. In respect of performers, producers of phonograms and broadcasting organizations, this obligation only applies in respect of the rights provided under this Agreement. Any Member availing itself of the possibilities provided in Article 6 of the Berne Convention (1971) or paragraph 1(b) of Article 16 of the Rome Convention shall make a notification as foreseen in those provisions to the Council for TRIPS.

2. Members may avail themselves of the exceptions permitted under paragraph 1 in relation to judicial and administrative procedures, including the designation of an address for service or the appointment of an agent within the jurisdiction of a Member, only where such exceptions are necessary to secure compliance with laws and regulations which are not inconsistent with the provisions of this Agreement and where such practices are not applied in a manner which would constitute a disguised restriction on trade.

Article 4

Most–Favoured–Nation Treatment

With regard to the protection of intellectual property, any advantage, favour, privilege or immunity granted by a Member to the nationals of any other country shall be accorded immediately and unconditionally to the nationals of all other Members. Exempted from this obligation are any advantage, favour, privilege or immunity accorded by a Member:

(a) deriving from international agreements on judicial assistance or law enforcement of a general nature and not particularly confined to the protection of intellectual property;

(b) granted in accordance with the provisions of the Berne Convention (1971) or the Rome Convention authorizing that the treatment accorded be a function not of national treatment but of the treatment accorded in another country;

---

3. For the purposes of Articles 3 and 4, "protection" shall include matters affecting the availability, acquisition, scope, maintenance and enforcement of intellectual property rights as well as those matters affecting the use of intellectual property rights specifically addressed in this Agreement.

(c) in respect of the rights of performers, producers of phonograms and broadcasting organizations not provided under this Agreement;

(d) deriving from international agreements related to the protection of intellectual property which entered into force prior to the entry into force of the WTO Agreement, provided that such agreements are notified to the Council for TRIPS and do not constitute an arbitrary or unjustifiable discrimination against nationals of other Members.

Article 5

Multilateral Agreements on Acquisition or Maintenance of Protection

The obligations under Articles 3 and 4 do not apply to procedures provided in multilateral agreements concluded under the auspices of WIPO relating to the acquisition or maintenance of intellectual property rights.

Article 6

Exhaustion

For the purposes of dispute settlement under this Agreement, subject to the provisions of Articles 3 and 4 nothing in this Agreement shall be used to address the issue of the exhaustion of intellectual property rights.

Article 7

Objectives

The protection and enforcement of intellectual property rights should contribute to the promotion of technological innovation and to the transfer and dissemination of technology, to the mutual advantage of producers and users of technological knowledge and in a manner conducive to social and economic welfare, and to a balance of rights and obligations.

Article 8

Principles

1. Members may, in formulating or amending their laws and regulations, adopt measures necessary to protect public health and nutrition, and to promote the public interest in sectors of vital importance to their socio-economic and technological development, provided that such measures are consistent with the provisions of this Agreement.

2. Appropriate measures, provided that they are consistent with the provisions of this Agreement, may be needed to prevent the abuse of intellectual property rights by right holders or the resort to practices which unreasonably restrain trade or adversely affect the international transfer of technology.

PART II

STANDARDS CONCERNING THE AVAILABILITY, SCOPE AND USE OF INTELLECTUAL PROPERTY RIGHTS

SECTION 1: COPYRIGHT AND RELATED RIGHTS

Article 9

Relation to the Berne Convention

1. Members shall comply with Articles 1 through 21 of the Berne Convention (1971) and the Appendix thereto. However, Members shall not have rights or obligations under this Agreement in respect of the rights conferred under Article 6 *bis* of that Convention or of the rights derived therefrom.

2. Copyright protection shall extend to expressions and not to ideas, procedures, methods of operation or mathematical concepts as such.

Article 10

Computer Programs and Compilations of Data

1. Computer programs, whether in source or object code, shall be protected as literary works under the Berne Convention (1971).

2. Compilations of data or other material, whether in machine readable or other form, which by reason of the selection or arrangement of their contents constitute intellectual creations shall be protected as such. Such protection, which shall not extend to the data or material itself, shall be without prejudice to any copyright subsisting in the data or material itself.

Article 11

Rental Rights

In respect of at least computer programs and cinematographic works, a Member shall provide authors and their successors in title the right to authorize or to prohibit the commercial rental to the public of originals or copies of their copyright works. A Member shall be excepted from this obligation in respect of cinematographic works unless such rental has led to widespread copying of such works which is materially impairing the exclusive right of reproduction conferred in that Member on authors and their successors in title. In respect of computer programs, this obligation does not apply to rentals where the program itself is not the essential object of the rental.

Article 12

Term of Protection

Whenever the term of protection of a work, other than a photographic work or a work of applied art, is calculated on a basis other than the life of a natural person, such term shall be no less than 50 years from the end of the calendar year of authorized publication, or, failing such authorized publication within 50 years from the making of the work, 50 years from the end of the calendar year of making.

Article 13

Limitations and Exceptions

Members shall confine limitations or exceptions to exclusive rights to certain special cases which do not conflict with a normal exploitation of the work and do not unreasonably prejudice the legitimate interests of the right holder.

Article 14

Protection of Performers, Producers of Phonograms (Sound Recordings) and Broadcasting Organizations

1. In respect of a fixation of their performance on a phonogram, performers shall have the possibility of preventing the following acts when undertaken without their authorization: the fixation of their unfixed performance and the reproduction of such fixation. Performers shall also have the possibility of preventing the following acts when undertaken without their authorization: the broadcasting by wireless means and the communication to the public of their live performance.

2. Producers of phonograms shall enjoy the right to authorize or prohibit the direct or indirect reproduction of their phonograms.

3. Broadcasting organizations shall have the right to prohibit the following acts when undertaken without their authorization: the fixation, the reproduction of fixations, and the rebroadcasting by wireless means of broadcasts, as well as the communication to the public of television broadcasts of the same. Where Members do not grant such rights to broadcasting organizations, they shall provide owners of copyright in the subject matter of broadcasts with the possibility of preventing the above acts, subject to the provisions of the Berne Convention (1971).

4. The provisions of Article 11 in respect of computer programs shall apply *mutatis mutandis* to producers of phonograms and any other right holders in phonograms as determined in a Member's law. If on 15 April 1994 a Member has in force a system of equitable remuneration of right holders in respect of the rental of phonograms, it may maintain such system provided that the commercial rental of phonograms is not giving rise to the material impairment of the exclusive rights of reproduction of right holders.

5. The term of the protection available under this Agreement to performers and producers of phonograms shall last at least until the end of a period of 50 years computed from the end of the calendar year in which the fixation was made or the performance took place. The term of protection granted pursuant to paragraph 3 shall last for at least 20 years from the end of the calendar year in which the broadcast took place.

6. Any Member may, in relation to the rights conferred under paragraphs 1, 2 and 3, provide for conditions, limitations, exceptions and reservations to the extent permitted by the Rome Convention. However, the provisions of Article 18 of the Berne Convention (1971) shall also apply, *mutatis mutandis,* to the rights of performers and producers of phonograms in phonograms.

SECTION 2: TRADEMARKS

Article 15

Protectable Subject Matter

1. Any sign, or any combination of signs, capable of distinguishing the goods or services of one undertaking from those of other undertakings, shall be capable of constituting a trademark. Such signs, in particular words including personal names, letters, numerals, figurative elements and combinations of colours as well as any combination of such signs, shall be eligible for registration as trademarks. Where signs are not inherently capable of distinguishing the relevant goods or services, Members may make registrability depend on distinctiveness acquired through use. Members may require, as a condition of registration, that signs be visually perceptible.

2. Paragraph 1 shall not be understood to prevent a Member from denying registration of a trademark on other grounds, provided that they do not derogate from the provisions of the Paris Convention (1967).

3. Members may make registrability depend on use. However, actual use of a trademark shall not be a condition for filing an application for registration. An application shall not be refused solely on the ground that intended use has not taken place before the expiry of a period of three years from the date of application.

4. The nature of the goods or services to which a trademark is to be applied shall in no case form an obstacle to registration of the trademark.

5. Members shall publish each trademark either before it is registered or promptly after it is registered and shall afford a reasonable opportunity for petitions to cancel the registration. In addition, Members may afford an opportunity for the registration of a trademark to be opposed.

Article 16

Rights Conferred

1. The owner of a registered trademark shall have the exclusive right to prevent all third parties not having the owner's consent from using in the course of trade identical or similar signs for goods or services which are identical or similar to those in respect of which the trademark is registered where such use would result in a likelihood of confusion. In case of the use of an identical sign for identical goods or services, a likelihood of confusion shall be presumed. The rights described above

shall not prejudice any existing prior rights, nor shall they affect the possibility of Members making rights available on the basis of use.

2. Article 6 *bis* of the Paris Convention (1967) shall apply, *mutatis mutandis,* to services. In determining whether a trademark is well-known, Members shall take account of the knowledge of the trademark in the relevant sector of the public, including knowledge in the Member concerned which has been obtained as a result of the promotion of the trademark.

3. Article 6 *bis* of the Paris Convention (1967) shall apply, *mutatis mutandis,* to goods or services which are not similar to those in respect of which a trademark is registered, provided that use of that trademark in relation to those goods or services would indicate a connection between those goods or services and the owner of the registered trademark and provided that the interests of the owner of the registered trademark are likely to be damaged by such use.

Article 17

Exceptions

Members may provide limited exceptions to the rights conferred by a trademark, such as fair use of descriptive terms, provided that such exceptions take account of the legitimate interests of the owner of the trademark and of third parties.

Article 18

Term of Protection

Initial registration, and each renewal of registration, of a trademark shall be for a term of no less than seven years. The registration of a trademark shall be renewable indefinitely.

Article 19

Requirement of Use

1. If use is required to maintain a registration, the registration may be cancelled only after an uninterrupted period of at least three years of non-use, unless valid reasons based on the existence of obstacles to such use are shown by the trademark owner. Circumstances arising independently of the will of the owner of the trademark which constitute an obstacle to the use of the trademark, such as import restrictions on or other government requirements for goods or services protected by the trademark, shall be recognized as valid reasons for non-use.

2. When subject to the control of its owner, use of a trademark by another person shall be recognized as use of the trademark for the purpose of maintaining the registration.

Article 20

Other Requirements

The use of a trademark in the course of trade shall not be unjustifiably encumbered by special requirements, such as use with another trademark, use in a special form or use in a manner detrimental to its capability to distinguish the goods or services of one undertaking from those of other undertakings. This will not preclude a requirement prescribing the use of the trademark identifying the undertaking producing the goods or services along with, but without linking it to, the trademark distinguishing the specific goods or services in question of that undertaking.

Article 21

Licensing and Assignment

Members may determine conditions on the licensing and assignment of trademarks, it being understood that the compulsory licensing of trademarks shall not be permitted and that the owner of a registered trademark shall have the right to assign the trademark with or without the transfer of the business to which the trademark belongs.

SECTION 3. GEOGRAPHICAL INDICATIONS (omitted)

* * *

SECTION 4: INDUSTRIAL DESIGNS (omitted)

* * *

Requirements for Protection

SECTION 5: PATENTS

Article 27

Patentable Subject Matter

1. Subject to the provisions of paragraphs 2 and 3, patents shall be available for any inventions, whether products or processes, in all fields of technology, provided that they are new, involve an inventive step and are capable of industrial application.[5] Subject to paragraph 4 of Article 65, paragraph 8 of Article 70 and paragraph 3 of this Article, patents shall be available and patent rights enjoyable without discrimination as to the place of invention, the field of technology and whether products are imported or locally produced.

2. Members may exclude from patentability inventions, the prevention within their territory of the commercial exploitation of which is necessary to protect *ordre public* or morality, including to protect human, animal or plant life or health or to avoid serious prejudice to the environment, provided that such exclusion is not made merely because the exploitation is prohibited by their law.

3. Members may also exclude from patentability:

---

5. For the purposes of this Article, the terms "inventive step" and "capable of industrial application" may be deemed by a Member to be synonymous with the terms "non-obvious" and "useful" respectively.

(a) diagnostic, therapeutic and surgical methods for the treatment of humans or animals;

(b) plants and animals other than micro-organisms, and essentially biological processes for the production of plants or animals other than non-biological and microbiological processes. However, Members shall provide for the protection of plant varieties either by patents or by an effective *sui generis* system or by any combination thereof. The provisions of this subparagraph shall be reviewed four years after the date of entry into force of the WTO Agreement.

Article 28

Rights Conferred

1. A patent shall confer on its owner the following exclusive rights:

(a) where the subject matter of a patent is a product, to prevent third parties not having the owner's consent from the acts of: making, using, offering for sale, selling, or importing[6] for these purposes that product;

(b) where the subject matter of a patent is a process, to prevent third parties not having the owner's consent from the act of using the process, and from the acts of: using, offering for sale, selling, or importing for these purposes at least the product obtained directly by that process.

2. Patent owners shall also have the right to assign, or transfer by succession, the patent and to conclude licensing contracts.

Article 29

Conditions on Patent Applicants

1. Members shall require that an applicant for a patent shall disclose the invention in a manner sufficiently clear and complete for the invention to be carried out by a person skilled in the art and may require the applicant to indicate the best mode for carrying out the invention known to the inventor at the filing date or, where priority is claimed, at the priority date of the application.

2. Members may require an applicant for a patent to provide information concerning the applicant's corresponding foreign applications and grants.

Article 30

Exceptions to Rights Conferred

Members may provide limited exceptions to the exclusive rights conferred by a patent, provided that such exceptions do not unreasonably

6. This right, like all other rights conferred under this Agreement in respect of the use, sale, importation or other distribution of goods, is subject to the provisions of Article 6.

conflict with a normal exploitation of the patent and do not unreasonably prejudice the legitimate interests of the patent owner, taking account of the legitimate interests of third parties.

Article 31

Other Use Without Authorization of the Right Holder

Where the law of a Member allows for other use[7] of the subject matter of a patent without the authorization of the right holder, including use by the government or third parties authorized by the government, the following provisions shall be respected:

(a) authorization of such use shall be considered on its individual merits;

(b) such use may only be permitted if, prior to such use, the proposed user has made efforts to obtain authorization from the right holder on reasonable commercial terms and conditions and that such efforts have not been successful within a reasonable period of time. This requirement may be waived by a Member in the case of a national emergency or other circumstances of extreme urgency or in cases of public non-commercial use. In situations of national emergency or other circumstances of extreme urgency, the right holder shall, nevertheless, be notified as soon as reasonably practicable. In the case of public non-commercial use, where the government or contractor, without making a patent search, knows or has demonstrable grounds to know that a valid patent is or will be used by or for the government, the right holder shall be informed promptly;

(c) the scope and duration of such use shall be limited to the purpose for which it was authorized, and in the case of semi-conductor technology shall only be for public non-commercial use or to remedy a practice determined after judicial or administrative process to be anti-competitive;

(d) such use shall be non-exclusive;

(e) such use shall be non-assignable, except with that part of the enterprise or goodwill which enjoys such use;

(f) any such use shall be authorized predominantly for the supply of the domestic market of the Member authorizing such use;

(g) authorization for such use shall be liable, subject to adequate protection of the legitimate interests of the persons so authorized, to be terminated if and when the circumstances which led to it cease to exist and are unlikely to recur. The competent authority shall have the authority to review, upon motivated request, the continued existence of these circumstances;

---

7. "Other use" refers to other than that allowed under Article 30.

(h) the right holder shall be paid adequate remuneration in the circumstances of each case, taking into account the economic value of the authorization;

(i) the legal validity of any decision relating to the authorization of such use shall be subject to judicial review or other independent review by a distinct higher authority in that Member;

(j) any decision relating to the remuneration provided in respect of such use shall be subject to judicial review or other independent review by a distinct higher authority in that Member;

(k) Members are not obliged to apply the conditions set forth in subparagraphs (b) and (f) where such use is permitted to remedy a practice determined after judicial or administrative process to be anti-competitive. The need to correct anti-competitive practices may be taken into account in determining the amount of remuneration in such cases. Competent authorities shall have the authority to refuse termination of authorization if and when the conditions which led to such authorization are likely to recur;

(*l*) where such use is authorized to permit the exploitation of a patent ("the second patent") which cannot be exploited without infringing another patent ("the first patent"), the following additional conditions shall apply:

(i) the invention claimed in the second patent shall involve an important technical advance of considerable economic significance in relation to the invention claimed in the first patent;

(ii) the owner of the first patent shall be entitled to a cross-licence on reasonable terms to use the invention claimed in the second patent; and

(iii) the use authorized in respect of the first patent shall be non-assignable except with the assignment of the second patent.

Article 32

Revocation/Forfeiture

An opportunity for judicial review of any decision to revoke or forfeit a patent shall be available.

Article 33

Term of Protection

The term of protection available shall not end before the expiration of a period of twenty years counted from the filing date.[8]

8. It is understood that those Members which do not have a system of original grant may provide that the term of protection shall be computed from the filing date in the system of original grant.

Article 34

Process Patents: Burden of Proof

1. For the purposes of civil proceedings in respect of the infringement of the rights of the owner referred to in paragraph 1(b) of Article 28, if the subject matter of a patent is a process for obtaining a product, the judicial authorities shall have the authority to order the defendant to prove that the process to obtain an identical product is different from the patented process. Therefore, Members shall provide, in at least one of the following circumstances, that any identical product when produced without the consent of the patent owner shall, in the absence of proof to the contrary, be deemed to have been obtained by the patented process:

(a) if the product obtained by the patented process is new;

(b) if there is a substantial likelihood that the identical product was made by the process and the owner of the patent has been unable through reasonable efforts to determine the process actually used.

2. Any Member shall be free to provide that the burden of proof indicated in paragraph 1 shall be on the alleged infringer only if the condition referred to in subparagraph (a) is fulfilled or only if the condition referred to in subparagraph (b) is fulfilled.

3. In the adduction of proof to the contrary, the legitimate interests of defendants in protecting their manufacturing and business secrets shall be taken into account.

SECTION 6: LAYOUT–DESIGNS (TOPOGRAPHIES) OF INTEGRATED CIRCUITS (omitted)

* * *

SECTION 7: PROTECTION OF UNDISCLOSED INFORMATION

Article 39

1. In the course of ensuring effective protection against unfair competition as provided in Article 10 *bis* of the Paris Convention (1967), Members shall protect undisclosed information in accordance with paragraph 2 and data submitted to governments or governmental agencies in accordance with paragraph 3.

2. Natural and legal persons shall have the possibility of preventing information lawfully within their control from being disclosed to, acquired by, or used by others without their consent in a manner contrary to honest commercial practices[10] so long as such information:

(a) is secret in the sense that it is not, as a body or in the precise configuration and assembly of its components, generally known

10. For the purpose of this provision, "a manner contrary to honest commercial practices" shall mean at least practices such as breach of contract, breach of confidence and inducement to breach, and includes the acquisition of undisclosed information by third parties who knew, or were grossly negligent in failing to know, that such practices were involved in the acquisition.

among or readily accessible to persons within the circles that normally deal with the kind of information in question;

(b) has commercial value because it is secret; and

(c) has been subject to reasonable steps under the circumstances, by the person lawfully in control of the information, to keep it secret.

3. Members, when requiring, as a condition of approving the marketing of pharmaceutical or of agricultural chemical products which utilize new chemical entities, the submission of undisclosed test or other data, the origination of which involves a considerable effort, shall protect such data against unfair commercial use. In addition, Members shall protect such data against disclosure, except where necessary to protect the public, or unless steps are taken to ensure that the data are protected against unfair commercial use.

SECTION 8: CONTROL OF ANTI–COMPETITIVE PRACTICES IN CONTRACTUAL LICENSES

Article 40

1. Members agree that some licensing practices or conditions pertaining to intellectual property rights which restrain competition may have adverse effects on trade and may impede the transfer and dissemination of technology.

2. Nothing in this Agreement shall prevent Members from specifying in their legislation licensing practices or conditions that may in particular cases constitute an abuse of intellectual property rights having an adverse effect on competition in the relevant market. As provided above, a Member may adopt, consistently with the other provisions of this Agreement, appropriate measures to prevent or control such practices, which may include for example exclusive grantback conditions, conditions preventing challenges to validity and coercive package licensing, in the light of the relevant laws and regulations of that Member.

3. Each Member shall enter, upon request, into consultations with any other Member which has cause to believe that an intellectual property right owner that is a national or domiciliary of the Member to which the request for consultations has been addressed is undertaking practices in violation of the requesting Member's laws and regulations on the subject matter of this Section, and which wishes to secure compliance with such legislation, without prejudice to any action under the law and to the full freedom of an ultimate decision of either Member. The Member addressed shall accord full and sympathetic consideration to, and shall afford adequate opportunity for, consultations with the requesting Member, and shall cooperate through supply of publicly available non-confidential information of relevance to the matter in question and of other information available to the Member, subject to domestic law and to the conclusion of

mutually satisfactory agreements concerning the safeguarding of its confidentiality by the requesting Member.

4. A Member whose nationals or domiciliaries are subject to proceedings in another Member concerning alleged violation of that other Member's laws and regulations on the subject matter of this Section shall, upon request, be granted an opportunity for consultations by the other Member under the same conditions as those foreseen in paragraph 3.

PART III

ENFORCEMENT OF INTELLECTUAL PROPERTY RIGHTS

SECTION 1: GENERAL OBLIGATIONS

Article 41

1. Members shall ensure that enforcement procedures as specified in this Part are available under their law so as to permit effective action against any act of infringement of intellectual property rights covered by this Agreement, including expeditious remedies to prevent infringements and remedies which constitute a deterrent to further infringements. These procedures shall be applied in such a manner as to avoid the creation of barriers to legitimate trade and to provide for safeguards against their abuse.

2. Procedures concerning the enforcement of intellectual property rights shall be fair and equitable. They shall not be unnecessarily complicated or costly, or entail unreasonable time-limits or unwarranted delays.

3. Decisions on the merits of a case shall preferably be in writing and reasoned. They shall be made available at least to the parties to the proceeding without undue delay. Decisions on the merits of a case shall be based only on evidence in respect of which parties were offered the opportunity to be heard.

4. Parties to a proceeding shall have an opportunity for review by a judicial authority of final administrative decisions and, subject to jurisdictional provisions in a Member's law concerning the importance of a case, of at least the legal aspects of initial judicial decisions on the merits of a case. However, there shall be no obligation to provide an opportunity for review of acquittals in criminal cases.

5. It is understood that this Part does not create any obligation to put in place a judicial system for the enforcement of intellectual property rights distinct from that for the enforcement of law in general, nor does it affect the capacity of Members to enforce their law in general. Nothing in this Part creates any obligation with respect to the distribution of resources as between enforcement of intellectual property rights and the enforcement of law in general.

SECTION 2: CIVIL AND ADMINISTRATIVE PROCEDURES AND REMEDIES

Article 42

Fair and Equitable Procedures

Members shall make available to right holders[11] civil judicial procedures concerning the enforcement of any intellectual property right covered by this Agreement. Defendants shall have the right to written notice which is timely and contains sufficient detail, including the basis of the claims. Parties shall be allowed to be represented by independent legal counsel, and procedures shall not impose overly burdensome requirements concerning mandatory personal appearances. All parties to such procedures shall be duly entitled to substantiate their claims and to present all relevant evidence. The procedure shall provide a means to identify and protect confidential information, unless this would be contrary to existing constitutional requirements.

Article 43

Evidence

1. The judicial authorities shall have the authority, where a party has presented reasonably available evidence sufficient to support its claims and has specified evidence relevant to substantiation of its claims which lies in the control of the opposing party, to order that this evidence be produced by the opposing party, subject in appropriate cases to conditions which ensure the protection of confidential information.

2. In cases in which a party to a proceeding voluntarily and without good reason refuses access to, or otherwise does not provide necessary information within a reasonable period, or significantly impedes a procedure relating to an enforcement action, a Member may accord judicial authorities the authority to make preliminary and final determinations, affirmative or negative, on the basis of the information presented to them, including the complaint or the allegation presented by the party adversely affected by the denial of access to information, subject to providing the parties an opportunity to be heard on the allegations or evidence.

Article 44

Injunctions

1. The judicial authorities shall have the authority to order a party to desist from an infringement, *inter alia* to prevent the entry into the channels of commerce in their jurisdiction of imported goods that involve the infringement of an intellectual property right, immediately after customs clearance of such goods. Members are not obliged to accord such authority in respect of protected subject matter acquired or ordered by a person prior to knowing or having reasonable grounds to know that

11. For the purpose of this Part, the term "right holder" includes federations and associations having legal standing to assert such rights.

dealing in such subject matter would entail the infringement of an intellectual property right.

2. Notwithstanding the other provisions of this Part and provided that the provisions of Part II specifically addressing use by governments, or by third parties authorized by a government, without the authorization of the right holder are complied with, Members may limit the remedies available against such use to payment of remuneration in accordance with subparagraph (h) of Article 31. In other cases, the remedies under this Part shall apply or, where these remedies are inconsistent with a Member's law, declaratory judgments and adequate compensation shall be available.

Article 45

Damages

1. The judicial authorities shall have the authority to order the infringer to pay the right holder damages adequate to compensate for the injury the right holder has suffered because of an infringement of that person's intellectual property right by an infringer who knowingly, or with reasonable grounds to know, engaged in infringing activity.

2. The judicial authorities shall also have the authority to order the infringer to pay the right holder expenses, which may include appropriate attorney's fees. In appropriate cases, Members may authorize the judicial authorities to order recovery of profits and/or payment of pre-established damages even where the infringer did not knowingly, or with reasonable grounds to know, engage in infringing activity.

Article 46

Other Remedies

In order to create an effective deterrent to infringement, the judicial authorities shall have the authority to order that goods that they have found to be infringing be, without compensation of any sort, disposed of outside the channels of commerce in such a manner as to avoid any harm caused to the right holder, or, unless this would be contrary to existing constitutional requirements, destroyed. The judicial authorities shall also have the authority to order that materials and implements the predominant use of which has been in the creation of the infringing goods be, without compensation of any sort, disposed of outside the channels of commerce in such a manner as to minimize the risks of further infringements. In considering such requests, the need for proportionality between the seriousness of the infringement and the remedies ordered as well as the interests of third parties shall be taken into account. In regard to counterfeit trademark goods, the simple removal of the trademark unlawfully affixed shall not be sufficient, other than in exceptional cases, to permit release of the goods into the channels of commerce.

Article 47

Right of Information

Members may provide that the judicial authorities shall have the authority, unless this would be out of proportion to the seriousness of the infringement, to order the infringer to inform the right holder of the identity of third persons involved in the production and distribution of the infringing goods or services and of their channels of distribution.

Article 48

Indemnification of the Defendant

1. The judicial authorities shall have the authority to order a party at whose request measures were taken and who has abused enforcement procedures to provide to a party wrongfully enjoined or restrained adequate compensation for the injury suffered because of such abuse. The judicial authorities shall also have the authority to order the applicant to pay the defendant expenses, which may include appropriate attorney's fees.

2. In respect of the administration of any law pertaining to the protection or enforcement of intellectual property rights, Members shall only exempt both public authorities and officials from liability to appropriate remedial measures where actions are taken or intended in good faith in the course of the administration of that law.

Article 49

Administrative Procedures

To the extent that any civil remedy can be ordered as a result of administrative procedures on the merits of a case, such procedures shall conform to principles equivalent in substance to those set forth in this Section.

SECTION 3: PROVISIONAL MEASURES

Article 50

1. The judicial authorities shall have the authority to order prompt and effective provisional measures:

(a) to prevent an infringement of any intellectual property right from occurring, and in particular to prevent the entry into the channels of commerce in their jurisdiction of goods, including imported goods immediately after customs clearance;

(b) to preserve relevant evidence in regard to the alleged infringement.

2. The judicial authorities shall have the authority to adopt provisional measures *inaudita altera parte* where appropriate, in particular where any delay is likely to cause irreparable harm to the right holder, or where there is a demonstrable risk of evidence being destroyed.

3. The judicial authorities shall have the authority to require the applicant to provide any reasonably available evidence in order to satisfy themselves with a sufficient degree of certainty that the applicant is the right holder and that the applicant's right is being infringed or that such infringement is imminent, and to order the applicant to provide a security or equivalent assurance sufficient to protect the defendant and to prevent abuse.

4. Where provisional measures have been adopted *inaudita altera parte,* the parties affected shall be given notice, without delay after the execution of the measures at the latest. A review, including a right to be heard, shall take place upon request of the defendant with a view to deciding, within a reasonable period after the notification of the measures, whether these measures shall be modified, revoked or confirmed.

5. The applicant may be required to supply other information necessary for the identification of the goods concerned by the authority that will execute the provisional measures.

6. Without prejudice to paragraph 4, provisional measures taken on the basis of paragraphs 1 and 2 shall, upon request by the defendant, be revoked or otherwise cease to have effect, if proceedings leading to a decision on the merits of the case are not initiated within a reasonable period, to be determined by the judicial authority ordering the measures where a Member's law so permits or, in the absence of such a determination, not to exceed 20 working days or 31 calendar days, whichever is the longer.

7. Where the provisional measures are revoked or where they lapse due to any act or omission by the applicant, or where it is subsequently found that there has been no infringement or threat of infringement of an intellectual property right, the judicial authorities shall have the authority to order the applicant, upon request of the defendant, to provide the defendant appropriate compensation for any injury caused by these measures.

8. To the extent that any provisional measure can be ordered as a result of administrative procedures, such procedures shall conform to principles equivalent in substance to those set forth in this Section.

SECTION 4: SPECIAL REQUIREMENTS RELATED TO BORDER MEASURES[12]

Article 51

Suspension of Release by Customs Authorities

Members shall, in conformity with the provisions set out below, adopt procedures[13] to enable a right holder, who has valid grounds for suspect-

12. Where a Member has dismantled substantially all controls over movement of goods across its border with another Member with which it forms part of a customs union, it shall not be required to apply the provisions of this Section at that border.

13. It is understood that there shall be no obligation to apply such procedures to imports of goods put on the market in another country by or with the consent of the right holder, or to goods in transit.

ing that the importation of counterfeit trademark or pirated copyright goods[14] may take place, to lodge an application in writing with competent authorities, administrative or judicial, for the suspension by the customs authorities of the release into free circulation of such goods. Members may enable such an application to be made in respect of goods which involve other infringements of intellectual property rights, provided that the requirements of this Section are met. Members may also provide for corresponding procedures concerning the suspension by the customs authorities of the release of infringing goods destined for exportation from their territories.

Article 52

Application

Any right holder initiating the procedures under Article 51 shall be required to provide adequate evidence to satisfy the competent authorities that, under the laws of the country of importation, there is *prima facie* an infringement of the right holder's intellectual property right and to supply a sufficiently detailed description of the goods to make them readily recognizable by the customs authorities. The competent authorities shall inform the applicant within a reasonable period whether they have accepted the application and, where determined by the competent authorities, the period for which the customs authorities will take action.

Article 53

Security or Equivalent Assurance

1. The competent authorities shall have the authority to require an applicant to provide a security or equivalent assurance sufficient to protect the defendant and the competent authorities and to prevent abuse. Such security or equivalent assurance shall not unreasonably deter recourse to these procedures.

2. Where pursuant to an application under this Section the release of goods involving industrial designs, patents, layout-designs or undisclosed information into free circulation has been suspended by customs authorities on the basis of a decision other than by a judicial or other independent authority, and the period provided for in Article 55 has expired without the granting of provisional relief by the duly empowered authority, and provided that all other conditions for importation have

---

14. For the purposes of this Agreement:

(a) "counterfeit trademark goods" shall mean any goods, including packaging, bearing without authorization a trademark which is identical to the trademark validly registered in respect of such goods, or which cannot be distinguished in its essential aspects from such a trademark, and which thereby infringes the rights of the owner of the trademark in question under the law of the country of importation;

(b) "pirated copyright goods" shall mean any goods which are copies made without the consent of the right holder or person duly authorized by the right holder in the country of production and which are made directly or indirectly from an article where the making of that copy would have constituted an infringement of a copyright or a related right under the law of the country of importation.

been complied with, the owner, importer, or consignee of such goods shall be entitled to their release on the posting of a security in an amount sufficient to protect the right holder for any infringement. Payment of such security shall not prejudice any other remedy available to the right holder, it being understood that the security shall be released if the right holder fails to pursue the right of action within a reasonable period of time.

Article 54

Notice of Suspension

The importer and the applicant shall be promptly notified of the suspension of the release of goods according to Article 51.

Article 55

Duration of Suspension

If, within a period not exceeding 10 working days after the applicant has been served notice of the suspension, the customs authorities have not been informed that proceedings leading to a decision on the merits of the case have been initiated by a party other than the defendant, or that the duly empowered authority has taken provisional measures prolonging the suspension of the release of the goods, the goods shall be released, provided that all other conditions for importation or exportation have been complied with; in appropriate cases, this time-limit may be extended by another 10 working days. If proceedings leading to a decision on the merits of the case have been initiated, a review, including a right to be heard, shall take place upon request of the defendant with a view to deciding, within a reasonable period, whether these measures shall be modified, revoked or confirmed. Notwithstanding the above, where the suspension of the release of goods is carried out or continued in accordance with a provisional judicial measure, the provisions of paragraph 6 of Article 50 shall apply.

Article 56

Indemnification of the Importer and of the Owner of the Goods

Relevant authorities shall have the authority to order the applicant to pay the importer, the consignee and the owner of the goods appropriate compensation for any injury caused to them through the wrongful detention of goods or through the detention of goods released pursuant to Article 55.

Article 57

Right of Inspection and Information

Without prejudice to the protection of confidential information, Members shall provide the competent authorities the authority to give the right holder sufficient opportunity to have any goods detained by the customs authorities inspected in order to substantiate the right holder's claims.

The competent authorities shall also have authority to give the importer an equivalent opportunity to have any such goods inspected. Where a positive determination has been made on the merits of a case, Members may provide the competent authorities the authority to inform the right holder of the names and addresses of the consignor, the importer and the consignee and of the quantity of the goods in question.

Article 58

Ex Officio Action

Where Members require competent authorities to act upon their own initiative and to suspend the release of goods in respect of which they have acquired *prima facie* evidence that an intellectual property right is being infringed:

(a) the competent authorities may at any time seek from the right holder any information that may assist them to exercise these powers;

(b) the importer and the right holder shall be promptly notified of the suspension. Where the importer has lodged an appeal against the suspension with the competent authorities, the suspension shall be subject to the conditions, *mutatis mutandis,* set out at Article 55;

(c) Members shall only exempt both public authorities and officials from liability to appropriate remedial measures where actions are taken or intended in good faith.

Article 59

Remedies

Without prejudice to other rights of action open to the right holder and subject to the right of the defendant to seek review by a judicial authority, competent authorities shall have the authority to order the destruction or disposal of infringing goods in accordance with the principles set out in Article 46. In regard to counterfeit trademark goods, the authorities shall not allow the re-exportation of the infringing goods in an unaltered state or subject them to a different customs procedure, other than in exceptional circumstances.

Article 60

De Minimis Imports

Members may exclude from the application of the above provisions small quantities of goods of a non-commercial nature contained in travellers' personal luggage or sent in small consignments.

SECTION 5: CRIMINAL PROCEDURES

Article 61

Members shall provide for criminal procedures and penalties to be applied at least in cases of wilful trademark counterfeiting or copyright piracy on a commercial scale. Remedies available shall include imprisonment and/or monetary fines sufficient to provide a deterrent, consistently with the level of penalties applied for crimes of a corresponding gravity. In appropriate cases, remedies available shall also include the seizure, forfeiture and destruction of the infringing goods and of any materials and implements the predominant use of which has been in the commission of the offence. Members may provide for criminal procedures and penalties to be applied in other cases of infringement of intellectual property rights, in particular where they are committed wilfully and on a commercial scale.

PART IV

ACQUISITION AND MAINTENANCE OF INTELLECTUAL PROPERTY RIGHTS AND RELATED *INTER-PARTES* PROCEDURES

Article 62

1. Members may require, as a condition of the acquisition or maintenance of the intellectual property rights provided for under Sections 2 through 6 of Part II, compliance with reasonable procedures and formalities. Such procedures and formalities shall be consistent with the provisions of this Agreement.

2. Where the acquisition of an intellectual property right is subject to the right being granted or registered, Members shall ensure that the procedures for grant or registration, subject to compliance with the substantive conditions for acquisition of the right, permit the granting or registration of the right within a reasonable period of time so as to avoid unwarranted curtailment of the period of protection.

3. Article 4 of the Paris Convention (1967) shall apply *mutatis mutandis* to service marks.

4. Procedures concerning the acquisition or maintenance of intellectual property rights and, where a Member's law provides for such procedures, administrative revocation and *inter partes* procedures such as opposition, revocation and cancellation, shall be governed by the general principles set out in paragraphs 2 and 3 of Article 41.

5. Final administrative decisions in any of the procedures referred to under paragraph 4 shall be subject to review by a judicial or quasi-judicial authority. However, there shall be no obligation to provide an opportunity for such review of decisions in cases of unsuccessful opposition or administrative revocation, provided that the grounds for such procedures can be the subject of invalidation procedures.

PART V

DISPUTE PREVENTION AND SETTLEMENT

Article 63

Transparency

1. Laws and regulations, and final judicial decisions and administrative rulings of general application, made effective by a Member pertaining

to the subject matter of this Agreement (the availability, scope, acquisition, enforcement and prevention of the abuse of intellectual property rights) shall be published, or where such publication is not practicable made publicly available, in a national language, in such a manner as to enable governments and right holders to become acquainted with them. Agreements concerning the subject matter of this Agreement which are in force between the government or a governmental agency of a Member and the government or a governmental agency of another Member shall also be published.

2. Members shall notify the laws and regulations referred to in paragraph 1 to the Council for TRIPS in order to assist that Council in its review of the operation of this Agreement. The Council shall attempt to minimize the burden on Members in carrying out this obligation and may decide to waive the obligation to notify such laws and regulations directly to the Council if consultations with WIPO on the establishment of a common register containing these laws and regulations are successful. The Council shall also consider in this connection any action required regarding notifications pursuant to the obligations under this Agreement stemming from the provisions of Article 6 *ter* of the Paris Convention (1967).

3. Each Member shall be prepared to supply, in response to a written request from another Member, information of the sort referred to in paragraph 1. A Member, having reason to believe that a specific judicial decision or administrative ruling or bilateral agreement in the area of intellectual property rights affects its rights under this Agreement, may also request in writing to be given access to or be informed in sufficient detail of such specific judicial decisions or administrative rulings or bilateral agreements.

4. Nothing in paragraphs 1, 2 and 3 shall require Members to disclose confidential information which would impede law enforcement or otherwise be contrary to the public interest or would prejudice the legitimate commercial interests of particular enterprises, public or private.

Article 64

Dispute Settlement

1. The provisions of Articles XXII and XXIII of GATT 1994 as elaborated and applied by the Dispute Settlement Understanding shall apply to consultations and the settlement of disputes under this Agreement except as otherwise specifically provided herein.

2. Subparagraphs 1(b) and 1(c) of Article XXIII of GATT 1994 shall not apply to the settlement of disputes under this Agreement for a period of five years from the date of entry into force of the WTO Agreement.

3. During the time period referred to in paragraph 2, the Council for TRIPS shall examine the scope and modalities for complaints of the type provided for under subparagraphs 1(b) and 1(c) of Article XXIII of GATT 1994 made pursuant to this Agreement, and submit its recommendations

to the Ministerial Conference for approval. Any decision of the Ministerial Conference to approve such recommendations or to extend the period in paragraph 2 shall be made only by consensus, and approved recommendations shall be effective for all Members without further formal acceptance process.

PART VI

TRANSITIONAL ARRANGEMENTS

Article 65

Transitional Arrangements

1. Subject to the provisions of paragraphs 2, 3 and 4, no Member shall be obliged to apply the provisions of this Agreement before the expiry of a general period of one year following the date of entry into force of the WTO Agreement.

2. A developing country Member is entitled to delay for a further period of four years the date of application, as defined in paragraph 1, of the provisions of this Agreement other than Articles 3, 4 and 5.

3. Any other Member which is in the process of transformation from a centrally-planned into a market, free-enterprise economy and which is undertaking structural reform of its intellectual property system and facing special problems in the preparation and implementation of intellectual property laws and regulations, may also benefit from a period of delay as foreseen in paragraph 2.

4. To the extent that a developing country Member is obliged by this Agreement to extend product patent protection to areas of technology not so protectable in its territory on the general date of application of this Agreement for that Member, as defined in paragraph 2, it may delay the application of the provisions on product patents of Section 5 of Part II to such areas of technology for an additional period of five years.

5. A Member availing itself of a transitional period under paragraphs 1, 2, 3 or 4 shall ensure that any changes in its laws, regulations and practice made during that period do not result in a lesser degree of consistency with the provisions of this Agreement.

Article 66

Least–Developed Country Members

1. In view of the special needs and requirements of least-developed country Members, their economic, financial and administrative constraints, and their need for flexibility to create a viable technological base, such Members shall not be required to apply the provisions of this Agreement, other than Articles 3, 4 and 5, for a period of 10 years from the date of application as defined under paragraph 1 of Article 65. The Council for TRIPS shall, upon duly motivated request by a least-developed country Member, accord extensions of this period.

2. Developed country Members shall provide incentives to enterprises and institutions in their territories for the purpose of promoting and encouraging technology transfer to least-developed country Members in order to enable them to create a sound and viable technological base.

Article 67

Technical Cooperation

In order to facilitate the implementation of this Agreement, developed country Members shall provide, on request and on mutually agreed terms and conditions, technical and financial cooperation in favour of developing and least-developed country Members. Such cooperation shall include assistance in the preparation of laws and regulations on the protection and enforcement of intellectual property rights as well as on the prevention of their abuse, and shall include support regarding the establishment or reinforcement of domestic offices and agencies relevant to these matters, including the training of personnel.

PART VII

INSTITUTIONAL ARRANGEMENTS; FINAL PROVISIONS (omitted)

* * *

DOCUMENT 10

WTO AGREEMENT ON TRADE-RELATED INVESTMENT MEASURES

* * *

Article 1

Coverage

This Agreement applies to investment measures related to trade in goods only (referred to in this Agreement as "TRIMs").

Article 2

National Treatment and Quantitative Restrictions

1. Without prejudice to other rights and obligations under GATT 1994, no Member shall apply any TRIM that is inconsistent with the provisions of Article III or Article XI of GATT 1994.

2. An illustrative list of TRIMs that are inconsistent with the obligation of national treatment provided for in paragraph 4 of Article III of GATT 1994 and the obligation of general elimination of quantitative restrictions provided for in paragraph 1 of Article XI of GATT 1994 is contained in the Annex to this Agreement.

Article 3

Exceptions

All exceptions under GATT 1994 shall apply, as appropriate, to the provisions of this Agreement.

Article 4

Developing Country Members

A developing country Member shall be free to deviate temporarily from the provisions of Article 2 to the extent and in such a manner as Article XVIII of GATT 1994, the Understanding on the Balance-of-Payments Provisions of GATT 1994, and the Declaration on Trade Measures Taken for Balance-of-Payments Purposes adopted on 28 November 1979 (BISD 26S/205–209) permit the Member to deviate from the provisions of Articles III and XI of GATT 1994.

Article 5

Notification and Transitional Arrangements

1. Members, within 90 days of the date of entry into force of the WTO Agreement, shall notify the Council for Trade in Goods of all TRIMs they are applying that are not in conformity with the provisions of this Agreement. Such TRIMs of general or specific application shall be notified, along with their principal features.[1]

2. Each Member shall eliminate all TRIMs which are notified under paragraph 1 within two years of the date of entry into force of the WTO Agreement in the case of a developed country Member, within five years in the case of a developing country Member, and within seven years in the case of a least-developed country Member.

3. On request, the Council for Trade in Goods may extend the transition period for the elimination of TRIMs notified under paragraph 1 for a developing country Member, including a least-developed country Member, which demonstrates particular difficulties in implementing the provisions of this Agreement. In considering such a request, the Council for Trade in Goods shall take into account the individual development, financial and trade needs of the Member in question.

4. During the transition period, a Member shall not modify the terms of any TRIM which it notifies under paragraph 1 from those prevailing at the date of entry into force of the WTO Agreement so as to increase the degree of inconsistency with the provisions of Article 2. TRIMs introduced less than 180 days before the date of entry into force of the WTO Agreement shall not benefit from the transitional arrangements provided in paragraph 2.

5. Notwithstanding the provisions of Article 2, a Member, in order not to disadvantage established enterprises which are subject to a TRIM notified under paragraph 1, may apply during the transition period the same TRIM to a new investment (*i*) where the products of such investment are like products to those of the established enterprises, and (*ii*) where necessary to avoid distorting the conditions of competition between the new investment and the established enterprises. Any TRIM so applied to a new investment shall be notified to the Council for Trade in Goods. The terms of such a TRIM shall be equivalent in their competitive effect to those applicable to the established enterprises, and it shall be terminated at the same time.

Article 6

Transparency

1. Members reaffirm, with respect to TRIMs, their commitment to obligations on transparency and notification in Article X of GATT 1994, in

---

1. In the case of TRIMs applied under discretionary authority, each specific application shall be notified. Information that would prejudice the legitimate commercial interests of particular enterprises need not be disclosed.

the undertaking on "Notification" contained in the Understanding Regarding Notification, Consultation, Dispute Settlement and Surveillance adopted on 28 November 1979 and in the Ministerial Decision on Notification Procedures adopted on 15 April 1994.

2. Each Member shall notify the Secretariat of the publications in which TRIMs may be found, including those applied by regional and local governments and authorities within their territories.

3. Each Member shall accord sympathetic consideration to requests for information, and afford adequate opportunity for consultation, on any matter arising from this Agreement raised by another Member. In conformity with Article X of GATT 1994 no Member is required to disclose information the disclosure of which would impede law enforcement or otherwise be contrary to the public interest or would prejudice the legitimate commercial interests of particular enterprises, public or private.

Article 7

Committee on Trade–Related Investment Measures

1. A Committee on Trade–Related Investment Measures (referred to in this Agreement as the "Committee") is hereby established, and shall be open to all Members. The Committee shall elect its own Chairman and Vice–Chairman, and shall meet not less than once a year and otherwise at the request of any Member.

2. The Committee shall carry out responsibilities assigned to it by the Council for Trade in Goods and shall afford Members the opportunity to consult on any matters relating to the operation and implementation of this Agreement.

3. The Committee shall monitor the operation and implementation of this Agreement and shall report thereon annually to the Council for Trade in Goods.

Article 8

Consultation and Dispute Settlement

The provisions of Articles XXII and XXIII of GATT 1994, as elaborated and applied by the Dispute Settlement Understanding, shall apply to consultations and the settlement of disputes under this Agreement.

* * *

ANNEX

Illustrative List

1. TRIMs that are inconsistent with the obligation of national treatment provided for in paragraph 4 of Article III of GATT 1994 include those which are mandatory or enforceable under domestic law or under administrative rulings, or compliance with which is necessary to obtain an advantage, and which require:

(a) the purchase or use by an enterprise of products of domestic origin or from any domestic source, whether specified in terms of particular products, in terms of volume or value of products, or in terms of a proportion of volume or value of its local production; or

(b) that an enterprise's purchases or use of imported products be limited to an amount related to the volume or value of local products that it exports.

2. TRIMs that are inconsistent with the obligation of general elimination of quantitative restrictions provided for in paragraph 1 of Article XI of GATT 1994 include those which are mandatory or enforceable under domestic law or under administrative rulings, or compliance with which is necessary to obtain an advantage, and which exports;

(a) the importation by an enterprise of products used in or related to its local production, generally or to an amount related to the volume or value of local production that it exports;

(b) the importation by an enterprise of products used in or related to its local production by restricting its access to foreign exchange to an amount related to the foreign exchange inflows attributable to the enterprise; or

(c) the exportation or sale for export by an enterprise of products, whether specified in terms of particular products, in terms of volume or value of products, or in terms of a proportion of volume or value of its local production.

DOCUMENT 11

NORTH AMERICAN FREE TRADE AGREEMENT BETWEEN THE GOVERNMENT OF THE UNITED STATES OF AMERICA, THE GOVERNMENT OF CANADA AND THE GOVERNMENT OF THE UNITED MEXICAN STATES

(1993)

TABLE OF CONTENTS

PART FOUR: GOVERNMENT PROCUREMENT

PART FIVE: INVESTMENT, SERVICES AND RELATED MATTERS

Article 1213: Definitions (omitted)
Annexes

Chapter Thirteen: Telecommunications (omitted)

Chapter Fourteen: Financial Services (omitted)

Chapter Fifteen: Competition Policy, Monopolies and State Enterprises (omitted)

Chapter Sixteen: Temporary Entry for Business Persons (omitted)

PART SIX: INTELLECTUAL PROPERTY

Chapter Seventeen: Intellectual Property

Article 1701: Nature and Scope of Obligations
Article 1702: More Extensive Protection
Article 1703: National Treatment
Article 1704: Control of Abusive or Anticompetitive Practices or Conditions
Article 1705: Copyright
Article 1706: Sound Recordings (omitted)
Article 1707: Protection of Encrypted Program–Carrying Satellite Signals (omitted)
Article 1708: Trademarks
Article 1709: Patents
Article 1710: Layout Designs of Semiconductor Integrated Circuits (omitted)
Article 1711: Trade Secrets
Article 1712: Geographical Indications (omitted)
Article 1713: Industrial Designs (omitted)
Article 1714: Enforcement of Intellectual Property Rights: General Provisions
Article 1715: Specific Procedural and Remedial Aspects of Civil and Administrative Procedures
Article 1716: Provisional Measures
Article 1717: Criminal Procedures and Penalties
Article 1718: Enforcement of Intellectual Property Rights at the Border
Article 1719: Cooperation and Technical Assistance (omitted)
Article 1720: Protection of Existing Subject Matter (omitted)
Article 1721: Definitions
Annexes (omitted)

PART SEVEN: ADMINISTRATIVE AND INSTITUTIONAL PROVISIONS

Chapter Eighteen: Publication, Notification and Administration of Laws (omitted)

Article 1801: Contact Points (omitted)

PART ONE

GENERAL PART

Chapter One

Objectives

Article 101: Establishment of the Free Trade Area

The Parties to this Agreement, consistent with Article XXIV of the *General Agreement on Tariffs and Trade,* hereby establish a free trade area.

Article 102: Objectives

1. The objectives of this Agreement, as elaborated more specifically through its principles and rules, including national treatment, most-favored-nation treatment and transparency, are to:

(a) eliminate barriers to trade in, and facilitate the cross-border movement of, goods and services between the territories of the Parties;

(b) promote conditions of fair competition in the free trade area;

(c) increase substantially investment opportunities in the territories of the Parties;

(d) provide adequate and effective protection and enforcement of intellectual property rights in each Party's territory;

(e) create effective procedures for the implementation and application of this Agreement, for its joint administration and for the resolution of disputes; and

(f) establish a framework for further trilateral, regional and multilateral cooperation to expand and enhance the benefits of this Agreement.

2. The Parties shall interpret and apply the provisions of this Agreement in the light of its objectives set out in paragraph 1 and in accordance with applicable rules of international law.

Article 103: Relation to Other Agreements

1. The Parties affirm their existing rights and obligations with respect to each other under the *General Agreement on Tariffs and Trade* and other agreements to which such Parties are party.

2. In the event of any inconsistency between this Agreement and such other agreements, this Agreement shall prevail to the extent of the inconsistency, except as otherwise provided in this Agreement.

Article 104: Relation to Environmental and Conservation Agreements

1. In the event of any inconsistency between this Agreement and the specific trade obligations set out in:

(a) the *Convention on International Trade in Endangered Species of Wild Fauna and Flora,* done at Washington, March 3, 1973, as amended June 22, 1979,

(b) the *Montreal Protocol on Substances that Deplete the Ozone Layer,* done at Montreal, September 16, 1987, as amended June 29, 1990,

(c) the *Basel Convention on the Control of Transboundary Movements of Hazardous Wastes and Their Disposal,* done at Basel, March 22, 1989, on its entry into force for Canada, Mexico and the United States, or

(d) the agreements set out in Annex 104.1,

such obligations shall prevail to the extent of the inconsistency, provided that where a Party has a choice among equally effective and reasonably available means of complying with such obligations, the Party chooses the alternative that is the least inconsistent with the other provisions of this Agreement.

* * *

Article 105: Extent of Obligations

The Parties shall ensure that all necessary measures are taken in order to give effect to the provisions of this Agreement, including their observance, except as otherwise provided in this Agreement, by state and provincial governments.

Annex 104.1

Bilateral and Other Environmental and Conservation Agreements

1. The *Agreement Between the Government of Canada and the Government of the United States of America Concerning the Transboundary Movement of Hazardous Waste,* signed at Ottawa, October 28, 1986.

2. The *Agreement Between the United States of America and the United Mexican States on Cooperation for the Protection and Improvement of the Environment in the Border Area,* signed at La Paz, Baja California Sur, August 14, 1983.

PART TWO

TRADE IN GOODS

Chapter Three

National Treatment and Market Access for Goods

* * *

Section A—National Treatment

Article 301: National Treatment

1. Each Party shall accord national treatment to the goods of another Party in accordance with Article III of the *General Agreement on Tariffs and Trade* (GATT), including its interpretative notes, and to this end Article III of the GATT and its interpretative notes, or any equivalent provision of a successor agreement to which all Parties are party, are incorporated into and made part of this Agreement.

2. The provisions of paragraph 1 regarding national treatment shall mean, with respect to a state or province, treatment no less favorable than the most favorable treatment accorded by such state or province to any like, directly competitive or substitutable goods, as the case may be, of the Party of which it forms a part.

* * *

Section B—Tariffs

Article 302: Tariff Elimination

1. Except as otherwise provided in this Agreement, no Party may increase any existing customs duty, or adopt any customs duty, on an originating good.

2. Except as otherwise provided in this Agreement, each Party shall progressively eliminate its customs duties on originating goods in accordance with its Schedule to Annex 302.2.

3. On the request of any Party, the Parties shall consult to consider accelerating the elimination of customs duties set out in their Schedules. * * *

* * *

Article 303: Restriction on Drawback and Duty Deferral Programs

1. Except as otherwise provided in this Article, no Party may refund the amount of customs duties paid, or waive or reduce the amount of customs duties owed, on a good imported into its territory, on condition that the good is:

(a) subsequently exported to the territory of another Party,

(b) used as a material in the production of another good that is subsequently exported to the territory of another Party, or

(c) substituted by an identical or similar good used as a material in the production of another good that is subsequently exported to the territory of another Party, in an amount that exceeds the lesser of the total amount of customs duties paid or owed on the good on importation into its territory and the total amount of customs duties paid to another Party on the good that has been subsequently exported to the territory of that other Party.

2. No Party may, on condition of export, refund, waive or reduce:

(a) an antidumping or countervailing duty that is applied pursuant to a Party's domestic law and that is not applied inconsistently with Chapter Nineteen (Review and Dispute Settlement in Antidumping and Countervailing Duty Matters);

(b) a premium offered or collected on an imported good arising out of any tendering system in respect of the administration of quantitative import restrictions, tariff rate quotas or tariff preference levels;

(c) a fee applied pursuant to section 22 of the U.S. *Agricultural Adjustment Act,* subject to Chapter Seven (Agriculture and Sanitary and Phytosanitary Measures); or

(d) customs duties paid or owed on a good imported into its territory and substituted by an identical or similar good that is subsequently exported to the territory of another Party.

3. Where a good is imported into the territory of a Party pursuant to a duty deferral program and is subsequently exported to the territory of another Party, or is used as a material in the production of another good that is subsequently exported to the territory of another Party, or is substituted by an identical or similar good used as a material in the production of another good that is subsequently exported to the territory of another Party, the Party from whose territory the good is exported:

(a) shall assess the customs duties as if the exported good had been withdrawn for domestic consumption; and

(b) may waive or reduce such customs duties to the extent permitted under paragraph 1.

* * *

Article 304: Waiver of Customs Duties

1. Except as set out in Annex 304.1, no Party may adopt any new waiver of customs duties, or expand with respect to existing recipients or extend to any new recipient the application of an existing waiver of customs duties, where the waiver is conditioned, explicitly or implicitly, on the fulfillment of a performance requirement.

2. Except as set out in Annex 304.2, no Party may, explicitly or implicitly, condition on the fulfillment of a performance requirement the continuation of any existing waiver of customs duties.

3. If a waiver or a combination of waivers of customs duties granted by a Party with respect to goods for commercial use by a designated person can be shown by another Party to have an adverse impact on the commercial interests of a person of that Party, or of a person owned or controlled by a person of that Party that is located in the territory of the Party granting the waiver, or on the other Party's economy, the Party granting the waiver shall either cease to grant it or make it generally available to any importer.

4. This Article shall not apply to measures subject to Article 303.

Article 305: Temporary Admission of Goods

1. Each Party shall grant duty-free temporary admission for:

(a) professional equipment necessary for carrying out the business activity, trade or profession of a business person who qualifies for temporary entry pursuant to Chapter Sixteen (Temporary Entry for Business Persons),

(b) equipment for the press or for sound or television broadcasting and cinematographic equipment,

(c) goods imported for sports purposes and goods intended for display or demonstration, and

(d) commercial samples and advertising films,

imported from the territory of another Party, regardless of their origin and regardless of whether like, directly competitive or substitutable goods are available in the territory of the Party.

* * *

Section C—Non-Tariff Measures

Article 309: Import and Export Restrictions

1. Except as otherwise provided in this Agreement, no Party may adopt or maintain any prohibition or restriction on the importation of any good

of another Party or on the exportation or sale for export of any good destined for the territory of another Party, except in accordance with Article XI of the GATT, including its interpretative notes, and to this end Article XI of the GATT and its interpretative notes, or any equivalent provision of a successor agreement to which all Parties are party, are incorporated into and made a part of this Agreement.

2. The Parties understand that the GATT rights and obligations incorporated by paragraph 1 prohibit, in any circumstances in which any other form of restriction is prohibited, export price requirements and, except as permitted in enforcement of countervailing and antidumping orders and undertakings, import price requirements.

* * *

Article 311: Country of Origin Marking

Annex 311 applies to measures relating to country of origin marking.

Article 314: Export Taxes

Except as set out in Annex 314, no Party may adopt or maintain any duty, tax or other charge on the export of any good to the territory of another Party, unless such duty, tax or charge is adopted or maintained on:

(a) exports of any such good to the territory of all other Parties; and

(b) any such good when destined for domestic consumption.

* * *

Annex 302.2

Tariff Elimination

1. Except as otherwise provided in a Party's Schedule attached to this Annex, the following staging categories apply to the elimination of customs duties by each Party pursuant to Article 302(2):

(a) duties on goods provided for in the items in staging category A in a Party's Schedule shall be eliminated entirely and such goods shall be duty-free, effective January 1, 1994;

(b) duties on goods provided for in the items in staging category B in a Party's Schedule shall be removed in five equal annual stages beginning on January 1, 1994, and such goods shall be duty-free, effective January 1, 1998;

(c) duties on goods provided for in the items in staging category C in a Party's Schedule shall be removed in 10 equal annual stages beginning on January 1, 1994, and such goods shall be duty-free, effective January 1, 2003;

(d) duties on goods provided for in the items in staging category C+ in a Party's Schedule shall be removed in 15 equal annual stages beginning on January 1, 1994, and such goods shall be duty-free, effective January 1, 2008; and

(e) goods provided for in the items in staging category D in a Party's Schedule shall continue to receive duty-free treatment.

2. The base rate of customs duty and staging category for determining the interim rate of customs duty at each stage of reduction for an item are indicated for the item in each Party's Schedule attached to this Annex. These rates generally reflect the rate of duty in effect on July 1, 1991, including rates under the U.S. Generalized System of Preferences and the General Preferential Tariff of Canada.

* * *

Annex 311

Country of Origin Marking

1. The Parties shall establish by January 1, 1994, rules for determining whether a good is a good of a Party ("Marking Rules") for purposes of this Annex, Annex 300–B and Annex 302.2, and for such other purposes as the Parties may agree.

2. Each Party may require that a good of another Party, as determined in accordance with the Marking Rules, bear a country of origin marking, when imported into its territory, that indicates to the ultimate purchaser of that good the name of its country of origin.

3. Each Party shall permit the country of origin marking of a good of another Party to be indicated in English, French or Spanish, except that a Party may, as part of its general consumer information measures, require that an imported good be marked with its country of origin in the same manner as prescribed for goods of that Party.

4. Each Party shall, in adopting, maintaining and applying any measure relating to country of origin marking, minimize the difficulties, costs and inconveniences that the measure may cause to the commerce and industry of the other Parties.

* * *

Annex 313

Distinctive Products

1. Canada and Mexico shall recognize Bourbon Whiskey and Tennessee Whiskey, which is a straight Bourbon Whiskey authorized to be produced only in the State of Tennessee, as distinctive products of the United States. Accordingly, Canada and Mexico shall not permit the sale of any product as Bourbon Whiskey or Tennessee Whiskey, unless it has been manufactured in the United States in accordance with the laws and regulations of the United States governing the manufacture of Bourbon Whiskey and Tennessee Whiskey.

2. Mexico and the United States shall recognize Canadian Whisky as a distinctive product of Canada. Accordingly, Mexico and the United States shall not permit the sale of any product as Canadian Whisky, unless it has been manufactured in Canada in accordance with the laws and regulations of Canada governing the manufacture of Canadian Whisky for consumption in Canada.

3. Canada and the United States shall recognize Tequila and Mezcal as distinctive products of Mexico. Accordingly, Canada and the United States shall not permit the sale of any product as Tequila or Mezcal, unless it has been manufactured in Mexico in accordance with the laws and regulations of Mexico governing the manufacture of Tequila and Mezcal. This provision shall apply to Mezcal, either on the date of entry into force of this Agreement, or 90 days after the date when the official standard for this product is made obligatory by the Government of Mexico, whichever is later.

Annex 300–A

Trade and Investment in the Automotive Sector

1. Each Party shall accord to all existing producers of vehicles in its territory treatment no less favorable than it accords to any new producer of vehicles in its territory under the measures referred to in this Annex, except that this obligation shall not be construed to apply to any differences in treatment specifically provided for in the Appendices to this Annex.

* * *

Annex 300–B

Textile and Apparel Goods

Section 1: Scope and Coverage

1. This Annex applies to the textile and apparel goods set out in Appendix 1.1.

2. In the event of any inconsistency between this Agreement and the *Arrangement Regarding International Trade in Textiles* (Multifiber Arrangement), as amended and extended, including any amendment or extension after January 1, 1994, or any other existing or future agreement applicable to trade in textile or apparel goods, this Agreement shall prevail to the extent of the inconsistency, unless the Parties agree otherwise.

Section 2: Tariff Elimination

1. Except as otherwise provided in this Agreement, each Party shall progressively eliminate its customs duties on originating textile and apparel goods in accordance with its Schedule to Annex 302.2 (Tariff Elimination), and as set out for ease of reference in Appendix 2.1.

* * *

Chapter Four

Rules of Origin

Article 401: Originating Goods

Except as otherwise provided in this Chapter, a good shall originate in the territory of a Party where:

(a) the good is wholly obtained or produced entirely in the territory of one or more of the Parties, as defined in Article 415;

(b) each of the non-originating materials used in the production of the good undergoes an applicable change in tariff classification set out in Annex 401 as a result of production occurring entirely in the territory of one or more of the Parties, or the good otherwise satisfies the applicable requirements of that Annex where no change in tariff classification is required, and the good satisfies all other applicable requirements of this Chapter;

(c) the good is produced entirely in the territory of one or more of the Parties exclusively from originating materials; or

(d) except for a good provided for in Chapters 61 through 63 of the Harmonized System, the good is produced entirely in the territory of one or more of the Parties but one or more of the non-originating materials provided for as parts under the Harmonized System that are used in the production of the good does not undergo a change in tariff classification because

(i) the good was imported into the territory of a Party in an unassembled or a disassembled form but was classified as an assembled good pursuant to General Rule of Interpretation 2(a) of the Harmonized System, or

(ii) the heading for the good provides for and specifically describes both the good itself and its parts and is not further subdivided into subheadings, or the subheading for the good provides for and specifically describes both the good itself and its parts,

provided that the regional value content of the good, determined in accordance with Article 402, is not less than 60 percent where the transaction value method is used, or is not less than 50 percent where the net cost method is used, and that the good satisfies all other applicable requirements of this Chapter.

Article 402: Regional Value Content

1. Except as provided in paragraph 5, each Party shall provide that the regional value content of a good shall be calculated, at the choice of the exporter or producer of the good, on the basis of either the transaction value method set out in paragraph 2 or the net cost method set out in paragraph 3.

2. Each Party shall provide that an exporter or producer may calculate the regional value content of a good on the basis of the following transaction value method:

$$RVC = \frac{TV - VNM}{TV} \times 100$$

where

RVC is the regional value content, expressed as a percentage;

TV is the transaction value of the good adjusted to a F.O.B. basis; and

VNM is the value of non-originating materials used by the producer in the production of the good.

3. Each Party shall provide that an exporter or producer may calculate the regional value content of a good on the basis of the following net cost method:

$$RVC = \frac{NC - VNM}{NC} \times 100$$

where

RVC is the regional value content, expressed as a percentage;

NC is the net cost of the good; and

VNM is the value of non-originating materials used by the producer in the production of the good.

4. Except as provided in Article 403(1) and for a motor vehicle identified in Article 403(2) or a component identified in Annex 403.2, the value of non-originating materials used by the producer in the production of a good shall not, for purposes of calculating the regional value content of the good under paragraph 2 or 3, include the value of non-originating materials used to produce originating materials that are subsequently used in the production of the good.

5. *Net Cost Method Must be Used in Certain Cases.*—An exporter or producer shall calculate the regional value-content of a good solely on the basis of the net cost method described in paragraph (3), if—

(A) there is no transaction value for the good;

(B) the transaction value of the good is unacceptable under Article 1 of the Customs Valuation Code;

(C) the good is sold by the producer to a related person and the volume, by units of quantity, of sales of identical or similar goods to related persons during the six-month period immediately preceding the month in which the good is sold exceeds 85 percent of the producer's total sales of such goods during that period;

(D) the good is—

(i) a motor vehicle provided for in heading 8701 or 8702, subheadings 8703.21 through 8703.90, or heading 8704, 8705, or 8706;

(ii) identified in Annex 403.1 or 403.2 of the Agreement and is for use in a motor vehicle provided for in heading 8701 or 8702, subheadings 8703.21 through 8703.90, or heading 8704, 8705, or 8706;

(iii) provided for in subheadings 6401.10 through 6406.10; or

(iv) a word processing machine provided for in subheading 8469.10.00;

(E) the exporter or producer chooses to accumulate the regional value-content of the good in accordance with subsection (d); or

(F) the good is designated as an intermediate material under paragraph (10) and is subject to a regional value-content requirement.

6. *Net Cost Method Allowed for Adjustments.*—If an exporter or producer of a good calculates the regional value-content of the good on the basis of the transaction value method and a NAFTA country subsequently notifies the exporter or producer, during the course of a verification conducted in accordance with chapter 5 of the Agreement, that the transaction value of the good or the value of any material used in the production of the good must be adjusted or is unacceptable under Article 1 of the Customs Valuation Code, the exporter or producer may calculate the regional value-content of the good on the basis of the net cost method.

7. *Review of Adjustment.*—Nothing in paragraph (6) shall be construed to prevent any review or appeal available in accordance with article 510 of the Agreement with respect to an adjustment to or a rejection of—

(A) the transaction value of a good; or

(B) the value of any material used in the production of a good.

8. *Calculating Net Cost.*—The producer may, consistent with regulations implementing this section, calculate the net cost of a good under paragraph (3), by—

(A) calculating the total cost incurred with respect to all goods produced by that producer, subtracting any sales promotion, marketing and after-sales service costs, royalties, shipping and packing costs, and nonallowable interest costs that are included in the total cost of all such goods, and reasonably allocating the resulting net cost of those goods to the good;

(B) calculating the total cost incurred with respect to all goods produced by that producer, reasonably allocating the total cost to the good, and subtracting any sales promotion, marketing and after-sales service costs, royalties, shipping and packing costs, and nonallowable interest costs that are included in the portion of the total cost allocated to the good; or

(C) reasonably allocating each cost that is part of the total cost incurred with respect to the good so that the aggregate of these costs does not include any sales promotion, marketing and after-sales service costs, royalties, shipping and packing costs, or nonallowable interest costs.

9. *Value of Material Used in Production.*—Except as provided in paragraph (11), the value of a material used in the production of a good—

(A) shall—

(i) be the transaction value of the material determined in accordance with Article 1 of the Customs Valuation Code; or

(ii) in the event that there is no transaction value or the transaction value of the material is unacceptable under Article 1 of the Customs Valuation Code, be determined in accordance with Articles 2 through 7 of the Customs Valuation Code; and

(B) if not included under clause (i) or (ii) of subparagraph (A), shall include—

(i) freight, insurance, packing, and all other costs incurred in transporting the material to the location of the producer;

(ii) duties, taxes, and customs brokerage fees paid on the material in the territory of one or more of the NAFTA countries; and

(iii) the cost of waste and spoilage resulting from the use of the material in the production of the good, less the value of renewable scrap or by-product.

10. *Intermediate Material.*—Except for goods described in subsection (c)(1), any self-produced material, other than a component identified in Annex 403.2 of the Agreement, that is used in the production of a good may be designated by the producer of the good as an intermediate material for the purpose of calculating the regional value-content of the good under paragraph (2) or (3); provided that if the intermediate material is subject to a regional value-content requirement, no other self-produced material that is subject to a regional value-content requirement and is used in the production of the intermediate material may be designated by the producer as an intermediate material.

11. *Value of Intermediate Material.*—The value of an intermediate material shall be—

(A) the total cost incurred with respect to all goods produced by the producer of the good that can be reasonably allocated to the intermediate material; or

(B) the aggregate of each cost that is part of the total cost incurred with respect to the intermediate material that can be reasonably allocated to that intermediate material.

12. *Indirect Material.*—The value of an indirect material shall be based on the Generally Accepted Accounting Principles applicable in the territory of the NAFTA country in which the good is produced.

(c) Automotive Goods.—

1. *Passenger Vehicles and Light Trucks, and their Automotive Parts.*—For purposes of calculating the regional value-content under the net cost method for—

(A) a good that is a motor vehicle for the transport of 15 or fewer persons provided for in subheading 8702.10.00 or 8702.90.00, or a motor vehicle provided for in subheadings 8703.21 through 8703.90, or subheading 8704.21 or 8704.31, or

(B) a good provided for in the tariff provisions listed in Annex 403.1 of the Agreement, that is subject to a regional value-content requirement and is for use as original equipment in the production of a motor vehicle for the transport of 15 or fewer persons provided for in subheading 8702.10.00 or 8702.90.00, or a motor vehicle provided for in subheadings 8703.21 through 8703.90, or subheading 8704.21 or 8704.31,

the value of nonoriginating materials used by the producer in the production of the good shall be the sum of the values of all nonoriginating materials, determined in accordance with subsection (b)(9) at the time the nonoriginating materials are received by the first person in the territory of a NAFTA country who takes title to them, that are imported from outside the territories of the NAFTA countries under the tariff provisions listed in Annex 403.1 of the Agreement and are used in the production of the good or that are used in the production of any material used in the production of the good.

2. *Other Vehicles and their Automotive Parts.*—For purposes of calculating the regional value-content under the net cost method for a good that is a motor vehicle provided for in heading 8701, subheading 8704.10, 8704.22, 8704.23, 8704.32, or 8704.90, or heading 8705 or 8706, a motor vehicle for the transport of 16 or more persons provided for in subheading 8702.10.00 or 8702.90.00, or a component identified in Annex 403.2 of the Agreement for use as original equipment in the production of the motor vehicle, the value of nonoriginating materials used by the producer in the production of the good shall be the sum of—

(A) for each material used by the producer listed in Annex 403.2 of the Agreement, whether or not produced by the producer, at the choice of the producer and determined in accordance with subsection (b), either—

(i) the value of such material that is nonoriginating, or

(ii) the value of nonoriginating materials used in the production of such material; and

(B) the value of any other nonoriginating material used by the producer that is not listed in Annex 403.2 of the Agreement determined in accordance with subsection (b).

3. *Averaging Permitted.*—

(A) In General.—For purposes of calculating the regional value-content of a motor vehicle described in paragraph (1) or (2), the producer may average its calculation over its fiscal year, using any of the categories described in subparagraph (B), on the basis of either all motor vehicles in the category or on the basis of only the motor vehicles in the category that are exported to the territory of one or more of the other NAFTA countries.

(B) Category Described.—A category is described in this subparagraph if it is—

(i) the same model line of motor vehicles in the same class of vehicles produced in the same plant in the territory of a NAFTA country;

(ii) the same class of motor vehicles produced in the same plant in the territory of a NAFTA country;

(iii) the same model line of motor vehicles produced in the territory of a NAFTA country; or

(iv) if applicable, the basis set out in Annex 403.3 of the Agreement.

4. *Annex 403.1 and Annex 403.2.*—For purposes of calculating the regional value-content for any or all goods provided for in a tariff provision listed in Annex 403.1 of the Agreement, or a component or material identified in Annex 403.2 of the Agreement, produced in the same plant, the producer of the good may—

(A) average its calculation—

(i) over the fiscal year of the motor vehicle producer to whom the good is sold;

(ii) over any quarter or month; or

(iii) over its fiscal year, if the good is sold as an aftermarket part;

(B) calculate the average referred to in subparagraph (A) separately for any or all goods sold to one or more motor vehicle producers; or

(C) with respect to any calculation under this paragraph, make a separate calculation for goods that are exported to the territory of one or more NAFTA countries.

5. *Phase-in of Regional Value-Content Requirement.*—Notwithstanding Annex 401 of the Agreement, and except as provided in paragraph (6), the regional value-content requirement shall be—

(A) for a producer's fiscal year beginning on the day closest to January 1, 1998, and thereafter, 56 percent calculated under the net cost method, and for a producer's fiscal year beginning on the day closest to January 1, 2002, and thereafter, 62.5 percent calculated under the net cost method, for—

(i) a good that is a motor vehicle for the transport of 15 or fewer persons provided for in subheading 8702.10.00 or 8702.90.00, or a motor vehicle provided for in subheadings 8703.21 through 8703.90, or subheading 8704.21 or 8704.31; and

(ii) a good provided for in heading 8407 or 8408, or subheading 8708.40, that is for use in a motor vehicle identified in clause (i); and

(B) for a producer's fiscal year beginning on the day closest to January 1, 1998, and thereafter, 55 percent calculated under the net cost method, and for a producer's fiscal year beginning on the day closest to January 1, 2002, and thereafter, 60 percent calculated under the net cost method, for—

(i) a good that is a motor vehicle provided for in heading 8701, subheading 8704.10, 8704.22, 8704.23, 8704.32, or 8704.90, or heading 8705 or 8706, or a motor vehicle for the transport of 16 or more persons provided for in subheading 8702.10.00 or 8702.90.00;

(ii) a good provided for in heading 8407 or 8408, or subheading 8708.40 that is for use in a motor vehicle identified in clause (i); and

(iii) except for a good identified in subparagraph (A)(ii) or a good provided for in subheadings 8482.10 through 8482.80, or subheading 8483.20 or 8483.30, a good identified in Annex 403.1 of the Agreement that is subject to a regional value-content requirement and is for use in a motor vehicle identified in subparagraph (A)(i) or (B)(i).

6. *New and Refitted Plants.*—The regional value-content requirement for a motor vehicle identified in paragraph (1) or (2) shall be—

(A) 50 percent for 5 years after the date on which the first motor vehicle prototype is produced in a plant by a motor vehicle assembler, if—

(i) it is a motor vehicle of a class, or marque, or, except for a motor vehicle identified in paragraph (2), size category and underbody, not previously produced by the motor vehicle assembler in the territory of any of the NAFTA countries;

(ii) the plant consists of a new building in which the motor vehicle is assembled; and

(iii) the plant contains substantially all new machinery that is used in the assembly of the motor vehicle; or

(B) 50 percent for 2 years after the date on which the first motor vehicle prototype is produced at a plant following a refit, if it is a motor vehicle of a class, or marque, or, except for a motor vehicle identified in paragraph (2), size category and underbody, different from that assembled by the motor vehicle assembler in the plant before the refit.

* * *

Article 403: Automotive Goods

1. For purposes of calculating the regional value content under the net cost method set out in Article 402(3) for:

(a) a good that is a motor vehicle provided for in tariff item 8702.10.bb or 8702.90.bb (vehicles for the transport of 15 or fewer persons), or subheading 8703.21 through 8703.90, 8704.21 or 8704.31, or

(b) a good provided for in the tariff provisions listed in Annex 403.1 where the good is subject to a regional value-content requirement and is for use as original equipment in the production of a good provided for in tariff item 8702.10.bb or 8702.90.bb (vehicles for the transport of 15 or fewer persons), or subheading 8702.xx, 8703.21 through 8703.90, 8704.21 or 8704.31, the value of non-originating materials used by the producer in the production of the good shall be the sum of the values of non-originating materials, determined in accordance with Article 402(9) at the time the non-originating materials are received by the first person in the territory of a Party who takes title to them, that are imported from outside the territories of the Parties under the tariff provisions listed in Annex 403.1 and that are used in the production of the good or that are used in the production of any material used in the production of the good.

2. For purposes of calculating the regional value content under the net cost method set out in Article 402(3) for a good that is a motor vehicle provided for in heading 87.01, tariff item 8702.10.aa or 8702.90.aa (vehicles for the transport of 16 or more persons), subheading 8704.10, 8704.22, 8704.23, 8704.32 or 8704.90, or heading 87.05 or 87.06, or for a component identified in Annex 403.2 for use as original equipment in the production of the motor vehicle, the value of non-originating materials used by the producer in the production of the good shall be the sum of:

(a) for each material used by the producer listed in Annex 403.2, whether or not produced by the producer, at the choice of the producer and determined in accordance with Article 402, either

(i) the value of such material that is non-originating, or

(ii) the value of non-originating materials used in the production of such material; and

(b) the value of any other non-originating material used by the producer that is not listed in Annex 403.2, determined in accordance with Article 402.

3. For purposes of calculating the regional value content of a motor vehicle identified in paragraph 1 or 2, the producer may average its

calculation over its fiscal year, using any one of the following categories, on the basis of either all motor vehicles in the category or only those motor vehicles in the category that are exported to the territory of one or more of the other Parties:

(a) the same model line of motor vehicles in the same class of vehicles produced in the same plant in the territory of a Party:

(b) the same class of motor vehicles produced in the same plant in the territory of a Party;

(c) the same model line of motor vehicles produced in the territory of a Party; or

(d) if applicable, the basis set out in Annex 403.3.

4. For purposes of calculating the regional value content for any or all goods provided for in a tariff provision listed in Annex 403.1, or a component or material identified in Annex 403.2, produced in the same plant, the producer of the good may:

(a) average its calculation

(i) over the fiscal year of the motor vehicle producer to whom the good is sold.

(ii) over any quarter or month, or

(iii) over its fiscal year, if the good is sold as an aftermarket part;

(b) calculate the average referred to in subparagraph (a) separately for any or all goods sold to one or more motor vehicle producers; or

(c) with respect to any calculation under this paragraph, calculate separately those goods that are exported to the territory of one or more of the Parties.

5. Notwithstanding Annex 401, and except as provided in paragraph 6, the regional value-content requirement shall be:

(a) for a producer's fiscal year beginning on the day closest to January 1, 1998 and thereafter, 56 percent under the net cost method, and for a producer's fiscal year beginning on the day closest to January 1, 2002 and thereafter, 62.5 percent under the net cost method, for

(i) a good that is a motor vehicle provided for in tariff item 8702.10.bb or 8702.90.bb (vehicles for the transport of 15 or fewer persons), or subheading 8703.21 through 8703.90, 8704.21 or 8704.31, and

(ii) a good provided for in heading 84.07 or 84.08, or subheading 8708.40, that is for use in a motor vehicle identified in subparagraph (a)(i); and

(b) for a producer's fiscal year beginning on the day closest to January 1, 1998 and thereafter, 55 percent under the net cost method, and for a producer's fiscal year beginning on the day closest to January 1, 2002 and thereafter, 60 percent under the net cost method, for

(i) a good that is a motor vehicle provided for in heading 87.01, subheading 8702.yy (vehicles for the transport of 16 or more persons), 8704.10, 8704.22, 8704.23, 8704.32 or 8704.90, or heading 87.05 or 87.06,

(ii) a good provided for in heading 84.07 or 84.08 or subheading 8708.40 that is for use in a motor vehicle identified in subparagraph (b)(i), and

(iii) except for a good identified in subparagraph (a)(ii) or provided for in subheading 8482.10 through 8482.80, 8483.20 or 8483.30, a good identified in Annex 403.1 that is subject to a regional value content requirement and that is for use in a motor vehicle identified in subparagraphs (a)(i) or (b)(i).

6. The regional value-content requirement for a motor vehicle identified in Article 403(1) or 403(2) shall be:

(a) 50 percent for five years after the date on which the first motor vehicle prototype is produced in a plant by a motor vehicle assembler, if

(i) it is a motor vehicle of a class, or marque, or, except for a motor vehicle identified in Article 403(2), size category and underbody, not previously produced by the motor vehicle assembler in the territory of any of the Parties,

(ii) the plant consists of a new building in which the motor vehicle is assembled, and

(iii) the plant contains substantially all new machinery that is used in the assembly of the motor vehicle; or

(b) 50 percent for two years after the date on which the first motor vehicle prototype is produced at a plant following a refit, if it is a different motor vehicle of a class, or marque, or, except for a motor vehicle identified in Article 403(2), size category and underbody, than was assembled by the motor vehicle assembler in the plant before the refit.

Article 404: Accumulation

1. For purposes of determining whether a good is an originating good, the production of the good in the territory of one or more of the Parties by one or more producers shall, at the choice of the exporter or producer of the good for which preferential tariff treatment is claimed, be considered to have been performed in the territory of any of the Parties by that exporter or producer, provided that:

(a) all non-originating materials used in the production of the good undergo an applicable tariff classification change set out in Annex 401, and the good satisfies any applicable regional value-content requirement, entirely in the territory of one or more of the Parties; and

(b) the good satisfies all other applicable requirements of this Chapter.

2. For purposes of Article 402(10), the production of a producer that chooses to accumulate its production with that of other producers under paragraph 1 shall be considered to be the production of a single producer.

Article 405: De Minimis

1. Except as provided in paragraphs 3 through 6, a good shall be considered to be an originating good if the value of all non-originating materials used in the production of the good that do not undergo an applicable change in tariff classification set out in Annex 401 is not more than seven percent of the transaction value of the good, adjusted to a F.O.B. basis, or, if the transaction value of the good is unacceptable under Article 1 of the Customs Valuation Code, the value of all such non-originating materials is not more than seven percent of the total cost of the good, provided that:

(a) if the good is subject to a regional value-content requirement, the value of such non-originating materials shall be taken into account in calculating the regional value content of the good; and

(b) the good satisfies all other applicable requirements of this Chapter.

* * *

Article 411: Transshipment

A good shall not be considered to be an originating good by reason of having undergone production that satisfies the requirements of Article 401 if, subsequent to that production, the good undergoes further production or any other operation outside the territories of the Parties, other than unloading, reloading or any other operation necessary to preserve it in good condition or to transport the good to the territory of a Party.

Article 412: Non–Qualifying Operations

A good shall not be considered to be an originating good merely by reason of:

(a) mere dilution with water or another substance that does not materially alter the characteristics of the good; or

(b) any production or pricing practice in respect of which it may be demonstrated, on the basis of a preponderance of evidence, that the object was to circumvent this Chapter.

Article 413: Interpretation and Application

For purposes of this Chapter:

(a) the basis for tariff classification in this Chapter is the Harmonized System;

(b) where a good referred to by a tariff item number is described in parentheses following the tariff item number, the description is provided for purposes of reference only;

(c) where applying Article 401(d), the determination of whether a heading or subheading under the Harmonized System provides for and specifically describes both a good and its parts shall be made on the basis of the nomenclature of the heading or subheading, or the General Rules of Interpretation, the Chapter Notes or the Section Notes of the Harmonized System;

(d) in applying the Customs Valuation Code under this Chapter,

(i) the principles of the Customs Valuation Code shall apply to domestic transactions, with such modifications as may be required by the circumstances, as would apply to international transactions,

(ii) the provisions of this Chapter shall take precedence over the Customs Valuation Code to the extent of any difference, and

(iii) the definitions in Article 415 shall take precedence over the definitions in the Customs Valuation Code to the extent of any difference; and

(e) all costs referred to in this Chapter shall be recorded and maintained in accordance with the Generally Accepted Accounting Principles applicable in the territory of the Party in which the good is produced.

* * *

Chapter Five

Customs Procedures

Section A—Certification of Origin

Article 501: Certificate of Origin

1. The Parties shall establish by January 1, 1994 a Certificate of Origin for the purpose of certifying that a good being exported from the territory of a Party into the territory of another Party qualifies as an originating good, and may thereafter revise the Certificate by agreement.

2. Each Party may require that a Certificate of Origin for a good imported into its territory be completed in a language required under its law.

3. Each Party shall:

(a) require an exporter in its territory to complete and sign a Certificate of Origin for any exportation of a good for which an importer may claim preferential tariff treatment on importation of the good into the territory of another Party; and

(b) provide that where an exporter in its territory is not the producer of the good, the exporter may complete and sign a Certificate on the basis of

(i) its knowledge of whether the good qualifies as an originating good,

(ii) its reasonable reliance on the producer's written representation that the good qualifies as an originating good, or

(iii) a completed and signed Certificate for the good voluntarily provided to the exporter by the producer.

4. Nothing in paragraph 3 shall be construed to require a producer to provide a Certificate of Origin to an exporter.

5. Each Party shall provide that a Certificate of Origin that has been completed and signed by an exporter or a producer in the territory of another Party that is applicable to:

(a) a single importation of a good into the Party's territory, or

(b) multiple importations of identical goods into the Party's territory that occur within a specified period, not exceeding 12 months, set out therein by the exporter or producer,

shall be accepted by its customs administration for four years after the date on which the Certificate was signed.

Article 502: Obligations Regarding Importations

1. Except as otherwise provided in this Chapter, each Party shall require an importer in its territory that claims preferential tariff treatment for a good imported into its territory from the territory of another Party to:

(a) make a written declaration, based on a valid Certificate of Origin, that the good qualifies as an originating good;

(b) have the Certificate in its possession at the time the declaration is made;

(c) provide, on the request of that Party's customs administration, a copy of the Certificate; and

(d) promptly make a corrected declaration and pay any duties owing where the importer has reason to believe that a Certificate on which a declaration was based contains information that is not correct.

2. Each Party shall provide that, where an importer in its territory claims preferential tariff treatment for a good imported into its territory from the territory of another Party:

(a) the Party may deny preferential tariff treatment to the good if the importer fails to comply with any requirement under this Chapter; and

(b) the importer shall not be subject to penalties for the making of an incorrect declaration, if it voluntarily makes a corrected declaration pursuant to paragraph 1(d).

3. Each Party shall provide that, where a good would have qualified as an originating good when it was imported into the territory of that Party

but no claim for preferential tariff treatment was made at that time, the importer of the good may, no later than one year after the date on which the good was imported, apply for a refund of any excess duties paid as the result of the good not having been accorded preferential tariff treatment, on presentation of:

(a) a written declaration that the good qualified as an originating good at the time of importation;

(b) a copy of the Certificate of Origin; and

(c) such other documentation relating to the importation of the good as that Party may require.

* * *

Section D—Review and Appeal of Origin Determinations and Advance Rulings

Article 510: Review and Appeal

1. Each Party shall grant substantially the same rights of review and appeal of marking determinations of origin, country of origin determinations and advance rulings by its customs administration as it provides to importers in its territory to any person:

(a) who completes and signs a Certificate of Origin for a good that has been the subject of a determination of origin;

(b) whose good has been the subject of a country of origin marking determination pursuant to Article 311 (Country of Origin Marking); or

(c) who has received an advance ruling pursuant to Article 509(1).

2. Further to Articles 1804 (Administrative Proceedings) and 1805 (Review and Appeal), each Party shall provide that the rights of review and appeal referred to in paragraph 1 shall include access to:

(a) at least one level of administrative review independent of the official or office responsible for the determination under review; and

(b) in accordance with its domestic law, judicial or quasi-judicial review of the determination or decision taken at the final level of administrative review.

Section E—Uniform Regulations

* * *

Chapter Six

Energy and Basic Petrochemicals

Article 601: Principles

1. The Parties confirm their full respect for their Constitutions.

2. The Parties recognize that it is desirable to strengthen the important role that trade in energy and basic petrochemical goods plays in the free trade area and to enhance this role through sustained and gradual liberalization.

3. The Parties recognize the importance of having viable and internationally competitive energy and petrochemical sectors to further their individual national interests.

Article 602: Scope and Coverage

1. This Chapter applies to measures relating to energy and basic petrochemical goods originating in the territories of the Parties and to measures relating to investment and to the cross-border trade in services associated with such goods, as set forth in this Chapter.

* * *

Article 603: Import and Export Restrictions

1. Subject to the further rights and obligations of this Agreement, the Parties incorporate the provisions of the *General Agreement on Tariffs and Trade* (GATT), with respect to prohibitions or restrictions on trade in energy and basic petrochemical goods. The Parties agree that this language does not incorporate their respective protocols of provisional application to the GATT.

2. The Parties understand that the provisions of the GATT incorporated in paragraph 1 prohibit, in any circumstances in which any other form of quantitative restriction is prohibited, minimum or maximum export-price requirements and, except as permitted in enforcement of countervailing and antidumping orders and undertakings, minimum or maximum import-price requirements.

3. In circumstances where a Party adopts or maintains a restriction on importation from or exportation to a non-Party of an energy or basic petrochemical good, nothing in this Agreement shall be construed to prevent the Party from:

(a) limiting or prohibiting the importation from the territory of any Party of such energy or basic petrochemical good of the non-Party; or

(b) requiring as a condition of export of such energy or basic petrochemical good of the Party to the territory of any other Party that the good be consumed within the territory of the other Party.

4. In the event that a Party adopts or maintains a restriction on imports of an energy or basic petrochemical good from non-Party countries, the Parties, on request of any Party, shall consult with a view to avoiding undue interference with or distortion of pricing, marketing and distribution arrangements in another Party.

5. Each Party may administer a system of import and export licensing for energy or basic petrochemical goods provided that such system is

operated in a manner consistent with the provisions of this Agreement, including paragraph 1 and Article 1502 (Monopolies and State Enterprises).

* * *

Article 604: Export Taxes

No Party may adopt or maintain any duty, tax or other charge on the export of any energy or basic petrochemical good to the territory of another Party, unless such duty, tax or charge is adopted or maintained on:

(a) exports of any such good to the territory of all other Parties; and

(b) any such good when destined for domestic consumption.

* * *

Annex 602.3

Reservations and Special Provisions

Reservations

1. The Mexican State reserves to itself the following strategic activities, including investment in such activities and the provision of services in such activities:

(a) exploration and exploitation of crude oil and natural gas; refining or processing of crude oil and natural gas; and production of artificial gas, basic petrochemicals and their feedstocks and pipelines;

(b) foreign trade; transportation, storage and distribution, up to and including the first hand sales of the following goods:

(i) crude oil,

(ii) natural and artificial gas,

(iii) goods covered by this Chapter obtained from the refining or processing of crude oil and natural gas, and

(iv) basic petrochemicals;

(c) the supply of electricity as a public service in Mexico, including, except as provided in paragraph 5, the generation, transmission, transformation, distribution and sale of electricity; and

(d) exploration, exploitation and processing of radioactive minerals, the nuclear fuel cycle, the generation of nuclear energy, the transportation and storage of nuclear waste, the use and reprocessing of nuclear fuel and the regulation of their applications for other purposes and the production of heavy water.

In the event of an inconsistency between this paragraph and another provision of this Agreement, this paragraph shall prevail to the extent of that inconsistency.

2. Pursuant to Article 1101(2) (Investment—Scope and Coverage), private investment is not permitted in the activities listed in paragraph 1.

Chapter Twelve (Cross–Border Trade in Services) shall only apply to activities involving the provision of services covered in paragraph 1 when Mexico permits a contract to be granted in respect of such activities and only to the extent of that contract.

Trade in Natural Gas and Basic Petrochemicals

3. Where end-users and suppliers of natural gas or basic petrochemical goods consider that cross-border trade in such goods may be in their interests, each Party shall permit such end-users and suppliers, and any state enterprise of that Party as may be required under its domestic law, to negotiate supply contracts.

Each Party shall leave the modalities of the implementation of any such contract to the end-users, suppliers, and any state enterprise of the Party as may be required under its domestic law, which may take the form of individual contracts between the state enterprise and each of the other entities. Such contracts may be subject to regulatory approval.

Performance Clauses

4. Each Party shall allow its state enterprises to negotiate performance clauses in their service contracts.

Activities and Investment in Electricity Generation Facilities

* * *

Chapter Seven

Agriculture and Sanitary and Phytosanitary Measures

Section A—Agriculture

Article 701: Scope and Coverage

1. This Section applies to measures adopted or maintained by a Party relating to agricultural trade.

2. In the event of any inconsistency between this Section and another provision of this Agreement, this Section shall prevail to the extent of the inconsistency.

Article 702: International Obligations

1. Annex 702.1 applies to the Parties specified in that Annex with respect to agricultural trade under certain agreements between them.

2. Prior to adopting pursuant to an intergovernmental commodity agreement, a measure that may affect trade in an agricultural good between the Parties, the Party proposing to adopt the measure shall consult with the other Parties with a view to avoiding nullification or impairment of a concession granted by that Party in its Schedule to Annex 302.2.

3. Annex 702.3 applies to the Parties specified in that Annex with respect to measures adopted or maintained pursuant to an intergovernmental coffee agreement.

Article 703: Market Access

1. The Parties shall work together to improve access to their respective markets through the reduction or elimination of import barriers to trade between them in agricultural goods.

* * *

Article 704: Domestic Support

The Parties recognize that domestic support measures can be of crucial importance to their agricultural sectors but may also have trade distorting and production effects and that domestic support reduction commitments may result from agricultural multilateral trade negotiations under the *General Agreement on Tariffs and Trade* (GATT). Accordingly, where a Party supports its agricultural producers, that Party should endeavor to work toward domestic support measures that:

(a) have minimal or no trade distorting or production effects; or

(b) are exempt from any applicable domestic support reduction commitments that may be negotiated under the GATT.

The Parties further recognize that a Party may change its domestic support measures, including those that may be subject to reduction commitments, at the Party's discretion, subject to its rights and obligations under the GATT.

Article 705: Export Subsidies

1. The Parties share the objective of the multilateral elimination of export subsidies for agricultural goods and shall cooperate in an effort to achieve an agreement under the GATT to eliminate those subsidies.

2. The Parties recognize that export subsidies for agricultural goods may prejudice the interests of importing and exporting Parties and, in particular, may disrupt the markets of importing Parties. Accordingly, in addition to the rights and obligations of the Parties specified in Annex 702.1, the Parties affirm that it is inappropriate for a Party to provide an export subsidy for an agricultural good exported to the territory of another Party where there are no other subsidized imports of that good into the territory of that other Party.

* * *

Section B—Sanitary and Phytosanitary Measures

Article 709: Scope and Coverage

In order to establish a framework of rules and disciplines to guide the development, adoption and enforcement of sanitary and phytosanitary measures, this Section applies to any such measure of a Party that may, directly or indirectly, affect trade between the Parties.

Article 710: Relation to Other Chapters

Articles 301 (National Treatment) and 309 (Import and Export Restrictions), and the provisions of Article XX(b) of the GATT as incorporated into Article 2101(1) (General Exceptions), do not apply to any sanitary or phytosanitary measure.

Article 711: Reliance on Non–Governmental Entities

Each Party shall ensure that any non-governmental entity on which it relies in applying a sanitary or phytosanitary measure acts in a manner consistent with this Section.

Article 712: Basic Rights and Obligations

Right to Take Sanitary and Phytosanitary Measures

1. Each Party may, in accordance with this Section, adopt, maintain or apply any sanitary or phytosanitary measure necessary for the protection of human, animal or plant life or health in its territory, including a measure more stringent than an international standard, guideline or recommendation.

Right to Establish Level of Protection

2. Notwithstanding any other provision of this Section, each Party may, in protecting human, animal or plant life or health, establish its appropriate levels of protection in accordance with Article 715.

Scientific Principles

3. Each Party shall ensure that any sanitary or phytosanitary measure that it adopts, maintains or applies is:

(a) based on scientific principles, taking into account relevant factors including, where appropriate, different geographic conditions;

(b) not maintained where there is no longer a scientific basis for it; and

(c) based on a risk assessment, as appropriate to the circumstances.

Non–Discriminatory Treatment

4. Each Party shall ensure that a sanitary or phytosanitary measure that it adopts, maintains or applies does not arbitrarily or unjustifiably discriminate between its goods and like goods of another Party, or between goods of another Party and like goods of any other country, where identical or similar conditions prevail.

Unnecessary Obstacles

5. Each Party shall ensure that any sanitary or phytosanitary measure that it adopts, maintains or applies is applied only to the extent necessary

to achieve its appropriate level of protection, taking into account technical and economic feasibility.

Disguised Restrictions

6. No Party may adopt, maintain or apply any sanitary or phytosanitary measure with a view to, or with the effect of, creating a disguised restriction on trade between the Parties.

Article 713: International Standards and Standardizing Organizations

1. Without reducing the level of protection of human, animal or plant life or health, each Party shall use, as a basis for its sanitary and phytosanitary measures, relevant international standards, guidelines or recommendations with the objective, among others, of making its sanitary and phytosanitary measures equivalent or, where appropriate, identical to those of the other Parties.

2. A Party's sanitary or phytosanitary measure that conforms to a relevant international standard, guideline or recommendation shall be presumed to be consistent with Article 712. A measure that results in a level of sanitary or phytosanitary protection different from that which would be achieved by a measure based on a relevant international standard, guideline or recommendation shall not for that reason alone be presumed to be inconsistent with this Section.

3. Nothing in Paragraph 1 shall be construed to prevent a Party from adopting, maintaining or applying, in accordance with the other provisions of this Section, a sanitary or phytosanitary measure that is more stringent than the relevant international standard, guideline or recommendation.

4. Where a Party has reason to believe that a sanitary or phytosanitary measure of another Party is adversely affecting or may adversely affect its exports and the measure is not based on a relevant international standard, guideline or recommendation, it may request, and the other Party shall provide in writing, the reasons for the measure.

5. Each Party shall, to the greatest extent practicable, participate in relevant international and North American standardizing organizations, including the *Codex Alimentarius Commission,* the *International Office of Epizootics,* the *International Plant Protection Convention,* and the *North American Plant Protection Organization,* with a view to promoting the development and periodic review of international standards, guidelines and recommendations.

Article 714: Equivalence

1. Without reducing the level of protection of human, animal or plant life or health, the Parties shall, to the greatest extent practicable and in accordance with this Section, pursue equivalence of their respective sanitary and phytosanitary measures.

* * *

Article 715: Risk Assessment and Appropriate Level of Protection

1. In conducting a risk assessment, each Party shall take into account:

(a) relevant risk assessment techniques and methodologies developed by international or North American standardizing organizations;

(b) relevant scientific evidence;

(c) relevant processes and production methods;

(d) relevant inspection, sampling and testing methods;

(e) the prevalence of relevant diseases or pests, including the existence of pest-free or disease-free areas or areas of low pest or disease prevalence;

(f) relevant ecological and other environmental conditions; and

(g) relevant treatments, such as quarantines.

2. Further to paragraph 1, each Party shall, in establishing its appropriate level of protection regarding the risk associated with the introduction, establishment or spread of an animal or plant pest or disease, and in assessing the risk, also take into account the following economic factors, where relevant:

(a) loss of production or sales that may result from the pest or disease;

(b) costs of control or eradication of the pest or disease in its territory; and

(c) the relative cost-effectiveness of alternative approaches to limiting risks.

3. Each Party, in establishing its appropriate level of protection:

(a) should take into account the objective of minimizing negative trade effects; and

(b) shall, with the objective of achieving consistency in such levels, avoid arbitrary or unjustifiable distinctions in such levels in different circumstances, where such distinctions result in arbitrary or unjustifiable discrimination against a good of another Party or constitute a disguised restriction on trade between the Parties.

4. Notwithstanding paragraphs (1) through (3) and Article 712(3)(c), where a Party conducting a risk assessment determines that available relevant scientific evidence or other information is insufficient to complete the assessment, it may adopt a provisional sanitary or phytosanitary measure on the basis of available relevant information, including from international or North American standardizing organizations and from sanitary or phytosanitary measures of other Parties. The Party shall, within a reasonable period after information sufficient to complete the assessment is presented to it, complete its assessment, review and, where appropriate, revise the provisional measure in the light of the assessment.

5. Where a Party is able to achieve its appropriate level of protection through the phased application of a sanitary or phytosanitary measure, it may, on the request of another Party and in accordance with this Section, allow for such a phased application, or grant specified exceptions for limited periods from the measure, taking into account the requesting Party's export interests.

Article 716: Adaptation to Regional Conditions

1. Each Party shall adapt any of its sanitary or phytosanitary measures relating to the introduction, establishment or spread of an animal or plant pest or disease, to the sanitary or phytosanitary characteristics of the area where a good subject to such a measure is produced and the area in its territory to which the good is destined, taking into account any relevant conditions, including those relating to transportation and handling, between those areas. In assessing such characteristics of an area, including whether an area is, and is likely to remain, a pest-free or disease-free area or an area of low pest or disease prevalence, each Party shall take into account, among other factors:

(a) the prevalence of relevant pests or diseases in that area;

(b) the existence of eradication or control programs in that area; and

(c) any relevant international standard, guideline or recommendation.

* * *

Chapter Eight

Emergency Action

Article 801: Bilateral Actions

1. Subject to paragraphs 2 through 4 and Annex 801.1, and during the transition period only, if a good originating in the territory of a Party, as a result of the reduction or elimination of a duty provided for in this Agreement, is being imported into the territory of another Party in such increased quantities, in absolute terms, and under such conditions that the imports of the good from that Party alone constitute a substantial cause of serious injury, or threat thereof, to a domestic industry producing a like or directly competitive good, the Party into whose territory the good is being imported may, to the minimum extent necessary to remedy or prevent the injury:

(a) suspend the further reduction of any rate of duty provided for under this Agreement on the good;

(b) increase the rate of duty on the good to a level not to exceed the lesser of

(i) the most-favored-nation (MFN) applied rate of duty in effect at the time the action is taken, and

(ii) the MFN applied rate of duty in effect on the day immediately preceding the date of entry into force of this Agreement; or

(c) in the case of a duty applied to a good on a seasonal basis, increase the rate of duty to a level not to exceed the MFN applied rate of duty that was in effect on the good for the corresponding season immediately preceding the date of entry into force of this Agreement.

2. The following conditions and limitations shall apply to a proceeding that may result in emergency action under paragraph 1: (a) a Party shall, without delay, deliver to any Party that may be affected written notice of, and a request for consultations regarding, the institution of a proceeding that could result in emergency action against a good originating in the territory of a Party; (b) any such action shall be initiated no later than one year after the date of institution of the proceeding; (c) no action may be maintained (i) for a period exceeding three years, except where the good against which the action is taken is provided for in the items in staging category C+ of the Schedule to Annex 302.2 of the Party taking the action and that Party determines that the affected industry has undertaken adjustment and requires an extension of the period of relief, in which case the period of relief may be extended for one year provided that the duty applied during the initial period of relief is substantially reduced at the beginning of the extension period, or (ii) beyond the expiration of the transition period, except with the consent of the Party against whose good the action is taken; (d) no action may be taken by a Party against any particular good originating in the territory of another Party more than once during the transition period; and (e) on the termination of the action, the rate of duty shall be the rate that, according to the Party's Schedule to Annex 302.2 for the staged elimination of the tariff, would have been in effect one year after the initiation of the action, and beginning January 1 of the year following the termination of the action, at the option of the Party that has taken the action (i) the rate of duty shall conform to the applicable rate set out in its Schedule to Annex 302.2, or (ii) the tariff shall be eliminated in equal annual stages ending on the date set out in its Schedule to Annex 302.2 for the elimination of the tariff.

3. A Party may take a bilateral emergency action after the expiration of the transition period to deal with cases of serious injury, or threat thereof, to a domestic industry arising from the operation of this Agreement only with the consent of the Party against whose good the action would be taken.

4. The Party taking an action under this Article shall provide to the Party against whose good the action is taken mutually agreed trade liberalizing compensation in the form of concessions having substantially equivalent trade effects or equivalent to the value of the additional duties expected to result from the action. If the Parties concerned are unable to agree on compensation, the Party against whose good the action is taken may take tariff action having trade effects substantially equivalent to the action taken under this Article. The Party taking the tariff action shall apply the action only for the minimum period necessary to achieve the substantially equivalent effects.

5. This Article does not apply to emergency actions respecting goods covered by Annex 300-B (Textile and Apparel Goods).

Annex 801.1

Bilateral Actions

1. Notwithstanding Article 801, bilateral emergency actions between Canada and the United States on goods originating in the territory of either Party, other than goods covered by Annex 300-B (Textile and Apparel Goods), shall be governed in accordance with the terms of Article 1101 of the Canada-United States Free Trade Agreement, which is hereby incorporated into and made a part of this Agreement for such purpose.

2. For such purposes, "good originating in the territory of one Party" means "good originating in the territory of a Party" as defined in Article 805.

Article 802

Global Actions

1. Each Party retains its rights and obligations under Article XIX of the GATT or any safeguard agreement pursuant thereto except those regarding compensation or retaliation and exclusion from an action to the extent that such rights or obligations are inconsistent with this Article. Any Party taking an emergency action under Article XIX or any such agreement shall exclude imports of a good from each other Party from the action unless: (a) imports from a Party, considered individually, account for a substantial share of total imports; and (b) imports from a Party, considered individually, or in exceptional circumstances imports from Parties considered collectively, contribute importantly to the serious injury, or threat thereof, caused by imports.

2. In determining whether: (a) imports from a Party, considered individually, account for a substantial share of total imports, those imports normally shall not be considered to account for a substantial share of total imports if that Party is not among the top five suppliers of the good subject to the proceeding, measured in terms of import share during the most recent three-year period; and (b) imports from a Party or Parties contribute importantly to the serious injury, or threat thereof, the competent investigating authority shall consider such factors as the change in the import share of each Party, and the level and change in the level of imports of each Party. In this regard, imports from a Party normally shall not be deemed to contribute importantly to serious injury, or the threat thereof, if the growth rate of imports from a Party during the period in which the injurious surge in imports occurred is appreciably lower than the growth rate of total imports from all sources over the same period.

3. A Party taking such action, from which a good from another Party or Parties is initially excluded pursuant to paragraph 1, shall have the right subsequently to include that good from the other Party or Parties in the action in the event that the competent investigating

authority determines that a surge in imports of such good from the other Party or Parties undermines the effectiveness of the action.

4. A Party shall, without delay, deliver written notice to the other Parties of the institution of a proceeding that may result in emergency action under paragraph 1 or 3.

5. No Party may impose restrictions on a good in an action under paragraph 1 or 3: (a) without delivery of prior written notice to the Commission, and without adequate opportunity for consultation with the Party or Parties against whose good the action is proposed to be taken, as far in advance of taking the action is practicable; and (b) that would have the effect of reducing imports of such good from a Party below the trend of imports of the good from that Party over a recent representative base period with allowance for reasonable growth.

6. The Party taking an action pursuant to this Article shall provide to the Party or Parties against whose good the action is taken mutually agreed trade liberalizing compensation in the form of concessions having substantially equivalent trade effects or equivalent to the value of the additional duties expected to result from the action. If the Parties concerned are unable to agree on compensation, the Party against whose good the action is taken may take action having trade effects substantially equivalent to the action taken under paragraph 1 or 3.

Article 803

Administration of Emergency Action Proceedings

1. Each Party shall ensure the consistent, impartial and reasonable administration of its laws, regulations, decisions and rulings governing all emergency action proceedings.

2. Each Party shall entrust determinations of serious injury, or threat thereof, in emergency action proceedings to a competent investigating authority, subject to review by judicial or administrative tribunals, to the extent provided by domestic law. Negative injury determinations shall not be subject to modification, except by such review. The competent investigating authority empowered under domestic law to conduct such proceedings should be provided with the necessary resources to enable it to fulfill its duties.

3. Each Party shall adopt or maintain equitable, timely, transparent and effective procedures for emergency action proceedings, in accordance with the requirements set out in Annex 803.3.

4. This Article does not apply to emergency actions taken under Annex 300-B (Textile and Apparel Goods).

Annex 803.3

Administration of Emergency Action Proceedings

Institution of a Proceeding

1. An emergency action proceeding may be instituted by a petition or complaint by entities specified in domestic law. The entity filing the

petition or complaint shall demonstrate that it is representative of the domestic industry producing a good like or directly competitive with the imported good.

2. A Party may institute a proceeding on its own motion or request the competent investigating authority to conduct a proceeding.

Contents of a Petition or Complaint

3. Where the basis for an investigation is a petition or complaint filed by an entity representative of a domestic industry, the petitioning entity shall, in its petition or complaint, provide the following information to the extent that such information is publicly available from governmental or other sources, or best estimates and the basis therefor if such information is not available: (a) product description—the name and description of the imported good concerned, the tariff subheading under which that good is classified, its current tariff treatment and the name and description of the like or directly competitive domestic good concerned; (b) representativeness—(i) the names and addresses of the entities filing the petition or complaint, and the locations of the establishments in which they produce the domestic good, (ii) the percentage of domestic production of the like or directly competitive good that such entities account for and the basis for claiming that they are representative of an industry, and (iii) the names and locations of all other domestic establishments in which the like or directly competitive good is produced; (c) import data—import data for each of the five most recent full years that form the basis of the claim that the good concerned is being imported in increased quantities, either in absolute terms or relative to domestic production as appropriate; (d) domestic production data—data on total domestic production of the like or directly competitive good for each of the five most recent full years; (e) data showing injury—quantitative and objective data indicating the nature and extent of injury to the concerned industry, such as data showing changes in the level of sales, prices, production, productivity, capacity utilization, market share, profits and losses, and employment; (f) cause of injury— an enumeration and description of the alleged causes of the injury, or threat thereof, and a summary of the basis for the assertion that increased imports, either actual or relative to domestic production, of the imported good are causing or threatening to cause serious injury, supported by pertinent data; and (g) criteria for inclusion—quantitative and objective data indicating the share of imports accounted for by imports from the territory of each other Party and the petitioner's views on the extent to which such imports are contributing importantly to the serious injury, or threat thereof, caused by imports of that good.

4. Petitions or complaints, except to the extent that they contain confidential business information, shall promptly be made available for public inspection on being filed.

Notice Requirement

5. On instituting an emergency action proceeding, the competent investigating authority shall publish notice of the institution of the proceeding in the official journal of the Party. The notice shall identify the petitioner or other requester, the imported good that is the subject of the proceeding and its tariff subheading, the nature and timing of the determination to be made, the time and place of the public hearing, dates of deadlines for filing briefs, statements and other documents, the place at which the petition and any other documents filed in the course of the proceeding may be inspected, and the name, address and telephone number of the office to be contacted for more information.

6. With respect to an emergency action proceeding instituted on the basis of a petition or complaint filed by an entity asserting that it is representative of the domestic industry, the competent investigating authority shall not publish the notice required by paragraph 5 without first assessing carefully that the petition or complaint meets the requirements of paragraph 3, including representativeness.

Public Hearing

7. In the course of each proceeding, the competent investigating authority shall: (a) hold a public hearing, after providing reasonable notice, to allow all interested parties, and any association whose purpose is to represent the interests of consumers in the territory of the Party instituting the proceeding, to appear in person or by counsel, to present evidence and to be heard on the questions of serious injury, or threat thereof, and the appropriate remedy; and (b) provide an opportunity to all interested parties and any such association appearing at the hearing to cross-question interested parties making presentations at that hearing.

Confidential Information

8. The competent investigating authority shall adopt or maintain procedures for the treatment of confidential information, protected under domestic law, that is provided in the course of a proceeding, including a requirement that interested parties and consumer associations providing such information furnish non-confidential written summaries thereof, or where they indicate that the information cannot be summarized, the reasons why a summary cannot be provided.

Evidence of Injury and Causation

9. In conducting its proceeding the competent investigating authority shall gather, to the best of its ability, all relevant information appropriate to the determination it must make. It shall evaluate all relevant factors of an objective and quantifiable nature having a bearing on the situation of that industry, including the rate and amount of the increase in imports of the good concerned, in absolute and relative terms as

appropriate, the share of the domestic market taken by increased imports, and changes in the level of sales, production, productivity, capacity utilization, profits and losses, and employment. In making its determination, the competent investigating authority may also consider other economic factors, such as changes in prices and inventories, and the ability of firms in the industry to generate capital.

10. The competent investigating authority shall not make an affirmative injury determination unless its investigation demonstrates, on the basis of objective evidence, the existence of a clear causal link between increased imports of the good concerned and serious injury, or threat thereof. Where factors other than increased imports are causing injury to the domestic industry at the same time, such injury shall not be attributed to increased imports.

Deliberation and Report

11. Except in critical circumstances and in global actions involving perishable agricultural goods, the competent investigating authority, before making an affirmative determination in an emergency action proceeding, shall allow sufficient time to gather and consider the relevant information, hold a public hearing and provide an opportunity for all interested parties and consumer associations to prepare and submit their views.

12. The competent investigating authority shall publish promptly a report, including a summary thereof in the official journal of the Party, setting out its findings and reasoned conclusions on all pertinent issues of law and fact. The report shall describe the imported good and its tariff item number, the standard applied and the finding made. The statement of reasons shall set out the basis for the determination, including a description of: (a) the domestic industry seriously injured or threatened with serious injury; (b) information supporting a finding that imports are increasing, the domestic industry is seriously injured or threatened with serious injury, and increasing imports are causing or threatening serious injury; and (c) if provided for by domestic law, any finding or recommendation regarding the appropriate remedy and the basis therefor.

13. In its report, the competent investigating authority shall not disclose any confidential information provided pursuant to any undertaking concerning confidential information that may have been made in the course of the proceedings.

Article 804

Dispute Settlement in Emergency Action Matters

No Party may request the establishment of an arbitral panel under Article 2008 (Request for an Arbitral Panel) regarding any proposed emergency action.

Article 805

Definitions

For purposes of this Chapter:

competent investigating authority means the "competent investigating authority" of a Party as defined in Annex 805;

contribute importantly means an important cause, but not necessarily the most important cause;

critical circumstances means circumstances where delay would cause damage that would be difficult to repair;

domestic industry means the producers as a whole of the like or directly competitive good operating in the territory of a Party;

emergency action does not include any emergency action pursuant to a proceeding instituted prior to January 1, 1994;

good originating in the territory of a Party means an originating good, except that in determining the Party in whose territory that good originates, the relevant rules of Annex 302.2 shall apply;

serious injury means a significant overall impairment of a domestic industry;

surge means a significant increase in imports over the trend for a recent representative base period;

threat of serious injury means serious injury that, on the basis of facts and not merely on allegation, conjecture or remote possibility, is clearly imminent; and

transition period means the 10-year period beginning on January 1, 1994, except where the good against which the action is taken is provided for in the items in staging category C+ of the Schedule to Annex 302.2 of the Party taking the action, in which case the transition period shall be the period of staged tariff elimination for that good.

Annex 805

Country-Specific Definitions

For purposes of this Chapter: **competent investigating authority** means: (a) in the case of Canada, the Canadian International Trade Tribunal, or its successor; (b) in the case of Mexico, the designated authority within the Ministry of Trade and Industrial Development ("Secretaria de Comercio y Fomento Industrial"), or its successor; and (c) in the case of the United States, the U.S. International Trade Commission, or its successor.

PART THREE

TECHNICAL BARRIERS TO TRADE

Chapter Nine

Standards–Related Measures

Article 901: Scope and Coverage

1. This Chapter applies to standards-related measures of a Party, other than those covered by Section B of Chapter Seven (Sanitary and Phyto-

sanitary Measures), that may, directly or indirectly, affect trade in goods or services between the Parties, and to measures of the Parties relating to such measures.

2. Technical specifications prepared by governmental bodies for production or consumption requirements of such bodies shall be governed exclusively by Chapter Ten (Government Procurement).

Article 902: Extent of Obligations

1. Article 105 (Extent of Obligations) does not apply to this Chapter.

2. Each Party shall seek, through appropriate measures, to ensure observance of Articles 904 through 908 by state or provincial governments and by non-governmental standardizing bodies in its territory.

Article 903: Affirmation of Agreement on Technical Barriers to Trade and Other Agreements

Further to Article 103 (Relation to Other Agreements), the Parties affirm with respect to each other their existing rights and obligations relating to standards-related measures under the *GATT Agreement on Technical Barriers to Trade* and all other international agreements, including environmental and conservation agreements, to which those Parties are party.

Article 904: Basic Rights and Obligations

Right to Take Standards–Related Measures

1. Each Party may, in accordance with this Agreement, adopt, maintain or apply any standards-related measure, including any such measure relating to safety, the protection of human, animal or plant life or health, the environment or consumers, and any measure to ensure its enforcement or implementation. Such measures include those to prohibit the importation of a good of another Party or the provision of a service by a service provider of another Party that fails to comply with the applicable requirements of those measures or to complete the Party's approval procedures.

Right to Establish Level of Protection

2. Notwithstanding any other provision of this Chapter, each Party may, in pursuing its legitimate objectives of safety or the protection of human, animal or plant life or health, the environment or consumers, establish the levels of protection that it considers appropriate in accordance with Article 907(2).

Non–Discriminatory Treatment

3. Each Party shall, in respect of its standards-related measures, accord to goods and service providers of another Party:

(a) national treatment in accordance with Article 301 (Market Access) or Article 1202 (Cross–Border Trade in Services); and

(b) treatment no less favorable than that it accords to like goods, or in like circumstances to service providers, of any other country.

Unnecessary Obstacles

4. No Party may prepare, adopt, maintain or apply any standards-related measure with a view to or with the effect of creating an unnecessary obstacle to trade between the Parties. An unnecessary obstacle to trade shall not be deemed to be created where:

(a) the demonstrable purpose of the measure is to achieve a legitimate objective; and

(b) the measure does not operate to exclude goods of another Party that meet that legitimate objective.

Article 905: Use of International Standards

1. Each Party shall use, as a basis for its standards-related measures, relevant international standards or international standards whose completion is imminent, except where such standards would be an ineffective or inappropriate means to fulfill its legitimate objectives, for example because of fundamental climatic, geographical, technological or infrastructural factors, scientific justification or the level of protection that the Party considers appropriate.

2. A Party's standards-related measure that conforms to an international standard shall be presumed to be consistent with Article 904(3) and (4).

3. Nothing in paragraph 1 shall be construed to prevent a Party, in pursuing its legitimate objectives, from adopting, maintaining or applying any standards-related measure that results in a higher level of protection than would be achieved if the measure were based on the relevant international standard.

Article 906: Compatibility and Equivalence

1. Recognizing the crucial role of standards-related measures in achieving legitimate objectives, the Parties shall, in accordance with this Chapter, work jointly to enhance the level of safety and of protection of human, animal and plant life and health, the environment and consumers.

2. Without reducing the level of safety or of protection of human, animal or plant life or health, the environment or consumers, without prejudice to the rights of any Party under this Chapter, and taking into account international standardization activities, the Parties shall, to the greatest extent practicable, make compatible their respective standards-related measures, so as to facilitate trade in a good or service between the Parties.

3. Further to Articles 902 and 905, a Party shall, on request of another Party, seek, through appropriate measures, to promote the compatibility of a specific standard or conformity assessment procedure that is maintained in its territory with the standards or conformity assessment procedures maintained in the territory of the other Party.

4. Each importing Party shall treat a technical regulation adopted or maintained by an exporting Party as equivalent to its own where the exporting Party, in cooperation with the importing Party, demonstrates to the satisfaction of the importing Party that its technical regulation adequately fulfills the importing Party's legitimate objectives.

5. The importing Party shall provide to the exporting Party, on request, its reasons in writing for not treating a technical regulation as equivalent under paragraph 4.

6. Each Party shall, wherever possible, accept the results of a conformity assessment procedure conducted in the territory of another Party, provided that it is satisfied that the procedure offers an assurance, equivalent to that provided by a procedure it conducts or a procedure conducted in its territory the results of which it accepts, that the relevant good or service complies with the applicable technical regulation or standard adopted or maintained in the Party's territory.

7. Prior to accepting the results of a conformity assessment procedure pursuant to paragraph 6, and to enhance confidence in the continued reliability of each other's conformity assessment results, the Parties may consult on such matters as the technical competence of the conformity assessment bodies involved, including verified compliance with relevant international standards through such means as accreditation.

Article 907: Assessment of Risk

1. A Party may, in pursuing its legitimate objectives, conduct an assessment of risk. In conducting an assessment, a Party may take into account, among other factors relating to a good or service:

(a) available scientific evidence or technical information;

(b) intended end uses;

(c) processes or production, operating, inspection, sampling or testing methods; or

(d) environmental conditions.

2. Where pursuant to Article 904(2) a Party establishes a level of protection that it considers appropriate and conducts an assessment of risk, it should avoid arbitrary or unjustifiable distinctions between similar goods or services in the level of protection it considers appropriate, where the distinctions:

(a) result in arbitrary or unjustifiable discrimination against goods or service providers of another Party;

(b) constitute a disguised restriction on trade between the Parties; or

(c) discriminate between similar goods or services for the same use under the same conditions that pose the same level of risk and provide similar benefits.

3. Where a Party conducting an assessment of risk determines that available scientific evidence or other information is insufficient to com-

plete the assessment, it may adopt a provisional technical regulation on the basis of available relevant information. The Party shall, within a reasonable period after information sufficient to complete the assessment of risk is presented to it, complete its assessment, review and, where appropriate, revise the provisional technical regulation in the light of that assessment.

Article 908: Conformity Assessment

1. The Parties shall, further to Article 906 and recognizing the existence of substantial differences in the structure, organization and operation of conformity assessment procedures in their respective territories, make compatible those procedures to the greatest extent practicable.

2. Recognizing that it should be to the mutual advantage of the Parties concerned and except as set out in Annex 908.2, each Party shall accredit, approve, license or otherwise recognize conformity assessment bodies in the territory of another Party on terms no less favorable than those accorded to conformity assessment bodies in its territory.

3. Each Party shall, with respect to its conformity assessment procedures:

(a) not adopt or maintain any such procedure that is stricter, nor apply the procedure more strictly, than necessary to give it confidence that a good or a service conforms with an applicable technical regulation or standard, taking into account the risks that non-conformity would create;

(b) initiate and complete the procedure as expeditiously as possible;

(c) in accordance with Article 904(3), undertake processing of applications in non-discriminatory order;

(d) publish the normal processing period for each such procedure or communicate the anticipated processing period to an applicant on request;

(e) ensure that the competent body

(i) on receipt of an application, promptly examines the completeness of the documentation and informs the applicant in a precise and complete manner of any deficiency,

(ii) transmits to the applicant as soon as possible the results of the conformity assessment procedure in a form that is precise and complete so that the applicant may take any necessary corrective action,

(iii) where the application is deficient, proceeds as far as practicable with the procedure where the applicant so requests, and

(iv) informs the applicant, on request, of the status of the application and the reasons for any delay;

(f) limit the information the applicant is required to supply to that necessary to conduct the procedure and to determine appropriate fees;

(g) accord confidential or proprietary information arising from, or supplied in connection with, the conduct of the procedure for a good of another Party or for a service provided by a person of another Party

(i) the same treatment as that for a good of the Party or a service provided by a person of the Party, and

(ii) in any event, treatment that protects an applicant's legitimate commercial interests to the extent provided under the Party's law;

(h) ensure that any fee it imposes for conducting the procedure is no higher for a good of another Party or a service provider of another Party than is equitable in relation to any such fee imposed for its like goods or service providers or for like goods or service providers of any other country, taking into account communication, transportation and other related costs;

(i) ensure that the location of facilities at which a conformity assessment procedure is conducted does not cause unnecessary inconvenience to an applicant or its agent;

(j) limit the procedure, for a good or service modified subsequent to a determination that the good or service conforms to the applicable technical regulation or standard, to that necessary to determine that the good or service continues to conform to the technical regulation or standard; and

(k) limit any requirement regarding samples of a good to that which is reasonable, and ensure that the selection of samples does not cause unnecessary inconvenience to an applicant or its agent.

4. Each Party shall apply, with such modifications as may be necessary, the relevant provisions of paragraph 3 to its approval procedures.

5. Each Party shall, on request of another Party, take such reasonable measures as may be available to it to facilitate access in its territory for conformity assessment activities.

6. Each Party shall give sympathetic consideration to a request by another Party to negotiate agreements for the mutual recognition of the results of that other Party's conformity assessment procedures.

* * *

Article 915: Definitions

1. For purposes of this Chapter:

* * *

legitimate objective includes an objective such as:

(a) safety,

(b) protection of human, animal or plant life or health, the environment or consumers, including matters relating to quality and identifiability of goods or services, and

(c) sustainable development,

considering, among other things, where appropriate, fundamental climatic or other geographical factors, technological or infrastructural factors, or scientific justification but does not include the protection of domestic production;

* * *

standard means a document, approved by a recognized body, that provides, for common and repeated use, rules, guidelines or characteristics for goods or related processes and production methods, or for services or related operating methods, with which compliance is not mandatory. It may also include or deal exclusively with terminology, symbols, packaging, marking or labelling requirements as they apply to a good, process, or production or operating method;

* * *

technical regulation means a document which lays down goods' characteristics or their related processes and production methods, or services' characteristics or their related operating methods, including the applicable administrative provisions, with which compliance is mandatory. It may also include or deal exclusively with terminology, symbols, packaging, marking or labelling requirements as they apply to a good, process, or production or operating method;

* * *

PART FOUR

GOVERNMENT PROCUREMENT

Chapter Ten

Government Procurement

Section A—Scope and Coverage and National Treatment

Article 1001: Scope and Coverage

1. This Chapter applies to measures adopted or maintained by a Party relating to procurement:

(a) by a federal government entity set out in Annex 1001.1a–1, a government enterprise set out in Annex 1001.1a–2, or a state or provincial government entity set out in Annex 1001.1a–3 in accordance with Article 1024;

(b) of goods in accordance with Annex 1001.1b–1, services in accordance with Annex 1001.1b–2, or construction services in accordance with Annex 1001.1b–3; and

(c) where the value of the contract to be awarded is estimated to be equal to or greater than a threshold, calculated and adjusted according to the U.S. inflation rate as set out in Annex 1001.1c, of

(i) for federal government entities, US$50,000 for contracts for goods, services or any combination thereof, and US$6.5 million for contracts for construction services,

(ii) for government enterprises, US$250,000 for contracts for goods, services or any combination thereof, and US$8.0 million for contracts for construction services, and

(iii) for state and provincial government entities, the applicable threshold, as set out in Annex 1001.1a–3 in accordance with Article 1024.

* * *

Article 1003: National Treatment and Non–Discrimination

1. With respect to measures covered by this Chapter, each Party shall accord to goods of another Party, to the suppliers of such goods and to service suppliers of another Party, treatment no less favorable than the most favorable treatment that the Party accords to:

(a) its own goods and suppliers; and

(b) goods and suppliers of another Party.

2. With respect to measures covered by this Chapter, no Party may:

(a) treat a locally established supplier less favorably than another locally established supplier on the basis of degree of foreign affiliation or ownership; or

(b) discriminate against a locally established supplier on the basis that the goods or services offered by that supplier for the particular procurement are goods or services of another Party.

3. Paragraph 1 does not apply to measures respecting customs duties or other charges of any kind imposed on or in connection with importation, the method of levying such duties or charges or other import regulations, including restrictions and formalities.

Article 1004: Rules of Origin

No Party may apply rules of origin to goods imported from another Party for purposes of government procurement covered by this Chapter that are different from or inconsistent with the rules of origin the Party applies in the normal course of trade, which may be the Marking Rules established under Annex 311 if they become the rules of origin applied by that Party in the normal course of its trade.

Article 1005: Denial of Benefits

1. Subject to prior notification and consultation in accordance with Articles 1803 (Notification and Provision of Information) and 2006 (Consultations), a Party may deny the benefits of this Chapter to a service supplier of another Party where the Party establishes that the service is being provided by an enterprise that is owned or controlled by persons of a non-Party and that has no substantial business activities in the territory of any Party.

2. A Party may deny to an enterprise of another Party the benefits of this Chapter if nationals of a non-Party own or control the enterprise and:

(a) the circumstance set out in Article 1113(1)(a) (Denial of Benefits) is met; or

(b) the denying Party adopts or maintains measures with respect to the non-Party that prohibit transactions with the enterprise or that would be violated or circumvented if the benefits of this Chapter were accorded to the enterprise.

Article 1006: Prohibition of Offsets

Each Party shall ensure that its entities do not, in the qualification and selection of suppliers, goods or services, in the evaluation of bids or the award of contracts, consider, seek or impose offsets. For purposes of this Article, offsets means conditions imposed or considered by an entity prior to or in the course of its procurement process that encourage local development or improve its Party's balance of payments accounts, by means of requirements of local content, licensing of technology, investment, counter-trade or similar requirements.

Article 1007: Technical Specifications

1. Each Party shall ensure that its entities do not prepare, adopt or apply any technical specification with the purpose or the effect of creating unnecessary obstacles to trade.

2. Each Party shall ensure that any technical specification prescribed by its entities is, where appropriate:

(a) specified in terms of performance criteria rather than design or descriptive characteristics; and

(b) based on international standards, national technical regulations, recognized national standards, or building codes.

3. Each Party shall ensure that the technical specifications prescribed by its entities do not require or refer to a particular trademark or name, patent, design or type, specific origin or producer or supplier unless there is no sufficiently precise or intelligible way of otherwise describing the procurement requirements and provided that, in such cases, words such as "or equivalent" are included in the tender documentation.

4. Each Party shall ensure that its entities do not seek or accept, in a manner that would have the effect of precluding competition, advice that may be used in the preparation or adoption of any technical specification for a specific procurement from a person that may have a commercial interest in that procurement.

Section B—Tendering Procedures (omitted)

* * *

Section C—Bid Challenge

Article 1017: Bid Challenge

1. In order to promote fair, open and impartial procurement procedures, each Party shall adopt and maintain bid challenge procedures for procurement covered by this Chapter in accordance with the following:

(a) each Party shall allow suppliers to submit bid challenges concerning any aspect of the procurement process, which for the purposes of this Article begins after an entity has decided on its procurement requirement and continues through the contract award;

(b) a Party may encourage a supplier to seek a resolution of any complaint with the entity concerned prior to initiating a bid challenge;

(c) each Party shall ensure that its entities accord fair and timely consideration to any complaint regarding procurement covered by this Chapter;

(d) whether or not a supplier has attempted to resolve its complaint with the entity, or following an unsuccessful attempt at such a resolution, no Party may prevent the supplier from initiating a bid challenge or seeking any other relief;

(e) a Party may require a supplier to notify the entity on initiation of a bid challenge;

(f) a Party may limit the period within which a supplier may initiate a bid challenge, but in no case shall the period be less than 10 working days from the time when the basis of the complaint became known or reasonably should have become known to the supplier;

(g) each Party shall establish or designate a reviewing authority with no substantial interest in the outcome of procurements to receive bid challenges and make findings and recommendations concerning them;

(h) on receipt of a bid challenge, the reviewing authority shall expeditiously investigate the challenge;

(i) a Party may require its reviewing authority to limit its considerations to the challenge itself;

(j) in investigating the challenge, the reviewing authority may delay the awarding of the proposed contract pending resolution of the challenge, except in cases of urgency or where the delay would be contrary to the public interest;

(k) the reviewing authority shall issue a recommendation to resolve the challenge, which may include directing the entity to re-evaluate offers, terminate or re-compete the contract in question;

(*l*) entities normally shall follow the recommendations of the reviewing authority;

(m) each Party should authorize its reviewing authority, following the conclusion of a bid challenge procedure, to make additional recommendations in writing to an entity respecting any facet of the entity's procurement process that is identified as problematic during the investigation of the challenge, including recommendations for changes in the procurement procedures of the entity to bring them into conformity with this Chapter;

(n) the reviewing authority shall provide its findings and recommendations respecting bid challenges in writing and in a timely manner, and shall make them available to the Parties and interested persons;

(*o*) each Party shall specify in writing and shall make generally available all its bid challenge procedures; and

(p) each Party shall ensure that each of its entities maintains complete documentation regarding each of its procurements, including a written record of all communications substantially affecting each procurement, for at least three years from the date the contract was awarded, to allow verification that the procurement process was carried out in accordance with this Chapter.

PART FIVE

INVESTMENT, SERVICES AND RELATED MATTERS

Chapter Eleven

Investment

Section A—Investment

Article 1101: Scope and Coverage

1. This Chapter applies to measures adopted or maintained by a Party relating to:

(a) investors of another Party;

(b) investments of investors of another Party in the territory of the Party; and

(c) with respect to Articles 1106 and 1114, all investments in the territory of the Party.

2. A Party has the right to perform exclusively the economic activities set out in Annex III and to refuse to permit the establishment of investment in such activities.

3. This Chapter does not apply to measures adopted or maintained by a Party to the extent that they are covered by Chapter Fourteen (Financial Services).

4. Nothing in this Chapter shall be construed to prevent a Party from providing a service or performing a function such as law enforcement, correctional services, income security or insurance, social security or

insurance, social welfare, public education, public training, health, and child care, in a manner that is not inconsistent with this Chapter.

Article 1102: National Treatment

1. Each Party shall accord to investors of another Party treatment no less favorable than that it accords, in like circumstances, to its own investors with respect to the establishment, acquisition, expansion, management, conduct, operation, and sale or other disposition of investments.

2. Each Party shall accord to investments of investors of another Party treatment no less favorable than that it accords, in like circumstances, to investments of its own investors with respect to the establishment, acquisition, expansion, management, conduct, operation, and sale or other disposition of investments.

3. The treatment accorded by a Party under paragraphs 1 and 2 means, with respect to a state or province, treatment no less favorable than the most favorable treatment accorded, in like circumstances, by that state or province to investors, and to investments of investors, of the Party of which it forms a part.

4. For greater certainty, no Party may:

(a) impose on an investor of another Party a requirement that a minimum level of equity in an enterprise in the territory of the Party be held by its nationals, other than nominal qualifying shares for directors or incorporators of corporations; or

(b) require an investor of another Party, by reason of its nationality, to sell or otherwise dispose of an investment in the territory of the Party.

Article 1103: Most–Favored–Nation Treatment

1. Each Party shall accord to investors of another Party treatment no less favorable than that it accords, in like circumstances, to investors of any other Party or of a non-Party with respect to the establishment, acquisition, expansion, management, conduct, operation, and sale or other disposition of investments.

2. Each Party shall accord to investments of investors of another Party treatment no less favorable than that it accords, in like circumstances, to investments of investors of any other Party or of a non-Party with respect to the establishment, acquisition, expansion, management, conduct, operation, and sale or other disposition of investments.

Article 1104: Standard of Treatment

Each Party shall accord to investors of another Party and to investments of investors of another Party the better of the treatment required by Articles 1102 and 1103.

Article 1105: Minimum Standard of Treatment

1. Each Party shall accord to investments of investors of another Party treatment in accordance with international law, including fair and equitable treatment and full protection and security.

2. Without prejudice to paragraph 1 and notwithstanding Article 1108(7)(b), each Party shall accord to investors of another Party, and to investments of investors of another Party, non-discriminatory treatment with respect to measures it adopts or maintains relating to losses suffered by investments in its territory owing to armed conflict or civil strife.

3. Paragraph 2 does not apply to existing measures relating to subsidies or grants that would be inconsistent with Article 1102 but for Article 1108(7)(b).

Article 1106: Performance Requirements

1. No Party may impose or enforce any of the following requirements, or enforce any commitment or undertaking, in connection with the establishment, acquisition, expansion, management, conduct or operation of an investment of an investor of a Party or of a non-Party in its territory:

(a) to export a given level or percentage of goods or services;

(b) to achieve a given level or percentage of domestic content;

(c) to purchase, use or accord a preference to goods produced or services provided in its territory, or to purchase goods or services from persons in its territory;

(d) to relate in any way the volume or value of imports to the volume or value of exports or to the amount of foreign exchange inflows associated with such investment;

(e) to restrict sales of goods or services in its territory that such investment produces or provides by relating such sales in any way to the volume or value of its exports or foreign exchange earnings;

(f) to transfer technology, a production process or other proprietary knowledge to a person in its territory, except when the requirement is imposed or the commitment or undertaking is enforced by a court, administrative tribunal or competition authority to remedy an alleged violation of competition laws or to act in a manner not inconsistent with other provisions of this Agreement; or

(g) to act as the exclusive supplier of the goods it produces or services it provides to a specific region or world market.

2. A measure that requires an investment to use a technology to meet generally applicable health, safety or environmental requirements shall not be construed to be inconsistent with paragraph 1(f). For greater certainty, Articles 1102 and 1103 apply to the measure.

3. No Party may condition the receipt or continued receipt of an advantage, in connection with an investment in its territory of an investor of a

Party or of a non-Party, on compliance with any of the following requirements:

(a) to achieve a given level or percentage of domestic content;

(b) to purchase, use or accord a preference to goods produced in its territory, or to purchase goods from producers in its territory;

(c) to relate in any way the volume or value of imports to the volume or value of exports or to the amount of foreign exchange inflows associated with such investment; or

(d) to restrict sales of goods or services in its territory that such investment produces or provides by relating such sales in any way to the volume or value of its exports or foreign exchange earnings.

4. Nothing in paragraph 3 shall be construed to prevent a Party from conditioning the receipt or continued receipt of an advantage, in connection with an investment in its territory of an investor of a Party or of a non-Party, on compliance with a requirement to locate production, provide a service, train or employ workers, construct or expand particular facilities, or carry out research and development, in its territory.

5. Paragraphs 1 and 3 do not apply to any requirement other than the requirements set out in those paragraphs.

6. Provided that such measures are not applied in an arbitrary or unjustifiable manner, or do not constitute a disguised restriction on international trade or investment, nothing in paragraph 1(b) or (c) or 3(a) or (b) shall be construed to prevent any Party from adopting or maintaining measures, including environmental measures:

(a) necessary to secure compliance with laws and regulations that are not inconsistent with the provisions of this Agreement;

(b) necessary to protect human, animal or plant life or health; or

(c) necessary for the conservation of living or non-living exhaustable natural resources.

Article 1107: Senior Management and Boards of Directors

1. No Party may require that an enterprise of that Party that is an investment of an investor of another Party appoint to senior management positions individuals of any particular nationality.

2. A Party may require that a majority of the board of directors, or any committee thereof, of an enterprise of that Party that is an investment of an investor of another Party, be of a particular nationality, or resident in the territory of the Party, provided that the requirement does not materially impair the ability of the investor to exercise control over its investment.

Article 1108: Reservation and Exceptions

1. Articles 1102, 1103, 1106 and 1107 do not apply to:

(a) any existing non-conforming measure that is maintained by

(i) a Party at the federal level, as set out in its Schedule to Annex I or III,

(ii) a state or province, for two years after the date of entry into force of this Agreement, and thereafter as set out by a Party in its Schedule to Annex I in accordance with paragraph 2, or

(iii) a local government;

(b) the continuation or prompt renewal of non-conforming measure referred to in subparagraph (a); or

(c) an amendment to any non-conforming measure referred to in subparagraph (a) to the extent that the amendment does not decrease the conformity of the measure, as it existed immediately before the amendment, with Articles 1102, 1103, 1106 and 1107.

2. Each Party may set out in its Schedule to Annex I, within two years of the date of entry into force of this Agreement, any existing non-conforming measure maintained by a state or province, not including a local government.

3. Articles 1102, 1103, 1106 and 1107 do not apply to any measure that a Party adopts or maintains with respect to sectors, subsectors or activities, as set out in its Schedule to Annex II.

4. No Party may, under any measure adopted after the date of entry into force of this Agreement and covered by its Schedule to Annex II, require an investor of another Party, by reason of its nationality, to sell or otherwise dispose of an investment existing at the time the measure becomes effective.

5. Articles 1102 and 1103 do not apply to any measure that is an exception to, or derogation from, the obligations under Article 1703 (Intellectual Property—National Treatment) as specifically provided for in that Article.

6. Article 1103 does not apply to treatment accorded by a Party pursuant to agreements, or with respect to sectors, set out in its Schedule to Annex IV.

7. Articles 1102, 1103 and 1107 do not apply to:

(a) procurement by a Party or a State enterprise; or

(b) subsidies or grants provided by a Party or a state enterprise, including government-supported loans, guarantees and insurance.

8. The provisions of:

(a) Article 1106(1)(a), (b) and (c), and (3)(a) and (b) do not apply to qualification requirements for goods or services with respect to export promotion and foreign aid programs;

(b) Article 1106(1)(b), (c) (f) and (g), and 3(a) and (b) do not apply to procurement by a Party or a state enterprise; and

(c) Article 1106(3)(a) and (b) do not apply to requirements imposed by an importing Party relating to the content of goods necessary to qualify for preferential tariffs or preferential quotas.

Article 1109: Transfers

1. Each Party shall permit all transfers relating to an investment of an investor of another Party in the territory of the Party to be made freely and without delay. Such transfers include:

(a) profits, dividends, interest, capital gains, royalty payments, management fees, technical assistance and other fees, returns in kind and other amounts derived from the investment;

(b) proceeds from the sale of all or any part of the investment or from the partial or complete liquidation of the investment;

(c) payments made under a contract entered into by the investor, or its investment, including payments made pursuant to a loan agreement;

(d) payments made pursuant to Article 1110; and

(e) payments arising under Section B.

2. Each Party shall permit transfers to be made in a freely usable currency at the market rate of exchange prevailing on the date of transfer with respect to spot transactions in the currency to be transferred.

3. No Party may require its investors to transfer, or penalize its investors that fail to transfer, the income, earnings, profits or other amounts derived from, or attributable to, investments in the territory of another Party.

4. Notwithstanding paragraphs 1 and 2, a Party may prevent a transfer through the equitable, non-discriminatory and good faith application of its laws relating to:

(a) bankruptcy, insolvency or the protection of the rights of creditors;

(b) issuing, trading or dealing in securities;

(c) criminal or penal offenses;

(d) reports of transfers of currency or other monetary instruments; or

(e) ensuring the satisfaction of judgments in adjudicatory proceedings.

5. Paragraph 3 shall not be construed to prevent a Party from imposing any measure through the equitable, non-discriminatory and good faith application of its laws relating to the matters set out in subparagraphs (a) through (e) of paragraph 4.

6. Notwithstanding paragraph 1, a Party may restrict transfers of returns in kind in circumstances where it could otherwise restrict such transfers under this Agreement, including as set out in paragraph 4.

Article 1110: Expropriation and Compensation

1. No Party may directly or indirectly nationalize or expropriate an investment of an investor of another Party in its territory or take a measure tantamount to nationalization or expropriation of such an investment ("expropriation"), except:

(a) for a public purpose;

(b) on a non-discriminatory basis;

(c) in accordance with due process of law and Article 1105(1); and

(d) on payment of compensation in accordance with paragraphs 2 through 6.

2. Compensation shall be equivalent to the fair market value of the expropriated investment immediately before the expropriation took place ("date of expropriation"), and shall not reflect any change in value occurring because the intended expropriation had become known earlier. Valuation criteria shall include going concern value, asset value including declared tax value of tangible property, and other criteria, as appropriate, to determine fair market value.

3. Compensation shall be paid without delay and be fully realizable.

4. If payment is made in a G7 currency, compensation shall include interest at a commercially reasonable rate for that currency from the date of expropriation until the date of actual payment.

5. If a Party elects to pay in a currency other than a G7 currency, the amount paid on the date of payment, if converted into a G7 currency at the market rate of exchange prevailing on that date, shall be no less than if the amount of compensation owed on the date of expropriation had been converted into that G7 currency at the market rate of exchange prevailing on that date, and interest had accrued at a commercially reasonable rate for that G7 currency from the date of expropriation until the date of payment.

6. On payment, compensation shall be freely transferable as provided in Article 1109.

7. This Article does not apply to the issuance of compulsory licenses granted in relation to intellectual property rights, or to the revocation, limitation or creation of intellectual property rights, to the extent that such issuance, revocation, limitation or creation is consistent with Chapter Seventeen (Intellectual Property).

8. For purposes of this Article and for greater certainty, a non-discriminatory measure of general application shall not be considered a measure tantamount to an expropriation of a debt security or loan covered by this Chapter solely on the ground that the measure imposes costs on the debtor that cause it to default on the debt.

* * *

Article 1112: Relation to Other Chapters

1. In the event of any inconsistency between this Chapter and another Chapter, the other Chapter shall prevail to the extent of the inconsistency.

2. A requirement by a Party that a service provider of another Party post a bond or other form of financial security as a condition of providing a service into its territory does not of itself make this Chapter applicable to the provision of that cross-border service. This Chapter applies to that Party's treatment of the posted bond or financial security.

Article 1113: Denial of Benefits

1. A Party may deny the benefits of this Chapter to an investor of another Party that is an enterprise of such Party and to investments of such investor if investors of a non-Party own or control the enterprise and the denying Party:

(a) does not maintain diplomatic relations with the non-Party; or

(b) adopts or maintains measures with respect to the non-Party that prohibit transactions with the enterprise or that would be violated or circumvented if the benefits of this Chapter were accorded to the enterprise or to its investments.

* * *

Article 1114: Environmental Measures

1. Nothing in this Chapter shall be construed to prevent a Party from adopting, maintaining or enforcing any measure otherwise consistent with this Chapter that it considers appropriate to ensure that investment activity in its territory is undertaken in a manner sensitive to environmental concerns.

2. The Parties recognize that it is inappropriate to encourage investment by relaxing domestic health, safety or environmental measures. Accordingly, a Party should not waive or otherwise derogate from, or offer to waive or otherwise derogate from, such measures as an encouragement for the establishment, acquisition, expansion or retention in its territory of an investment of an investor. If a Party considers that another Party has offered such an encouragement, it may request consultations with the other Party and the two Parties shall consult with a view to avoiding any such encouragement.

Section B—Settlement of Disputes Between a Party and an Investor of Another Party

Article 1115: Purpose

Without prejudice to the rights and obligations of the Parties under Chapter Twenty (Institutional Arrangements and Dispute Settlement Procedures), this Section establishes a mechanism for the settlement of investment disputes that assures both equal treatment among investors of the Parties in accordance with the principle of international reciprocity and due process before an impartial tribunal.

Article 1116: Claim by an Investor of a Party on Its Own Behalf

1. An investor of a Party may submit to arbitration under this Section a claim that another Party has breached an obligation under:

(a) Section A or Article 1503(2) (State Enterprises), or

(b) Article 1502(3)(a) (Monopolies and State Enterprises) where the monopoly has acted in a manner inconsistent with the Party's obligations under Section A,

and that the investor has incurred loss or damage by reason of, or arising out of, that breach.

* * *

Article 1117: Claim by an Investor of a Party on Behalf of an Enterprise

1. An investor of a Party, on behalf of an enterprise of another Party that is a juridical person that the investor owns or controls directly or indirectly, may submit to arbitration under this Section a claim that the other Party has breached an obligation under:

(a) Section A or Article 1503(2) (State Enterprises), or

(b) Article 1502(3)(a) (Monopolies and State Enterprises) where the monopoly has acted in a manner inconsistent with the Party's obligations under Section A,

and that the enterprise has incurred loss or damage by reason of, or arising out of, that breach.

* * *

Article 1118: Settlement of a Claim through Consultation and Negotiation

The disputing parties should first attempt to settle a claim through consultation or negotiation.

* * *

Article 1120: Submission of a Claim to Arbitration

1. Except as provided in Annex 1120.1, and provided that six months have elapsed since the events giving rise to a claim, a disputing investor may submit the claim to arbitration under:

(a) the ICSID Convention, provided that both the disputing Party and the Party of the investor are parties to the Convention;

(b) the Additional Facility Rules of ICSID, provided that either the disputing Party or the Party of the investor, but not both, is a party to the ICSID Convention; or

(c) the UNCITRAL Arbitration Rules.

* * *

Article 1121: Conditions Precedent to Submission of a Claim to Arbitration

1. A disputing investor may submit a claim under Article 1116 to arbitration only if:

(a) the investor consents to arbitration in accordance with the procedures set out in this Agreement; and

(b) the investor and, where the claim is for loss or damage to an interest in an enterprise of another Party that is a juridical person that the investor owns or controls directly or indirectly, the enterprise, waive their right to initiate or continue before any administrative tribunal or court under the law of any Party, or other dispute settlement procedures, any proceedings with respect to the measure of the disputing Party that is alleged to be a breach referred to in Article 1116, except for proceedings for injunctive, declaratory or other extraordinary relief, not involving the payment of damages, before an administrative tribunal or court under the law of the disputing Party.

2. A disputing investor may submit a claim under Article 1117 to arbitration only if both the investor and the enterprise:

(a) consent to arbitration in accordance with the procedures set out in this Agreement; and

(b) waive their right to initiate or continue before any administrative tribunal or court under the law of any Party, or other dispute settlement procedures, any proceedings with respect to the measure of the disputing Party that is alleged to be a breach referred to in Article 1117, except for proceedings for injunctive, declaratory or other extraordinary relief, not involving the payment of damages, before an administrative tribunal or court under the law of the disputing Party.

* * *

Article 1122: Consent to Arbitration

1. Each Party consents to the submission of a claim to arbitration in accordance with the procedures set out in this Agreement.

* * *

Article 1123: Number of Arbitrators and Method of Appointment

Except in respect of a Tribunal established under Article 1126, and unless the disputing parties otherwise agree, the Tribunal shall comprise three arbitrators, one arbitrator appointed by each of the disputing parties and the third, who shall be the presiding arbitrator, appointed by agreement of the disputing parties.

* * *

Article 1125: Agreement to Appointment of Arbitrators

For purposes of Article 39 of the ICSID Convention and Article 7 of Schedule C to the ICSID Additional Facility Rules, and without prejudice to an objection to an arbitrator based on Article 1124(3) or on a ground other than nationality:

(a) the disputing Party agrees to the appointment of each individual member of a Tribunal established under the ICSID Convention or the ICSID Additional Facility Rules;

(b) a disputing investor referred to in Article 1116 may submit a claim to arbitration, or continue a claim, under the ICSID Convention or the ICSID Additional Facility Rules, only on condition that the disputing investor agrees in writing to the appointment of each individual member of the Tribunal; and

(c) a disputing investor referred to in Article 1117(1) may submit a claim to arbitration, or continue a claim, under the ICSID Convention or the ICSID Additional Facility Rules, only on condition that the disputing investor and the enterprise agree in writing to the appointment of each individual member of the Tribunal.

* * *

Article 1130: Place of Arbitration

Unless the disputing parties agree otherwise, a Tribunal shall hold an arbitration in the territory of a Party that is a party to the New York Convention, selected in accordance with:

(a) the ICSID Additional Facility Rules if the arbitration is under those Rules or the ICSID Convention; or

(b) the UNCITRAL Arbitration Rules if the arbitration is under those Rules.

Article 1131: Governing Law

1. A Tribunal established under this Section shall decide the issues in dispute in accordance with this Agreement and applicable rules of international law.

2. An interpretation by the Commission of a provision of this Agreement shall be binding on a Tribunal established under this Section.

* * *

Article 1135: Final Award

1. Where a Tribunal makes a final award against a Party, the Tribunal may award, separately or in combination, only:

(a) monetary damages and any applicable interest;

(b) restitution of property, in which case the award shall provide that the disputing Party may pay monetary damages and any applicable interest in lieu of restitution.

A tribunal may also award costs in accordance with the applicable arbitration rules.

2. Subject to paragraph 1, where a claim is made under Article 1117(1):

(a) an award of restitution of property shall provide that restitution be made to the enterprise;

(b) an award of monetary damages and any applicable interest shall provide that the sum be paid to the enterprise; and

(c) the award shall provide that it is made without prejudice to any right that any person may have in the relief under applicable domestic law.

3. A Tribunal may not order a Party to pay punitive damages.

Article 1136: Finality and Enforcement of an Award

1. An award made by a Tribunal shall have no binding force except between the disputing parties and in respect of the particular case.

2. Subject to paragraph 3 and the applicable review procedure for an interim award, a disputing party shall abide by and comply with an award without delay.

3. A disputing party may not seek enforcement of a final award until:

(a) in the case of a final award made under the ICSID Convention

(i) 120 days have elapsed from the date the award was rendered and no disputing party has requested revision or annulment of the award, or

(ii) revision or annulment proceedings have been completed; and

(b) in the case of a final award under the ICSID Additional Facility Rules or the UNCITRAL Arbitration Rules

(i) three months have elapsed from the date the award was rendered and no disputing party has commenced a proceeding to revise, set aside or annul the award, or

(ii) a court has dismissed or allowed an application to revise, set aside or annul the award and there is no further appeal.

4. Each Party shall provide for the enforcement of an award in its territory.

5. If a disputing Party fails to abide by or comply with a final award, the Commission, on delivery of a request by a Party whose investor was a party to the arbitration, shall establish a panel under Article 2008 (Request for an Arbitral Panel). The requesting Party may seek in such proceedings:

(a) a determination that the failure to abide by or comply with the final award is inconsistent with the obligations of this Agreement; and

(b) a recommendation that the Party abide by or comply with the final award.

6. A disputing investor may seek enforcement of an arbitration award under the ICSID Convention, the New York Convention or the Inter–American Convention regardless of whether proceedings have been taken under paragraph 5.

7. A claim that is submitted to arbitration under this Section shall be considered to arise out of a commercial relationship or transaction for purposes of Article I of the New York Convention and Article I of the Inter–American Convention.

* * *

Annex 1120.1

Submission of a Claim to Arbitration

Mexico

With respect to the submission of a claim to arbitration:

(a) an investor of another Party may not allege that Mexico has breached an obligation under:

(i) Section A or Article 1503(2) (State Enterprises), or

(ii) Article 1502(3)(a) (Monopolies and State Enterprises) where the monopoly has acted in a manner inconsistent with the Party's obligations under Section A, both in an arbitration under this Section and in proceedings before a Mexican court or administrative tribunal; and

(b) where an enterprise of Mexico that is a juridical person that an investor of another Party owns or controls directly or indirectly alleges in proceedings before a Mexican court or administrative tribunal that Mexico has breached an obligation under:

(i) Section A or Article 1503(2) (State Enterprises), or

(ii) Article 1502(3)(a) (Monopolies and State Enterprises) where the monopoly has acted in a manner inconsistent with the Party's obligations under Section A, the investor may not allege the breach in an arbitration under this Section.

Annex 1138.2

Exclusions From Dispute Settlement

Canada

A decision by Canada following a review under the Investment Canada Act, with respect to whether or not to permit an acquisition that is subject to review, shall not be subject to the dispute settlement provisions of Section B or of Chapter Twenty (Institutional Arrangements and Dispute Settlement Procedures).

Mexico

A decision by the National Commission on Foreign Investment ("Comision Nacional de Inversiones Extranjeras") following a review pursuant to Annex I, page I-M-4, with respect to whether or not to permit an acquisition that is subject to review, shall not be subject to the dispute settlement provisions of Section B or of Chapter Twenty.

Section C—Definitions

Article 1139

Definitions

For purposes of this Chapter:

disputing investor means an investor that makes a claim under Section B;

disputing parties means the disputing investor and the disputing Party;

disputing party means the disputing investor or the disputing Party;

disputing Party means a Party against which a claim is made under Section B;

enterprise means an "enterprise" as defined in Article 201 (Definitions of General Application), and a branch of an enterprise;

enterprise of a Party means an enterprise constituted or organized under the law of a Party, and a branch located in the territory of a Party and carrying out business activities there.

equity or debt securities includes voting and non-voting shares, bonds, convertible debentures, stock options and warrants;

G7 Currency means the currency of Canada, France, Germany, Italy, Japan, the United Kingdom of Great Britain and Northern Ireland or the United States;

ICSID means the International Centre for Settlement of Investment Disputes;

ICSID Convention means the Convention on the Settlement of Investment Disputes between States and Nationals of other States, done at Washington, March 18, 1965;

Inter-American Convention means the Inter-American Convention on International Commercial Arbitration, done at Panama, January 30, 1975;

investment means: (a) an enterprise; (b) an equity security of an enterprise; (c) a debt security of an enterprise (i) where the enterprise is an affiliate of the investor, or (ii) where the original maturity of the debt security is at least three years, but does not include a debt security, regardless of original maturity, of a state enterprise; (d) a loan to an enterprise (i) where the enterprise is an affiliate of the investor, or (ii) where the original maturity of the loan is at least three years, but does not include a loan, regardless of original maturity, to a state enterprise; (e) an interest in an enterprise that entitles the owner to share in income or profits of the enterprise; (f) an interest in an enterprise that entitles the owner to share in the assets of that enterprise on dissolution, other than a debt security or a loan excluded from subparagraph (c) or (d); (g) real estate or other property, tangible or intangible, acquired in the expectation or used for the purpose of economic benefit or other business purposes; and (h) interests arising from the commitment of capital or other resources in the territory of a Party to economic activity in such territory, such as under (i) contracts involving the presence of an investor's property in the territory of the Party, including turnkey or construction contracts, or concessions, or (ii) contracts where remuneration depends substantially on the production, revenues or profits of an enterprise; but investment does not mean, (i) claims to money that arise solely from (i) commercial contracts for the sale of goods or services by a national or enterprise in the territory of a Party to an enterprise in the territory of another Party, or (ii) the extension of credit in connection with a commercial transaction, such as trade financing, other than a loan covered by subparagraph (d); or (j) any other claims to money, that do not involve the kinds of interests set out in subparagraphs (a) through (h);

investment of an investor of a Party means an investment owned or controlled directly or indirectly by an investor of such Party;

investor of a Party means a Party or state enterprise thereof, or a national or an enterprise of such Party, that seeks to make, is making or has made an investment;

investor of a non-Party means an investor other than an investor of a Party, that seeks to make, is making or has made an investment;

New York Convention means the United Nations Convention on the Recognition and Enforcement of Foreign Arbitral Awards, done at New York, June 10, 1958;

Secretary-General means the Secretary-General of ICSID;

transfers means transfers and international payments;

Tribunal means an arbitration tribunal established under Article 1120 or 1126; and

UNCITRAL Arbitration Rules means the arbitration rules of the United Nations Commission on International Trade Law, approved by the United Nations General Assembly on December 15, 1976.

Chapter Twelve

Cross–Border Trade in Services

Article 1201: Scope and Coverage*

1. This Chapter applies to measures adopted or maintained by a Party relating to cross-border trade in services by service providers of another Party, including measures respecting:

(a) the production, distribution, marketing, sale and delivery of a service;

(b) the purchase or use of, or payment for, a service;

(c) the access to and use of distribution and transportation systems in connection with the provision of a service;

(d) the presence in its territory of a service provider of another Party; and

(e) the provision of a bond or other form of financial security as a condition for the provision of a service.

2. This Chapter does not apply to:

(a) financial services, as defined in Chapter Fourteen (Financial Services);

(b) air services, including domestic and international air transportation services, whether scheduled or non-scheduled, and related services in support of air services, other than

(i) aircraft repair and maintenance services during which an aircraft is withdrawn from service, and

(ii) specialty air services;

(c) procurement by a Party or a state enterprise; or

(d) subsidies or grants provided by a Party or a state enterprise, including government-supported loans, guarantees and insurance.

3. Nothing in this Chapter shall be construed to:

(a) impose any obligation on a Party with respect to a national of another Party seeking access to its employment market, or employed on a permanent basis in its territory, or to confer any right on that national with respect to that access or employment; or

(b) prevent a Party from providing a service or performing a function such as law enforcement, correctional services, income security or insurance, social security or insurance, social welfare, public education, public training, health, and child care, in a manner that is not inconsistent with this Chapter.

Article 1202: National Treatment

1. Each Party shall accord to service providers of another Party treatment no less favorable than that it accords, in like circumstances, to its own service providers.

* For a list of covered services, see Chapter 4.

2. The treatment accorded by a Party under paragraph 1 means, with respect to a state or province, treatment no less favorable than the most favorable treatment accorded, in like circumstances, by that state or province to service providers of the Party of which it forms a part.

Article 1203: Most–Favored–Nation Treatment

Each Party shall accord to service providers of another Party treatment no less favorable than that it accords, in like circumstances, to service providers of any other Party or of a non–Party.

Article 1204: Standard of Treatment

Each Party shall accord to service providers of any other Party the better of the treatment required by Articles 1202 and 1203.

Article 1205: Local Presence

No Party may require a service provider of another Party to establish or maintain a representative office or any form of enterprise, or to be resident, in its territory as a condition for the cross-border provision of a service.

* * *

Article 1210: Licensing and Certification

1. With a view to ensuring that any measure adopted or maintained by a Party relating to the licensing or certification of nationals of another Party does not constitute an unnecessary barrier to trade, each Party shall endeavor to ensure that any such measure:

(a) is based on objective and transparent criteria, such as competence and the ability to provide a service;

(b) is not more burdensome than necessary to ensure the quality of a service; and

(c) does not constitute a disguised restriction on the cross-border provision of a service.

2. Where a Party recognizes, unilaterally or by agreement, education, experience, licenses or certifications obtained in the territory of another Party or of a non-Party:

(a) nothing in Article 1203 shall be construed to require the Party to accord such recognition to education, experience, licenses or certifications obtained in the territory of another Party; and

(b) the Party shall afford another Party an adequate opportunity to demonstrate that education, experience, licenses or certifications obtained in that other Party's territory should also be recognized or to conclude an agreement or arrangement of comparable effect.

3. Each Party shall, within two years of the date of entry into force of this Agreement, eliminate any citizenship or permanent residency require-

ment set out in its Schedule to Annex I that it maintains for the licensing or certification of professional service providers of another Party. Where a Party does not comply with this obligation with respect to a particular sector, any other Party may, in the same sector and for such period as the non-complying Party maintains its requirement, solely have recourse to maintaining an equivalent requirement set out in its Schedule to Annex I or reinstating:

(a) any such requirement at the federal level that it eliminated pursuant to this Article; or

(b) on notification to the non-complying Party, any such requirement at the state or provincial level existing on the date of entry into force of this Agreement.

* * *

Article 1211: Denial of Benefits

1. A Party may deny the benefits of this Chapter to a service provider of another Party where the Party establishes that:

(a) the service is being provided by an enterprise owned or controlled by nationals of a non-Party, and

(i) the denying Party does not maintain diplomatic relations with the non-Party, or

(ii) the denying Party adopts or maintains measures with respect to the non-Party that prohibit transactions with the enterprise or that would be violated or circumvented if the benefits of this Chapter were accorded to the enterprise; or

(b) the cross-border provision of a transportation service covered by this Chapter is provided using equipment not registered by any Party.

2. Subject to prior notification and consultation in accordance with Articles 1803 (Notification and Provision of Information) and 2006 (Consultations), a Party may deny the benefits of this Chapter to a service provider of another Party where the Party establishes that the service is being provided by an enterprise that is owned or controlled by persons of a non-Party and that has no substantial business activities in the territory of any Party.

* * *

Annex 1210.5

Professional Services

Section A—General Provisions

Processing of Applications for Licenses and Certifications

* * *

Development of Professional Standards

2. The Parties shall encourage the relevant bodies in their respective territories to develop mutually acceptable standards and criteria for licensing and certification of professional service providers and to provide recommendations on mutual recognition to the Commission.

3. The standards and criteria referred to in paragraph 2 may be developed with regard to the following matters:

(a) education—accreditation of schools or academic programs;

(b) examinations—qualifying examinations for licensing, including alternative methods of assessment such as oral examinations and interviews;

(c) experience—length and nature of experience required for licensing;

(d) conduct and ethics—standards of professional conduct and the nature of disciplinary action for non-conformity with those standards;

(e) professional development and re-certification—continuing education and ongoing requirements to maintain professional certification;

(f) scope of practice—extent of, or limitations on, permissible activities;

(g) local knowledge—requirements for knowledge of such matters as local laws, regulations, language, geography or climate; and

(h) consumer protection—alternatives to residency requirements, including bonding, professional liability insurance and client restitution funds, to provide for the protection of consumers.

* * *

Section B—Foreign Legal Consultants

1. Each Party shall, in implementing its obligations and commitments regarding foreign legal consultants as set out in its relevant Schedules and subject to any reservations therein, ensure that a national of another Party is permitted to practice or advise on the law of any country in which that national is authorized to practice as a lawyer.

Consultations With Professional Bodies

2. Each Party shall consult with its relevant professional bodies to obtain their recommendations on:

(a) the form of association or partnership between lawyers authorized to practice in its territory and foreign legal consultants;

(b) the development of standards and criteria for the authorization of foreign legal consultants in conformity with Article 1210; and

(c) other matters relating to the provision of foreign legal consultancy services.

* * *

Future Liberalization

4. Each Party shall establish a work program to develop common procedures throughout its territory for the authorization of foreign legal consultants.

* * *

PART SIX

INTELLECTUAL PROPERTY

Chapter Seventeen

Intellectual Property

Article 1701: Nature and Scope of Obligations

1. Each Party shall provide in its territory to the nationals of another Party adequate and effective protection and enforcement of intellectual property rights, while ensuring that measures to enforce intellectual property rights do not themselves become barriers to legitimate trade.

2. To provide adequate and effective protection and enforcement of intellectual property rights, each Party shall, at a minimum, give effect to this Chapter and to the substantive provisions of:

(a) the *Geneva Convention for the Protection of Producers of Phonograms Against Unauthorized Duplication of their Phonograms,* 1971 (Geneva Convention);

(b) the *Berne Convention for the Protection of Literary and Artistic Works,* 1971 (Berne Convention);

(c) the *Paris Convention for the Protection of Industrial Property,* 1967 (Paris Convention); and

(d) the *International Convention for the Protection of New Varieties of Plants,* 1978 (UPOV Convention), or the *International Convention for the Protection of New Varieties of Plants,* 1991 (UPOV Convention).

If a Party has not acceded to the specified text of any such Conventions on or before the date of entry into force of this Agreement, it shall make every effort to accede.

* * *

Article 1702: More Extensive Protection

A Party may implement in its domestic law more extensive protection of intellectual property rights than is required under this Agreement, provided that such protection is not inconsistent with this Agreement.

Article 1703: National Treatment

1. Each Party shall accord to nationals of another Party treatment no less favorable than that it accords to its own nationals with regard to the protection and enforcement of all intellectual property rights. In respect of sound recordings, each Party shall provide such treatment to producers and performers of another Party, except that a Party may limit rights of performers of another Party in respect of secondary uses of sound recordings to those rights its nationals are accorded in the territory of such other Party.

2. No Party may, as a condition of according national treatment under this Article, require right holders to comply with any formalities or conditions in order to acquire rights in respect of copyright and related rights.

3. A Party may derogate from paragraph 1 in relation to its judicial and administrative procedures for the protection or enforcement of intellectual property rights, including any procedure requiring a national of another Party to designate for service of process an address in the Party's territory or to appoint an agent in the Party's territory, if the derogation is consistent with the relevant Convention listed in Article 1701(2), provided that such derogation:

(a) is necessary to secure compliance with measures that are not inconsistent with this Chapter; and

(b) is not applied in a manner that would constitute a disguised restriction on trade.

4. No Party shall have any obligation under this Article with respect to procedures provided in multilateral agreements concluded under the auspices of the World Intellectual Property Organization relating to the acquisition or maintenance of intellectual property rights.

Article 1704: Control of Abusive or Anticompetitive Practices or Conditions

Nothing in this Chapter shall prevent a Party from specifying in its domestic law licensing practices or conditions that may in particular cases constitute an abuse of intellectual property rights having an adverse effect on competition in the relevant market. A Party may adopt or maintain, consistent with the other provisions of this Agreement, appropriate measures to prevent or control such practices or conditions.

Article 1705: Copyright

1. Each Party shall protect the works covered by Article 2 of the Berne Convention, including any other works that embody original expression within the meaning of that Convention. In particular:

(a) all types of computer programs are literary works within the meaning of the Berne Convention and each Party shall protect them as such; and

(b) compilations of data or other material, whether in machine readable or other form, which by reason of the selection or arrangement of their contents constitute intellectual creations, shall be protected as such.

The protection a Party provides under subparagraph (b) shall not extend to the data or material itself, or prejudice any copyright subsisting in that data or material.

2. Each Party shall provide to authors and their successors in interest those rights enumerated in the Berne Convention in respect of works covered by paragraph 1, including the right to authorize or prohibit:

(a) the importation into the Party's territory of copies of the work made without the right holder's authorization;

(b) the first public distribution of the original and each copy of the work by sale, rental or otherwise;

(c) the communication of a work to the public; and

(d) the commercial rental of the original or a copy of a computer program.

Subparagraph (d) shall not apply where the copy of the computer program is not itself an essential object of the rental. Each Party shall provide that putting the original or a copy of a computer program on the market with the right holder's consent shall not exhaust the rental right.

3. Each Party shall provide that for copyright and related rights:

(a) any person acquiring or holding economic rights may freely and separately transfer such rights by contract for purposes of their exploitation and enjoyment by the transferee; and

(b) any person acquiring or holding such economic rights by virtue of a contract, including contracts of employment underlying the creation of works and sound recordings, shall be able to exercise those rights in its own name and enjoy fully the benefits derived from those rights.

4. Each Party shall provide that, where the term of protection of a work, other than a photographic work or a work of applied art, is to be calculated on a basis other than the life of a natural person, the term shall be not less than 50 years from the end of the calendar year of the first authorized publication of the work or, failing such authorized publication within 50 years from the making of the work, 50 years from the end of the calendar year of making.

5. Each Party shall confine limitations or exceptions to the rights provided for in this Article to certain special cases that do not conflict with a normal exploitation of the work and do not unreasonably prejudice the legitimate interests of the right holder.

6. No Party may grant translation and reproduction licenses permitted under the Appendix to the Berne Convention where legitimate needs in that Party's territory for copies or translations of the work could be met

by the right holder's voluntary actions but for obstacles created by the Party's measures.

* * *

Article 1708: Trademarks

1. For purposes of this Agreement, a trademark consists of any sign, or any combination of signs, capable of distinguishing the goods or services of one person from those of another, including personal names, designs, letters, numerals, colors, figurative elements, or the shape of goods or of their packaging. Trademarks shall include service marks and collective marks, and may include certification marks. A Party may require, as a condition for registration, that a sign be visually perceptible.

2. Each Party shall provide to the owner of a registered trademark the right to prevent all persons not having the owner's consent from using in commerce identical or similar signs for goods or services that are identical or similar to those goods or services in respect of which the owner's trademark is registered, where such use would result in a likelihood of confusion. In the case of the use of an identical sign for identical goods or services, a likelihood of confusion shall be presumed. The rights described above shall not prejudice any prior rights, nor shall they affect the possibility of a Party making rights available on the basis of use.

3. A Party may make registrability depend on use. However, actual use of a trademark shall not be a condition for filing an application for registration. No Party may refuse an application solely on the ground that intended use has not taken place before the expiry of a period of three years from the date of application for registration.

4. Each Party shall provide a system for the registration of trademarks, which shall include:

(a) examination of applications;

(b) notice to be given to an applicant of the reasons for the refusal to register a trademark;

(c) a reasonable opportunity for the applicant to respond to the notice;

(d) publication of each trademark either before or promptly after it is registered; and

(e) a reasonable opportunity for interested persons to petition to cancel the registration of a trademark.

A Party may provide for a reasonable opportunity for interested persons to oppose the registration of a trademark.

5. The nature of the goods or services to which a trademark is to be applied shall in no case form an obstacle to the registration of the trademark.

6. Article 6bis of the Paris Convention shall apply, with such modifications as may be necessary, to services. In determining whether a trademark is well-known, account shall be taken of the knowledge of the trademark in the relevant sector of the public, including knowledge in the Party's territory obtained as a result of the promotion of the trademark. No Party may require that the reputation of the trademark extend beyond the sector of the public that normally deals with the relevant goods or services.

7. Each Party shall provide that the initial registration of a trademark be for a term of at least 10 years and that the registration be indefinitely renewable for terms of not less than 10 years when conditions for renewal have been met.

8. Each Party shall require the use of a trademark to maintain a registration. The registration may be canceled for the reason of non-use only after an uninterrupted period of at least two years of non-use, unless valid reasons based on the existence of obstacles to such use are shown by the trademark owner. Each Party shall recognize, as valid reasons for non-use, circumstances arising independently of the will of the trademark owner that constitute an obstacle to the use of the trademark, such as import restrictions on, or other government requirements for, goods or services identified by the trademark.

9. Each Party shall recognize use of a trademark by a person other than the trademark owner, where such use is subject to the owner's control, as use of the trademark for purposes of maintaining the registration.

10. No Party may encumber the use of a trademark in commerce by special requirements, such as a use that reduces the trademark's function as an indication of source or a use with another trademark.

11. A Party may determine conditions on the licensing and assignment of trademarks, it being understood that the compulsory licensing of trademarks shall not be permitted and that the owner of a registered trademark shall have the right to assign its trademark with or without the transfer of the business to which the trademark belongs.

12. A Party may provide limited exceptions to the rights conferred by a trademark, such as fair use of descriptive terms, provided that such exceptions take into account the legitimate interests of the trademark owner and of other persons.

13. Each Party shall prohibit the registration as a trademark of words, at least in English, French or Spanish, that generically designate goods or services or types of goods or services to which the trademark applies.

14. Each Party shall refuse to register trademarks that consist of or comprise immoral, deceptive or scandalous matter, or matter that may disparage or falsely suggest a connection with persons, living or dead, institutions, beliefs or any Party's national symbols, or bring them into contempt or disrepute.

Article 1709: Patents

1. Subject to paragraphs 2 and 3, each Party shall make patents available for any inventions, whether products or processes, in all fields of technology, provided that such inventions are new, result from an inventive step and are capable of industrial application. For purposes of this Article, a Party may deem the terms "inventive step" and "capable of industrial application" to be synonymous with the terms "non-obvious" and "useful", respectively.

2. A Party may exclude from patentability inventions if preventing in its territory the commercial exploitation of the inventions is necessary to protect *ordre public* or morality, including to protect human, animal or plant life or health or to avoid serious prejudice to nature or the environment, provided that the exclusion is not based solely on the ground that the Party prohibits commercial exploitation in its territory of the subject matter of the patent.

3. A Party may also exclude from patentability:

(a) diagnostic, therapeutic and surgical methods for the treatment of humans or animals;

(b) plants and animals other than microorganisms; and

(c) essentially biological processes for the production of plants or animals, other than non-biological and microbiological processes for such production.

Notwithstanding subparagraph (b), each Party shall provide for the protection of plant varieties through patents, an effective scheme of *sui generis* protection, or both.

4. If a Party has not made available product patent protection for pharmaceutical or agricultural chemicals commensurate with paragraph 1:

(a) as of January 1, 1992, for subject matter that relates to naturally occurring substances prepared or produced by, or significantly derived from, microbiological processes and intended for food or medicine, and

(b) as of July 1, 1991, for any other subject matter,

that Party shall provide to the inventor of any such product or its assignee the means to obtain product patent protection for such product for the unexpired term of the patent for such product granted in another Party, as long as the product has not been marketed in the Party providing protection under this paragraph and the person seeking such protection makes a timely request.

5. Each Party shall provide that:

(a) where the subject matter of a patent is a product, the patent shall confer on the patent owner the right to prevent other persons from making, using or selling the subject matter of the patent, without the patent owner's consent; and

(b) where the subject matter of a patent is a process, the patent shall confer on the patent owner the right to prevent other persons from using that process and from using, selling, or importing at least the product obtained directly by that process, without the patent owner's consent.

6. A Party may provide limited exceptions to the exclusive rights conferred by a patent, provided that such exceptions do not unreasonably conflict with a normal exploitation of the patent and do not unreasonably prejudice the legitimate interests of the patent owner, taking into account the legitimate interests of other persons.

7. Subject to paragraphs 2 and 3, patents shall be available and patent rights enjoyable without discrimination as to the field of technology, the territory of the Party where the invention was made and whether products are imported or locally produced.

8. A Party may revoke a patent only when:

(a) grounds exist that would have justified a refusal to grant the patent; or

(b) the grant of a compulsory license has not remedied the lack of exploitation of the patent.

9. Each Party shall permit patent owners to assign and transfer by succession their patents, and to conclude licensing contracts.

10. Where the law of a Party allows for use of the subject matter of a patent, other than that use allowed under paragraph 6, without the authorization of the right holder, including use by the government or other persons authorized by the government, the Party shall respect the following provisions:

(a) authorization of such use shall be considered on its individual merits;

(b) such use may only be permitted if, prior to such use, the proposed user has made efforts to obtain authorization from the right holder on reasonable commercial terms and conditions and such efforts have not been successful within a reasonable period of time. The requirement to make such efforts may be waived by a Party in the case of a national emergency or other circumstances of extreme urgency or in cases of public non-commercial use. In situations of national emergency or other circumstances of extreme urgency, the right holder shall, nevertheless, be notified as soon as reasonably practicable. In the case of public non-commercial use, where the government or contractor, without making a patent search, knows or has demonstrable grounds to know that a valid patent is or will be used by or for the government, the right holder shall be informed promptly;

(c) the scope and duration of such use shall be limited to the purpose for which it was authorized;

(d) such use shall be non-exclusive;

(e) such use shall be non-assignable, except with that part of the enterprise or goodwill that enjoys such use;

(f) any such use shall be authorized predominantly for the supply of the Party's domestic market;

(g) authorization for such use shall be liable, subject to adequate protection of the legitimate interests of the persons so authorized, to be terminated if and when the circumstances that led to it cease to exist and are unlikely to recur. The competent authority shall have the authority to review, on motivated request, the continued existence of these circumstances;

(h) the right holder shall be paid adequate remuneration in the circumstances of each case, taking into account the economic value of the authorization;

(i) the legal validity of any decision relating to the authorization shall be subject to judicial or other independent review by a distinct higher authority;

(j) any decision relating to the remuneration provided in respect of such use shall be subject to judicial or other independent review by a distinct higher authority;

(k) the Party shall not be obliged to apply the conditions set out in subparagraphs (b) and (f) where such use is permitted to remedy a practice determined after judicial or administrative process to be anticompetitive. The need to correct anticompetitive practices may be taken into account in determining the amount of remuneration in such cases. Competent authorities shall have the authority to refuse termination of authorization if and when the conditions that led to such authorization are likely to recur;

(*l*) the Party shall not authorize the use of the subject matter of a patent to permit the exploitation of another patent except as a remedy for an adjudicated violation of domestic laws regarding anticompetitive practices.

11. Where the subject matter of a patent is a process for obtaining a product, each Party shall, in any infringement proceeding, place on the defendant the burden of establishing that the allegedly infringing product was made by a process other than the patented process in one of the following situations:

(a) the product obtained by the patented process is new; or

(b) a substantial likelihood exists that the allegedly infringing product was made by the process and the patent owner has been unable through reasonable efforts to determine the process actually used.

In the gathering and evaluation of evidence, the legitimate interests of the defendant in protecting its trade secrets shall be taken into account.

12. Each Party shall provide a term of protection for patents of at least 20 years from the date of filing or 17 years from the date of grant. A Party may extend the term of patent protection, in appropriate cases, to compensate for delays caused by regulatory approval processes.

* * *

Article 1711: Trade Secrets

1. Each Party shall provide the legal means for any person to prevent trade secrets from being disclosed to, acquired by, or used by others without the consent of the person lawfully in control of the information in a manner contrary to honest commercial practices, in so far as:

(a) the information is secret in the sense that it is not, as a body or in the precise configuration and assembly of its components, generally known among or readily accessible to persons that normally deal with the kind of information in question;

(b) the information has actual or potential commercial value because it is secret; and

(c) the person lawfully in control of the information has taken reasonable steps under the circumstances to keep it secret.

2. A Party may require that to qualify for protection a trade secret must be evidenced in documents, electronic or magnetic means, optical discs, microfilms, films or other similar instruments.

3. No Party may limit the duration of protection for trade secrets, so long as the conditions in paragraph 1 exist.

4. No Party may discourage or impede the voluntary licensing of trade secrets by imposing excessive or discriminatory conditions on such licenses or conditions that dilute the value of the trade secrets.

5. If a Party requires, as a condition for approving the marketing of pharmaceutical or agricultural chemical products that utilize new chemical entities, the submission of undisclosed test or other data necessary to determine whether the use of such products is safe and effective, the Party shall protect against disclosure of the data of persons making such submissions, where the origination of such data involves considerable effort, except where the disclosure is necessary to protect the public or unless steps are taken to ensure that the data is protected against unfair commercial use.

6. Each Party shall provide that for data subject to paragraph 5 that are submitted to the Party after the date of entry into force of this Agreement, no person other than the person that submitted them may, without the latter's permission, rely on such data in support of an application for product approval during a reasonable period of time after their submission. For this purpose, a reasonable period shall normally mean not less than five years from the date on which the Party granted approval to the person that produced the data for approval to market its product, taking

account of the nature of the data and the person's efforts and expenditures in producing them. Subject to this provision, there shall be no limitation on any Party to implement abbreviated approval procedures for such products on the basis of bioequivalence and bioavailability studies.

7. Where a Party relies on a marketing approval granted by another Party, the reasonable period of exclusive use of the data submitted in connection with obtaining the approval relied on shall begin with the date of the first marketing approval relied on.

* * *

Article 1714: Enforcement of Intellectual Property Rights: General Provisions

1. Each Party shall ensure that enforcement procedures, as specified in this Article and Articles 1715 through 1718, are available under its domestic law so as to permit effective action to be taken against any act of infringement of intellectual property rights covered by this Chapter, including expeditious remedies to prevent infringements and remedies to deter further infringements. Such enforcement procedures shall be applied so as to avoid the creation of barriers to legitimate trade and to provide for safeguards against abuse of the procedures.

2. Each Party shall ensure that its procedures for the enforcement of intellectual property rights are fair and equitable, are not unnecessarily complicated or costly, and do not entail unreasonable time limits or unwarranted delays.

3. Each Party shall provide that decisions on the merits of a case in judicial and administrative enforcement proceedings shall:

(a) preferably be in writing and preferably state the reasons on which the decisions are based;

(b) be made available at least to the parties in a proceeding without undue delay; and

(c) be based only on evidence in respect of which such parties were offered the opportunity to be heard.

4. Each Party shall ensure that parties in a proceeding have an opportunity to have final administrative decisions reviewed by a judicial authority of that Party and, subject to jurisdictional provisions in its domestic laws concerning the importance of a case, to have reviewed at least the legal aspects of initial judicial decisions on the merits of a case. Notwithstanding the above, no Party shall be required to provide for judicial review of acquittals in criminal cases.

* * *

Article 1715: Specific Procedural and Remedial Aspects of Civil and Administrative Procedures

1. Each Party shall make available to right holders civil judicial procedures for the enforcement of any intellectual property right provided in this Chapter. Each Party shall provide that:

(a) defendants have the right to written notice that is timely and contains sufficient detail, including the basis of the claims;

(b) parties in a proceeding are allowed to be represented by independent legal counsel;

(c) the procedures do not include imposition of overly burdensome requirements concerning mandatory personal appearances;

(d) all parties in a proceeding are duly entitled to substantiate their claims and to present relevant evidence; and

(e) the procedures include a means to identify and protect confidential information.

2. Each Party shall provide that its judicial authorities shall have the authority:

(a) where a party in a proceeding has presented reasonably available evidence sufficient to support its claims and has specified evidence relevant to the substantiation of its claims that is within the control of the opposing party, to order the opposing party to produce such evidence, subject in appropriate cases to conditions that ensure the protection of confidential information;

(b) where a party in a proceeding voluntarily and without good reason refuses access to, or otherwise does not provide relevant evidence under that party's control within a reasonable period, or significantly impedes a proceeding relating to an enforcement action, to make preliminary and final determinations, affirmative or negative, on the basis of the evidence presented, including the complaint or the allegation presented by the party adversely affected by the denial of access to evidence, subject to providing the parties an opportunity to be heard on the allegations or evidence;

(c) to order a party in a proceeding to desist from an infringement, including to prevent the entry into the channels of commerce in their jurisdiction of imported goods that involve the infringement of an intellectual property right, which order shall be enforceable at least immediately after customs clearance of such goods;

(d) to order the infringer of an intellectual property right to pay the right holder damages adequate to compensate for the injury the right holder has suffered because of the infringement where the infringer knew or had reasonable grounds to know that it was engaged in an infringing activity;

(e) to order an infringer of an intellectual property right to pay the right holder's expenses, which may include appropriate attorney's fees; and

(f) to order a party in a proceeding at whose request measures were taken and who has abused enforcement procedures to provide adequate compensation to any party wrongfully enjoined or restrained in the proceeding for the injury suffered because of such abuse and to pay that party's expenses, which may include appropriate attorney's fees.

3. With respect to the authority referred to in subparagraph 2(c), no Party shall be obliged to provide such authority in respect of protected subject matter that is acquired or ordered by a person before that person knew or had reasonable grounds to know that dealing in that subject matter would entail the infringement of an intellectual property right.

4. With respect to the authority referred to in subparagraph 2(d), a Party may, at least with respect to copyrighted works and sound recordings, authorize the judicial authorities to order recovery of profits or payment of pre-established damages, or both, even where the infringer did not know or had no reasonable grounds to know that it was engaged in an infringing activity.

5. Each Party shall provide that, in order to create an effective deterrent to infringement, its judicial authorities shall have the authority to order that:

(a) goods that they have found to be infringing be, without compensation of any sort, disposed of outside the channels of commerce in such a manner as to avoid any injury caused to the right holder or, unless this would be contrary to existing constitutional requirements, destroyed; and

(b) materials and implements the predominant use of which has been in the creation of the infringing goods be, without compensation of any sort, disposed of outside the channels of commerce in such a manner as to minimize the risks of further infringements.

In considering whether to issue such an order, judicial authorities shall take into account the need for proportionality between the seriousness of the infringement and the remedies ordered as well as the interests of other persons. In regard to counterfeit goods, the simple removal of the trademark unlawfully affixed shall not be sufficient, other than in exceptional cases, to permit release of the goods into the channels of commerce.

6. In respect of the administration of any law pertaining to the protection or enforcement of intellectual property rights, each Party shall only exempt both public authorities and officials from liability to appropriate remedial measures where actions are taken or intended in good faith in the course of the administration of such laws.

7. Notwithstanding the other provisions of Articles 1714 through 1718, where a Party is sued with respect to an infringement of an intellectual property right as a result of its use of that right or use on its behalf, that Party may limit the remedies available against it to the payment to the right holder of adequate remuneration in the circumstances of each case, taking into account the economic value of the use.

8. Each Party shall provide that, where a civil remedy can be ordered as a result of administrative procedures on the merits of a case, such procedures shall conform to principles equivalent in substance to those set out in this Article.

Article 1716: Provisional Measures

1. Each Party shall provide that its judicial authorities shall have the authority to order prompt and effective provisional measures:

(a) to prevent an infringement of any intellectual property right, and in particular to prevent the entry into the channels of commerce in their jurisdiction of allegedly infringing goods, including measures to prevent the entry of imported goods at least immediately after customs clearance; and

(b) to preserve relevant evidence in regard to the alleged infringement.

2. Each Party shall provide that its judicial authorities shall have the authority to require any applicant for provisional measures to provide to the judicial authorities any evidence reasonably available to that applicant that the judicial authorities consider necessary to enable them to determine with a sufficient degree of certainty whether:

(a) the applicant is the right holder;

(b) the applicant's right is being infringed or such infringement is imminent; and

(c) any delay in the issuance of such measures is likely to cause irreparable harm to the right holder, or there is a demonstrable risk of evidence being destroyed.

Each Party shall provide that its judicial authorities shall have the authority to require the applicant to provide a security or equivalent assurance sufficient to protect the interests of the defendant and to prevent abuse.

3. Each Party shall provide that its judicial authorities shall have the authority to require an applicant for provisional measures to provide other information necessary for the identification of the relevant goods by the authority that will execute the provisional measures.

4. Each Party shall provide that its judicial authorities shall have the authority to order provisional measures on an *ex parte* basis, in particular where any delay is likely to cause irreparable harm to the right holder, or where there is a demonstrable risk of evidence being destroyed.

5. Each Party shall provide that where provisional measures are adopted by that Party's judicial authorities on an *ex parte* basis:

(a) a person affected shall be given notice of those measures without delay but in any event no later than immediately after the execution of the measures;

(b) a defendant shall, on request, have those measures reviewed by that Party's judicial authorities for the purpose of deciding, within a reasonable period after notice of those measures is given, whether the measures shall be modified, revoked or confirmed, and shall be given an opportunity to be heard in the review proceedings.

6. Without prejudice to paragraph 5, each Party shall provide that, on the request of the defendant, the Party's judicial authorities shall revoke or otherwise cease to apply the provisional measures taken on the basis of paragraphs 1 and 4 if proceedings leading to a decision on the merits are not initiated:

(a) within a reasonable period as determined by the judicial authority ordering the measures where the Party's domestic law so permits; or

(b) in the absence of such a determination, within a period of no more than 20 working days or 31 calendar days, whichever is longer.

7. Each Party shall provide that, where the provisional measures are revoked or where they lapse due to any act or omission by the applicant, or where the judicial authorities subsequently find that there has been no infringement or threat of infringement of an intellectual property right, the judicial authorities shall have the authority to order the applicant, on request of the defendant, to provide the defendant appropriate compensation for any injury caused by these measures.

8. Each Party shall provide that, where a provisional measure can be ordered as a result of administrative procedures, such procedures shall conform to principles equivalent in substance to those set out in this Article.

Article 1717: Criminal Procedures and Penalties

1. Each Party shall provide criminal procedures and penalties to be applied at least in cases of willful trademark counterfeiting or copyright piracy on a commercial scale. Each Party shall provide that penalties available include imprisonment or monetary fines, or both, sufficient to provide a deterrent, consistent with the level of penalties applied for crimes of a corresponding gravity.

2. Each Party shall provide that, in appropriate cases, its judicial authorities may order the seizure, forfeiture and destruction of infringing goods and of any materials and implements the predominant use of which has been in the commission of the offense.

3. A Party may provide criminal procedures and penalties to be applied in cases of infringement of intellectual property rights, other than those in paragraph 1, where they are committed wilfully and on a commercial scale.

Article 1718: Enforcement of Intellectual Property Rights at the Border

1. Each Party shall, in conformity with this Article, adopt procedures to enable a right holder, who has valid grounds for suspecting that the importation of counterfeit trademark goods or pirated copyright goods may take place, to lodge an application in writing with its competent authorities, whether administrative or judicial, for the suspension by the customs administration of the release of such goods into free circulation. No Party shall be obligated to apply such procedures to goods in transit. A Party may permit such an application to be made in respect of goods that involve other infringements of intellectual property rights, provided that the requirements of this Article are met. A Party may also provide for corresponding procedures concerning the suspension by the customs administration of the release of infringing goods destined for exportation from its territory.

2. Each Party shall require any applicant who initiates procedures under paragraph 1 to provide adequate evidence:

(a) to satisfy that Party's competent authorities that, under the domestic laws of the country of importation, there is *prima facie* an infringement of its intellectual property right; and

(b) to supply a sufficiently detailed description of the goods to make them readily recognizable by the customs administration.

The competent authorities shall inform the applicant within a reasonable period whether they have accepted the application and, if so, the period for which the customs administration will take action.

3. Each Party shall provide that its competent authorities shall have the authority to require an applicant under paragraph 1 to provide a security or equivalent assurance sufficient to protect the defendant and the competent authorities and to prevent abuse. Such security or equivalent assurance shall not unreasonably deter recourse to these procedures.

4. Each Party shall provide that, where pursuant to an application under procedures adopted pursuant to this Article, its customs administration suspends the release of goods involving industrial designs, patents, integrated circuits or trade secrets into free circulation on the basis of a decision other than by a judicial or other independent authority, and the period provided for in paragraphs 6 through 8 has expired without the granting of provisional relief by the duly empowered authority, and provided that all other conditions for importation have been complied with, the owner, importer or consignee of such goods shall be entitled to their release on the posting of a security in an amount sufficient to protect the right holder against any infringement. Payment of such security shall not prejudice any other remedy available to the right holder, it being understood that the security shall be released if the right holder fails to pursue its right of action within a reasonable period of time.

5. Each Party shall provide that its customs administration shall promptly notify the importer and the applicant when the customs administration suspends the release of goods pursuant to paragraph 1.

6. Each Party shall provide that its customs administration shall release goods from suspension if, within a period not exceeding 10 working days after the applicant under paragraph 1 has been served notice of the suspension, the customs administration has not been informed that:

(a) a party other than the defendant has initiated proceedings leading to a decision on the merits of the case, or

(b) a competent authority has taken provisional measures prolonging the suspension,

provided that all other conditions for importation or exportation have been met. Each Party shall provide that, in appropriate cases, the customs administration may extend the suspension by another 10 working days.

7. Each Party shall provide that if proceedings leading to a decision on the merits of the case have been initiated, a review, including a right to be heard, shall take place on request of the defendant with a view to deciding, within a reasonable period, whether these measures shall be modified, revoked or confirmed.

8. Notwithstanding paragraphs 6 and 7, where the suspension of the release of goods is carried out or continued in accordance with a provisional judicial measure, Article 1716(6) shall apply.

9. Each Party shall provide that its competent authorities shall have the authority to order the applicant under paragraph 1 to pay the importer, the consignee and the owner of the goods appropriate compensation for any injury caused to them through the wrongful detention of goods or through the detention of goods released pursuant to paragraph 6.

10. Without prejudice to the protection of confidential information, each Party shall provide that its competent authorities shall have the authority to give the right holder sufficient opportunity to have any goods detained by the customs administration inspected in order to substantiate the right holder's claims. Each Party shall also provide that its competent authorities have the authority to give the importer an equivalent opportunity to have any such goods inspected. Where the competent authorities have made a positive determination on the merits of a case, a Party may provide the competent authorities the authority to inform the right holder of the names and addresses of the consignor, the importer and the consignee, and of the quantity of the goods in question.

11. Where a Party requires its competent authorities to act on their own initiative and to suspend the release of goods in respect of which they have acquired *prima facie* evidence that an intellectual property right is being infringed:

(a) the competent authorities may at any time seek from the right holder any information that may assist them to exercise these powers;

(b) the importer and the right holder shall be promptly notified of the suspension by the Party's competent authorities, and where the importer lodges an appeal against the suspension with competent authorities, the suspension shall be subject to the conditions, with such modifications as may be necessary, set out in paragraphs 6 through 8; and

(c) the Party shall only exempt both public authorities and officials from liability to appropriate remedial measures where actions are taken or intended in good faith.

12. Without prejudice to other rights of action open to the right holder and subject to the defendant's right to seek judicial review, each Party shall provide that its competent authorities shall have the authority to order the destruction or disposal of infringing goods in accordance with the principles set out in Article 1715(5). In regard to counterfeit goods, the authorities shall not allow the re-exportation of the infringing goods in an unaltered state or subject them to a different customs procedure, other than in exceptional circumstances.

13. A Party may exclude from the application of paragraphs 1 through 12 small quantities of goods of a non-commercial nature contained in travellers' personal luggage or sent in small consignments that are not repetitive.

14. Annex 1718.14 applies to the Parties specified in that Annex.

* * *

Article 1721: Definitions

1. For purposes of this Chapter:

confidential information includes trade secrets, privileged information and other materials exempted from disclosure under the Party's domestic law.

2. For purposes of this Agreement:

encrypted program-carrying satellite signal means a program-carrying satellite signal that is transmitted in a form whereby the aural or visual characteristics, or both, are modified or altered for the purpose of preventing the unauthorized reception, by persons without the authorized equipment that is designed to eliminate the effects of such modification or alteration, of a program carried in that signal;

geographical indication means any indication that identifies a good as originating in the territory of a Party, or a region or locality in that territory, where a particular quality, reputation or other characteristic of the good is essentially attributable to its geographical origin;

in a manner contrary to honest commercial practices means at least practices such as breach of contract, breach of confidence and inducement to breach, and includes the acquisition of undisclosed information by other persons who knew, or were grossly negligent in failing to know, that such practices were involved in the acquisition;

intellectual property rights refers to copyright and related rights, trademark rights, patent rights, rights in layout designs of semiconductor integrated circuits, trade secret rights, plant breeders' rights, rights in geographical indications and industrial design rights;

nationals of another Party means, in respect of the relevant intellectual property right, persons who would meet the criteria for eligibility for protection provided for in the Paris Convention (1967), the Berne Convention (1971), the Geneva Convention (1971), the International Convention for the Protection of Performers, Producers of Phonograms and Broadcasting Organizations (1961), the UPOV Convention (1978), the UPOV Convention (1991) or the *Treaty on Intellectual Property in Respect of Integrated Circuits*, as if each Party were a party to those Conventions, and with respect to intellectual property rights that are not the subject of these Conventions, "nationals of another Party" shall be understood to be at least individuals who are citizens or permanent residents of that Party and also includes any other natural person referred to in Annex 201.1 (Country-Specific Definitions);

public includes, with respect to rights of communication and performance of works provided for under Articles 11, 11*bis* (1) and 14(1)(ii) of the Berne Convention, with respect to dramatic, dramatico-musical, musical and cinematographic works, at least, any aggregation of individuals intended to be the object of, and capable of perceiving, communications or performances of works, regardless of whether they can do so at the same or different times or in the same or different places, provided that such an aggregation is larger than a family and its immediate circle of acquaintances or is not a group comprising a limited number of individuals having similarly close ties that has not been formed for the principal purpose of receiving such performances and communications of works; and

secondary uses of sound recordings means the use directly for broadcasting or for any other public communication of a sound recording.

* * *

PART SEVEN

ADMINISTRATIVE AND INSTITUTIONAL PROVISIONS

Chapter Nineteen

Review and Dispute Settlement in Antidumping and Countervailing Duty Matters

Article 1901: General Provisions

1. Article 1904 applies only with respect to goods that the competent investigating authority of the importing Party, applying the importing

Party's antidumping or countervailing duty law to the facts of a specific case, determines are goods of another Party.

2. For purposes of Articles 1903 and 1904, panels shall be established in accordance with Annex 1901.2.

3. Except for Article 2203 (Entry into Force), no provision of any other Chapter of this Agreement shall be construed as imposing obligations on a Party with respect to the Party's antidumping law or countervailing duty law.

Article 1902: Retention of Domestic Antidumping Law and Countervailing Duty Law

1. Each Party reserves the right to apply its antidumping law and countervailing duty law to goods imported from the territory of any other Party. Antidumping law and countervailing duty law include, as appropriate for each Party, relevant statutes, legislative history, regulations, administrative practice and judicial precedents.

* * *

Article 1904: Review of Final Antidumping and Countervailing Duty Determinations

1. As provided in this Article, each Party shall replace judicial review of final antidumping and countervailing duty determinations with binational panel review.

2. An involved Party may request that a panel review, based on the administrative record, a final antidumping or countervailing duty determination of a competent investigating authority of an importing Party to determine whether such determination was in accordance with the antidumping or countervailing duty law of the importing Party. For this purpose, the antidumping or countervailing duty law consists of the relevant statutes, legislative history, regulations, administrative practice and judicial precedents to the extent that a court of the importing Party would rely on such materials in reviewing a final determination of the competent investigating authority. Solely for purposes of the panel review provided for in this Article, the antidumping and countervailing duty statutes of the Parties, as those statutes may be amended from time to time, are incorporated into and made a part of this Agreement.

3. The panel shall apply the standard of review set out in Annex 1911 and the general legal principles that a court of the importing Party otherwise would apply to a review of a determination of the competent investigating authority.

* * *

8. The panel may uphold a final determination, or remand it for action not inconsistent with the panel's decision. Where the panel remands a final determination, the panel shall establish as brief a time as is reasonable for compliance with the remand, taking into account the complexity

of the factual and legal issues involved and the nature of the panel's decision. In no event shall the time permitted for compliance with a remand exceed an amount of time equal to the maximum amount of time (counted from the date of the filing of a petition, complaint or application) permitted by statute for the competent investigating authority in question to make a final determination in an investigation. If review of the action taken by the competent investigating authority on remand is needed, such review shall be before the same panel, which shall normally issue a final decision within 90 days of the date on which such remand action is submitted to it.

9. The decision of a panel under this Article shall be binding on the involved Parties with respect to the particular matter between the Parties that is before the panel.

10. This Agreement shall not affect:

(a) the judicial review procedures of any Party, or

(b) cases appealed under those procedures,

with respect to determinations other than final determinations.

11. A final determination shall not be reviewed under any judicial review procedures of the importing Party if an involved Party requests a panel with respect to that determination within the time limits set out in this Article. No Party may provide in its domestic legislation for an appeal from a panel decision to its domestic courts.

12. This Article shall not apply where:

(a) neither involved Party seeks panel review of a final determination;

(b) a revised final determination is issued as a direct result of judicial review of the original final determination by a court of the importing Party in cases where neither involved Party sought panel review of that original final determination; or

(c) a final determination is issued as a direct result of judicial review that was commenced in a court of the importing Party before the date of entry into force of this Agreement.

13. Where, within a reasonable time after the panel decision is issued, an involved Party alleges that:

(a) (i) a member of the panel was guilty of gross misconduct, bias, or a serious conflict of interest, or otherwise materially violated the rules of conduct,

(ii) the panel seriously departed from a fundamental rule of procedure, or

(iii) the panel manifestly exceeded its powers, authority or jurisdiction set out in this Article, for example by failing to apply the appropriate standard of review, and

(b) any of the actions set out in subparagraph (a) has materially affected the panel's decision and threatens the integrity of the binational panel review process, that Party may avail itself of the extraordinary challenge procedure set out in Annex 1904.13.

* * *

Article 1905: Safeguarding the Panel Review System

1. Where a Party alleges that the application of another Party's domestic law:

(a) has prevented the establishment of a panel requested by the complaining Party;

(b) has prevented a panel requested by the complaining Party from rendering a final decision;

(c) has prevented the implementation of the decision of a panel requested by the complaining Party or denied it binding force and effect with respect to the particular matter that was before the panel; or

(d) has resulted in a failure to provide opportunity for review of a final determination by a panel or court of competent jurisdiction that is independent of the competent investigating authorities, that examines the basis for the competent investigating authority's determination and whether the competent investigating authority properly applied domestic antidumping and countervailing duty law in reaching the challenged determination, and that employs the relevant standard of review identified in Article 1911,

the Party may request in writing consultations with the other Party regarding the allegations. The consultations shall begin within 15 days of the date of the request.

* * *

Annex 1901.2

Establishment of Binational Panels

1. On the date of entry into force of this Agreement, the Parties shall establish and thereafter maintain a roster of individuals to serve as panelists in disputes under this Chapter. The roster shall include judges or former judges to the fullest extent practicable. The Parties shall consult in developing the roster, which shall include at least 75 candidates. Each Party shall select at least 25 candidates, and all candidates shall be citizens of Canada, Mexico or the United States. Candidates shall be of good character, high standing and repute, and shall be chosen strictly on the basis of objectivity, reliability, sound judgment and general familiarity with international trade law. Candidates shall not be affiliated with a Party, and in no event shall a candidate take instructions from a Party. The Parties shall maintain the roster, and may amend it, when necessary, after consultations.

2. A majority of the panelists on each panel shall be lawyers in good standing. Within 30 days of a request for a panel, each involved Party shall appoint two panelists, in consultation with the other involved Party. The involved Parties normally shall appoint panelists from the roster. If a panelist is not selected from the roster, the panelist shall be chosen in accordance with and be subject to the criteria of paragraph 1. Each involved Party shall have the right to exercise four peremptory challenges, to be exercised simultaneously and in confidence, disqualifying from appointment to the panel up to four candidates proposed by the other involved Party. Peremptory challenges and the selection of alternative panelists shall occur within 45 days of the request for the panel. If an involved Party fails to appoint its members to a panel within 30 days or if a panelist is struck and no alternative panelist is selected within 45 days, such panelist shall be selected by lot on the 31st or 46th day, as the case may be, from that Party's candidates on the roster.

3. Within 55 days of the request for a panel, the involved Parties shall agree on the selection of a fifth panelist. If the involved Parties are unable to agree, they shall decide by lot which of them shall select, by the 61st day, the fifth panelist from the roster, excluding candidates eliminated by peremptory challenges.

4. On appointment of the fifth panelist, the panelists shall promptly appoint a chair from among the lawyers on the panel by majority vote of the panelists. If there is no majority vote, the chair shall be appointed by lot from among the lawyers on the panel.

5. Decisions of the panel shall be by majority vote and based on the votes of all members of the panel. The panel shall issue a written decision with reasons, together with any dissenting or concurring opinions of panelists.

* * *

Annex 1904.13

Extraordinary Challenge Procedure

1. The involved Parties shall establish an extraordinary challenge committee, comprising three members, within 15 days of a request pursuant to Article 1904(13). The members shall be selected from a 15–person roster comprised of judges or former judges of a federal judicial court of the United States or a judicial court of superior jurisdiction of Canada, or a federal judicial court of Mexico. Each Party shall name five persons to this roster. Each involved Party shall select one member from this roster and the involved Parties shall decide by lot which of them shall select the third member from the roster.

2. The Parties shall establish by the date of entry into force of the Agreement rules of procedure for committees. The rules shall provide for a decision of a committee within 90 days of its establishment.

3. Committee decisions shall be binding on the Parties with respect to the particular matter between the Parties that was before the panel.

After examination of the legal and factual analysis underlying the findings and conclusions of the panel's decision in order to determine whether one of the grounds set out in Article 1904(13) has been established, and on finding that one of those grounds has been established, the committee shall vacate the original panel decision or remand it to the original panel for action not inconsistent with the committee's decision; if the grounds are not established, it shall deny the challenge and, therefore, the original panel decision shall stand affirmed. If the original decision is vacated, a new panel shall be established pursuant to Annex 1901.2.

Annex 1911

Country–Specific Definitions

For purposes of this Chapter:

antidumping statute means:

(a) in the case of Canada, the relevant provisions of the *Special Import Measures Act,* as amended, and any successor statutes;

(b) in the case of the United States, the relevant provisions of Title VII of the *Tariff Act of 1930,* as amended, and any successor statutes:

(c) in the case of Mexico, the relevant provisions of the *Foreign Trade Act Implementing Article 131 of the Constitution of the United Mexican States* ("Ley Reglamentaria del Artículo 131 de la Constitución Política de los Estados Unidos Mexicanos en Materia de Comercio Exterior"), as amended, and any successor statutes; and

(d) the provisions of any other statute that provides for judicial review of final determinations under subparagraph (a), (b) or (c), or indicates the standard of review to be applied to such determinations;

competent investigating authority means:

(a) in the case of Canada,

(i) the Canadian International Trade Tribunal, or its successor, or

(ii) the Deputy Minister of National Revenue for Customs and Excise as defined in the *Special Import Measures Act,* as amended, or the Deputy Minister's successor;

(b) in the case of the United States,

(i) the International Trade Administration of the U.S. Department of Commerce, or its successor, or

(ii) the U.S. International Trade Commission, or its successor; and

(c) in the case of Mexico, the designated authority within the Secretariat of Trade and Industrial Development ("Secretaría de Comercio y Fomento Industrial"), or its successor;

countervailing duty statute means:

(a) in the case of Canada, the relevant provisions of the *Special Import Measures Act,* as amended, and any successor statutes;

(b) in the case of the United States, section 303 and the relevant provisions of Title VII of the *Tariff Act of 1930,* as amended, and any successor statutes;

(c) in the case of Mexico, the relevant provisions of the *Foreign Trade Act Implementing Article 131 of the Constitution of the United Mexican States* ("Ley Reglamentaria del Artículo 131 de la Constitución Política de los Estados Unidos Mexicanos en Materia de Comercio Exterior"), as amended, and any successor statutes; and

(d) the provisions of any other statute that provides for judicial review of final determinations under subparagraph (a), (b) or (c), or indicates the standard of review to be applied to such determinations;

final determination means:

(a) in the case of Canada,

(i) an order or finding of the Canadian International Trade Tribunal under subsection 43(1) of the *Special Import Measures Act,*

(ii) an order by the Canadian International Trade Tribunal under subsection 76(4) of the *Special Import Measures Act,* as amended, continuing an order or finding made under subsection 43(1) of the Act with or without amendment,

(iii) a determination by the Deputy Minister of National Revenue for Customs and Excise pursuant to section 41 of the *Special Import Measures Act,* as amended,

(iv) a re-determination by the Deputy Minister pursuant to section 59 of the *Special Import Measures Act,* as amended,

(v) a decision by the Canadian International Trade Tribunal pursuant to subsection 76(3) of the *Special Import Measures Act,* as amended, not to initiate a review,

(vi) a reconsideration by the Canadian International Trade Tribunal pursuant to subsection 91(3) of the *Special Import Measures Act,* as amended, and

(vii) a review by the Deputy Minister of an undertaking pursuant to subsection 53(1) of the *Special Import Measures Act,* as amended;

(b) in the case of the United States,

(i) a final affirmative determination by the International Trade Administration of the U.S. Department of Commerce or by the U.S. International Trade Commission under section 705 or 735 of the *Tariff Act of 1930,* as amended, including any negative part of such a determination,

(ii) a final negative determination by the International Trade Administration of the U.S. Department of Commerce or by the U.S. International Trade Commission under section 705 or 735 of the *Tariff Act of 1930,* as amended, including any affirmative part of such a determination,

(iii) a final determination, other than a determination in (iv), under section 751 of the *Tariff Act of 1930,* as amended,

(iv) a determination by the U.S. International Trade Commission under section 751(b) of the *Tariff Act of 1930,* as amended, not to review a determination based on changed circumstances, and

(v) a final determination by the International Trade Administration of the U.S. Department of Commerce as to whether a particular type of merchandise is within the class or kind of merchandise described in an existing finding of dumping or antidumping or countervailing duty order; and

(c) in the case of Mexico,

(i) a final resolution regarding antidumping or countervailing duties investigations by the Secretariat of Trade and Industrial Development ("Secretaría de Comercio y Fomento Industrial"), pursuant to Article 13 of the *Foreign Trade Act Implementing Article 131 of the Constitution of the United Mexican States* ("Ley Reglamentaria del Artículo 131 de la Constitución Política de los Estados Unidos Mexicanos en Materia de Comercio Exterior"), as amended,

(ii) a final resolution regarding an annual administrative review of antidumping or countervailing duties by the Secretariat of Trade and Industrial Development ("Secretaría de Comercio y Fomento Industrial"), as described in paragraph (*o*) of its Schedule to Annex 1904.15, and

(iii) a final resolution by the Secretariat of Trade and Industrial Development ("Secretaría de Comercio y Fomento Industrial") as to whether a particular type of merchandise is within the class or kind of merchandise described in an existing antidumping or countervailing duty resolution; and

standard of review means the following standards, as may be amended from time to time by the relevant Party:

(a) in the case of Canada, the grounds set out in subsection 18.1(4) of the *Federal Court Act,* as amended, with respect to all final determinations;

(b) in the case of the United States,

(i) the standard set out in section 516A(b)(1)(B) of the *Tariff Act of 1930,* as amended, with the exception of a determination referred to in (ii), and

(ii) the standard set out in section 516A(b)(1)(A) of the *Tariff Act of 1930,* as amended, with respect to a determination by the U.S. International Trade Commission not to initiate a review pursuant to section 751(b) of the *Tariff Act of 1930,* as amended; and

(c) in the case of Mexico, the standard set out in Article 238 of the *Federal Fiscal Code* ("Código Fiscal de la Federación"), or any successor statutes, based solely on the administrative record.

Chapter Twenty

Institutional Arrangements and Dispute Settlement Procedures

Section A—Institutions

Article 2001: The Free Trade Commission

1. The Parties hereby establish the Free Trade Commission, comprising cabinet-level representatives of the Parties or their designees.

2. The Commission shall:

(a) supervise the implementation of this Agreement;

(b) oversee its further elaboration;

(c) resolve disputes that may arise regarding its interpretation or application;

(d) supervise the work of all committees and working groups established under this Agreement, referred to in Annex 2001.2; and

(e) consider any other matter that may affect the operation of this Agreement.

3. The Commission may:

(a) establish, and delegate responsibilities to, ad hoc or standing committees, working groups or expert groups;

(b) seek the advice of non-governmental persons or groups; and

(c) take such other action in the exercise of its functions as the Parties may agree.

4. The Commission shall establish its rules and procedures. All decisions of the Commission shall be taken by consensus, except as the Commission may otherwise agree.

5. The Commission shall convene at least once a year in regular session. Regular sessions of the Commission shall be chaired successively by each Party.

Article 2002: The Secretariat

1. The Commission shall establish and oversee a Secretariat comprising national Sections.

2. Each Party shall:

(a) establish a permanent office of its Section;

(b) be responsible for

(i) the operation and costs of its Section, and

(ii) the remuneration and payment of expenses of panelists and members of committees and scientific review boards established under this Agreement, as set out in Annex 2002.2;

(c) designate an individual to serve as Secretary for its Section, who shall be responsible for its administration and management; and

(d) notify the Commission of the location of its Section's office.

3. The Secretariat shall:

(a) provide assistance to the Commission;

(b) provide administrative assistance to

(i) panels and committees established under Chapter Nineteen (Review and Dispute Settlement in Antidumping and Countervailing Duty Matters), in accordance with the procedures established pursuant to Article 1908, and

(ii) panels established under this Chapter, in accordance with procedures established pursuant to Article 2012; and

(c) as the Commission may direct

(i) support the work of other committees and groups established under this Agreement, and

(ii) otherwise facilitate the operation of this Agreement.

Section B—Dispute Settlement

Article 2003: Cooperation

The Parties shall at all times endeavor to agree on the interpretation and application of this Agreement, and shall make every attempt through cooperation and consultations to arrive at a mutually satisfactory resolution of any matter that might affect its operation.

Article 2004: Recourse to Dispute Settlement Procedures

Except for the matters covered in Chapter Nineteen (Review and Dispute Settlement in Antidumping and Countervailing Duty Matters) and as otherwise provided in this Agreement, the dispute settlement provisions of this Chapter shall apply with respect to the avoidance or settlement of all disputes between the Parties regarding the interpretation or application of this Agreement or wherever a Party considers that an actual or proposed measure of another Party is or would be inconsistent with the obligations of this Agreement or cause nullification or impairment in the sense of Annex 2004.

Article 2005: GATT Dispute Settlement

1. Subject to paragraphs 2, 3 and 4, disputes regarding any matter arising under both this Agreement and the *General Agreement on Tariffs and Trade* (GATT), any agreement negotiated thereunder, or any successor agreement, may be settled in either forum at the discretion of the complaining Party.

2. Before a Party initiates a dispute settlement proceeding in the GATT against another Party on grounds that are substantially equivalent to

those available to that Party under this Agreement, that Party shall notify any third Party of its intention. If a third Party wishes to have recourse to dispute settlement procedures under this Agreement regarding the matter, it shall inform promptly the notifying Party and those Parties shall consult with a view to agreement on a single forum. If those Parties cannot agree, the dispute normally shall be settled under this Agreement.

3. In any dispute referred to in paragraph 1 where the responding Party claims that its action is subject to Article 104 (Relation to Environmental and Conservation Agreements) and requests in writing that the matter be considered under this Agreement, the complaining Party may, in respect of that matter, thereafter have recourse to dispute settlement procedures solely under this Agreement.

4. In any dispute referred to in paragraph 1 that arises under Section B of Chapter Seven (Sanitary and Phytosanitary Measures) or Chapter Nine (Standards–Related Measures):

(a) concerning a measure adopted or maintained by a Party to protect its human, animal or plant life or health, or to protect its environment, and

(b) that raises factual issues concerning the environment, health, safety or conservation, including directly related scientific matters,

where the responding Party requests in writing that the matter be considered under this Agreement, the complaining Party may, in respect of that matter, thereafter have recourse to dispute settlement procedures solely under this Agreement.

5. The responding Party shall deliver a copy of a request made pursuant to paragraph 3 or 4 to the other Parties and to its Section of the Secretariat. Where the complaining Party has initiated dispute settlement proceedings regarding any matter subject to paragraph 3 or 4, the responding Party shall deliver its request no later than 15 days thereafter. On receipt of such request, the complaining Party shall promptly withdraw from participation in those proceedings and may initiate dispute settlement procedures under Article 2007.

6. Once dispute settlement procedures have been initiated under Article 2007 or dispute settlement proceedings have been initiated under the GATT, the forum selected shall be used to the exclusion of the other, unless a Party makes a request pursuant to paragraph 3 or 4.

7. For purposes of this Article, dispute settlement proceedings under the GATT are deemed to be initiated by a Party's request for a panel, such as under Article XXIII:2 of the *General Agreement on Tariffs and Trade 1947,* or for a committee investigation, such as under Article 20.1 of the Customs Valuation Code.

Consultations

Article 2006: Consultations

1. Any Party may request in writing consultations with any other Party regarding any actual or proposed measure or any other matter that it considers might affect the operation of this Agreement.

2. The requesting Party shall deliver the request to the other Parties and to its Section of the Secretariat.

3. Unless the Commission otherwise provides in its rules and procedures established under Article 2001(4), a third Party that considers it has a substantial interest in the matter shall be entitled to participate in the consultations on delivery of written notice to the other Parties and to its Section of the Secretariat.

4. Consultations on matters regarding perishable agricultural goods shall commence within 15 days of the date of delivery of the request.

5. The consulting Parties shall make every attempt to arrive at a mutually satisfactory resolution of any matter through consultations under this Article or other consultative provisions of this Agreement. To this end, the consulting Parties shall:

(a) provide sufficient information to enable a full examination of how the actual or proposed measure or other matter might affect the operation of this Agreement;

(b) treat any confidential or proprietary information exchanged in the course of consultations on the same basis as the Party providing the information; and

(c) seek to avoid any resolution that adversely affects the interests under this Agreement of any other Party.

Initiation of Procedures

Article 2007: Commission—Good Offices, Conciliation and Mediation

1. If the consulting Parties fail to resolve a matter pursuant to Article 2006 within:

(a) 30 days of delivery of a request for consultations,

(b) 45 days of delivery of such request if any other Party has subsequently requested or has participated in consultations regarding the same matter,

(c) 15 days of delivery of a request for consultations in matters regarding perishable agricultural goods, or

(d) such other period as they may agree,

any such Party may request in writing a meeting of the Commission.

2. A Party may also request in writing a meeting of the Commission where:

(a) it has initiated dispute settlement proceedings under the GATT regarding any matter subject to Article 2005(3) or (4), and has received a request pursuant to Article 2005(5) for recourse to dispute settlement procedures under this Chapter; or

(b) consultations have been held pursuant to Article 513 (Working Group on Rules of Origin), Article 723 (Sanitary and Phytosanitary Measures—Technical Consultations) and Article 914 (Standards–Related Measures—Technical Consultations).

3. The requesting Party shall state in the request the measure or other matter complained of and indicate the provisions of this Agreement that it considers relevant, and shall deliver the request to the other Parties and to its Section of the Secretariat.

4. Unless it decides otherwise, the Commission shall convene within 10 days of delivery of the request and shall endeavor to resolve the dispute promptly.

5. The Commission may:

(a) call on such technical advisers or create such working groups or expert groups as it deems necessary,

(b) have recourse to good offices, conciliation, mediation or such other dispute resolution procedures, or

(c) make recommendations,

as may assist the consulting Parties to reach a mutually satisfactory resolution of the dispute.

6. Unless it decides otherwise, the Commission shall consolidate two or more proceedings before it pursuant to this Article regarding the same measure. The Commission may consolidate two or more proceedings regarding other matters before it pursuant to this Article that it determines are appropriate to be considered jointly.

Panel Proceedings

Article 2008: Request for an Arbitral Panel

1. If the Commission has convened pursuant to Article 2007(4), and the matter has not been resolved within:

(a) 30 days thereafter,

(b) 30 days after the Commission has convened in respect of the matter most recently referred to it, where proceedings have been consolidated pursuant to Article 2007(6), or

(c) such other period as the consulting Parties may agree,

any consulting Party may request in writing the establishment of an arbitral panel. The requesting Party shall deliver the request to the other Parties and to its Section of the Secretariat.

2. On delivery of the request, the Commission shall establish an arbitral panel.

3. A third Party that considers it has a substantial interest in the matter shall be entitled to join as a complaining Party on delivery of written notice of its intention to participate to the disputing Parties and its Section of the Secretariat. The notice shall be delivered at the earliest possible time, and in any event no later than seven days after the date of delivery of a request by a Party for the establishment of a panel.

4. If a third Party does not join as a complaining Party in accordance with paragraph 3, it normally shall refrain thereafter from initiating or continuing:

(a) a dispute settlement procedure under this Agreement, or

(b) a dispute settlement proceeding in the GATT on grounds that are substantially equivalent to those available to that Party under this Agreement,

regarding the same matter in the absence of a significant change in economic or commercial circumstances.

5. Unless otherwise agreed by the disputing Parties, the panel shall be established and perform its functions in a manner consistent with the provisions of this Chapter.

Article 2009: Roster

1. The Parties shall establish by January 1, 1994 and maintain a roster of up to 30 individuals who are willing and able to serve as panelists. The roster members shall be appointed by consensus for terms of three years, and may be reappointed.

2. Roster members shall:

(a) have expertise or experience in law, international trade, other matters covered by this Agreement or the resolution of disputes arising under international trade agreements, and shall be chosen strictly on the basis of objectivity, reliability and sound judgment;

(b) be independent of, and not be affiliated with or take instructions from, any Party; and

(c) comply with a code of conduct to be established by the Commission.

Article 2010: Qualifications of Panelists

1. All panelists shall meet the qualifications set out in Article 2009(2).

2. Individuals may not serve as panelists for a dispute in which they have participated pursuant to Article 2007(5).

Article 2011: Panel Selection

1. Where there are two disputing Parties, the following procedures shall apply:

(a) The panel shall comprise five members.

(b) The disputing Parties shall endeavor to agree on the chair of the panel within 15 days of the delivery of the request for the establishment of the panel. If the disputing Parties are unable to agree on the chair within this period, the disputing Party chosen by lot shall select within five days as chair an individual who is not a citizen of that Party.

(c) Within 15 days of selection of the chair, each disputing Party shall select two panelists who are citizens of the other disputing Party.

(d) If a disputing Party fails to select its panelists within such period, such panelists shall be selected by lot from among the roster members who are citizens of the other disputing Party.

2. Where there are more than two disputing Parties, the following procedures shall apply:

(a) The panel shall comprise five members.

(b) The disputing Parties shall endeavor to agree on the chair of the panel within 15 days of the delivery of the request for the establishment of the panel. If the disputing Parties are unable to agree on the chair within this period, the Party or Parties on the side of the dispute chosen by lot shall select within 10 days a chair who is not a citizen of such Party or Parties.

(c) Within 15 days of selection of the chair, the Party complained against shall select two panelists, one of whom is a citizen of a complaining Party, and the other of whom is a citizen of another complaining Party. The complaining Parties shall select two panelists who are citizens of the Party complained against.

(d) If a disputing Party fails to select a panelist within such period, such panelist shall be selected by lot in accordance with the citizenship criteria of subparagraph (c).

3. Panelists shall normally be selected from the roster. Any disputing Party may exercise a peremptory challenge against any individual not on the roster who is proposed as a panelist by a disputing Party within 15 days after the individual has been proposed.

4. If a disputing Party believes that a panelist is in violation of the code of conduct, the disputing Parties shall consult and if they agree, the panelist shall be removed and a new panelist shall be selected in accordance with this Article.

* * *

Article 2017: Final Report

1. The panel shall present to the disputing Parties a final report, including any separate opinions on matters not unanimously agreed, within 30 days of presentation of the initial report, unless the disputing Parties otherwise agree.

2. No panel may, either in its initial report or its final report, disclose which panelists are associated with majority or minority opinions.

3. The disputing Parties shall transmit to the Commission the final report of the panel, including any report of a scientific review board established under Article 2015, as well as any written views that a disputing Party desires to be appended, on a confidential basis within a reasonable period of time after it is presented to them.

4. Unless the Commission decides otherwise, the final report of the panel shall be published 15 days after it is transmitted to the Commission.

Implementation of Panel Reports

Article 2018: Implementation of Final Report

1. On receipt of the final report of a panel, the disputing Parties shall agree on the resolution of the dispute, which normally shall conform with the determinations and recommendations of the panel, and shall notify their Sections of the Secretariat of any agreed resolution of any dispute.

2. Wherever possible, the resolution shall be non-implementation or removal of a measure not conforming with this Agreement or causing nullification or impairment in the sense of Annex 2004 or, failing such a resolution, compensation.

Article 2019: Non–Implementation—Suspension of Benefits

1. If in its final report a panel has determined that a measure is inconsistent with the obligations of this Agreement or causes nullification or impairment in the sense of Annex 2004 and the Party complained against has not reached agreement with any complaining Party on a mutually satisfactory resolution pursuant to Article 2018(1) within 30 days of receiving the final report, such complaining Party may suspend the application to the Party complained against of benefits of equivalent effect until such time as they have reached agreement on a resolution of the dispute.

2. In considering what benefits to suspend pursuant to paragraph 1:

(a) a complaining Party should first seek to suspend benefits in the same sector or sectors as that affected by the measure or other matter that the panel has found to be inconsistent with the obligations of this Agreement or to have caused nullification or impairment in the sense of Annex 2004; and

(b) a complaining Party that considers it is not practicable or effective to suspend benefits in the same sector or sectors may suspend benefits in other sectors.

3. On the written request of any disputing Party delivered to the other Parties and its Section of the Secretariat, the Commission shall establish a panel to determine whether the level of benefits suspended by a Party pursuant to paragraph 1 is manifestly excessive.

4. The panel proceedings shall be conducted in accordance with the Model Rules of Procedure. The panel shall present its determination within 60 days after the last panelist is selected or such other period as the disputing Parties may agree.

Section C—Domestic Proceedings and Private Commercial Dispute Settlement

Article 2020: Referrals of Matters From Judicial or Administrative Proceedings

1. If an issue of interpretation or application of this Agreement arises in any domestic judicial or administrative proceeding of a Party that any Party considers would merit its intervention, or if a court or administrative body solicits the views of a Party, that Party shall notify the other Parties and its Section of the Secretariat. The Commission shall endeavor to agree on an appropriate response as expeditiously as possible.

2. The Party in whose territory the court or administrative body is located shall submit any agreed interpretation of the Commission to the court or administrative body in accordance with the rules of that forum.

3. If the Commission is unable to agree, any Party may submit its own views to the court or administrative body in accordance with the rules of that forum.

Article 2021: Private Rights

No Party may provide for a right of action under its domestic law against any other Party on the ground that a measure of another Party is inconsistent with this Agreement.

Article 2022: Alternative Dispute Resolution

1. Each Party shall, to the maximum extent possible, encourage and facilitate the use of arbitration and other means of alternative dispute resolution for the settlement of international commercial disputes between private parties in the free trade area.

2. To this end, each Party shall provide appropriate procedures to ensure observance of agreements to arbitrate and for the recognition and enforcement of arbitral awards in such disputes.

3. A Party shall be deemed to be in compliance with paragraph 2 if it is a party to and is in compliance with the 1958 *United Nations Convention on the Recognition and Enforcement of Foreign Arbitral Awards* or the 1975 *Inter-American Convention on International Commercial Arbitration.*

4. The Commission shall establish an Advisory Committee on Private Commercial Disputes comprising persons with expertise or experience in the resolution of private international commercial disputes. The Committee shall report and provide recommendations to the Commission on general issues referred to it by the Commission respecting the availability,

use and effectiveness of arbitration and other procedures for the resolution of such disputes in the free trade area.

Annex 2004

Nullification and Impairment

1. If any Party considers that any benefit it could reasonably have expected to accrue to it under any provision of:

(a) Part Two (Trade in Goods), except for those provisions of Annex 300–A (Automotive Sector) or Chapter Six (Energy) relating to investment,

(b) Part Three (Technical Barriers to Trade),

(c) Chapter Twelve (Cross–Border Trade in Services), or

(d) Part Six (Intellectual Property),

is being nullified or impaired as a result of the application of any measure that is not inconsistent with this Agreement, the Party may have recourse to dispute settlement under this Chapter.

2. A Party may not invoke:

(a) paragraph 1(a) or (b), to the extent that the benefit arises from any cross-border trade in services provision of Part Two or Three, or

(b) paragraph 1(c) or (d),

with respect to any measure subject to an exception under Article 2101 (General Exceptions).

PART EIGHT

OTHER PROVISIONS

Chapter Twenty–One

Exceptions

Article 2101: General Exceptions

1. For purposes of:

(a) Part Two (Trade in Goods), except to the extent that a provision of that Part applies to services or investment, and

(b) Part Three (Technical Barriers to Trade), except to the extent that a provision of that Part applies to services,

GATT Article XX and its interpretative notes, or any equivalent provision of a successor agreement to which all Parties are party, are incorporated into and made part of this Agreement. The Parties understand that the measures referred to in GATT Article XX(b) include environmental measures necessary to protect human, animal or plant life or health, and that GATT Article XX(g) applies to measures relating to the conservation of living and non-living exhaustible natural resources.

2. Provided that such measures are not applied in a manner that would constitute a means of arbitrary or unjustifiable discrimination between countries where the same conditions prevail or a disguised restriction on trade between the Parties, nothing in:

(a) Part Two (Trade in Goods), to the extent that a provision of that Part applies to services,

(b) Part Three (Technical Barriers to Trade), to the extent that a provision of that Part applies to services,

(c) Chapter Twelve (Cross–Border Trade in Services), and

(d) Chapter Thirteen (Telecommunications),

shall be construed to prevent the adoption or enforcement by any Party of measures necessary to secure compliance with laws or regulations that are not inconsistent with the provisions of this Agreement, including those relating to health and safety and consumer protection.

Article 2102: National Security

1. Subject to Articles 607 (Energy—National Security Measures) and 1018 (Government Procurement—Exceptions), nothing in this Agreement shall be construed:

(a) to require any Party to furnish or allow access to any information the disclosure of which it determines to be contrary to its essential security interests;

(b) to prevent any Party from taking any actions that it considers necessary for the protection of its essential security interests

(i) relating to the traffic in arms, ammunition and implements of war and to such traffic and transactions in other goods, materials, services and technology undertaken directly or indirectly for the purpose of supplying a military or other security establishment,

(ii) taken in time of war or other emergency in international relations, or

(iii) relating to the implementation of national policies or international agreements respecting the non-proliferation of nuclear weapons or other nuclear explosive devices; or

(c) to prevent any Party from taking action in pursuance of its obligations under the United Nations Charter for the maintenance of international peace and security.

Article 2103: Taxation

1. Except as set out in this Article, nothing in this Agreement shall apply to taxation measures.

* * *

Article 2104: Balance of Payments

1. Nothing in this Agreement shall be construed to prevent a Party from adopting or maintaining measures that restrict transfers where the Party

experiences serious balance of payments difficulties, or the threat thereof, and such restrictions are consistent with paragraphs 2 through 4 and are:

(a) consistent with paragraph 5 to the extent they are imposed on transfers other than cross-border trade in financial services; or

(b) consistent with paragraphs 6 and 7 to the extent they are imposed on cross-border trade in financial services.

General Rules

2. As soon as practicable after a Party imposes a measure under this Article, the Party shall:

(a) submit any current account exchange restrictions to the IMF for review under Article VIII of the Articles of Agreement of the IMF;

(b) enter into good faith consultations with the IMF on economic adjustment measures to address the fundamental underlying economic problems causing the difficulties; and

(c) adopt or maintain economic policies consistent with such consultations.

3. A measure adopted or maintained under this Article shall:

(a) avoid unnecessary damage to the commercial, economic or financial interests of another Party;

(b) not be more burdensome than necessary to deal with the balance of payments difficulties or threat thereof;

(c) be temporary and be phased out progressively as the balance of payments situation improves;

(d) be consistent with paragraph 2(c) and with the Articles of Agreement of the IMF; and

(e) be applied on a national treatment or most-favored-nation treatment basis, whichever is better.

4. A Party may adopt or maintain a measure under this Article that gives priority to services that are essential to its economic program, provided that a Party may not impose a measure for the purpose of protecting a specific industry or sector unless the measure is consistent with paragraph 2(c) and with Article VIII(3) of the Articles of Agreement of the IMF.

* * *

Article 2105: Disclosure of Information

Nothing in this Agreement shall be construed to require a Party to furnish or allow access to information the disclosure of which would impede law enforcement or would be contrary to the Party's law protecting personal privacy or the financial affairs and accounts of individual customers of financial institutions.

Article 2106: Cultural Industries

Annex 2106 applies to the Parties specified in that Annex with respect to cultural industries.

Annex 2106

Cultural Industries

Notwithstanding any other provision of this Agreement, as between Canada and the United States, any measure adopted or maintained with respect to cultural industries, except as specifically provided in Article 302 (Market Access—Tariff Elimination), and any measure of equivalent commercial effect taken in response, shall be governed under this Agreement exclusively in accordance with the provisions of the *Canada—United States Free Trade Agreement.* The rights and obligations between Canada and any other Party with respect to such measures shall be identical to those applying between Canada and the United States.

Chapter Twenty–Two

Final Provisions

Article 2201: Annexes

The Annexes to this Agreement constitute an integral part of this Agreement.

Article 2202: Amendments

1. The Parties may agree on any modification of or addition to this Agreement.

2. When so agreed, and approved in accordance with the applicable legal procedures of each Party, a modification or addition shall constitute an integral part of this Agreement.

Article 2203: Entry Into Force

This Agreement shall enter into force on January 1, 1994, on an exchange of written notifications certifying the completion of necessary legal procedures.

Article 2204: Accession

1. Any country or group of countries may accede to this Agreement subject to such terms and conditions as may be agreed between such country or countries and the Commission and following approval in accordance with the applicable legal procedures of each country.

2. This Agreement shall not apply as between any Party and any acceding country or group of countries if, at the time of accession, either does not consent to such application.

Article 2205: Withdrawal

A Party may withdraw from this Agreement six months after it provides written notice of withdrawal to the other Parties. If a Party withdraws, the Agreement shall remain in force for the remaining Parties.

Article 2206: Authentic Texts

The English, French and Spanish texts of this Agreement are equally authentic.

DOCUMENT 12

OMNIBUS TRADE AND COMPETITIVENESS ACT OF 1988 (SELECTED PROVISIONS)

Public Law 100–418, Aug. 23, 1988, 102 Stat. 1107

This Act includes amendments to numerous American trade laws. Such amendments have been integrated into the laws that appear in this documents supplement. The following are provisions of the 1988 Act which are not amendments to earlier laws.

Table of Contents (Selected Provisions Only)

* See Document 39.

TITLE I—TRADE, CUSTOMS, AND TARIFF LAWS

SUBTITLE A—UNITED STATES TRADE AGREEMENTS

Part 1—Negotiation and Implementation of Trade Agreements

19 U.S.C. § 2901

Sec. 1101. Overall and principal trade negotiating objectives of the United States

(a) Overall trade negotiating objectives. The overall trade negotiating objectives of the United States are to obtain—

(1) more open, equitable, and reciprocal market access;

(2) the reduction or elimination of barriers and other trade-distorting policies and practices; and

(3) a more effective system of international trading disciplines and procedures.

(b) Principal trade negotiating objectives.

(1) Dispute settlement. The principal negotiating objectives of the United States with respect to dispute settlement are—

(A) to provide for more effective and expeditious dispute settlement mechanisms and procedures; and

(B) to ensure that such mechanisms within the GATT and GATT agreements provide for more effective and expeditious resolution of disputes and enable better enforcement of United States rights.

(2) Improvement of the GATT and multilateral trade negotiation agreements. The principal negotiating objectives of the United States regarding the improvement of GATT and multilateral trade negotiation agreements are—

(A) to enhance the status of the GATT;

** Integrated into Buy American Act. See Document 34.

(B) to improve the operation and extend the coverage of the GATT and such agreements and arrangements to products, sectors, and conditions of trade not adequately covered; and

(C) to expand country participation in particular agreements or arrangements, where appropriate.

(3) Transparency. The principal negotiating objective of the United States regarding transparency is to obtain broader application of the principle of transparency and clarification of the costs and benefits of trade policy actions through the observance of open and equitable procedures in trade matters by Contracting Parties to the GATT.

(4) Developing countries. The principal negotiating objectives of the United States regarding developing countries are—

(A) to ensure that developing countries promote economic development by assuming the fullest possible measure of responsibility for achieving and maintaining an open international trading system by providing reciprocal benefits and assuming equivalent obligations with respect to their import and export practices; and

(B) to establish procedures for reducing nonreciprocal trade benefits for the more advanced developing countries.

(5) Current account surpluses. The principal negotiating objective of the United States regarding current account surpluses is to develop rules to address large and persistent global current account imbalances of countries, including imbalances which threaten the stability of the international trading system, by imposing greater responsibility on such countries to undertake policy changes aimed at restoring current account equilibrium, including expedited implementation of trade agreements where feasible and appropriate.

(6) Trade and monetary coordination. The principal negotiating objective of the United States regarding trade and monetary coordination is to develop mechanisms to assure greater coordination, consistency, and cooperation between international trade and monetary systems and institutions.

(7) Agriculture. The principal negotiating objectives of the United States with respect to agriculture are to achieve, on an expedited basis to the maximum extent feasible, more open and fair conditions of trade in agricultural commodities by—

(A) developing, strengthening, and clarifying rules for agricultural trade, including disciplines on restrictive or trade-distorting import and export practices;

(B) increasing United States agricultural exports by eliminating barriers to trade (including transparent and nontransparent barriers) and reducing or eliminating the subsidization of agricultural production consistent with the United States policy of agricultural stabilization in cyclical and unpredictable markets;

(C) creating a free and more open world agricultural trading system by resolving questions pertaining to export and other trade-distorting subsidies, market pricing and market access and eliminating and reducing substantially other specific constraints to fair trade and more open market access, such as tariffs, quotas, and other nontariff practices, including unjustified phytosanitary and sanitary restrictions; and

(D) seeking agreements by which the major agricultural exporting nations agree to pursue policies to reduce excessive production of agricultural commodities during periods of oversupply, with due regard for the fact that the United States already undertakes such policies, and without recourse to arbitrary schemes to divide market shares among major exporting countries.

(8) Unfair trade practices. The principal negotiating objectives of the United States with respect to unfair trade practices are—

(A) to improve the provisions of the GATT and nontariff measure agreements in order to define, deter, discourage the persistent use of, and otherwise discipline unfair trade practices having adverse trade effects, including forms of subsidy and dumping and other practices not adequately covered such as resource input subsidies, diversionary dumping, dumped or subsidized inputs, and export targeting practices;

(B) to obtain the application of similar rules to the treatment of primary and nonprimary products in the Agreement on Interpretation and Application of Articles VI, XVI, and XXIII of the GATT (relating to subsidies and countervailing measures); and

(C) to obtain the enforcement of GATT rules against—

(i) state trading enterprises, and

(ii) the acts, practices, or policies of any foreign government which, as a practical matter, unreasonably require that—

(I) substantial direct investment in the foreign country be made,

(II) intellectual property be licensed to the foreign country or to any firm of the foreign country, or

(III) other collateral concessions be made,

as a condition for the importation of any product or service of the United States into the foreign country or as a condition for carrying on business in the foreign country.

(9) Trade in services.

(A) The principal negotiating objectives of the United States regarding trade in services are—

(i) to reduce or to eliminate barriers to, or other distortions of, international trade in services, including barriers that deny national treatment and restrictions on establishment and operation in such markets; and

(ii) to develop internationally agreed rules, including dispute settlement procedures, which—

(I) are consistent with the commercial policies of the United States, and

(II) will reduce or eliminate such barriers or distortions, and help ensure fair, equitable opportunities for foreign markets.

(B) In pursuing the negotiating objectives described in subparagraph (A), United States negotiators shall take into account legitimate United States domestic objectives including, but not limited to, the protection of legitimate health or safety, essential security, environmental, consumer or employment opportunity interests and the law and regulations related thereto.

(10) Intellectual property. The principal negotiating objectives of the United States regarding intellectual property are—

(A) to seek the enactment and effective enforcement by foreign countries of laws which—

(i) recognize and adequately protect intellectual property, including copyrights, patents, trademarks, semiconductor chip layout designs, and trade secrets, and

(ii) provide protection against unfair competition,

(B) to establish in the GATT obligations—

(i) to implement adequate substantive standards based on—

(I) the standards in existing international agreements that provide adequate protection, and

(II) the standards in national laws if international agreement standards are inadequate or do not exist,

(ii) to establish effective procedures to enforce, both internally and at the border, the standards implemented under clause (i), and

(iii) to implement effective dispute settlement procedures that improve on existing GATT procedures;

(C) to recognize that the inclusion in the GATT of—

(i) adequate and effective substantive norms and standards for the protection and enforcement of intellectual property rights, and

(ii) dispute settlement provisions and enforcement procedures,

is without prejudice to other complementary initiatives undertaken in other international organizations; and

(D) to supplement and strengthen standards for protection and enforcement in existing international intellectual property conventions administered by other international organizations, including their expansion to cover new and emerging technologies and elimination of discrimination or unreasonable exceptions or preconditions to protection.

(11) Foreign direct investment.

(A) The principal negotiating objectives of the United States regarding foreign direct investment are—

(i) to reduce or to eliminate artificial or trade-distorting barriers to foreign direct investment, to expand the principle of national treatment, and to reduce unreasonable barriers to establishment; and

(ii) to develop internationally agreed rules, including dispute settlement procedures, which—

(I) will help ensure a free flow of foreign direct investment, and

(II) will reduce or eliminate the trade distortive effects of certain trade-related investment measures.

(B) In pursuing the negotiating objectives described in subparagraph (A), United States negotiators shall take into account legitimate United States domestic objectives including, but not limited to, the protection of legitimate health or safety, essential security, environmental, consumer or employment opportunity interests and the law and regulations related thereto.

(12) Safeguards. The principal negotiating objectives of the United States regarding safeguards are—

(A) to improve and expand rules and procedures covering safeguard measures;

(B) to ensure that safeguard measures are—

(i) transparent,

(ii) temporary,

(iii) degressive, and

(iv) subject to review and termination when no longer necessary to remedy injury and to facilitate adjustment; and

(C) to require notification of, and to monitor the use by, GATT Contracting Parties of import relief actions for their domestic industries.

(13) Specific barriers. The principal negotiating objective of the United States regarding specific barriers is to obtain competitive opportunities for United States exports in foreign markets substantially equivalent to the competitive opportunities afforded foreign exports to United

States markets, including the reduction or elimination of specific tariff and nontariff trade barriers, particularly—

(A) measures identified in the annual report prepared under section 181 of the Trade Act of 1974 (19 U.S.C. § 2241) and

(B) foreign tariffs and nontariff barriers on competitive United States exports when like or similar products enter the United States at low rates of duty or are duty-free, and other tariff disparities that impede access to particular export markets.

(14) Worker rights. The principal negotiating objectives of the United States regarding worker rights are—

(A) to promote respect for worker rights;

(B) to secure a review of the relationship of worker rights to GATT articles, objectives, and related instruments with a view to ensuring that the benefits of the trading system are available to all workers; and

(C) to adopt, as a principle of the GATT, that the denial of worker rights should not be a means for a country or its industries to gain competitive advantage in international trade.

(15) Access to high technology.

(A) The principal negotiating objective of the United States regarding access to high technology is to obtain the elimination or reduction of foreign barriers to, and acts, policies, or practices by foreign governments which limit equitable access by United States persons to foreign developed technology, including barriers, acts, policies, or practices which have the effect of—

(i) restricting the participation of United States persons in government-supported research and development projects;

(ii) denying equitable access by United States persons to government-held patents;

(iii) requiring the approval or agreement of government entities, or imposing other forms of government interventions, as a condition for the granting of licenses to United States persons by foreign persons (except for approval or agreement which may be necessary for national security purposes to control the export of critical military technology); and

(iv) otherwise denying equitable access by United States persons to foreign-developed technology or contributing to the inequitable flow of technology between the United States and its trading partners.

(B) In pursuing the negotiating objective described in subparagraph (A), the United States negotiators shall take into account United States Government policies in licensing or otherwise making available to foreign persons technology and other information developed by United States laboratories.

(16) Border taxes. The principal negotiating objective of the United States regarding border taxes is to obtain a revision of the GATT with respect to the treatment of border adjustments for internal taxes to redress the disadvantage to countries relying primarily for revenue on direct taxes rather than indirect taxes.

19 U.S.C. § 2902

Sec. 1102. Trade agreement negotiating authority

(a) Agreements regarding tariff barriers.

(1) Whenever the President determines that one or more existing duties or other import restrictions of any foreign country or the United States are unduly burdening and restricting the foreign trade of the United States and that the purposes, policies, and objectives of this title will be promoted thereby, the President—

(A) before June 1, 1993, may enter into trade agreements with foreign countries; and

(B) may, subject to paragraphs (2) through (5), proclaim—

(i) such modification or continuance of any existing duty,

(ii) such continuance of existing duty-free or excise treatment, or

(iii) such additional duties;

as he determines to be required or appropriate to carry out any such trade agreement.

(2) No proclamation may be made under subsection (a) that—

(A) reduces any rate of duty (other than a rate of duty that does not exceed 5 percent ad valorem on the date of enactment of this Act) to a rate which is less than 50 percent of the rate of such duty that applies on such date of enactment; or

(B) increases any rate of duty above the rate that applies on such date of enactment.

(3)(A) Except as provided in subparagraph (B), the aggregate reduction in the rate of duty on any article which is in effect on any day pursuant to a trade agreement entered into under paragraph (1) shall not exceed the aggregate reduction which would have been in effect on such day if a reduction of 3 percent ad valorem or a reduction of one-tenth of the total reduction, whichever is greater, had taken effect on the effective date of the first reduction proclaimed in paragraph (1) to carry out such agreement with respect to such article.

(B) No staging under subparagraph (A) is required with respect to a rate reduction that is proclaimed under paragraph (1) for an article of a kind that is not produced in the United States. The United States International Trade Commission shall advise the President of the identity of articles that may be exempted from staging under this subparagraph.

(4) If the President determines that such action will simplify the computation of reductions under paragraph (3), the President may round an annual reduction by the lesser of—

(A) the difference between the reduction without regard to this paragraph and the next lower whole number; or

(B) one-half of 1 percent ad valorem.

(5) No reduction in a rate of duty under a trade agreement entered into under subsection (a) on any article may take effect more than 10 years after the effective date of the first reduction under paragraph (1) that is proclaimed to carry out the trade agreement with respect to such article.

(6) A rate of duty reduction or increase that may not be proclaimed by reason of paragraph (2) may take effect only if a provision authorizing such reduction or increase is included within an implementing bill provided for under section 1103 and that bill is enacted into law.

(b) Agreements regarding nontariff barriers.

(1) Whenever the President determines that any barrier to, or other distortion of, international trade—

(A) unduly burdens or restricts the foreign trade of the United States or adversely affects the United States economy; or

(B) the imposition of any such barrier or distortion is likely to result in such a burden, restriction, or effect;

and that the purposes, policies, and objectives of this title will be promoted thereby, the President may, before June 1, 1993, enter into a trade agreement with foreign countries providing for—

(i) the reduction or elimination of such barrier or other distortion; or

(ii) the prohibition of, or limitations on the imposition of, such barrier or other distortion.

(2) A trade agreement may be entered into under this subsection only if such agreement makes progress in meeting the applicable objectives described in section 1101.

(c) Bilateral agreements regarding tariff and nontariff barriers.

(1) Before June 1, 1993, the President may enter into bilateral trade agreements with foreign countries that provide for the elimination or reduction of any duty imposed by the United States. A trade agreement entered into under this paragraph may also provide for the reduction or elimination of barriers to, or other distortions of, the international trade of the foreign country or the United States.

(2) Notwithstanding any other provision of law, no trade benefit shall be extended to any country by reason of the extension of any trade benefit to another country under a trade agreement entered into under paragraph (1) with such other country.

(3) A trade agreement may be entered into under paragraph (1) with any foreign country only if—

(A) the agreement makes progress in meeting the applicable objectives described in section 1101;

(B) such foreign country requests the negotiation of such an agreement; and

(C) the President, at least 60 days before the date notice is provided under section 1103(a)(1)(A)—

(i) provides written notice of such negotiations to the Committee on Finance of the Senate and the Committee on Ways and Means of the House of Representatives, and

(ii) consults with such committees regarding the negotiation of such agreement.

(4) The 60-day period of time described in paragraph (3)(C) shall be computed in accordance with section 1103(f).

(5) In any case in which there is an inconsistency between any provision of this Act and any bilateral free trade area agreement that entered into force and effect with respect to the United States before January 1, 1987, the provision shall not apply with respect to the foreign country that is party to that agreement.

(d) Consultation with Congress before agreements entered into.

(1) Before the President enters into any trade agreement under subsection (b) or (c), the President shall consult with—

(A) the Committee on Ways and Means of the House of Representatives and the Committee on Finance of the Senate; and

(B) each other committee of the House and the Senate, and each joint committee of the Congress, which has jurisdiction over legislation involving subject matters which would be affected by the trade agreement.

(2) The consultation under paragraph (1) shall include—

(A) the nature of the agreement;

(B) how and to what extent the agreement will achieve the applicable purposes, policies, and objectives of this title; and

(C) all matters relating to the implementation of the agreement under section 1103.

(3) If it is proposed to implement two or more trade agreements in a single implementing bill under section 1103, the consultation under para-

graph (1) shall include the desirability and feasibility of such proposed implementation.

(e) Special provisions regarding Uruguay Round trade negotiations.

(1) In general

Notwithstanding the time limitations in subsections (a) and (b) of this section, if the Uruguay Round of multilateral trade negotiations under the auspices of the General Agreement on Tariffs and Trade has not resulted in trade agreements by May 31, 1993, the President may, during the period after May 31, 1993, and before April 16, 1994, enter into, under subsections (a) and (b) of this section, trade agreements resulting from such negotiations.

(2) Application of tariff proclamation authority

No proclamation under subsection (a) of this section to carry out the provisions regarding tariff barriers of a trade agreement that is entered into pursuant to paragraph (1) may take effect before the effective date of a bill that implements the provisions regarding nontariff barriers of a trade agreement that is entered into under such paragraph.

(3) Application of implementing and "fast track" procedures

Section 1103 applies to any trade agreement negotiated under subsection (b) of this section pursuant to paragraph (1), except that—

(A) in applying subsection (a)(1)(A) of section 1103 to any such agreement, the phrase "at least 120 calendar days before the day on which he enters into the trade agreement (but not later than December 15, 1993)," shall be substituted for the phrase "at least 90 calendar days before the day on which he enters into the trade agreement,"; and

(B) no provision of subsection (b) of section 1103 other than paragraph (1)(A) applies to any such agreement and in applying such paragraph, "April 16, 1994;" shall be substituted for "June 1, 1991;".

(4) Advisory committee reports

The report required under section 135(e)(1) of the Trade Act of 1974 (19 U.S.C. § 2155) regarding any trade agreement provided for under paragraph (1) shall be provided to the President, the Congress, and the United States Trade Representative not later than 30 days after the date on which the President notifies the Congress under section 1103(a)(1)(A) of this title of his intention to enter into the agreement (but before January 15, 1994).

19 U.S.C. § 2903

Sec. 1103. Implementation of trade agreements

(a) In general.

(1) Any agreement entered into under section 1102(b) or (c) shall enter into force with respect to the United States if (and only if)—

(A) the President, at least 90 calendar days before the day on which he enters into the trade agreement, notifies the House of Representatives and the Senate of his intention to enter into the agreement, and promptly thereafter publishes notice of such intention in the Federal Register;

(B) after entering into the agreement, the President submits a document to the House of Representatives and to the Senate containing a copy of the final legal text of the agreement, together with—

(i) a draft of an implementing bill,

(ii) a statement of any administrative action proposed to implement the trade agreement, and

(iii) the supporting information described in paragraph (2); and

(C) the implementing bill is enacted into law.

(2) The supporting information required under paragraph (1)(B)(iii) consists of—

(A) an explanation as to how the implementing bill and proposed administrative action will change or affect existing law; and

(B) a statement—

(i) asserting that the agreement makes progress in achieving the applicable purposes, policies, and objectives of this title,

(ii) setting forth the reasons of the President regarding—

(I) how and to what extent the agreement makes progress in achieving the applicable purposes, policies, and objectives referred to in clause (i), and why and to what extent the agreement does not achieve other applicable purposes, policies, and objectives,

(II) how the agreement serves the interests of United States commerce, and

(III) why the implementing bill and proposed administrative action is required or appropriate to carry out the agreement;

(iii) describing the efforts made by the President to obtain international exchange rate equilibrium and any effect the agreement may have regarding increased international monetary stability; and

(iv) describing the extent, if any, to which—

(I) each foreign country that is a party to the agreement maintains non-commercial state trading enterprises that may adversely affect, nullify, or impair the benefits to the United States under the agreement, and

(II) the agreement applies to or affects purchases and sales by such enterprises.

(3) To ensure that a foreign country which receives benefits under a trade agreement entered into under section 1102(b) or (c) is subject to the obligations imposed by such agreement, the President shall recommend to Congress in the implementing bill and statement of administrative action submitted with respect to such agreement that the benefits and obligations of such agreement apply solely to the parties to such agreement, if such application is consistent with the terms of such agreement. The President may also recommend with respect to any such agreement that the benefits and obligations of such agreement not apply uniformly to all parties to such agreement, if such application is consistent with the terms of such agreement.

(b) Application of Congressional "fast track" procedures to implementing bills.

(1) Except as provided in subsection (c)—

(A) the provisions of section 151 of the Trade Act of 1974 (19 U.S.C. 2191) (hereinafter in this section referred to as "fast track procedures") apply to implementing bills submitted with respect to trade agreements entered into under section 1102(b) or (c) before June 1, 1991; and

(B) such fast track procedures shall be extended to implementing bills submitted with respect to trade agreements entered into under section 1102(b) or (c) after May 31, 1991, and before June 1, 1993, if (and only if)—

(i) the President requests such extension under paragraph (2); and

(ii) neither House of the Congress adopts an extension disapproval resolution under paragraph (5) before June 1, 1991.

(2) If the President is of the opinion that the fast track procedures should be extended to implementing bills described in paragraph (1)(B), the President must submit to the Congress, no later than March 1, 1991, a written report that contains a request for such extension, together with—

(A) a description of all trade agreements that have been negotiated under section 1102(b) or (c) and the anticipated schedule for submitting such agreements to the Congress for approval;

(B) a description of the progress that has been made in multilateral and bilateral negotiations to achieve the purposes, policies, and objectives of this title, and a statement that such progress justifies the continuation of negotiations; and

(C) a statement of the reasons why the extension is needed to complete the negotiations.

(3) The President shall promptly inform the Advisory Committee for Trade Policy and Negotiations established under section 135 of the Trade

Act of 1974 (19 U.S.C. 2155) of his decision to submit a report to Congress under paragraph (2). The Advisory Committee shall submit to the Congress as soon as practicable, but no later than March 1, 1991, a written report that contains—

(A) its views regarding the progress that has been made in multilateral and bilateral negotiations to achieve the purposes, policies, and objectives of this title; and

(B) a statement of its views, and the reasons therefor, regarding whether the extension requested under paragraph (2) should be approved or disapproved.

(4) The reports submitted to the Congress under paragraphs (2) and (3), or any portion of the reports, may be classified to the extent the President determines appropriate.

(5)(A) For purposes of this subsection, the term "extension disapproval resolution" means a resolution of either House of the Congress, the sole matter after the resolving clause of which is as follows: "That the disapproves the request of the President for the extension, under section 1103(b)(1)(B)(i) of the Omnibus Trade and Competitiveness Act of 1988 [subsec. (b)(1)(B)(i) of this section], of the provisions of section 151 of the Trade Act of 1974 to any implementing bill submitted with respect to any trade agreement entered into under section 1102(b) or (c) of such Act after May 31, 1991, because sufficient tangible progress has not been made in trade negotiations.", with the blank space being filled with the name of the resolving House of the Congress.

(B) Extension disapproval resolutions—

(i) may be introduced in either House of the Congress by any member of such House; and

(ii) shall be jointly referred, in the House of Representatives, to the Committee on Ways and Means and the Committee on Rules.

(C) The provisions of section 152 (d) and (e) of the Trade Act of 1974 (19 U.S.C. 2192 (d) and (e)) (relating to the floor consideration of certain resolutions in the House and Senate) apply to extension disapproval resolutions.

(D) It is not in order for—

(i) the Senate to consider any extension disapproval resolution not reported by the Committee on Finance;

(ii) the House of Representatives to consider any extension disapproval resolution not reported by the Committee on Ways and Means and the Committee on Rules; or

(iii) either House of the Congress to consider an extension disapproval resolution that is reported to such House after May 15, 1991.

(c) Limitations on use of "fast track" procedures.

(1)(A) The fast track procedures shall not apply to any implementing bill submitted with respect to a trade agreement entered into under section 1102(b) or (c) if both Houses of the Congress separately agree to procedural disapproval resolutions within any 60-day period.

(B) Procedural disapproval resolutions—

(i) in the House of Representatives—

(I) shall be introduced by the chairman or ranking minority member of the Committee on Ways and Means or the chairman or ranking minority member of the Committee on Rules,

(II) shall be jointly referred to the Committee on Ways and Means and the Committee on Rules, and

(III) may not be amended by either Committee; and

(ii) in the Senate shall be original resolutions of the Committee on Finance.

(C) The provisions of section 152(d) and (e) of the Trade Act of 1974 (19 U.S.C. 2192(d) and (e)) (relating to the floor consideration of certain resolutions in the House and Senate) apply to procedural disapproval resolutions.

(D) It is not in order for the House of Representatives to consider any procedural disapproval resolution not reported by the Committee on Ways and Means and the Committee on Rules.

(E) For purposes of this subsection, the term "procedural disapproval resolution" means a resolution of either House of the Congress, the sole matter after the resolving clause of which is as follows: "That the President has failed or refused to consult with Congress on trade negotiations and trade agreements in accordance with the provisions of the Omnibus Trade and Competitiveness Act of 1988, and, therefore, the provisions of section 151 of the Trade Act of 1974 shall not apply to any implementing bill submitted with respect to any trade agreement entered into under section 1102(b) or (c) of such Act of 1988, if, during the 60-day period beginning on the date on which this resolution is agreed to by the * * *, the * * * agrees to a procedural disapproval resolution (within the meaning of section 1103(c)(1)(E) of such Act of 1988 [subsec. (c)(1)(E) of this section])", with the first blank space being filled with the name of the resolving House of the Congress and the second blank space being filled with the name of the other House of the Congress.

(2) The fast track procedures shall not apply to any implementing bill that contains a provision approving of any trade agreement which is entered into under section 1102(c) with any foreign country if either—

(A) the requirements of section 1102(c)(3) are not met with respect to the negotiation of such agreement; or

(B) the Committee on Finance of the Senate or the Committee on Ways and Means of the House of Representatives disapproves of the negotiation of such agreement before the close of the 60-day period which begins on the date notice is provided under section 1102(c)(3)(C)(i) with respect to the negotiation of such agreement.

(d) Rules of House of Representatives and Senate. Subsections (b) and (c) are enacted by the Congress—

(1) as an exercise of the rulemaking power of the House of Representatives and the Senate, respectively, and as such is deemed a part of the rules of each House, respectively, and such procedures supersede other rules only to the extent that they are inconsistent with such other rules; and

(2) with the full recognition of the constitutional right of either House to change the rules (so far as relating to the procedures of that House) at any time, in the same manner, and to the same extent as any other rule of that House.

(e) Computation of certain periods of time. Each period of time described in subsection (c)(1) (A) and (E) and (2) of this section shall be computed without regard to—

(1) the days on which either House of Congress is not in session because of an adjournment of more than 3 days to a day certain or an adjournment of the Congress sine die; and

(2) any Saturday and Sunday, not excluded under paragraph (1), when either House of the Congress is not in session.

* * *

SUBTITLE B—IMPLEMENTATION OF THE HARMONIZED TARIFF SCHEDULE

19 U.S.C. § 3001

Sec. 1201. Purposes

The purposes of this subtitle are—

(1) to approve the International Convention on the Harmonized Commodity Description and Coding System;

(2) to implement in United States law the nomenclature established internationally by the Convention; and

(3) to provide that the Convention shall be treated as a trade agreement obligation of the United States.

19 U.S.C. § 3002

Sec. 1202. Definitions

As used in this subtitle:

(1) The term "Commission" means the United States International Trade Commission.

(2) The term "Convention" means the International Convention on the Harmonized Commodity Description and Coding System, done at Brussels on June 14, 1983, and the Protocol thereto, done at Brussels on June 24, 1986, submitted to the Congress on June 15, 1987.

(3) The term "entered" means entered, or withdrawn from warehouse for consumption, in the customs territory of the United States.

(4) The term "Federal agency" means any establishment in the executive branch of the United States Government.

(5) The term "old Schedules" means title I of the Tariff Act of 1930 (19 U.S.C. § 1202) as in effect on the day before the effective date of the amendment to such title under section 1204(a).

(6) The term "technical rectifications" means rectifications of an editorial character or minor technical or clerical changes which do not affect the substance or meaning of the text, such as—

(A) errors in spelling, numbering, or punctuation;

(B) errors in indentation;

(C) errors (including inadvertent omissions) in cross-references to headings or subheadings or notes; and

(D) other clerical or typographical errors.

19 U.S.C. § 3003

§ 3003. Congressional approval of United States accession to the Convention

(a) Congressional approval

The Congress approves the accession by the United States of America to the Convention.

* * *

§ 3004. Enactment of Harmonized Tariff Schedule

* * *

(1) The following shall be considered to be statutory provisions of law for all purposes:

(A) The provisions of the Harmonized Tariff Schedule as enacted by this chapter.

(B) Each statutory amendment to the Harmonized Tariff Schedule.

(C) Each modification or change made to the Harmonized Tariff Schedule by the President under authority of law (including section 604 of the Trade Act of 1974 [19 U.S.C.A. § 2483]).

* * *

§ 3005. Commission review of, and recommendations regarding, Harmonized Tariff Schedule

(a) In general

The Commission shall keep the Harmonized Tariff Schedule under continuous review and periodically, at such time as amendments to the Convention are recommended by the Customs Cooperation Council for adoption, and as other circumstances warrant, shall recommend to the President such modifications in the Harmonized Tariff Schedule as the Commission considers necessary or appropriate—

(1) to conform the Harmonized Tariff Schedule with amendments made to the Convention;

(2) to promote the uniform application of the Convention and particularly the Annex thereto;

(3) to ensure that the Harmonized Tariff Schedule is kept up-to-date in light of changes in technology or in patterns of international trade;

* * *

§ 3006. Presidential action on Commission recommendations

(a) In general

The President may proclaim modifications, based on the recommendations by the Commission under section 3005 of this title, to the Harmonized Tariff Schedule if the President determines that the modifications—

(1) are in conformity with United States obligations under the Convention; and

(2) do not run counter to the national economic interest of the United States.

* * *

§ 3007. Publication of Harmonized Tariff Schedule

(a) In general

The Commission shall compile and publish, at appropriate intervals, and keep up to date the Harmonized Tariff Schedule and related information in the form of printed copy; and, if, in its judgment, such format would serve the public interest and convenience—

(1) in the form of microfilm images; or

(2) in the form of electronic media.

* * *

HISTORY; ANCILLARY LAWS AND DIRECTIVES

References in text:

"The Harmonized Tariff Schedule", referred to in subsec. (a), is not published in the Code. A current version of the Harmonized Tariff Schedule is maintained and published periodically by the United States International Trade Commission and is available for sale by the Superintendent of Documents, U.S. Government Printing Office, Washington, D.C. 20402; such Schedule is also available via the Internet at http://www.customs.treas.gov.

* * *

HARMONIZED TARIFF SCHEDULE OF THE UNITED STATES

GENERAL NOTES

1. *Tariff Treatment of Imported Goods and of Vessel Equipments, Parts and Repairs.* All goods provided for in this schedule and imported into the customs territory of the United States from outside thereof, and all vessel equipments, parts, materials and repairs covered by the provisions of subchapter XVIII to chapter 98 of this schedule, are subject to duty or exempt therefrom as prescribed in general notes 3 through 18, inclusive.
2. *Customs Territory of the United States.* The term "*customs territory of the United States*", as used in the tariff schedule, includes only the States, the District of Columbia and Puerto Rico.
3. *Rates of Duty.* The rates of duty in the "Rates of Duty" columns designated 1 ("General" and "Special") and 2 of the tariff schedule apply to goods imported into the customs territory of the United States as hereinafter provided in this note:

    (a) *Rate of Duty Column 1.*

    (i) Except as provided in subparagraph (iv) of this paragraph, the rates of duty in column 1 are rates which are applicable to all products other than those of countries enumerated in paragraph (b) of this note. Column 1 is divided into two subcolumns, "General" and "Special", which are applicable as provided below.

    (ii) The "*General*" subcolumn sets forth the general or normal trade relations (NTR) rates which are applicable to products of those countries described in subparagraph (i) above which are not entitled to special tariff treatment as set forth below.

    (iii) The "*Special*" subcolumn reflects rates of duty under one or more special tariff treatment programs described in paragraph (c) of this note and identified in parentheses immediately following the duty rate specified in such subcolumn. These rates apply to those products which are properly classified under a provision for which a special rate is indicated and for which all of the legal requirements for eligibility for such program or programs have been met. Where a product is eligible for special treatment under more than one program, the lowest rate of duty provided for any applicable program shall be imposed. Where no special rate of duty is provided for a provision, or where the country from which a product otherwise eligible for special treatment was imported is not designated as a beneficiary country under a program appearing with the appropriate provision, the rates of duty in the "General" subcolumn of column 1 shall apply.

* * *

(b) *Rate of Duty Column 2.* Notwithstanding any of the foregoing provisions of this note, the rates of duty shown in column 2 shall apply to products, whether imported directly or indirectly, of the following countries and areas pursuant to section 401 of the Tariff Classification Act of 1962, to section 231 or 257(e)(2) of the Trade Expansion Act of 1962, to section 404(a) of the Trade Act of 1974 or to any other applicable section of law, or to action taken by the President thereunder:

Cuba North Korea

* * *

GENERAL RULES OF INTERPRETATION

Classification of goods in the tariff schedule shall be governed by the following principles:

1. The table of contents, alphabetical index, and titles of sections, chapters and sub-chapters are provided for ease of reference only; for legal purposes, classification shall be determined according to the terms of the headings and any relative section or chapter notes and, provided such headings or notes do not otherwise require, according to the following provisions:
2. (a) Any reference in a heading to an article shall be taken to include a reference to that article incomplete or unfinished, provided that, as entered, the incomplete or unfinished article has the essential character of the complete or finished article. It shall also include a reference to that article complete or finished (or failing to be classified as complete or finished by virtue of this rule), entered unassembled or disassembled.

   (b) Any reference in a heading to a material or substance shall be taken to include a reference to mixtures or combinations of that material or substance with other materials or substances. Any reference to goods of a given material or substance shall be taken to include a reference to goods consisting wholly or partly of such material or substance. The classification of goods consisting of more than one material or substance shall be according to the principles of rule 3.
3. When, by application of rule 2(b) or for any other reason, goods are, *prima facie,* classifiable under two or more headings, classification shall be effected as follows:

(a) The heading which provides the most specific description shall be preferred to headings providing a more general description. However, when two or more headings each refer to part only of the materials or substances contained in mixed or composite goods or to part only of the items in a set put up for retail sale, those headings are to be regarded as equally specific in relation to those goods, even if one of them gives a more complete or precise description of the goods.

(b) Mixtures, composite goods consisting of different materials or made up of different components, and goods put up in sets for retail sale, which cannot be classified by reference to 3(a), shall be classified as if they consisted of the material or component which gives them their essential character, insofar as this criterion is applicable.

(c) When goods cannot be classified by reference to 3(a) or 3(b), they shall be classified under the heading which occurs last in numerical order among those which equally merit consideration.

4. Goods which cannot be classified in accordance with the above rules shall be classified under the heading appropriate to the goods to which they are most akin.

5. In addition to the foregoing provisions, the following rules shall apply in respect of the goods referred to therein:

(a) Camera cases, musical instrument cases, gun cases, drawing instrument cases, necklace cases and similar containers, specially shaped or fitted to contain a specific article or set of articles, suitable for long-term use and entered with the articles for which they are intended, shall be classified with such articles when of a kind normally sold therewith. The rule does not, however, apply to containers which give the whole its essential character;

(b) Subject to the provisions of rule 5(a) above, packing materials and packing containers entered with the goods therein shall be classified with the goods if they are of a kind normally used for packing such goods. However, this provision is not binding when such packing materials or packing containers are clearly suitable for repetitive use.

6. For legal purposes, the classification of goods in the subheadings of a heading shall be determined according to the terms of those subheadings and any related subheading notes and, *mutatis mutandis,* to the above rules, on the understanding that only subheadings at the same level are comparable. For the purposes of this rule, the relative section, chapter and subchapter notes also apply, unless the context otherwise requires.

ADDITIONAL U.S. RULES OF INTERPRETATION

1. In the absence of special language or context which otherwise requires—

(a) a tariff classification controlled by use (other than actual use) is to be determined in accordance with the use in the United

States at, or immediately prior to, the date of importation, of goods of that class or kind to which the imported goods belong, and the controlling use is the principal use;

(b) a tariff classification controlled by the actual use to which the imported goods are put in the United States is satisfied only if such use is intended at the time of importation, the goods are so used and proof thereof is furnished within 3 years after the date the goods are entered;

(c) a provision for parts of an article covers products solely or principally used as a part of such articles but a provision for "parts" or "parts and accessories" shall not prevail over a specific provision for such part or accessory; and

(d) the principles of section XI regarding mixtures of two or more textile materials shall apply to the classification of goods in any provision in which a textile material is named.

* * *

SUBTITLE C—RESPONSE TO UNFAIR INTERNATIONAL TRADE PRACTICES

Part 1—Enforcement of United States Rights Under Trade Agreements and Response to Certain Foreign Trade Practices

* * *

Part 2—Improvement in the Enforcement of the Antidumping and Countervailing Duty Laws

Part 3—Protection of Intellectual Property Rights

Part 4—Telecommunications Trade

SUBTITLE D—ADJUSTMENT TO IMPORT COMPETITION

SUBTITLE E—NATIONAL SECURITY

SUBTITLE F—TRADE AGENCIES

SUBTITLE G—TARIFF PROVISIONS

* * *

TITLE II—EXPORT ENHANCEMENT

SUBTITLE B—EXPORT ENHANCEMENT

SUBTITLE C—EXPORT PROMOTION

SUBTITLE D—EXPORT CONTROLS

Part I—Export Controls Generally

Part II—Multilateral Export Control Enhancement

Sec. 2441. Short title

This part may be cited as the "Multilateral Export Control Enhancement Amendments Act".

Sec. 2442. Findings

The Congress makes the following findings:

(1) The diversion of advanced milling machinery to the Soviet Union by the Toshiba Machine Company and Kongsberg Trading Company has had a serious impact on United States and Western security interests.

(2) United States and Western security is undermined without the cooperation of the governments and nationals of all countries participating in the group known as the Coordinating Committee (hereafter in this part referred to as "COCOM") in enforcing the COCOM agreement.

(3) It is the responsibility of all governments participating in COCOM to place in effect strong national security export control laws, to license strategic exports carefully, and to enforce those export control laws strictly, since the COCOM system is only as strong as the national laws and enforcement on which it is based.

(4) It is also important for corporations to implement effective internal control systems to ensure compliance with export control laws.

(5) In order to protect United States national security, the United States must take steps to ensure the compliance of foreign companies with COCOM controls, including, where necessary conditions have been met, the imposition of sanctions against violators of controls commensurate with the severity of the violation.

Sec. 2443. Mandatory sanctions against Toshiba and Kongsberg

(a) Sanctions against Toshiba Machine Company, Kongsberg Trading Company, and Certain other Foreign Persons. (1) The President shall impose, for a period of 3 years—

(1) a prohibition on contracting with, and procurement of products and services from—

(A) Toshiba Machine Company and Kongsberg Trading Company, and

(B) any other foreign person whom the President finds to have knowingly facilitated the diversion of advanced milling machinery by

Toshiba Machine Company and Kongsberg Trading Company to the Soviet Union, by any department, agency, or instrumentality of the United States Government; and

(2) a prohibition on the importation into the United States of all products produced by Toshiba Machine Company, Kongsberg Trading Company, and any foreign person described in paragraph (1)(B).

(b) Sanctions against Toshiba Corporation and Kongsberg Vaapenfabrikk. The President shall impose, for a period of 3 years, a prohibition on contracting with, and procurement of products and services from, the Toshiba Corporation and Kongsberg Vaapenfabrikk, by any department, agency, or instrumentality of the United States Government.

(c) Exceptions. The President shall not apply sanctions under this section—

(1) in the case of procurement of defense articles or defense services—

(A) under existing contracts or subcontracts, including exercise of options for production quantities to satisfy United States operational military requirements;

(B) if the President determines that the company or foreign person to whom the sanctions would otherwise be applied is a sole source supplier of essential defense articles or services and no alternative supplier can be identified; or

(C) if the President determines that such articles or services are essential to the national security under defense coproduction agreements; or

(2) to—

(A) products or services provided under contracts or other binding agreements (as such terms are defined by the President in regulations) entered into before June 30, 1987;

(B) spare parts;

(C) component parts, but not finished products, essential to United States products or production;

(D) routine servicing and maintenance of products; or

(E) information and technology.

(d) Definitions. For purposes of this section—

(1) the term "component part" means any article which is not usable for its intended functions without being imbedded or integrated into any other product and which, if used in production of a finished product, would be substantially transformed in that process;

(2) the term "finished product" means any article which is usable for its intended functions without being imbedded in or integrated into any other product, but in no case shall such term be deemed to include an article produced by a person other than a sanctioned person that contains

parts or components of the sanctioned person if the parts or components have been substantially transformed during production of the finished product; and

(3) the term "sanctioned person" means a company or other foreign person upon whom prohibitions have been imposed under subsection (a) or (b).

* * *

TITLE III—INTERNATIONAL FINANCIAL POLICY

* * *

TITLE V—FOREIGN CORRUPT PRACTICES AMENDMENTS; INVESTMENT; AND TECHNOLOGY

SUBTITLE A—FOREIGN CORRUPT PRACTICES ACT AMENDMENTS; REVIEW OF CERTAIN ACQUISITIONS

Part I—Foreign Corrupt Practices Act Amendments [included as a separate document]

Part II—Review of Certain Mergers, Acquisitions, and Takeovers

Sec. 5021. Authority to Review Certain Mergers, Acquisitions, and Takeovers [Exon–Florio Provision]

Title VII of the Defense Production Act of 1950 (50 U.S.C.App. § 2158 et seq.) is amended by adding at the end thereof the following:

AUTHORITY TO REVIEW CERTAIN MERGERS, ACQUISITIONS, AND TAKEOVERS

Sec. 721. (a) Investigations. The President or the President's designee may make an investigation to determine the effects on national security of mergers, acquisitions, and takeovers proposed or pending on or after the date of enactment of this section by or with foreign persons which could result in foreign control of persons engaged in interstate commerce in the United States. If it is determined that an investigation should be undertaken, it shall commence no later than 30 days after receipt by the President or the President's designee of written notification of the proposed or pending merger, acquisition, or takeover as prescribed by regulations promulgated pursuant to this section. Such investigation shall be completed no later than 45 days after such determination.

(b) Mandatory investigations. The President or the President's designee shall make an investigation, as described in subsection (a), in any instance in which an entity controlled by or acting on behalf of a foreign government seeks to engage in any merger, acquisition, or takeover which could result in control of a person engaged in interstate commerce in the United States that could affect the national security of the United States. Such investigation shall—

(1) commence not later than 30 days after receipt by the President or the President's designee of written notification of the proposed or pending merger, acquisition, or takeover, as prescribed by regulations promulgated pursuant to this section; and

(2) shall be completed not later than 45 days after its commencement.

(c) Confidentiality of information. Any information or documentary material filed with the President or the President's designee pursuant to this section shall be exempt from disclosure under section 552 of title 5, United States Code, and no such information or documentary material may be made public, except as may be relevant to any administrative or judicial action or proceeding. Nothing in this subsection shall be construed to prevent disclosure to either House of Congress or to any duly authorized committee or subcommittee of the Congress.

(d) Action by the President. Subject to subsection (e), the President may take such action for such time as the President considers appropriate to suspend or prohibit any acquisition, merger, or takeover, of a person engaged in interstate commerce in the United States proposed or pending on or after the date of enactment of this section by or with foreign persons so that such control will not threaten to impair the national security. The President shall announce the decision to take action pursuant to this subsection not later than 15 days after the investigation described in subsection (a) is completed. The President may direct the Attorney General to seek appropriate relief, including divestment relief, in the district courts of the United States in order to implement and enforce this section.

(e) Findings of the President. The President may exercise the authority conferred by subsection (d) only if the President finds that—

(1) there is credible evidence that leads the President to believe that the foreign interest exercising control might take action that threatens to impair the national security, and

(2) provisions of law, other than this section, and the International Emergency Economic Powers Act (50 U.S.C. §§ 1701–1706), do not in the President's judgment provide adequate and appropriate authority for the President to protect the national security in the matter before the President.

The provisions of subsection (e) of this section shall not be subject to judicial review.

(f) Factors to be considered. For purposes of this section, the President or the President's designee may, taking into account the requirements of national security, consider among other factors—

(1) domestic production needed for projected national defense requirements,

(2) the capability and capacity of domestic industries to meet national defense requirements, including the availability of human resources, products, technology, materials, and other supplies and services, and

(3) the control of domestic industries and commercial activity by foreign citizens as it affects the capability and capacity of the United States to meet the requirements of national security,

(4) the potential effects of the proposed or pending transaction on sales of military goods, equipment, or technology to any country—

(A) identified by the Secretary of State—

(i) under section 6(j) of the Export Administration Act of 1979 [section 2405(j) of this Appendix], as a country that supports terrorism;

(ii) under section 6(*l*) of the Export Administration Act of 1979 [section 2405(*l*) of this Appendix], as a country of concern regarding missile proliferation; or

(iii) under section 6(m) of the Export Administration Act of 1979 [section 2405(m) of this Appendix], as a country of concern regarding the proliferation of chemical and biological weapons; or

(B) listed under section 309(c) of the Nuclear Non–Proliferation Act of 1978 on the "Nuclear Non–Proliferation–Special Country List" (15 C.F.R. Part 778, Supplement No. 4) or any successor list; and

(5) the potential effects of the proposed or pending transaction on United States international technological leadership in areas affecting United States national security.

(g) Report to the Congress. The President shall immediately transmit to the Secretary of the Senate and the Clerk of the House of Representatives a written report of the President's determination of whether or not to take action under subsection (d), including a detailed explanation of the findings made under subsection (e) and the factors considered under subsection (f). Such report shall be consistent with the requirements of subsection (c) of this Act [subsection (c) of this section].

* * *

SUBTITLE B—TECHNOLOGY

SUBTITLE C—COMPETITIVENESS POLICY COUNCIL ACT

SUBTITLE D—FEDERAL BUDGET COMPETITIVENESS IMPACT STATEMENT

SUBTITLE E—TRADE DATA AND STUDIES

TITLE VI—EDUCATION AND TRAINING FOR AMERICAN COMPETITIVENESS

* * *

DOCUMENT 13

NORTH AMERICAN FREE TRADE AGREEMENT IMPLEMENTATION ACT (1993) (SELECTED PROVISIONS)

PUBLIC LAW 103–182 of December 8, 1993, 107 Stat. 2060

An Act to implement the North American Free Trade Agreement.

Be it enacted by the Senate and House of Representatives of the United States of America in Congress assembled,

SECTION 1. SHORT TITLE AND TABLE OF CONTENTS.

19 U.S.C. § 3301 NOTE

(a) Short Title.—This Act may be cited as the "North American Free Trade Agreement Implementation Act". (omitted)

(b) Table of Contents. (omitted)

* * *

19 U.S.C. § 3301

Sec. 2. Definitions

For purposes of this Act:

(1) Agreement.—The term "Agreement" means the North American Free Trade Agreement approved by the Congress under section 101(a).

(2) HTS.—The term "HTS" means the Harmonized Tariff Schedule of the United States.

(3) Mexico.—Any reference to Mexico shall be considered to be a reference to the United Mexican States.

(4) NAFTA Country.—Except as provided in section 202, the term "NAFTA country" means—

(A) Canada for such time as the Agreement is in force with respect to, and the United States applies the Agreement to, Canada; and

(B) Mexico for such time as the Agreement is in force with respect to, and the United States applies the Agreement to, Mexico.

(5) International Trade Commission.—The term "International Trade Commission" means the United States International Trade Commission.

(6) Trade Representative.—The term "Trade Representative" means the United States Trade Representative.

TITLE I—APPROVAL OF, AND GENERAL PROVISIONS RELATING TO, THE NORTH AMERICAN FREE TRADE AGREEMENT

19 U.S.C. § 3311

Sec. 101. Approval and Entry into Force of the North American Free Trade Agreement

(a) Approval of agreement and statement of administrative action.—Pursuant to section 1103 of the Omnibus Trade and Competitiveness Act of 1988 (19 U.S.C. § 2903) and section 151 of the Trade Act of 1974 (19 U.S.C. § 2191), the Congress approves—

(1) the North American Free Trade Agreement entered into on December 17, 1992, with the Governments of Canada and Mexico and submitted to the Congress on November 4, 1993; * * *

19 U.S.C. § 3312

Sec. 102. Relationship of the Agreement to United States and State law

(a) Relationship of Agreement to United States Law.—

(1) United States law to Prevail in Conflict.—No provision of the Agreement, nor the application of any such provision to any person or circumstance, which is inconsistent with any law of the United States shall have effect.

(2) Construction.—Nothing in this Act shall be construed—

(A) to amend or modify any law of the United States, including any law regarding—

(i) the protection of human, animal, or plant life or health,

(ii) the protection of the environment, or

(iii) motor carrier or worker safety; or

(B) to limit any authority conferred under any law of the United States, including section 301 of the Trade Act of 1974;

unless specifically provided for in this Act.

(b) Relationship of Agreement to State Law.—

(1) Federal–State Consultation.—

(A) In General.—Upon the enactment of this Act, the President shall, through the intergovernmental policy advisory committees on trade established under section 306(c)(2)(A) of the Trade and Tariff Act of 1984, consult with the States for the purpose of achieving conformity of State laws and practices with the Agreement.

(B) Federal–State Consultation Process.—The Trade Representative shall establish within the Office of the United States Trade Representative a Federal–State consultation process for addressing issues relating to the Agreement that directly relate to, or will potentially have a direct impact on, the States. The Federal–State consultation process shall include procedures under which—

(i) the Trade Representative will assist the States in identifying those State laws that may not conform with the Agreement but may be maintained under the Agreement by reason of being in effect before the Agreement entered into force;

(ii) the States will be informed on a continuing basis of matters under the Agreement that directly relate to, or will potentially have a direct impact on, the States;

(iii) the States will be provided opportunity to submit, on a continuing basis, to the Trade Representative information and advice with respect to matters referred to in clause (ii);

(iv) the Trade Representative will take into account the information and advice received from the States under clause (iii) when formulating United States positions regarding matters referred to in clause (ii); and

(v) the States will be involved (including involvement through the inclusion of appropriate representatives of the States) to the greatest extent practicable at each stage of the development of United States positions regarding matters referred to in clause (ii) that will be addressed by committees, subcommittees, or working groups established under the Agreement or through dispute settlement processes provided for under the Agreement.

The Federal Advisory Committee Act (5 U.S.C.App.) shall not apply to the Federal–State consultation process established by this paragraph.

(2) Legal Challenge.—No State law, or the application thereof, may be declared invalid as to any person or circumstance on the ground that the provision or application is inconsistent with the Agreement, except in an action brought by the United States for the purpose of declaring such law or application invalid.

(3) Definition of State law.—For purposes of this subsection, the term "State law" includes—

(A) any law of a political subdivision of a State; and

(B) any State law regulating or taxing the business of insurance.

(c) Effect of Agreement with Respect to Private Remedies.—No person other than the United States—

(1) shall have any cause of action or defense under—

(A) the Agreement or by virtue of Congressional approval thereof, or

(B) the North American Agreement on Environmental Cooperation or the North American Agreement on Labor Cooperation; or

(2) may challenge, in any action brought under any provision of law, any action or inaction by any department, agency, or other instrumentality of the United States, any State, or any political subdivision of a State on the ground that such action or inaction is inconsistent with the Agreement, the North American Agreement on Environmental Cooperation, or the North American Agreement on Labor Cooperation.

* * *

TITLE II—CUSTOMS PROVISIONS

19 U.S.C. § 3331

Sec. 201. Tariff Modifications

(a) Tariff Modifications Provided for in the Agreement.—

(1) Proclamation Authority.—The President may proclaim—

(A) such modifications or continuation of any duty,

(B) such continuation of duty-free or excise treatment, or

(C) such additional duties,

as the President determines to be necessary or appropriate to carry out or apply articles 302, 305, 307, 308, and 703 and Annexes 302.2, 307.1, 308.1, 308.2, 300–B, 703.2, and 703.3 of the Agreement.

(2) Effect on Mexican GSP Status.—Notwithstanding section 502(a)(2) of the Trade Act of 1974 (19 U.S.C. § 2462(a)(2)), the President shall terminate the designation of Mexico as a beneficiary developing country for purposes of title V of the Trade Act of 1974 on the date of entry into force of the Agreement between the United States and Mexico.

* * *

19 U.S.C. § 3332

Sec. 202. Rules of Origin

(a) Originating Goods.—

(1) In General.—For purposes of implementing the tariff treatment and quantitative restrictions provided for under the Agreement, except as otherwise provided in this section, a good originates in the territory of a NAFTA country if—

(A) the good is wholly obtained or produced entirely in the territory of one or more of the NAFTA countries;

(B)(i) each nonoriginating material used in the production of the good—

(I) undergoes an applicable change in tariff classification set out in Annex 401 of the Agreement as a result of production occurring entirely in the territory of one or more of the NAFTA countries; or

(II) where no change in tariff classification is required, the good otherwise satisfies the applicable requirements of such Annex; and

(ii) the good satisfies all other applicable requirements of this section;

(C) the good is produced entirely in the territory of one or more of the NAFTA countries exclusively from originating materials; or

(D) except for a good provided for in chapters 61 through 63 of the HTS, the good is produced entirely in the territory of one or more of the NAFTA countries, but one or more of the nonoriginating materials, that are provided for as parts under the HTS and are used in the production of the good, does not undergo a change in tariff classification because—

(i) the good was imported into the territory of a NAFTA country in an unassembled or a disassembled form but was classified as an assembled good pursuant to General Rule of Interpretation 2(a) of the HTS; or

(ii)(I) the heading for the good provides for and specifically describes both the good itself and its parts and is not further subdivided into subheadings; or

(II) the subheading for the good provides for and specifically describes both the good itself and its parts.

(2) Special Rules.—

(A) Foreign–Trade Zones.—Subparagraph (B) of paragraph (1) shall not apply to a good produced in a foreign-trade zone or subzone (established pursuant to the Act of June 18, 1934, commonly known as the Foreign Trade Zones Act) that is entered for consumption in the customs territory of the United States.

(B) Regional Value–Content Requirement.—For purposes of subparagraph (D) of paragraph (1), a good shall be treated as originating in a NAFTA country if the regional value-content of the good, determined in accordance with subsection (b), is not less than 60 percent where the transaction value method is used, or not less than 50 percent where the net cost method is used, and the good satisfies all other applicable requirements of this section.

(b) Regional Value–Content.—

(1) In General.—Except as provided in paragraph (5), the regional value-content of a good shall be calculated, at the choice of the exporter or producer of the good, on the basis of—

(A) the transaction value method described in paragraph (2); or

(B) the net cost method described in paragraph (3).

(2) Transaction Value Method.—

(A) In General.—An exporter or producer may calculate the regional value-content of a good on the basis of the following transaction value method:

$$RVC = \frac{TV - VNM}{TV} \times 100$$

(B) Definitions.—For purposes of subparagraph (A):

(i) The term "RVC" means the regional value-content, expressed as a percentage.

(ii) The term "TV" means the transaction value of the good adjusted to a F.O.B. basis.

(iii) The term "VNM" means the value of nonoriginating materials used by the producer in the production of the good.

(3) Net Cost Method.—

(A) In General.—An exporter or producer may calculate the regional value-content of a good on the basis of the following net cost method:

$$RVC = \frac{NC - VNM}{NC} \times 100$$

(B) Definitions.—For purposes of subparagraph (A):

(i) The term "RVC" means the regional value-content, expressed as a percentage.

(ii) The term "NC" means the net cost of the good.

(iii) The term "VNM" means the value of nonoriginating materials used by the producer in the production of the good.

(4) Value of Nonoriginating Materials Used in Originating Materials.—Except as provided in subsection (c)(1), and for a motor vehicle identified in subsection (c)(2) or a component identified in Annex 403.2 of the Agreement, the value of nonoriginating materials used by the producer in the production of a good shall not, for purposes of calculating the regional value-content of the good under paragraph (2) or (3), include the value of nonoriginating materials used to produce originating materials that are subsequently used in the production of the good.

(5) Net Cost Method Must be Used in Certain Cases.—An exporter or producer shall calculate the regional value-content of a good solely on the basis of the net cost method described in paragraph (3), if—

(A) there is no transaction value for the good;

(B) the transaction value of the good is unacceptable under Article 1 of the Customs Valuation Code;

(C) the good is sold by the producer to a related person and the volume, by units of quantity, of sales of identical or similar goods to related persons during the six-month period immediately preceding the month in which the good is sold exceeds 85 percent of the producer's total sales of such goods during that period;

(D) the good is—

(i) a motor vehicle provided for in heading 8701 or 8702, subheadings 8703.21 through 8703.90, or heading 8704, 8705, or 8706;

(ii) identified in Annex 403.1 or 403.2 of the Agreement and is for use in a motor vehicle provided for in heading 8701 or 8702, subheadings 8703.21 through 8703.90, or heading 8704, 8705, or 8706;

(iii) provided for in subheadings 6401.10 through 6406.10; or

(iv) a word processing machine provided for in subheading 8469.10.00;

(E) the exporter or producer chooses to accumulate the regional value-content of the good in accordance with subsection (d); or

(F) the good is designated as an intermediate material under paragraph (10) and is subject to a regional value-content requirement.

(6) Net Cost Method Allowed for Adjustments.—If an exporter or producer of a good calculates the regional value-content of the good on the basis of the transaction value method and a NAFTA country subsequently notifies the exporter or producer, during the course of a verification conducted in accordance with chapter 5 of the Agreement, that the transaction value of the good or the value of any material used in the production of the good must be adjusted or is unacceptable under Article 1 of the Customs Valuation Code, the exporter or producer may calculate the regional value-content of the good on the basis of the net cost method.

(7) Review of Adjustment.—Nothing in paragraph (6) shall be construed to prevent any review or appeal available in accordance with article 510 of the Agreement with respect to an adjustment to or a rejection of—

(A) the transaction value of a good; or

(B) the value of any material used in the production of a good.

(8) Calculating Net Cost.—The producer may, consistent with regulations implementing this section, calculate the net cost of a good under paragraph (3), by—

(A) calculating the total cost incurred with respect to all goods produced by that producer, subtracting any sales promotion, marketing and after-sales service costs, royalties, shipping and packing costs, and nonallowable interest costs that are included in the total cost of all such goods, and reasonably allocating the resulting net cost of those goods to the good;

(B) calculating the total cost incurred with respect to all goods produced by that producer, reasonably allocating the total cost to the good, and subtracting any sales promotion, marketing and after-sales service costs, royalties, shipping and packing costs, and nonallowable interest costs that are included in the portion of the total cost allocated to the good; or

(C) reasonably allocating each cost that is part of the total cost incurred with respect to the good so that the aggregate of these costs does not include any sales promotion, marketing and after-sales service costs, royalties, shipping and packing costs, or nonallowable interest costs.

(9) Value of Material Used in Production.—Except as provided in paragraph (11), the value of a material used in the production of a good—

(A) shall—

(i) be the transaction value of the material determined in accordance with Article 1 of the Customs Valuation Code; or

(ii) in the event that there is no transaction value or the transaction value of the material is unacceptable under Article 1 of the Customs Valuation Code, be determined in accordance with Articles 2 through 7 of the Customs Valuation Code; and

(B) if not included under clause (i) or (ii) of subparagraph (A), shall include—

(i) freight, insurance, packing, and all other costs incurred in transporting the material to the location of the producer;

(ii) duties, taxes, and customs brokerage fees paid on the material in the territory of one or more of the NAFTA countries; and

(iii) the cost of waste and spoilage resulting from the use of the material in the production of the good, less the value of renewable scrap or by-product.

(10) Intermediate Material.—Except for goods described in subsection (c)(1), any self-produced material, other than a component identified in Annex 403.2 of the Agreement, that is used in the production of a good may be designated by the producer of the good as an intermediate material for the purpose of calculating the regional value-content of the good under paragraph (2) or (3); provided that if the intermediate material is subject to a regional value-content requirement, no other self-produced material that is subject to a regional value-content requirement, and is used in the production of the intermediate material may be designated by the producer as an intermediate material.

(11) Value of Intermediate Material.—The value of an intermediate material shall be—

(A) the total cost incurred with respect to all goods produced by the producer of the good that can be reasonably allocated to the intermediate material; or

(B) the aggregate of each cost that is part of the total cost incurred with respect to the intermediate material that can be reasonably allocated to that intermediate material.

(12) Indirect Material.—The value of an indirect material shall be based on the Generally Accepted Accounting Principles applicable in the territory of the NAFTA country in which the good is produced.

(c) Automotive Goods.—

* * *

(m) Interpretation and Application.—For purposes of this section:

(1) The basis for any tariff classification is the HTS.

(2) Except as otherwise expressly provided, whenever in this section there is a reference to a heading or subheading such reference shall be a reference to a heading or subheading of the HTS.

(3) In applying subsection (a)(4), the determination of whether a heading or subheading under the HTS provides for and specifically describes both a good and its parts shall be made on the basis of the

nomenclature of the heading or subheading, the rules of interpretation, or notes of the HTS.

(4) In applying the Customs Valuation Code—

(A) the principles of the Customs Valuation Code shall apply to domestic transactions, with such modifications as may be required by the circumstances, as would apply to international transactions;

(B) the provisions of this section shall take precedence over the Customs Valuation Code to the extent of any difference; and

(C) the definitions in subsection (*o*) shall take precedence over the definitions in the Customs Valuation Code to the extent of any difference.

(5) All costs referred to in this section shall be recorded and maintained in accordance with the Generally Accepted Accounting Principles applicable in the territory of the NAFTA country in which the good is produced.

* * *

TITLE IV—DISPUTE SETTLEMENT IN ANTIDUMPING AND COUNTERVAILING DUTY CASES

Subtitle A—Organizational, Administrative, and Procedural Provisions Regarding the Implementation of Chapter 19 of the Agreement

* * *

19 U.S.C. § 3432

Sec. 402. Organizational and Administrative Provisions

(a) Criteria for Selection of Individuals to Serve on Panels and Committees.—

(1) In General.—The selection of individuals under this section for—

(A) placement on lists prepared by the interagency group under subsection (c)(2)(B)(i) and (ii);

(B) placement on preliminary candidate lists under subsection (c)(3)(A);

(C) placement on final candidate lists under subsection (c)(4)(A);

(D) placement by the Trade Representative on the rosters described in paragraph 1 of Annex 1901.2 and paragraph 1 of Annex 1904.13; and

(E) appointment by the Trade Representative for service on the panels and committees convened under chapter 19;

shall be made on the basis of the criteria provided in paragraph 1 of Annex 1901.2 and paragraph 1 of Annex 1904.13 and shall be made without regard to political affiliation.

(2) Additional Criteria for Roster Placements and Appointments Under Paragraph 1 of Annex 1901.2.—Rosters described in paragraph 1 of Annex 1901.2 shall include, to the fullest extent practicable, judges and former judges who meet the criteria referred to in paragraph (1). The Trade Representative shall, subject to subsection (b), appoint judges to binational panels convened under chapter 19, extraordinary challenge committees convened under chapter 19, and special committees established under article 1905, where such judges offer and are available to serve and such service is authorized by the chief judge of the court on which they sit.

(b) Selection of Certain Judges to Serve on Panels and Committees.—

(1) Applicability.—This subsection applies only with respect to the selection of individuals for binational panels convened under chapter 19, extraordinary challenge committees convened under chapter 19, and special committees established under article 1905, who are judges of courts created under article III of the Constitution of the United States.

(2) Consultation with Chief Judges.—The Trade Representative shall consult, from time to time, with the chief judges of the Federal judicial circuits regarding the interest in, and availability for, participation in binational panels, extraordinary challenge committees, and special committees, of judges within their respective circuits. If the chief judge of a Federal judicial circuit determines that it is appropriate for one or more judges within that circuit to be included on a roster described in subsection (a)(1)(D), the chief judge shall identify all such judges for the Chief Justice of the United States who may, upon his or her approval, submit the names of such judges to the Trade Representative. The Trade Representative shall include the names of such judges on the roster.

(3) Submission of Lists to Congress.—The Trade Representative shall submit to the Committee on the Judiciary and the Committee on Ways and Means of the House of Representatives and to the Committee on Finance and the Committee on the Judiciary of the Senate a list of all judges included on a roster under paragraph (2). Such list shall be submitted at the same time as the final candidate lists are submitted under subsection (c)(4)(A) and the final forms of amendments are submitted under subsection (c)(4)(C)(iv).

(4) Appointment of Judges to Panels or Committees.—At such time as the Trade Representative proposes to appoint a judge described in paragraph (1) to a binational panel, an extraordinary challenge committee, or a special committee, the Trade Representative shall consult with that judge in order to ascertain whether the judge is available for such appointment.

(c) Selection of Other Candidates.—

(1) Applicability.—This subsection applies only with respect to the selection of individuals for binational panels convened under chapter 19, extraordinary challenge committees convened under chapter 19, and spe-

cial committees established under article 1905, other than those individuals to whom subsection (b) applies.

(2) Interagency Group.—

(A) Establishment.—There is established within the interagency organization established under section 242 of the Trade Expansion Act of 1962 (19 U.S.C. § 1872) an interagency group which shall—

(i) be chaired by the Trade Representative; and

(ii) consist of such officers (or the designees thereof) of the United States Government as the Trade Representative considers appropriate.

(B) Functions.—The interagency group established under subparagraph (A) shall, in a manner consistent with chapter 19—

(i) prepare by January 3 of each calendar year—

(I) a list of individuals who are qualified to serve as members of binational panels convened under chapter 19; and

(II) a list of individuals who are qualified to serve on extraordinary challenge committees convened under chapter 19 and special committees established under article 1905;

(ii) if the Trade Representative makes a request under paragraph (4)(C)(i) with respect to a final candidate list during any calendar year, prepare by July 1 of such calendar year a list of those individuals who are qualified to be added to that final candidate list;

(iii) exercise oversight of the administration of the United States Section that is authorized to be established under section 105; and

(iv) make recommendations to the Trade Representative regarding the convening of extraordinary challenge committees and special committees under chapter 19.

(3) Preliminary Candidate Lists.—

(A) In General.—The Trade Representative shall select individuals from the respective lists prepared by the interagency group under paragraph (2)(B)(i) for placement on—

(i) a preliminary candidate list of individuals eligible to serve as members of binational panels under Annex 1901.2; and

(ii) a preliminary candidate list of individuals eligible for selection as members of extraordinary challenge committees under Annex 1904.13 and special committees under article 1905.

(B) Submission of Lists to Congressional Committees.—

(i) In General.—No later than January 3 of each calendar year, the Trade Representative shall submit to the Committee on

Finance of the Senate and the Committee on Ways and Means of the House of Representatives (hereafter in this section referred to as the "appropriate Congressional Committees") the preliminary candidate lists of those individuals selected by the Trade Representative under subparagraph (A) to be candidates eligible to serve on panels or committees convened pursuant to chapter 19 during the 1–year period beginning on April 1 of such calendar year.

(ii) Additional Information.—At the time the candidate lists are submitted under clause (i), the Trade Representative shall submit for each individual on the list a statement of professional qualifications.

(C) Consultation.—Upon submission of the preliminary candidate lists under subparagraph (B) to the appropriate Congressional Committees, the Trade Representative shall consult with such Committees with regard to the individuals included on the preliminary candidate lists.

(D) Revision of Lists.—The Trade Representative may add and delete individuals from the preliminary candidate lists submitted under subparagraph (B) after consultation with the appropriate Congressional Committees regarding the additions and deletions. The Trade Representative shall provide to the appropriate Congressional Committees written notice of any addition or deletion of an individual from the preliminary candidate lists, along with the information described in subparagraph (B)(ii) with respect to any proposed addition.

(4) Final Candidate Lists.—

(A) Submission of Lists to Congressional Committees.—No later than March 31 of each calendar year, the Trade Representative shall submit to the appropriate Congressional Committees the final candidate lists of those individuals selected by the Trade Representative to be candidates eligible to serve on panels and committees convened under chapter 19 during the 1–year period beginning on April 1 of such calendar year. An individual may be included on a final candidate list only if such individual was included in the preliminary candidate list or if written notice of the addition of such individual to the preliminary candidate list was submitted to the appropriate Congressional Committees at least 15 days before the date on which that final candidate list is submitted to such Committees under this subparagraph.

(B) Finality of Lists.—Except as provided in subparagraph (C), no additions may be made to the final candidate lists after the final candidate lists are submitted to the appropriate Congressional Committees under subparagraph (A).

(C) Amendment of Lists.—

(i) In General.—If, after the Trade Representative has submitted the final candidate lists to the appropriate Congressional Committees under subparagraph (A) for a calendar year and before July 1 of such calendar year, the Trade Representative determines that additional individuals need to be added to a final candidate list, the Trade Representative shall—

(I) request the interagency group established under paragraph (2)(A) to prepare a list of individuals who are qualified to be added to such candidate list;

(II) select individuals from the list prepared by the interagency group under paragraph (2)(B)(ii) to be included in a proposed amendment to such final candidate list; and

(III) by no later than July 1 of such calendar year, submit to the appropriate Congressional Committees the proposed amendments to such final candidate list developed by the Trade Representative under subclause (II), along with the information described in paragraph (3)(B)(ii).

(ii) Consultation with Congressional Committees. Upon submission of a proposed amendment under clause (i)(III) to the appropriate Congressional Committees, the Trade Representative shall consult with the appropriate Congressional Committees with regard to the individuals included in the proposed amendment.

(iii) Adjustment of Proposed Amendment.—The Trade Representative may add and delete individuals from any proposed amendment submitted under clause (i)(III) after consulting with the appropriate Congressional Committees with regard to the additions and deletions. The Trade Representative shall provide to the appropriate Congressional Committees written notice of any addition or deletion of an individual from the proposed amendment.

(iv) Final Amendment.—

(I) In General.—If the Trade Representative submits under clause (i)(III) in any calendar year a proposed amendment to a final candidate list, the Trade Representative shall, no later than September 30 of such calendar year, submit to the appropriate Congressional Committees the final form of such amendment. On October 1 of such calendar year, such amendment shall take effect and, subject to subclause (II), the individuals included in the final form of such amendment shall be added to the final candidate list.

(II) Inclusion of Individuals.—An individual may be included in the final form of an amendment submitted under subclause (I) only if such individual was included in the proposed form of such amendment or if written notice of the addition of such individual to the proposed form of such amendment was submitted to the appropriate Congressional Committees at least 15 days before the date on which the final form of such amendment is submitted to such Committees under subclause (I).

(III) Eligibility for Service.—Individuals added to a final candidate list under subclause (I) shall be eligible to serve on panels or committees convened under chapter 19 during the 6–month period beginning on October 1 of the calendar year in which such addition occurs.

(IV) Finality of Amendment.—No additions may be made to the final form of an amendment described in subclause (I) after the final form of such amendment is submitted to the appropriate Congressional Committees under subclause (I).

(5) Treatment of Responses.—For purposes of applying section 1001 of title 18, United States Code, the written or oral responses of individuals to inquiries of the interagency group established under paragraph (2)(A) or of the Trade Representative regarding their personal and professional qualifications, and financial and other relevant interests, that bear on their suitability for the placements and appointments described in subsection (a)(1), shall be treated as matters within the jurisdiction of an agency of the United States.

(d) Selection and Appointment.—

(1) Authority of Trade Representative.—The Trade Representative is the only officer of the United States Government authorized to act on behalf of the United States Government in making any selection or appointment of an individual to—

(A) the rosters described in paragraph 1 of Annex 1901.2 and paragraph 1 of Annex 1904.13; or

(B) the panels or committees convened under chapter 19;

that is to be made solely or jointly by the United States Government under the terms of the Agreement.

(2) Restrictions on Selection and Appointment.—Except as provided in paragraph (3)—

(A) the Trade Representative may—

(i) select an individual for placement on the rosters described in paragraph 1 of Annex 1901.2 and paragraph 1 of Annex 1904.13 during the 1–year period beginning on April 1 of any calendar year;

(ii) appoint an individual to serve as one of those members of any panel or committee convened under chapter 19 during such 1–year period who, under the terms of the Agreement, are to be appointed solely by the United States Government; or

(iii) act to make a joint appointment with the Government of a NAFTA country, under the terms of the Agreement, of any individual who is a citizen or national of the United States to serve as any other member of such a panel or committee;

only if such individual is on the appropriate final candidate list that was submitted to the appropriate Congressional Committees under subsection (c)(4)(A) during such calendar year or on such list as it may be amended under subsection (c)(4)(C)(iv)(I), or on the list submitted under subsection (b)(3) to the congressional committees referred to in such subsection; and

(B) no individual may—

(i) be selected by the United States Government for placement on the rosters described in paragraph 1 of Annex 1901.2 and paragraph 1 of Annex 1904.13; or

(ii) be appointed solely or jointly by the United States Government to serve as a member of a panel or committee convened under chapter 19;

during the 1–year period beginning on April 1 of any calendar year for which the Trade Representative has not met the requirements of subsection (a), and of subsection (b) or (c) (as the case may be).

(3) Exceptions.—Notwithstanding subsection (c)(3) (other than subparagraph (B)), (c)(4), or paragraph (2)(A) of this subsection, individuals included on the preliminary candidate lists submitted to the appropriate Congressional Committees under subsection (c)(3)(B) may—

(A) be selected by the Trade Representative for placement on the rosters described in paragraph 1 of Annex 1901.2 and paragraph 1 of Annex 1904.13 during the 3–month period beginning on the date on which the Agreement enters into force with respect to the United States; and

(B) be appointed solely or jointly by the Trade Representative under the terms of the Agreement to serve as members of panels or committees that are convened under chapter 19 during such 3–month period.

(e) Transition.—If the Agreement enters into force between the United States and a NAFTA country after January 3, 1994, the provisions of subsection (c) shall be applied with respect to the calendar year in which such entering into force occurs—

(1) by substituting "the date that is 30 days after the date on which the Agreement enters into force with respect to the United States" for "January 3 of each calendar year" in subsections (c)(2)(B)(i) and (c)(3)(B)(i); and

(2) by substituting "the date that is 3 months after the date on which the Agreement enters into force with respect to the United States" for "March 31 of each calendar year" in subsection (c)(4)(A).

(f) Immunity.—With the exception of acts described in section 777(f)(3) of the Tariff Act of 1930 (19 U.S.C. § 1677f(f)(3)), individuals serving on panels or committees convened pursuant to chapter 19, and individuals designated to assist the individuals serving on such panels or committees, shall be immune from suit and legal process relating to acts performed by such individuals in their official capacity and within the scope of their functions as such panelists or committee members or assistants to such panelists or committee members.

(g) Regulations.—The administering authority under title VII of the Tariff Act of 1930, the International Trade Commission, and the Trade Representative may promulgate such regulations as are necessary or appropriate to carry out actions in order to implement their respective responsibilities under chapter 19. Initial regulations to carry out such functions shall be issued before the date on which the Agreement enters into force with respect to the United States.

(h) Report to Congress.—At such time as the final candidate lists are submitted under subsection (c)(4)(A) and the final forms of amendments are submitted under subsection (c)(4)(C)(iv), the Trade Representative shall submit to the Committee on the Judiciary and the Committee on Ways and Means of the House of Representatives, and to the Committee on Finance and the Committee on the Judiciary of the Senate, a report regarding the efforts made to secure the participation of judges and former judges on binational panels, extraordinary challenge committees, and special committees established under chapter 19.

19 U.S.C. § 3433

Sec. 403. Testimony and Production of Papers in Extraordinary Challenges

(a) Authority of Extraordinary Challenge Committee to Obtain Information.—If an extraordinary challenge committee (hereafter in this section referred to as the "committee") is convened under paragraph 13 of article 1904, and the allegations before the committee include a matter referred to in paragraph 13(a)(i) of article 1904, for the purposes of carrying out its functions and duties under Annex 1904.13, the committee—

(1) shall have access to, and the right to copy, any document, paper, or record pertinent to the subject matter under consideration, in the possession of any individual, partnership, corporation, association, organization, or other entity;

(2) may summon witnesses, take testimony, and administer oaths;

(3) may require any individual, partnership, corporation, association, organization, or other entity to produce documents, books, or records relating to the matter in question; and

(4) may require any individual, partnership, corporation, association, organization, or other entity to furnish in writing, in such detail and in

such form as the committee may prescribe, information in its possession pertaining to the matter.

Any member of the committee may sign subpoenas, and members of the committee, when authorized by the committee, may administer oaths and affirmations, examine witnesses, take testimony, and receive evidence.

(b) Witnesses and Evidence.—The attendance of witnesses who are authorized to be summoned, and the production of documentary evidence authorized to be ordered, under subsection (a) may be required from any place in the United States at any designated place of hearing. In the case of disobedience to a subpoena authorized under subsection (a), the committee may request the Attorney General of the United States to invoke the aid of any district or territorial court of the United States in requiring the attendance and testimony of witnesses and the production of documentary evidence. Such court, within the jurisdiction of which such inquiry is carried on, may, in case of contumacy or refusal to obey a subpoena issued to any individual, partnership, corporation, association, organization, or other entity, issue an order requiring such individual or entity to appear before the committee, or to produce documentary evidence if so ordered or to give evidence concerning the matter in question. Any failure to obey such order of the court may be punished by such court as a contempt thereof.

(c) Mandamus.—Any court referred to in subsection (b) shall have jurisdiction to issue writs of mandamus commanding compliance with the provisions of this section or any order of the committee made in pursuance thereof.

(d) Depositions.—The committee may order testimony to be taken by deposition at any stage of the committee review. Such deposition may be taken before any person designated by the committee and having power to administer oaths. Such testimony shall be reduced to writing by the person taking the deposition, or under the direction of such person, and shall then be subscribed by the deponent. Any individual, partnership, corporation, association, organization, or other entity may be compelled to appear and be deposed and to produce documentary evidence in the same manner as witnesses may be compelled to appear and testify and produce documentary evidence before the committee, as provided in this section.

19 U.S.C. § 3434

Sec. 404. Requests for Review of Determinations by Competent Investigating Authorities of NAFTA Countries

(a) Definitions.—As used in this section:

(1) Competent Investigating Authority.—The term "competent investigating authority" means the competent investigating authority, as defined in article 1911, of a NAFTA country.

(2) United States Secretary.—The term "United States Secretary" means that officer of the United States referred to in article 1908.

(b) Requests for Review by the United States.—In the case of a final determination of a competent investigating authority, requests by the United States for binational panel review of such determination under article 1904 shall be made by the United States Secretary.

(c) Requests for Review by a Person.—In the case of a final determination of a competent investigating authority, a person, within the meaning of paragraph 5 of article 1904, may request a binational panel review of such determination by filing such a request with the United States Secretary within the time limit provided for in paragraph 4 of article 1904. The receipt of such request by the United States Secretary shall be deemed to be a request for binational panel review within the meaning of article 1904. The request for such panel review shall be without prejudice to any challenge before a binational panel of the basis for a particular request for review.

(d) Service of Request for Review.—Whenever binational panel review of a final determination made by a competent investigating authority is requested under this section, the United States Secretary shall serve a copy of the request on all persons who would otherwise be entitled under the law of the importing country to commence proceedings for judicial review of the determination.

19 U.S.C. § 3435

Sec. 405. Rules of Procedure for Panels and Committees

(a) Rules of Procedure for Binational Panels.—The administering authority shall prescribe rules, negotiated in accordance with paragraph 14 of article 1904, governing, with respect to binational panel reviews—

* * *

(b) Rules of Procedure for Extraordinary Challenge Committees.—The administering authority shall prescribe rules, negotiated in accordance with paragraph 2 of Annex 1904.13, governing the procedures for reviews by extraordinary challenge committees.

(c) Rules of Procedure for Safeguarding the Panel Review System.—The administering authority shall prescribe rules, negotiated in accordance with Annex 1905.6, governing the procedures for special committees described in such Annex.

* * *

Document 14

Foreign Sovereign Immunities Act of 1976 (Selected Provisions)

90 Stat. 2891, 28 U.S.C.A. §§ 1330, 1332, 1391, 1441, 1602–1611 (1976), as amended by Public Law 100–640, 102 Stat. 3333 (1988); Public Law 100–669, 102 Stat. 3969 (1988); Public Law 104-132, 110 Stat. 1241 (1986); and Public Law 105-11, 111 Stat. 22 (1997).

An Act to define the jurisdiction of United States courts in suits against foreign states, the circumstances in which foreign states are immune from suit and in which execution may not be levied on their property, and for other purposes.

Be it enacted by the Senate and House of Representatives of the United States of America in Congress assembled, That this Act may be cited as the "Foreign Sovereign Immunities Act of 1976."

Sec. 2. (a) That chapter 85 of title 28, United States Code, is amended by inserting immediately before section 1331 the following new section:

"§ 1330. Actions Against Foreign States

"(a) The district courts shall have original jurisdiction without regard to amount in controversy of any nonjury civil action against a foreign state as defined in section 1603(a) of this title as to any claim for relief in personam with respect to which the foreign state is not entitled to immunity either under sections 1605–1607 of this title or under any applicable international agreement.

"(b) Personal jurisdiction over a foreign state shall exist as to every claim for relief over which the district courts have jurisdiction under subsection (a) where service has been made under section 1608 of this title.

"(c) For purposes of subsection (b), an appearance by a foreign state does not confer personal jurisdiction with respect to any claim for relief not arising out of any transaction or occurrence enumerated in sections 1605–1607 of this title."

Sec. 4. (a) That title 28, United States Code, is amended by inserting after chapter 95 the following new chapter:

CHAPTER 97—JURISDICTIONAL IMMUNITIES OF FOREIGN STATES

"§ 1602. Findings and Declaration of Purpose

"The Congress finds that the determination by United States courts of the claims of foreign states to immunity from the jurisdiction of such courts would serve the interests of justice and would protect the rights of both foreign states and litigants in United States courts. Under international law, states are not immune from the jurisdiction of foreign courts insofar as their commercial activities are concerned, and their commercial property may be levied upon for the satisfaction of judgments rendered against them in connection with their commercial activities. Claims of foreign states to immunity should henceforth be decided by courts of the United States and of the States in conformity with the principles set forth in this chapter.

"§ 1603. Definitions

"For purposes of this chapter—

"(a) A 'foreign state' except as used in section 1608 of this title, includes a political subdivision of a foreign state or an agency or instrumentality of a foreign state as defined in subsection (b).

"(b) An 'agency or instrumentality of a foreign state' means any entity—

"(1) which is a separate legal person, corporate or otherwise, and

"(2) which is an organ of a foreign state or political subdivision thereof, or a majority of whose shares or other ownership interest is owned by a foreign state or political subdivision thereof, and

"(3) which is neither a citizen of a State of the United States as defined in section 1332(c) and (d) of this title, nor created under the laws of any third country.

"(c) The 'United States' includes all territory and waters, continental or insular, subject to the jurisdiction of the United States.

"(d) A 'commercial activity' means either a regular course of commercial conduct or a particular commercial transaction or act. The commercial character of an activity shall be determined by reference to the nature of the course of conduct or particular transaction or act, rather than by reference to its purpose.

"(e) A 'commercial activity carried on in the United States by a foreign state' means commercial activity carried on by such state and having substantial contact with the United States.

"§ 1604. Immunity of a Foreign State From Jurisdiction

"Subject to existing international agreements to which the United States is a party at the time of enactment of this Act a foreign state shall be immune from the jurisdiction of the courts of the United States and of the States except as provided in sections 1605 to 1607 of this chapter.

"§ 1605. General Exceptions to the Jurisdictional Immunity of a Foreign State

"(a) A foreign state shall not be immune from the jurisdiction of courts of the United States or of the States in any case—

"(1) in which the foreign state has waived its immunity either explicitly or by implication, notwithstanding any withdrawal of the waiver which the foreign state may purport to effect except in accordance with the terms of the waiver;

"(2) in which the action is based upon a commercial activity carried on in the United States by the foreign state; or upon an act performed in the United States in connection with a commercial activity of the foreign state elsewhere; or upon an act outside the territory of the United States in connection with a commercial activity of the foreign state elsewhere and that act causes a direct effect in the United States;

"(3) in which rights in property taken in violation of international law are in issue and that property or any property exchanged for such property is present in the United States in connection with a commercial activity carried on in the United States by the foreign state; or that property or any property exchanged for such property is owned or operated by an agency or instrumentality of the foreign state and that agency or instrumentality is engaged in a commercial activity in the United States;

"(4) in which rights in property in the United States acquired by succession or gift or rights in immovable property situated in the United States are in issue;

"(5) not otherwise encompassed in paragraph (2) above, in which money damages are sought against a foreign state for personal injury or death, or damage to or loss of property, occurring in the United States and caused by the tortious act or omission of that foreign state or of any official or employee of that foreign state while acting within the scope of his office or employment; except this paragraph shall not apply to—

"(A) any claim based upon the exercise or performance or the failure to exercise or perform a discretionary function regardless of whether the discretion be abused, or

"(B) any claim arising out of malicious prosecution, abuse of process, libel, slander, misrepresentation, deceit, or interference with contract rights;

"(6) in which the action is brought, either to enforce an agreement made by the foreign State with or for the benefit of a private party to submit to arbitration all or any differences which have arisen or which may arise between the parties with respect to a defined legal relationship, whether contractual or not, concerning a subject matter capable of settlement by arbitration under the laws of the United States, or to confirm an award made pursuant to such an agreement to arbitrate, if (A) the arbitration takes place or is intended to take place in the United States, (B) the agreement or award is or may be governed by a treaty or other international agreement in force for the United States calling for the recognition and enforcement of arbitral awards, (C) the underlying claim, save for the agreement to arbitrate, could have been brought in a United States court under this section or section 1607, or (D) paragraph (1) of this subsection is otherwise applicable; or

"(7) not otherwise covered by paragraph (2), in which money damages are sought against a foreign state for personal injury or death that was caused by an act of torture, extrajudicial killing, aircraft sabotage, hostage taking, or the provision of material support or resources (as defined in section 2339A of title 18) for such an act if such act or provision of material support is engaged in by an official, employee, or agent of such foreign state while acting within the scope of his or her office, employment, or agency, except that the court shall decline to hear a claim under this paragraph—

"(A) if the foreign state was not designated as a state sponsor of terrorism under section 6(j) of the Export Administration Act of 1979 (50 U.S.C. App. 2405(j)) or section 620A of the Foreign Assistance Act of 1961 (22 U.S.C. 2371) at the time the act occurred, unless later so designated as a result of such act; and

"(B) even if the foreign state is or was so designated, if—

"(i) the act occurred in the foreign state against which the claim has been brought and the claimant has not afforded the foreign state a reasonable opportunity to arbitrate the claim in accordance with accepted international rules of arbitration; or

"(ii) neither the claimant nor the victim was a national of the United States (as that term is defined in section 101(a)(22) of the Immigration and Nationality Act) when the act upon which the claim is based occurred.

"(b) A foreign state shall not be immune from the jurisdiction of the courts of the United States in any case in which a suit in admiralty is brought to enforce a maritime lien against a vessel or cargo of the foreign state, which maritime lien is based upon a commercial activity of the foreign state: *Provided,* That—

"(1) notice of the suit is given by delivery of a copy of the summons and of the complaint to the person, or his agent, having possession of the vessel or cargo against which the maritime lien is asserted; and if the vessel or cargo is arrested pursuant to process obtained on behalf of the party bringing the suit, the service of process of arrest shall be deemed to constitute valid delivery of such notice, but the party bringing the suit shall be liable for any damages sustained by the foreign state as a result of the arrest if the party bringing the suit had actual or constructive knowledge that the vessel or cargo of a foreign state was involved; and

"(2) notice to the foreign state of the commencement of suit as provided in section 1608 of this title is initiated within ten days either of the delivery of notice as provided in paragraph (1) of this subsection or, in the case of a party who was unaware that the vessel or cargo of a foreign state was involved, of the date such party determined the existence of the foreign state's interest.

"(c) Whenever notice is delivered under subsection (b)(1), the suit to enforce a maritime lien shall thereafter proceed and shall be heard and determined according to the principles of law and rules of practice of suits in rem whenever it appears that, had the vessel been privately owned and possessed, a suit in rem might have been maintained. A decree against the foreign state may include costs of the suit and, if the decree is for a money judgment, interest as ordered by the court, except that the court may not award judgment against the foreign state in an amount greater than the value of the vessel or cargo upon which the maritime lien arose. Such value shall be determined as of the time notice is served under subsection (b)(1). Decrees shall be subject to appeal and revision as provided in other cases of admiralty and maritime jurisdiction. Nothing shall preclude the plaintiff in any proper case from seeking relief in personam in the same action brought to enforce a maritime lien as provided in this section.

"(d) A foreign state shall not be immune from the jurisdiction of the courts of the United States in any action brought to foreclose a preferred mortgage, as defined in the Ship Mortgage Act 1920, (46 U.S.C. § 911 and following). Such action shall be brought, heard, and determined in accordance with the provisions of that Act and in accordance with the principles of law and rules of practice of suits in rem, whenever it appears that had the vessel been privately owned and possessed a suit in rem might have been maintained.

"(e) For purposes of paragraph (7) of subsection (a)—

"(1) the terms 'torture' and 'extrajudicial killing' have the meaning given those terms in section 3 of the Torture Victim Protection Act of 1991;

"(2) the term 'hostage taking' has the meaning given that term in Article 1 of the International Convention Against the Taking of Hostages; and

"(3) the term 'aircraft sabotage' has the meaning given that term in Article 1 of the Convention for the Suppression of Unlawful Acts Against the Safety of Civil Aviation.

"(f) No action shall be maintained under subsection (a)(7) unless the action is commenced not later than 10 years after the date on which the cause of action arose. All principles of equitable tolling, including the period during which the foreign state was immune from suit, shall apply in calculating this limitation period.

"(g) Limitation on discovery.—

"**(1) In general.—(A)** Subject to paragraph (2), if an action is filed that would otherwise be barred by section 1604, but for subsection (a)(7), the court, upon request of the Attorney General, shall stay any request, demand, or order for discovery on the United States that the Attorney General certifies would significantly interfere with a criminal investigation or prosecution, or a national security operation, related to the incident that gave rise to the cause of action, until such time as the Attorney General advises the court that such request, demand, or order will no longer so interfere.

"(B) A stay under this paragraph shall be in effect during the 12-month period beginning on the date on which the court issues the order to stay discovery. The court shall renew the order to stay discovery for additional 12-month periods upon motion by the United States if the Attorney General certifies that discovery would significantly interfere with a criminal investigation or prosecution, or a national security operation, related to the incident that gave rise to the cause of action.

"**(2) Sunset.—(A)** Subject to subparagraph (B), no stay shall be granted or continued in effect under paragraph (1) after the date that is 10 years after the date on which the incident that gave rise to the cause of action occurred.

"(B) After the period referred to in subparagraph (A), the court, upon request of the Attorney General, may stay any request, demand, or order for discovery on the United States that the court finds a substantial likelihood would—

"(i) create a serious threat of death or serious bodily injury to any person;

"(ii) adversely affect the ability of the United States to work in cooperation with foreign and international law enforcement agencies in investigating violations of United States law; or

"(iii) obstruct the criminal case related to the incident that gave rise to the cause of action or undermine the potential for a conviction in such case.

* * *

"§ 1606. Extent of Liability

"As to any claim for relief with respect to which a foreign state is not entitled to immunity under section 1605 or 1607 of this chapter, the foreign state shall be liable in the same manner and to the same extent as a private individual under like circumstances; but a foreign state except for an agency or instrumentality thereof shall not be liable for punitive damages; if, however, in any case wherein death was caused, the law of the place where the action or omission occurred provides, or has been construed to provide, for damages only punitive in nature, the foreign state shall be liable for actual or compensatory damages measured by the pecuniary injuries resulting from such death which were incurred by the persons for whose benefit the action was brought.

"§ 1607. Counterclaims

"In any action brought by a foreign state, or in which a foreign state intervenes, in a court of the United States or of a State, the foreign state shall not be accorded immunity with respect to any counterclaim—

"(a) for which a foreign state would not be entitled to immunity under section 1605 of this chapter had such claim been brought in a separate action against the foreign state; or

"(b) arising out of the transaction or occurrence that is the subject matter of the claim of the foreign state; or

"(c) to the extent that the counterclaim does not seek relief exceeding in amount or differing in kind from that sought by the foreign state.

* * *

"§ 1609. Immunity From Attachment and Execution of Property of a Foreign State

"Subject to existing international agreements to which the United States is a party at the time of enactment of this Act the property in the United States of a foreign state shall be immune from attachment arrest and execution except as provided in sections 1610 and 1611 of this chapter.

"§ 1610. Exceptions to the Immunity From Attachment or Execution

"(a) The property in the United States of a foreign state, as defined in section 1603(a) of this chapter, used for a commercial activity in the United States, shall not be immune from attachment in aid of execution, or from execution, upon a judgment entered by a court of the United States or of a State after the effective date of this Act, if—

"(1) the foreign state has waived its immunity from attachment in aid of execution or from execution either explicitly or by implication, notwithstanding any withdrawal of the waiver the foreign state may purport to effect except in accordance with the terms of the waiver, or

"(2) the property is or was used for the commercial activity upon which the claim is based, or

"(3) the execution relates to a judgment establishing rights in property which has been taken in violation of international law or which has been exchanged for property taken in violation of international law, or

"(4) the execution relates to a judgment establishing rights in property—

"(A) which is acquired by succession or gift, or

"(B) which is immovable and situated in the United States: *Provided,* That such property is not used for purposes of maintaining a diplomatic or consular mission or the residence of the Chief of such mission, or

"(5) the property consists of any contractual obligation or any proceeds from such a contractual obligation to indemnify or hold harmless the foreign state or its employees under a policy of automobile or other liability or casualty insurance covering the claim which merged into the judgment;

"(6) the judgment is based on an order confirming an arbitral award rendered against the foreign State, provided that attachment in aid of execution, or execution, would not be inconsistent with any provision in the arbitral agreement, or

"(7) the judgment relates to a claim for which the foreign state is not immune under section 1605(a)(7), regardless of whether the property is or was involved with the act upon which the claim is based.

"(b) In addition to subsection (a), any property in the United States of an agency or instrumentality of a foreign state engaged in commercial activity in the United States shall not be immune from attachment in aid of execution, or from execution, upon a judgment entered by a court of the United States or of a State after the effective date of this Act, if—

"(1) the agency or instrumentality has waived its immunity from attachment in aid of execution or from execution either explicitly or implicitly, notwithstanding any withdrawal of the waiver the agency or instrumentality may purport to effect except in accordance with the terms of the waiver, or

"(2) the judgment relates to a claim for which the agency or instrumentality is not immune by virtue of section 1605(a)(2), (3), (5) or (7) 1605(b) of this chapter, regardless of whether the property is or was used for the activity upon which the claim is based.

"(c) No attachment or execution referred to in subsections (a) and (b) of this section shall be permitted until the court has ordered such attachment and execution after having determined that a reasonable period of time has elapsed following the entry of judgment and the giving of any notice required under section 1608(e) of this chapter.

"(d) The property of a foreign state, as defined in section 1603(a) of this chapter, used for a commercial activity in the United States, shall not be immune from attachment prior to the entry of judgment in any action brought in a court of the United States or of a State, or prior to the elapse of the period of time provided in subsection (c) of this section, if—

"(1) the foreign state has explicitly waived its immunity from attachment prior to judgment, notwithstanding any withdrawal of the waiver the foreign state may purport to effect except in accordance with the terms of the waiver, and

"(2) the purpose of the attachment is to secure satisfaction of a judgment that has been or may ultimately be entered against the foreign state, and not to obtain jurisdiction.

"(e) The vessels of a foreign State shall not be immune from arrest in rem, interlocutory sale, and execution in actions brought to foreclose a preferred mortgage as provided in section 1605(d).

"§ 1611. Certain Types of Property Immune From Execution

"(a) Notwithstanding the provisions of section 1610 of this chapter, the property of those organizations designated by the President as being entitled to enjoy the privileges, exemptions and immunities provided by the International Organizations Immunities Act shall not be subject to attachment or any other judicial process impeding the disbursement of funds to, or on the order of, a foreign state as the result of an action brought in the courts of the United States or of the States.

"(b) Notwithstanding the provisions of section 1610 of this chapter, the property of a foreign state shall be immune from attachment and from execution, if—

"(1) the property is that of a foreign central bank or monetary authority held for its own account, unless such bank or authority, or its parent foreign government, has explicitly waived its immunity from attachment in aid of execution, or from execution, notwithstanding any withdrawal of the waiver which the bank, authority or government may purport to effect except in accordance with the terms of the waiver; or

"(2) the property is, or is intended to be, used in connection with a military activity and

"(A) is of a military character, or

"(B) is under the control of a military authority or defense agency."

"(c) Notwithstanding the provisions of section 1610 of this chapter, the property of a foreign state shall be immune from attachment and from execution in an action brought under section 302 of the Cuban Liberty and Democratic Solidarity (LIBERTAD) Act of 1996 to the extent that the property is a facility or installation used by an accredited diplomatic mission for official purposes.

(b) That the analysis of "Part IV.—JURISDICTION AND VENUE" of title 28, United States Code, is amended by inserting after—

"95. Customs Court.",

the following new item:

"97. Jurisdictional Immunities of Foreign States."

Sec. 5. That section 1391 of title 28, United States Code, is amended by adding at the end thereof the following new subsection:

"(f) A civil action against a foreign state as defined in section 1603(a) of this title may be brought—

"(1) in any judicial district in which a substantial part of the events or omissions giving rise to the claim occurred, or a substantial part of property that is the subject of the action is situated;

"(2) in any judicial district in which the vessel or cargo of a foreign state is situated, if the claim is asserted under section 1605(b) of this title;

"(3) in any judicial district in which the agency or instrumentality is licensed to do business or is doing business, if the action is brought against an agency or instrumentality of a foreign state as defined in section 1603(b) of this title; or

"(4) in the United States District Court for the District of Columbia if the action is brought against a foreign state or political subdivision thereof."

Sec. 6. That section 1441 of title 28, United States Code, is amended by adding at the end thereof the following new subsection:

"(d) Any civil action brought in a State court against a foreign state as defined in section 1603(a) of this title may be removed by the foreign state to the district court of the United States for the district and division embracing the place where such action is pending. Upon removal the action shall be tried by the court without jury. Where removal is based upon this subsection, the time limitations of section 1446(b) of this chapter may be enlarged at any time for cause shown."

DOCUMENT 15

ALIEN TORT CLAIMS ACT AND TORTURE VICTIMS PROTECTION ACT

28 U.S.C. § 1350

§ 1350. Alien's action for tort

The district courts shall have original jurisdiction of any civil action by an alien for a tort only, committed in violation of the law of nations or a treaty of the United States.

TORTURE VICTIM PROTECTION

Pub.L. 102–256, Mar. 12, 1992, 106 Stat. 73, provided that:

Section 1. Short Title.

This Act may be cited as the 'Torture Victim Protection Act of 1991'.

Section 2. Establishment of Civil Action.

(a) Liability.—An individual who, under actual or apparent authority, or color of law, of any foreign nation—

(1) subjects an individual to torture shall, in a civil action, be liable for damages to that individual; or

(2) subjects an individual to extrajudicial killing shall, in a civil action, be liable for damages to the individual's legal representative, or to any person who may be a claimant in an action for wrongful death.

(b) Exhaustion of remedies.—A court shall decline to hear a claim under this section if the claimant has not exhausted adequate and available remedies in the place in which the conduct giving rise to the claim occurred.

(c) Statute of limitations.—No action shall be maintained under this section unless it is commenced within 10 years after the cause of action arose.

Section 3. Definitions.

(a) Extrajudicial killing.—For the purposes of this Act, the term 'extrajudicial killing' means a deliberated killing not authorized by a previous judgment pronounced by a regularly constituted court affording all the judicial guarantees which are recognized as indispensable by civilized peoples. Such term, however, does not include any such killing that, under international law, is lawfully carried out under the authority of a foreign nation.

(b) Torture.—For the purposes of this Act—

(1) the term 'torture' means any act, directed against an individual in the offender's custody or physical control, by which severe pain or suffering (other than pain or suffering arising only from or inherent in, or incidental to, lawful sanctions), whether physical or mental, is intentionally inflicted on that individual for such purposes as obtaining from that individual or a third person information or a confession, punishing that individual for an act that individual or a third person has committed or is suspected of having committed, intimidating or coercing that individual or a third person, or for any reason based on discrimination of any kind; and

(2) mental pain or suffering refers to prolonged mental harm caused by or resulting from—

(A) the intentional infliction or threatened infliction of severe physical pain or suffering;

(B) the administration or application, or threatened administration or application, of mind altering substances or other procedures calculated to disrupt profoundly the senses or the personality;

(C) the threat of imminent death; or

(D) the threat that another individual will imminently be subjected to death, severe physical pain or suffering, or the administration or application of mind altering substances or other procedures calculated to disrupt profoundly the senses or personality."

Document 16

Harter Act and COGSA (U.S.) (Selected Provisions)

Harter Act

46 USC 190. *"Stipulations relieving from liability for negligence"*

It shall not be lawful for the manager, agent, master, or owner of any vessel transporting merchandise or property from or between ports of the United States and foreign ports to insert in any bill of lading or shipping document any clause, covenant, or agreement whereby it, he, or they shall be relieved from liability for loss or damage arising from negligence, fault, or failure in proper loading, stowage, custody, care, or proper delivery of any and all lawful merchandise or property committed to its or their charge. Any and all words or clauses of such import inserted in bills of lading or shipping receipts shall be null and void and of no effect.

(Feb. 13, 1893, ch. 105, § 1, 27 Stat. 445.)

SHORT TITLE

Act Feb. 13, 1893, enacting this section and sections 191 to 196 of this Appendix, is popularly known as the "Harter Act".

46 USC 191. *"Stipulations relieving from exercise of due diligence in equipping vessels"*

It shall not be lawful for any vessel transporting merchandise or property from or between ports of the United States of America and foreign ports, her owner, master, agent, or manager, to insert in any bill of lading or shipping document any covenant or agreement whereby the obligations of the owner or owners of said vessel to exercise due diligence[1] properly equip, man, provision, and outfit said vessel, and to make said vessel seaworthy and capable of performing her intended voyage, or whereby the obligations of the master, officers, agents, or servants to carefully handle and stow her cargo and to care for and properly deliver same, shall in any wise be lessened, weakened, or avoided.

(Feb. 13, 1893, ch. 105, § 2, 27 Stat. 445.)

COGSA (U.S.)

46 USC 1303 *"Responsibilities and liabilities of carrier and ship"*

1. So in original. Probably should be followed by "to".

(1) Seaworthiness

The carrier shall be bound, before and at the beginning of the voyage, to exercise due diligence to—

(a) Make the ship seaworthy;

(b) Properly man, equip, and supply the ship;

(c) Make the holds, refrigerating and cooling chambers, and all other parts of the ship in which goods are carried, fit and safe for their reception, carriage, and preservation.

(2) Cargo

The carrier shall properly and carefully load, handle, stow, carry, keep, care for, and discharge the goods carried.

(3) Contents of bill

After receiving the goods into his charge the carrier, or the master or agent of the carrier, shall, on demand of the shipper, issue to the shipper a bill of lading showing among other things—

(a) The leading marks necessary for identification of the goods as the same are furnished in writing by the shipper before the loading of such goods starts, provided such marks are stamped or otherwise shown clearly upon the goods if uncovered, or on the cases or coverings in which such goods are contained, in such a manner as should ordinarily remain legible until the end of the voyage.

(b) Either the number of packages or pieces, or the quantity or weight, as the case may be, as furnished in writing by the shipper.

(c) The apparent order and condition of the goods: Provided, That no carrier, master, or agent of the carrier, shall be bound to state or show in the bill of lading any marks, number, quantity, or weight which he has reasonable ground for suspecting not accurately to represent the goods actually received, or which he has had no reasonable means of checking.

(4) Bill as prima facie evidence

Such a bill of lading shall be prima facie evidence of the receipt by the carrier of the goods as therein described in accordance with paragraphs (3)(a), (b), and (c), of this section: Provided, That nothing in this chapter shall be construed as repealing or limiting the application of any part of chapter 801 of title 49.

(5) Guaranty of statements

The shipper shall be deemed to have guaranteed to the carrier the accuracy at the time of shipment of the marks, number, quantity, and weight, as furnished by him; and the shipper shall indemnify the carrier against all loss, damages, and expenses arising or resulting from inaccuracies in such particulars. The right of the carrier to such indemnity shall in no way limit his responsibility and liability under the contract of carriage to any person other than the shipper.

(6) Notice of loss or damage; limitation of actions

Unless notice of loss or damage and the general nature of such loss or damage be given in writing to the carrier or his agent at the port of discharge before or at the time of the removal of the goods into the custody of the person entitled to delivery thereof under the contract of carriage, such removal shall be prima facie evidence of the delivery by the carrier of the goods as described in the bill of lading. If the loss or damage is not apparent, the notice must be given within three days of the delivery.

Said notice of loss or damage may be endorsed upon the receipt for the goods given by the person taking delivery thereof.

The notice in writing need not be given if the state of the goods has at the time of their receipt been the subject of joint survey or inspection.

In any event the carrier and the ship shall be discharged from all liability in respect of loss or damage unless suit is brought within one year after delivery of the goods or the date when the goods should have been delivered: Provided, That if a notice of loss or damage, either apparent or concealed, is not given as provided for in this section, that fact shall not affect or prejudice the right of the shipper to bring suit within one year after the delivery of the goods or the date when the goods should have been delivered.

In the case of any actual or apprehended loss or damage the carrier and the receiver shall give all reasonable facilities to each other for inspecting and tallying the goods.

(7) "Shipped" bill of lading

After the goods are loaded the bill of lading to be issued by the carrier, master, or agent of the carrier to the shipper shall, if the shipper so demands, be a "shipped" bill of lading: Provided, That if the shipper shall have previously taken up any document of title to such goods, he shall surrender the same as against the issue of the "shipped" bill of lading, but at the option of the carrier such document of title may be noted at the port of shipment by the carrier, master, or agent with the name or names of the ship or ships upon which the goods have been shipped and the date or dates of shipment, and when so noted the same shall for the purpose of this section be deemed to constitute a "shipped" bill of lading.

(8) Limitation of liability for negligence

Any clause, covenant, or agreement in a contract of carriage relieving the carrier or the ship from liability for loss or damage to or in connection with the goods, arising from negligence, fault, or failure in the duties and obligations provided in this section, or lessening such liability otherwise than as provided in this chapter, shall be null and void and of no effect. A benefit of insurance in favor of the carrier, or similar clause, shall be deemed to be a clause relieving the carrier from liability.

(Apr. 16, 1936, ch. 229, title I, § 3, 49 Stat. 1208.)

Codification

In par. (4), "chapter 801 of title 49" substituted for "the Act of August 29, 1916, commonly known as the 'Pomerene Bills of Lading Act' [49 App. U.S.C. 81 et seq.]" on authority of Pub. L. 103–272, § 6(b), July 5, 1994, 108 Stat. 1378, the first section of which enacted subtitles II, III, and V to X of Title 49, Transportation.

DOCUMENT 17

ELECTRONIC RECORDS AND SIGNATURES IN COMMERCE (E-SIGN) ACT (SELECTED PROVISIONS)

Section 1. Short Title.

This Act may be cited as the 'Electronic Signatures in Global and National Commerce Act'.

TITLE I—ELECTRONIC RECORDS AND SIGNATURES IN COMMERCE

15 U.S.C. § 7001

Sec. 101. General Rule of Validity.

(a) In General—Notwithstanding any statute, regulation, or other rule of law (other than this title and title II), with respect to any transaction in or affecting interstate or foreign commerce—

(1) a signature, contract, or other record relating to such transaction may not be denied legal effect, validity, or enforceability solely because it is in electronic form; and

(2) a contract relating to such transaction may not be denied legal effect, validity, or enforceability solely because an electronic signature or electronic record was used in its formation.

(b) Preservation of Rights and Obligations—This title does not—

(1) limit, alter, or otherwise affect any requirement imposed by a statute, regulation, or rule of law relating to the rights and obligations of persons under such statute, regulation, or rule of law other than a requirement that contracts or other records be written, signed, or in nonelectronic form; or

(2) require any person to agree to use or accept electronic records or electronic signatures, other than a governmental agency with respect to a record other than a contract to which it is a party.

(c) Consumer Disclosures—

(1) Consent to Electronic Records—Notwithstanding subsection (a), if a statute, regulation, or other rule of law requires that information relating to a transaction or transactions in or affecting interstate or foreign commerce be provided or made available to a consumer in

writing, the use of an electronic record to provide or make available (whichever is required) such information satisfies the requirement that such information be in writing if—

(A) the consumer has affirmatively consented to such use and has not withdrawn such consent;

(B) the consumer, prior to consenting, is provided with a clear and conspicuous statement—

(i) informing the consumer of (I) any right or option of the consumer to have the record provided or made available on paper or in nonelectronic form, and (II) the right of the consumer to withdraw the consent to have the record provided or made available in an electronic form and of any conditions, consequences (which may include termination of the parties' relationship), or fees in the event of such withdrawal;

(ii) informing the consumer of whether the consent applies (I) only to the particular transaction which gave rise to the obligation to provide the record, or (II) to identified categories of records that may be provided or made available during the course of the parties' relationship;

(iii) describing the procedures the consumer must use to withdraw consent as provided in clause (i) and to update information needed to contact the consumer electronically; and

(iv) informing the consumer (I) how, after the consent, the consumer may, upon request, obtain a paper copy of an electronic record, and (II) whether any fee will be charged for such copy;

(C) the consumer—

(i) prior to consenting, is provided with a statement of the hardware and software requirements for access to and retention of the electronic records; and

(ii) consents electronically, or confirms his or her consent electronically, in a manner that reasonably demonstrates that the consumer can access information in the electronic form that will be used to provide the information that is the subject of the consent; and

(D) after the consent of a consumer in accordance with subparagraph (A), if a change in the hardware or software requirements needed to access or retain electronic records creates a material risk that the consumer will not be able to access or retain a subsequent electronic record that was the subject of the consent, the person providing the electronic record—

(i) provides the consumer with a statement of (I) the revised hardware and software requirements for access to and retention of the electronic records, and (II) the right to withdraw consent without the imposition of any fees for such withdrawal and without the imposition of any condition or consequence that was not disclosed under subparagraph (B)(i); and

(ii) again complies with subparagraph (C).

(2) Other Rights—

(A) Preservation of Consumer Protections—Nothing in this title affects the content or timing of any disclosure or other record required to be provided or made available to any consumer under any statute, regulation, or other rule of law.

(B) Verification or Acknowledgment—If a law that was enacted prior to this Act expressly requires a record to be provided or made available by a specified method that requires verification or acknowledgment of receipt, the record may be provided or made available electronically only if the method used provides verification or acknowledgment of receipt (whichever is required).

(3) Effect of Failure to Obtain Electronic Consent or Confirmation of Consent—The legal effectiveness, validity, or enforceability of any contract executed by a consumer shall not be denied solely because of the failure to obtain electronic consent or confirmation of consent by that consumer in accordance with paragraph (1)(C)(ii).

(4) Prospective Effect—Withdrawal of consent by a consumer shall not affect the legal effectiveness, validity, or enforceability of electronic records provided or made available to that consumer in accordance with paragraph (1) prior to implementation of the consumer's withdrawal of consent. A consumer's withdrawal of consent shall be effective within a reasonable period of time after receipt of the withdrawal by the provider of the record. Failure to comply with paragraph (1)(D) may, at the election of the consumer, be treated as a withdrawal of consent for purposes of this paragraph.

(5) Prior consent—This subsection does not apply to any records that are provided or made available to a consumer who has consented prior to the effective date of this title to receive such records in electronic form as permitted by any statute, regulation, or other rule of law.

(6) Oral Communications—An oral communication or a recording of an oral communication shall not qualify as an electronic record for purposes of this subsection except as otherwise provided under applicable law.

(d) Retention of Contracts and Records—

(1) Accuracy and Accessibility—If a statute, regulation, or other rule of law requires that a contract or other record relating to a

transaction in or affecting interstate or foreign commerce be retained, that requirement is met by retaining an electronic record of the information in the contract or other record that—

(A) accurately reflects the information set forth in the contract or other record; and

(B) remains accessible to all persons who are entitled to access by statute, regulation, or rule of law, for the period required by such statute, regulation, or rule of law, in a form that is capable of being accurately reproduced for later reference, whether by transmission, printing, or otherwise.

(2) Exception—A requirement to retain a contract or other record in accordance with paragraph (1) does not apply to any information whose sole purpose is to enable the contract or other record to be sent, communicated, or received.

(3) Originals—If a statute, regulation, or other rule of law requires a contract or other record relating to a transaction in or affecting interstate or foreign commerce to be provided, available, or retained in its original form, or provides consequences if the contract or other record is not provided, available, or retained in its original form, that statute, regulation, or rule of law is satisfied by an electronic record that complies with paragraph (1).

(4) Checks—If a statute, regulation, or other rule of law requires the retention of a check, that requirement is satisfied by retention of an electronic record of the information on the front and back of the check in accordance with paragraph (1).

(e) Accuracy and Ability to Retain Contracts and Other Records— Notwithstanding subsection (a), if a statute, regulation, or other rule of law requires that a contract or other record relating to a transaction in or affecting interstate or foreign commerce be in writing, the legal effect, validity, or enforceability of an electronic record of such contract or other record may be denied if such electronic record is not in a form that is capable of being retained and accurately reproduced for later reference by all parties or persons who are entitled to retain the contract or other record.

(f) Proximity—Nothing in this title affects the proximity required by any statute, regulation, or other rule of law with respect to any warning, notice, disclosure, or other record required to be posted, displayed, or publicly affixed.

(g) Notarization and Acknowledgment—If a statute, regulation, or other rule of law requires a signature or record relating to a transaction in or affecting interstate or foreign commerce to be notarized, acknowledged, verified, or made under oath, that requirement is satisfied if the electronic signature of the person authorized to perform those acts, together with all other information required to be included by other applicable statute, regulation, or rule of law, is attached to or logically associated with the signature or record.

(h) Electronic Agents—A contract or other record relating to a transaction in or affecting interstate or foreign commerce may not be denied legal effect, validity, or enforceability solely because its formation, creation, or delivery involved the action of one or more electronic agents so long as the action of any such electronic agent is legally attributable to the person to be bound.

* * *

15 U.S.C. § 7002

Sec. 102. Exemption to Preemption.

(a) In General—A State statute, regulation, or other rule of law may modify, limit, or supersede the provisions of section 101 with respect to State law only if such statute, regulation, or rule of law—

(1) constitutes an enactment or adoption of the Uniform Electronic Transactions Act as approved and recommended for enactment in all the States by the National Conference of Commissioners on Uniform State Laws in 1999, except that any exception to the scope of such Act enacted by a State under section 3(b)(4) of such Act shall be preempted to the extent such exception is inconsistent with this title or title II, or would not be permitted under paragraph (2)(A)(ii) of this subsection; or

(2) (A) specifies the alternative procedures or requirements for the use or acceptance (or both) of electronic records or electronic signatures to establish the legal effect, validity, or enforceability of contracts or other records, if—

(i) such alternative procedures or requirements are consistent with this title and title II; and

(ii) such alternative procedures or requirements do not require, or accord greater legal status or effect to, the implementation or application of a specific technology or technical specification for performing the functions of creating, storing, generating, receiving, communicating, or authenticating electronic records or electronic signatures; and

(B) if enacted or adopted after the date of the enactment of this Act, makes specific reference to this Act.

(b) Exceptions for Actions by States as Market Participants—Subsection (a)(2)(A)(ii) shall not apply to the statutes, regulations, or other rules of law governing procurement by any State, or any agency or instrumentality thereof.

(c) Prevention of Circumvention—Subsection (a) does not permit a State to circumvent this title or title II through the imposition of nonelectronic delivery methods under section 8(b)(2) of the Uniform Electronic Transactions Act.

* * *

15 U.S.C. § 7006

Sec. 106. Definitions.

For purposes of this title:

(1) Consumer—The term 'consumer' means an individual who obtains, through a transaction, products or services which are used primarily for personal, family, or household purposes, and also means the legal representative of such an individual.

(2) Electronic—The term 'electronic' means relating to technology having electrical, digital, magnetic, wireless, optical, electromagnetic, or similar capabilities.

(3) Electronic Agent—The term 'electronic agent' means a computer program or an electronic or other automated means used independently to initiate an action or respond to electronic records or performances in whole or in part without review or action by an individual at the time of the action or response.

(4) Electronic Record—The term 'electronic record' means a contract or other record created, generated, sent, communicated, received, or stored by electronic means.

(5) Electronic Signature—The term 'electronic signature' means an electronic sound, symbol, or process, attached to or logically associated with a contract or other record and executed or adopted by a person with the intent to sign the record.

(6) Federal Regulatory Agency—The term 'Federal regulatory agency' means an agency, as that term is defined in section 552(f) of title 5, United States Code.

(7) Information—The term 'information' means data, text, images, sounds, codes, computer programs, software, databases, or the like.

(8) Person—The term 'person' means an individual, corporation, business trust, estate, trust, partnership, limited liability company, association, joint venture, governmental agency, public corporation, or any other legal or commercial entity.

(9) Record—the term 'record' means information that is inscribed on a tangible medium or that is stored in an electronic or other medium and is retrievable in perceivable form.

(10) Requirement—The term 'requirement' includes a prohibition.

(11) Self–Regulatory Organization—The term "self-regulatory organization" means an organization or entity that is not a Federal

regulatory agency or a State, but that is under the supervision of a Federal regulatory agency and is authorized under Federal law to adopt and administer rules applicable to its members that are enforced by such organization or entity, by a Federal regulatory agency, or by another self-regulatory organization.

(12) State—The term "State" includes the District of Columbia and the territories and possessions of the United States.

(13) Transaction—The term 'transaction' means an action or set of actions relating to the conduct of business, consumer, or commercial affairs between two or more persons, including any of the following types of conduct—

(A) the sale, lease, exchange, licensing, or other disposition of (i) personal property, including goods and intangibles, (ii) services, and (iii) any combination thereof; and

(B) the sale, lease, exchange, or other disposition of any interest in real property, or any combination thereof.

DOCUMENT 18

FEDERAL BILLS OF LADING ACT (SELECTED PROVISIONS)

49 U.S.C. § 80101. Definitions

In this chapter—

(1) "consignee" means the person named in a bill of lading as the person to whom the goods are to be delivered.

(2) "consignor" means the person named in a bill of lading as the person from whom the goods have been received for shipment.

(3) "goods" means merchandise or personal property that has been, is being, or will be transported.

(4) "holder" means a person having possession of, and a property right in, a bill of lading.

(5) "order" means an order by indorsement on a bill of lading.

(6) "purchase" includes taking by mortgage or pledge.

(7) "State" means a State of the United States, the District of Columbia, and a territory or possession of the United States.

49 U.S.C. § 80102. Application

This chapter applies to a bill of lading when the bill is issued by a common carrier for the transportation of goods—

(1) between a place in the District of Columbia and another place in the District of Columbia;

(2) between a place in a territory or possession of the United States and another place in the same territory or possession;

(3) between a place in a State and a place in another State;

(4) between a place in a State and a place in the same State through another State or a foreign country; or

(5) from a place in a State to a place in a foreign country.

49 U.S.C. § 80103. Negotiable and nonnegotiable bills

(a) Negotiable bills.—(1) A bill of lading is negotiable if the bill—

(A) states that the goods are to be delivered to the order of a consignee; and

(B) does not contain on its face an agreement with the shipper that the bill is not negotiable.

(2) Inserting in a negotiable bill of lading the name of a person to be notified of the arrival of goods—

(A) does not limit its negotiability; and

(B) is not notice to the purchaser of the goods of a right the named person has to the goods.

(b) Nonnegotiable bills.—(1) A bill of lading is nonnegotiable if the bill states that the goods are to be delivered to a consignee. The indorsement of a negotiable bill does not—

(A) make the bill negotiable; or

(B) give the transferee any additional right.

(2) A common carrier issuing a nonnegotiable bill of lading must put "nonnegotiable" or "not negotiable" on the bill. This paragraph does not apply to an informal memorandum or acknowledgment.

49 U.S.C. § 80104. Form and requirements for negotiation

(a) General Rules.—(1) A negotiable bill of lading may be negotiated by indorsement. An indorsement may be made in blank or to a specified person. If the goods are deliverable to the order of a specified person, then the bill must be indorsed by that person.

(2) A negotiable bill of lading may be negotiated by delivery when the common carrier, under the terms of the bill, undertakes to deliver the goods to the order of a specified person and that person or a subsequent indorsee has indorsed the bill in blank.

(3) A negotiable bill of lading may be negotiated by a person possessing the bill, regardless of the way in which the person got possession, if—

(A) a common carrier, under the terms of the bill, undertakes to deliver the goods to that person; or

(B) when the bill is negotiated, it is in a form that allows it to be negotiated by delivery.

(b) Validity not affected.— The validity of a negotiation of a bill of lading is not affected by the negotiation having been a breach of duty by the person making the negotiation, or by the owner of the bill having been deprived of possession by fraud, accident, mistake, duress, loss, theft, or conversion, if the person to whom the bill is negotiated, or a person to whom the bill is subsequently negotiated, gives value for the bill in good faith and without notice of the breach of duty, fraud, accident, mistake, duress, loss, theft, or conversion.

(c) Negotiation by seller, mortgagor, or pledgor to person without notice.— When goods for which a negotiable bill of lading has been issued are in a common carrier's possession, and the person to whom the bill has been issued retains possession of the bill after selling, mortgaging, or pledging the goods or bill, the subsequent negotiation of the bill by that person to another person receiving the bill for value, in good faith, and without notice of the prior sale, mortgage, or pledge has the same effect as if the first purchaser of the goods or bill had expressly authorized the subsequent negotiation.

* * *

49 U.S.C. § 80107. Warranties and liability

(a) General rule.—Unless a contrary intention appears, a person negotiating or transferring a bill of lading for value warrants that—

(1) the bill is genuine;

(2) the person has the right to transfer the bill and the title to the goods described in the bill;

(3) the person does not know of a fact that would affect the validity or worth of the bill; and

(4) the goods are merchantable or fit for a particular purpose when merchantability or fitness would have been implied if the agreement of the parties had been to transfer the goods without a bill of lading.

(b) Security for debt.—A person holding a bill of lading as security for a debt and in good faith demanding or receiving payment of the debt from another person does not warrant by the demand or receipt—

(1) the genuineness of the bill; or

(2) the quantity or quality of the goods described in the bill.

(c) Duplicates.—A common carrier issuing a bill of lading, on the face of which is the word "duplicate" or another word indicating that the bill is not an original bill, is liable the same as a person that represents and warrants that the bill is an accurate copy of an original bill properly issued. The carrier is not otherwise liable under the bill.

(d) Indorser liability.—Indorsement of a bill of lading does not make the indorser liable for failure of the common carrier or a previous indorser to fulfill its obligations.

* * *

49 U.S.C. § 80110. Duty to deliver goods

(a) General rules.—Except to the extent a common carrier establishes an excuse provided by law, the carrier must deliver goods covered by a bill of lading on demand of the consignee named in a nonnegotiable bill or the holder of a negotiable bill for the goods when the consignee or holder—

(1) offers in good faith to satisfy the lien of the carrier on the goods;

(2) has possession of the bill and, if a negotiable bill, offers to indorse and give the bill to the carrier; and

(3) agrees to sign, on delivery of the goods, a receipt for delivery if requested by the carrier.

(b) Persons to whom goods may be delivered.—Subject to section 80111 of this title, a common carrier may deliver the goods covered by a bill of lading to—

(1) a person entitled to their possession;

(2) the consignee named in a nonnegotiable bill; or

(3) a person in possession of a negotiable bill if—

(A) the goods are deliverable to the order of that person; or

(B) the bill has been indorsed to that person or in blank by the consignee or another indorsee.

(c) Common carrier claims of title and possession.—A claim by a common carrier that the carrier has title to goods or right to their possession is an excuse for nondelivery of the goods only if the title or right is derived from—

(1) a transfer made by the consignor or consignee after the shipment; or

(2) the carrier's lien.

(d) Adverse claims.—If a person other than the consignee or the person in possession of a bill of lading claims title to or possession of goods and the common carrier knows of the claim, the carrier is not required to deliver the goods to any claimant until the carrier has had a reasonable time to decide the validity of the adverse claim or to bring a civil action to require all claimants to interplead.

(e) Interpleader.—If at least 2 persons claim title to or possession of the goods, the common carrier may—

(1) bring a civil action to interplead all known claimants to the goods; or

(2) require those claimants to interplead as a defense in an action brought against the carrier for nondelivery.

(f) Third person claims not a defense.—Except as provided in subsections (b), (d), and (e) of this section, title or a right of a third person is not a defense to an action brought by the consignee of a nonnegotiable bill of lading or by the holder of a negotiable bill against the common carrier for failure to deliver the goods on demand unless enforced by legal process.

49 U.S.C. § 80111. Liability for delivery of goods

(a) General rules.—A common carrier is liable for damages to a person having title to, or right to possession of, goods when—

(1) the carrier delivers the goods to a person not entitled to their possession unless the delivery is authorized under section 80110(b)(2) or (3) of this title;

(2) the carrier makes a delivery under section 80110(b)(2) or (3) of this title after being requested by or for a person having title to, or right to possession of, the goods not to make the delivery; or

(3) at the time of delivery under section 80110(b)(2) or (3) of this title, the carrier has information it is delivering the goods to a person not entitled to their possession.

(b) Effectiveness of request or information.—A request or information is effective under subsection (a)(2) or (3) of this section only if—

(1) an officer or agent of the carrier, whose actual or apparent authority includes acting on the request or information, has been given the request or information; and

(2) the officer or agent has had time, exercising reasonable diligence, to stop delivery of the goods.

(c) Failure to take and cancel bills.—Except as provided in subsection (d) of this section, if a common carrier delivers goods for which a negotiable bill of lading has been issued without taking and canceling the bill, the carrier is liable for damages for failure to deliver the goods to a person purchasing the bill for value in good faith whether the purchase was before or after delivery and even when delivery was made to the person entitled to the goods. The carrier also is liable under this paragraph if part of the goods are delivered without taking and canceling the bill or plainly noting on the bill that a partial delivery was made and generally describing the goods or the remaining goods kept by the carrier.

(d) Exceptions to liability.—A common carrier is not liable for failure to deliver goods to the consignee or owner of the goods or a holder of the bill if—

(1) a delivery described in subsection (c) of this section was compelled by legal process;

(2) the goods have been sold lawfully to satisfy the carrier's lien;

(3) the goods have not been claimed; or

(4) the goods are perishable or hazardous.

* * *

49 U.S.C. § 80113. Liability for nonreceipt, misdescription, and improper loading

(a) Liability for nonreceipt and misdescription.—Except as provided in this section, a common carrier issuing a bill of lading is liable for damages caused by nonreceipt by the carrier of any part of the goods by the date shown in the bill or by failure of the goods to correspond with the description contained in the bill. The carrier is liable to the owner of goods transported under a nonnegotiable bill (subject to the right of stoppage in transit) or to the holder of a negotiable bill if the owner or holder gave value in good faith relying on the description of the goods in the bill or on the shipment being made on the date shown in the bill.

(b) Nonliability of carriers.—A common carrier issuing a bill of lading is not liable under subsection (a) of this section—

(1) when the goods are loaded by the shipper;

(2) when the bill—

(A) describes the goods in terms of marks or labels, or in a statement about kind, quantity, or condition; or

(B) is qualified by "contents or condition of contents of packages unknown", "said to contain", "shipper's weight, load, and count", or words of the same meaning; and

(3) to the extent the carrier does not know whether any part of the goods were received or conform to the description.

(c) Liability for improper loading.—A common carrier issuing a bill of lading is not liable for damages caused by improper loading if—

(1) the shipper loads the goods; and

(2) the bill contains the words "shipper's weight, load, and count", or words of the same meaning indicating the shipper loaded the goods.

(d) Carrier's duty to determine kind, quantity, and number.—(1) When bulk freight is loaded by a shipper that makes available to the common carrier adequate facilities for weighing the freight, the carrier must determine the kind and quantity of the freight within a reasonable time after receiving the written request of the shipper to make the determination. In that situation, inserting the words "shipper's weight" or words of the same meaning in the bill of lading has no effect.

(2) When goods are loaded by a common carrier, the carrier must count the packages of goods, if package freight, and determine the kind and quantity, if bulk freight. In that situation, inserting in the bill of lading or in a notice, receipt, contract, rule, or tariff, the words "shipper's weight, load, and count" or words indicating that the shipper described and loaded the goods, has no effect except for freight concealed by packages.

DOCUMENT 19

FOREIGN INVESTMENT AND NATIONAL SECURITY ACT OF 2007

Amending Section 721 of the Defense Production Act of 1950 (50 U.S.C. App. 2170)

SECTION 1. SHORT TITLE; TABLE OF CONTENTS.

(a) Short Title—This Act may be cited as the 'Foreign Investment and National Security Act of 2007'.

(b) Table of Contents—* * *

SEC. 2. UNITED STATES SECURITY IMPROVEMENT AMENDMENTS; CLARIFICATION OF REVIEW AND INVESTIGATION PROCESS.

Section 721 of the Defense Production Act of 1950 (50 U.S.C. App. 2170) is amended by striking subsections (a) and (b) and inserting the following:

'(a) Definitions—For purposes of this section, the following definitions shall apply:

'(1) COMMITTEE; CHAIRPERSON—The terms 'Committee' and 'chairperson' mean the Committee on Foreign Investment in the United States and the chairperson thereof, respectively.

'(2) CONTROL—The term 'control' has the meaning given to such term in regulations which the Committee shall prescribe.

'(3) COVERED TRANSACTION—The term 'covered transaction' means any merger, acquisition, or takeover that is proposed or pending after August 23, 1988, by or with any foreign person which could result in foreign control of any person engaged in interstate commerce in the United States.

'(4) FOREIGN GOVERNMENT–CONTROLLED TRANSACTION—The term 'foreign government—controlled transaction' means any covered transaction that could result in the control of any person engaged in interstate commerce in the United States by a foreign government or an entity controlled by or acting on behalf of a foreign government.

'(5) CLARIFICATION—The term 'national security' shall be construed so as to include those issues relating to 'homeland security', including its application to critical infrastructure.

'(6) CRITICAL INFRASTRUCTURE—The term 'critical infrastructure' means, subject to rules issued under this section, systems and assets, whether physical or virtual, so vital to the United States that the incapacity or destruction of such systems or assets would have a debilitating impact on national security.

'(7) CRITICAL TECHNOLOGIES—The term 'critical technologies' means critical technology, critical components, or critical technology items essential to national defense, identified pursuant to this section, subject to regulations issued at the direction of the President, in accordance with subsection (h).

'(8) LEAD AGENCY—The term 'lead agency' means the agency, or agencies, designated as the lead agency or agencies pursuant to subsection (k)(5) for the review of a transaction.

'(b) National Security Reviews and Investigations—

'(1) NATIONAL SECURITY REVIEWS—

'(A) IN GENERAL—Upon receiving written notification under subparagraph (C) of any covered transaction, or pursuant to a unilateral notification initiated under subparagraph (D) with respect to any covered transaction, the President, acting through the Committee—

'(i) shall review the covered transaction to determine the effects of the transaction on the national security of the United States; and

'(ii) shall consider the factors specified in subsection (f) for such purpose, as appropriate.

'(B) CONTROL BY FOREIGN GOVERNMENT—If the Committee determines that the covered transaction is a foreign government—controlled transaction, the Committee shall conduct an investigation of the transaction under paragraph (2).

'(C) WRITTEN NOTICE—

'(i) IN GENERAL—Any party or parties to any covered transaction may initiate a review of the transaction under this paragraph by submitting a written notice of the transaction to the Chairperson of the Committee. * * *

'(D) UNILATERAL INITIATION OF REVIEW—Subject to subparagraph (F), the President or the Committee may initiate a review under subparagraph (A) of—

'(i) any covered transaction;

'(ii) any covered transaction that has previously been reviewed or investigated under this section, if any party to the transaction submitted false or misleading material information to the Committee in connection with the review or investigation or omitted material information, including material documents, from information submitted to the Committee; or

'(iii) any covered transaction that has previously been reviewed or investigated under this section, if—

'(I) any party to the transaction or the entity resulting from consummation of the transaction intentionally materially breaches a mitigation agreement or condition described in subsection (*l*)(1)(A);

'(II) such breach is certified to the Committee by the lead department or agency monitoring and enforcing such agreement or condition as an intentional material breach; and

'(III) the Committee determines that there are no other remedies or enforcement tools available to address such breach.

'(E) TIMING—Any review under this paragraph shall be completed before the end of the 30–day period beginning on the date of the acceptance of written notice under subparagraph (C) by the chairperson, or beginning on the date of the initiation of the review in accordance with subparagraph (D), as applicable.

'(F) LIMIT ON DELEGATION OF CERTAIN AUTHORITY—The authority of the Committee to initiate a review under subparagraph (D) may not be delegated to any person, other than the Deputy Secretary or an appropriate Under Secretary of the department or agency represented on the Committee.

'(2) NATIONAL SECURITY INVESTIGATIONS—

'(A) IN GENERAL—In each case described in subparagraph (B), the Committee shall immediately conduct an investigation of the effects of a covered transaction on the national security of the United States, and take any necessary actions in connection with the transaction to protect the national security of the United States.

'(B) APPLICABILITY—Subparagraph (A) shall apply in each case in which—

'(i) a review of a covered transaction under paragraph (1) results in a determination that—

'(I) the transaction threatens to impair the national security of the United States and that threat has not been mitigated during or prior to the review of a covered transaction under paragraph (1);

'(II) the transaction is a foreign government—controlled transaction; or

'(III) the transaction would result in control of any critical infrastructure of or within the United States by or on behalf of any foreign person, if the Committee determines that the transaction could impair national security, and that such impairment to national security has not been mitigated by assurances provided or renewed with the approval of the Committee, as described in subsection (*l*), during the review period under paragraph (1); or

'(ii) the lead agency recommends, and the Committee concurs, that an investigation be undertaken.

'(C) TIMING—Any investigation under subparagraph (A) shall be completed before the end of the 45-day period beginning on the date on which the investigation commenced.

'(D) EXCEPTION—

'(i) IN GENERAL—Notwithstanding subparagraph (B)(i), an investigation of a foreign government—controlled transaction described in subclause (II) of subparagraph (B)(i) or a transaction involving critical infrastructure described in subclause (III) of subparagraph (B)(i) shall not be required under this paragraph, if the Secretary of the Treasury and the head of the lead agency jointly determine, on the basis of the review of the transaction under paragraph (1), that the transaction will not impair the national security of the United States.

* * *

'(E) GUIDANCE ON CERTAIN TRANSACTIONS WITH NATIONAL SECURITY IMPLICATIONS—The Chairperson shall, not later than 180 days after the effective date of the Foreign Investment and National Security Act of 2007, publish in the Federal Register guidance on the types of transactions that the Committee has reviewed and that have presented national security considerations, including transactions that may constitute covered transactions that would result in control of critical infrastructure relating to United States national security by a foreign government or an entity controlled by or acting on behalf of a foreign government.

'(3) CERTIFICATIONS TO CONGRESS—

'(A) CERTIFIED NOTICE AT COMPLETION OF REVIEW—Upon completion of a review under subsection (b) that concludes action under this section, the chairperson and the head of the lead agency shall transmit a certified notice to the members of Congress. . . .

'(B) CERTIFIED REPORT AT COMPLETION OF INVESTIGATION—As soon as is practicable after completion of an investigation under subsection (b) that concludes action under this section, the chairperson and the head of the lead agency shall transmit to the members of Congress. . . .

* * *

'(4) ANALYSIS BY DIRECTOR OF NATIONAL INTELLIGENCE—

'(A) IN GENERAL—The Director of National Intelligence shall expeditiously carry out a thorough analysis of any threat to the national security of the United States posed by any covered transaction. The Director of National Intelligence shall also seek and incorporate the views of all affected or appropriate intelligence agencies with respect to the transaction.

'(B) TIMING—The analysis required under subparagraph (A) shall be provided by the Director of National Intelligence to the Committee not later than 20 days after the date on which notice of the transaction is accepted by the Committee. . . .

'(C) INTERACTION WITH INTELLIGENCE COMMUNITY—The Director of National Intelligence shall ensure that the intelligence community remains engaged in the collection, analysis, and dissemination to the Committee of any additional relevant information that may become available during the course of any investigation conducted under subsection (b) with respect to a transaction.

'(D) INDEPENDENT ROLE OF DIRECTOR—The Director of National Intelligence shall be a nonvoting, ex officio member of the Committee, and shall be provided with all notices received by the Committee . . . regarding covered transactions, but shall serve no policy role on the Committee, other than to provide analysis under subparagraphs (A) and (C) in connection with a covered transaction.

* * *

SEC. 3. STATUTORY ESTABLISHMENT OF THE COMMITTEE ON FOREIGN INVESTMENT IN THE UNITED STATES.

'(1) ESTABLISHMENT—The Committee on Foreign Investment in the United States, established pursuant to Executive Order No. 11858, shall be a multi agency committee to carry out this section and such other assignments as the President may designate.

'(2) MEMBERSHIP—The Committee shall be comprised of the following members or the designee of any such member:

'(A) The Secretary of the Treasury.

'(B) The Secretary of Homeland Security.

'(C) The Secretary of Commerce.

'(D) The Secretary of Defense.

'(E) The Secretary of State.

'(F) The Attorney General of the United States.

'(G) The Secretary of Energy.

'(H) The Secretary of Labor (nonvoting, ex officio).

'(I) The Director of National Intelligence (nonvoting, ex officio).

'(J) The heads of any other executive department, agency, or office, as the President determines appropriate, generally or on a case-by-case basis.

'(3) CHAIRPERSON—The Secretary of the Treasury shall serve as the chairperson of the Committee.

'(4) ASSISTANT SECRETARY FOR THE DEPARTMENT OF THE TREASURY—There shall be established an additional position of Assistant Secretary of the Treasury, who shall be appointed by the President, by and with the advice and consent of the Senate. The Assistant Secretary appointed under this paragraph shall report directly to the Undersecretary of the Treasury for International Affairs. The duties of the Assistant Secretary shall include duties related to the Committee on Foreign Investment in the United States, as delegated by the Secretary of the Treasury under this section.

'(5) DESIGNATION OF LEAD AGENCY—The Secretary of the Treasury shall designate, as appropriate, a member or members of the Committee to be the lead agency or agencies on behalf of the Committee—

'(A) for each covered transaction, and for negotiating any mitigation agreements or other conditions necessary to protect national security; and

'(B) for all matters related to the monitoring of the completed transaction, to ensure compliance with such agreements or conditions and with this section.

'(6) OTHER MEMBERS—The chairperson shall consult with the heads of such other Federal departments, agencies, and independent establishments in any review or investigation under subsection (a), as the chairperson determines to be appropriate, on the basis of the facts and circumstances of the covered transaction under review or investigation (or the designee of any such department or agency head).

* * *

SEC. 4. ADDITIONAL FACTORS FOR CONSIDERATION.

* * * '(6) the potential national security—related effects on United States critical infrastructure, including major energy assets;

'(7) the potential national security-related effects on United States critical technologies;

'(8) whether the covered transaction is a foreign government—controlled transaction, as determined under subsection (b)(1)(B);

* * *

'(10) the long-term projection of United States requirements for sources of energy and other critical resources and material;* * *

SEC. 5. MITIGATION, TRACKING, AND POSTCONSUMMATION MONITORING AND ENFORCEMENT.

'* * *(1) MITIGATION—

'(A) IN GENERAL—The Committee or a lead agency may, on behalf of the Committee, negotiate, enter into or impose, and enforce any agreement or condition with any party to the covered transaction in order to mitigate any threat to the national security of the United States that arises as a result of the covered transaction.

'(B) RISK-BASED ANALYSIS REQUIRED—Any agreement entered into or condition imposed under subparagraph (A) shall be based on a risk-based analysis, conducted by the Committee, of the threat to national security of the covered transaction.

* * *

SEC. 6. ACTION BY THE PRESIDENT.

* * *

'(1) IN GENERAL—Subject to paragraph (4), the President may take such action for such time as the President considers appropriate to suspend or prohibit any covered transaction that threatens to impair the national security of the United States.

'(2) ANNOUNCEMENT BY THE PRESIDENT—The President shall announce the decision on whether or not to take action pursuant to paragraph (1) not later than 15 days after the date on which an investigation described in subsection (b) is completed. '(3) ENFORCEMENT—The President may direct the Attorney General of the United States to seek appropriate relief, including divestment relief, in the district courts of the United States, in order to implement and enforce this subsection.

'(4) FINDINGS OF THE PRESIDENT—The President may exercise the authority conferred by paragraph (1), only if the President finds that—

'(A) there is credible evidence that leads the President to believe that the foreign interest exercising control might take action that threatens to impair the national security; and

'(B) provisions of law, other than this section and the International Emergency Economic Powers Act, do not, in the judgment of the President, provide adequate and appropriate authority for the President to protect the national security in the matter before the President.

'(5) FACTORS TO BE CONSIDERED—For purposes of determining whether to take action under paragraph (1), the President shall consider, among other factors each of the factors described in subsection (f), as appropriate.

'(e) Actions and Findings Nonreviewable—The actions of the President under paragraph (1) of subsection (d) and the findings of the President under paragraph (4) of subsection (d) shall not be subject to judicial review.'.

SEC. 7. INCREASED OVERSIGHT BY CONGRESS.

(g) Additional Information to Congress; Confidentiality—

'(1) BRIEFING REQUIREMENT ON REQUEST—The Committee shall, upon request from any Member of Congress specified in subsection (b)(3)(C)(iii), provide briefings on a covered transaction for which all action has concluded under this section, or on compliance with a mitigation agreement or condition imposed with respect to such transaction, on a classified basis, if deemed necessary by the sensitivity of the information. Briefings under this paragraph may be provided to the congressional staff of such a Member of Congress having appropriate security clearance.

'(2) APPLICATION OF CONFIDENTIALITY PROVISIONS—

'(A) IN GENERAL—The disclosure of information under this subsection shall be consistent with the requirements of subsection (c). Members of Congress and staff of either House of Congress or any committee of Congress, shall be subject to the same limitations on disclosure of information as are applicable under subsection (c).

'(B) PROPRIETARY INFORMATION—Proprietary information which can be associated with a particular party to a covered transaction shall be furnished in accordance with subparagraph (A) only to a committee of Congress, and only when the committee provides assurances of confidentiality, unless such party otherwise consents in writing to such disclosure.'.

* * * '(m) Annual Report to Congress—

(1) IN GENERAL—The chairperson shall transmit a report to the chairman and ranking member of the committee of jurisdiction in the Senate and the House of Representatives, before July 31 of each year on all of the reviews and investigations of covered transactions completed . . . during the 12–month period covered by the report.

* * *

(3) CONTENTS OF REPORT RELATING TO CRITICAL TECHNOLOGIES—

'(A) IN GENERAL—In order to assist Congress in its oversight responsibilities with respect to this section, the President and such agencies as the President shall designate shall include in the annual report submitted under paragraph (1)—

'(i) an evaluation of whether there is credible evidence of a coordinated strategy by 1 or more countries or companies to acquire United States companies involved in research, development, or production of critical technologies for which the United States is a leading producer; and

'(ii) an evaluation of whether there are industrial espionage activities directed or directly assisted by foreign governments against private United States companies aimed at obtaining commercial secrets related to critical technologies.

'(B) RELEASE OF UNCLASSIFIED STUDY—All appropriate portions of the annual report under paragraph (1) may be classified. An unclassified version of the report, as appropriate, consistent with safeguarding national security and privacy, shall be made available to the public.'.

(c) Study and Report—

(1) STUDY REQUIRED—Before the end of the 120–day period beginning on the date of enactment of this Act and annually thereafter, the Secretary of the Treasury, in consultation with the Secretary of State and the Secretary of Commerce, shall conduct a study on foreign direct investments in the United States, especially investments in critical infrastructure and industries affecting national security, by—

(A) foreign governments, entities controlled by or acting on behalf of a foreign government, or persons of foreign countries which comply with any boycott of Israel; or

(B) foreign governments, entities controlled by or acting on behalf of a foreign government, or persons of foreign countries which do not ban organizations designated by the Secretary of State as foreign terrorist organizations.

* * *

DOCUMENT 20

UNIFORM COMMERCIAL CODE (SELECTED PROVISIONS)

Table of Contents

Section

ARTICLE 1. GENERAL PROVISIONS

§ 1–102. Purposes; Rules of Construction; Variation by Agreement.

(1) This Act shall be liberally construed and applied to promote its underlying purposes and policies.

(2) Underlying purposes and policies of this Act are

(a) to simplify, clarify and modernize the law governing commercial transactions;

(b) to permit the continued expansion of commercial practices through custom, usage and agreement of the parties;

(c) to make uniform the law among the various jurisdictions.

(3) The effect of provisions of this Act may be varied by agreement, except as otherwise provided in this Act and except that the obligations of good faith, diligence, reasonableness and care prescribed by this Act may not be disclaimed by agreement but the parties may by agreement determine the standards by which the performance of such obligations is to be measured if such standards are not manifestly unreasonable.

(4) The presence in certain provisions of this Act of the words "unless otherwise agreed" or words of similar import does not imply that the effect of other provisions may not be varied by agreement under subsection (3).

(5) In this Act unless the context otherwise requires

(a) words in the singular number include the plural, and in the plural include the singular;

(b) words of the masculine gender include the feminine and the neuter, and when the sense so indicates words of the neuter gender may refer to any gender.

Official Comment

1. Subsections (1) and (2) are intended to make it clear that:

This Act is drawn to provide flexibility so that, since it is intended to be a semi-permanent piece of legislation, it will provide its own machinery for expansion of commercial practices. It is intended to make it possible for the law embodied in this Act to be developed by the courts in the light of unforeseen and new circumstances and practices. However, the proper construction of the Act requires that its interpretation and application be limited to its reason.

* * *

The Act should be construed in accordance with its underlying purposes and policies. The text of each section should be read in the light of the purpose and policy of the rule or principle in question, as also of the Act as a whole, and the application of the language should be construed narrowly or broadly, as the case may be, in conformity with the purposes and policies involved.

* * *

§ 1–105. Territorial Application of the Act; Parties' Power to Choose Applicable Law.

(1) Except as provided hereafter in this section, when a transaction bears a reasonable relation to this state and also to another state or nation the parties may agree that the law either of this state or of such other state or nation shall govern their rights and duties. Failing such agreement this Act applies to transactions bearing an appropriate relation to this state.

* * *

Official Comment

1. Subsection (1) states affirmatively the right of the parties to a multi-state transaction or a transaction involving foreign trade to choose their own law. That right is subject to the firm rules stated in the five sections listed in subsection (2), and is limited to jurisdictions to which the transaction bears a "reasonable relation." In general, the test of "reasonable relation" is similar to that laid down by the Supreme Court in Seeman v. Philadelphia Warehouse Co., 274 U.S. 403, 47 S.Ct. 626, 71 L.Ed. 1123 (1927). Ordinarily the law chosen must be that of a jurisdiction where a significant enough portion of the making or performance of the contract is to occur or occurs. But an agreement as to choice of law may sometimes take effect as a shorthand expression of the intent of the parties as to matters governed by their agreement, even though the transaction has no significant contact with the jurisdiction chosen.

2. Where there is no agreement as to the governing law, the Act is applicable to any transaction having an "appropriate" relation to any state which enacts it. Of course, the Act applies to any transaction which takes place in its entirety in a state which has enacted the Act. But the mere fact that suit is brought in a state does not make it appropriate to apply the

substantive law of that state. Cases where a relation to the enacting state is not "appropriate" include, for example, those where the parties have clearly contracted on the basis of some other law, as where the law of the place of contracting and the law of the place of contemplated performance are the same and are contrary to the law under the Code.

3. Where a transaction has significant contacts with a state which has enacted the Act and also with other jurisdictions, the question what relation is "appropriate" is left to judicial decision. In deciding that question, the court is not strictly bound by precedents established in other contexts. Thus a conflict-of-laws decision refusing to apply a purely local statute or rule of law to a particular multi-state transaction may not be valid precedent for refusal to apply the Code in an analogous situation. Application of the Code in such circumstances may be justified by its comprehensiveness, by the policy of uniformity, and by the fact that it is in large part a reformulation and restatement of the law merchant and of the understanding of a business community which transcends state and even national boundaries. Compare Global Commerce Corp. v. Clark-Babbitt Industries, Inc., 239 F.2d 716, 719 (2d Cir. 1956). In particular, where a transaction is governed in large part by the Code, application of another law to some detail of performance because of an accident of geography may violate the commercial understanding of the parties.

4. The Act does not attempt to prescribe choice-of-law rules for states which do not enact it, but this section does not prevent application of the Act in a court of such a state. Common-law choice of law often rests on policies of giving effect to agreements and of uniformity of result regardless of where suit is brought. To the extent that such policies prevail, the relevant considerations are similar in such a court to those outlined above.

5. Subsection (2) spells out essential limitations on the parties' right to choose the applicable law. Especially in Article 9 parties taking a security interest or asked to extend credit which may be subject to a security interest must have sure ways to find out whether and where to file and where to look for possible existing filings.

6. Section 9–103 should be consulted as to the rules for perfection of security interests and the effects of perfection and nonperfection.

* * *

§ 1–201. General Definitions.

Subject to additional definitions contained in the subsequent Articles of this Act which are applicable to specific Articles or Parts thereof, and unless the context otherwise requires, in this Act:

* * *

(39) "Signed" includes any symbol executed or adopted by a party with present intention to authenticate a writing.

* * *

(46) "Written" or "writing" includes printing, typewriting or any other intentional reduction to tangible form.

Official Comment

* * *

39. "Signed". New. The inclusion of authentication in the definition of "signed" is to make clear that as the term is used in this Act a complete signature is not necessary. Authentication may be printed, stamped or written; it may be by initials or by thumbprint. It may be on any part of the document and in appropriate cases may be found in a billhead or letterhead. No catalog of possible authentications can be complete and the court must use common sense and commercial experience in passing upon these matters. The question always is whether the symbol was executed or adopted by the party with present intention to authenticate the writing.

* * *

46. "Written" or "writing". This is a broadening of the definition contained in Section 191 of the Uniform Negotiable Instruments Law.

* * *

§ 1–205. Course of Dealing and Usage of Trade.

(1) A course of dealing is a sequence of previous conduct between the parties to a particular transaction which is fairly to be regarded as establishing a common basis of understanding for interpreting their expressions and other conduct.

(2) A usage of trade is any practice or method of dealing having such regularity of observance in a place, vocation or trade as to justify an expectation that it will be observed with respect to the transaction in question. The existence and scope of such a usage are to be proved as facts. If it is established that such a usage is embodied in a written trade code or similar writing the interpretation of the writing is for the court.

(3) A course of dealing between parties and any usage of trade in the vocation or trade in which they are engaged or of which they are or should be aware give particular meaning to and supplement or qualify terms of an agreement.

(4) The express terms of an agreement and an applicable course of dealing or usage of trade shall be construed wherever reasonable as consistent with each other; but when such construction is unreasonable express terms control both course of dealing and usage of trade and course of dealing controls usage of trade.

(5) An applicable usage of trade in the place where any part of performance is to occur shall be used in interpreting the agreement as to that part of the performance.

* * *

Official Comment

1. This Act rejects both the "lay-dictionary" and the "conveyancer's" reading of a commercial agreement. Instead the meaning of the agreement of the parties is to be determined by the language used by them and by their

action, read and interpreted in the light of commercial practices and other surrounding circumstances. The measure and background for interpretation are set by the commercial context, which may explain and supplement even the language of a formal or final writing.

* * *

4. This Act deals with "usage of trade" as a factor in reaching the commercial meaning of the agreement which the parties have made. The language used is to be interpreted as meaning what it may fairly be expected to mean to parties involved in the particular commercial transaction in a given locality or in a given vocation or trade. By adopting in this context the term "usage of trade" this Act expresses its intent to reject those cases which see evidence of "custom" as representing an effort to displace or negate "established rules of law". A distinction is to be drawn between mandatory rules of law such as the Statute of Frauds provisions of Article 2 on Sales whose very office is to control and restrict the actions of the parties, and which cannot be abrogated by agreement, or by a usage of trade, and those rules of law (such as those in Part 3 of Article 2 on Sales) which fill in points which the parties have not considered and in fact agreed upon. The latter rules hold "unless otherwise agreed" but yield to the contrary agreement of the parties. Part of the agreement of the parties to which such rules yield is to be sought for in the usages of trade which furnish the background and give particular meaning to the language used, and are the framework of common understanding controlling any general rules of law which hold only when there is no such understanding.

5. A usage of trade under subsection (2) must have the "regularity of observance" specified. The ancient English tests for "custom" are abandoned in this connection. Therefore, it is not required that a usage of trade be "ancient or immemorial", "universal" or the like. Under the requirement of subsection (2) full recognition is thus available for new usages and for usages currently observed by the great majority of decent dealers, even though dissidents ready to cut corners do not agree. There is room also for proper recognition of usage agreed upon by merchants in trade codes.

6. The policy of this Act controlling explicit unconscionable contracts and clauses (Sections 1–203, 2–302) applies to implicit clauses which rest on usage of trade and carries forward the policy underlying the ancient requirement that a custom or usage must be "reasonable". However, the emphasis is shifted. The very fact of commercial acceptance makes out a prima facie case that the usage is reasonable, and the burden is no longer on the usage to establish itself as being reasonable. But the anciently established policing of usage by the courts is continued to the extent necessary to cope with the situation arising if an unconscionable or dishonest practice should become standard.

7. Subsection (3), giving the prescribed effect to usages of which the parties "are or should be aware", reinforces the provision of subsection (2) requiring not universality but only the described "regularity of observance" of the practice or method. This subsection also reinforces the point of subsec-

tion (2) that such usages may be either general to trade or particular to a special branch of trade.

* * *

9. In cases of a well established line of usage varying from the general rules of this Act where the precise amount of the variation has not been worked out into a single standard, the party relying on the usage is entitled, in any event, to the minimum variation demonstrated. The whole is not to be disregarded because no particular line of detail has been established. In case a dominant pattern has been fairly evidenced, the party relying on the usage is entitled under this section to go to the trier of fact on the question of whether such dominant pattern has been incorporated into the agreement.

* * *

ARTICLE 2. SALES

§ 2–201. Formal Requirements; Statute of Frauds.

(1) Except as otherwise provided in this section a contract for the sale of goods for the price of $500 or more is not enforceable by way of action or defense unless there is some writing sufficient to indicate that a contract for sale has been made between the parties and signed by the party against whom enforcement is sought or by his authorized agent or broker. A writing is not insufficient because it omits or incorrectly states a term agreed upon but the contract is not enforceable under this paragraph beyond the quantity of goods shown in such writing.

(2) Between merchants if within a reasonable time a writing in confirmation of the contract and sufficient against the sender is received and the party receiving it has reason to know its contents, it satisfies the requirements of subsection (1) against such party unless written notice of objection to its contents is given within 10 days after it is received.

(3) A contract which does not satisfy the requirements of subsection (1) but which is valid in other respects is enforceable

(a) if the goods are to be specially manufactured for the buyer and are not suitable for sale to others in the ordinary course of the seller's business and the seller, before notice of repudiation is received and under circumstances which reasonably indicate that the goods are for the buyer, has made either a substantial beginning of their manufacture or commitments for their procurement; or

(b) if the party against whom enforcement is sought admits in his pleading, testimony or otherwise in court that a contract for sale was made, but the contract is not enforceable under this provision beyond the quantity of goods admitted; or

(c) with respect to goods for which payment has been made and accepted or which have been received and accepted (Sec. 2–606).

Official Comment

1. The required writing need not contain all the material terms of the contract and such material terms as are stated need not be precisely stated. All that is required is that the writing afford a basis for believing that the offered oral evidence rests on a real transaction. It may be written in lead pencil on a scratch pad. It need not indicate which party is the buyer and which the seller. The only term which must appear is the quantity term which need not be accurately stated but recovery is limited to the amount stated. The price, time and place of payment or delivery, the general quality of the goods, or any particular warranties may all be omitted.

Special emphasis must be placed on the permissibility of omitting the price term in view of the insistence of some courts on the express inclusion of this term even where the parties have contracted on the basis of a published price list. In many valid contracts for sale the parties do not mention the price in express terms, the buyer being bound to pay and the seller to accept a reasonable price which the trier of the fact may well be trusted to determine. Again, frequently the price is not mentioned since the parties have based their agreement on a price list or catalogue known to both of them and this list serves as an efficient safeguard against perjury. Finally, "market" prices and valuations that are current in the vicinity constitute a similar check. Thus if the price is not stated in the memorandum it can normally be supplied without danger of fraud. Of course if the "price" consists of goods rather than money the quantity of goods must be stated.

Only three definite and invariable requirements as to the memorandum are made by this subsection. First, it must evidence a contract for the sale of goods; second, it must be "signed", a word which includes any authentication which identifies the party to be charged; and third, it must specify a quantity.

2. "Partial performance" as a substitute for the required memorandum can validate the contract only for the goods which have been accepted or for which payment has been made and accepted.

* * *

3. Between merchants, failure to answer a written confirmation of a contract within ten days of receipt is tantamount to a writing under subsection (2) and is sufficient against both parties under subsection (1). The only effect, however, is to take away from the party who fails to answer the defense of the Statute of Frauds; the burden of persuading the trier of fact that a contract was in fact made orally prior to the written confirmation is unaffected. Compare the effect of a failure to reply under Section 2–207.

4. Failure to satisfy the requirements of this section does not render the contract void for all purposes, but merely prevents it from being judicially enforced in favor of a party to the contract. For example, a buyer who takes possession of goods as provided in an oral contract which the seller has not meanwhile repudiated, is not a trespasser. Nor would the Statute of Frauds provisions of this section be a defense to a third person who wrongfully induces a party to refuse to perform an oral contract, even though the injured party cannot maintain an action for damages against the party so refusing to perform.

5. The requirement of "signing" is discussed in the comment to Section 1–201.

6. It is not necessary that the writing be delivered to anybody. It need not be signed or authenticated by both parties but it is, of course, not sufficient against one who has not signed it. Prior to a dispute no one can determine which party's signing of the memorandum may be necessary but from the time of contracting each party should be aware that to him it is signing by the other which is important.

* * *

§ 2–207. Additional Terms in Acceptance or Confirmation.

(1) A definite and seasonable expression of acceptance or a written confirmation which is sent within a reasonable time operates as an acceptance even though it states terms additional to or different from those offered or agreed upon, unless acceptance is expressly made conditional on assent to the additional or different terms.

(2) The additional terms are to be construed as proposals for addition to the contract. Between merchants such terms become part of the contract unless:

(a) the offer expressly limits acceptance to the terms of the offer;

(b) they materially alter it; or

(c) notification of objection to them has already been given or is given within a reasonable time after notice of them is received.

(3) Conduct by both parties which recognizes the existence of a contract is sufficient to establish a contract for sale although the writings of the parties do not otherwise establish a contract. In such case the terms of the particular contract consist of those terms on which the writings of the parties agree, together with any supplementary terms incorporated under any other provisions of this Act.

Official Comment

1. This section is intended to deal with two typical situations. The one is the written confirmation, where an agreement has been reached either orally or by informal correspondence between the parties and is followed by one or both of the parties sending formal memoranda embodying the terms so far as agreed upon and adding terms not discussed. The other situation is offer and acceptance, in which a wire or letter expressed and intended as an acceptance or the closing of an agreement adds further minor suggestions or proposals such as "ship by Tuesday," "rush," "ship draft against bill of lading inspection allowed," or the like. A frequent example of the second situation is the exchange of printed purchase order and acceptance (sometimes called "acknowledgment") forms. Because the forms are oriented to the thinking of the respective drafting parties, the terms contained in them often do not correspond. Often the seller's form contains terms different from or additional to those set forth in the buyer's form. Nevertheless, the parties proceed with the transaction. [Comment 1 was amended in 1966.]

2. Under this Article a proposed deal which in commercial understanding has in fact been closed is recognized as a contract. Therefore, any additional matter contained in the confirmation or in the acceptance falls within subsection (2) and must be regarded as a proposal for an added term unless the acceptance is made conditional on the acceptance of the additional or different terms. [Comment 2 was amended in 1966.]

3. Whether or not additional or different terms will become part of the agreement depends upon the provisions of subsection (2). If they are such as materially to alter the original bargain, they will not be included unless expressly agreed to by the other party. If, however, they are terms which would not so change the bargain they will be incorporated unless notice of objection to them has already been given or is given within a reasonable time.

4. Examples of typical clauses which would normally "materially alter" the contract and so result in surprise or hardship if incorporated without express awareness by the other party are: a clause negating such standard warranties as that of merchantability or fitness for a particular purpose in circumstances in which either warranty normally attaches; a clause requiring a guaranty of 90% or 100% deliveries in a case such as a contract by cannery, where the usage of the trade allows greater quantity leeways; a clause reserving to the seller the power to cancel upon the buyer's failure to meet any invoice when due; a clause requiring that complaints be made in a time materially shorter than customary or reasonable.

5. Examples of clauses which involve no element of unreasonable surprise and which therefore are to be incorporated in the contract unless notice of objection is seasonably given are: a clause setting forth and perhaps enlarging slightly upon the seller's exemption due to supervening causes beyond his control, similar to those covered by the provision of this Article on merchant's excuse by failure of presupposed conditions or a clause fixing in advance any reasonable formula of proration under such circumstances; a clause fixing a reasonable time for complaints within customary limits, or in the case of a purchase for sub-sale, providing for inspection by the sub-purchaser; a clause providing for interest on overdue invoices or fixing the seller's standard credit terms where they are within the range of trade practice and do not limit any credit bargained for; a clause limiting the right of rejection for defects which fall within the customary trade tolerances for acceptance "with adjustment" or otherwise limiting remedy in a reasonable manner (see Sections 2–718 and 2–719).

6. If no answer is received within a reasonable time after additional terms are proposed, it is both fair and commercially sound to assume that their inclusion has been assented to. Where clauses on confirming forms sent by both parties conflict each party must be assumed to object to a clause of the other conflicting with one on the confirmation sent by himself. As a result the requirement that there be notice of objection which is found in subsection (2) is satisfied and the conflicting terms do not become a part of the contract. The contract then consists of the terms originally expressly agreed to, terms on which the confirmations agree, and terms supplied by this Act, including subsection (2). The written confirmation is also subject to Section 2–201. Under that section a failure to respond permits enforcement

of a prior oral agreement; under this section a failure to respond permits additional terms to become part of the agreement. [Comment 6 was amended in 1966.]

7. In many cases, as where goods are shipped, accepted and paid for before any dispute arises, there is no question whether a contract has been made. In such cases, where the writings of the parties do not establish a contract, it is not necessary to determine which act or document constituted the offer and which the acceptance. See Section 2–204. The only question is what terms are included in the contract, and subsection (3) furnishes the governing rule. [Comment 7 was added in 1966.]

* * *

§ 2–305. Open Price Term.

(1) The parties if they so intend can conclude a contract for sale even though the price is not settled. In such a case the price is a reasonable price at the time for delivery if

(a) nothing is said as to price; or

(b) the price is left to be agreed by the parties and they fail to agree; or

(c) the price is to be fixed in terms of some agreed market or other standard as set or recorded by a third person or agency and it is not so set or recorded.

(2) A price to be fixed by the seller or by the buyer means a price for him to fix in good faith.

(3) When a price left to be fixed otherwise than by agreement of the parties fails to be fixed through fault of one party the other may at his option treat the contract as cancelled or himself fix a reasonable price.

(4) Where, however, the parties intend not to be bound unless the price be fixed or agreed and it is not fixed or agreed there is no contract. In such a case the buyer must return any goods already received or if unable so to do must pay their reasonable value at the time of delivery and the seller must return any portion of the price paid on account.

Official Comment

1. This section applies when the price term is left open on the making of an agreement which is nevertheless intended by the parties to be a binding agreement. This Article rejects in these instances the formula that "an agreement to agree is unenforceable" if the case falls within subsection (1) of this section, and rejects also defeating such agreements on the ground of "indefiniteness". Instead this Article recognizes the dominant intention of the parties to have the deal continue to be binding upon both. As to future performance, since this Article recognizes remedies such as cover (Section 2–712), resale (Section 2–706) and specific performance (Section 2–716) which go beyond any mere arithmetic as between contract price and market price, there is usually a "reasonably certain basis for granting an appropriate remedy for breach" so that the contract need not fail for indefiniteness.

2. Under some circumstances the postponement of agreement on price will mean that no deal has really been concluded, and this is made express in the preamble of subsection (1) ("The parties *if they so intend*") and in subsection (4). Whether or not this is so is, in most cases, a question to be determined by the trier of fact.

3. Subsection (2), dealing with the situation where the price is to be fixed by one party rejects the uncommercial idea that an agreement that the seller may fix the price means that he may fix any price he may wish by the express qualification that the price so fixed must be fixed in good faith. Good faith includes observance of reasonable commercial standards of fair dealing in the trade if the party is a merchant. (Section 2–103). But in the normal case a "posted price" or a future seller's or buyer's "given price," "price in effect," "market price," or the like satisfies the good faith requirement.

* * *

§ 2–306. Output, Requirements and Exclusive Dealings.

(1) A term which measures the quantity by the output of the seller or the requirements of the buyer means such actual output or requirements as may occur in good faith, except that no quantity unreasonably disproportionate to any stated estimate or in the absence of a stated estimate to any normal or otherwise comparable prior output or requirements may be tendered or demanded.

(2) A lawful agreement by either the seller or the buyer for exclusive dealing in the kind of goods concerned imposes unless otherwise agreed an obligation by the seller to use best efforts to supply the goods and by the buyer to use best efforts to promote their sale.

Official Comment

1. Subsection (1) of this section, in regard to output and requirements, applies to this specific problem the general approach of this Act which requires the reading of commercial background and intent into the language of any agreement and demands good faith in the performance of that agreement. It applies to such contracts of nonproducing establishments such as dealers or distributors as well as to manufacturing concerns.

2. Under this Article, a contract for output or requirements is not too indefinite since it is held to mean the actual good faith output or requirements of the particular party. Nor does such a contract lack mutuality of obligation since, under this section, the party who will determine quantity is required to operate his plant or conduct his business in good faith and according to commercial standards of fair dealing in the trade so that his output or requirements will approximate a reasonably foreseeable figure. Reasonable elasticity in the requirements is expressly envisaged by this section and good faith variations from prior requirements are permitted even when the variation may be such as to result in discontinuance. A shut-down by a requirements buyer for lack of orders might be permissible when a shut-down merely to curtail losses would not. The essential test is whether the party is acting in good faith. Similarly, a sudden expansion of the plant by which requirements are to be measured would not be included within the

scope of the contract as made but normal expansion undertaken in good faith would be within the scope of this section. One of the factors in an expansion situation would be whether the market price had risen greatly in a case in which the requirements contract contained a fixed price. Reasonable variation of an extreme sort is exemplified in Southwest Natural Gas Co. v. Oklahoma Portland Cement Co., 102 F.2d 630 (C.C.A.10, 1939). This Article takes no position as to whether a requirements contract is a provable claim in bankruptcy.

3. If an estimate of output or requirements is included in the agreement, no quantity unreasonably disproportionate to it may be tendered or demanded. Any minimum or maximum set by the agreement shows a clear limit on the intended elasticity. In similar fashion, the agreed estimate is to be regarded as a center around which the parties intend the variation to occur.

* * *

5. Subsection (2), on exclusive dealing, makes explicit the commercial rule embodied in this Act under which the parties to such contracts are held to have impliedly, even when not expressly, bound themselves to use reasonable diligence as well as good faith in their performance of the contract. Under such contracts the exclusive agent is required, although no express commitment has been made, to use reasonable effort and due diligence in the expansion of the market or the promotion of the product, as the case may be. The principal is expected under such a contract to refrain from supplying any other dealer or agent within the exclusive territory. An exclusive dealing agreement brings into play all of the good faith aspects of the output and requirement problems of subsection (1). It also raises questions of insecurity and right to adequate assurance under this Article.

* * *

§ 2–314. Implied Warranty: Merchantability; Usage of Trade.

(1) Unless excluded or modified (Section 2–316), a warranty that the goods shall be merchantable is implied in a contract for their sale if the seller is a merchant with respect to goods of that kind. Under this section the serving for value of food or drink to be consumed either on the premises or elsewhere is a sale.

(2) Goods to be merchantable must be at least such as

(a) pass without objection in the trade under the contract description; and

(b) in the case of fungible goods, are of fair average quality within the description; and

(c) are fit for the ordinary purposes for which such goods are used; and

(d) run, within the variations permitted by the agreement, of even kind, quality and quantity within each unit and among all units involved; and

(e) are adequately contained, packaged, and labeled as the agreement may require; and

(f) conform to the promise or affirmations of fact made on the container or label if any.

(3) Unless excluded or modified (Section 2–316) other implied warranties may arise from course of dealing or usage of trade.

Official Comment

* * *

3. A specific designation of goods by the buyer does not exclude the seller's obligation that they be fit for the general purposes appropriate to such goods. A contract for the sale of second-hand goods, however, involves only such obligation as is appropriate to such goods for that is their contract description. A person making an isolated sale of goods is not a "merchant" within the meaning of the full scope of this section and, thus, no warranty of merchantability would apply. His knowledge of any defects not apparent on inspection would, however, without need for express agreement and in keeping with the underlying reason of the present section and the provisions on good faith, impose an obligation that known material but hidden defects be fully disclosed.

* * *

8. Fitness for the ordinary purposes for which goods of the type are used is a fundamental concept of the present section and is covered in paragraph (c). As stated above, merchantability is also a part of the obligation owing to the purchaser for use. Correspondingly, protection, under this aspect of the warranty, of the person buying for resale to the ultimate consumer is equally necessary, and merchantable goods must therefore be "honestly" resalable in the normal course of business because they are what they purport to be.

* * *

11. Exclusion or modification of the warranty of merchantability, or of any part of it, is dealt with in the section to which the text of the present section makes explicit precautionary references. That section must be read with particular reference to its subsection (4) on limitation of remedies. The warranty of merchantability, wherever it is normal, is so commonly taken for granted that its exclusion from the contract is a matter threatening surprise and therefore requiring special precaution.

12. Subsection (3) is to make explicit that usage of trade and course of dealing can create warranties and that they are implied rather than express warranties and thus subject to exclusion or modification under Section 2–316. A typical instance would be the obligation to provide pedigree papers to evidence conformity of the animal to the contract in the case of a pedigreed dog or blooded bull.

§ 2–315. Implied Warranty: Fitness for Particular Purpose.

Where the seller at the time of contracting has reason to know any particular purpose for which the goods are required and that the buyer is relying on the seller's skill or judgment to select or furnish suitable goods, there is unless excluded or modified under the next section an implied warranty that the goods shall be fit for such purpose.

Official Comment

1. Whether or not this warranty arises in any individual case is basically a question of fact to be determined by the circumstances of the contracting. Under this section the buyer need not bring home to the seller actual knowledge of the particular purpose for which the goods are intended or of his reliance on the seller's skill and judgment, if the circumstances are such that the seller has reason to realize the purpose intended or that the reliance exists. The buyer, of course, must actually be relying on the seller.

2. A "particular purpose" differs from the ordinary purpose for which the goods are used in that it envisages a specific use by the buyer which is peculiar to the nature of his business whereas the ordinary purposes for which goods are used are those envisaged in the concept of merchantability and go to uses which are customarily made of the goods in question. For example, shoes are generally used for the purpose of walking upon ordinary ground, but a seller may know that a particular pair was selected to be used for climbing mountains.

A contract may of course include both a warranty of merchantability and one of fitness for a particular purpose.

The provisions of this Article on the cumulation and conflict of express and implied warranties must be considered on the question of inconsistency between or among warranties. In such a case any question of fact as to which warranty was intended by the parties to apply must be resolved in favor of the warranty of fitness for particular purpose as against all other warranties except where the buyer has taken upon himself the responsibility of furnishing the technical specifications.

3. In connection with the warranty of fitness for a particular purpose the provisions of this Article on the allocation or division of risks are particularly applicable in any transaction in which the purpose for which the goods are to be used combines requirements both as to the quality of the goods themselves and compliance with certain laws or regulations. How the risks are divided is a question of fact to be determined, where not expressly contained in the agreement, from the circumstances of contracting, usage of trade, course of performance and the like, matters which may constitute the "otherwise agreement" of the parties by which they may divide the risk or burden.

* * *

6. The specific reference forward in the present section to the following section on exclusion or modification of warranties is to call attention to the possibility of eliminating the warranty in any given case. However it must be noted that under the following section the warranty of fitness for a particular purpose must be excluded or modified by a conspicuous writing.

§ 2–316. Exclusion or Modification of Warranties.

(1) Words or conduct relevant to the creation of an express warranty and words or conduct tending to negate or limit warranty shall be construed wherever reasonable as consistent with each other; but subject to the provisions of this Article on parol or extrinsic evidence (Section 2–202) negation or limitation is inoperative to the extent that such construction is unreasonable.

(2) Subject to subsection (3), to exclude or modify the implied warranty of merchantability or any part of it the language must mention merchantability and in case of a writing must be conspicuous, and to exclude or modify any implied warranty of fitness the exclusion must be by a writing and conspicuous. Language to exclude all implied warranties of fitness is sufficient if it states, for example, that "There are no warranties which extend beyond the description on the face hereof."

(3) Notwithstanding subsection (2)

(a) unless the circumstances indicate otherwise, all implied warranties are excluded by expressions like "as is", "with all faults" or other language which in common understanding calls the buyer's attention to the exclusion of warranties and makes plain that there is no implied warranty; and

(b) when the buyer before entering into the contract has examined the goods or the sample or model as fully as he desired or has refused to examine the goods there is no implied warranty with regard to defects which an examination ought in the circumstances to have revealed to him; and

(c) an implied warranty can also be excluded or modified by course of dealing or course of performance or usage of trade.

(4) Remedies for breach of warranty can be limited in accordance with the provisions of this Article on liquidation or limitation of damages and on contractual modification of remedy (Sections 2–718 and 2–719).

Official Comment

1. This section is designed principally to deal with those frequent clauses in sales contracts which seek to exclude "all warranties, express or implied." It seeks to protect a buyer from unexpected and unbargained language of disclaimer by denying effect to such language when inconsistent with language of express warranty and permitting the exclusion of implied warranties only by conspicuous language or other circumstances which protect the buyer from surprise.

* * *

3. Disclaimer of the implied warranty of merchantability is permitted under subsection (2), but with the safeguard that such disclaimers must mention merchantability and in case of a writing must be conspicuous.

4. Unlike the implied warranty of merchantability, implied warranties of fitness for a particular purpose may be excluded by general language, but only if it is in writing and conspicuous.

5. Subsection (2) presupposes that the implied warranty in question exists unless excluded or modified. Whether or not language of disclaimer satisfies the requirements of this section, such language may be relevant under other sections to the question whether the warranty was ever in fact created. Thus, unless the provisions of this Article on parol and extrinsic evidence prevent, oral language of disclaimer may raise issues of fact as to whether reliance by the buyer occurred and whether the seller had "reason to know" under the section on implied warranty of fitness for a particular purpose.

6. The exceptions to the general rule set forth in paragraphs (a), (b) and (c) of subsection (3) are common factual situations in which the circumstances surrounding the transaction are in themselves sufficient to call the buyer's attention to the fact that no implied warranties are made or that a certain implied warranty is being excluded.

* * *

9. The situation in which the buyer gives precise and complete specifications to the seller is not explicitly covered in this section, but this is a frequent circumstance by which the implied warranties may be excluded. The warranty of fitness for a particular purpose would not normally arise since in such a situation there is usually no reliance on the seller by the buyer. The warranty of merchantability in such a transaction, however, must be considered in connection with the next section on the cumulation and conflict of warranties. Under paragraph (c) of that section in case of such an inconsistency the implied warranty of merchantability is displaced by the express warranty that the goods will comply with the specifications. Thus, where the buyer gives detailed specifications as to the goods, neither of the implied warranties as to quality will normally apply to the transaction unless consistent with the specifications.

* * *

§ 2–319. F.O.B. and F.A.S. Terms.

(1) Unless otherwise agreed the term F.O.B. (which means "free on board") at a named place, even though used only in connection with the stated price, is a delivery term under which

(a) when the term is F.O.B. the place of shipment, the seller must at that place ship the goods in the manner provided in this Article (Section 2–504) and bear the expense and risk of putting them into the possession of the carrier; or

(b) when the term is F.O.B. the place of destination, the seller must at his own expense and risk transport the goods to that place and there tender delivery of them in the manner provided in this Article (Section 2–503);

(c) when under either (a) or (b) the term is also F.O.B. vessel, car or other vehicle, the seller must in addition at his own expense and risk load the goods on board. If the term is F.O.B. vessel the buyer must name the vessel and in an appropriate case the seller must comply with the provisions of this Article on the form of bill of lading (Section 2–323).

(2) Unless otherwise agreed the term F.A.S. vessel (which means "free alongside") at a named port, even though used only in connection with the stated price, is a delivery term under which the seller must

(a) at his own expense and risk deliver the goods alongside the vessel in the manner usual in that port or on a dock designated and provided by the buyer; and

(b) obtain and tender a receipt for the goods in exchange for which the carrier is under a duty to issue a bill of lading.

(3) Unless otherwise agreed in any case falling within subsection (1)(a) or (c) or subsection (2) the buyer must seasonably give any needed instructions for making delivery, including when the term is F.A.S. or F.O.B. the loading berth of the vessel and in an appropriate case its name and sailing date. The seller may treat the failure of needed instructions as a failure of cooperation under this Article (Section 2–311). He may also at his option move the goods in any reasonable manner preparatory to delivery or shipment.

(4) Under the term F.O.B. vessel or F.A.S. unless otherwise agreed the buyer must make payment against tender of the required documents and the seller may not tender nor the buyer demand delivery of the goods in substitution for the documents.

Official Comment

1. This section is intended to negate the uncommercial line of decision which treats an "F.O.B." term as "merely a price term." The distinctions taken in subsection (1) handle most of the issues which have on occasion led to the unfortunate judicial language just referred to. Other matters which have led to sound results being based on unhappy language in regard to F.O.B. clauses are dealt with in this Act by Section 2–311(2) (seller's option re arrangements relating to shipment) and Sections 2–614 and 615 (substituted performance and seller's excuse).

2. Subsection (1)(c) not only specifies the duties of a seller who engages to deliver "F.O.B. vessel," or the like, but ought to make clear that no agreement is soundly drawn when it looks to reshipment from San Francisco or New York, but speaks merely of "F.O.B." the place.

3. The buyer's obligations stated in subsection (1)(c) and subsection (3) are, as shown in the text, obligations of cooperation. The last sentence of subsection (3) expressly, though perhaps unnecessarily, authorizes the seller, pending instructions, to go ahead with such preparatory moves as shipment from the interior to the named point of delivery. The sentence presupposes the usual case in which instructions "fail"; a prior repudiation by the buyer, giving notice that breach was intended, would remove the reason for the

sentence, and would normally bring into play, instead, the second sentence of Section 2–704, which duly calls for lessening damages.

4. The treatment of "F.O.B. vessel" in conjunction with F.A.S. fits, in regard to the need for payment against documents, with standard practice and case-law; but "F.O.B. vessel" is a term which by its very language makes express the need for an "on board" document. In this respect, that term is stricter than the ordinary overseas "shipment" contract (C.I.F., etc., Section 2–320).

§ 2–320. C.I.F. and C. & F. Terms.

(1) The term C.I.F. means that the price includes in a lump sum the cost of the goods and the insurance and freight to the named destination. The term C. & F. or C.F. means that the price so includes cost and freight to the named destination.

(2) Unless otherwise agreed and even though used only in connection with the stated price and destination, the term C.I.F. destination or its equivalent requires the seller at his own expense and risk to

(a) put the goods into the possession of a carrier at the port for shipment and obtain a negotiable bill or bills of lading covering the entire transportation to the named destination; and

(b) load the goods and obtain a receipt from the carrier (which may be contained in the bill of lading) showing that the freight has been paid or provided for; and

(c) obtain a policy or certificate of insurance, including any war risk insurance, of a kind and on terms then current at the port of shipment in the usual amount, in the currency of the contract, shown to cover the same goods covered by the bill of lading and providing for payment of loss to the order of the buyer or for the account of whom it may concern; but the seller may add to the price the amount of the premium for any such war risk insurance; and

(d) prepare an invoice of the goods and procure any other documents required to effect shipment or to comply with the contract; and

(e) forward and tender with commercial promptness all the documents in due form and with any indorsement necessary to perfect the buyer's rights.

(3) Unless otherwise agreed the term C. & F. or its equivalent has the same effect and imposes upon the seller the same obligations and risks as a C.I.F. term except the obligation as to insurance.

(4) Under the term C.I.F. or C. & F. unless otherwise agreed the buyer must make payment against tender of the required documents and the seller may not tender nor the buyer demand delivery of the goods in substitution for the documents.

Official Comment

1. The C.I.F. contract is not a destination but a shipment contract with risk of subsequent loss or damage to the goods passing to the buyer upon shipment if the seller has properly performed all his obligations with respect to the goods. Delivery to the carrier is delivery to the buyer for purposes of risk and "title". Delivery of possession of the goods is accomplished by delivery of the bill of lading, and upon tender of the required documents the buyer must pay the agreed price without awaiting the arrival of the goods and if they have been lost or damaged after proper shipment he must seek his remedy against the carrier or insurer. The buyer has no right of inspection prior to payment or acceptance of the documents.

2. The seller's obligations remain the same even though the C.I.F. term is "used only in connection with the stated price and destination".

3. The insurance stipulated by the C.I.F. term is for the buyer's benefit, to protect him against the risk of loss or damage to the goods in transit. A clause in a C.I.F. contract "insurance—for the account of sellers" should be viewed in its ordinary mercantile meaning that the sellers must pay for the insurance and not that it is intended to run to the seller's benefit.

4. A bill of lading covering the entire transportation from the port of shipment is explicitly required but the provision on this point must be read in the light of its reason to assure the buyer of as full protection as the conditions of shipment reasonably permit, remembering always that this type of contract is designed to move the goods in the channels commercially available. To enable the buyer to deal with the goods while they are afloat the bill of lading must be one that covers only the quantity of goods called for by the contract. The buyer is not required to accept his part of the goods without a bill of lading because the latter covers a larger quantity, nor is he required to accept a bill of lading for the whole quantity under a stipulation to hold the excess for the owner. Although the buyer is not compelled to accept either goods or documents under such circumstances he may of course claim his rights in any goods which have been identified to his contract.

* * *

6. The requirement that unless otherwise agreed the seller must procure insurance "of a kind and on terms then current at the port for shipment in the usual amount, in the currency of the contract, sufficiently shown to cover the same goods covered by the bill of lading", applies to both marine and war risk insurance. As applied to marine insurance, it means such insurance as is usual or customary at the port for shipment with reference to the particular kind of goods involved, the character and equipment of the vessel, the route of the voyage, the port of destination and any other considerations that affect the risk. It is the substantial equivalent of the ordinary insurance in the particular trade and on the particular voyage and is subject to agreed specifications of type or extent of coverage. The language does not mean that the insurance must be adequate to cover all risks to which the goods may be subject in transit. There are some types of loss or damage that are not covered by the usual marine insurance and are excepted in bills of lading or in applicable statutes from the causes of loss or damage for which

the carrier or the vessel is liable. Such risks must be borne by the buyer under this Article.

Insurance secured in compliance with a C.I.F. term must cover the entire transportation of the goods to the named destination.

7. An additional obligation is imposed upon the seller in requiring him to procure customary war risk insurance at the buyer's expense. This changes the common law on the point. The seller is not required to assume the risk of including in the C.I.F. price the cost of such insurance, since it often fluctuates rapidly, but is required to treat it simply as a necessary for the buyer's account. What war risk insurance is "current" or usual turns on the standard forms of policy or rider in common use.

8. The C.I.F. contract calls for insurance covering the value of the goods at the time and place of shipment and does not include any increase in market value during transit or any anticipated profit to the buyer on a sale by him.

The contract contemplates that before the goods arrive at their destination they may be sold again and again on C.I.F. terms and that the original policy of insurance and bill of lading will run with the interest in the goods by being transferred to each successive buyer. A buyer who becomes the seller in such an intermediate contract for sale does not thereby, if his sub-buyer knows the circumstances, undertake to insure the goods again at an increased price fixed in the new contract or to cover the increase in price by additional insurance, and his buyer may not reject the documents on the ground that the original policy does not cover such higher price. If such a sub-buyer desires additional insurance he must procure it for himself.

* * *

12. Under a C.I.F. contract the buyer, as under the common law, must pay the price upon tender of the required documents without first inspecting the goods, but his payment in these circumstances does not constitute an acceptance of the goods nor does it impair his right of subsequent inspection or his options and remedies in the case of improper delivery. All remedies and rights for the seller's breach are reserved to him. The buyer must pay before inspection and assert his remedy against the seller afterward unless the nonconformity of the goods amounts to a real failure of consideration, since the purpose of choosing this form of contract is to give the seller protection against the buyer's unjustifiable rejection of the goods at a distant port of destination which would necessitate taking possession of the goods and suing the buyer there.

13. A valid C.I.F. contract may be made which requires part of the transportation to be made on land and part on the sea, as where the goods are to be brought by rail from an inland point to a seaport and thence transported by vessel to the named destination under a "through" or combination bill of lading issued by the railroad company. In such a case shipment by rail from the inland point within the contract period is a timely shipment notwithstanding that the loading of the goods on the vessel is delayed by causes beyond the seller's control.

14. Although subsection (2) stating the legal effects of the C.I.F. term is an "unless otherwise agreed" provision, the express language used in an

agreement is frequently a precautionary, fuller statement of the normal C.I.F. terms and hence not intended as a departure or variation from them. Moreover, the dominant outlines of the C.I.F. term are so well understood commercially that any variation should, whenever reasonably possible, be read as falling within those dominant outlines rather than as destroying the whole meaning of a term which essentially indicates a contract for proper shipment rather than one for delivery at destination. Particularly careful consideration is necessary before a printed form or clause is construed to mean agreement otherwise and where a C.I.F. contract is prepared on a printed form designed for some other type of contract, the C.I.F. terms must prevail over printed clauses repugnant to them.

* * *

17. It is to be remembered that in a French contract the term "C.A.F." does not mean "Cost and Freight" but has exactly the same meaning as the term "C.I.F." since it is merely the French equivalent of that term. The "A" does not stand for "and" but for "assurance" which means insurance.

* * *

§ 2–403. Power to Transfer; Good Faith Purchase of Goods; "Entrusting".

(1) A purchaser of goods acquires all title which his transferor had or had power to transfer except that a purchaser of a limited interest acquires rights only to the extent of the interest purchased. A person with voidable title has power to transfer a good title to a good faith purchaser for value. When goods have been delivered under a transaction of purchase the purchaser has such power even though

(a) the transferor was deceived as to the identity of the purchaser, or

(b) the delivery was in exchange for a check which is later dishonored, or

(c) it was agreed that the transaction was to be a "cash sale", or

(d) the delivery was procured through fraud punishable as larcenous under the criminal law.

(2) Any entrusting of possession of goods to a merchant who deals in goods of that kind gives him power to transfer all rights of the entruster to a buyer in ordinary course of business.

(3) "Entrusting" includes any delivery and any acquiescence in retention of possession regardless of any condition expressed between the parties to the delivery or acquiescence and regardless of whether the procurement of the entrusting or the possessor's disposition of the goods have been such as to be larcenous under the criminal law.

(4) The rights of other purchasers of goods and of lien creditors are governed by the Articles on Secured Transactions (Article 9), Bulk Sales (Article 6) and Documents of Title (Article 7).

§ 2–504. Shipment by Seller.

Where the seller is required or authorized to send the goods to the buyer and the contract does not require him to deliver them at a particular destination, then unless otherwise agreed he must

(a) put the goods in the possession of such a carrier and make such a contract for their transportation as may be reasonable having regard to the nature of the goods and other circumstances of the case; and

(b) obtain and promptly deliver or tender in due form any document necessary to enable the buyer to obtain possession of the goods or otherwise required by the agreement or by usage of trade; and

(c) promptly notify the buyer of the shipment.

Failure to notify the buyer under paragraph (c) or to make a proper contract under paragraph (a) is a ground for rejection only if material delay or loss ensues.

Official Comment

1. The section is limited to "shipment" contracts as contrasted with "destination" contracts or contracts for delivery at the place where the goods are located. The general principles embodied in this section cover the special cases of F.O.B. point of shipment contracts and C.I.F. and C. & F. contracts. Under the preceding section on manner of tender of delivery, due tender by the seller requires that he comply with the requirements of this section in appropriate cases.

2. The contract to be made with the carrier under paragraph (a) must conform to all express terms of the agreement, subject to any substitution necessary because of failure of agreed facilities as provided in the later provision on substituted performance. However, under the policies of this Article on good faith and commercial standards and on buyer's rights on improper delivery, the requirements of explicit provisions must be read in terms of their commercial and not their literal meaning. This policy is made express with respect to bills of lading in a set in the provision of this Article on form of bills of lading required in overseas shipment.

3. In the absence of agreement, the provision of this Article on options and cooperation respecting performance gives the seller the choice of any reasonable carrier, routing and other arrangements. Whether or not the shipment is at the buyer's expense the seller must see to any arrangements, reasonable in the circumstances, such as refrigeration, watering of live stock, protection against cold, the sending along of any necessary help, selection of specialized cars and the like for paragraph (a) is intended to cover all necessary arrangements whether made by contract with the carrier or otherwise. There is, however, a proper relaxation of such requirements if the buyer is himself in a position to make the appropriate arrangements and the seller gives him reasonable notice of the need to do so. It is an improper contract under paragraph (a) for the seller to agree with the carrier to a limited valuation below the true value and thus cut off the buyer's opportuni-

ty to recover from the carrier in the event of loss, when the risk of shipment is placed on the buyer by his contract with the seller.

* * *

In this connection, in the case of pool car shipments a delivery order furnished by the seller on the pool car consignee, or on the carrier for delivery out of a larger quantity, satisfies the requirements of paragraph (b) unless the contract requires some other form of document.

5. This Article, unlike the prior uniform statutory provision, makes it the seller's duty to notify the buyer of shipment in all cases. The consequences of his failure to do so, however, are limited in that the buyer may reject on this ground only where material delay or loss ensues.

A standard and acceptable manner of notification in open credit shipments is the sending of an invoice and in the case of documentary contracts is the prompt forwarding of the documents as under paragraph (b) of this section. It is also usual to send on a straight bill of lading but this is not necessary to the required notification. However, should such a document prove necessary or convenient to the buyer, as in the case of loss and claim against the carrier, good faith would require the seller to send it on request.

* * *

§ 2–513. Buyer's Right to Inspection of Goods.

(1) Unless otherwise agreed and subject to subsection (3), where goods are tendered or delivered or identified to the contract for sale, the buyer has a right before payment or acceptance to inspect them at any reasonable place and time and in any reasonable manner. When the seller is required or authorized to send the goods to the buyer, the inspection may be after their arrival.

(2) Expenses of inspection must be borne by the buyer but may be recovered from the seller if the goods do not conform and are rejected.

(3) Unless otherwise agreed and subject to the provisions of this Article on C.I.F. contracts (subsection (3) of Section 2–321), the buyer is not entitled to inspect the goods before payment of the price when the contract provides

(a) for delivery "C.O.D." or on other like terms; or

(b) for payment against documents of title, except where such payment is due only after the goods are to become available for inspection.

(4) A place or method of inspection fixed by the parties is presumed to be exclusive but unless otherwise expressly agreed it does not postpone identification or shift the place for delivery or for passing the risk of loss. If compliance becomes impossible, inspection shall be as provided in this section unless the place or method fixed was clearly intended as an indispensable condition failure of which avoids the contract.

Official Comment

1. The buyer is entitled to inspect goods as provided in subsection (1) unless it has been otherwise agreed by the parties. The phrase "unless otherwise agreed" is intended principally to cover such situations as those outlined in subsections (3) and (4) and those in which the agreement of the parties negates inspection before tender of delivery. However, no agreement by the parties can displace the entire right of inspection except where the contract is simply for the sale of "this thing." Even in a sale of boxed goods "as is" inspection is a right of the buyer, since if the boxes prove to contain some other merchandise altogether the price can be recovered back; nor do the limitations of the provision on effect of acceptance apply in such a case.

2. The buyer's right of inspection is available to him upon tender, delivery or appropriation of the goods with notice to him. Since inspection is available to him on tender, where payment is due against delivery he may, unless otherwise agreed, make his inspection before payment of the price. It is also available to him after receipt of the goods and so may be postponed after receipt for a reasonable time. Failure to inspect before payment does not impair the right to inspect after receipt of the goods unless the case falls within subsection (4) on agreed and exclusive inspection provisions. The right to inspect goods which have been appropriated with notice to the buyer holds whether or not the sale was by sample.

3. The buyer may exercise his right of inspection at any reasonable time or place and in any reasonable manner. It is not necessary that he select the most appropriate time, place or manner to inspect or that his selection be the customary one in the trade or locality. Any reasonable time, place or manner is available to him and the reasonableness will be determined by trade usages, past practices between the parties and the other circumstances of the case.

The last sentence of subsection (1) makes it clear that the place of arrival of shipped goods is a reasonable place for their inspection.

4. Expenses of an inspection made to satisfy the buyer of the seller's performance must be assumed by the buyer in the first instance. Since the rule provides merely for an allocation of expense there is no policy to prevent the parties from providing otherwise in the agreement. Where the buyer would normally bear the expenses of the inspection but the goods are rightly rejected because of what the inspection reveals, demonstrable and reasonable costs of the inspection are part of his incidental damage caused by the seller's breach.

5. In the case of payment against documents, subsection (3) requires payment before inspection, since shipping documents against which payment is to be made will commonly arrive and be tendered while the goods are still in transit. This Article recognizes no exception in any peculiar case in which the goods happen to arrive before the documents. However, where by the agreement payment is to await the arrival of the goods, inspection before payment becomes proper since the goods are then "available for inspection."

Where by the agreement the documents are to be held until arrival the buyer is entitled to inspect before payment since the goods are then "available for inspection". Proof of usage is not necessary to establish this right, but if inspection before payment is disputed the contrary must be established by usage or by an explicit contract term to that effect.

For the same reason, that the goods are available for inspection, a term calling for payment against storage documents or a delivery order does not normally bar the buyer's right to inspection before payment under subsection (3)(b). This result is reinforced by the buyer's right under subsection (1) to inspect goods which have been appropriated with notice to him.

* * *

§ 2–615. Excuse by Failure of Presupposed Conditions.

Except so far as a seller may have assumed a greater obligation and subject to the preceding section on substituted performance:

(a) Delay in delivery or non-delivery in whole or in part by a seller who complies with paragraphs (b) and (c) is not a breach of his duty under a contract for sale if performance as agreed has been made impracticable by the occurrence of a contingency the non-occurrence of which was a basic assumption on which the contract was made or by compliance in good faith with any applicable foreign or domestic governmental regulation or order whether or not it later proves to be invalid.

(b) Where the causes mentioned in paragraph (a) affect only a part of the seller's capacity to perform, he must allocate production and deliveries among his customers but may at his option include regular customers not then under contract as well as his own requirements for further manufacture. He may so allocate in any manner which is fair and reasonable.

(c) The seller must notify the buyer seasonably that there will be delay or non-delivery and, when allocation is required under paragraph (b), of the estimated quota thus made available for the buyer.

Official Comment

1. This section excuses a seller from timely delivery of goods contracted for, where his performance has become commercially impracticable because of unforeseen supervening circumstances not within the contemplation of the parties at the time of contracting. The destruction of specific goods and the problem of the use of substituted performance on points other than delay or quantity, treated elsewhere in this Article, must be distinguished from the matter covered by this section.

2. The present section deliberately refrains from any effort at an exhaustive expression of contingencies and is to be interpreted in all cases sought to be brought within its scope in terms of its underlying reason and purpose.

3. The first test for excuse under this Article in terms of basic assumption is a familiar one. The additional test of commercial impracticability (as contrasted with "impossibility," "frustration of performance" or "frustration

of the venture") has been adopted in order to call attention to the commercial character of the criterion chosen by this Article.

4. Increased cost alone does not excuse performance unless the rise in cost is due to some unforeseen contingency which alters the essential nature of the performance. Neither is a rise or a collapse in the market in itself a justification, for that is exactly the type of business risk which business contracts made at fixed prices are intended to cover. But a severe shortage of raw materials or of supplies due to a contingency such as war, embargo, local crop failure, unforeseen shutdown of major sources of supply or the like, which either causes a marked increase in cost or altogether prevents the seller from securing supplies necessary to his performance, is within the contemplation of this section. (See Ford & Sons, Ltd., v. Henry Leetham & Sons, Ltd., 21 Com.Cas. 55 (1915, K.B.D.).)

5. Where a particular source of supply is exclusive under the agreement and fails through casualty, the present section applies rather than the provision on destruction or deterioration of specific goods. The same holds true where a particular source of supply is shown by the circumstances to have been contemplated or assumed by the parties at the time of contracting. There is no excuse under this section, however, unless the seller has employed all due measures to assure himself that his source will not fail.

In the case of failure of production by an agreed source for causes beyond the seller's control, the seller should, if possible, be excused since production by an agreed source is without more a basic assumption of the contract. Such excuse should not result in relieving the defaulting supplier from liability nor in dropping into the seller's lap an unearned bonus of damages over. The flexible adjustment machinery of this Article provides the solution under the provision on the obligation of good faith. A condition to his making good the claim of excuse is the turning over to the buyer of his rights against the defaulting source of supply to the extent of the buyer's contract in relation to which excuse is being claimed.

6. In situations in which neither sense nor justice is served by either answer when the issue is posed in flat terms of "excuse" or "no excuse," adjustment under the various provisions of this Article is necessary, especially the sections on good faith, on insecurity and assurance and on the reading of all provisions in the light of their purposes, and the general policy of this Act to use equitable principles in furtherance of commercial standards and good faith.

7. The failure of conditions which go to convenience or collateral values rather than to the commercial practicability of the main performance does not amount to a complete excuse. However, good faith and the reason of the present section and of the preceding one may properly be held to justify and even to require any needed delay involved in a good faith inquiry seeking a readjustment of the contract terms to meet the new conditions.

8. The provisions of this section are made subject to assumption of greater liability by agreement and such agreement is to be found not only in the expressed terms of the contract but in the circumstances surrounding the contracting, in trade usage and the like. Thus the exemptions of this section do not apply when the contingency in question is sufficiently foreshadowed at

the time of contracting to be included among the business risks which are fairly to be regarded as part of the dickered terms, either consciously or as a matter of reasonable, commercial interpretation from the circumstances. The exemption otherwise present through usage of trade under the present section may also be expressly negated by the language of the agreement. Generally, express agreements as to exemptions designed to enlarge upon or supplant the provisions of this section are to be read in the light of mercantile sense and reason, for this section itself sets up the commercial standard for normal and reasonable interpretation and provides a minimum beyond which agreement may not go.

Agreement can also be made in regard to the consequences of exemption as laid down in paragraphs (b) and (c) and the next section on procedure on notice claiming excuse.

* * *

Exemption of the buyer in the case of a "requirements" contract is covered by the "Output and Requirements" section both as to assumption and allocation of the relevant risks. But when a contract by a manufacturer to buy fuel or raw material makes no specific reference to a particular venture and no such reference may be drawn from the circumstances, commercial understanding views it as a general deal in the general market and not conditioned on any assumption of the continuing operation of the buyer's plant. Even when notice is given by the buyer that the supplies are needed to fill a specific contract of a normal commercial kind, commercial understanding does not see such a supply contract as conditioned on the continuance of the buyer's further contract for outlet. On the other hand, where the buyer's contract is in reasonable commercial understanding conditioned on a definite and specific venture or assumption as, for instance, a war procurement subcontract known to be based on a prime contract which is subject to termination, or a supply contract for a particular construction venture, the reason of the present section may well apply and entitle the buyer to the exemption.

10. Following its basic policy of using commercial practicability as a test for excuse, this section recognizes as of equal significance either a foreign or domestic regulation and disregards any technical distinctions between "law," "regulation," "order" and the like. Nor does it make the present action of the seller depend upon the eventual judicial determination of the legality of the particular governmental action. The seller's good faith belief in the validity of the regulation is the test under this Article and the best evidence of his good faith is the general commercial acceptance of the regulation. However, governmental interference cannot excuse unless it truly "supervenes" in such a manner as to be beyond the seller's assumption of risk. And any action by the party claiming excuse which causes or colludes in inducing the governmental action preventing his performance would be in breach of good faith and would destroy his exemption.

11. An excused seller must fulfill his contract to the extent which the supervening contingency permits, and if the situation is such that his customers are generally affected he must take account of all in supplying one. Subsections (a) and (b), therefore, explicitly permit in any proration a fair and

reasonable attention to the needs of regular customers who are probably relying on spot orders for supplies. Customers at different stages of the manufacturing process may be fairly treated by including the seller's manufacturing requirements. A fortiori, the seller may also take account of contracts later in date than the one in question. The fact that such spot orders may be closed at an advanced price causes no difficulty, since any allocation which exceeds normal past requirements will not be reasonable. However, good faith requires, when prices have advanced, that the seller exercise real care in making his allocations, and in case of doubt his contract customers should be favored and supplies prorated evenly among them regardless of price. Save for the extra care thus required by changes in the market, this section seeks to leave every reasonable business leeway to the seller.

* * *

[REVISED] ARTICLE 5. LETTERS OF CREDIT

§ 5–101. Short Title.

This article may be cited as Uniform Commercial Code—Letters of Credit.

Official Comment

The Official Comment to the original Section 5–101 was a remarkably brief inaugural address. Noting that letters of credit had not been the subject of statutory enactment and that the law concerning them had been developed in the cases, the Comment stated that Article 5 was intended "within its limited scope" to set an independent theoretical frame for the further development of letters of credit. That statement addressed accurately conditions as they existed when the statement was made, nearly half a century ago. Since Article 5 was originally drafted, the use of letters of credit has expanded and developed, and the case law concerning these developments is, in some respects, discordant.

Revision of Article 5 therefore has required reappraisal both of the statutory goals and of the extent to which particular statutory provisions further or adversely affect achievement of those goals.

The statutory goal of Article 5 was originally stated to be: (1) to set a substantive theoretical frame that describes the function and legal nature of letters of credit; and (2) to preserve procedural flexibility in order to accommodate further development of the efficient use of letters of credit. A letter of credit is an idiosyncratic form of undertaking that supports performance of an obligation incurred in a separate financial, mercantile, or other transaction or arrangement. The objectives of the original and revised Article 5 are best achieved (1) by defining the peculiar characteristics of a letter of credit that distinguish it and the legal consequences of its use from other forms of assurance such as secondary guarantees, performance bonds, and insurance policies, and from ordinary contracts, fiduciary engagements, and escrow arrangements; and (2) by preserving flexibility through variation by agreement in order to respond to and accommodate developments in custom and usage that are not inconsistent with the essential definitions and substantive mandates of the statute. No statute can, however, prescribe the manner in which such substantive rights and duties are to be enforced or imposed without risking stultification of wholesome developments in the letter of credit mechanism. Letter of credit law should remain responsive to commercial reality and in particular to the customs and expectations of the international banking and mercantile community. Courts should read the terms of this article in a manner consistent with these customs and expectations.

The subject matter in Article 5, letters of credit, may also be governed by an international convention that is now being drafted by UNCITRAL, the draft Convention on Independent Guarantees and Standby Letters of Credit. The Uniform Customs and Practice is an international body of trade practice that is commonly adopted by international and domestic letters of credit and as such is the "law of the transaction" by agreement of the parties. Article 5 is consistent with and was influenced by the rules in the existing version of the UCP. In addition to the UCP and the international convention, other bodies of law apply to letters of credit. For example, the federal bankruptcy law applies to letters of credit with respect to applicants and beneficiaries that are in bankruptcy; regulations of the Federal Reserve Board and the Comptroller of the Currency lay out requirements for banks that issue letters of credit and describe how letters of credit are to be treated for calculating asset risk and for the purpose of loan limitations. In addition there is an array of anti-boycott and other similar laws that may affect the issuance and performance of letters of credit. All of these laws are beyond the scope of Article 5, but in certain circumstances they will override Article 5.

§ 5–102. Definitions.

(a) In this article:

(1) "Adviser" means a person who, at the request of the issuer, a confirmer, or another adviser, notifies or requests another adviser to notify the beneficiary that a letter of credit has been issued, confirmed, or amended.

(2) "Applicant" means a person at whose request or for whose account a letter of credit is issued. The term includes a person who requests an issuer to issue a letter of credit on behalf of another if the person making the request undertakes an obligation to reimburse the issuer.

(3) "Beneficiary" means a person who under the terms of a letter of credit is entitled to have its complying presentation honored. The term includes a person to whom drawing rights have been transferred under a transferable letter of credit.

(4) "Confirmer" means a nominated person who undertakes, at the request or with the consent of the issuer, to honor a presentation under a letter of credit issued by another.

(5) "Dishonor" of a letter of credit means failure timely to honor or to take an interim action, such as acceptance of a draft, that may be required by the letter of credit.

(6) "Document" means a draft or other demand, document of title, investment security, certificate, invoice, or other rec-

ord, statement, or representation of fact, law, right, or opinion (i) which is presented in a written or other medium permitted by the letter of credit or, unless prohibited by the letter of credit, by the standard practice referred to in Section 5–108(e) and (ii) which is capable of being examined for compliance with the terms and conditions of the letter of credit. A document may not be oral.

(7) "Good faith" means honesty in fact in the conduct or transaction concerned.

(8) "Honor" of a letter of credit means performance of the issuer's undertaking in the letter of credit to pay or deliver an item of value. Unless the letter of credit otherwise provides, "honor" occurs

(i) upon payment,

(ii) if the letter of credit provides for acceptance, upon acceptance of a draft and, at maturity, its payment, or

(iii) if the letter of credit provides for incurring a deferred obligation, upon incurring the obligation and, at maturity, its performance.

(9) "Issuer" means a bank or other person that issues a letter of credit, but does not include an individual who makes an engagement for personal, family, or household purposes.

(10) "Letter of credit" means a definite undertaking that satisfies the requirements of Section 5–104 by an issuer to a beneficiary at the request or for the account of an applicant or, in the case of a financial institution, to itself or for its own account, to honor a documentary presentation by payment or delivery of an item of value.

(11) "Nominated person" means a person whom the issuer (i) designates or authorizes to pay, accept, negotiate, or otherwise give value under a letter of credit and (ii) undertakes by agreement or custom and practice to reimburse.

(12) "Presentation" means delivery of a document to an issuer or nominated person for honor or giving of value under a letter of credit.

(13) "Presenter" means a person making a presentation as or on behalf of a beneficiary or nominated person.

(14) "Record" means information that is inscribed on a tangible medium, or that is stored in an electronic or other medium and is retrievable in perceivable form.

(15) "Successor of a beneficiary" means a person who succeeds to substantially all of the rights of a beneficiary by operation of law, including a corporation with or into which the beneficiary has been merged or consolidated, an administrator, executor, personal representative, trustee in bankruptcy, debtor in possession, liquidator, and receiver.

* * *

Official Comment

1. Since no one can be a confirmer unless that person is a nominated person as defined in Section 5–102(a)(11), those who agree to "confirm"

without the designation or authorization of the issuer are not confirmers under Article 5. Nonetheless, the undertakings to the beneficiary of such persons may be enforceable by the beneficiary as letters of credit issued by the "confirmer" for its own account or as guarantees or contracts outside of Article 5.

2. The definition of "document" contemplates and facilitates the growing recognition of electronic and other nonpaper media as "documents," however, for the time being, data in those media constitute documents only in certain circumstances. For example, a facsimile received by an issuer would be a document only if the letter of credit explicitly permitted it, if the standard practice authorized it and the letter did not prohibit it, or the agreement of the issuer and beneficiary permitted it. The fact that data transmitted in a nonpaper (unwritten) medium can be recorded on paper by a recipient's computer printer, facsimile machine, or the like does not under current practice render the data so transmitted a "document." A facsimile or S.W.I.F.T. message received directly by the issuer is in an electronic medium when it crosses the boundary of the issuer's place of business. One wishing to make a presentation by facsimile (an electronic medium) will have to procure the explicit agreement of the issuer (assuming that the standard practice does not authorize it). Where electronic transmissions are authorized neither by the letter of credit nor by the practice, the beneficiary may transmit the data electronically to its agent who may be able to put it in written form and make a conforming presentation.

3. "Good faith" continues in revised Article 5 to be defined as "honesty in fact." "Observance of reasonable standards of fair dealing" has not been added to the definition. The narrower definition of "honesty in fact" reinforces the "independence principle" in the treatment of "fraud," "strict compliance," "preclusion," and other tests affecting the performance of obligations that are unique to letters of credit. This narrower definition—which does not include "fair dealing"—is appropriate to the decision to honor or dishonor a presentation of documents specified in a letter of credit. The narrower definition is also appropriate for other parts of revised Article 5 where greater certainty of obligations is necessary and is consistent with the goals of speed and low cost. It is important that U.S. letters of credit have continuing vitality and competitiveness in international transactions.

For example, it would be inconsistent with the "independence" principle if any of the following occurred: (i) the beneficiary's failure to adhere to the standard of "fair dealing" in the underlying transaction or otherwise in presenting documents were to provide applicants and issuers with an "unfairness" defense to dishonor even when the documents complied with the terms of the letter of credit; (ii) the issuer's obligation to honor in "strict compliance in accordance with standard practice" were changed to "reasonable compliance" by use of the "fair dealing" standard, or (iii) the preclusion against the issuer (Section 5–108(d)) were modified under the "fair dealing" standard to enable the issuer later to raise additional deficiencies in the presentation. The rights and obligations arising from presentation, honor, dishonor and reimbursement, are independent and strict, and thus "honesty in fact" is an appropriate standard.

The contract between the applicant and beneficiary is not governed by Article 5, but by applicable contract law, such as Article 2 or the general law of contracts. "Good faith" in that contract is defined by other law, such as Section 2–103(1)(b) or Restatement of Contracts 2d, § 205, which incorporate the principle of "fair dealing" in most cases, or a State's common law or other statutory provisions that may apply to that contract.

The contract between the applicant and the issuer (sometimes called the "reimbursement" agreement) is governed in part by this article (e.g., Sections 5–108(i), 5–111(b), and 5–103(c)) and partly by other law (e.g., the general law of contracts). The definition of good faith in Section 5–102(a)(7) applies only to the extent that the reimbursement contract is governed by provisions in this article; for other purposes good faith is defined by other law.

* * *

6. The label on a document is not conclusive; certain documents labelled "guarantees" in accordance with European (and occasionally, American) practice are letters of credit. On the other hand, even documents that are labelled "letter of credit" may not constitute letters of credit under the definition in Section 5–102(a). When a document labelled a letter of credit requires the issuer to pay not upon the presentation of documents, but upon the determination of an extrinsic fact such as applicant's failure to perform a construction contract, and where that condition appears on its face to be fundamental and would, if ignored, leave no obligation to the issuer under the document labelled letter of credit, the issuer's undertaking is not a letter of credit. It is probably some form of suretyship or other contractual arrangement and may be enforceable as such. See Sections 5–102(a)(10) and 5–103(d). Therefore, undertakings whose fundamental term requires an issuer to look beyond documents and beyond conventional reference to the clock, calendar, and practices concerning the form of various documents are not governed by Article 5. Although Section 5–108(g) recognizes that certain nondocumentary conditions can be included in a letter of credit without denying the undertaking the status of letter of credit, that section does not apply to cases where the nondocumentary condition is fundamental to the issuer's obligation. The rules in Sections 5–102(a)(10), 5–103(d), and 5–108(g) approve the conclusion in Wichita Eagle & Beacon Publishing Co. v. Pacific Nat. Bank, 493 F.2d 1285 (9th Cir.1974).

A financial institution may be both the issuer and the applicant or the issuer and the beneficiary. Such letters are sometimes issued by a bank in support of the bank's own lease obligations or on behalf of one of its divisions as an applicant or to one of its divisions as beneficiary, such as an overseas branch. Because wide use of letters of credit in which the issuer and the applicant or the issuer and the beneficiary are the same would endanger the unique status of letters of credit, only financial institutions are authorized to issue them.

In almost all cases the ultimate performance of the issuer under a letter of credit is the payment of money. In rare cases the issuer's obligation is to deliver stock certificates or the like. The definition of letter of credit in Section 5–102(a)(10) contemplates those cases.

7. Under the UCP any bank is a nominated bank where the letter of credit is "freely negotiable." A letter of credit might also nominate by the following: "We hereby engage with the drawer, indorsers, and bona fide holders of drafts drawn under and in compliance with the terms of this credit that the same will be duly honored on due presentation" or "available with any bank by negotiation." A restricted negotiation credit might be "available with x bank by negotiation" or the like.

Several legal consequences may attach to the status of nominated person. First, when the issuer nominates a person, it is authorizing that person to pay or give value and is authorizing the beneficiary to make presentation to that person. Unless the letter of credit provides otherwise, the beneficiary need not present the documents to the issuer before the letter of credit expires; it need only present those documents to the nominated person. Secondly, a nominated person that gives value in good faith has a right to payment from the issuer despite fraud. Section 5–109(a)(1).

8. A "record" must be in or capable of being converted to a perceivable form. For example, an electronic message recorded in a computer memory that could be printed from that memory could constitute a record. Similarly, a tape recording of an oral conversation could be a record.

* * *

§ 5–103. Scope.

(a) This article applies to letters of credit and to certain rights and obligations arising out of transactions involving letters of credit.

(b) The statement of a rule in this article does not by itself require, imply, or negate application of the same or a different rule to a situation not provided for, or to a person not specified, in this article.

(c) With the exception of this subsection, subsections (a) and (d), Sections 5–102(a)(9) and (10), 5–106(d), and 5–114(d), and except to the extent prohibited in Sections 1–102(3) and 5–117(d), the effect of this article may be varied by agreement or by a provision stated or incorporated by reference in an undertaking. A term in an agreement or undertaking generally excusing liability or generally limiting remedies for failure to perform obligations is not sufficient to vary obligations prescribed by this article.

(d) Rights and obligations of an issuer to a beneficiary or a nominated person under a letter of credit are independent of the existence, performance, or nonperformance of a contract or arrangement out of which the letter of credit arises or which underlies it, including contracts or arrangements between the issuer and the applicant and between the applicant and the beneficiary.

Official Comment

1. Sections 5–102(a)(10) and 5–103 are the principal limits on the scope of Article 5. Many undertakings in commerce and contract are similar, but not identical to the letter of credit. Principal among those are "secondary," "accessory," or "suretyship" guarantees. Although the word "guarantee" is

sometimes used to describe an independent obligation like that of the issuer of a letter of credit (most often in the case of European bank undertakings but occasionally in the case of undertakings of American banks), in the United States the word "guarantee" is more typically used to describe a suretyship transaction in which the "guarantor" is only secondarily liable and has the right to assert the underlying debtor's defenses. This article does not apply to secondary or accessory guarantees and it is important to recognize the distinction between letters of credit and those guarantees. It is often a defense to a secondary or accessory guarantor's liability that the underlying debt has been discharged or that the debtor has other defenses to the underlying liability. In letter of credit law, on the other hand, the independence principle recognized throughout Article 5 states that the issuer's liability is independent of the underlying obligation. That the beneficiary may have breached the underlying contract and thus have given a good defense on that contract to the applicant against the beneficiary is no defense for the issuer's refusal to honor. Only staunch recognition of this principle by the issuers and the courts will give letters of credit the continuing vitality that arises from the certainty and speed of payment under letters of credit. To that end, it is important that the law not carry into letter of credit transactions rules that properly apply only to secondary guarantees or to other forms of engagement.

2. Like all of the provisions of the Uniform Commercial Code, Article 5 is supplemented by Section 1–103 and, through it, by many rules of statutory and common law. Because this article is quite short and has no rules on many issues that will affect liability with respect to a letter of credit transaction, law beyond Article 5 will often determine rights and liabilities in letter of credit transactions. Even within letter of credit law, the article is far from comprehensive; it deals only with "certain" rights of the parties. Particularly with respect to the standards of performance that are set out in Section 5–108, it is appropriate for the parties and the courts to turn to customs and practice such as the Uniform Customs and Practice for Documentary Credits, currently published by the International Chamber of Commerce as I.C.C. Pub. No. 500 (hereafter UCP). Many letters of credit specifically adopt the UCP as applicable to the particular transaction. Where the UCP are adopted but conflict with Article 5 and except where variation is prohibited, the UCP terms are permissible contractual modifications under Sections 1–102(3) and 5–103(c). See Section 5–116(c). Normally Article 5 should not be considered to conflict with practice except when a rule explicitly stated in the UCP or other practice is different from a rule explicitly stated in Article 5.

Except by choosing the law of a jurisdiction that has not adopted the Uniform Commercial Code, it is not possible entirely to escape the Uniform Commercial Code. Since incorporation of the UCP avoids only "conflicting" Article 5 rules, parties who do not wish to be governed by the nonconflicting provisions of Article 5 must normally either adopt the law of a jurisdiction other than a State of the United States or state explicitly the rule that is to govern. When rules of custom and practice are incorporated by reference, they are considered to be explicit terms of the agreement or undertaking.

Neither the obligation of an issuer under Section 5–108 nor that of an adviser under Section 5–107 is an obligation of the kind that is invariable under Section 1–102(3). Section 5–103(c) and Comment 1 to Section 5–108 make it clear that the applicant and the issuer may agree to almost any provision establishing the obligations of the issuer to the applicant. The last sentence of subsection (c) limits the power of the issuer to achieve that result by a nonnegotiated disclaimer or limitation of remedy.

What the issuer could achieve by an explicit agreement with its applicant or by a term that explicitly defines its duty, it cannot accomplish by a general disclaimer. The restriction on disclaimers in the last sentence of subsection (c) is based more on procedural than on substantive unfairness. Where, for example, the reimbursement agreement provides explicitly that the issuer need not examine any documents, the applicant understands the risk it has undertaken. A term in a reimbursement agreement which states generally that an issuer will not be liable unless it has acted in "bad faith" or committed "gross negligence" is ineffective under Section 5–103(c). On the other hand, less general terms such as terms that permit issuer reliance on an oral or electronic message believed in good faith to have been received from the applicant or terms that entitle an issuer to reimbursement when it honors a "substantially" though not "strictly" complying presentation, are effective. In each case the question is whether the disclaimer or limitation is sufficiently clear and explicit in reallocating a liability or risk that is allocated differently under a variable Article 5 provision.

Of course, no term in a letter of credit, whether incorporated by reference to practice rules or stated specifically, can free an issuer from a conflicting contractual obligation to its applicant. If, for example, an issuer promised its applicant that it would pay only against an inspection certificate of a particular company but failed to require such a certificate in its letter of credit or made the requirement only a nondocumentary condition that had to be disregarded, the issuer might be obliged to pay the beneficiary even though its payment might violate its contract with its applicant.

3. Parties should generally avoid modifying the definitions in Section 5–102. The effect of such an agreement is almost inevitably unclear. To say that something is a "guarantee" in the typical domestic transaction is to say that the parties intend that particular legal rules apply to it. By acknowledging that something is a guarantee, but asserting that it is to be treated as a "letter of credit," the parties leave a court uncertain about where the rules on guarantees stop and those concerning letters of credit begin.

* * *

§ 5–104. Formal Requirements.

A letter of credit, confirmation, advice, transfer, amendment, or cancellation may be issued in any form that is a record and is authenticated (i) by a signature or (ii) in accordance with the agreement of the parties or the standard practice referred to in Section 5–108(e).

Official Comment

1. Neither Section 5–104 nor the definition of letter of credit in Section 5–102(a)(10) requires inclusion of all the terms that are normally contained in a letter of credit in order for an undertaking to be recognized as a letter of

credit under Article 5. For example, a letter of credit will typically specify the amount available, the expiration date, the place where presentation should be made, and the documents that must be presented to entitle a person to honor. Undertakings that have the formalities required by Section 5–104 and meet the conditions specified in Section 5–102(a)(10) will be recognized as letters of credit even though they omit one or more of the items usually contained in a letter of credit.

2. The authentication specified in this section is authentication only of the identity of the issuer, confirmer, or adviser.

An authentication agreement may be by system rule, by standard practice, or by direct agreement between the parties. The reference to practice is intended to incorporate future developments in the UCP and other practice rules as well as those that may arise spontaneously in commercial practice.

3. Many banking transactions, including the issuance of many letters of credit, are now conducted mostly by electronic means. For example, S.W.I.F.T. is currently used to transmit letters of credit from issuing to advising banks. The letter of credit text so transmitted may be printed at the advising bank, stamped "original" and provided to the beneficiary in that form. The printed document may then be used as a way of controlling and recording payments and of recording and authorizing assignments of proceeds or transfers of rights under the letter of credit. Nothing in this section should be construed to conflict with that practice.

To be a record sufficient to serve as a letter of credit or other undertaking under this section, data must have a durability consistent with that function. Because consideration is not required for a binding letter of credit or similar undertaking (Section 5–105) yet those undertakings are to be strictly construed (Section 5–108), parties to a letter of credit transaction are especially dependent on the continued availability of the terms and conditions of the letter of credit or other undertaking. By declining to specify any particular medium in which the letter of credit must be established or communicated, Section 5–104 leaves room for future developments.

* * *

§ 5–106. Issuance, Amendment, Cancellation, and Duration.

(a) A letter of credit is issued and becomes enforceable according to its terms against the issuer when the issuer sends or otherwise transmits it to the person requested to advise or to the beneficiary. A letter of credit is revocable only if it so provides.

(b) After a letter of credit is issued, rights and obligations of a beneficiary, applicant, confirmer, and issuer are not affected by an amendment or cancellation to which that person has not consented except to the extent the letter of credit provides that it is revocable or that the issuer may amend or cancel the letter of credit without that consent.

* * *

§ 5–107. Confirmer, Nominated Person, and Adviser.

(a) A confirmer is directly obligated on a letter of credit and has the rights and obligations of an issuer to the extent of its confirmation. The confirmer also has rights against and obligations to the issuer as if the issuer were an applicant and the confirmer had issued the letter of credit at the request and for the account of the issuer.

(b) A nominated person who is not a confirmer is not obligated to honor or otherwise give value for a presentation.

(c) A person requested to advise may decline to act as an adviser. An adviser that is not a confirmer is not obligated to honor or give value for a presentation. An adviser undertakes to the issuer and to the beneficiary accurately to advise the terms of the letter of credit, confirmation, amendment, or advice received by that person and undertakes to the beneficiary to check the apparent authenticity of the request to advise. Even if the advice is inaccurate, the letter of credit, confirmation, or amendment is enforceable as issued.

(d) A person who notifies a transferee beneficiary of the terms of a letter of credit, confirmation, amendment, or advice has the rights and obligations of an adviser under subsection (c). The terms in the notice to the transferee beneficiary may differ from the terms in any notice to the transferor beneficiary to the extent permitted by the letter of credit, confirmation, amendment, or advice received by the person who so notifies.

Official Comment

1. A confirmer has the rights and obligations identified in Section 5–108. Accordingly, unless the context otherwise requires, the terms "confirmer" and "confirmation" should be read into this article wherever the terms "issuer" and "letter of credit" appear.

A confirmer that has paid in accordance with the terms and conditions of the letter of credit is entitled to reimbursement by the issuer even if the beneficiary committed fraud (see Section 5–109(a)(1)(ii)) and, in that sense, has greater rights against the issuer than the beneficiary has. To be entitled to reimbursement from the issuer under the typical confirmed letter of credit, the confirmer must submit conforming documents, but the confirmer's presentation to the issuer need not be made before the expiration date of the letter of credit.

A letter of credit confirmation has been analogized to a guarantee of issuer performance, to a parallel letter of credit issued by the confirmer for the account of the issuer or the letter of credit applicant or both, and to a back-to-back letter of credit in which the confirmer is a kind of beneficiary of the original issuer's letter of credit. Like letter of credit undertakings, confirmations are both unique and flexible, so that no one of these analogies is perfect, but unless otherwise indicated in the letter of credit or confirmation, a confirmer should be viewed by the letter of credit issuer and the beneficiary as an issuer of a parallel letter of credit for the account of the original letter of credit issuer. Absent a direct agreement between the applicant and a confirmer, normally the obligations of a confirmer are to the issuer not the applicant, but the applicant might have a right to injunction against a confirmer under Section 5–109 or warranty claim under Section 5–110, and either might have claims against the other under Section 5–117.

2. * * * By advising or agreeing to advise a letter of credit, the adviser assumes a duty to the issuer and to the beneficiary accurately to report what it has received from the issuer, but, beyond determining the apparent authenticity of the letter, an adviser has no duty to investigate the accuracy of the message it has received from the issuer. "Checking" the apparent authenticity of the request to advise means only that the prospective adviser must attempt to authenticate the message (e.g., by "testing" the telex that comes from the purported issuer), and if it is unable to authenticate the message must report that fact to the issuer and, if it chooses to advise the message, to the beneficiary. By proper agreement, an adviser may disclaim its obligation under this section.

3. An issuer may issue a letter of credit which the adviser may advise with different terms. The issuer may then believe that it has undertaken a certain engagement, yet the text in the hands of the beneficiary will contain different terms, and the beneficiary would not be entitled to honor if the documents it submitted did not comply with the terms of the letter of credit as originally issued. On the other hand, if the adviser also confirmed the letter of credit, then as a confirmer it will be independently liable on the letter of credit as advised and confirmed. If in that situation the beneficiary's ultimate presentation entitled it to honor under the terms of the confirmation but not under those in the original letter of credit, the confirmer would have to honor but might not be entitled to reimbursement from the issuer.

4. When the issuer nominates another person to "pay," "negotiate," or otherwise to take up the documents and give value, there can be confusion about the legal status of the nominated person. In rare cases the person might actually be an agent of the issuer and its act might be the act of the issuer itself. In most cases the nominated person is not an agent of the issuer and has no authority to act on the issuer's behalf. * * *

§ 5–108. Issuer's Rights and Obligations.

(a) Except as otherwise provided in Section 5–109, an issuer shall honor a presentation that, as determined by the standard practice referred to in subsection (e), appears on its face strictly to comply with the terms and conditions of the letter of credit. Except as otherwise provided in Section 5–113 and unless otherwise agreed with the applicant, an issuer shall dishonor a presentation that does not appear so to comply.

(b) An issuer has a reasonable time after presentation, but not beyond the end of the seventh business day of the issuer after the day of its receipt of documents:

(1) to honor,

(2) if the letter of credit provides for honor to be completed more than seven business days after presentation, to accept a draft or incur a deferred obligation, or

(3) to give notice to the presenter of discrepancies in the presentation.

(c) Except as otherwise provided in subsection (d), an issuer is precluded from asserting as a basis for dishonor any discrepancy if timely notice is not given, or any discrepancy not stated in the notice if timely notice is given.

(d) Failure to give the notice specified in subsection (b) or to mention fraud, forgery, or expiration in the notice does not preclude the issuer from asserting as a basis for dishonor fraud or forgery as described in Section 5–109(a) or expiration of the letter of credit before presentation.

(e) An issuer shall observe standard practice of financial institutions that regularly issue letters of credit. Determination of the issuer's observance of the standard practice is a matter of interpretation for the court. The court shall offer the parties a reasonable opportunity to present evidence of the standard practice.

(f) An issuer is not responsible for:

(1) the performance or nonperformance of the underlying contract, arrangement, or transaction,

(2) an act or omission of others, or

(3) observance or knowledge of the usage of a particular trade other than the standard practice referred to in subsection (e).

(g) If an undertaking constituting a letter of credit under Section 5–102(a)(10) contains nondocumentary conditions, an issuer shall disregard the nondocumentary conditions and treat them as if they were not stated.

(h) An issuer that has dishonored a presentation shall return the documents or hold them at the disposal of, and send advice to that effect to, the presenter.

(i) An issuer that has honored a presentation as permitted or required by this article:

(1) is entitled to be reimbursed by the applicant in immediately available funds not later than the date of its payment of funds;

(2) takes the documents free of claims of the beneficiary or presenter;

(3) is precluded from asserting a right of recourse on a draft under Sections 3–414 and 3–415;

(4) except as otherwise provided in Sections 5–110 and 5–117, is precluded from restitution of money paid or other value given by mistake to the extent the mistake concerns discrepancies in the documents or tender which are apparent on the face of the presentation; and

(5) is discharged to the extent of its performance under the letter of credit unless the issuer honored a presentation in which a required signature of a beneficiary was forged.

Official Comment

1. * * * Because a confirmer has the rights and duties of an issuer, this section applies equally to a confirmer and an issuer.

The standard of strict compliance governs the issuer's obligation to the beneficiary and to the applicant. By requiring that a "presentation" appear strictly to comply, the section requires not only that the documents themselves appear on their face strictly to comply, but also that the other terms of the letter of credit such as those dealing with the time and place of presentation are strictly complied with. Typically, a letter of credit will provide that presentation is timely if made to the issuer, confirmer, or any other nominated person prior to expiration of the letter of credit. Accordingly, a nominated person that has honored a demand or otherwise given value before expiration will have a right to reimbursement from the issuer even though presentation to the issuer is made after the expiration of the letter of credit. Conversely, where the beneficiary negotiates documents to one who is not a nominated person, the beneficiary or that person acting on behalf of the beneficiary must make presentation to a nominated person, confirmer, or issuer prior to the expiration date.

This section does not impose a bifurcated standard under which an issuer's right to reimbursement might be broader than a beneficiary's right to honor. However, the explicit deference to standard practice in Section 5–108(a) and (e) and elsewhere expands issuers' rights of reimbursement where that practice so provides. Also, issuers can and often do contract with their applicants for expanded rights of reimbursement. Where that is done, the beneficiary will have to meet a more stringent standard of compliance as to the issuer than the issuer will have to meet as to the applicant. Similarly, a nominated person may have reimbursement and other rights against the issuer based on this article, the UCP, bank-to-bank reimbursement rules, or other agreement or undertaking of the issuer. These rights may allow the nominated person to recover from the issuer even when the nominated person would have no right to obtain honor under the letter of credit.

The section adopts strict compliance, rather than the standard that commentators have called "substantial compliance," the standard arguably applied in Banco Español de Credito v. State Street Bank and Trust Company, 385 F.2d 230 (1st Cir.1967) and Flagship Cruises Ltd. v. New England Merchants Nat. Bank, 569 F.2d 699 (1st Cir.1978). Strict compliance does not mean slavish conformity to the terms of the letter of credit. For example, standard practice (what issuers do) may recognize certain presentations as complying that an unschooled layman would regard as discrepant. By adopting standard practice as a way of measuring strict compliance, this article indorses the conclusion of the court in New Braunfels Nat. Bank v. Odiorne, 780 S.W.2d 313 (Tex.Ct.App. 1989) (beneficiary could collect when draft requested payment on "Letter of Credit No. 86–122–5" and letter of credit specified "Letter of Credit No. 86–122–S" holding strict compliance does not demand oppressive perfectionism). The section also indorses the result in

Tosco Corp. v. Federal Deposit Insurance Corp., 723 F.2d 1242 (6th Cir.1983). The letter of credit in that case called for "drafts Drawn under Bank of Clarksville Letter of Credit Number 105." The draft presented stated "drawn under Bank of Clarksville, Clarksville, Tennessee letter of Credit No. 105." The court correctly found that despite the change of upper case "L" to a lower case "l" and the use of the word "No." instead of "Number," and despite the addition of the words "Clarksville, Tennessee," the presentation conformed. Similarly a document addressed by a foreign person to General Motors as "Jeneral Motors" would strictly conform in the absence of other defects.

Identifying and determining compliance with standard practice are matters of interpretation for the court, not for the jury. As with similar rules in Sections 4A–202(c) and 2–302, it is hoped that there will be more consistency in the outcomes and speedier resolution of disputes if the responsibility for determining the nature and scope of standard practice is granted to the court, not to a jury. Granting the court authority to make these decisions will also encourage the salutary practice of courts' granting summary judgment in circumstances where there are no significant factual disputes. The statute encourages outcomes such as American Coleman Co. v. Intrawest Bank, 887 F.2d 1382 (10th Cir.1989), where summary judgment was granted.

In some circumstances standards may be established between the issuer and the applicant by agreement or by custom that would free the issuer from liability that it might otherwise have. For example, an applicant might agree that the issuer would have no duty whatsoever to examine documents on certain presentations (e.g., those below a certain dollar amount). Where the transaction depended upon the issuer's payment in a very short time period (e.g., on the same day or within a few hours of presentation), the issuer and the applicant might agree to reduce the issuer's responsibility for failure to discover discrepancies. By the same token, an agreement between the applicant and the issuer might permit the issuer to examine documents exclusively by electronic or electro-optical means. Neither those agreements nor others like them explicitly made by issuers and applicants violate the terms of Section 5–108(a) or (b) or Section 5–103(c).

2. Section 5–108(a) balances the need of the issuer for time to examine the documents against the possibility that the examiner (at the urging of the applicant or for fear that it will not be reimbursed) will take excessive time to search for defects. What is a "reasonable time" is not extended to accommodate an issuer's procuring a waiver from the applicant. See Article 14c of the UCP.

Under both the UCC and the UCP the issuer has a reasonable time to honor or give notice. The outside limit of that time is measured in business days under the UCC and in banking days under the UCP, a difference that will rarely be significant. Neither business nor banking days are defined in Article 5, but a court may find useful analogies in Regulation CC, 12 CFR 229.2, in state law outside of the Uniform Commercial Code, and in Article 4.

Examiners must note that the seven-day period is not a safe harbor. The time within which the issuer must give notice is the lesser of a reasonable time or seven business days. Where there are few documents (as, for example, with the mine run standby letter of credit), the reasonable time would be less than seven days. If more than a reasonable time is consumed in examination, no timely notice is possible. What is a "reasonable time" is to be determined by examining the behavior of those in the business of examining documents, mostly banks. Absent prior agreement of the issuer, one could not expect a bank issuer to examine documents while the beneficiary waited in the lobby if the normal practice was to give the documents to a person who had the opportunity to examine those together with many others in an orderly process. That the applicant has not yet paid the issuer or that the applicant's account with the issuer is insufficient to cover the amount of the draft is not a basis for extension of the time period.

This section does not preclude the issuer from contacting the applicant during its examination; however, the decision to honor rests with the issuer, and it has no duty to seek a waiver from the applicant or to notify the applicant of receipt of the documents. If the issuer dishonors a conforming presentation, the beneficiary will be entitled to the remedies under Section 5–111, irrespective of the applicant's views.

* * *

Failure of the issuer to act within the time permitted by subsection (b) constitutes dishonor. Because of the preclusion in subsection (c) and the liability that the issuer may incur under Section 5–111 for wrongful dishonor, the effect of such a silent dishonor may ultimately be the same as though the issuer had honored, i.e., it may owe damages in the amount drawn but unpaid under the letter of credit.

3. The requirement that the issuer send notice of the discrepancies or be precluded from asserting discrepancies is new to Article 5. It is taken from the similar provision in the UCP and is intended to promote certainty and finality.

The section thus substitutes a strict preclusion principle for the doctrines of waiver and estoppel that might otherwise apply under Section 1–103. * * *

4. To act within a reasonable time, the issuer must normally give notice without delay after the examining party makes its decision. If the examiner decides to dishonor on the first day, it would be obliged to notify the beneficiary shortly thereafter, perhaps on the same business day. This rule accepts the reasoning in cases such as Datapoint Corp. v. M & I Bank, 665 F.Supp. 722 (W.D.Wis.1987) and Esso Petroleum Canada, Div. of Imperial Oil, Ltd. v. Security Pacific Bank, 710 F.Supp. 275 (D.Or.1989).

The section deprives the examining party of the right simply to sit on a presentation that is made within seven days of expiration. The section requires the examiner to examine the documents and make a decision and, having made a decision to dishonor, to communicate promptly with the presenter. Nevertheless, a beneficiary who presents documents shortly before the expiration of a letter of credit runs the risk that it will never have the opportunity to cure any discrepancies.

5. Confirmers, other nominated persons, and collecting banks acting for beneficiaries can be presenters and, when so, are entitled to the notice provided in subsection (b). * * *

6. In many cases a letter of credit authorizes presentation by the beneficiary to someone other than the issuer. Sometimes that person is identified as a "payor" or "paying bank," or as an "acceptor" or "accepting bank," in other cases as a "negotiating bank," and in other cases there will be no specific designation. The section does not impose any duties on a person other than the issuer or confirmer, however a nominated person or other person may have liability under this article or at common law if it fails to perform an express or implied agreement with the beneficiary.

7. The issuer's obligation to honor runs not only to the beneficiary but also to the applicant. It is possible that an applicant who has made a favorable contract with the beneficiary will be injured by the issuer's wrongful dishonor. Except to the extent that the contract between the issuer and the applicant limits that liability, the issuer will have liability to the applicant for wrongful dishonor under Section 5–111 as a matter of contract law. A good faith extension of the time in Section 5–108(b) by agreement between the issuer and beneficiary binds the applicant even if the applicant is not consulted or does not consent to the extension.

The issuer's obligation to dishonor when there is no apparent compliance with the letter of credit runs only to the applicant. * * *

8. The standard practice referred to in subsection (e) includes (i) international practice set forth in or referenced by the Uniform Customs and Practice, (ii) other practice rules published by associations of financial institutions, and (iii) local and regional practice. It is possible that standard practice will vary from one place to another. Where there are conflicting practices, the parties should indicate which practice governs their rights. A practice may be overridden by agreement or course of dealing. See Section 1–205(4).

* * *

10. Subsection (f) condones an issuer's ignorance of "any usage of a particular trade"; that trade is the trade of the applicant, beneficiary, or others who may be involved in the underlying transaction. The issuer is expected to know usage that is commonly encountered in the course of document examination. For example, an issuer should know the common usage with respect to documents in the maritime shipping trade but would not be expected to understand synonyms used in a particular trade for product descriptions appearing in a letter of credit or an invoice.

* * *

13. The last clause of Section 5–108(i)(5) deals with a special case in which the fraud is not committed by the beneficiary, but is committed by a stranger to the transaction who forges the beneficiary's signature. If the issuer pays against documents on which a required signature of the beneficiary is forged, it remains liable to the true beneficiary.

§ 5–109. Fraud and Forgery.

(a) If a presentation is made that appears on its face strictly to comply with the terms and conditions of the letter of credit, but a required document is forged or materially fraudulent, or honor of the presentation would facilitate a material fraud by the beneficiary on the issuer or applicant:

(1) the issuer shall honor the presentation, if honor is demanded by (i) a nominated person who has given value in good faith and without notice of forgery or material fraud, (ii) a confirmer who has honored its confirmation in good faith, (iii) a holder in due course of a draft drawn under the letter of credit which was taken after acceptance by the issuer or nominated person, or (iv) an assignee of the issuer's or nominated person's deferred obligation that was taken for value and without notice of forgery or material fraud after the obligation was incurred by the issuer or nominated person; and

(2) the issuer, acting in good faith, may honor or dishonor the presentation in any other case.

(b) If an applicant claims that a required document is forged or materially fraudulent or that honor of the presentation would facilitate a material fraud by the beneficiary on the issuer or applicant, a court of competent jurisdiction may temporarily or permanently enjoin the issuer from honoring a presentation or grant similar relief against the issuer or other persons only if the court finds that:

(1) the relief is not prohibited under the law applicable to an accepted draft or deferred obligation incurred by the issuer;

(2) a beneficiary, issuer, or nominated person who may be adversely affected is adequately protected against loss that it may suffer because the relief is granted;

(3) all of the conditions to entitle a person to the relief under the law of this State have been met; and

(4) on the basis of the information submitted to the court, the applicant is more likely than not to succeed under its claim of forgery or material fraud and the person demanding honor does not qualify for protection under subsection (a)(1).

Official Comment

1. This recodification makes clear that fraud must be found either in the documents or must have been committed by the beneficiary on the issuer or applicant. See Cromwell v. Commerce & Energy Bank, 464 So.2d 721 (La.1985).

Secondly, it makes clear that fraud must be "material." Necessarily courts must decide the breadth and width of "materiality." The use of the word requires that the fraudulent aspect of a document be material to a purchaser of that document or that the fraudulent act be significant to the participants in the underlying transaction. Assume, for example, that the beneficiary has a contract to deliver 1,000 barrels of salad oil. Knowing that it has delivered only 998, the beneficiary nevertheless submits an invoice showing 1,000 barrels. If two barrels in a 1,000 barrel shipment would be an insubstantial and immaterial breach of the underlying contract, the beneficiary's act, though possibly fraudulent, is not materially so and would not justify an injunction. Conversely, the knowing submission of those invoices upon delivery of only five barrels would be materially fraudulent. The courts must examine the underlying transaction when there is an allegation of material fraud, for only by examining that transaction can one determine whether a document is fraudulent or the beneficiary has committed fraud and, if so, whether the fraud was material.

Material fraud by the beneficiary occurs only when the beneficiary has no colorable right to expect honor and where there is no basis in fact to support such a right to honor. The section indorses articulations such as those stated in Intraworld Indus. v. Girard Trust Bank, 336 A.2d 316 (Pa.1975), Roman Ceramics Corp. v. People's Nat. Bank, 714 F.2d 1207 (3d Cir.1983), and similar decisions and embraces certain decisions under Section 5–114 that relied upon the phrase "fraud in the transaction." Some of these decisions have been summarized as follows in Ground Air Transfer v. Westates Airlines, 899 F.2d 1269, 1272–73 (1st Cir.1990):

We have said throughout that courts may not "*normally*" issue an injunction because of an important exception to the general "no injunction" rule. The exception, as we also explained in Itek, 730 F.2d at 24–25, concerns "fraud" so serious as to make it obviously pointless and unjust to permit the beneficiary to obtain the money. Where the circumstances "*plainly*" show that the underlying contract forbids the beneficiary to call a letter of credit, Itek, 730 F.2d at 24; where they show that the contract deprives the beneficiary of even a "*colorable*" right to do so, id., at 25; where the contract and circumstances reveal that the beneficiary's demand for payment has "absolutely no basis in fact," id.; see Dynamics Corp. of America, 356 F.Supp. at 999; where the beneficiary's conduct has "so vitiated the entire transaction that the legitimate purposes of the independence of the issuer's obligation would no longer be served," Itek, 730 F.2d at 25 (quoting Roman Ceramics Corp. v. Peoples National Bank, 714 F.2d 1207, 1212 n.12, 1215 (3d Cir.1983) (quoting Intraworld Indus., 336 A.2d at 324–25)); *then* a court may enjoin payment.

2. Subsection (a)(2) makes clear that the issuer may honor in the face of the applicant's claim of fraud. The subsection also makes clear what was not stated in former Section 5–114, that the issuer may dishonor and defend that dishonor by showing fraud or forgery of the kind stated in subsection (a). Because issuers may be liable for wrongful dishonor if they are unable to prove forgery or material fraud, presumably most issuers will choose to honor despite applicant's claims of fraud or forgery unless the applicant procures an injunction. Merely because the issuer has a right to dishonor and to defend that dishonor by showing forgery or material fraud does not mean it has a duty to the applicant to dishonor. The applicant's normal recourse is to procure an injunction, if the applicant is unable to procure an injunction, it will have a claim against the issuer only in the rare case in which it can show that the issuer did not honor in good faith.

3. Whether a beneficiary can commit fraud by presenting a draft under a clean letter of credit (one calling only for a draft and no other documents)

has been much debated. Under the current formulation it would be possible but difficult for there to be fraud in such a presentation. If the applicant were able to show that the beneficiary were committing material fraud on the applicant in the underlying transaction, then payment would facilitate a material fraud by the beneficiary on the applicant and honor could be enjoined. The courts should be skeptical of claims of fraud by one who has signed a "suicide" or clean credit and thus granted a beneficiary the right to draw by mere presentation of a draft.

4. The standard for injunctive relief is high, and the burden remains on the applicant to show, by evidence and not by mere allegation, that such relief is warranted. Some courts have enjoined payments on letters of credit on insufficient showing by the applicant. For example, in Griffin Cos. v. First Nat. Bank, 374 N.W.2d 768 (Minn.App.1985), the court enjoined payment under a standby letter of credit, basing its decision on plaintiff's allegation, rather than competent evidence, of fraud.

There are at least two ways to prohibit injunctions against honor under this section after acceptance of a draft by the issuer. First is to define honor (see Section 5–102(a)(8)) in the particular letter of credit to occur upon acceptance and without regard to later payment of the acceptance. Second is explicitly to agree that the applicant has no right to an injunction after acceptance—whether or not the acceptance constitutes honor.

5. Although the statute deals principally with injunctions against honor, it also cautions against granting "similar relief" and the same principles apply when the applicant or issuer attempts to achieve the same legal outcome by injunction against presentation (see Ground Air Transfer Inc. v. Westates Airlines, Inc., 899 F.2d 1269 (1st Cir.1990)), interpleader, declaratory judgment, or attachment. These attempts should face the same obstacles that face efforts to enjoin the issuer from paying. Expanded use of any of these devices could threaten the independence principle just as much as injunctions against honor. For that reason courts should have the same hostility to them and place the same restrictions on their use as would be applied to injunctions against honor. Courts should not allow the "sacred cow of equity to trample the tender vines of letter of credit law."

6. Section 5–109(a)(1) also protects specified third parties against the risk of fraud. By issuing a letter of credit that nominates a person to negotiate or pay, the issuer (ultimately the applicant) induces that nominated person to give value and thereby assumes the risk that a draft drawn under the letter of credit will be transferred to one with a status like that of a holder in due course who deserves to be protected against a fraud defense.

7. The "loss" to be protected against—by bond or otherwise under subsection (b)(2)—includes incidental damages. Among those are legal fees that might be incurred by the beneficiary or issuer in defending against an injunction action.

§ 5–110. Warranties.

(a) If its presentation is honored, the beneficiary warrants:

(1) to the issuer, any other person to whom presentation is made, and the applicant that there is no fraud or forgery of the kind described in Section 5–109(a); and

(2) to the applicant that the drawing does not violate any agreement between the applicant and beneficiary or any other agreement intended by them to be augmented by the letter of credit.

(b) The warranties in subsection (a) are in addition to warranties arising under Article 3, 4, 7, and 8 because of the presentation or transfer of documents covered by any of those articles.

Official Comment

1. Since the warranties in subsection (a) are not given unless a letter of credit has been honored, no breach of warranty under this subsection can be a defense to dishonor by the issuer. Any defense must be based on Section 5–108 or 5–109 and not on this section. Also, breach of the warranties by the beneficiary in subsection (a) cannot excuse the applicant's duty to reimburse.

2. The warranty in Section 5–110(a)(2) assumes that payment under the letter of credit is final. It does not run to the issuer, only to the applicant. In most cases the applicant will have a direct cause of action for breach of the underlying contract. This warranty has primary application in standby letters of credit or other circumstances where the applicant is not a party to an underlying contract with the beneficiary. It is not a warranty that the statements made on the presentation of the documents presented are truthful nor is it a warranty that the documents strictly comply under Section 5–108(a). It is a warranty that the beneficiary has performed all the acts expressly and implicitly necessary under any underlying agreement to entitle the beneficiary to honor. If, for example, an underlying sales contract authorized the beneficiary to draw only upon "due performance" and the beneficiary drew even though it had breached the underlying contract by delivering defective goods, honor of its draw would break the warranty. By the same token, if the underlying contract authorized the beneficiary to draw only upon actual default or upon its or a third party's determination of default by the applicant and if the beneficiary drew in violation of its authorization, then upon honor of its draw the warranty would be breached. In many cases, therefore, the documents presented to the issuer will contain inaccurate statements (concerning the goods delivered or concerning default or other matters), but the breach of warranty arises not because the statements are untrue but because the beneficiary's drawing violated its express or implied obligations in the underlying transaction.

* * *

§ 5–116. Choice of Law and Forum.

(a) The liability of an issuer, nominated person, or adviser for action or omission is governed by the law of the jurisdiction chosen by an agreement in the form of a record signed or otherwise authenticated by the affected parties in the manner provided in Section 5–104 or by a provision in the person's letter of credit, confirmation, or other undertaking. The jurisdiction whose law is chosen need not bear any relation to the transaction.

(b) Unless subsection (a) applies, the liability of an issuer, nominated person, or adviser for action or omission is governed by the law of the jurisdiction in which the person is located. The person is considered to be located at the address indicated in the person's undertaking. If more than one address is indicated, the person is considered to be located at the address from which the person's undertaking was issued. For the purpose of jurisdiction, choice of law, and recognition of interbranch letters of credit, but not enforcement of a judgment, all branches of a bank are considered separate juridical entities and a bank is considered to be located at the place where its relevant branch is considered to be located under this subsection.

(c) Except as otherwise provided in this subsection, the liability of an issuer, nominated person, or adviser is governed by any rules of custom or practice, such as the Uniform Customs and Practice for Documentary Credits, to which the letter of credit, confirmation, or other undertaking is expressly made subject. If (i) this article would govern the liability of an issuer, nominated person, or adviser under subsection (a) or (b), (ii) the relevant undertaking incorporates rules of custom or practice, and (iii) there is conflict between this article and those rules as applied to that undertaking, those rules govern except to the extent of any conflict with the nonvariable provisions specified in Section 5–103(c).

* * *

Official Comment

1. Although it would be possible for the parties to agree otherwise, the law normally chosen by agreement under subsection (a) and that provided in the absence of agreement under subsection (b) is the substantive law of a particular jurisdiction not including the choice of law principles of that jurisdiction. Thus, two parties, an issuer and an applicant, both located in Oklahoma might choose the law of New York. Unless they agree otherwise, the section anticipates that they wish the substantive law of New York to apply to their transaction and they do not intend that a New York choice of law principle might direct a court to Oklahoma law. By the same token, the liability of an issuer located in New York is governed by New York substantive law—in the absence of agreement—even in circumstances in which choice of law principles found in the common law of New York might direct one to the law of another State. Subsection (b) states the relevant choice of law principles and it should not be subordinated to some other choice of law rule. Within the States of the United States *renvoi* will not be a problem once every jurisdiction has enacted Section 5–116 because every jurisdiction will then have the same choice of law rule and in a particular case all choice of law rules will point to the same substantive law.

Subsection (b) does not state a choice of law rule for the "liability of an applicant." However, subsection (b) does state a choice of law rule for the liability of an issuer, nominated person, or adviser, and since some of the issues in suits by applicants against those persons involve the "liability of an issuer, nominated person, or adviser," subsection (b) states the choice of law rule for those issues. Because an issuer may have liability to a confirmer both as an issuer (Section 5–108(a), Comment 5 to Section 5–108) and as an applicant (Section 5–107(a), Comment 1 to Section 5–107, Section 5–108(i)), subsection (b) may state the choice of law rule for some but not all of the issuer's liability in a suit by a confirmer.

2. Because the confirmer or other nominated person may choose different law from that chosen by the issuer or may be located in a different jurisdiction and fail to choose law, it is possible that a confirmer or nominated person may be obligated to pay (under their law) but will not be entitled to payment from the issuer (under its law). Similarly, the rights of an unreimbursed issuer, confirmer, or nominated person against a beneficiary under Section 5–109, 5–110, or 5–117, will not necessarily be governed by the same law that applies to the issuer's or confirmer's obligation upon presentation. Because the UCP and other practice are incorporated in most international letters of credit, disputes arising from different legal obligations to honor have not been frequent. Since Section 5–108 incorporates standard practice, these problems should be further minimized—at least to the extent that the same practice is and continues to be widely followed.

3. This section does not permit what is now authorized by the nonuniform Section 5–102(4) in New York. Under the current law in New York a letter of credit that incorporates the UCP is not governed in any respect by Article 5. Under revised Section 5–116 letters of credit that incorporate the UCP or similar practice will still be subject to Article 5 in certain respects. First, incorporation of the UCP or other practice does not override the nonvariable terms of Article 5. Second, where there is no conflict between Article 5 and the relevant provision of the UCP or other practice, both apply. Third, practice provisions incorporated in a letter of credit will not be effective if they fail to comply with Section 5–103(c). Assume, for example, that a practice provision purported to free a party from any liability unless it were "grossly negligent" or that the practice generally limited the remedies that one party might have against another. Depending upon the circumstances, that disclaimer or limitation of liability might be ineffective because of Section 5–103(c).

Even though Article 5 is generally consistent with UCP 500, it is not necessarily consistent with other rules or with versions of the UCP that may be adopted after Article 5's revision, or with other practices that may develop. Rules of practice incorporated in the letter of credit or other undertaking are those in effect when the letter of credit or other undertaking is issued. Except in the unusual cases discussed in the immediately preceding paragraph, practice adopted in a letter of credit will override the rules of Article 5 and the parties to letter of credit transactions must be familiar with practice (such as future versions of the UCP) that is explicitly adopted in letters of credit.

* * *

ARTICLE 7. WAREHOUSE RECEIPTS, BILLS OF LADING AND OTHER DOCUMENTS OF TITLE

PART 1

GENERAL

§ 7–103. Relation of Article to Treaty, Statute, Tariff, Classification or Regulation.

To the extent that any treaty or statute of the United States, regulatory statute of this State or tariff, classification or regulation filed or issued pursuant thereto is applicable, the provisions of this Article are subject thereto.

§ 7–104. Negotiable and Non-negotiable Warehouse Receipt, Bill of Lading or Other Document of Title.

(1) A warehouse receipt, bill of lading or other document of title is negotiable

(a) if by its terms the goods are to be delivered to bearer or to the order of a named person; or

(b) where recognized in overseas trade, if it runs to a named person or assigns.[a]

(2) Any other document is non-negotiable. A bill of lading in which it is stated that the goods are consigned to a named person is not made negotiable by a provision that the goods are to be delivered only against a written order signed by the same or another named person.

* * *

PART 5

WAREHOUSE RECEIPTS AND BILLS OF LADING: NEGOTIATION AND TRANSFER

§ 7–501. Form of Negotiation and Requirements of "Due Negotiation".

(1) A negotiable document of title running to the order of a named person is negotiated by his indorsement and delivery. After his indorsement in blank or to bearer any person can negotiate it by delivery alone.

(2)(a) A negotiable document of title is also negotiated by delivery alone when by its original terms it runs to bearer.

(b) When a document running to the order of a named person is delivered to him the effect is the same as if the document had been negotiated.

a. Author's Note: UCC § 7–104(1)(b) is omitted in Revised UCC Article 7.

(3) Negotiation of a negotiable document of title after it has been indorsed to a specified person requires indorsement by the special indorsee as well as delivery.

(4) A negotiable document of title is "duly negotiated" when it is negotiated in the manner stated in this section to a holder who purchases it in good faith without notice of any defense against or claim to it on the part of any person and for value, unless it is established that the negotiation is not in the regular course of business or financing or involves receiving the document in settlement or payment of a money obligation.

(5) Indorsement of a non-negotiable document neither makes it negotiable nor adds to the transferee's rights.

(6) The naming in a negotiable bill of a person to be notified of the arrival of the goods does not limit the negotiability of the bill nor constitute notice to a purchaser thereof of any interest of such person in the goods.

Official Comment

1. In general this section is intended to clarify the language of the old acts and to restate the effect of the better decisions thereunder. An important new concept is added, however, in the requirement of "regular course of business or financing" to effect the "due negotiation" which will transfer greater rights than those held by the person negotiating. The foundation of the mercantile doctrine of good faith purchase for value has always been, as shown by the case situations, the furtherance and protection of the regular course of trade. The reason for allowing a person, in bad faith or in error, to convey away rights which are not his own has from the beginning been to make possible the speedy handling of that great run of commercial transactions which are patently usual and normal.

There are two aspects to the usual and normal course of mercantile dealings, namely, the person making the transfer and the nature of the transaction itself. The first question which arises is: Is the transferor a person with whom it is reasonable to deal as having full powers? In regard to documents of title the only holder whose possession appears, commercially, to be in order is almost invariably a person in the trade. No commercial purpose is served by allowing a tramp or a professor to "duly negotiate" an order bill of lading for hides or cotton not his own, and since such a transfer is obviously not in the regular course of business, it is excluded from the scope of the protection of subsection (4).

§ 7–502. Rights Acquired by Due Negotiation.

(1) Subject to the following section and to the provisions of Section 7–205 on fungible goods, a holder to whom a negotiable document of title has been duly negotiated acquires thereby:

(a) title to the document;

(b) title to the goods;

(c) all rights accruing under the law of agency or estoppel, including rights to goods delivered to the bailee after the document was issued; and

(d) the direct obligation of the issuer to hold or deliver the goods according to the terms of the document free of any defense or claim by him except those arising under the terms of the document or under this Article. In the case of a delivery order the bailee's obligation accrues only upon acceptance and the obligation acquired by the holder is that the issuer and any indorser will procure the acceptance of the bailee.

(2) Subject to the following section, title and rights so acquired are not defeated by any stoppage of the goods represented by the document or by surrender of such goods by the bailee, and are not impaired even though the negotiation or any prior negotiation constituted a breach of duty or even though any person has been deprived of possession of the document by misrepresentation, fraud, accident, mistake, duress, loss, theft or conversion, or even though a previous sale or other transfer of the goods or document has been made to a third person.

§ 7–503. Document of Title to Goods Defeated in Certain Cases.

(1) A document of title confers no right in goods against a person who before issuance of the document had a legal interest or a perfected security interest in them and who neither

(a) delivered or entrusted them or any document of title covering them to the bailor or his nominee with actual or apparent authority to ship, store or sell or with power to obtain delivery under this Article (Section 7–403) or with power of disposition under this Act (Sections 2–403 and 9–320) or other statute or rule of law: nor

(b) acquiesced in the procurement by the bailor or his nominee, of any document of title.

(2) Title to goods based upon an unaccepted delivery order is subject to the rights of anyone to whom a negotiable warehouse receipt or bill of lading covering the goods has been duly negotiated. Such a title may be defeated under the next section to the same extent as the rights of the issuer or a transferee from the issuer.

(3) Title to goods based upon a bill of lading issued to a freight forwarder is subject to the rights of anyone to whom a bill issued by the freight forwarder is duly negotiated; but delivery by the carrier in accordance with Part 4 of this Article pursuant to its own bill of lading discharges the carrier's obligation to deliver.

* * *

§ 7–507. Warranties on Negotiation or Transfer of Receipt or Bill.

Where a person negotiates or transfers a document of title for value otherwise than as a mere intermediary under the next following section, then unless otherwise agreed he warrants to his immediate purchaser only in addition to any warranty made in selling the goods

(a) that the document is genuine; and

(b) that he has no knowledge of any fact which would impair its validity or worth; and

(c) that his negotiation or transfer is rightful and fully effective with respect to the title to the document and the goods it represents.

Official Comment

1. This section omits provisions of the prior acts on warranties as to the goods as unnecessary and incomplete. It is unnecessary because such warranties derive from the contract of sale and not from the transfer of the documents. The fact that transfer of control occurs by way of a document of title does not limit or displace the ordinary obligations of a seller. The former provision, moreover, was incomplete because it did not expressly include all of the warranties which might rest upon a seller under such circumstances. This Act handles the problem by means of the precautionary reference to "any warranty made in selling the goods." If the transfer of documents attends or follows the making of a contract for the sale of goods, the general obligations on warranties as to the goods (Sections 2–312 through 2–318) are brought to bear as well as the special warranties under this section.

2. The limited warranties of a delivering or collecting intermediary are stated in Section 7–508.

§ 7–508. Warranties of Collecting Bank as to Documents.

A collecting bank or other intermediary known to be entrusted with documents on behalf of another or with collection of a draft or other claim against delivery of documents warrants by such delivery of the documents only its own good faith and authority. This rule applies even though the intermediary has purchased or made advances against the claim or draft to be collected.

Official Comment

1. To state the limited warranties given with respect to the documents accompanying a documentary draft.

2. In warranting its authority a bank only warrants its authority from its transferor. See Section 4–203. It does not warrant the genuineness or effectiveness of the document. Compare Section 7–507.

DOCUMENT 21

UNIFORM COMMERCIAL CODE [REVISED] ARTICLE 1

GENERAL PROVISIONS

[Author's Note: Revised Article 1 was approved by the Uniform Commissioners and the ALI in 2001. Dozens of states have enacted it and the U.S. Virgin Islands. However, the enacting states have not adopted Revised § 1–301 on choice of law. Instead they have replaced the language in Revised § 1–301 with the language in original UCC § 1–105. Only the U.S., Virgin Islands has enacted Revised § 1–301]

PART 2

GENERAL DEFINITIONS AND PRINCIPLES OF INTERPRETATION

§ 1–201. General Definitions.

(a) Unless the context otherwise requires, words or phrases defined in this section, or in the additional definitions contained in other articles of [the Uniform Commercial Code] that apply to particular articles or parts thereof, have the meanings stated.

(b) Subject to definitions contained in other articles of [the Uniform Commercial Code] that apply to particular articles or parts thereof:

(31) "Record" means information that is inscribed on a tangible medium or that is stored in an electronic or other medium and is retrievable in perceivable form.

(43) "Writing" includes printing, typewriting, or any other intentional reduction to tangible form. "Written" has a corresponding meaning.

Official Comments

43. "Written" or "writing." Unchanged from former Section 1–201.

PART 3

TERRITORIAL APPLICABILITY AND GENERAL RULES

§ 1–301. Territorial Applicability; Parties' Power to Choose Applicable Law.

[*Author's Note: No state has enacted Revised § 1–301. Instead, they substituted original § 1–105 in its place.*]

(a) In this section:

(1) "Domestic transaction" means a transaction other than an international transaction.

(2) "International transaction" means a transaction that bears a reasonable relation to a country other than the United States.

(b) This section applies to a transaction to the extent that it is governed by another article of the [Uniform Commercial Code].

(c) Except as otherwise provided in this section:

(1) an agreement by parties to a domestic transaction that any or all of their rights and obligations are to be determined by the law of this State or of another State is effective, whether or not the transaction bears a relation to the State designated; and

(2) an agreement by parties to an international transaction that any or all of their rights and obligations are to be determined by the law of this State or of another State or country is effective, whether or not the transaction bears a relation to the State or country designated.

(d) In the absence of an agreement effective under subsection (c), and except as provided in subsections (e) and (g), the rights and obligations of the parties are determined by the law that would be selected by application of this State's conflict of laws principles.

(e) If one of the parties to a transaction is a consumer, the following rules apply:

(1) An agreement referred to in subsection (c) is not effective unless the transaction bears a reasonable relation to the State or country designated.

(2) Application of the law of the State or country determined pursuant to subsection (c) or (d) may not deprive the consumer of the protection of any rule of law governing a matter within the scope of this section, which both is protective of consumers and may not be varied by agreement:

(A) of the State or country in which the consumer principally resides, unless subparagraph (B) applies; or

(B) if the transaction is a sale of goods, of the State or country in which the consumer both makes the contract and takes delivery of those goods, if such State or country is not the State or country in which the consumer principally resides.

(f) An agreement otherwise effective under subsection (c) is not effective to the extent that application of the law of the State or country designated would be contrary to a fundamental policy of the State or country whose law would govern in the absence of agreement under subsection (d).

(g) To the extent that [the Uniform Commercial Code] governs a transaction, if one of the following provisions of [the Uniform Commercial Code] specifies the applicable law, that provision governs and a contrary agreement is effective only to the extent permitted by the law so specified:

(1) Section 2–402; * * *

Official Comments

Source: Former Section 1–105.

Summary of changes from former law: Section 1–301, which replaces former Section 1–105, represents a significant rethinking of choice of law issues addressed in that section. The new section reexamines both the power of parties to select the jurisdiction whose law will govern their transaction and the determination of the governing law in the absence of such selection by the parties. With respect to the power to select governing law, the draft affords greater party autonomy than former Section 1–105, but with important safeguards protecting consumer interests and fundamental policies.

Section 1–301 addresses contractual designation of governing law somewhat differently than does former Section 1–105. Former law allowed the parties to any transaction to designate a jurisdiction whose law governs if the transaction bears a "reasonable relation" to that jurisdiction. Section 1–301 deviates from this approach by providing different rules for transactions involving a consumer than for non-consumer transactions, such as "business to business" transactions.

In the context of consumer transactions, the language of Section 1–301, unlike that of former Section 1–105, protects consumers against the possibility of losing the protection of consumer protection rules applicable to the aspects of the transaction governed by the Uniform Commercial Code. In most situations, the relevant consumer protection rules will be those of the consumer's home jurisdiction. A special rule, however, is provided for certain face-to-face sales transactions. (See Comment 3.)

In the context of business-to-business transactions, Section 1–301 generally provides the parties with greater autonomy to designate a jurisdiction whose law will govern than did former Section 1–105, but also provides safeguards against abuse that did not appear in former Section 1–105. In the non-consumer context, following emerging international norms, greater autonomy is provided in subsections (c)(1) and (c)(2) by deleting the former requirement that the transaction bear a "reasonable relation" to the jurisdiction. In the case of wholly domestic transactions, however, the jurisdiction designated must be a State. (See Comment 4.)

An important safeguard not present in former Section 1–105 is found in subsection (f). Subsection (f) provides that the designation of a jurisdiction's law is not effective (even if the transaction bears a reasonable relation to that jurisdiction) to the extent that application of that law would be contrary to a fundamental policy of the jurisdiction whose law would govern in the absence of contractual designation. Application of the law designated may be contrary to a fundamental policy of the State or country whose law would otherwise govern either because of the nature of the law designated or because of the "mandatory" nature of the law that would otherwise apply. (See Comment 6.)

In the absence of an effective contractual designation of governing law, former Section 1–105(1) directed the forum to apply its own law if the transaction bore "an appropriate relation to this state." This direction, however, was frequently ignored by courts. Section 1–301(d) provides that, in the absence of an effective contractual designation, the forum should apply the forum's general choice of law principles, subject to certain special rules in consumer transactions. (See Comments 3 and 7).

1. *Applicability of section.* This section is neither a complete restatement of choice of law principles nor a free-standing choice of law statute. Rather, it is a provision of Article 1 of the Uniform Commercial Code. As such, the scope of its application is limited in two significant ways.

First, this section is subject to Section 1–102, which states the scope of Article 1. As that section indicates, Article 1, and the rules contained therein, apply to transactions to the extent that they are governed by one of the other Articles of the Uniform Commercial Code. Thus, this section does not apply to matters outside the scope of the Uniform Commercial Code, such as a services contract, a credit card agreement, or a contract for the sale of real estate. This limitation was implicit in former Section 1–105, and is made explicit in Section 1–301(b).

Second, subsection (g) provides that this section is subject to the specific choice of law provisions contained in other Articles of the Uniform Commercial Code. Thus, to the extent that a transaction otherwise within the scope of this section also is within the scope of one of those provisions, the rules of that specific provision, rather than of this section, apply.

The following cases illustrate these two limitations on the scope of Section 1–301:

Example 1: A, a resident of Indiana, enters into an agreement with Credit Card Company, a Delaware corporation with its chief executive office located in New York, pursuant to which A agrees to pay Credit Card Company for purchases charged to A's credit card. The agreement contains a provision stating that it is governed by the law of South Dakota. The choice of law rules in Section 1–301 do not apply to this agreement because the agreement is not governed by any of the other Articles of the Uniform Commercial Code.

Example 2: A, a resident of Indiana, maintains a checking account with Bank B, an Ohio banking corporation located in Ohio. At the time that the account was established, Bank B and A entered into a "Bank–Customer Agreement" governing their relationship with respect to the account. The Bank–Customer Agreement contains some provisions that purport to limit the liability of Bank B with respect to its decisions whether to honor or dishonor checks purporting to be drawn on A's account. The Bank–Customer Agreement also contains a provision stating that it is governed by the law of Ohio. The provisions purporting to limit the liability of Bank B deal with issues governed by Article 4. Therefore, determination of the law applicable to those issues (including determination of the effectiveness of the choice of law clause as it applies to those issues) is within the scope of Section 1–301 as provided in subsection (b). Nonetheless, the rules of Section 1–301 would not apply to that determination because of subsection (g), which states that the choice of law rules in Section 4–102 govern instead.

2. *Contractual choice of law.* This section allows parties broad autonomy, subject to several important limitations, to select the law governing their transaction, even if the transaction does not bear a relation to the State or country whose law is selected. This recognition of party autonomy with respect to governing law has already been established in several Articles of the Uniform Commercial Code (see Sections 4A–507, 5–116, and 8–110) and is consistent with international norms. See, e.g., Inter–American Convention on the Law Applicable to International Contracts, Article 7 (Mexico City 1994); Convention on the Law Applicable to Contracts for the International Sale of Goods, Article 7(1) (The Hague 1986); EC Convention on the Law Applicable to Contractual Obligations, Article 3(1) (Rome 1980).

There are three important limitations on this party autonomy to select governing law. First, a different, and more protective, rule applies in the context of consumer transactions. (See Comment 3). Second, in an entirely domestic transaction, this section does not validate the selection of foreign law. (See Comment 4.) Third, contractual choice of law will not be given effect to the extent that application of the law designated would be contrary to a fundamental policy of the State or country whose law would be applied in the absence of such contractual designation. (See Comment 6).

This Section does not address the ability of parties to designate non-legal codes such as trade codes as the set of rules governing their transaction. The power of parties to make such a designation as part of their agreement is found in the principles of Section 1–302. That Section, allowing parties broad freedom of contract to structure their relations, is adequate for this purpose. This is also the case with respect to the ability of the parties to designate recognized bodies of rules or principles applicable to commercial transactions that are promulgated by intergovernmental organizations such as UNCITRAL or Unidroit. See, e.g., Unidroit Principles of International Commercial Contracts.

* * *

4. *Wholly domestic transactions.* While this Section provides parties broad autonomy to select governing law, that autonomy is limited in the case of wholly domestic transactions. In a "domestic transaction," subsection (c)(1) validates only the designation of the law of a State. A "domestic transaction"

is a transaction that does not bear a reasonable relation to a country other than the United States. (See subsection (a)). Thus, in a wholly domestic non-consumer transaction, parties may (subject to the limitations set out in subsections (f) and (g)) designate the law of any State but not the law of a foreign country.

5. *International transactions.* This section provides greater autonomy in the context of international transactions. As defined in subsection (a)(2), a transaction is an "international transaction" if it bears a reasonable relation to a country other than the United States. In a non-consumer international transaction, subsection (c)(2) provides that a designation of the law of any State or country is effective (subject, of course, to the limitations set out in subsections (f) and (g)). It is important to note that the transaction need not bear a relation to the State or country designated if the transaction is international. Thus, for example, in a non-consumer lease of goods in which the lessor is located in Mexico and the lessee is located in Louisiana, a designation of the law of Ireland to govern the transaction would be given effect under this section even though the transaction bears no relation to Ireland. The ability to designate the law of any country in non-consumer international transactions is important in light of the common practice in many commercial contexts of designating the law of a "neutral" jurisdiction or of a jurisdiction whose law is well-developed. If a country has two or more territorial units in which different systems of law relating to matters within the scope of this section are applicable (as is the case, for example, in Canada and the United Kingdom), subsection (c)(2) should be applied to designation by the parties of the law of one of those territorial units. Thus, for example, subsection (c)(2) should be applied if the parties to a non-consumer international transaction designate the laws of Ontario or Scotland as governing their transaction.

6. *Fundamental policy.* Subsection (f) provides that an agreement designating the governing law will not be given effect to the extent that application of the designated law would be contrary to a fundamental policy of the State or country whose law would otherwise govern. This rule provides a narrow exception to the broad autonomy afforded to parties in subsection (c). One of the prime objectives of contract law is to protect the justified expectations of the parties and to make it possible for them to foretell with accuracy what will be their rights and liabilities under the contract. In this way, certainty and predictability of result are most likely to be secured. See Restatement (Second) Conflict of Laws, Section 187, comment *e*.

Under the fundamental policy doctrine, a court should not refrain from applying the designated law merely because application of that law would lead to a result different than would be obtained under the local law of the State or country whose law would otherwise govern. Rather, the difference must be contrary to a public policy of that jurisdiction that is so substantial that it justifies overriding the concerns for certainty and predictability underlying modern commercial law as well as concerns for judicial economy generally. Thus, application of the designated law will rarely be found to be contrary to a fundamental policy of the State or country whose law would otherwise govern when the difference between the two concerns a requirement, such as a statute of frauds, that relates to formalities, or general rules of contract law, such as those concerned with the need for consideration.

The opinion of Judge Cardozo in *Loucks v. Standard Oil Co. of New York*, 120 N.E. 198 (1918), regarding the related issue of when a state court may decline to apply the law of another state, is a helpful touchstone here:

Our own scheme of legislation may be different. We may even have no legislation on the subject. That is not enough to show that public policy forbids us to enforce the foreign right. A right of action is property. If a foreign statute gives the right, the mere fact that we do not give a like right is no reason for refusing to help the plaintiff in getting what belongs to him. We are not so provincial as to say that every solution of a problem is wrong because we deal with it otherwise at home. Similarity of legislation has indeed this importance; its presence shows beyond question that the foreign statute does not offend the local policy. But its absence does not prove the contrary. It is not to be exalted into an indispensable condition. The misleading word 'comity' has been responsible for much of the trouble. It has been fertile in suggesting a discretion unregulated by general principles.

* * *

The courts are not free to refuse to enforce a foreign right at the pleasure of the judges, to suit the individual notion of expediency or fairness. They do not close their doors, unless help would violate some fundamental principle of justice, some prevalent conception of good morals, some deep-rooted tradition of the common weal.

120 N.E. at 201–02 (citations to authorities omitted).

Application of the designated law may be contrary to a fundamental policy of the State or country whose law would otherwise govern either (i) because the substance of the designated law violates a fundamental principle of justice of that State or country or (ii) because it differs from a rule of that State or country that is "mandatory" in that it *must* be applied in the courts of that State or country without regard to otherwise-applicable choice of law rules of that State or country and without regard to whether the designated law is otherwise offensive. The mandatory rules concept appears in international conventions in this field, *e.g.*, EC Convention on the Law Applicable to Contractual Obligations, although in some cases the concept is applied to authorize the *forum* state to apply *its* mandatory rules, rather than those of the State or country whose law would otherwise govern. The latter situation is not addressed by this section. (See Comment 9.)

It is obvious that a rule that is freely changeable by agreement of the parties under the law of the State or country whose law would otherwise govern cannot be construed as a mandatory rule of that State or country. This does not mean, however, that rules that cannot be changed by agreement under that law are, for that reason alone, mandatory rules. Otherwise, contractual choice of law in the context of the Uniform Commercial Code would be illusory and redundant; the parties would be able to accomplish by choice of law no more than can be accomplished under Section 1–302, which allows variation of otherwise applicable rules by agreement. (Under Section 1–302, the parties could agree to vary the rules that would otherwise govern their transaction by substituting for those rules the rules that would apply if the transaction were governed by the law of the designated State or country without designation of governing law.) Indeed, other than cases in which a mandatory choice of law rule is established by statute (see, *e.g.*, Sections 9–301 through 9–307, explicitly preserved in subsection (g)), cases in which courts have declined to follow the designated law solely because a rule of the State or country whose law would otherwise govern is mandatory are rare.

7. *Choice of law in the absence of contractual designation.* Subsection (d), which replaces the second sentence of former Section 1–105(1), determines which jurisdiction's law governs a transaction in the absence of an effective contractual choice by the parties. Former Section 1–105(1) provided that the law of the forum (*i.e.*, the Uniform Commercial Code) applied if the transaction bore "an appropriate relation to this state." By using an "appropriate relation" test, rather than, for example, a "most significant relationship" test, Section 1–105(1) expressed a bias in favor of applying the forum's law. This bias, while not universally respected by the courts, was justifiable in light of the uncertainty that existed at the time of drafting as to whether the Uniform Commercial Code would be adopted by all the states; the pro-forum bias would assure that the Uniform Commercial Code would be applied so long as the transaction bore an "appropriate" relation to the forum. Inasmuch as the Uniform Commercial Code has been adopted, at least in part, in all U.S. jurisdictions, the vitality of this point is minimal in the domestic context, and international comity concerns militate against continuing the pro-forum, pro-UCC bias in transnational transactions. Whether the choice is between the law of two jurisdictions that have adopted the Uniform Commercial Code, but whose law differs (because of differences in enacted language or differing judicial interpretations), or between the Uniform Commercial Code and the law of another country, there is no strong justification for directing a court to apply different choice of law principles to that determination than it would apply if the matter were not governed by the Uniform Commercial Code. Similarly, given the variety of choice of law principles applied by the states, it would not be prudent to designate only one such principle as the proper one for transactions governed by the Uniform Commercial Code. Accordingly, in cases in which the parties have not made an effective choice of law, Section 1–301(d) simply directs the forum to apply its ordinary choice of law principles to determine which jurisdiction's law governs, subject to the special rules of Section 1–301(e)(2) with regard to consumer transactions.

* * *

9. *Matters not addressed by this section.* As noted in Comment 1, this section is not a complete statement of conflict of laws doctrines applicable in commercial cases. Among the issues this section does not address, and leaves to other law, three in particular deserve mention. First, a forum will occasionally decline to apply the law of a different jurisdiction selected by the parties when application of that law would be contrary to a fundamental policy of the forum jurisdiction, even if it would not be contrary to a fundamental policy of the State or country whose law would govern in the absence of contractual designation. Standards for application of this doctrine relate primarily to concepts of sovereignty rather than commercial law and are thus left to the

courts. Second, in determining whether to give effect to the parties' agreement that the law of a particular State or country will govern their relationship, courts must, of necessity, address some issues as to the basic validity of that agreement. These issues might relate, for example, to capacity to contract and absence of duress. This section does not address these issues. Third, this section leaves to other choice of law principles of the forum the issues of whether, and to what extent, the forum will apply the same law to the non-UCC aspects of a transaction that it applies to the aspects of the transaction governed by the Uniform Commercial Code.

§ 1–302. Variation by Agreement.

(a) Except as otherwise provided in subsection (b) or elsewhere in [the Uniform Commercial Code], the effect of provisions of [the Uniform Commercial Code] may be varied by agreement.

(b) The obligations of good faith, diligence, reasonableness, and care prescribed by [the Uniform Commercial Code] may not be disclaimed by agreement. The parties, by agreement, may determine the standards by which the performance of those obligations is to be measured if those standards are not manifestly unreasonable. Whenever [the Uniform Commercial Code] requires an action to be taken within a reasonable time, a time that is not manifestly unreasonable may be fixed by agreement.

(c) The presence in certain provisions of [the Uniform Commercial Code] of the phrase "unless otherwise agreed", or words of similar import, does not imply that the effect of other provisions may not be varied by agreement under this section.

Official Comments

Source: Former Sections 1–102(3)-(4) and 1–204(1).

Changes: This section combines the rules from subsections (3) and (4) of former Section 1–102 and subsection (1) of former Section 1–204. No substantive changes are made.

1. Subsection (a) states affirmatively at the outset that freedom of contract is a principle of the Uniform Commercial Code: "the effect" of its provisions may be varied by "agreement." The meaning of the statute itself must be found in its text, including its definitions, and in appropriate extrinsic aids; it cannot be varied by agreement. * * * But an agreement can change the legal consequences that would otherwise flow from the provisions of the Uniform Commercial Code. "Agreement" here includes the effect given to course of dealing, usage of trade and course of performance by Sections 1–201 and 1–303; the effect of an agreement on the rights of third parties is left to specific provisions of the Uniform Commercial Code and to supplementary principles applicable under Section 1–103. The rights of third parties under Section 9–317 when a security interest is unperfected, for example, cannot be destroyed by a clause in the security agreement.

This principle of freedom of contract is subject to specific exceptions found elsewhere in the Uniform Commercial Code and to the general exception stated here. The specific exceptions vary in explicitness: the statute of frauds found in Section 2–201, for example, does not explicitly preclude oral waiver of the requirement of a writing, but a fair reading denies enforcement to such a waiver as part of the "contract" made unenforceable; Section 9–602, on the other hand, is a quite explicit limitation on freedom of contract. Under the exception for "the obligations of good faith, diligence, reasonableness and care prescribed by [the Uniform Commercial Code]," provisions of the Uniform Commercial Code prescribing such obligations are not to be disclaimed. However, the section also recognizes the prevailing practice of having agreements set forth standards by which due diligence is measured and explicitly provides that, in the absence of a showing that the standards manifestly are unreasonable, the agreement controls. In this connection, Section 1–303 incorporating into the agreement prior course of dealing and usages of trade is of particular importance.

Subsection (b) also recognizes that nothing is stronger evidence of a reasonable time than the fixing of such time by a fair agreement between the parties. However, provision is made for disregarding a clause which whether by inadvertence or overreaching fixes a time so unreasonable that it amounts to eliminating all remedy under the contract. The parties are not required to fix the most reasonable time but may fix any time which is not obviously unfair as judged by the time of contracting.

2. An agreement that varies the effect of provisions of the Uniform Commercial Code may do so by stating the rules that will govern in lieu of the provisions varied. Alternatively, the parties may vary the effect of such provisions by stating that their relationship will be governed by recognized bodies of rules or principles applicable to commercial transactions. Such bodies of rules or principles may include, for example, those that are promulgated by intergovernmental authorities such as UNCITRAL or Unidroit (*see, e.g.*, Unidroit Principles of International Commercial Contracts), or non-legal codes such as trade codes.

3. Subsection (c) is intended to make it clear that, as a matter of drafting, phrases such as "unless otherwise agreed" have been used to avoid controversy as to whether the subject matter of a particular section does or does not fall within the exceptions to subsection (b), but absence of such words contains no negative implication since under subsection (b) the general and residual rule is that the effect of all provisions of the Uniform Commercial Code may be varied by agreement.

§ 1–303. Course of Performance, Course of Dealing, and Usage of Trade.

(a) A "course of performance" is a sequence of conduct between the parties to a particular transaction that exists if:

(1) the agreement of the parties with respect to the transaction involves repeated occasions for performance by a party; and

(2) the other party, with knowledge of the nature of the performance and opportunity for objection to it, accepts the performance or acquiesces in it without objection.

(b) A "course of dealing" is a sequence of conduct concerning previous transactions between the parties to a particular transaction that is fairly to be regarded as establishing a common basis of understanding for interpreting their expressions and other conduct.

(c) A "usage of trade" is any practice or method of dealing having such regularity of observance in a place, vocation, or trade as to justify an expectation that it will be observed with respect to the transaction in question. The existence and scope of such a usage must be proved as facts. If it is established that such a usage is embodied in a trade code or similar record, the interpretation of the record is a question of law.

(d) A course of performance or course of dealing between the parties or usage of trade in the vocation or trade in which they are engaged or of which they are or should be aware is relevant in ascertaining the meaning of the parties' agreement, may give particular meaning to specific terms of the agreement, and may supplement or qualify the terms of the agreement. A usage of trade applicable in the place in which part of the performance under the agreement is to occur may be so utilized as to that part of the performance.

(e) Except as otherwise provided in subsection (f), the express terms of an agreement and any applicable course of performance, course of dealing, or usage of trade must be construed whenever reasonable as consistent with each other. If such a construction is unreasonable:

(1) express terms prevail over course of performance, course of dealing, and usage of trade;

(2) course of performance prevails over course of dealing and usage of trade; and

(3) course of dealing prevails over usage of trade.

(f) Subject to Section 2–209, a course of performance is relevant to show a waiver or modification of any term inconsistent with the course of performance.

(g) Evidence of a relevant usage of trade offered by one party is not admissible unless that party has given the other party notice that the court finds sufficient to prevent unfair surprise to the other party.

Official Comments

Source: Former Sections 1–205, 2–208, and Section 2A–207.

Changes from former law: This section integrates the "course of performance" concept from Articles 2 and 2A into the principles of former Section 1–205, which deals with course of dealing and usage of trade. In so doing, the section slightly modifies the articulation of the course of performance rules to fit more comfortably with the approach and structure of former Section 1–205.

DOCUMENT 22

(2003) AMENDMENTS TO UNIFORM COMMERCIAL CODE ARTICLE 2—SALES

[*Author's note: These Amendments to UCC Article 2 were approved by the American Law Institute and the National Conference of Commissioners on Uniform State Laws during 2002–2003. However, to date no state has enacted these Amendments.*]

ARTICLE 2

SALES

TABLE OF CONTENTS

PART 2

FORM, FORMATION, TERMS AND READJUSTMENT OF CONTRACT; ELECTRONIC CONTRACTING

§ 2–201. Formal Requirements; Statute of Frauds.

(1) ~~Except as otherwise provided in this section a~~ A contract for the sale of goods for the price of ~~$500~~ $5,000 or more is not enforceable by way of action or defense unless there is some ~~writing~~ record sufficient to indicate that a contract for sale has been made between the parties and signed by the party against ~~whom~~ which enforcement is sought or by ~~his~~ the party's authorized agent or broker. A ~~writing~~ record is not insufficient because it omits or incorrectly states a term agreed upon but the contract is not enforceable under this subsection beyond the quantity of goods shown in ~~such~~ the ~~writing~~ record.

(2) Between merchants if within a reasonable time a ~~writing~~ record in confirmation of the contract and sufficient against the sender is received and the party receiving it has reason to know its contents, it satisfies the requirements of subsection (1) against ~~such party~~ the recipient unless ~~written~~ notice of objection to its contents is given in a record within 10 days after it is received.

(3) A contract which does not satisfy the requirements of subsection (1) but which is valid in other respects is enforceable

(a) if the goods are to be specially manufactured for the buyer and are not suitable for sale to others in the ordinary course of the seller's business and the seller, before notice of repudiation is received and under circumstances which reasonably indicate that the goods are for the buyer, has made either a substantial beginning of their manufacture or commitments for their procurement; or

(b) if the party against ~~whom~~ which enforcement is sought admits in ~~his~~ the party's pleading, or in the party's testimony or otherwise ~~in court~~ under oath that a contract for sale was made, but the contract is not enforceable under this ~~provision~~ paragraph beyond the quantity of goods admitted; or

(c) with respect to goods for which payment has been made and accepted or which have been received and accepted (Sec. 2–606).

(4) A contract that is enforceable under this section is not unenforceable merely because it is not capable of being performed within one year or any other period after its making.

§ 2–206. Offer and Acceptance in Formation of Contract.

(1) Unless otherwise unambiguously indicated by the language or circumstances

(a) an offer to make a contract shall be construed as inviting acceptance in any manner and by any medium reasonable in the circumstances;

(b) an order or other offer to buy goods for prompt or current shipment shall be construed as inviting acceptance either by a prompt promise to ship or by the prompt or current shipment of conforming or nonconforming goods, but ~~such a~~ the shipment of nonconforming goods is not an acceptance if the seller seasonably notifies the buyer that the shipment is offered only as an accommodation to the buyer.

(2) Where the beginning of a requested performance is a reasonable mode of acceptance an offeror ~~who~~ that is not notified of acceptance within a reasonable time may treat the offer as having lapsed before acceptance.

(3) A definite and seasonable expression of acceptance in a record operates as an acceptance even if it contains terms additional to or different from the offer.

§ 2–207. ~~Additional Terms in Acceptance or~~ Terms of Contract; Effect of Confirmation.

Subject to Section 2–202, if (i) conduct by both parties recognizes the existence of a contract although their records do not otherwise establish a contract, (ii) a contract is formed by an offer and acceptance, or (iii) a contract formed in any manner is confirmed by a record that contains terms additional to or different from those in the contract being confirmed, the terms of the contract, are:

(a) terms that appear in the records of both parties;

(b) terms, whether in a record or not, to which both parties agree; and

(c) terms supplied or incorporated under any provision of this Act.

§ 2–316. Exclusion or Modification of Warranties.

(1) Words or conduct relevant to the creation of an express warranty and words or conduct tending to negate or limit warranty shall be construed wherever reasonable as consistent with each other; but subject to the provisions of this Article on parol or extrinsic evidence (Section 2–202) negation or limitation is inoperative to the extent that such construction is unreasonable.

(2) Subject to subsection (3), to exclude or modify the implied warranty of merchantability or any part of it in a consumer contract the language must be in a record, be conspicuous, and state "The seller undertakes no responsibility for the quality of the goods except as otherwise provided in this contract," and in any other contract the language must mention merchantability and in case of a ~~writing~~ record must be conspicuous~~, and to~~. Subject to subsection (3), to exclude or modify the implied warranty of fitness, the exclusion must be ~~by a writing~~ in a record and be conspicuous. Language to exclude all implied warranties of fitness in a consumer contract must state "The seller assumes no responsibility that the goods will be fit for any particular purpose for which you may be buying these

goods, except as otherwise provided in the contract," and in any other contract the language is sufficient if it states, for example, that "There are no warranties that extend beyond the description on the face hereof." Language that satisfies the requirements of this subsection for the exclusion and modification of a warranty in a consumer contract also satisfies the requirements for any other contract.

(3) Notwithstanding subsection (2):

(a) unless the circumstances indicate otherwise, all implied warranties are excluded by expressions like "as is", "with all faults" or other language which in common understanding calls the buyer's attention to the exclusion of warranties ~~and~~, makes plain that there is no implied warranty, and, in a consumer contract evidenced by a record, is set forth conspicuously in the record; and

(b) when the buyer before entering into the contract has examined the goods or the sample or model as fully as ~~he~~ desired or has refused to examine the goods after a demand by the seller there is no implied warranty with regard to defects which an examination ought in the circumstances to have revealed to ~~him~~ the buyer; and

(c) an implied warranty can also be excluded or modified by course of dealing or course of performance or usage of trade.

(4) Remedies for breach of warranty can be limited in accordance with the provisions of this article on liquidation or limitation of damages and on contractual modification of remedy (Sections 2–718 and 2–719).

§ 2–319. ~~F.O.B. And F.A.S. Terms~~ Reserved.

§ 2–320. ~~C.I.F. And C. & F. Terms~~ Reserved.

PART 5

PERFORMANCE

§ 2–504. Shipment by Seller.

Where the seller is required or authorized to send the goods to the buyer and the contract does not require ~~him~~ the seller to deliver them at a particular destination, then unless otherwise agreed ~~he~~ the seller must

(a) put ~~the~~ conforming goods in the possession of ~~such~~ a carrier and make ~~such~~ a proper contract for their transportation, ~~as may be reasonable~~ having regard to the nature of the goods and other circumstances of the case; and

(b) obtain and promptly deliver or tender in due form any document necessary to enable the buyer to obtain possession of the goods or otherwise required by the agreement or by usage of trade; and

(c) promptly notify the buyer of the shipment.

Failure to notify the buyer under paragraph (c) or to make a proper contract under paragraph (a) is a ground for rejection only if material delay or loss ensues.

§ 2–513. Buyer's Right to Inspection of Goods.

(1) Unless otherwise agreed and subject to subsection (3), where goods are tendered or delivered or identified to the contract for sale, the buyer has a right before payment or acceptance to inspect them at any reasonable place and time and in any reasonable manner. When the seller is required or authorized to send the goods to the buyer, the inspection may be after their arrival.

(2) Expenses of inspection must be borne by the buyer but may be recovered from the seller if the goods do not conform and are rejected.

(3) Unless otherwise agreed ~~and subject to the provisions of this Article on C.I.F. contracts (subsection (3) of Section 2–321),~~ the buyer is not entitled to inspect the goods before payment of the price when the contract provides

(a) for delivery ~~"C.O.D." or on other like terms~~ on terms that under applicable course of performance, course of dealing, or usage of trade are interpreted to preclude inspection before payment; or

(b) for payment against documents of title, except where such payment is due only after the goods are to become available for inspection.

(4) A place ~~or method~~, method or standard of inspection fixed by the parties is presumed to be exclusive but unless otherwise expressly agreed it does not postpone identification or shift the place for delivery or for passing the risk of loss. If compliance becomes impossible, inspection shall be as provided in this section unless the place ~~or method~~, method or standard fixed was clearly intended as an indispensable condition failure of which avoids the contract.

PART 6

BREACH, REPUDIATION AND EXCUSE

§ 2–615. Excuse by Failure of Presupposed Conditions.

Except so far as a seller may have assumed a greater obligation and subject to the preceding section on substituted performance:

(a) Delay in ~~delivery or non-delivery~~ performance or non-performance in whole or in part by a seller ~~who~~ that complies with paragraphs (b) and(c) is not a breach of ~~his~~ the seller's duty under a contract for sale if performance as agreed has been made impracticable by the occurrence of a contingency the non-occurrence of which was a basic assumption on which the contract was made or by compliance in good faith with any applicable foreign or domestic governmental regulation or order whether or not it later proves to be invalid.

(b) Where the causes mentioned in paragraph (a) affect only a part of the seller's capacity to perform, ~~he~~ the seller must allocate production and deliveries among ~~his~~ its customers but may at ~~his~~ its option include regular customers not then under contract as well as ~~his~~ its own requirements for further manufacture. ~~He~~ The seller may so allocate in any manner which is fair and reasonable.

(c) The seller must notify the buyer seasonably that there will be delay or non-delivery and, when allocation is required under paragraph (b), of the estimated quota thus made available for the buyer.

DOCUMENT 23

UNIFORM COMPUTER INFORMATION TRANSACTIONS ACT

PART 1

GENERAL PROVISIONS

[SUBPART A. SHORT TITLE AND DEFINITIONS]

Section 101. Short Title. This [Act] may be cited as the Uniform Computer Information Transactions Act.

Section 102. Definitions.

(a) In this [Act]:

* * *

(4) "Agreement" means the bargain of the parties in fact as found in their language or by implication from other circumstances, including course of performance, course of dealing, and usage of trade as provided in this [Act].

(5) "Attribution procedure" means a procedure to verify that an electronic authentication, display, message, record, or performance is that of a particular person or to detect changes or errors in information. The term includes a procedure that requires the use of algorithms or other codes, identifying words or numbers, encryption, or callback or other acknowledgment.

(6) "Authenticate" means:

(A) to sign; or

(B) with the intent to sign a record, otherwise to execute or adopt an electronic symbol, sound, message, or process referring to, attached to, included in, or logically associated or linked with, that record.

(7) "Automated transaction" means a transaction in which a contract is formed in whole or part by electronic actions of one or both parties which are not previously reviewed by an individual in the ordinary course.

(8) "Cancellation" means the ending of a contract by a party because of breach of contract by another party.

(9) "Computer" means an electronic device that accepts information in digital or similar form and manipulates it for a result based on a sequence of instructions.

(10) "Computer information" means information in electronic form which is obtained from or through the use of a computer or which is in a form capable of being processed by a computer. The term includes a copy of the information and any documentation or packaging associated with the copy.

(11) "Computer information transaction" means an agreement or the performance of it to create, modify, transfer, or license computer information or informational rights in computer information. The term includes a support contract under Section 612. The term does not include a transaction merely because the parties' agreement provides that their communications about the transaction will be in the form of computer information.

(12) "Computer program" means a set of statements or instructions to be used directly or indirectly in a computer to bring about a certain result. The term does not include separately identifiable informational content.

(13) "Consequential damages" resulting from breach of contract includes (i) any loss resulting from general or particular requirements and needs of which the breaching party at the time of contracting had reason to know and which could not reasonably be prevented and (ii) any injury to an individual or damage to property other than the subject matter of the transaction proximately resulting from breach of warranty. The term does not include direct damages or incidental damages.

(14) "Conspicuous", with reference to a term, means so written, displayed, or presented that a reasonable person against which it is to operate ought to have noticed it. A term in an electronic record intended to evoke a response by an electronic agent is conspicuous if it is presented in a form that would enable a reasonably configured electronic agent to take it into account or react to it without review of the record by an individual. Conspicuous terms include the following:

(A) with respect to a person:

(i) a heading in capitals in a size equal to or greater than, or in contrasting type, font, or color to, the surrounding text;

(ii) language in the body of a record or display in larger or other contrasting type, font, or color or set off from the surrounding text by symbols or other marks that draw attention to the language; and

(iii) a term prominently referenced in an electronic record or display which is readily accessible or reviewable from the record or display; and

(B) with respect to a person or an electronic agent, a term or reference to a term that is so placed in a record or display that the person or electronic agent cannot proceed without taking action with respect to the particular term or reference.

(15) "Consumer" means an individual who is a licensee of information or informational rights that the individual at the time of contracting intended to be used primarily for personal, family, or household purposes. The term does not include an individual who is a licensee primarily for professional or commercial purposes, including agriculture, business management, and investment management other than management of the individual's personal or family investments.

(16) "Consumer contract" means a contract between a merchant licensor and a consumer.

(17) "Contract" means the total legal obligation resulting from the parties' agreement as affected by this [Act] and other applicable law.

(18) "Contract fee" means the price, fee, rent, or royalty payable in a contract under this [Act] or any part of the amount payable.

(19) "Contractual use term" means an enforceable term that defines or limits the use, disclosure of, or access to licensed information or informational rights, including a term that defines the scope of a license.

(20) "Copy" means the medium on which information is fixed on a temporary or permanent basis and from which it can be perceived, reproduced, used, or communicated, either directly or with the aid of a machine or device.

(21) "Course of dealing" means a sequence of previous conduct between the parties to a particular transaction which establishes a common basis of understanding for interpreting their expressions and other conduct.

(22) "Course of performance" means repeated performances, under a contract that involves repeated occasions for performance, which are accepted or acquiesced in without objection by a party having knowledge of the nature of the performance and an opportunity to object to it.

* * *

(24) "Delivery", with respect to a copy, means the voluntary physical or electronic transfer of possession or control.

* * *

(26) "Electronic" means relating to technology having electrical, digital, magnetic, wireless, optical, electromagnetic, or similar capabilities.

(27) "Electronic agent" means a computer program, or electronic or other automated means, used by a person to initiate an action, or to respond to electronic messages or performances, on the person's behalf without review or action by an individual at the time of the action or response to the message or performance.

(28) "Electronic message" means a record or display that is stored, generated, or transmitted by electronic means for the purpose of communication to another person or electronic agent.

* * *

(32) "Good faith" means honesty in fact and the observance of reasonable commercial standards of fair dealing.

(33) "Goods" means all things that are movable at the time relevant to the computer information transaction. The term includes the unborn young of animals, growing crops, and other identified things to be severed from realty which are covered by [Section 2–107 of the Uniform Commercial Code]. The term does not include computer information, money, the subject matter of foreign exchange transactions, documents, letters of credit, letter-of-credit rights, instruments, investment property, accounts, chattel paper, deposit accounts, or general intangibles.

* * *

(35) "Information" means data, text, images, sounds, mask works, or computer programs, including collections and compilations of them.

(36) "Information processing system" means an electronic system for creating, generating, sending, receiving, storing, displaying, or processing information.

(37) "Informational content" means information that is intended to be communicated to or perceived by an individual in the ordinary use of the information, or the equivalent of that information.

(38) "Informational rights" include all rights in information created under laws governing patents, copyrights, mask works, trade secrets, trademarks, publicity rights, or any other law that gives a person, independently of contract, a right to control or preclude another person's use of or access to the information on the basis of the rights holder's interest in the information.

(39) "Knowledge", with respect to a fact, means actual knowledge of the fact.

(40) "License" means a contract that authorizes access to, or use, distribution, performance, modification, or reproduction of, information or informational rights, but expressly limits the access or uses authorized or expressly grants fewer than all rights in the information, whether or not the transferee has title to a licensed copy. The term includes an access contract, a lease of a computer program, and a consignment of a copy. The term does not include a reservation or creation of a security interest to the extent the interest is governed by [Article 9 of the Uniform Commercial Code].

(41) "Licensee" means a person entitled by agreement to acquire or exercise rights in, or to have access to or use of, computer information under an agreement to which this [Act] applies. A licensor is not a licensee with respect to rights reserved to it under the agreement.

(42) "Licensor" means a person obligated by agreement to transfer or create rights in, or to give access to or use of, computer information or informational rights in it under an agreement to which this [Act] applies. Between the provider of access and a provider of the informational content

to be accessed, the provider of content is the licensor. In an exchange of information or informational rights, each party is a licensor with respect to the information, informational rights, or access it gives.

(43) "Mass-market license" means a standard form used in a mass-market transaction.

(44) "Mass-market transaction" means a transaction that is:

(A) a consumer contract; or

(B) any other transaction with an end-user licensee if:

(i) the transaction is for information or informational rights directed to the general public as a whole, including consumers, under substantially the same terms for the same information;

(ii) the licensee acquires the information or informational rights in a retail transaction under terms and in a quantity consistent with an ordinary transaction in a retail market; and

(iii) the transaction is not:

(I) a contract for redistribution or for public performance or public display of a copyrighted work;

(II) a transaction in which the information is customized or otherwise specially prepared by the licensor for the licensee, other than minor customization using a capability of the information intended for that purpose;

(III) a site license; or

(IV) an access contract.

(45) "Merchant" means a person:

(A) that deals in information or informational rights of the kind involved in the transaction;

(B) that by the person's occupation holds itself out as having knowledge or skill peculiar to the relevant aspect of the business practices or information involved in the transaction; or

(C) to which the knowledge or skill peculiar to the practices or information involved in the transaction may be attributed by the person's employment of an agent or broker or other intermediary that by its occupation holds itself out as having the knowledge or skill.

(46) "Nonexclusive license" means a license that does not preclude the licensor from transferring to other licensees the same information, informational rights, or contractual rights within the same scope. The term includes a consignment of a copy.

(47) "Notice" of a fact means knowledge of the fact, receipt of notification of the fact, or reason to know the fact exists.

(48) "Notify", or "give notice", means to take such steps as may be reasonably required to inform the other person in the ordinary course, whether or not the other person actually comes to know of it.

(49) "Party" means a person that engages in a transaction or makes an agreement under this [Act].

(50) "Person" means an individual, corporation, business trust, estate, trust, partnership, limited liability company, association, joint venture, governmental subdivision, instrumentality, or agency, public corporation, or any other legal or commercial entity.

(51) "Published informational content" means informational content prepared for or made available to recipients generally, or to a class of recipients, in substantially the same form. The term does not include informational content that is:

(A) customized for a particular recipient by one or more individuals acting as or on behalf of the licensor, using judgment or expertise; or

(B) provided in a special relationship of reliance between the provider and the recipient.

(52) "Receipt" means:

(A) with respect to a copy, taking delivery; or

(B) with respect to a notice:

(i) coming to a person's attention; or

(ii) being delivered to and available at a location or system designated by agreement for that purpose or, in the absence of an agreed location or system:

(I) being delivered at the person's residence, or the person's place of business through which the contract was made, or at any other place held out by the person as a place for receipt of communications of the kind; or

(II) in the case of an electronic notice, coming into existence in an information processing system or at an address in that system in a form capable of being processed by or perceived from a system of that type by a recipient, if the recipient uses, or otherwise has designated or holds out, that place or system for receipt of notices of the kind to be given and the sender does not know that the notice cannot be accessed from that place.

(53) "Receive" means to take receipt.

(54) "Record" means information that is inscribed on a tangible medium or that is stored in an electronic or other medium and is retrievable in perceivable form.

(55) "Release" means an agreement by a party not to object to, or exercise any rights or pursue any remedies to limit, the use of information or informational rights which agreement does not require an affirmative act by the party to enable or support the other party's use of the

information or informational rights. The term includes a waiver of informational rights.

(56) "Return", with respect to a record containing contractual terms that were rejected, refers only to the computer information and means:

(A) in the case of a licensee that rejects a record regarding a single information product transferred for a single contract fee, a right to reimbursement of the contract fee paid from the person to which it was paid or from another person that offers to reimburse that fee, on:

(i) submission of proof of purchase; and

(ii) proper redelivery of the computer information and all copies within a reasonable time after initial delivery of the information to the licensee;

(B) in the case of a licensee that rejects a record regarding an information product provided as part of multiple information products integrated into and transferred as a bundled whole but retaining their separate identity:

(i) a right to reimbursement of any portion of the aggregate contract fee identified by the licensor in the initial transaction as charged to the licensee for all bundled information products which was actually paid, on:

(I) rejection of the record before or during the initial use of the bundled product;

(II) proper redelivery of all computer information products in the bundled whole and all copies of them within a reasonable time after initial delivery of the information to the licensee; and

(III) submission of proof of purchase; or

(ii) a right to reimbursement of any separate contract fee identified by the licensor in the initial transaction as charged to the licensee for the separate information product to which the rejected record applies, on:

(I) submission of proof of purchase; and

(II) proper redelivery of that computer information product and all copies within a reasonable time after initial delivery of the information to the licensee; or

(C) in the case of a licensor that rejects a record proposed by the licensee, a right to proper redelivery of the computer information and all copies from the licensee, to stop delivery or access to the information by the licensee, and to reimbursement from the licensee of amounts paid by the licensor with respect to the rejected record, on reimbursement to the licensee of contract fees that it paid with respect to the rejected record, subject to recoupment and setoff.

(57) "Scope", with respect to terms of a license, means:

(A) the licensed copies, information, or informational rights involved;

(B) the use or access authorized, prohibited, or controlled;

(C) the geographic area, market, or location; or

(D) the duration of the license.

(58) "Seasonable", with respect to an act, means taken within the time agreed or, if no time is agreed, within a reasonable time.

(59) "Send" means, with any costs provided for and properly addressed or directed as reasonable under the circumstances or as otherwise agreed, to deposit a record in the mail or with a commercially reasonable carrier, to deliver a record for transmission to or re-creation in another location or information processing system, or to take the steps necessary to initiate transmission to or re-creation of a record in another location or information processing system. In addition, with respect to an electronic message, the message must be in a form capable of being processed by or perceived from a system of the type the recipient uses or otherwise has designated or held out as a place for the receipt of communications of the kind sent. Receipt within the time in which it would have arrived if properly sent, has the effect of a proper sending.

(60) "Standard form" means a record or a group of related records containing terms prepared for repeated use in transactions and so used in a transaction in which there was no negotiated change of terms by individuals except to set the price, quantity, method of payment, selection among standard options, or time or method of delivery.

* * *

[SUBPART B. GENERAL SCOPE AND TERMS]

Section 103. Scope; Exclusions.

(a) This [Act] applies to computer information transactions.

(b) Except for subject matter excluded in subsection (d) and as otherwise provided in Section 104, if a computer information transaction includes subject matter other than computer information or subject matter excluded under subsection (d), the following rules apply:

(1) If a transaction includes computer information and goods, this [Act] applies to the part of the transaction involving computer information, informational rights in it, and creation or modification of it. However, if a copy of a computer program is contained in and sold or leased as part of goods, this [Act] applies to the copy and the computer program only if:

(A) the goods are a computer or computer peripheral; or

(B) giving the buyer or lessee of the goods access to or use of the program is ordinarily a material purpose of transactions in goods of the type sold or leased.

(2) In all other cases, this [Act] applies to the entire transaction if the computer information and informational rights, or access to them, is the primary subject matter, but otherwise applies only to the part of the transaction involving computer information, informational rights in it, and creation or modification of it.

(c) To the extent of a conflict between this [Act] and [Article 9 of the Uniform Commercial Code], [Article 9] governs.

(d) This [Act] does not apply to:

(1) a financial services transaction;

(2) an agreement to create, perform or perform in, include information in, acquire, use, distribute, modify, reproduce, have access to, adapt, make available, transmit, license, or display:

(A) audio or visual programming that is provided by broadcast, satellite, or cable as defined or used in the Federal Communications Act and related regulations as they existed on July 1, 1999, or by similar methods of delivering that programming; or

(B) a motion picture, sound recording, musical work, or phonorecord as defined or used in Title 17 of the United States Code as of July 1, 1999, or an enhanced sound recording.

(3) a compulsory license; or

(4) a contract of employment of an individual, other than an individual hired as an independent contractor to create or modify computer information, unless the independent contractor is a freelancer in the news reporting industry as that term is commonly understood in that industry;

(5) a contract that does not require that information be furnished as computer information or a contract in which, under the agreement, the form of the information as computer information is otherwise insignificant with respect to the primary subject matter of the part of the transaction pertaining to the information; or

(6) subject matter within the scope of [Article 3, 4, 4A, 5, [6,] 7, or 8 of the Uniform Commercial Code].

(e) As used in subsection (d)(2)(B), "enhanced sound recording" means a separately identifiable product or service the dominant character of which consists of recorded sounds but which includes (i) statements or instructions whose purpose is to allow or control the perception, reproduction, or communication of those sounds or (ii) other information so long as recorded sounds constitute the dominant character of the product or service despite the inclusion of the other information.

Section 104. Mixed Transactions: Agreement to Opt–in or Opt–Out. The parties may agree that this [Act], including contract-formation rules, governs the transaction, in whole or part, or that other law governs the transaction and this [Act] does not apply, if a material part of the subject matter to which the agreement applies is computer information or informational rights in it that are within the scope of this [Act], or is subject matter within this [Act] under Section 103(b), or is subject matter excluded by Section 103(d)(1) or (2). However, any agreement to do so is subject to the following rules:

(1) An agreement that this [Act] governs a transaction does not alter the applicability of any rule or procedure that may not be varied by agreement of the parties or that may be varied only in a manner specified by the rule or procedure, including a consumer protection statute [or administrative rule]. In addition, in a mass-market transaction, the agreement does not alter the applicability of a law applicable to a copy of information in printed form.

(2) An agreement that this [Act] does not govern a transaction:

(A) does not alter the applicability of Section 214 or 816; and

(B) in a mass-market transaction, does not alter the applicability under [this Act] of the doctrine of unconscionability or fundamental public policy or the obligation of good faith.

(3) In a mass-market transaction, any term under this section which changes the extent to which this [Act] governs the transaction must be conspicuous.

(4) A copy of a computer program contained in and sold or leased as part of goods and which is excluded from this [Act] by Section 103(b)(1) cannot provide the basis for an agreement under this section that this [Act] governs the transaction.

Section 105. Relation to Federal Law; Fundamental Public Policy; Transactions Subject to Other State Law.

(a) A provision of this [Act] which is preempted by federal law is unenforceable to the extent of the preemption.

(b) If a term of a contract violates a fundamental public policy, the court may refuse to enforce the contract, enforce the remainder of the contract without the impermissible term, or limit the application of the impermissible term so as to avoid a result contrary to public policy, in each case to the extent that the interest in enforcement is clearly outweighed by a public policy against enforcement of the term.

(c) Except as otherwise provided in subsection (d), if this [Act] or a term of a contract under this [Act] conflicts with a consumer protection statute [or administrative rule], the consumer protection statute [or rule] governs.

(d) If a law of this State in effect on the effective date of this [Act] applies to a transaction governed by this [Act], the following rules apply:

(1) A requirement that a term, waiver, notice, or disclaimer be in a writing is satisfied by a record.

(2) A requirement that a record, writing, or term be signed is satisfied by an authentication.

(3) A requirement that a term be conspicuous, or the like, is satisfied by a term that is conspicuous under this [Act].

(4) A requirement of consent or agreement to a term is satisfied by a manifestation of assent to the term in accordance with this [Act].

[(e) The following laws govern in the case of a conflict between this [Act] and the other law: [List laws establishing a digital signature and similar form of attribution procedure.]]

Legislative Note: If there are any consumer protection laws that should be excepted from the electronic commerce rules in subsection (d), those laws should be excluded from the operation of that subsection.

Section 107. Legal Recognition of Electronic Record and Authentication; Use of Electronic Agents.

(a) A record or authentication may not be denied legal effect or enforceability solely because it is in electronic form.

(b) This [Act] does not require that a record or authentication be generated, stored, sent, received, or otherwise processed by electronic means or in electronic form.

(c) In any transaction, a person may establish requirements regarding the type of authentication or record acceptable to it.

(d) A person that uses an electronic agent that it has selected for making an authentication, performance, or agreement, including manifestation of assent, is bound by the operations of the electronic agent, even if no individual was aware of or reviewed the agent's operations or the results of the operations.

Section 108. Proof and Effect of Authentication.

(a) Authentication may be proven in any manner, including a showing that a party made use of information or access that could have been available only if it engaged in conduct or operations that authenticated the record or term.

(b) Compliance with a commercially reasonable attribution procedure agreed to or adopted by the parties or established by law for authenticating a record authenticates the record as a matter of law.

Section 109. Choice of Law.

(a) The parties in their agreement may choose the applicable law. However, the choice is not enforceable in a consumer contract to the extent it would vary a rule that may not be varied by agreement under the law of the jurisdiction whose law would apply under subsections (b) and (c) in the absence of the agreement.

(b) In the absence of an enforceable agreement on choice of law, the following rules determine which jurisdiction's law governs in all respects for purposes of contract law:

(1) An access contract or a contract providing for electronic delivery of a copy is governed by the law of the jurisdiction in which the licensor was located when the agreement was entered into.

(2) A consumer contract that requires delivery of a copy on a tangible medium is governed by the law of the jurisdiction in which the copy is or should have been delivered to the consumer.

(3) In all other cases, the contract is governed by the law of the jurisdiction having the most significant relationship to the transaction.

(c) In cases governed by subsection (b), if the jurisdiction whose law governs is outside the United States, the law of that jurisdiction governs only if it provides substantially similar protections and rights to a party not located in that jurisdiction as are provided under this [Act]. Otherwise, the law of the State that has the most significant relationship to the transaction governs.

(d) For purposes of this section, a party is located at its place of business if it has one place of business, at its chief executive office if it has more than one place of business, or at its place of incorporation or primary registration if it does not have a physical place of business. Otherwise, a party is located at its primary residence.

Section 110. Contractual Choice of Forum.

(a) The parties in their agreement may choose an exclusive judicial forum unless the choice is unreasonable and unjust.

(b) A judicial forum specified in an agreement is not exclusive unless the agreement expressly so provides.

Section 111. Unconscionable Contract or Term.

(a) If a court as a matter of law finds a contract or a term thereof to have been unconscionable at the time it was made, the court may refuse to enforce the contract, enforce the remainder of the contract without the unconscionable term, or limit the application of the unconscionable term so as to avoid an unconscionable result.

(b) If it is claimed or appears to the court that a contract or term thereof may be unconscionable, the parties must be afforded a reasonable opportunity to present evidence as to its commercial setting, purpose, and effect to aid the court in making the determination.

Section 112. Manifesting Assent; Opportunity to Review.

(a) A person manifests assent to a record or term if the person, acting with knowledge of, or after having an opportunity to review the record or term or a copy of it:

(1) authenticates the record or term with intent to adopt or accept it; or

(2) intentionally engages in conduct or makes statements with reason to know that the other party or its electronic agent may infer

from the conduct or statement that the person assents to the record or term.

(b) An electronic agent manifests assent to a record or term if, after having an opportunity to review it, the electronic agent:

(1) authenticates the record or term; or

(2) engages in operations that in the circumstances indicate acceptance of the record or term.

(c) If this [Act] or other law requires assent to a specific term, a manifestation of assent must relate specifically to the term.

(d) Conduct or operations manifesting assent may be proved in any manner, including a showing that a person or an electronic agent obtained or used the information or informational rights and that a procedure existed by which a person or an electronic agent must have engaged in the conduct or operations in order to do so. Proof of compliance with subsection (a)(2) is sufficient if there is conduct that assents and subsequent conduct that reaffirms assent by electronic means.

(e) With respect to an opportunity to review, the following rules apply:

(1) A person has an opportunity to review a record or term only if it is made available in a manner that ought to call it to the attention of a reasonable person and permit review.

(2) An electronic agent has an opportunity to review a record or term only if it is made available in manner that would enable a reasonably configured electronic agent to react to the record or term.

(3) If a record or term is available for review only after a person becomes obligated to pay or begins its performance, the person has an opportunity to review only if it has a right to a return if it rejects the record. However, a right to a return is not required if:

(A) the record proposes a modification of contract or provides particulars of performance under Section 305; or

(B) the primary performance is other than delivery or acceptance of a copy, the agreement is not a mass-market transaction, and the parties at the time of contracting had reason to know that a record or term would be presented after performance, use, or access to the information began.

(4) The right to a return under paragraph (3) may arise by law or by agreement.

(f) The effect of provisions of this section may be modified by an agreement setting out standards applicable to future transactions between the parties.

Section 113. variation by agreement; commercial practice.

(a) The effect of any provision of this [Act], including an allocation of risk or imposition of a burden, may be varied by agreement of the parties. However, the following rules apply:

(1) Obligations of good faith, diligence, reasonableness, and care imposed by this [Act] may not be disclaimed by agreement, but the parties by agreement may determine the standards by which the performance of the obligation is to be measured if the standards are not manifestly unreasonable.

(2) The limitations on enforceability imposed by unconscionability under Section 111 and fundamental public policy under Section 105(b) may not be varied by agreement.

(3) Limitations on enforceability of, or agreement to, a contract, term, or right expressly stated in the sections listed in the following subparagraphs may not be varied by agreement except to the extent provided in each section:

(A) the limitations on agreed choice of law in Section 109(a);

(B) the limitations on agreed choice of forum in Section 110;

(C) the requirements for manifesting assent and opportunity for review in Section 112;

(D) the limitations on enforceability in Section 201;

(E) the limitations on a mass-market license in Section 209;

(F) the consumer defense arising from an electronic error in Section 214;

(G) the requirements for an enforceable term in Sections 303(b), 307(g), 406(b) and (c), and 804(a);

(H) the limitations on a financier in Sections 507 through 511;

(I) the restrictions on altering the period of limitations in Section 805(a) and (b); and

(J) the limitations on self-help repossession in Sections 815(b) and 816.

(b) Any usage of trade of which the parties are or should be aware and any course of dealing or course of performance between the parties are relevant to determining the existence or meaning of an agreement.

Section 114. Supplemental Principles; Good Faith; Decision for Court; Reasonable Time; Reason to Know.

(a) Unless displaced by this [Act], principles of law and equity, including the law merchant and the common law of this State relative to capacity to contract, principal and agent, estoppel, fraud, misrepresentation, duress, coercion, mistake, and other validating or invalidating cause, supplement this [Act]. Among the laws supplementing and not displaced by this [Act] are trade secret laws and unfair competition laws.

(b) Every contract or duty within the scope of this [Act] imposes an obligation of good faith in its performance or enforcement.

(c) Whether a term is conspicuous or is unenforceable under Section 105(a) or (b), 111, or 209(a) and whether an attribution procedure is commercially reasonable or effective under Section 108, 212, or 213 are questions to be determined by the court.

(d) Whether an agreement has legal consequences is determined by this [Act].

(e) Whenever this [Act] requires any action to be taken within a reasonable time, the following rules apply:

(1) What is a reasonable time for taking the action depends on the nature, purpose, and circumstances of the action.

(2) Any time that is not manifestly unreasonable may be fixed by agreement.

(f) A person has reason to know a fact if the person has knowledge of the fact or, from all the facts and circumstances known to the person without investigation, the person should be aware that the fact exists.

PART 2

FORMATION AND TERMS

[SUBPART A. FORMATION OF CONTRACT]

Section 201. Formal Requirements.

(a) Except as otherwise provided in this section, a contract requiring payment of a contract fee of $5,000 or more is not enforceable by way of action or defense unless:

(1) the party against which enforcement is sought authenticated a record sufficient to indicate that a contract has been formed and which reasonably identifies the copy or subject matter to which the contract refers; or

(2) the agreement is a license for an agreed duration of one year or less or which may be terminated at will by the party against which the contract is asserted.

(b) A record is sufficient under subsection (a) even if it omits or incorrectly states a term, but the contract is not enforceable under that subsection beyond the number of copies or subject matter shown in the record.

(c) A contract that does not satisfy the requirements of subsection (a) is nevertheless enforceable under that subsection if:

(1) a performance was tendered or the information was made available by one party and the tender was accepted or the information accessed by the other; or

(2) the party against which enforcement is sought admits in court, by pleading or by testimony or otherwise under oath, facts

sufficient to indicate a contract has been made, but the agreement is not enforceable under this paragraph beyond the number of copies or the subject matter admitted.

(d) Between merchants, if, within a reasonable time, a record in confirmation of the contract and sufficient against the sender is received and the party receiving it has reason to know its contents, the record satisfies subsection (a) against the party receiving it unless notice of objection to its contents is given in a record within 10 days after the confirming record is received.

(e) An agreement that the requirements of this section need not be satisfied as to future transactions is effective if evidenced in a record authenticated by the person against which enforcement is sought.

(f) A transaction within the scope of this [Act] is not subject to a statute of frauds contained in another law of this State.

Section 202. Formation in General.

(a) A contract may be formed in any manner sufficient to show agreement, including offer and acceptance or conduct of both parties or operations of electronic agents which recognize the existence of a contract.

(b) If the parties so intend, an agreement sufficient to constitute a contract may be found even if the time of its making is undetermined, one or more terms are left open or to be agreed on, the records of the parties do not otherwise establish a contract, or one party reserves the right to modify terms.

(c) Even if one or more terms are left open or to be agreed upon, a contract does not fail for indefiniteness if the parties intended to make a contract and there is a reasonably certain basis for giving an appropriate remedy.

(d) In the absence of conduct or performance by both parties to the contrary, a contract is not formed if there is a material disagreement about a material term, including a term concerning scope.

(e) If a term is to be adopted by later agreement and the parties intend not to be bound unless the term is so adopted, a contract is not formed if the parties do not agree to the term. In that case, each party shall deliver to the other party, or with the consent of the other party destroy, all copies of information, access materials, and other materials received or made, and each party is entitled to a return with respect to any contract fee paid for which performance has not been received, has not been accepted, or has been redelivered without any benefit being retained. The parties remain bound by any restriction in a contractual use term with respect to information or copies received or made from copies received pursuant to the agreement, but the contractual use term does not apply to information or copies properly received or obtained from another source.

Section 203. Offer and Acceptance in General. Unless Otherwise Unambiguously Indicated by the Language or the Circumstances:

(1) An offer to make a contract invites acceptance in any manner and by any medium reasonable under the circumstances.

(2) An order or other offer to acquire a copy for prompt or current delivery invites acceptance by either a prompt promise to ship or a prompt or current shipment of a conforming or nonconforming copy. However, a shipment of a nonconforming copy is not an acceptance if the licensor seasonably notifies the licensee that the shipment is offered only as an accommodation to the licensee.

(3) If the beginning of a requested performance is a reasonable mode of acceptance, an offeror that is not notified of acceptance or performance within a reasonable time may treat the offer as having lapsed before acceptance.

(4) If an offer in an electronic message evokes an electronic message accepting the offer, a contract is formed:

(A) when an electronic acceptance is received; or

(B) if the response consists of beginning performance, full performance, or giving access to information, when the performance is received or the access is enabled and necessary access materials are received.

Section 204. Acceptance With Varying Terms.

(a) In this section, an acceptance materially alters an offer if it contains a term that materially conflicts with or varies a term of the offer or that adds a material term not contained in the offer.

(b) Except as otherwise provided in Section 205, a definite and seasonable expression of acceptance operates as an acceptance, even if the acceptance contains terms that vary from the terms of the offer, unless the acceptance materially alters the offer.

(c) If an acceptance materially alters the offer, the following rules apply:

(1) A contract is not formed unless:

(A) a party agrees, such as by manifesting assent, to the other party's offer or acceptance; or

(B) all the other circumstances, including the conduct of the parties, establish a contract.

(2) If a contract is formed by the conduct of both parties, the terms of the contract are determined under Section 210.

(d) If an acceptance varies from but does not materially alter the offer, a contract is formed based on the terms of the offer. In addition, the following rules apply:

(1) Terms in the acceptance which conflict with terms in the offer are not part of the contract.

(2) An additional nonmaterial term in the acceptance is a proposal for an additional term. Between merchants, the proposed additional term becomes part of the contract unless the offeror gives notice of objection before, or within a reasonable time after, it receives the proposed terms.

Section 205. Conditional Offer or Acceptance.

(a) In this section, an offer or acceptance is conditional if it is conditioned on agreement by the other party to all the terms of the offer or acceptance.

(b) Except as otherwise provided in subsection (c), a conditional offer or acceptance precludes formation of a contract unless the other party agrees to its terms, such as by manifesting assent.

(c) If an offer and acceptance are in standard forms and at least one form is conditional, the following rules apply:

(1) Conditional language in a standard term precludes formation of a contract only if the actions of the party proposing the form are consistent with the conditional language, such as by refusing to perform, refusing to permit performance, or refusing to accept the benefits of the agreement, until its proposed terms are accepted.

(2) A party that agrees, such as by manifesting assent, to a conditional offer that is effective under paragraph (1) adopts the terms of the offer under Section 208 or 209, except a term that conflicts with an expressly agreed term regarding price or quantity.

Section 206. Offer and Acceptance: Electronic Agents.

(a) A contract may be formed by the interaction of electronic agents. If the interaction results in the electronic agents' engaging in operations that under the circumstances indicate acceptance of an offer, a contract is formed, but a court may grant appropriate relief if the operations resulted from fraud, electronic mistake, or the like.

(b) A contract may be formed by the interaction of an electronic agent and an individual acting on the individual's own behalf or for another person. A contract is formed if the individual takes an action or makes a statement that the individual can refuse to take or say and that the individual has reason to know will:

(1) cause the electronic agent to perform, provide benefits, or allow the use or access that is the subject of the contract, or send instructions to do so; or

(2) indicate acceptance, regardless of other expressions or actions by the individual to which the individual has reason to know the electronic agent cannot react.

(c) The terms of a contract formed under subsection (b) are determined under Section 208 or 209 but do not include a term provided by the individual if the individual had reason to know that the electronic agent could not react to the term.

Section 207. Formation: Releases of Informational Rights.

(a) A release is effective without consideration if it is:

(1) in a record to which the releasing party agrees, such as by manifesting assent, and which identifies the informational rights released; or

(2) enforceable under estoppel, implied license, or other law.

(b) A release continues for the duration of the informational rights released if the release does not specify its duration and does not require affirmative performance after the grant of the release by:

(1) the party granting the release; or

(2) the party receiving the release, except for relatively insignificant acts.

(c) In cases not governed by subsection (b), the duration of a release is governed by Section 308.

* * *

Section 209. Mass–market License.

(a) A party adopts the terms of a mass-market license for purposes of Section 208 only if the party agrees to the license, such as by manifesting assent, before or during the party's initial performance or use of or access to the information. A term is not part of the license if:

(1) the term is unconscionable or is unenforceable under Section 105(a) or (b); or

(2) subject to Section 301, the term conflicts with a term to which the parties to the license have expressly agreed.

(b) If a mass-market license or a copy of the license is not available in a manner permitting an opportunity to review by the licensee before the licensee becomes obligated to pay and the licensee does not agree, such as by manifesting assent, to the license after having an opportunity to review, the licensee is entitled to a return under Section 112 and, in addition, to:

(1) reimbursement of any reasonable expenses incurred in complying with the licensor's instructions for returning or destroying the computer information or, in the absence of instructions, expenses incurred for return postage or similar reasonable expense in returning the computer information; and

(2) compensation for any reasonable and foreseeable costs of restoring the licensee's information processing system to reverse changes in the system caused by the installation, if:

(A) the installation occurs because information must be installed to enable review of the license; and

(B) the installation alters the system or information in it but does not restore the system or information after removal of the installed information because the licensee rejected the license.

(c) In a mass-market transaction, if the licensor does not have an opportunity to review a record containing proposed terms from the licensee before the licensor delivers or becomes obligated to deliver the information, and if the licensor does not agree, such as by manifesting assent, to those terms after having that opportunity, the licensor is entitled to a return.

* * *

Section 214. Electronic Error: Consumer Defenses.

(a) In this section, "electronic error" means an error in an electronic message created by a consumer using an information processing system if a reasonable method to detect and correct or avoid the error was not provided.

(b) In an automated transaction, a consumer is not bound by an electronic message that the consumer did not intend and which was caused by an electronic error, if the consumer:

(1) promptly on learning of the error:

(A) notifies the other party of the error; and

(B) causes delivery to the other party or, pursuant to reasonable instructions received from the other party, delivers to another person or destroys all copies of the information; and

(2) has not used, or received any benefit or value from, the information or caused the information or benefit to be made available to a third party.

(c) If subsection (b) does not apply, the effect of an electronic error is determined by other law.

Section 215. Electronic Message: When Effective; Effect of Acknowledgment.

(a) Receipt of an electronic message is effective when received even if no individual is aware of its receipt.

(b) Receipt of an electronic acknowledgment of an electronic message establishes that the message was received but by itself does not establish that the content sent corresponds to the content received.

* * *

DOCUMENT 24

UNIFORM ELECTRONIC TRANSACTIONS ACT (1999) (SELECTED PROVISIONS)

Section 1. Short Title. This [Act] may be cited as the Uniform Electronic Transactions Act.

Section 2. Definitions. In this [Act]:

(1) "Agreement" means the bargain of the parties in fact, as found in their language or inferred from other circumstances and from rules, regulations, and procedures given the effect of agreements under laws otherwise applicable to a particular transaction.

(2) "Automated transaction" means a transaction conducted or performed, in whole or in part, be electronic means or electronic records, in which the acts or records of one or both parties are not reviewed by an individual in the ordinary course in forming a contract, performing under an existing contract, or fulfilling an obligation required by the transaction.

(3) "Computer program" means a set of statements or instructions to be used directly or indirectly in an information processing system in order to bring about a certain result.

(4) "Contract" means the total legal obligation resulting from the parties' agreement as affected by this [Act] and other applicable law.

(5) "Electronic" means relating to technology having electrical, digital, magnetic, wireless, optical, electromagnetic, or similar capabilities.

(6) "Electronic Agent" means a computer program or an electronic or other automated means used independently to initiate an action or respond to electronic records or performances in whole or in part, without review or action by an individual.

(7) "Electronic record" means a record created, generated, sent, communicated, received, or stored by electronic means.

(8) "Electronic signature" means an electronic sound, symbol, or process attached to or logically associated with a record and executed or adopted by a person with the intent to sign the record.

(9) "Government agency" means an executive, legislative, or judicial agency, department, board, commission, authority, institution, or instrumentality of the federal government or of a State or of a county, municipality, or other political subdivision of a State.

(10) "Information" means data, text, images, sounds, codes, computer programs, software, databases, or the like.

(11) "Information processing system" means an electronic system for creating, generating, sending, receiving, storing, displaying, or processing information.

(12) "Person" means an individual, corporation, business trust, estate, trust, partnership, limited liability company, association, joint venture, governmental agency, public corporation, or any other legal or commercial entity.

(13) "Record" means information that is inscribed on a tangible medium or that is stored in an electronic or other medium and is retrievable in perceivable form.

(14) "Security procedure" means a procedure employed for the purpose of verifying that an electronic signature, record, or performance is that of a specific person or for detecting changes or errors in the information in an electronic record. The terms includes a procedure that requires the use of algorithms or other codes, identifying words or numbers, encryption, or callback or other acknowledgment procedures.

(15) "State" means a State of the United States, the District of Columbia, Puerto Rico, the United States Virgin Islands, or any territory or insular possession subject to the jurisdiction of the United States. The term includes an Indian Tribe or band, or Alaskan native village, which is recognized by federal law or formally acknowledged by a State.

(16) "Transaction" means an action or set of actions occurring between two or more persons relating to the conduct of business, commercial, or governmental affairs.

Section 3. Scope.

(a) Except as otherwise provided in subsection (b), this [Act] applies to electronic records and electronic signatures relating to a transaction.

(b) This [Act] does not apply to a transaction to the extent it is governed by:

(1) a law governing the creation and execution of wills, codicils, or testamentary trusts;

(2) [The Uniform Commercial Code other than Sections 1–107 and 1–206, Article 2, and Article 2A];

(3) [the Uniform Computer Information Transactions Act]; land

(4) [other laws, if any, identified by State].

(c) This [Act] applies to an electronic record or electronic signature otherwise excluded from the application of this [Act] under subsection (b) to the extent it is governed by a law other than those specified in subsection (b).

(d) A transaction subject to this [Act] is also subject to other applicable substantive law.

Section 4. Prospective Application. This [Act] applies to any electronic record or electronic signature created, generated, sent, communicated, received, or stored on or after the effective date of this [Act].

Section 5. Use of Electronic Records and Electronic Signatures; Variation by Agreement.

(a) This [Act] does not require a record or signature to be created, generated, sent, communicated, received, stored, or otherwise processed or used by electronic means or in electronic form.

(b) This [Act] applies only to transactions between parties each of which has agreed to conduct transactions by electronic means. Whether the parties agree to conduct a transaction by electronic means is determined from the context and surrounding circumstances, including the parties' conduct.

(c) A party that agrees to conduct a transaction by electronic means may refuse to conduct other transactions by electronic means. The right granted by this subsection may not be waived by agreement.

(d) Except as otherwise provided in this [Act], the effect of any of its provisions may be varied by agreement. The presence in certain provisions of this [Act] of the words "unless otherwise agreed", or words of similar import, does not imply that the effect of other provisions may not be varied by agreement.

(e) Whether an electronic record or electronic signature has legal consequences is determined by this [Act] and other applicable law.

Section 6. Construction and Application. This [Act] must be construed and applied:

(1) to facilitate electronic transactions consistent with other applicable law:

(2) to be consistent with reasonable practices concerning electronic transactions and with the continued expansion of those practices; and

(3) to effectuate its general purpose to make uniform the law with respect to the subject of this [Act] among States enacting it.

Section 7. Legal Recognition of Electronic Records, Electronic Signatures, and Electronic Contracts.

(a) A record or signature may not be denied legal effect or enforceability solely because it is in electronic form.

(b) A contract may not be denied legal effect or enforceability solely because an electronic record was used in its formation.

(c) If a law requires a record to be in writing, an electronic record satisfies the law.

(d) If a law requires a signature, an electronic signature satisfies the law.

Section 8. Provision of Information in Writing: Presentation of Records.

(a) If parties have agreed to conduct a transaction by electronic means and a law requires a person to provide, send, or deliver information in writing to another person, the requirement is satisfied if the information is provided, sent, or delivered, as the case may be, in an electronic record capable of retention by the recipient at the time of receipt. An electronic record is not capable of retention by the recipient if the sender or its information processing system inhibits the ability of the recipient to print or store the electronic record.

(b) If a law other than this [Act] requires a record (i) to be posted or displayed in a certain manner, (ii) to be sent, communicated, or transmitted by a specified method, or (iii) to contain information that is formatted in a certain manner, the following rules apply:

(1) The record must be posted displayed in the manner specified in the other law.

(2) Except, as otherwise provided in subsection (d)(2), the record must be sent, communicated, or transmitted by the method specified in the other law.

(3) The record must contain the information formatted in the manner specified in the other law.

(c) If a sender inhibits the ability of a recipient to store or print an electronic record, the electronic record is not enforceable against the recipient.

(d) The requirements of this section may not be varied by agreement, but:

(1) to the extent a law other than this [Act] requires information to be provided, sent, or delivered in writing but permits that requirement to be varied by agreement, the requirement under subsection (a) that the information be in the form of an electronic record capable of retention may also be varied by agreement; and

(2) a requirement under a law other than this [Act] to send, communicate, or transmit a record by [first-class mail, postage prepaid] [regular United States mail], may be varied by agreement to the extent permitted by the other law.

Section 9. Attribution and Effect of Electronic Record and Electronic Signature.

(a) An electronic record or electronic signature is attributable to a person if it was the act of the person. The act of the person may be shown in any manner, including a showing of the efficacy of any security procedure applied to determine the person to which the electronic record or electronic signature was attributable.

(b) The effect of an electronic record or electronic signature attributed to a person under subsection (a) is determined from the context and surrounding circumstances at the time of its creation, execution, or adoption, including the parties agreement, if any, and otherwise provided by law.

Section 10. Effect of Change or Error. If a change or error in an electronic record occurs in a transmission between parties to a transaction, the following rules apply:

(1) If the parties have agreed to use a security procedure to detect changes or errors and one party has conformed to the procedure, but the other party has not, and the nonconforming party would have detected the change or error had that party also conformed, the conforming party may avoid the effect of the changed or erroneous electronic record.

(2) In an automated transaction involving an individual, the individual may avoid the effect of an electronic record that resulted from an error made by the individual in dealing with the electronic agent of another person if the electronic did not provide an opportunity for the prevention or correction of the error and, at the time the individual learns of the error, the individual:

(A) promptly notifies the other person of the error and that the individual did not intend to be bound by the electronic record received by the other person:

(B) takes reasonable steps, including steps that conform to the other person's reasonable instructions, to return to the other person or, if instructed by the other person, to destroy the consideration received, if any, as a result of the erroneous electronic record; and

(C) has not used or received any benefit or value from the consideration, if any, received from the other person

(3) If neither paragraph (1) nor paragraph (2) applies, the change or error has the effect provided by other law, including the law of mistake, and the parties' contract, if any.

(4) Paragraphs (2) and (3) may not be varied by agreement.

Section 11. Notarization and Acknowledgment. If a law requires a signature or record to be notarized, acknowledged, verified, or made under oath, the requirement is satisfied if the electronic signature of the person authorized to perform those acts, together with all other information required to be included by other applicable law, is attached to or logically associated with the signature or record.

Section 12. Retention of Electronic Records; Originals.

(a) If a law requires that a record be retained, the requirement is satisfied by retaining an electronic record of the information in the record which:

(1) accurately reflects the information set forth in the record after it was first generated in its final form as an electronic record or otherwise; and

(2) remains accessible for later reference.

(b) A requirement to retain a record in accordance with subsection (a) does not apply to any information the sole purpose of which is to enable the record to be sent, communicated, or received.

(c) A person may satisfy subsection (a) by using the services of another person if the requirements of that subsection are satisfied.

(d) If a law requires a record to be presented or retained in its original form, or provides consequences if the record is not presented or retained in its original form, that law is satisfied by an electronic record retained in accordance with subsection (a)

(e) If a law requires retention of a check, that requirement is satisfied by retention of an electronic record of the information on the front and back of the check in accordance with subsection (a).

(f) A record retained as an electronic record in accordance with subsection (a) satisfies a law requiring a person to retain a record for evidentiary, audit, or like purposes, unless a law enacted after the effective date of this [Act] specifically prohibits the use of an electronic record for the specified purpose.

(g) This section does not preclude a governmental agency of this State from specifying additional requirements for the retention of a record subject to the agency's jurisdiction.

Section 13. Admissibility in Evidence. In a proceeding, evidence of a record or signature may not be excluded solely because it is an electronic form.

Section 14. Automated Transaction. In an automated transaction, the following rules apply:

(1) A contract may be formed by the interaction of electronic agents of the parties, even if no individual was aware of or reviewed the electronic agents' actions or the resulting terms and agreements.

(2) A contract may be formed by the interaction of an electronic agent and an individual, acting on the individual's own behalf or for another person, including by an interaction in which the individual performs actions that the individual is free to refuse to perform and which the individual knows or has reason to know will cause the electronic agent to complete the transaction or performance.

(3) The terms of the contract are determined by the substantive law applicable to it.

Section 15. Time and Place of Sending and Receipt.

(a) Unless otherwise agreed between the sender and the recipient, an electronic record is sent when it:

(1) is addressed properly or otherwise directed properly to an information processing system that the recipient has designated or uses for the purpose of receiving electronic records or information of the type sent and from which the recipient is able to retrieve the electronic record;

(2) is in a form capable of being processed by that system; and

(3) enters an information processing system outside the control of the sender or of a person that sent the electronic record on behalf of the sender or enters a region of the information processing system designated or used by the recipient which is under the control of the recipient.

(b) Unless otherwise agreed between a sender and the recipient, an electronic record is received when:

(1) it enters an information processing system that the recipient has designated or uses for the purpose of receiving electronic records or information of the type sent and from which the recipient is able to retrieve the electronic record; and

(2) it is in a form capable of being processed by that system.

(c) Subsection (b) applies even if the place the information processing system is located is different from the place the electronic record is deemed to be received under subsection (d).

(d) Unless otherwise expressly provided in the electronic record or agreed between the sender and the recipient, an electronic record is deemed to be sent from the senders place of business and to be received at the recipient's place of business, For purposes of this subsection, the following rules apply:

(1) If the sender or recipient has more than one place of business, the place of business of that person is the place having the closest relationship to the underlying transaction.

(2) If the sender or the recipient does not have a place of business, the place of business is the sender's or recipient's residence, as the case may be.

(e) An electronic record is received under subsection (b) even if no individual is aware of its receipt.

(f) Receipt of an electronic acknowledgment from an information processing system described in subsection (b) establishes that a record was received but, by itself, does not establish that the content sent corresponds to the content received.

(g) If a person is aware that an electronic record purportedly sent under subsection (a), or purportedly received under subsection (b), was not actually sent or received, the legal effect of the sending or receipt is determined by other applicable law. Except to the extent permitted by the other law, the requirements of this subsection may not be varied by agreement.

Section 16. Transferable Records

(a) In this section, "transferable record" means an electronic record that:

(1) would be a note under [Article 3 of the Uniform Commercial Code] or a document under [Article 7 of the Uniform Commercial Code] if the electronic record were in writing; and

(2) the issuer of the electronic record expressly has agreed is a transferable record.

(b) A person has control of transferable record if a system employed for evidencing the transfer of interests in the transferable record reliably establishes that person as the person to which the transferable record was issued or transferred.

(c) A system satisfies subsection (b), and a person is deemed to have control of a transferable record, if the transferable record is created, stored, and assigned in such a manner that:

(1) a single authoritative copy of the transferable record exists which is unique, identifiable, and except as otherwise provided in paragraphs (4), (5), and (6), unalterable;

(2) the authoritative copy identifies the person asserting control as:

(A) the person to which the transferable record was issued; or

(B) if the authoritative copy indicates that the transferable record has been transferred, the person to which the transferable record was most recently transferred;

(3) the authoritative copy is communicated to and maintained by the person asserting control or its designated custodian;

(4) copies or revisions that add or change an identified assignee of the authoritative copy can be made only with the consent of the person asserting control;

(5) each copy of the authoritative copy and any copy of a copy is readily identifiable as a copy that is not the authoritative copy; and

(6) any revision of the authoritative copy is readily identifiable as authorized or unauthorized.

(d) Except as otherwise agreed, a person having control of a transferable record is the holder, as defined in [Section 1–201(20) of the Uniform Commercial Code], of the transferable record and has the same rights and defenses as a holder of an equivalent record or writing under [the Uniform Commercial Code], including, if the applicable statutory requirements under [Section 3–802(a), 7–501, or 9–308 of the Uniform Commercial Code] are satisfied the rights and defenses of a holder in due course, a holder to which a negotiable document of title has been duly negotiated, or a purchaser respectively. Delivery, possession; and indorsement are not required to obtain or exercise any of the rights under this subsection.

(e) Except as otherwise agreed an obligor under a transferable record has the same rights and defenses as an equivalent obligor under equivalent records or writings under [Uniform Commercial Code].

(f) If requested by a person against which enforcement is sought, the person seeking to enforce the transferable record shall provide reasonable proof that the person is in control of the transferable record. Proof may include access to the authoritative copy of the transferable record and related business records sufficient to review the terms of the transferable record and to establish the identity of the person having control of the transferable record.

DOCUMENT 25

UNIFORM FOREIGN MONEY-JUDGMENTS RECOGNITION ACT*

§ 1. [Definitions]

As used in this Act:

(1) "foreign state" means any governmental unit other than the United States, or any state, district, commonwealth, territory, insular possession thereof, or the Panama Canal Zone, the Trust Territory of the Pacific Islands, or the Ryukyu Islands;

(2) "foreign judgment" means any judgment of a foreign state granting or denying recovery of a sum of money, other than a judgment for taxes, a fine or other penalty, or a judgment for support in matrimonial or family matters.

§ 2. [Applicability]

This Act applies to any foreign judgment that is final and conclusive and enforceable where rendered even though an appeal therefrom is pending or it is subject to appeal.

§ 3. [Recognition and Enforcement]

Except as provided in section 4, a foreign judgment meeting the requirements of section 2 is conclusive between the parties to the extent that it grants or denies recovery of a sum of money. The foreign judgment is enforceable in the same manner as the judgment of a sister state which is entitled to full faith and credit.

§ 4. [Grounds for Non-recognition]

(a) A foreign judgment is not conclusive if

(1) the judgment was rendered under a system which does not provide impartial tribunals or procedures compatible with the requirements of due process of law;

(2) the foreign court did not have personal jurisdiction over the defendant; or

(3) the foreign court did not have jurisdiction over the subject matter.

(b) A foreign judgment need not be recognized if

---

* Reprinted with permission of the National Conference of Commissioners on Uniform State Laws and West Group.

(1) the defendant in the proceedings in the foreign court did not receive notice of the proceedings in sufficient time to enable him to defend;

(2) the judgment was obtained by fraud;

(3) the [cause of action] [claim for relief] on which the judgment is based is repugnant to the public policy of this state;

(4) the judgment conflicts with another final and conclusive judgment;

(5) the proceeding in the foreign court was contrary to an agreement between the parties under which the dispute in question was to be settled otherwise than by proceedings in that court; or

(6) in the case of jurisdiction based only on personal service, the foreign court was a seriously inconvenient forum for the trial of the action.

§ 5. [Personal Jurisdiction]

(a) The foreign judgment shall not be refused recognition for lack of personal jurisdiction if

(1) the defendant was served personally in the foreign state;

(2) the defendant voluntarily appeared in the proceedings, other than for the purpose of protecting property seized or threatened with seizure in the proceedings or of contesting the jurisdiction of the court over him;

(3) the defendant prior to the commencement of the proceedings had agreed to submit to the jurisdiction of the foreign court with respect to the subject matter involved;

(4) the defendant was domiciled in the foreign state when the proceedings were instituted or, being a body corporate had its principal place of business, was incorporated, or had otherwise acquired corporate status, in the foreign state;

(5) the defendant had a business office in the foreign state and the proceedings in the foreign court involved a [cause of action] [claim for relief] arising out of business done by the defendant through that office in the foreign state; or

(6) the defendant operated a motor vehicle or airplane in the foreign state and the proceedings involved a [cause of action] [claim for relief] arising out of such operation.

(b) The courts of this state may recognize other bases of jurisdiction.

§ 6. [Stay in Case of Appeal]

If the defendant satisfies the court either that an appeal is pending or that he is entitled and intends to appeal from the foreign judgment, the court may stay the proceedings until the appeal has been determined or until the expiration of a period of time sufficient to enable the defendant to prosecute the appeal.

§ 7. [Saving Clause]

This Act does not prevent the recognition of a foreign judgment in situations not covered by this Act.

§ 8. [Uniformity of Interpretation]

This Act shall be so construed as to effectuate its general purpose to make uniform the law of those states which enact it.

§ 9. [Short Title]

This Act may be cited as the Uniform Foreign Money–Judgments Recognition Act.

DOCUMENT 26

UNIFORM FOREIGN-MONEY CLAIMS ACT* (SELECTED PROVISIONS)

Table of Contents

§ 1. Definitions

In this [Act]:

(1) "Action" means a judicial proceeding or arbitration in which a payment in money may be awarded or enforced with respect to a foreign-money claim.

(2) "Bank-offered spot rate" means the spot rate of exchange at which a bank will sell foreign money at a spot rate.

(3) "Conversion date" means the banking day next preceding the date on which money, in accordance with this [Act], is:

(i) paid to a claimant in an action or distribution proceeding;

(ii) paid to the official designated by law to enforce a judgment or award on behalf of a claimant; or

(iii) used to recoup, set-off, or counterclaim in different moneys in an action or distribution proceeding.

(4) "Distribution proceeding" means a judicial or nonjudicial proceeding for the distribution of a fund in which one or more foreign-money claims is asserted and includes an accounting, an assignment for the benefit of creditors, a foreclosure, the liquidation or rehabilitation of a corporation or other entity, and the distribution of an estate, trust, or other fund.

(5) "Foreign money" means money other than money of the United States of America.

(6) "Foreign-money claim" means a claim upon an obligation to pay, or a claim for recovery of a loss, expressed in or measured by a foreign money.

(7) "Money" means a medium of exchange for the payment of obligations or a store of value authorized or adopted by a government or by inter-governmental agreement.

(8) "Money of the claim" means the money determined as proper pursuant to Section 4.

(9) "Person" means an individual, a corporation, government or governmental subdivision or agency, business trust, estate, trust, joint venture, partnership, association, two or more persons having a joint or common interest, or any other legal or commercial entity.

(10) "Rate of exchange" means the rate at which money of one country may be converted into money of another country in a free financial market convenient to or reasonably usable by a person obligated to pay or to state a rate of conversion. If separate rates of exchange apply to different kinds of transactions, the term means the rate applicable to the particular transaction giving rise to the foreign-money claim.

(11) "Spot rate" means the rate of exchange at which foreign money is sold by a bank or other dealer in foreign exchange for immediate or next day availability or for settlement by immediate payment in cash or equivalent, by charge to an account, or by an agreed delayed settlement not exceeding two days.

(12) "State" means a State of the United States, the District of Columbia, the Commonwealth of Puerto Rico, or a territory or insular possession subject to the jurisdiction of the United States.

§ 2. Scope

(a) This [Act] applies only to a foreign-money claim in an action or distribution proceeding.

(b) This [Act] applies to foreign-money issues even if other law under the conflict of laws rules of this State applies to other issues in the action or distribution proceeding.

§ 3. Variation by Agreement

(a) The effect of this [Act] may be varied by agreement of the parties made before or after commencement of an action or distribution proceeding or the entry of judgment.

(b) Parties to a transaction may agree upon the money to be used in a transaction giving rise to a foreign-money claim and may agree to use different moneys for different aspects of the transaction. Stating the price in a foreign money for one aspect of a transaction does not alone require the use of that money for other aspects of the transaction.

§ 4. Determining Money of the Claim

(a) The money in which the parties to a transaction have agreed that payment is to be made is the proper money of the claim for payment.

(b) If the parties to a transaction have not otherwise agreed, the proper money of the claim, as in each case may be appropriate, is the money:

(1) regularly used between the parties as a matter of usage or course of dealing;

(2) used at the time of a transaction in international trade, by trade usage or common practice, for valuing or settling transactions in the particular commodity or service involved; or

(3) in which the loss was ultimately felt or will be incurred by the party claimant.

§ 5. Determining Amount of the Money of Certain Contract Claims

(a) If an amount contracted to be paid in a foreign money is measured by a specified amount of a different money, the amount to be paid is determined on the conversion date.

(b) If an amount contracted to be paid in a foreign money is to be measured by a different money at the rate of exchange prevailing on a date before default, that rate of exchange applies only to payments made within a reasonable time after default, not exceeding 30 days. Thereafter, conversion is made at the bank-offered spot rate on the conversion date.

(c) A monetary claim is neither usurious nor unconscionable because the agreement on which it is based provides that the amount of the debtor's obligation to be paid in the debtor's money, when received by the creditor, must equal a specified amount of the foreign money of the country of the creditor. If, because of unexcused delay in payment of a judgment or award, the amount received by the creditor does not equal the amount of the foreign money specified in the agreement, the court or arbitrator shall amend the judgment or award accordingly.

§ 6. Asserting and Defending Foreign–Money Claim

(a) A person may assert a claim in a specified foreign money. If a foreign-money claim is not asserted, the claimant makes the claim in United States dollars.

(b) An opposing party may allege and prove that a claim, in whole or in part, is in a different money than that asserted by the claimant.

(c) A person may assert a defense, set-off, recoupment, or counterclaim in any money without regard to the money of other claims.

(d) The determination of the proper money of the claim is a question of law.

§ 7. Judgments and Awards on Foreign–Money Claims; Times of Money Conversion; Form of Judgment

(a) Except as provided in subsection (c), a judgment or award on a foreign-money claim must be stated in an amount of the money of the claim.

(b) A judgment or award on a foreign-money claim is payable in that foreign money or, at the option of the debtor, in the amount of United States dollars which will purchase that foreign money on the conversion date at a bank-offered spot rate.

(c) Assessed costs must be entered in United States dollars.

(d) Each payment in United States dollars must be accepted and credited on a judgment or award on a foreign-money claim in the amount of the foreign money that could be purchased by the dollars at a bank-offered spot rate of exchange at or near the close of business on the conversion date for that payment.

(e) A judgment or award made in an action or distribution proceeding on both (i) a defense, set-off, recoupment, or counterclaim and (ii) the adverse party's claim, must be netted by converting the money of the smaller into the money of the larger, and by subtracting the smaller from the larger, and specify the rates of exchange used.

(f) A judgment substantially in the following form complies with subsection (a):

[IT IS ADJUDGED AND ORDERED, that Defendant (*insert name*) pay to Plaintiff (*insert name*) the sum of (*insert amount in the foreign money*) plus interest on that sum at the rate of (*insert rate—see Section 9*) percent a year or, at the option of the judgment debtor, the number of United States dollars which will purchase the (*insert name of foreign money*) with interest due, at a bank-offered spot rate at or near the close of business on the banking day next before the day of payment, together with assessed costs of (*insert amount*) United States dollars.]

[Note: States should insert their customary forms of judgment with appropriate modifications.]

(g) If a contract claim is of the type covered by Section 5(a) or (b), the judgment or award must be entered for the amount of money stated to measure the obligation to be paid in the money specified for payment or, at the option of the debtor, the number of United States dollars which will purchase the computed amount of the money of payment on the conversion date at a bank-offered spot rate.

(h) A judgment must be [filed] [docketed] [recorded] and indexed in foreign money in the same manner, and has the same effect as a lien, as other judgments. It may be discharged by payment.

§ 8. Conversions of Foreign Money in Distribution Proceeding

The rate of exchange prevailing at or near the close of business on the day the distribution proceeding is initiated governs all exchanges of foreign money in a distribution proceeding. A foreign-money claimant in a distribution proceeding shall assert its claim in the named foreign money and show the amount of United States dollars resulting from a conversion as of the date the proceeding was initiated.

§ 9. Pre-judgment and Judgment Interest

(a) With respect to a foreign-money claim, recovery of pre-judgment or pre-award interest and the rate of interest to be applied in the action or distribution proceeding, except as provided in subsection (b), are matters of the substantive law governing the right to recovery under the conflict-of-laws rules of this State.

(b) The court or arbitrator shall increase or decrease the amount of pre-judgment or pre-award interest otherwise payable in a judgment or award in foreign-money to the extent required by the law of this State governing a failure to make or accept an offer of settlement or offer of judgment, or conduct by a party or its attorney causing undue delay or expense.

(c) A judgment or award on a foreign-money claim bears interest at the rate applicable to judgments of this State.

§ 10. Enforcement of Foreign Judgments

(a) If an action is brought to enforce a judgment of another jurisdiction expressed in a foreign money and the judgment is recognized in this State as enforceable, the enforcing judgment must be entered as provided in Section 7, whether or not the foreign judgment confers an option to pay in an equivalent amount of United States dollars.

(b) A foreign judgment may be [filed] [docketed] [recorded] in accordance with any rule or statute of this State providing a procedure for its recognition and enforcement.

(c) A satisfaction or partial payment made upon the foreign judgment, on proof thereof, must be credited against the amount of foreign money specified in the judgment, notwithstanding the entry of judgment in this State.

(d) A judgment entered on a foreign-money claim only in United States dollars in another state must be enforced in this State in United States dollars only.

§ 11. Determining United States Dollar Value of Foreign-Money Claims for Limited Purposes

(a) Computations under this section are for the limited purposes of the section and do not affect computation of the United States dollar equivalent of the money of the judgment for the purpose of payment.

(b) For the limited purpose of facilitating the enforcement of provisional remedies in an action, the value in United States dollars of assets to be seized or restrained pursuant to a writ of attachment, garnishment, execution, or other legal process, the amount of United States dollars at issue for assessing costs, or the amount of United States dollars involved for a surety bond or other court-required undertaking, must be ascertained as provided in subsections (c) and (d).

(c) A party seeking process, costs, bond, or other undertaking under subsection (b) shall compute in United States dollars the amount of the foreign money claimed from a bank-offered spot rate prevailing at or near the close of business on the banking day next preceding the filing of a request or application for the issuance of process or for the determination of costs, or an application for a bond or other court-required undertaking.

(d) A party seeking the process, costs, bond, or other undertaking under subsection (b) shall file with each request or application an affidavit or certificate executed in good faith by its counsel or a bank officer, stating the market quotation used and how it was obtained, and setting forth the calculation. Affected court officials incur no liability, after a filing of the affidavit or certificate, for acting as if the judgment were in the amount of United States dollars stated in the affidavit or certificate.

§ 12. Effect of Currency Revalorization

(a) If, after an obligation is expressed or a loss is incurred in a foreign money, the country issuing or adopting that money substitutes a new money in place of that money, the obligation or the loss is treated as if expressed or incurred in the new money at the rate of conversion the issuing country establishes for the payment of like obligations or losses denominated in the former money.

(b) If substitution under subsection (a) occurs after a judgment or award is entered on a foreign-money claim, the court or arbitrator shall amend the judgment or award by a like conversion of the former money.

§ 13. Supplementary General Principles of Law

Unless displaced by particular provisions of this [Act], the principles of law and equity, including the law merchant, and the law relative to capacity to contract, principal and agent, estoppel, fraud, misrepresentation, duress, coercion, mistake, bankruptcy, or other validating or invalidating causes supplement its provisions.

§ 14. Uniformity of Application and Construction

This [Act] shall be applied and construed to effectuate its general purpose to make uniform the law with respect to the subject of this [Act] among states enacting it.

§ 15. Short Title

This [Act] may be cited as the Uniform Foreign–Money Claims Act.

§ 16. Severability Clause

If any provision of this [Act] or its application to any person or circumstance is held invalid, the invalidity does not affect other provisions or applications of this [Act] which can be given effect without the invalid provision or application, and to this end the provisions of this [Act] are severable.

DOCUMENT 27

UNIFORM FOREIGN-COUNTRY MONEY JUDGMENTS RECOGNITION ACT (2005)

TABLE OF CONTENTS

UNIFORM FOREIGN-COUNTRY MONEY JUDGMENTS RECOGNITION ACT

PREFATORY NOTE

This Act is a revision of the Uniform Foreign Money-Judgments Recognition Act of 1962. That Act codified the most prevalent common law rules with regard to the recognition of money judgments rendered in other countries. The hope was that codification by a state of its rules on the recognition of foreign-country money judgments, by satisfying reciprocity concerns of foreign courts, would make it more likely that money judgments rendered in that state would be recognized in other countries. Towards this end, the Act sets out the circumstances in which the courts in states that have adopted the Act must recognize foreign-country money judgments. It delineates a minimum of foreign-country judgments that must be recognized by the courts of adopting states, leaving those courts free to recognize other foreign-country judgments not covered by the Act under principles of comity or otherwise. Since its promulgation over forty years ago, the 1962 Act has been adopted in a majority of the states and has been in large part successful in carrying out it purpose of establishing uniform and clear standards under which state courts will enforce the foreign-country money judgments that come within its scope.

This Act continues the basic policies and approach of the 1962 Act. Its purpose is not to depart from the basic rules or approach of the 1962 Act, which have withstood well the test of time, but rather to update the 1962 Act, to clarify its provisions, and to correct problems created by the interpretation of the provisions of that Act by the courts over the years since its promulgation. Among the more significant issues that have arisen under the 1962 Act which are addressed in this Revised Act are (1) the need to update and clarify the definitions section; (2) the need to reorganize and clarify the scope provisions, and to allocate the burden of proof with regard to establishing application of the Act; (3) the need to set out the procedure by which recognition of a foreign-country money judgment under the Act must be sought; (4) the need to clarify and, to a limited extent, expand upon the grounds for denying recognition in light of differing interpretations of those provisions in the current case law; (5) the need to expressly allocate the burden of proof with regard to the grounds for denying recognition; and (6) the need to establish a statute of limitations for recognition actions.

In the course of drafting this Act, the drafters revisited the decision made in the 1962 Act not to require reciprocity as a condition to recognition of the foreign-country money judgments covered by the Act. After much discussion, the drafters decided that the approach of the 1962 Act continues to be the wisest course with regard to this issue. While recognition of U.S. judgments continues to be problematic in a number of foreign countries, there was insufficient evidence to establish that a reciprocity requirement would have a greater effect on encouraging foreign recognition of U.S. judgments than does the approach taken by the Act. At the same time, the certainty and uniformity provided by the approach of the 1962 Act, and continued in this Act, creates a stability in this area that facilitates international commercial transactions.

UNIFORM FOREIGN–COUNTRY MONEY JUDGMENTS RECOGNITION ACT

SECTION 1. SHORT TITLE. This [act] may be cited as the [Uniform Foreign–Country Money Judgments Recognition Act].

COMMENT

Source: This section is an updated version of Section 9 of the Uniform Foreign Money–Judgments Recognition Act of 1962.

SECTION 2. DEFINITIONS. In this [act]:

(1) "Foreign country" means a government other than:

(A) the United States;

(B) a state, district, commonwealth, territory, or insular possession of the United States; or

(C) any other government with regard to which the decision in this state as to whether to recognize a judgment of that government's courts is initially subject to determination under the Full Faith and Credit Clause of the United States Constitution.

(2) "Foreign-country judgment" means a judgment of a court of a foreign country.

COMMENT

Source: This section is derived from Section 1 of the Uniform Foreign Money–Judgments Recognition Act of 1962.

1. The defined terms "foreign state" and "foreign judgment" in the 1962 Act have been changed to "foreign country" and "foreign-country judgment" in order to make it clear that the Act does not apply to recognition of sister-state judgments. Some courts have noted that the "foreign state" and "foreign judgment" definitions of the 1962 Act have caused confusion as to whether the Act should apply to sister-state judgments because "foreign state" and "foreign judgment" are terms of art generally used in connection with recognition and enforcement of sister-state judgments. *See, e.g.,* Eagle Leasing v. Amandus, 476 N.W.2d 35 (S.Ct. Iowa 1991) (reversing lower court's application of UFMJRA to a sister-state judgment, but noting lower court's confusion was understandable as "foreign judgment" is term of art normally applied to sister-state judgments). *See also,* Uniform Enforcement of Foreign Judgments Act § 1 (defining "foreign judgment" as the judgment of a sister state or federal court).

The 1962 Act defines a "foreign state" as "any governmental unit other than the United States, or any state, district, commonwealth, territory, insular possession thereof, or the Panama Canal Zone, the Trust Territory of the Pacific Islands, or the Ryuku Islands." Rather than simply updating the list in the 1962 Act's definition of "foreign state," the new definition of "foreign country" in this Act combines the "listing" approach of the 1962 Act's "foreign state" definition with a provision that defines "foreign country" in terms of whether the judgments of the particular government's courts are initially subject to the Full Faith and Credit Clause standards for determining whether those judgments will be recognized. Under this new definition, a governmental unit is a "foreign country" if it is (1) not the United States or a state, district, commonwealth, territory or insular possession of the United States; and (2) its judgments are not initially subject to Full Faith and Credit Clause standards.

The Full Faith and Credit Clause, Art. IV, section 1, provides that "Full Faith and Credit shall be given in each State to the public Acts, Records, and judicial Proceedings of every other State. And the Congress may by general Laws prescribe the Manner in which such Acts, Records, and Proceedings shall be proved, and the Effect thereof." Whether the judgments of a governmental unit are subject to the Full Faith and Credit Clause may be determined by judicial interpretation of the Full Faith and Credit Clause or by statute, or by a combination of these two sources. For example, pursuant to the authority granted by the second sentence of the Full Faith and Credit Clause, Congress has passed 28 U.S.C.A. § 1738, which provides *inter alia* that court records from "any State, Territory, or Possession of the United States" are entitled to full faith and credit under the Full Faith and Credit Clause. In *Stoll v. Gottlieb*, 305 U.S. 165, 170 (1938), the United States Supreme Court held that this statute also requires that full faith and credit be given to judgments of federal courts. States also have made determinations as to whether certain types of judgments are subject to the Full Faith and Credit Clause. *E.g.* Day v. Montana Dept. Of Social & Rehab. Servs., 900 P.2d 296 (Mont. 1995) (tribal court judgment not subject to Full Faith and Credit, and should be treated with same deference shown foreign-country judgments). Under the definition of "foreign country" in this Act, the determination as to whether a governmental unit's judgments are subject to full faith and credit standards should be made by reference to any relevant law, whether statutory or decisional, that is applicable "in this state."

The definition of "foreign country" in terms of those judgments not subject to Full Faith and Credit standards also has the advantage of more effectively coordinating the Act with the Uniform Enforcement of Foreign Judgments Act. That Act, which establishes a registration procedure for the enforcement of sister state and equivalent judgments, defines a "foreign judgment" as "any judgment, decree, or order of a court of the United States or of any other court which is entitled to full faith and credit in this state." Uniform Enforcement of Foreign Judgments Act, § 1 (1964). By defining "foreign country" in the Recognition Act in terms of those judgments not subject to full faith and credit standards, this Act makes it clear that the Enforcement Act and the Recognition Act are mutually exclusive–if a foreign money judgment is subject to full faith and credit standards, then the Enforcement Act's registration procedure is available with regard to its enforcement; if the foreign money judgment is not subject to full faith and credit standards, then the foreign money judgment may not be enforced until recognition of it has been obtained in accordance with the provisions of the Recognition Act.

2. The definition of "foreign-country judgment" in this Act differs significantly from the 1962 Act's definition of "foreign judgment." The 1962 Act's definition served in large part as a scope provision for the Act. The part of the definition defining the scope of the Act has been moved to section 3, which is the scope section.

3. The definition of "foreign-country judgment" in this Act refers to "a judgment" of "a court" of the foreign country. The foreign-country judgment need not take a particular form—any order or decree that meets the requirements of this section and comes within the scope of the Act under Section 3 is subject to the Act. Similarly, any competent government tribunal that issues such a "judgment" comes within the term "court" for purposes of this Act. The judgment, however, must be a judgment of an adjudicative body of the foreign country, and not the result of an alternative dispute mechanism chosen by the parties. Thus, foreign arbitral awards and agreements to arbitrate are not covered by this Act. They are governed instead by federal law, Chapter 2 of the U.S. Arbitration Act, 9 U.S.C. §§ 201–208, implementing the United Nations Convention on the Recognition and Enforcement of Foreign Arbitral Awards and Chapter 3 of the U.S. Arbitration Act, 9 U.S.C. §§ 301–307, implementing the Inter–American Convention on International Commercial Arbitration. A judgment of a foreign court confirming or setting aside an arbitral award, however, would be covered by this Act.

4. The definition of "foreign-country judgment" does not limit foreign-country judgments to those rendered in litigation between private parties. Judgments in which a governmental entity is a party also are included, and are subject to this Act if they meet the requirements of this section and are within the scope of the Act under Section 3.

SECTION 3. APPLICABILITY.

(a) Except as otherwise provided in subsection (b), this [act] applies to a foreign-country judgment to the extent that the judgment:

(1) grants or denies recovery of a sum of money; and

(2) under the law of the foreign country where rendered, is final, conclusive, and enforceable.

(b) This [act] does not apply to a foreign-country judgment, even if the judgment grants or denies recovery of a sum of money, to the extent that the judgment is:

(1) a judgment for taxes;

(2) a fine or other penalty; or

(3) a judgment for divorce, support, or maintenance, or other judgment rendered in connection with domestic relations.

(c) A party seeking recognition of a foreign-country judgment has the burden of establishing that this [act] applies to the foreign-country judgment.

COMMENT

Source: This section is based on Section 2 of the 1962 Act. Subsection (b) contains material that was included as part of the definition of "foreign judgment" in Section 1(2) of the 1962 Act. Subsection (c) is new.

1. Like the 1962 Act, this Act sets out in subsection 3(a) two basic requirements that a foreign-country judgment must meet before it comes

within the scope of this Act—the foreign-country judgment must (1) grant or deny recovery of a sum of money and (2) be final, conclusive and enforceable under the law of the foreign country where it was rendered. Subsection 3(b) then sets out three types of foreign-country judgments that are excluded from the coverage of this Act, even though they meet the criteria of subsection 3(a)—judgments for taxes, judgments constituting fines and other penalties, and judgments in domestic relations matters. These exclusions are comparable to those contained in Section 1(2) of the 1962 Act.

2. This Act applies to a foreign-country judgment only to the extent the foreign-country judgment grants or denies recovery of a sum of money. If a foreign-country judgment both grants or denies recovery of a sum money and provides for some other form of relief, this Act would apply to the portion of the judgment that grants or denies monetary relief, but not to the portion that provides for some other form of relief. The U.S. court, however, would be left free to decide to recognize and enforce the non-monetary portion of the judgment under principles of comity or other applicable law. See Section 11.

3. In order to come within the scope of this Act, a foreign-country judgment must be final, conclusive, and enforceable under the law of the foreign country in which it was rendered. This requirement contains three distinct, although inter-related concepts. A judgment is final when it is not subject to additional proceedings in the rendering court other than execution. A judgment is conclusive when it is given effect between the parties as a determination of their legal rights and obligations. A judgment is enforceable when the legal procedures of the state to ensure that the judgment debtor complies with the judgment are available to the judgment creditor to assist in collection of the judgment.

While the first two of these requirements—finality and conclusiveness—will apply with regard to every foreign-country money judgment, the requirement of enforceability is only relevant when the judgment is one granting recovery of a sum of money. A judgment denying a sum of money obviously is not subject to enforcement procedures, as there is no monetary award to enforce. This Act, however, covers both judgments granting and those denying recovery of a sum of money. Thus, the fact that a foreign-country judgment denying recovery of a sum of money is not enforceable does not mean that such judgments are not within the scope of the Act. Instead, the requirement that the judgment be enforceable should be read to mean that, if the foreign-country judgment grants recovery of a sum of money, it must be enforceable in the foreign country in order to be within the scope of the Act.

Like the 1962 Act, subsection 3(b) requires that the determinations as to finality, conclusiveness and enforceability be made using the law of the foreign country in which the judgment was rendered. Unless the foreign-country judgment is final, conclusive, and (to the extent it grants recovery of a sum of money) enforceable in the foreign country where it was rendered, it will not be within the scope of this Act.

4. Subsection 3(b) follows the 1962 Act by excluding three categories of foreign-country money judgments from the scope of the Act–judgments for taxes, judgments that constitute fines and penalties, and judgments in domestic relations matters. The domestic relations exclusion has been redrafted to

make it clear that all judgments in domestic relations matters are excluded from the Act, not just judgments "for support" as provided in the 1962 Act. This is consistent with interpretation of the 1962 Act by the courts, which extended the "support" exclusion in the 1962 Act beyond its literal wording to exclude other money judgments in connection with domestic matters. *E.g.*, Wolff v. Wolff, 389 A.2d 413 (My. App. 1978) ("support" includes alimony).

Recognition and enforcement of domestic relations judgments traditionally has been treated differently from recognition and enforcement of other judgments. The considerations with regard to those judgments, particularly with regard to jurisdiction and finality, differ from those with regard to other money judgments. Further, national laws with regard to domestic relations vary widely, and recognition and enforcement of such judgments thus is more appropriately handled through comity than through use of this uniform Act. Finally, other statutes, such as the Uniform Interstate Family Support Act and the federal International Child Support Enforcement Act, 42 U.S.C. § 659a (1996), address various aspects of the recognition and enforcement of domestic relations awards. Under Section 11 of this Act, courts are free to recognize money judgments in domestic relations matters under principles of comity or otherwise, and U.S. courts routinely enforce money judgments in domestic relations matters under comity principles.

Foreign-country judgments for taxes and judgments that constitute fines or penalties traditionally have not been recognized and enforced in U.S. courts. *See, e.g.*, Restatement Third of the Foreign Relations Law of the United States § 483 (1986). Both the "revenue rule," under which the courts of one country will not enforce the revenue laws of another country, and the prohibition on enforcement of penal judgments seem to be grounded in the idea that one country does not enforce the public laws of another. *See id.* Reporters' Note 2. The exclusion of tax judgments and judgments constituting fines or penalties from the scope of the Act reflects this tradition. Under Section 11, however, courts remain free to consider whether such judgments should be recognized and enforced under comity or other principles.

A judgment for taxes is a judgment in favor of a foreign country or one of its subdivisions based on a claim for an assessment of a tax. Thus, a judgment awarding a plaintiff restitution of the purchase price paid for an item would not be considered in any part a judgment for taxes, even though one element of the recovery was the sales tax paid by the plaintiff at the time of purchase. Such a judgment would not be one designed to enforce the revenue laws of the foreign country, but rather one designed to compensate the plaintiff. Courts generally hold that the test for whether a judgment is a fine or penalty is determined by whether its purpose is remedial in nature, with its benefits accruing to private individuals, or it is penal in nature, punishing an offense against public justice. *E.g.*, Chase Manhattan Bank, N.A. v. Hoffman, 665 F.Supp 73 (D. Mass. 1987) (finding that Belgium judgment was not penal even though the proceeding forming the basis of the suit was primarily criminal where Belgium court considered damage petition a civil remedy, the judgment did not constitute punishment for an offense against public justice of Belgium, and benefit of the judgment accrued to private judgment creditor, not Belgium). Thus, a judgment that awards compensation or restitution for the benefit of private individuals should not automatically be considered penal in nature and therefore outside the scope of the Act simply because the action is brought on behalf of the private individuals by a government entity. *Cf.* U.S.-Australia Free Trade Agreement, art.14.7.2, U.S.-Austl., May 18, 2004 (providing that when government agency obtains a civil monetary judgment for purpose of providing restitution to consumers, investors, or customers who suffered economic harm due to fraud, judgment generally should not be denied recognition and enforcement on ground that it is penal or revenue in nature, or based on other foreign public law).

5. Under subsection 3(b), a foreign-country money judgment is not within the scope of this Act "to the extent" that it comes within one of the excluded categories. Therefore, if a foreign-country money judgment is only partially within one of the excluded categories, the non-excluded portion will be subject to this Act.

6. Subsection 3(c) is new. The 1962 Act does not expressly allocate the burden of proof with regard to establishing whether a foreign-country judgment is within the scope of the Act. Courts applying the 1962 Act generally have held that the burden of proof is on the person seeking recognition to establish that the judgment is final, conclusive and enforceable where rendered. *E.g.*, Mayekawa Mfg. Co. Ltd. v. Sasaki, 888 P.2d 183, 189 (Wash. App. 1995) (burden of proof on creditor to establish judgment is final, conclusive, and enforceable where rendered); Bridgeway Corp. v. Citibank, 45 F.Supp.2d 276, 285 (S.D.N.Y. 1999) (party seeking recognition must establish that there is a final judgment, conclusive and enforceable where rendered); S.C.Chimexim S.A. v. Velco Enterprises, Ltd., 36 F. Supp.2d 206, 212 (S.D.N.Y. 1999) (Plaintiff has the burden of establishing conclusive effect). Subsection (3)(c) places the burden of proof to establish whether a foreign-country judgment is within the scope of the Act on the party seeking recognition of the foreign-country judgment with regard to both subsection (a) and subsection (b).

SECTION 4. STANDARDS FOR RECOGNITION OF FOREIGN-COUNTRY JUDGMENT.

(a) Except as otherwise provided in subsections (b) and (c), a court of this state shall recognize a foreign-country judgment to which this [act] applies.

(b) A court of this state may not recognize a foreign-country judgment if:

(1) the judgment was rendered under a judicial system that does not provide impartial tribunals or procedures compatible with the requirements of due process of law;

(2) the foreign court did not have personal jurisdiction over the defendant; or

(3) the foreign court did not have jurisdiction over the subject matter.

(c) A court of this state need not recognize a foreign-country judgment if:

(1) the defendant in the proceeding in the foreign court did not receive notice of the proceeding in sufficient time to enable the defendant to defend;

(2) the judgment was obtained by fraud that deprived the losing party of an adequate opportunity to present its case;

(3) the judgment or the [cause of action] [claim for relief] on which the judgment is based is repugnant to the public policy of this state or of the United States;

(4) the judgment conflicts with another final and conclusive judgment;

(5) the proceeding in the foreign court was contrary to an agreement between the parties under which the dispute in question was to be determined otherwise than by proceedings in that foreign court;

(6) in the case of jurisdiction based only on personal service, the foreign court was a seriously inconvenient forum for the trial of the action;

(7) the judgment was rendered in circumstances that raise substantial doubt about the integrity of the rendering court with respect to the judgment; or

(8) the specific proceeding in the foreign court leading to the judgment was not compatible with the requirements of due process of law.

(d) A party resisting recognition of a foreign-country judgment has the burden of establishing that a ground for nonrecognition stated in subsection (b) or (c) exists.

Comment

Source: This section is based on Section 4 of the 1962 Act.

1. This Section provides the standards for recognition of a foreign-country money judgment. Section 7 sets out the effect of recognition of a foreign-country money judgment under this Act.

2. Recognition of a judgment means that the forum court accepts the determination of legal rights and obligations made by the rendering court in the foreign country. *See, e.g.* Restatement (Second) of Conflicts of Laws, Ch. 5, Topic 3, Introductory Note (recognition of foreign judgment occurs to the extent the forum court gives the judgment "the same effect with respect to the parties, the subject matter of the action and the issues involved that it has in the state where it was rendered.") Recognition of a foreign-country judgment must be distinguished from enforcement of that judgment. Enforcement of the foreign-country judgment involves the application of the legal procedures of the state to ensure that the judgment debtor obeys the foreign-country judgment. Recognition of a foreign-country money judgment often is associated with enforcement of the judgment, as the judgment creditor usually

seeks recognition of the foreign-country judgment primarily for the purpose of invoking the enforcement procedures of the forum state to assist the judgment creditor's collection of the judgment from the judgment debtor. Because the forum court cannot enforce the foreign-country judgment until it has determined that the judgment will be given effect, recognition is a prerequisite to enforcement of the foreign-country judgment. Recognition, however, also has significance outside the enforcement context because a foreign-country judgment also must be recognized before it can be given preclusive effect under res judicata and collateral estoppel principles. The issue of whether a foreign-country judgment will be recognized is distinct from both the issue of whether the judgment will be enforced, and the issue of the extent to which it will be given preclusive effect.

3. Subsection 4(a) places an affirmative duty on the forum court to recognize a foreign-country money judgment unless one of the grounds for nonrecognition stated in subsection (b) or (c) applies. Subsection (b) states three mandatory grounds for denying recognition to a foreign-country money judgment. If the forum court finds that one of the grounds listed in subsection (b) exists, then it must deny recognition to the foreign-country money judgment. Subsection (c) states eight nonmandatory grounds for denying recognition. The forum court has discretion to decide whether or not to refuse recognition based on one of these grounds. Subsection (d) places the burden of proof on the party resisting recognition of the foreign-country judgment to establish that one of the grounds for nonrecognition exists.

4. The mandatory grounds for nonrecognition stated in subsection (b) are identical to the mandatory grounds stated in Section 4 of the 1962 Act. The discretionary grounds stated in subsection 4(c)(1) through (6) are based on subsection 4(b)(1) through (6) of the 1962 Act. The discretionary grounds stated in subsection 4(c)(7) and (8) are new.

5. Under subsection (b)(1), the forum court must deny recognition to the foreign-country money judgment if that judgment was "rendered under a judicial system that does not provide impartial tribunals or procedures compatible with the requirements of due process of law." The standard for this ground for nonrecognition "has been stated authoritatively by the Supreme Court of the United States in *Hilton v. Guyot*, 159 U.S.113, 205 (1895). As indicated in that decision, a mere difference in the procedural system is not a sufficient basis for nonrecognition. A case of serious injustice must be involved." Cmt § 4, Uniform Foreign Money–Judgment Recognition Act (1962). The focus of inquiry is not whether the procedure in the rendering country is similar to U.S. procedure, but rather on the basic fairness of the foreign-country procedure. Kam–Tech Systems, Ltd. V. Yardeni, 74 A.2d 644, 649 (N.J. App. 2001) (interpreting the comparable provision in the 1962 Act); *accord*, Society of Lloyd's v. Ashenden, 233 F.3d 473 (7th Cir. 2000) (procedures need not meet all the intricacies of the complex concept of due process that has emerged from U.S. case law, but rather must be fair in the broader international sense) (interpreting comparable provision in the 1962 Act). Procedural differences, such as absence of jury trial or different evidentiary rules are not sufficient to justify denying recognition under subsection (b)(1), so long as the essential elements of impartial administration and basic

procedural fairness have been provided in the foreign proceeding. As the U.S. Supreme Court stated in *Hilton*:

> Where there has been opportunity for a full and fair trial abroad before a court of competent jurisdiction conducting the trial upon regular proceedings, after due citation or voluntary appearance of the defendant, and under a system of jurisprudence likely to secure an impartial administration of justice between the citizens of its own country and those of other countries, and there is nothing to show either prejudice in the court, or in the system of laws under which it was sitting, or fraud in procuring the judgment, or any other special reason why the comity of this nation should not allow it full effect then a foreign-country judgment should be recognized. *Hilton*, 159 U.S. at 202.

6. Under section 4(b)(2), the forum court must deny recognition to the foreign-country judgment if the foreign court did not have personal jurisdiction over the defendant. Section 5(a) lists six bases for personal jurisdiction that are adequate as a matter of law to establish that the foreign court had personal jurisdiction. Section 5(b) makes clear that other grounds for personal jurisdiction may be found sufficient.

7. Subsection 4(c)(2) limits the type of fraud that will serve as a ground for denying recognition to extrinsic fraud. This provision is consistent with the interpretation of the comparable provision in subsection 4(b)(2) of the 1962 Act by the courts, which have found that only extrinsic fraud—conduct of the prevailing party that deprived the losing party of an adequate opportunity to present its case—is sufficient under the 1962 Act. Examples of extrinsic fraud would be when the plaintiff deliberately had the initiating process served on the defendant at the wrong address, deliberately gave the defendant wrong information as to the time and place of the hearing, or obtained a default judgment against the defendant based on a forged confession of judgment. When this type of fraudulent action by the plaintiff deprives the defendant of an adequate opportunity to present its case, then it provides grounds for denying recognition of the foreign-country judgment. Extrinsic fraud should be distinguished from intrinsic fraud, such as false testimony of a witness or admission of a forged document into evidence during the foreign proceeding. Intrinsic fraud does not provide a basis for denying recognition under subsection 4(c)(2), as the assertion that intrinsic fraud has occurred should be raised and dealt with in the rendering court.

8. The public policy exception in subsection 4(c)(3) is based on the public policy exception in subsection 4(b)(3) of the 1962 Act, with one difference. The public policy exception in the 1962 Act states that the relevant inquiry is whether "the [cause of action] [claim for relief] on which the judgment is based" is repugnant to public policy. Based on this "cause of action" language, some courts interpreting the 1962 Act have refused to find that a public policy challenge based on something other than repugnancy of the foreign cause of action comes within this exception. *E.g.*, Southwest Livestock & Trucking Co., Inc. v. Ramon, 169 F.3d 317 (5th Cir. 1999) (refusing to deny recognition to Mexican judgment on promissory note with interest rate of 48% because cause of action to collect on promissory note does not violate public policy); Guinness PLC v. Ward, 955 F.2d 875 (4th Cir.

1992) (challenge to recognition based on post-judgment settlement could not be asserted under public policy exception); The Society of Lloyd's v. Turner, 303 F.3d 325 (5th Cir. 2002) (rejecting argument legal standards applied to establish elements of breach of contract violated public policy because cause of action for breach of contract itself is not contrary to state public policy); *cf.* Bachchan v. India Abroad Publications, Inc., 585 N.Y.S.2d 661 (N.Y. Sup. Ct. 1992) (judgment creditor argued British libel judgment should be recognized despite argument it violated First Amendment because New York recognizes a cause of action for libel). Subsection 4(c)(3) rejects this narrow focus by providing that the forum court may deny recognition if either the cause of action or the judgment itself violates public policy. *Cf.* Restatement (Third) of the Foreign Relations Law of the United States, § 482(2)(d) (1986) (containing a similarly-worded public policy exception to recognition).

Although subsection 4(c)(3) of this Act rejects the narrow focus on the cause of action under the 1962 Act, it retains the stringent test for finding a public policy violation applied by courts interpreting the 1962 Act. Under that test, a difference in law, even a marked one, is not sufficient to raise a public policy issue. Nor is it relevant that the foreign law allows a recovery that the forum state would not allow. Public policy is violated only if recognition or enforcement of the foreign-country judgment would tend clearly to injure the public health, the public morals, or the public confidence in the administration of law, or would undermine "that sense of security for individual rights, whether of personal liberty or of private property, which any citizen ought to feel." Hunt v. BP Exploration Co. (Libya) Ltd., 492 F. Supp. 885, 901 (N.D. Tex. 1980).

The language "or of the United States" in subsection 4(c)(3), which does not appear in the 1962 Act provision, makes it clear that the relevant public policy is that of both the State in which recognition is sought and that of the United States. This is the position taken by the vast majority of cases interpreting the 1962 public policy provision. *E.g.,* Bachchan v. India Abroad Publications, Inc., 585 N.Y.S.2d 661 (Sup.Ct. N.Y. 1992) (British libel judgment denied recognition because it violates First Amendment).

9. Subsection 4(c)(5) allows the forum court to refuse recognition of a foreign-country judgment when the parties had a valid agreement, such as a valid forum selection clause or agreement to arbitrate, providing that the relevant dispute would be resolved in a forum other than the forum issuing the foreign-country judgment. Under this provision, the forum court must find both the existence of a valid agreement and that the agreement covered the subject matter involved in the foreign litigation resulting in the foreign-country judgment.

10. Subsection 4(c)(6) authorizes the forum court to refuse recognition of a foreign-country judgment that was rendered in the foreign country solely on the basis of personal service when the forum court believes the original action should have been dismissed by the court in the foreign country on grounds of *forum non conveniens.*

11. Subsection 4(c)(7) is new. Under this subsection, the forum court may deny recognition to a foreign-country judgment if there are circumstances that raise substantial doubt about the integrity of the rendering court

with respect to that judgment. It requires a showing of corruption in the particular case that had an impact on the judgment that was rendered. This provision may be contrasted with subsection 4(b)(1) , which requires that the forum court refuse recognition to the foreign-country judgment if it was rendered under a judicial system that does not provide impartial tribunals. Like the comparable provision in subsection 4(a)(1) of the 1962 Act, subsection 4(b)(1) focuses on the judicial system of the foreign country as a whole, rather than on whether the particular judicial proceeding leading to the foreign-country judgment was impartial and fair. *See, e.g.*, The Society of Lloyd's v. Turner, 303 F.3d 325, 330 (5th Cir. 2002) (interpreting the 1962 Act); CIBC Mellon Trust Co. v. Mora Hotel Corp,. N.V., 743 N.Y.S.2d 408, 415 (N.Y. App. 2002) (interpreting the 1962 Act); Society of Lloyd's v. Ashenden, 233 F.3d 473, 477 (7th Cir. 2000) (interpreting the 1962 Act). On the other hand, subsection 4(c)(7) allows the court to deny recognition to the foreign-country judgment if it finds a lack of impartiality and fairness of the tribunal in the individual proceeding leading to the foreign-country judgment. Thus, the difference is that between showing, for example, that corruption and bribery is so prevalent throughout the judicial system of the foreign country as to make that entire judicial system one that does not provide impartial tribunals versus showing that bribery of the judge in the proceeding that resulted in the particular foreign-country judgment under consideration had a sufficient impact on the ultimate judgment as to call it into question.

12. Subsection 4(c)(8) also is new. It allows the forum court to deny recognition to the foreign-country judgment if the court finds that the specific proceeding in the foreign court was not compatible with the requirements of fundamental fairness. Like subsection 4(c)(7), it can be contrasted with subsection 4(b)(1), which requires the forum court to deny recognition to the foreign-country judgment if the forum court finds that the entire judicial system in the foreign country where the foreign-country judgment was rendered does not provide procedures compatible with the requirements of fundamental fairness. While the focus of subsection 4(b)(1) is on the foreign country's judicial system as a whole, the focus of subsection 4(c)(8) is on the particular proceeding that resulted in the specific foreign-country judgment under consideration. Thus, the difference is that between showing, for example, that there has been such a breakdown of law and order in the particular foreign country that judgments are rendered on the basis of political decisions rather than the rule of law throughout the judicial system versus a showing that for political reasons the particular party against whom the foreign-country judgment was entered was denied fundamental fairness in the particular proceedings leading to the foreign-country judgment.

Subsections 4(c)(7) and (8) both are discretionary grounds for denying recognition, while subsection 4(b)(1) is mandatory. Obviously, if the entire judicial system in the foreign country fails to satisfy the requirements of impartiality and fundamental fairness, a judgment rendered in that foreign country would be so compromised that the forum court should refuse to recognize it as a matter of course. On the other hand, if the problem is evidence of a lack of integrity or fundamental fairness with regard to the particular proceeding leading to the foreign-country judgment, then there may or may not be other factors in the particular case that would cause the forum court to decide to recognize the foreign-country judgment. For example, a forum court might decide not to exercise its discretion to deny recognition despite evidence of corruption or procedural unfairness in a particular case because the party resisting recognition failed to raise the issue on appeal from the foreign-country judgment in the foreign country, and the evidence establishes that, if the party had done so, appeal would have been an adequate mechanism for correcting the transgressions of the lower court.

13. Under subsection 4(d), the party opposing recognition of the foreign-country judgment has the burden of establishing that one of the grounds for nonrecognition set out in subsection 4(b) or (c) applies. The 1962 Act was silent as to who had the burden of proof to establish a ground for nonrecognition and courts applying the 1962 Act took different positions on the issue. *Compare* Bridgeway Corp. v. Citibank, 45 F.Supp. 2d 276, 285 (S.D.N.Y. 1999) (plaintiff has burden to show no mandatory basis under 4(a) for nonrecognition exists; defendant has burden regarding discretionary bases) *with* The Courage Co. LLC v. The ChemShare Corp., 93 S.W.3d 323, 331 (Tex. App. 2002) (party seeking to avoid recognition has burden to prove ground for nonrecognition). Because the grounds for nonrecognition in Section 4 are in the nature of defenses to recognition, the burden of proof is most appropriately allocated to the party opposing recognition of the foreign-country judgment.

SECTION 5. PERSONAL JURISDICTION.

(a) A foreign-country judgment may not be refused recognition for lack of personal jurisdiction if:

(1) the defendant was served with process personally in the foreign country;

(2) the defendant voluntarily appeared in the proceeding, other than for the purpose of protecting property seized or threatened with seizure in the proceeding or of contesting the jurisdiction of the court over the defendant;

(3) the defendant, before the commencement of the proceeding, had agreed to submit to the jurisdiction of the foreign court with respect to the subject matter involved;

(4) the defendant was domiciled in the foreign country when the proceeding was instituted or was a corporation or other form of business organization that had its principal place of business in, or was organized under the laws of, the foreign country;

(5) the defendant had a business office in the foreign country and the proceeding in the foreign court involved a [cause of action] [claim for relief] arising out of business done by the defendant through that office in the foreign country; or

(6) the defendant operated a motor vehicle or airplane in the foreign country and the proceeding involved a [cause of action] [claim for relief] arising out of that operation.

(b) The list of bases for personal jurisdiction in subsection (a) is not exclusive. The courts of this state may recognize bases of personal jurisdiction other than those listed in subsection(a) as sufficient to support a foreign-country judgment.

COMMENT

Source: This provision is based on Section 5 of the 1962 Act. Its substance is the same as that of Section 5 of the 1962 Act, except as noted in Comment 2 below with regard to subsection 5(a)(4).

1. Under section 4(b)(2), the forum court must deny recognition to the foreign-country judgment if the foreign court did not have personal jurisdiction over the defendant. Section 5(a) lists six bases for personal jurisdiction that are adequate as a matter of law to establish that the foreign court had personal jurisdiction. Section 5(b) makes it clear that these bases of personal jurisdiction are not exclusive. The forum court may find that the foreign court had personal jurisdiction over the defendant on some other basis.

2. Subsection 5(a)(4) of the 1962 Act provides that the foreign court had personal jurisdiction over the defendant if the defendant was "a body corporate" that "had its principal place of business, was incorporated, or had otherwise acquired corporate status, in the foreign state." Subsection 5(a)(4) of this Act extends that concept to forms of business organization other than corporations.

3. Subsection 5(a)(3) provides that the foreign court has personal jurisdiction over the defendant if the defendant agreed before commencement of the proceeding leading to the foreign-country judgment to submit to the jurisdiction of the foreign court with regard to the subject matter involved. Under this provision, the forum court must find both the existence of a valid agreement to submit to the foreign court's jurisdiction and that the agreement covered the subject matter involved in the foreign litigation resulting in the foreign-country judgment.

SECTION 6. PROCEDURE FOR RECOGNITION OF FOREIGN-COUNTRY JUDGMENT.

(a) If recognition of a foreign-country judgment is sought as an original matter, the issue of recognition shall be raised by filing an action seeking recognition of the foreign-country judgment.

(b) If recognition of a foreign-country judgment is sought in a pending action, the issue of recognition may be raised by counterclaim, cross-claim, or affirmative defense.

COMMENT

Source: This section is new.

1. Unlike the 1962 Act, which was silent as to the proper procedure for seeking recognition of a foreign-country judgment, Section 6 of this Act expressly sets out the ways in which the issue of recognition may be raised. Under section 6, the issue of recognition always must be raised in a court proceeding. Thus, section 6 rejects decisions under the 1962 Act holding that

the registration procedure found in the Uniform Enforcement of Foreign Judgments Act could be utilized with regard to recognition of a foreign-country judgment. *E.g.* Society of Lloyd's v. Ashenden, 233 F.3d 473 (7th Cir. 2000). The Enforcement Act deals solely with the *enforcement* of sister-state judgments and other judgments entitled to full faith and credit, not with the *recognition* of foreign-country judgments.

More broadly, section 6 rejects the use of any registration procedure in the context of the foreign-country judgments covered by this Act. A registration procedure represents a balance between the interest of the judgment creditor in obtaining quick and efficient recognition and enforcement of a judgment when the judgment debtor has already been provided with an opportunity to litigate the underlying issues, and the interest of the judgment debtor in being provided an adequate opportunity to raise and litigate issues regarding whether the foreign-country judgment should be recognized. In the context of sister-state judgments, this balance favors use of a truncated procedure such as that found in the Enforcement Act. Recognition of sister-state judgments normally is mandated by the Full Faith and Credit Clause. Courts recognize only a very limited number of grounds for denying full faith and credit to a sister-state judgment–that the rendering court lacked jurisdiction, that the judgment was procured by fraud, that the judgment has been satisfied, or that the limitations period has expired. Thus, the judgment debtor with regard to a sister-state judgment normally does not have any grounds for opposing recognition and enforcement of the judgment. The extremely limited grounds for denying full faith and credit to a sister-state judgment reflect the fact such judgments will have been rendered by a court that is subject to the same due process limitations and the same overlap of federal statutory and constitutional law as the forum state's courts, and, to a large extent, the same body of court precedent and socio-economic ideas as those shaping the law of the forum state. Therefore, there is a strong presumption of fairness and competence attached to a sister-state judgment that justifies use of a registration procedure.

The balance between the benefits and costs of a registration procedure is significantly different, however, in the context of recognition and enforcement of foreign-country judgments. Unlike the limited grounds for denying full faith and credit to a sister-state judgment, this Act provides a number of grounds upon which recognition of a foreign-country judgment may be denied. Determination of whether these grounds apply requires the forum court to look behind the foreign-country judgment to evaluate the law and the judicial system under which the foreign-country judgment was rendered. The existence of these grounds for nonrecognition reflects the fact there is less expectation that foreign-country courts will follow procedures comporting with U.S. notions of fundamental fairness and jurisdiction or that those courts will apply laws viewed as substantively tolerable by U.S. standards than there is with regard to sister-state courts. In some situations, there also may be suspicions of corruption or fraud in the foreign-country proceedings. These differences between sister-state judgments and foreign-country judgments provide a justification for requiring judicial involvement in the decision whether to recognize a foreign-country judgment in all cases in which that issue is raised. Although the threshold for establishing that a foreign-country judgment is not entitled to recognition under Section 4 is high, there is a sufficiently greater likelihood that significant recognition issues will be raised so as to require a judicial proceeding.

2. This Section contemplates that the issue of recognition may be raised either as an original matter or in the context of a pending proceeding. Subsection 6(a) provides that in order to raise the issue of recognition of a foreign-country judgment as an initial matter, the party seeking recognition must file an action for recognition of the foreign-country judgment. Subsection 6(b) provides that when the recognition issue is raised in a pending proceeding, it may be raised by counterclaim, cross-claim or affirmative defense, depending on the context in which it is raised. These rules are consistent with the way the issue of recognition most often was raised in most states under the 1962 Act.

3. An action seeking recognition of a foreign-country judgment under this Section is an action on the foreign-country judgment itself, not an action on the underlying cause of action that gave rise to that judgment. The parties to an action under Section 6 may not relitigate the merits of the underlying dispute that gave rise to the foreign-country judgment.

4. While this Section sets out the ways in which the issue of recognition of a foreign-country judgment may be raised, it is not intended to create any new procedure not currently existing in the state or to otherwise effect existing state procedural requirements. The parties to an action in which recognition of a foreign-country judgment is sought under Section 6 must comply with all state procedural rules with regard to that type of action. Nor does this Act address the question of what constitutes a sufficient basis for jurisdiction to adjudicate with regard to an action under Section 6. Courts have split over the issue of whether the presence of assets of the debtor in a state is a sufficient basis for jurisdiction in light of footnote 36 of the U.S. Supreme Court decision in Shaffer v. Heitner, 433 U.S. 186, 210 n.36 (1977). This Act takes no position on that issue.

5. In states that have adopted the Uniform Foreign–Money Claims Act, that Act will apply to the determination of the amount of a money judgment recognized under this Act.

SECTION 7. EFFECT OF RECOGNITION OF FOREIGN-COUNTRY JUDGMENT. If the court in a proceeding under Section 6 finds that the foreign-country judgment is entitled to recognition under this [act] then, to the extent that the foreign-country judgment grants or denies recovery of a sum of money, the foreign-country judgment is:

(1) conclusive between the parties to the same extent as the judgment of a sister state entitled to full faith and credit in this state would be conclusive; and

(2) enforceable in the same manner and to the same extent as a judgment rendered in this state.

COMMENT

Source: The substance of subsection 7(1) is based on Section 3 of the 1962 Act. Subsection 7(2) is new.

1. Section 5 of this Act sets out the standards for the recognition of foreign-country judgments within the scope of this Act, and places an affirmative duty on the forum court to recognize any foreign-country judgment that meets those standards. Section 6 of this Act sets out the procedures by which the issue of recognition may be raised. This Section sets out the consequences of the decision by the forum court that the foreign-country judgment is entitled to recognition.

2. Under subsection 7(1), the first consequence of recognition of a foreign-country judgment is that it is treated as conclusive between the parties in the forum state. Section 7(1) does not attempt to establish directly the extent of that conclusiveness. Instead, it provides that the foreign-country judgment is treated as conclusive to the same extent that a judgment of a sister state that had been determined to be entitled to full faith and credit would be conclusive. This means that the foreign-country judgment generally will be given the same effect in the forum state that it has in the foreign country where it was rendered. Subsection 7(1), however, sets out the minimum effect that must be given to the foreign-country judgment once recognized. The forum court remains free to give the foreign-country judgment a greater preclusive effect in the forum state than the judgment would have in the foreign country where it was rendered. *Cf.* Restatement (Third) of the Foreign Relations Law of the United States, § 481 cmt *c* (1986).

3. Under subsection 7(2), the second consequence of recognition of a foreign-country judgment is that, to the extent it grants a sum of money, it is enforceable in the forum state in accordance with the procedures for enforcement in the forum state and to the same extent that a judgment of the forum state would be enforceable. *Cf.* Restatement (Third) of the Foreign Relations Law of the United States § 481 (1986) (judgment entitled to recognition is enforceable in accordance with the procedure for enforcement of judgments applicable where enforcement is sought). Thus, under subsection 7(2), once recognized, the foreign-country judgment has the same effect and is subject to the same procedures, defenses and proceedings for reopening, vacating, or staying a judgment of a comparable court in the forum state, and can be enforced or satisfied in the same manner as such a judgment of the forum state.

SECTION 8. STAY OF PROCEEDINGS PENDING APPEAL OF FOREIGN-COUNTRY JUDGMENT. If a party establishes that an appeal from a foreign-country judgment is pending or will be taken, the court may stay any proceedings with regard to the foreign-country judgment until the appeal is concluded, the time for appeal expires, or the appellant has had sufficient time to prosecute the appeal and has failed to do so.

COMMENT

Source: This section is the same substantively as section 6 of the 1962 Act, except that it adds as an additional measure for the duration of the stay "the time for appeal expires."

1. Under Section 3 of this Act, a foreign-country judgment is not within the scope of this Act unless it is conclusive and enforceable where rendered. Thus, if the effect of appeal under the law of the foreign country in which the judgment was rendered is to prevent it from being conclusive or enforceable between the parties, the existence of a pending appeal in the foreign country would prevent the application of this Act. Section 8 addresses a different situation. It deals with the situation in which either (1) the party seeking a stay has demonstrated that it intends to file an appeal in the foreign country, although the appeal has not yet been filed or (2) an appeal has been filed in the foreign country, but under the law of the foreign country filing of an appeal does not affect the conclusiveness or enforceability of the judgment. Section 8 allows the forum court in those situations to determine in its discretion that a stay of proceedings is appropriate.

SECTION 9. STATUTE OF LIMITATIONS. An action to recognize a foreign-country judgment must be commenced within the earlier of the time during which the foreign-country judgment is effective in the foreign country or 15 years from the date that the foreign-country judgment became effective in the foreign country.

COMMENT

Source: This Section is new. The 1962 Act did not contain a statute of limitations. Some courts applying the 1962 Act have used the state's general statute of limitations, *e.g.*, Vrozos v. Sarantopoulos, 552 N.E.2d 1053 (Ill. App. 1990) (as Recognition Act contains no statute of limitations, general five-year statute of limitations applies), while others have used the statute of limitations applicable with regard to enforcement of a domestic judgment, *e.g.*, La Societe Anonyme Goro v. Conveyor Accessories, Inc., 677 N.E. 2d 30 (Ill. App. 1997).

1. Under Section 3 of this Act, this Act only applies to foreign-country judgments that are conclusive, and if the judgment grants recovery of a sum of money, enforceable where rendered. Thus, if the period of effectiveness of the foreign-country judgment has expired in the foreign country where the judgment was rendered, the foreign-country judgment would not be subject to this Act. This means that the period of time during which a foreign-country judgment may be recognized under this Act normally is measured by the period of time during which that judgment is effective (that is, conclusive and, if applicable, enforceable) in the foreign country that rendered the judgment. If, however, the foreign-country judgment remains effective for more than fifteen years after the date on which it became effective in the foreign country, Section 9 places an additional time limit on recognition of a foreign-country judgment. It provides that, if the foreign-country judgment remains effective between the parties for more than fifteen years, then an action to

recognize the foreign-country judgment under this Act must be commenced within that fifteen year period.

2. Section 9 does not address the issue of whether a foreign-country judgment that can no longer be the basis of a recognition action under this Act because of the application of the fifteen-year limitations period in Section 9 may be used for other purposes. For example, a common rule with regard to judgments barred by a statute of limitations is that they still may be used defensively for purposes of offset and for their preclusive effect. The extent to which a foreign-country judgment with regard to which a recognition action is barred by Section 9 may be used for these or other purposes is left to the other law of the forum state.

SECTION 10. UNIFORMITY OF INTERPRETATION. In applying and construing this uniform act, consideration must be given to the need to promote uniformity of the law with respect to its subject matter among states that enact it.

COMMENT

Source: This Section is substantively the same as Section 8 of the 1962 Act. The section has been rewritten to reflect current NCCUSL practice.

SECTION 11. SAVING CLAUSE. This [act] does not prevent the recognition under principles of comity or otherwise of a foreign-country judgment not within the scope of this [act].

COMMENT

Source: This section is based on Section 7 of the 1962 Act.

1. Section 3 of this Act provides that this Act applies only to certain foreign-country judgments that grant or deny recovery of a sum of money. The purpose of this Act is to establish the minimum standards for recognition of those judgments. Section 11 makes clear that no negative implication should be read from the fact that this Act does not provide for recognition of other foreign-country judgments. Rather, this Act simply does not address the issue of whether foreign-country judgments not within its scope under Section 3 should be recognized. Courts are free to recognize those foreign-country judgments not within the scope of this Act under common law principles of comity or other applicable law.

SECTION 12. EFFECTIVE DATE.

[(a) This [act] takes effect ________ .]

[(b) This [act] applies to all actions commenced on or after the effective date of this [act] in which the issue of recognition of a foreign-country judgment is raised.]

COMMENT

Source: Subsection 12(a) is the same as Section 11 of the 1962 Act. Subsection 12(b) is new.

1. Subsection 12(b) provides that this Act will apply to all actions in which the issue of recognition of a foreign-country judgment is raised that are commenced on or after the effective date of this Act. Thus, the application of this Act is measured not from the time the original action leading to the foreign-country judgment was commenced in the foreign country, but rather from the time the action in which the issue of recognition is raised is commenced in the forum court. Subsection 12(b) does not distinguish between whether the purpose of the action commenced in the forum court was to seek recognition as an original matter under Subsection 6(a) or was an action that was already pending when the issue of recognition was raised under Subsection 6(b).

SECTION 13. REPEAL. The following [acts] are repealed:

(a) Uniform Foreign Money–Judgments Recognition Act,

(b)

.]

COMMENT

Source: This Section is an updated version of Section 10 of the 1962 Act.

DOCUMENT 28

CONVENTION ON THE LAW APPLICABLE TO CONTRACTUAL OBLIGATIONS (EEC) (1980)* (ROME CONVENTION) (SELECTED PROVISIONS)

PREAMBLE

THE HIGH CONTRACTING PARTIES to the Treaty establishing the European Economic Community,

ANXIOUS to continue in the field of private international law the work of unification of law which has already been done within the Community, in particular in the field of jurisdiction and enforcement of judgments,

WISHING to establish uniform rules concerning the law applicable to contractual obligations,

HAVE AGREED AS FOLLOWS:

TITLE I. SCOPE OF THE CONVENTION

ARTICLE 1. SCOPE OF THE CONVENTION

1. The rules of this Convention shall apply to contractual obligations in any situation involving a choice between the laws of different countries.

22. They shall not apply to:

(a) questions involving the status or legal capacity of natural persons, without prejudice to Article 11;

(b) contractual obligations relating to:

— wills and succession,

— rights in property arising out of a matrimonial relationship,

— rights and duties arising out of a family relationship, parentage, marriage or affinity, including maintenance obligations in respect of children who are not legitimate;

* This Convention became effective April 1, 1991. EC regulation 593/2008 (the "Rome I regulation) largely replicates the 1980 Rome Convention. Articles 3 and 4 of the Rome I regulation are reproduced.

(c) obligations arising under bills of exchange, cheques and promissory notes and other negotiable instruments to the extent that the obligations under such other negotiable instruments arise out of their negotiable character;

(d) arbitration agreements and agreements on the choice of court;

(e) questions governed by the law of companies and other bodies corporate or unincorporate such as the creation, by registration or otherwise, legal capacity, internal organization or winding up of companies and other bodies corporate or unincorporate and the personal liability of officers and members as such for the obligations of the company or body;

(f) the question whether an agent is able to bind a principal, or an organ to bind a company or body corporate or unincorporate, to a third party;

(g) the constitution of trusts and the relationship between settlors, trustees and beneficiaries;

(h) evidence and procedure, without prejudice to Article 14.

3. The rules of this Convention do not apply to contracts of insurance which cover risks situated in the territories of the Member States of the European Economic Community. In order to determine whether a risk is situated in these territories the court shall apply its internal law.

4. The preceding paragraph does not apply to contracts of re-insurance.

ARTICLE 2. APPLICATION OF LAW OF NON–CONTRACTING STATES

Any law specified by this Convention shall be applied whether or not it is the law of a Contracting State.

TITLE II. UNIFORM RULES

ARTICLE 3. FREEDOM OF CHOICE

1. A contract shall be governed by the law chosen by the parties. The choice must be expressed or demonstrated with reasonable certainty by the terms of the contract or the circumstances of the case. By their choice the parties can select the law applicable to the whole or a part only of the contract.

2. The parties may at any time agree to subject the contract to a law other than that which previously governed it, whether as a result of an earlier choice under this Article or of other provisions of this Convention. Any variation by the parties of the law to be applied made after the conclusion of the contract shall not prejudice its formal validity under Article 9 or adversely affect the rights of third parties.

3. The fact that the parties have chosen a foreign law, whether or not accompanied by the choice of a foreign tribunal, shall not, where all the other elements relevant to the situation at the time of the choice are connected with one country only, prejudice the application of rules of the law of that country which cannot be derogated from by contract, hereinafter called "mandatory rules".

4. The existence and validity of the consent of the parties as to the choice of the applicable law shall be determined in accordance with the provisions of Articles 8, 9 and 11.

[ARTICLE 3. EC REGULATION 593/2008

FREEDOM OF CHOICE

1. A contract shall be governed by the law chosen by the parties. The choice shall be made expressly or clearly demonstrated by the terms of the contract or the circumstances of the case. By their choice the parties can select the law applicable to the whole or to part only of the contract.

2. The parties may at any time agree to subject the contract to a law other than that which previously governed it, whether as a result of an earlier choice made under this Article or of other provisions of this Regulation. Any change in the law to be applied that is made after the conclusion of the contract shall not prejudice its formal validity under Article 11 or adversely affect the rights of third parties.

3. Where all other elements relevant to the situation at the time of the choice are located in a country other than the country whose law has been chosen, the choice of the parties shall not prejudice the application of provisions of the law of that other country which cannot be derogated from by agreement.

4. Where all other elements relevant to the situation at the time of the choice are located in one or more Member States, the parties' choice of applicable law other than that of a Member State shall not prejudice the application of provisions of Community law, where appropriate as implemented in the Member State of the forum, which cannot be derogated from by agreement.

5. The existence and validity of the consent of the parties as to the choice of the applicable law shall be determined in accordance with the provisions of Articles 10, 11 and 13.]

ARTICLE 4. APPLICABLE LAW IN THE ABSENCE OF CHOICE

1. To the extent that the law applicable to the contract has not been chosen in accordance with Article 3, the contract shall be governed by the law of the country with which it is most closely connected. Nevertheless, a severable part of the contract which has a closer connection with another country may by way of exception be governed by the law of that other country.

2. Subject to the provisions of paragraph 5 of this Article, it shall be presumed that the contract is most closely connected with the country where the party who is to effect the performance which is characteristic of the contract has, at the time of conclusion of the contract, his habitual residence, or, in the case of a body corporate or unincorporate, its central administration. However, if the contract is entered into in the course of that party's trade or profession, that country shall be the country in which the principal place of business is situated or where under the terms of the contract the performance is to be effected through a place of business other than the principal place of business, the country in which that other place of business is situated.

3. Notwithstanding the provisions of paragraph 2 of this Article, to the extent that the subject matter of the contract is a right in immovable property or a right to use immovable property it shall be presumed that the contract is most closely connected with the country where the immovable property is situated.

4. A contract for the carriage of goods shall not be subject to the presumption in paragraph 2. In such a contract if the country in which, at the time the contract is concluded, the carrier has his principal place of business is also the country in which the place of loading or the place of discharge or the principal place of business of the consignor is situated, it shall be presumed that the contract is most closely connected with that country. In applying this paragraph single voyage charter-parties and other contracts the main purpose of which is the carriage of goods shall be treated as contracts for the carriage of goods.

5. Paragraph 2 shall not apply if the characteristic performance cannot be determined, and the presumptions in paragraphs 2, 3 and 4 shall be disregarded if it appears from the circumstances as a whole that the contract is more closely connected with another country.

[ARTICLE 4. EC REGULATION 593/2008

APPLICABLE LAW IN THE ABSENCE OF CHOICE

1. To the extent that the law applicable to the contract has not been chosen in accordance with Article 3 and without prejudice to Articles 5 to 8, the law governing the contract shall be determined as follows:

(a) a contract for the sale of goods shall be governed by the law of the country where the seller has his habitual residence;

(b) a contract for the provision of services shall be governed by the law of the country where the service provider has his habitual residence;

(c) a contract relating to a right in rem in immovable property or to a tenancy of immovable property shall be governed by the law of the country where the property is situated;

(d) notwithstanding point (c), a tenancy of immovable property concluded for temporary private use for a period of no more than six consecutive months shall be governed by the law of the country where the landlord has his habitual residence, provided that the tenant is a natural person and has his habitual residence in the same country;

(e) a franchise contract shall be governed by the law of the country where the franchisee has his habitual residence;

(f) a distribution contract shall be governed by the law of the country where the distributor has his habitual residence;

(g) a contract for the sale of goods by auction shall be governed by the law of the country where the auction takes place, if such a place can be determined;

(h) a contract concluded within a multilateral system which brings together or facilitates the bringing together of multiple third-party buying and selling interests in financial instruments, as defined by Article 4 (1), point (17) of Directive 2004/39/EC, in accordance with non-discretionary rules and governed by a single law, shall be governed by that law.

2. Where the contract is not covered by paragraph 1 or where the elements of the contract would be covered by more than one of points (a) to (h) of paragraph 1, the contract shall be governed by the law of the country where the party required to effect the characteristic performance of the contract has his habitual residence.

3. Where it is clear from all the circumstances of the case that the contract is manifestly more closely connected with a country other than that indicated in paragraphs 1 or 2, the law of that other country shall apply.

4. Where the law applicable cannot be determined pursuant to paragraphs 1 or 2, the contract shall be governed by the law of the country with which it is most closely connected.]

ARTICLE 7. MANDATORY RULES

1. When applying under this Convention the law of a country, effect may be given to the mandatory rules of the law of another country with which the situation has a close connection, if and in so far as, under the law of the latter country, those rules must be applied whatever the law applicable to the contract. In considering whether to give effect to these mandatory rules, regard shall be had to their nature and purpose and to the consequences of their application or non-application.

2. Nothing in this Convention shall restrict the application of the rules of the law of the forum in a situation where they are mandatory irrespective of the law otherwise applicable to the contract.

ARTICLE 8. MATERIAL VALIDITY

1. The existence and validity of a contract, or of any term of a contract, shall be determined by the law which would govern it under this Convention if the contract or term were valid.

2. Nevertheless a party may rely upon the law of the country in which he has his habitual residence to establish that he did not consent if it appears from the circumstances that it would not be reasonable to determine the effect of his conduct in accordance with the law specified in the preceding paragraph.

ARTICLE 9. FORMAL VALIDITY

1. A contract concluded between persons who are in the same country is formally valid if it satisfies the formal requirements of the law which governs it under this Convention or of the law of the country where it is concluded.

2. A contract concluded between persons who are in different countries is formally valid if it satisfies the formal requirements of the law which governs it under this Convention or of the law of one of those countries.

3. Where a contract is concluded by an agent, the country in which the agent acts is the relevant country for the purposes of paragraphs 1 and 2.

4. An act intended to have legal effect relating to an existing or contemplated contract is formally valid if it satisfies the formal requirements of the law which under this Convention governs or would govern the contract or of the law of the country where the act was done.

5. The provisions of the preceding paragraphs shall not apply to a contract to which Article 5 applies, concluded in the circumstances described in paragraph 2 of Article 5. The formal validity of such a contract is governed by the law of the country in which the consumer has his habitual residence.

6. Notwithstanding paragraphs 1 to 4 of this Article, a contract the subject matter of which is a right in immovable property or a right to use immovable property shall be subject to the mandatory requirements of form of the law of the country where the property is situated if by that law those requirements are imposed irrespective of the country where the contract is concluded and irrespective of the law governing the contract.

ARTICLE 10. SCOPE OF THE APPLICABLE LAW

1. The law applicable to a contract by virtue of Articles 3 to 5 and 12 of this Convention shall govern in particular:

(a) interpretation;

(b) performance;

(c) within the limits of the powers conferred on the court by its procedural law, the consequences of breach, including the assessment of damages in so far as it is governed by rules of law;

(d) the various ways of extinguishing obligations, and prescription and limitation of actions;

(e) the consequences of nullity of the contract.

2. In relation to the manner of performance and the steps to be taken in the event of defective performance regard shall be had to the law of the country in which performance takes place.

* * *

ARTICLE 15. EXCLUSION OF RENVOI

The application of the law of any country specified by this Convention means the application of the rules of law in force in that country other than its rules of private international law.

ARTICLE 16. "ORDRE PUBLIC"

The application of a rule of the law of any country specified by this Convention may be refused only if such application is manifestly incompatible with the public policy ("ordre public") of the forum.

* * *

ARTICLE 21. RELATIONSHIP WITH OTHER CONVENTIONS

This Convention shall not prejudice the application of international conventions to which a Contracting State is, or becomes, a party.

* * *

DOCUMENT 29

EU REGULATION ON JURISDICTION AND THE RECOGNITION AND ENFORCEMENT OF JUDGMENTS IN CIVIL AND COMMERCIAL MATTERS (BRUSSELS II)

COUNCIL REGULATION (EC) No 44/2001

CHAPTER I

SCOPE

Article 1

1. This Regulation shall apply in civil and commercial matters whatever the nature of the court or tribunal. It shall not extend, in particular, to revenue, customs or administrative matters.

2. The Regulation shall not apply to:

(a) the status or legal capacity of natural persons, rights in property arising out of a matrimonial relationship, wills and succession;

(b) bankruptcy, proceedings relating to the winding-up of insolvent companies or other legal persons, judicial arrangements, compositions and analogous proceedings;

(c) social security;

(d) arbitration.

3. In this Regulation, the term 'Member State' shall mean Member States with the exception of Denmark.

CHAPTER II

JURISDICTION

Section 1

General Provisions

Article 2

1. Subject to this Regulation, persons domiciled in a Member State shall, whatever their nationality, be sued in the courts of that Member State.

2. Persons who are not nationals of the Member State in which they are domiciled shall be governed by the rules of jurisdiction applicable to nationals of that State.

Article 3

1. Persons domiciled in a Member State may be sued in the courts of another Member State only by virtue of the rules set out in Sections 2 to 7 of this Chapter.

2. In particular the rules of national jurisdiction set out in Annex I shall not be applicable as against them.

Article 4

1. If the defendant is not domiciled in a Member State, the jurisdiction of the courts of each Member State shall, subject to Articles 22 and 23, be determined by the law of that Member State.

2. As against such a defendant, any person domiciled in a Member State may, whatever his nationality, avail himself in that State of the rules of jurisdiction there in force, and in particular those specified in Annex I, in the same way as the nationals of that State.

Section 2

Special Jurisdiction

Article 5

A person domiciled in a Member State may, in another Member State, be sued:

1. (a) in matters relating to a contract, in the courts for the place of performance of the obligation in question;

(b) for the purpose of this provision and unless otherwise agreed, the place of performance of the obligation in question shall be:

— in the case of the sale of goods, the place in the Member State where, under the contract, the goods were delivered or should have been delivered,

— in the case of the provision of services, the place in a Member State where, under the contract, the services were provided or should have been provided.

(c) if subparagraph (b) does not apply the subparagraph (a) applies;

* * *

Article 6

A person domiciled in a Member State may also be sued:

1. where he is one of a number of defendants, in the courts for the place where any one of them is domiciled, provided the claims are so

closely connected that it is expedient to hear and determine them together to avoid the risk of irreconcilable judgments resulting from separate proceedings;

2. as a third party in an action on a warranty or guarantee or in any other third party proceedings, in the court seised of the original proceedings, unless these were instituted solely with the object of removing him from the jurisdiction of the court which would be competent in his case;

3. on a counter-claim arising from the same contract or facts on which the original claim was based, in the court in which the original claim is pending;

4. in matters relating to a contract, if the action may be combined with an action against the same defendant in matters relating to right *in rem* in immovable property, in the court of the Member State in which the property is situated.

Article 7

Where by virtue of this Regulation a court of a Member State has jurisdiction in actions relating to liability from the use or operation of a ship, that court, or any other court substituted for this purpose by the internal law of that Member State, shall also have jurisdiction over claims for limitation of such liability.

* * *

Section 4

Jurisdiction Over Consumer Contracts

Article 15

1. In matters relating to a contract concluded by a person, the consumer, for a purpose which can be regarded as being outside his trade or profession, jurisdiction shall be determined by this Section, without prejudice to Article 4 and point 5 of Article 5, if:

(a) it is contract for the sale of goods on instalment credit terms; or

(b) it is a contract for a loan repayment by instalments, or for any other form of credit, made to finance the sale of goods; or

(c) in all other cases, the contract has been concluded with a person who pursues commercial or professional activities in the Member State of the consumer's domicile or, by any means, directs such activities to that Member State, and the contract falls within the scope of such activities.

2. Where a consumer enters into a contract with a party who is not domiciled in the Member State but has a branch, agency or other establishment in one of the Member States, that party shall, in disputes arising out of the operations of the branch, agency or establishment, be deemed to be domiciled in that State.

3. This Section shall not apply to a contract of transport other than a contract which, for an inclusive price, provides for a combination of travel and accommodation.

Article 16

1. A consumer may bring proceedings against the other party to a contract either in the courts of the Member State in which that party is domiciled or in the courts for the place where the consumer is domiciled.

2. Proceedings may be brought against a consumer by the other party to the contract only in the courts of the Member State in which the consumer is domiciled.

3. This Article shall not affect the right to bring a counter-claim in the court in which, in accordance with this Section, the original claim is pending.

Article 17

The provisions of this Section may be departed from only by an agreement:

1. which is entered into after the dispute has arisen; or

2. which allows the consumer to bring proceedings in courts other than those indicated in this Section; or

3. which is entered into by the consumer and the other party to the contract, both of whom are at the time of conclusion of the contract domiciled or habitually resident in the same Member State, and which confers jurisdiction on the courts of that Member State, provided that such an agreement is not contrary to the law of that Member State.

* * *

Section 6

Exclusive Jurisdiction

Article 22

The following courts shall have exclusive jurisdiction, regardless of domicile:

1. in proceedings which have as their object rights *in rem* in immovable property or tenancies of immovable property, the courts of the Member State in which the property is situated.

However, in proceedings which have as their object tenancies of immovable property concluded for temporary private use for a maximum period of six consecutive months, the courts of the Member State is which the defendant is domiciled shall also have jurisdiction, provided that the tenant is a natural person and that the landlord and the tenant are domiciled in the same Member State;

2. in proceedings which have their object the validity of the constitution, the nullity or the dissolution of companies or other legal persons or associations of natural or legal persons, or of the validity of the decisions of their organs, the courts of the Member States in which the company, legal person or association has its seat. In order to determine that seat, the court shall apply its rules of private international law;

3. in proceedings which have their object the validity of entries in public registers, the courts of the Member State in which the register is kept;

4. in proceedings concerned with the registration or validity of patents, trade marks, designs, or other similar rights required to be deposited or registered, the courts of the Member State in which the deposit or registration has been applied for, has taken place or if under the terms of a Community instrument or an international convention deemed to have taken place.

Without prejudice to the jurisdiction of the European Patent Office under the Convention on the Grant of European Patents, signed at Munich on 5 October 1973, the courts of each Member State shall have exclusive jurisdiction, regardless of domicile, in proceedings concerned with the registration or validity of any European patent granted for that State;

5. in proceedings concerned with the enforcement of judgments, the courts of the Member State in which the judgment has been or is to be enforced.

Section 7

Prorogation of Jurisdiction

Article 23

1. If the parties, one or more of whom is domiciled in a Member State, have agreed that a court or the courts of a Member State are to have jurisdiction to settle any disputes which have arisen or which may arise in connection with a particular legal relationship, that court or those courts shall have jurisdiction. Such jurisdiction shall be exclusive unless the parties have agreed otherwise. Such an agreement conferring jurisdiction shall be either:

(a) in writing or evidenced in writing; or

(b) in a form which accords with practices which the parties have established between themselves; or

(c) in international trade or commerce, in a form which accords with a usage of which the parties are or ought to have been aware and which in such trade or commerce is widely known to, and regularly observed by, parties to contracts of the type involved in the particular trade or commerce concerned.

2. Any communication by electronic means which provides a durable record of the agreement shall be equivalent to 'writing'.

3. Where such an agreement is concluded by partied, none of whom is domiciled in a Member State, the courts of other Member States shall have no jurisdiction over their disputes unless the court or courts chosen have declined jurisdiction.

* * *

Article 24

Apart from jurisdiction derived from other provisions of this Regulation, a court of a Member State before which a defendant entered an appearance shall have jurisdiction. This rule shall not apply where appearance was entered to contest the jurisdiction, or where another court has exclusive jurisdiction by virtue of Article 22.

* * *

CHAPTER III

RECOGNITION AND ENFORCEMENT

Article 32

For the purposes of this Regulation, 'judgment' means any judgment given by a court or tribunal of a Member State, whatever the judgment may be called, including a decree, order, decision or writ or execution, as well as the determination of costs or expenses by an officer of the court.

Section 1

Recognition

Article 33

1. A judgment given in a Member State shall be recognised in the other Member States without any special procedure being required.

2. Any interested party who raises the recognition of a judgment as the principal issue in a dispute may, in accordance with the procedure provided for in Sections 2 and 3 of this Chapter, apply for a decision that the judgment be recognised.

3. If the outcome of proceedings in a court of a Member State depends on the determination of an incidental question of recognition that court shall have jurisdiction over that question.

Article 34

A judgment shall not be recognised:

1. if such recognition is manifestly contrary to public policy in the Member State in which recognition is sought;

2. where it was given in default of appearance, if the defendant was not served with the document which instituted the proceedings or with an

equivalent document in sufficient time and in such a way as to enable him to arrange for his defence, unless the defendant failed to commence proceedings to challenge the judgment when it was possible for him to do so;

3. if it is irreconcilable with a judgment given in a dispute between the same parties in the Member State in which recognition is sought;

4. if it is irreconcilable with an earlier judgment given in another Member State or in a third State involving the same cause of action and between the same parties, provided that the earlier judgment fulfils the conditions necessary for its recognition in the Member State addressed.

Article 35

1. Moreover, a judgment shall not be recognised if it conflicts with Section 3, 4 or 6 of Chapter II, or in a case provided for in Article 72.

2. In its examination of the grounds of jurisdiction referred to in the foregoing paragraph, the court or authority applied to shall be bound by the findings of fact on which the court of the Member State of origin based its jurisdiction.

3. Subject to the paragraph 1, the jurisdiction of the court of the Member State of origin may not be reviewed. The test of public policy referred to in point 1 of Article 34 may not be applied to the rules relating to jurisdiction.

Article 36

Under no circumstances may a foreign judgment be reviewed as to its substance.

Article 37

1. A court of a Member State in which recognition is sought of a judgment given in another Member State may stay the proceedings if an ordinary appeal against the judgment has been lodged.

2. A court of a Member State in which recognition is sought of a judgment given in Ireland or the United Kingdom may stay the proceedings if enforcement is suspended in the State of origin, by reason of an appeal.

Section 2

Enforcement

Article 38

1. A judgment given in a Member State and enforceable in that State shall be enforced in another Member State when, on the application of any interested party, it has been declared enforceable there.

2. However, in the United Kingdom, such a judgment shall be enforced in England and Wales, in Scotland, or in Northern Ireland when,

on the application of any interested party, it has been registered for enforcement in that part of the United Kingdom.

Article 39

1. The application shall be submitted to the court or competent authority indicated in the list in Annex II.

2. The local jurisdiction shall be determined by reference to the place of domicile of the party against whom enforcement is sought, or to the place of enforcement.

Article 40

1. The procedure for making the application shall be governed by the law of the Member State in which enforcement is sought.

2. The applicant must give an address for service of process within the area of jurisdiction of the court applied to. However, if the law of the Member State in which enforcement is sought does not provide for the furnishing of such an address, the applicant shall appoint a representative *ad litem*.

3. The documents referred to in Article 53 shall be attached to the application.

Article 41

The judgment shall be declared enforceable immediately on completion of the formalities in Article 53 without any review under Articles 34 and 35. The party against whom enforcement is sought shall not at this stage of the proceedings be entitled to make any submissions on the application.

Article 42

1. The decision on the application for a declaration of enforceability shall forthwith be brought to the notice of the applicant in accordance with the procedure laid down by th law of the Member State in which enforcement is sought.

2. The declaration of enforceability shall be served on the party against whom enforcement is sought, accompanied by the judgment, if not already served on that party.

Article 43

1. The decision on the application for the declaration of enforceability may be appealed against by either party.

2. The appeal is to be lodged with the court indicated in the list in Annex III.

3. The appeal shall be dealt with in accordance with the rules governing procedure in contradictory matters.

4. If the party against whom enforcement is sought fails to appear before the appellate court in proceedings concerning an appeal brought by the applicant, Article 26(2) to (4) shall apply even where the party against whom enforcement is sought is not domiciled in any of the Member States.

5. An appeal against the declaration of enforceability is to be lodged within one month of service thereof. If the party against whom enforcement is sought is domiciled in a Member State other than that in which the declaration of enforceability was given, the time for appealing shall be two months and shall run from the date of service, either on him in person or at his residence. No extension of time may be granted on account of distance.

Article 44

The judgment given on the appeal may be contested only by the appeal referred to in Annex IV.

Article 45

1. The court with which an appeal is lodged under Article 43 or Article 44 shall refuse or revoke a declaration of enforceability only on one of the grounds specified in Articles 34 and 35. It shall give its decision without delay.

2. Under no circumstances may the foreign judgment be reviewed as to its substance.

* * *

Article 49

A foreign judgment which orders a periodic payment by way of a penalty shall be enforceable in the Member State in which enforcement is sought only if the amount of the payment has been finally determined by the courts of the Member State of origin.

ANNEX I

Rules of jurisdiction referred to in Article 3(2) and Article 4(2). The rules of jurisdiction referred to in Article 3(2) and Article 4(2) are the following:

— in Belgium: Article 15 of the Civil Code (Code civil/Burgerlijk Wetboek) and Article 638 of the Judicial Code (Code judiciaire/Gerechtelijk Wetboek);

— in Germany: Article 23 of the Code of Civil Procedure (Zivilprozessordnung),

— in Greece: Article 40 of the Code of Civil Procedure (. . .);

— in France: Articles 14 and 15 of the Civil Code (Code civil),

— in Ireland: the rules which enable jurisdiction to be founded on the document instituting the proceedings having been served on the defendant during his temporary presence in Ireland.

— in Italy: Articles 3 and 4 of Act 218 of 31 May 1995,

— in Luxembourg: Articles 14 and 15 of the Civil Code (Code civil),

— in the Netherlands: Articles 126(3) and 127 of the Code of Civil Procedure (wetboek van Burgerlijke Rechtsvordering),

— in Austria: Article 99 of the Court Jurisdiction Act (Jurisdiktionsnorm),

— in Portugal: Articles 65 and 65A of the Code of Civil Procedure (Codigo de Processo Civil) and Article 11 of the Code of Labour Procedure (Codigo de Processo de Trabalho),

— in Finland: the second, third and fourth sentences of the first paragraph of Section 1 of Chapter 10 of the Code of Judicial Procedure (oikeudenkaymiskaari/rattegangsbalken),

— in Sweden: the first sentence of the first paragraph of Section 3 of Chapter 10 of the Code of Judicial Procedure (rattegangsbalken),

— in the United Kingdom: rules which enable jurisdiction to be founded on:

(a) the document instituting the proceedings having been served on the defendant during his temporary presence in the United Kingdom; or

(b) the presence within the United Kingdom of property belonging to the defendant; or

(c) the seizure by the plaintiff of property situated in the United Kingdom.

DOCUMENT 30

EU REGULATION FOR A EUROPEAN COMPANY(SE) (SELECTED PROVISIONS)

Council Regulation (EC) No. 2157/2001

TITLE I

GENERAL PROVISIONS

Article 1

1. A company may be set up within the territory of the Community in the form of a European public limited-liability company (Societas Europaea or SE) on the conditions and in the manner laid down in this Regulation.

2. The capital of an SE shall be divided into shares. No shareholder shall be liable for more than the amount he has subscribed.

3. An SE shall have legal personality.

4. Employee involvement in an SE shall be governed by the provisions of Directive 2001/. . ./EC.

Article 2

1. Public limited-liability companies such as referred to in Annex I, formed under the law of a Member State, with registered offices and head offices within the Community may form an SE by means of a merger provided that at least two of them are governed by the law of different Member States.

2. Public and private limited-liability companies such as referred to in Annex II, formed under the law of a Member State, with registered offices and head offices within the Community may promote the formation of a holding SE provided that each of at least two of them:

(a) is governed by the law of a different Member State, or

(b) has for at least two years had a subsidiary company governed by the law of another Member State or an establishment situated in another Member State.

3. Companies and firms within the meaning of the second paragraph of Article 48 of the Treaty and other legal bodies governed by public or private law, formed under the law of a Member State, with registered

offices and head offices within the Community may form a subsidiary SE by subscribing for its shares, provided that each of at least two of them:

(a) is governed by the law of a different Member State, or

(b) has for at least two years had a subsidiary company governed by the law of another Member State or an establishment situated in another Member State.

4. A public limited-liability company, formed under the law of a Member State, which has its registered office and head office within the Community may be transformed into an SE if for at least two years it has had a subsidiary company governed by the law of another Member State.

5. A Member State may provide that a company the head office of which is not in the Community may participate in the formation of an SE provided that company is formed under the law of a Member State, has its registered office in that Member State and has a real and continuous link with a Member State's economy.

Article 3

1. For the purposes of Article 2(1), (2) and (3), an SE shall be regarded as a public limited-liability company governed by the law of the Member State in which it has its registered office.

2. An SE may itself set up one or more subsidiaries in the form of SEs. The provisions of the law of the Member State in which a subsidiary SE has its registered office that require a public limited-liability company to have more than one shareholder shall not apply in the case of the subsidiary SE. The provisions of national law implementing the Twelfth Council Company Law Directive (89/667/EEC) of 21 December 1989 on single-member private limited-liability companies shall apply to SEs "mutatis mutandis".

Article 4

1. The capital of an SE shall be expressed in euros.

2. The subscribed capital shall not be less than EUR 120,000.

3. The laws of a Member State requiring a greater subscribed capital for companies carrying on certain types of activity shall apply to SEs with registered offices in that Member State.

Article 5

Subject to Article 4(1) and (2), the capital of an SE, its maintenance and changes thereto, together with its shares, bonds and other similar securities shall be governed by the provisions which would apply to a public limited-liability company with a registered office in the Member State in which the SE is registered.

Article 6

For the purposes of this Regulation, "the statutes of the SE" shall mean both the instrument of incorporation and, where they are the subject of a separate document, the statutes of the SE.

Article 7

The registered office of an SE shall be located within the Community, in the same Member State as its head office. A Member State may in addition impose on SEs registered in its territory the obligation of locating their head office and their registered office in the same place.

Article 8

1. The registered office of an SE may be transferred to another Member State in accordance with paragraphs 2 to 13. Such a transfer shall not result in the winding up of the SE or in the creation of a new legal person.

* * *

Article 9

1. An SE shall be governed:

(a) by this Regulation,

(b) where expressly authorised by this Regulation, by the provisions of its statutes

or

(c) in the case of matters not regulated by this Regulation or, where matters are partly regulated by it, of those aspects not covered by it, by:

(i) the provisions of laws adopted by Member States in implementation of Community measures relating specifically to SEs;

(ii) the provisions of Member States' laws which would apply to a public limited-liability company formed in accordance with the law of the Member State in which the SE has its registered office;

(iii) the provisions of its statutes, in the same way as for a public limited-liability company formed in accordance with the law of the Member State in which the SE has its registered office.

2. The provisions of laws adopted by Member States specifically for the SE must be in accordance with Directives applicable to public limited-liability companies referred to in Annex I.

3. If the nature of the business carried out by an SE is regulated by specific provisions of national laws, those laws shall apply in full to the SE.

Article 10

Subject to this Regulation, an SE shall be treated in every Member State as if it were a public limited-liability company formed in accordance with the law of the Member State in which it has its registered office.

Article 11

1. The name of an SE shall be preceded or followed by the acronym "SE".

2. Only SEs may include the acronym "SE" in their name.

3. Nevertheless, companies, firms and other legal entities registered in a Member State before the date of entry into force of this Regulation in the names of which the acronym "SE" appears shall not be required to alter their names.

Article 12

1. Every SE shall be registered in the Member State in which it has its registered office in a register designated by the law of that Member State in accordance with Article 3 of the First Council Directive (68/151/EEC) of 9 March 1968 on coordination of safeguards which, for the protection of the interests of members and others, are required by Member States of companies within the meaning of the second paragraph of Article 58 of the Treaty, with a view to making such safeguards equivalent throughout the Community.

2. An SE may not be registered unless an agreement on arrangements for employee involvement pursuant to Article 4 of Directive 2001/ /EC has been concluded, or a decision pursuant to Article 3(6) of the Directive has been taken, or the period for negotiations pursuant to Article 5 of the Directive has expired without an agreement having been concluded.

3. In order for an SE to be registered in a Member State which has made use of the option referred to in Article 7(3) of Directive 2001/ /EC, either an agreement pursuant to Article 4 of the Directive must have been concluded on the arrangements for employee involvement, including participation, or none of the participating companies must have been governed by participation rules prior to the registration of the SE.

4. The statutes of the SE must not conflict at any time with the arrangements for employee involvement which have been so determined. Where new such arrangements determined pursuant to the Directive conflict with the existing statutes, the statutes shall to the extent necessary be amended.

In this case, a Member State may provide that the management organ or the administrative organ of the SE shall be entitled to proceed to amend the statutes without any further decision from the general shareholders meeting.

* * *

TITLE II
FORMATION
SECTION 1
General

Article 15

1. Subject to this Regulation, the formation of an SE shall be governed by the law applicable to public limited-liability companies in the State in which the SE establishes its registered office.

2. The registration of an SE shall be publicised in accordance with Article 13.

Article 16

1. An SE shall acquire legal personality on the date on which it is registered in the register referred to in Article 12.

2. If acts have been performed in an SE's name before its registration in accordance with Article 12 and the SE does not assume the obligations arising out of such acts after its registration, the natural persons, companies, firms or other legal entities which performed those acts shall be jointly and severally liable therefor, without limit, in the absence of agreement to the contrary.

SECTION 2

Formation by merger

Article 17

1. An SE may be formed by means of a merger in accordance with Article 2(1).

2. Such a merger may be carried out in accordance with:

(a) the procedure for merger by acquisition laid down in Article 3(1) of the Third Council Directive (78/855/EEC) of 9 October 1978 based on Article 54(3)(g) of the Treaty concerning mergers of public limited-liability companies or

(b) the procedure for merger by the formation of a new company laid down in Article 4(1) of the said Directive.

In the case of a merger by acquisition, the acquiring company shall take the form of an SE when the merger takes place. In the case of a merger by the formation of a new company, the SE shall be the newly formed company.

Article 18

For matters not covered by this section or, where a matter is partly covered by it, for aspects not covered by it, each company involved in the formation of an SE by merger shall be governed by the provisions of the law of the Member State to which it is subject that apply to mergers of public limited-liability companies in accordance with Directive 78/855/EEC.

Article 19

The laws of a Member State may provide that a company governed by the law of that Member State may not take part in the formation of an SE by merger if any of that Member State's competent authorities opposes it before the issue of the certificate referred to in Article 25(2).

Such opposition may be based only on grounds of public interest. Review by a judicial authority shall be possible.

* * *

Article 23

1. The general meeting of each of the merging companies shall approve the draft terms of merger.

2. Employee involvement in the SE shall be decided pursuant to Directive 2001/ /EC. The general meetings of each of the merging companies may reserve the right to make registration of the SE conditional upon its express ratification of the arrangements so decided.

* * *

SECTION 3

Formation of a holding SE

Article 32

1. A holding SE may be formed in accordance with Article 2(2).

A company promoting the formation of a holding SE in accordance with Article 2(2) shall continue to exist.

2. The management or administrative organs of the companies which promote such an operation shall draw up, in the same terms, draft terms for the formation of the holding SE. The draft terms shall include a report explaining and justifying the legal and economic aspects of the formation and indicating the implications for the shareholders and for the employees of the adoption of the form of a holding SE. The draft terms shall also set out the particulars provided for in Article 20(1)(a), (b), (c), (f), (g), (h) and (i) and shall fix the minimum proportion of the shares in each of the companies promoting the operation which the shareholders must contribute to the formation of the holding SE. That proportion shall be shares conferring more than 50% of the permanent voting rights.

3. For each of the companies promoting the operation, the draft terms for the formation of the holding SE shall be publicised in the manner laid down in each Member State's national law in accordance with Article 3 of Directive 68/151/EEC at least one month before the date of the general meeting called to decide thereon.

4. One or more experts independent of the companies promoting the operation, appointed or approved by a judicial or administrative authority in the Member State to which each company is subject in accordance with national provisions adopted in implementation of Directive 78/855/EEC, shall examine the draft terms of formation drawn up in accordance with paragraph 2 and draw up a written report for the shareholders of each company. By agreement between the companies promoting the operation, a single written report may be drawn up for the shareholders of all the companies by one or more independent experts, appointed or approved by

a judicial or administrative authority in the Member State to which one of the companies promoting the operation or the proposed SE is subject in accordance with national provisions adopted in implementation of Directive 78/855/EEC.

5. The report shall indicate any particular difficulties of valuation and state whether the proposed share-exchange ratio is fair and reasonable, indicating the methods used to arrive at it and whether such methods are adequate in the case in question.

6. The general meeting of each company promoting the operation shall approve the draft terms of formation of the holding SE.

Employee involvement in the holding SE shall be decided pursuant to Directive 2001/ /EC. The general meetings of each company promoting the operation may reserve the right to make registration of the holding SE conditional upon its express ratification of the arrangements so decided.

7. These provisions shall apply mutatis mutandis to private limited-liability companies.

Article 33

1. The shareholders of the companies promoting such an operation shall have a period of three months in which to inform the promoting companies whether they intend to contribute their shares to the formation of the holding SE. That period shall begin on the date upon which the terms for the formation of the holding SE have been finally determined in accordance with Article 32.

2. The holding SE shall be formed only if, within the period referred to in paragraph 1, the shareholders of the companies promoting the operation have assigned the minimum proportion of shares in each company in accordance with the draft terms of formation and if all the other conditions are fulfilled.

3. If the conditions for the formation of the holding SE are all fulfilled in accordance with paragraph 2, that fact shall, in respect of each of the promoting companies, be publicised in the manner laid down in the national law governing each of those companies adopted in implementation of Article 3 of Directive 68/151/EEC.

Shareholders of the companies promoting the operation who have not indicated whether they intend to make their shares available to the promoting companies for the purpose of forming the holding SE within the period referred to in paragraph 1 shall have a further month in which to do so.

4. Shareholders who have contributed their securities to the formation of the SE shall receive shares in the holding SE.

5. The holding SE may not be registered until it is shown that the formalities referred to in Article 32 have been completed and that the conditions referred to in paragraph 2 have been fulfilled.

Article 34

A Member State may, in the case of companies promoting such an operation, adopt provisions designed to ensure protection for minority shareholders who oppose the operation, creditors and employees.

SECTION 4

Formation of a subsidiary SE

Article 35

An SE may be formed in accordance with Article 2(3).

Article 36

Companies, firms and other legal entities participating in such an operation shall be subject to the provisions governing their participation in the formation of a subsidiary in the form of a public limited-liability company under national law.

SECTION 5

Conversion of an existing public-liability company into an SE.

Article 37

1. An SE may be formed in accordance with Article 2(4).

2. Without prejudice to Article 11 the conversion of a public limited-liability company into an SE shall not result in the winding up of the company or in the creation of a new legal person.

3. The registered office may not be transferred from one Member State to another pursuant to Article 8 at the same time as the conversion is effected.

4. The management or administrative organ of the company in question shall draw up draft terms of conversion and a report explaining and justifying the legal and economic aspects of the conversion and indicating the implications for the shareholders and for the employees of the adoption of the form of an SE.

5. The draft terms of conversion shall be publicised in the manner laid down in each Member State's law in accordance with Article 3 of Directive 68/151/EEC at least one month before the general meeting called upon to decide thereon.

6. Before the general meeting referred to in paragraph 7 one or more independent experts appointed or approved, in accordance with the national provisions adopted in implementation of Article 10 of Directive 78/855/EEC, by a judicial or administrative authority in the Member State to which the company being converted into an SE is subject shall certify in compliance with Directive (EEC) 77/91 mutatis mutandis that the company has net assets at least equivalent to its capital plus those reserves which must not be distributed under the law or the Statutes.

7. The general meeting of the company in question shall approve the draft terms of conversion together with the statutes of the SE. The decision of the general meeting shall be passed as laid down in the provisions of national law adopted in implementation of Article 7 of Directive 78/855/EEC.

8. Member States may condition a conversion to a favourable vote of a qualified majority or unanimity in the organ of the company to be converted within which employee participation is organised.

9. The rights and obligations of the company to be converted on terms and conditions of employment arising from national law, practice and individual employment contracts or employment relationships and existing at the date of the registration shall, by reason of such registration be transferred to the SE.

* * *

DOCUMENT 31

EU E–COMMERCE DIRECTIVE (SELECTED PROVISIONS)

DIRECTIVE 2000/31/EC OF THE EUROPEAN PARLIAMENT AND OF THE COUNCIL

GENERAL PROVISIONS

Article 1

Objective and scope

1. This Directive seeks to contribute to the proper functioning of the internal market by ensuring the free movement of information society services between the Member States.

2. This Directive approximates, to the extent necessary for the achievement of the objective set out in paragraph 1, certain national provisions on information society services relating to the internal market, the establishment of service providers, commercial communications, electronic contracts, the liability of intermediaries, codes of conduct, out-of-court dispute settlements, court actions and cooperation between Member States.

3. This Directive complements Community law applicable to information society services without prejudice to the level of protection for, in particular, public health and consumer interests, as established by Community acts and national legislation implementing them in so far as this does not restrict the freedom to provide information society services.

4. This Directive does not establish additional rules on private international law nor does it deal with the jurisdiction of Courts.

5. This Directive shall not apply to:

(a) the field of taxation;

(b) questions relating to information society services covered by Directives 95/46/EC and 97/66/EC;

(c) questions relating to agreements or practices governed by cartel law;

(d) the following activities of information society services:

— the activities of notaries or equivalent professions to the extent that they involve a direct and specific connection with the exercise of public authority,

— the representation of a client and defence of his interests before the courts,

— gambling activities which involve wagering a stake with monetary value in games of chance, including lotteries and betting transactions.

6. This Directive does not affect measures taken at Community or national level, in the respect of Community law, in order to promote cultural and linguistic diversity and to ensure the defence of pluralism.

Article 2

Definitions

For the purpose of this Directive, the following terms shall bear the following meanings:

(e) 'consumer': any natural person who is acting for purposes which are outside his or her trade, business or profession;

Article 3

Internal Market

* * *

2. Member States may not, for reasons falling within the coordinated field, restrict the freedom to provide information society services from another Member State.

* * *

4. Member States may take measures to derogate from paragraph 2 in respect of a given information society service if the following conditions are fulilled:

(i) necessary for one of the following reasons:

— public policy...,

— the protection of public health,

— public security, including the safeguarding of national security and defense,

— the protection of consumers, including investors;

* * *

(iii) proportionate to those objectives....

CHAPTER II

PRINCIPLES

* * *

Article 5

General information to be provided

1. In addition to other information requirements established by Community law, Member States shall ensure that the service provider shall render easily, directly and permanently accessible to the recipients of the service and competent authorities, at least the following information:

(a) the name of the service provider;

(b) the geographic address at which the service provider is established;

(c) the details of the service provider, including his electronic mail address, which allow him to be contacted rapidly and communicated with in a direct and effective manner;

(d) where the service provider is registered in a trade or similar public register, the trade register in which the service provider is entered and his registration number, or equivalent means of identification in that register;

(e) where the activity is subject to an authorisation scheme, the particulars of the relevant supervisory authority;

(f) as concerns the regulated professions:

— any professional body or similar institution with which the service provider is registered,

— the professional title and the Member State where it has been granted,

— a reference to the applicable professional rules in the Member State of establishment and the means to access them;

(g) where the service provider undertakes an activity that is subject to VAT, the identification number referred to in Article 22(1) of the sixth Council Directive 77/388/EEC of 17 May 1977 on the harmonisation of the laws of the Member States relating to turnover taxes—Common system of value added tax: uniform basis of assessment.

2. In addition to other information requirements established by Community law, Member States shall at least ensure that, where information society services refer to prices, these are to be indicated clearly and unambiguously and, in particular, must indicate whether they are inclusive of tax and delivery costs.

Section 2

Commercial Communications

Article 6

Information to be provided

In addition to other information requirements established by Community law, Member States shall ensure that commercial communications which are part of, or constitute, an information society service comply at least with the following conditions:

(a) the commercial communication shall be clearly identifiable as such;

(b) the natural or legal person on whose behalf the commercial communication is made shall be clearly identifiable;

(c) promotional offers, such as discounts, premiums and gifts, where permitted in the Member State where the service provider is established, shall be clearly identifiable as such, and the conditions which are to be met to qualify for them shall be easily accessible and be presented clearly and unambiguously;

(d) promotional competitions or games, where permitted in the Member State where the service provider is established, shall be clearly identifiable as such, and the conditions for participation shall be easily accessible and be presented clearly and unambiguously.

* * *

Section 3

Contracts Concluded by Electronic Means

Article 9

Treatment of contracts

1. Member States shall ensure that their legal system allows contracts to be concluded by electronic means. Member States shall in particular ensure that the legal requirements applicable to the contractual process neither create obstacles for the use of electronic contracts nor result in such contracts being deprived of legal effectiveness and validity on account of their having been made by electronic means.

2. Member States may lay down that paragraph 1 shall not apply to all or certain contracts falling into one of the following categories:

(a) contracts that create or transfer rights in real estate, except for rental rights;

(b) contracts requiring by law the involvement of courts, public authorities or professions exercising public authority;

(c) contracts of suretyship granted and on collateral securities furnished by persons acting for purposes outside their trade, business or profession;

(d) contracts governed by family law or by the law of succession.

3. Member States shall indicate to the Commission the categories referred to in paragraph 2 to which they do not apply paragraph 1. Member States shall submit to the Commission every five years a report on the application of paragraph 2 explaining the reasons why they consider it necessary to maintain the category referred to in paragraph 2(b) to which they do not apply paragraph 1.

Article 10

Information to be provided

1. In addition to other information requirements established by Community law, Member States shall ensure, except when otherwise agreed by parties who are not consumers, that at least the following information is given by the service provider clearly, comprehensibly and unambiguously and prior to the order being placed by the recipient of the service:

(a) the different technical steps to follow to conclude the contract;

(b) whether or not the concluded contract will be filed by the service provider and whether it will be accessible;

(c) the technical means for identifying and correcting input errors prior to the placing of the order;

(d) the languages offered for the conclusion of the contract.

2. Member States shall ensure that, except when otherwise agreed by parties who are not consumers, the service provider indicates any relevant codes of conduct to which he subscribes and information on how those codes can be consulted electronically.

3. Contract terms and general conditions provided to the recipient must be made available in a way that allows him to store and reproduce them.

4. Paragraphs 1 and 2 shall not apply to contracts concluded exclusively by exchange of electronic mail or by equivalent individual communications.

Article 11

Placing of the order

1. Member States shall ensure, except when otherwise agreed by parties who are not consumers, that in cases where the recipient of the service places his order through technological means, the following principles apply:

— the service provider has to acknowledge the receipt of the recipient's order without undue delay and by electronic means,

— the order and the acknowledgement of receipt are deemed to be received when the parties to whom they are addressed are able to access them.

2. Member States shall ensure that, except when otherwise agreed by parties who are not consumers, the service provider makes available to the recipient of the service appropriate, effective and accessible technical means allowing him to identify and correct input errors, prior to the placing of the order.

3. Paragraph 1, first indent, and paragraph 2 shall not apply to contracts concluded exclusively by exchange of electronic mail or by equivalent individual communications.

DOCUMENT 32

EU BUSINESS-TO-CONSUMER UNFAIR PRACTICES DIRECTIVE (SELECTED PROVISIONS)

DIRECTIVE 2005/29/EC OF THE EUROPEAN PARLIAMENT AND OF THE COUNCIL

CHAPTER 1

GENERAL PROVISIONS

Article 1

Purpose

The purpose of this Directive is to contribute to the proper functioning of the internal market and achieve a high level of consumer protection by approximating the laws, regulations and administrative provisions of the Member States on unfair commercial practices harming consumers' economic interests.

Article 2

Definitions

For the purposes of this Directive:

(a) 'consumer' means any natural person who, in commercial practices covered by this Directive, is acting for purposes which are outside his trade, business, craft or profession;

(b) 'trader' means any natural or legal person who, in commercial practices covered by this Directive, is acting for purposes relating to his trade, business, craft or profession and anyone acting in the name of or on behalf of a trader;

(c) 'product' means any goods or service including immovable property, rights and obligations;

(d) 'business-to-consumer commercial practices' (hereinafter also referred to as commercial practices) means any act, omission, course of conduct or representation, commercial communication including advertising and marketing, by a trader, directly connected with the promotion, sale or supply of a product to consumers;

(e) 'to materially distort the economic behaviour of consumers' means using a commercial practice to appreciably impair the consumer's ability to make an informed decision, thereby causing the consumer to take a transactional decision that he would not have taken otherwise;

(f) 'code of conduct' means an agreement or set of rules not imposed by law, regulation or administrative provision of a Member State which defines the behaviour of traders who undertake to be bound by the code in relation to one or more particular commercial practices or business sectors;

(g) 'code owner' means any entity, including a trader or group of traders, which is responsible for the formulation and revision of a code of conduct and/or for monitoring compliance with the code by those who have undertaken to be bound by it;

(h) 'professional diligence' means the standard of special skill and care which a trader may reasonably be expected to exercise towards consumers, commensurate with honest market practice and/or the general principle of good faith in the trader's field of activity;

(i) 'invitation to purchase' means a commercial communication which indicates characteristics of the product and the price in a way appropriate to the means of the commercial communication used and thereby enables the consumer to make a purchase;

(j) 'undue influence' means exploiting a position of power in relation to the consumer so as to apply pressure, even without using or threatening to use physical force, in a way which significantly limits the consumer's ability to make an informed decision;

(k) 'transactional decision' means any decision taken by a consumer concerning whether, how and on what terms to purchase, make payment in whole or in part for, retain or dispose of a product or to exercise a contractual right in relation to the product, whether the consumer decides to act or to refrain from acting;

(*l*) 'regulated profession' means a professional activity or a group of professional activities, access to which or the pursuit of which, or one of the modes of pursuing which, is conditional, directly or indirectly, upon possession of specific professional qualifications, pursuant to laws, regulations or administrative provisions.

Article 3

Scope

1. This Directive shall apply to unfair business-to-consumer commercial practices, as laid down in Article 5, before, during and after a commercial transaction in relation to a product.

2. This Directive is without prejudice to contract law and, in particular, to the rules on the validity, formation or effect of a contract.

3. This Directive is without prejudice to Community or national rules relating to the health and safety aspects of products.

4. In the case of conflict between the provisions of this Directive and other Community rules regulating specific aspects of unfair commercial practices, the latter shall prevail and apply to those specific aspects.

5. For a period of six years from 12 June 2007, Member States shall be able to continue to apply national provisions within the field approximated by this Directive which are more restrictive or prescriptive than this Directive and which implement directives containing minimum harmonisation clauses. These measures must be essential to ensure that consumers are adequately protected against unfair commercial practices and must be proportionate to the attainment of this objective. The review referred to in Article 18 may, if considered appropriate, include a proposal to prolong this derogation for a further limited period.

6. Member States shall notify the Commission without delay of any national provisions applied on the basis of paragraph 5.

7. This Directive is without prejudice to the rules determining the jurisdiction of the courts.

8. This Directive is without prejudice to any conditions of establishment or of authorisation regimes, or to the deontological codes of conduct or other specific rules governing regulated professions in order to uphold high standards of integrity on the part of the professional, which Member States may, in conformity with Community law, impose on professionals.

9. In relation to 'financial services', as defined in Directive 2002/65/EC, and immovable property, Member States may impose requirements which are more restrictive or prescriptive than this Directive in the field which it approximates.

10. This Directive shall not apply to the application of the laws, regulations and administrative provisions of Member States relating to the certification and indication of the standard of fineness of articles of precious metal.

Article 4

Internal market

Member States shall neither restrict the freedom to provide services nor restrict the free movement of goods for reasons falling within the field approximated by this Directive.

CHAPTER 2

UNFAIR COMMERCIAL PRACTICES

Article 5

Prohibition of unfair commercial practices

1. Unfair commercial practices shall be prohibited.

2. A commercial practice shall be unfair if:

(a) it is contrary to the requirements of professional diligence, and

(b) it materially distorts or is likely to materially distort the economic behaviour with regard to the product of the average consumer whom it reaches or to whom it is addressed, or of the average member of the group when a commercial practice is directed to a particular group of consumers.

3. Commercial practices which are likely to materially distort the economic behaviour only of a clearly identifiable group of consumers who are particularly vulnerable to the practice or the underlying product because of their mental or physical infirmity, age or credulity in a way which the trader could reasonably be expected to foresee, shall be assessed from the perspective of the average member of that group. This is without prejudice to the common and legitimate advertising practice of making exaggerated statements or statements which are not meant to be taken literally.

4. In particular, commercial practices shall be unfair which:

(a) are misleading as set out in Articles 6 and 7, or

(b) are aggressive as set out in Articles 8 and 9.

5. Annex I contains the list of those commercial practices which shall in all circumstances be regarded as unfair. The same single list shall apply in all Member States and may only be modified by revision of this Directive.

Section 1

Misleading commercial practices

Article 6

Misleading actions

1. A commercial practice shall be regarded as misleading if it contains false information and is therefore untruthful or in any way, including overall presentation, deceives or is likely to deceive the average consumer, even if the information is factually correct, in relation to one or more of the following elements, and in either case causes or is likely to cause him to take a transactional decision that he would not have taken otherwise:

(a) the existence or nature of the product;

(b) the main characteristics of the product, such as its availability, benefits, risks, execution, composition, accessories, aftersale customer assistance and complaint handling, method and date of manufacture or provision, delivery, fitness for purpose, usage, quantity, specification, geographical or commercial origin or the results to be expected from its use, or the results and material features of tests or checks carried out on the product;

(c) the extent of the trader's commitments, the motives for the commercial practice and the nature of the sales process, any statement or symbol in relation to direct or indirect sponsorship or approval of the trader or the product;

(d) the price or the manner in which the price is calculated, or the existence of a specific price advantage;

(e) the need for a service, part, replacement or repair;

(f) the nature, attributes and rights of the trader or his agent, such as his identity and assets, his qualifications, status, approval, affiliation or connection and ownership of industrial, commercial or intellectual property rights or his awards and distinctions;

(g) the consumer's rights, including the right to replacement or reimbursement under Directive 1999/44/EC of the European Parliament and of the Council of 25 May 1999 on certain aspects of the sale of consumer goods and associated guarantees, or the risks he may face.

2. A commercial practice shall also be regarded as misleading if, in its factual context, taking account of all its features and circumstances, it causes or is likely to cause the average consumer to take a transactional decision that he would not have taken otherwise, and it involves:

(a) any marketing of a product, including comparative advertising, which creates confusion with any products, trade marks, trade names or other distinguishing marks of a competitor;

(b) non-compliance by the trader with commitments contained in codes of conduct by which the trader has undertaken to be bound, where:

(i) the commitment is not aspirational but is firm and is capable of being verified, and

(ii) the trader indicates in a commercial practice that he is bound by the code.

Article 7

Misleading omissions

1. A commercial practice shall be regarded as misleading if, in its factual context, taking account of all its features and circumstances and the limitations of the communication medium, it omits material information that the average consumer needs, according to the context, to take an informed transactional decision and thereby causes or is likely to cause the average consumer to take a transactional decision that he would not have taken otherwise.

2. It shall also be regarded as a misleading omission when, taking account of the matters described in paragraph 1, a trader hides or provides in an unclear, unintelligible, ambiguous or untimely manner such material information as referred to in that paragraph or fails to identify the

commercial intent of the commercial practice if not already apparent from the context, and where, in either case, this causes or is likely to cause the average consumer to take a transactional decision that he would not have taken otherwise.

3. Where the medium used to communicate the commercial practice imposes limitations of space or time, these limitations and any measures taken by the trader to make the information available to consumers by other means shall be taken into account in deciding whether information has been omitted.

4. In the case of an invitation to purchase, the following information shall be regarded as material, if not already apparent from the context:

(a) the main characteristics of the product, to an extent appropriate to the medium and the product;

(b) the geographical address and the identity of the trader, such as his trading name and, where applicable, the geographical address and the identity of the trader on whose behalf he is acting;

(c) the price inclusive of taxes, or where the nature of the product means that the price cannot reasonably be calculated in advance, the manner in which the price is calculated, as well as, where appropriate, all additional freight, delivery or postal charges or, where these charges cannot reasonably be calculated in advance, the fact that such additional charges may be payable;

(d) the arrangements for payment, delivery, performance and the complaint handling policy, if they depart from the requirements of professional diligence;

(e) for products and transactions involving a right of withdrawal or cancellation, the existence of such a right.

5. Information requirements established by Community law in relation to commercial communication including advertising or marketing, a non-exhaustive list of which is contained in Annex II, shall be regarded as material.

* * *

Article 13

Penalties

Member States shall lay down penalties for infringements of national provisions adopted in application of this Directive and shall take all necessary measures to ensure that these are enforced. These penalties must be effective, proportionate and dissuasive.

* * *

ANNEX I

COMMERCIAL PRACTICES WHICH ARE IN ALL CIRCUMSTANCES CONSIDERED UNFAIR

Misleading commercial practices

1. Claiming to be a signatory to a code of conduct when the trader is not.

2. Displaying a trust mark, quality mark or equivalent without having obtained the necessary authorisation.

3. Claiming that a code of conduct has an endorsement from a public or other body which it does not have.

4. Claiming that a trader (including his commercial practices) or a product has been approved, endorsed or authorised by a public or private body when he/it has not or making such a claim without complying with the terms of the approval, endorsement or authorisation.

5. Making an invitation to purchase products at a specified price without disclosing the existence of any reasonable grounds the trader may have for believing that he will not be able to offer for supply or to procure another trader to supply, those products or equivalent products at that price for a period that is, and in quantities that are, reasonable having regard to the product, the scale of advertising of the product and the price offered (bait advertising).

6. Making an invitation to purchase products at a specified price and then:

(a) refusing to show the advertised item to consumers; or

(b) refusing to take orders for it or deliver it within a reasonable time; or

(c) demonstrating a defective sample of it, with the intention of promoting a different product (bait and switch)

7. Falsely stating that a product will only be available for a very limited time, or that it will only be available on particular terms for a very limited time, in order to elicit an immediate decision and deprive consumers of sufficient opportunity or time to make an informed choice.

8. Undertaking to provide after-sales service to consumers with whom the trader has communicated prior to a transaction in a language which is not an official language of the Member State where the trader is located and then making such service available only in another language without clearly disclosing this to the consumer before the consumer is committed to the transaction.

9. Stating or otherwise creating the impression that a product can legally be sold when it cannot.

10. Presenting rights given to consumers in law as a distinctive feature of the trader's offer.

11. Using editorial content in the media to promote a product where a trader has paid for the promotion without making that clear in the content or by images or sounds clearly identifiable by the consumer (advertorial). This is without prejudice to Council Directive 89/552/EEC (1).

12. Making a materially inaccurate claim concerning the nature and extent of the risk to the personal security of the consumer or his family if the consumer does not purchase the product.

13. Promoting a product similar to a product made by a particular manufacturer in such a manner as deliberately to mislead the consumer into believing that the product is made by that same manufacturer when it is not.

14. Establishing, operating or promoting a pyramid promotional scheme where a consumer gives consideration for the opportunity to receive compensation that is derived primarily from the introduction of other consumers into the scheme rather than from the sale or consumption of products.

15. Claiming that the trader is about to cease trading or move premises when he is not.

16. Claiming that products are able to facilitate winning in games of chance.

17. Falsely claiming that a product is able to cure illnesses, dysfunction or malformations.

18. Passing on materially inaccurate information on market conditions or on the possibility of finding the product with the intention of inducing the consumer to acquire the product at conditions less favourable than normal market conditions.

19. Claiming in a commercial practice to offer a competition or prize promotion without awarding the prizes described or a reasonable equivalent.

20. Describing a product as 'gratis', 'free', 'without charge' or similar if the consumer has to pay anything other than the unavoidable cost of responding to the commercial practice and collecting or paying for delivery of the item.

21. Including in marketing material an invoice or similar document seeking payment which gives the consumer the impression that he has already ordered the marketed product when he has not.

22. Falsely claiming or creating the impression that the trader is not acting for purposes relating to his trade, business, craft or profession, or falsely representing oneself as a consumer.

23. Creating the false impression that after-sales service in relation to a product is available in a Member State other than the one in which the product is sold.

Aggressive commercial practices

24. Creating the impression that the consumer cannot leave the premises until a contract is formed.

25. Conducting personal visits to the consumer's home ignoring the consumer's request to leave or not to return except in circumstances and

to the extent justified, under national law, to enforce a contractual obligation.

26. Making persistent and unwanted solicitations by telephone, fax, e-mail or other remote media except in circumstances and to the extent justified under national law to enforce a contractual obligation. This is without prejudice to Article 10 of Directive 97/7/EC and Directives 95/46/EC and 2002/58/EC.

27. Requiring a consumer who wishes to claim on an insurance policy to produce documents which could not reasonably be considered relevant as to whether the claim was valid, or failing systematically to respond to pertinent correspondence, in order to dissuade a consumer from exercising his contractual rights.

28. Including in an advertisement a direct exhortation to children to buy advertised products or persuade their parents or other adults to buy advertised products for them. This provision is without prejudice to Article 16 of Directive 89/552/EEC on television broadcasting.

29. Demanding immediate or deferred payment for or the return or safekeeping of products supplied by the trader, but not solicited by the consumer except where the product is a substitute supplied in conformity with Article 7(3) of Directive 97/7/EC (inertia selling).

30. Explicitly informing a consumer that if he does not buy the product or service, the trader's job or livelihood will be in jeopardy.

31. Creating the false impression that the consumer has already won, will win, or will on doing a particular act win, a prize or other equivalent benefit, when in fact either:

— there is no prize or other equivalent benefit, or

— taking any action in relation to claiming the prize or other equivalent benefit is subject to the consumer paying money or incurring a cost.

DOCUMENT 33

FOREIGN INVESTMENT LAW OF THE UNITED MEXICAN STATES

Published in the Official Gazette (Diario Oficial) of the Federation on December 27, 1993 and in force as of December 28, 1993, as amended December 24, 1996

TITLE FIRST

GENERAL PROVISIONS

Chapter I
Purpose of Law

* * *

ARTICLE 2

For purposes of this Law, the following definitions shall apply:

I. The Commission: The National Foreign Investments Commission;

II. Foreign Investment:

a. Participation of foreign investors in any proportion in the capital of Mexican corporations;

b. That done by Mexican corporations with majority foreign investment; and

c. The participation by foreign investors in the activities and acts included in this Law.

III. Foreign investor: The individual or corporate person with nationality other than Mexican and foreign entities without legal status.

IV. Registry: The National Foreign Investments Registry.

V. The Secretariat: The Secretariat of Commerce and Industrial Development.

VI. Restricted Zone: The strip of Mexican territory one hundred kilometers in depth from the borders and fifty kilometers in depth from the coast lines to which Article 27, paragraph I of the Political Constitution of the United Mexican States refers; and

VII. Exclusion of Foreigners Clause: The express agreement, or pact that forms an integral part of corporate by-laws by which it is provided that the companies at hand shall not admit directly or indirectly, foreign investors nor corporations with an admission of foreigners clause.

* * *

ARTICLE 4

Foreign investment may participate in any proportion in the capital of Mexican companies, acquire fixed assets, enter new fields of economic activity or manufacture new product lines, open and operate establishments, and expand or relocate existing establishments, except as otherwise provided herein.

* * *

Chapter II
Reserved Activities

ARTICLE 5

The functions determined by the laws in the following strategic areas are reserved exclusively to the State:

I. Petroleum and other hydrocarbons;
II. Basic petrochemicals;
III. Electricity;
IV. Generation of nuclear energy;
V. Radioactive minerals;
VI. Satellite communication;
VII. Telegraph;
VIII. Radiotelegraph;
IX. Mail;
X. Railroads;
XI. Issue of currency; and
XII. Minting of coins.
XIII. Control, supervision and oversight of ports, airports, and heliports; and
XIV. Such others as are expressly stated in the applicable legal provisions.

ARTICLE 6

The following economic activities and corporations hereinafter mentioned, are reserved exclusively to Mexicans or to Mexican companies with an Exclusion of Foreigners Clause:

I. National surface transportation of passengers, tourism, and freight, excluding messenger and package delivery service;
II. Retail trade in gasoline and liquid petroleum gas;
III. Radio broadcasting service and other radio and television services different from cable television;

IV. Credit unions;

V. Development banking institutions, pursuant to the provisions of the law on the subject; and

VI. Supply of professional and technical services expressly set forth in the applicable legal provisions.

Foreign investment may not participate in the aforesaid activities and corporations in this article directly or through trusts, agreements, corporate or shareholder pacts, pyramid schemes, or any other mechanism which grants any control or equity participation whatsoever, except as provided by Title Fifth hereof.

Chapter III
Activities and Acquisitions Subject to Specific Regulation

ARTICLE 7

In the economic activities and corporations mentioned hereafter, foreign investment may participate in the following percentages:

I. Up to 10% in:

Cooperative companies for production;

II. Up to 25% in:

- **a.** Domestic air transportation
- **b.** Air taxi transportation; and
- **c.** Specialized air transportation;

III. Up to 49% in:

- **a.** Holding companies for financial groups;
- **b.** Commercial (multiple) banking credit institutions;
- **c.** Securities brokerage firms; and
- **d.** Securities market specialists;
- **e.** Insurance institutions;
- **f.** Bonding institutions:
- **g.** Currency exchange houses;
- **h.** General deposit warehouses;
- **i.** Financial leasing companies;
- **j.** Financial factoring companies;
- **k.** Financial companies with purpose limited to those provided for in Article 103, paragraph IV, of the Law of Credit Institutions;
- **l.** Companies to which Article 12 Bis of the Securities Market Law refers;
- **m.** Shares representing the fixed capital in investment companies and operating companies of investment corporations;
- **n.** Manufacture and commercialization of explosives, firearms, cartridges, munitions and fireworks, excluding acquisition and use of explosives for industrial and extraction activities

or the preparation of explosive mixtures for use in said activities;

o. Printing and publication of newspapers for circulation solely throughout Mexico;

p. Series T shares in companies that own agricultural, ranching, and forestry lands;

q. Cable television;

r. Basic telephone services;

s. Fresh water, coastal, and exclusive economic zone fishing, excluding aquaculture;

t. Comprehensive port management services;

u. Piloting port services for vessels to carry out operations of inland navigation operations in the terms of the subject law;

v. Shipping companies engaged in commercial exploitation of ships for inland and coastal navigation, excluding tourism cruisers and exploitation of marine dredging and implements for port construction, conservation and operation;

w. Services connected to the railway sector that consist of passenger service, maintenance and rehabilitation of roads, rights of way, repair shops for tractive and hauling equipment, organization and commercialization of unit trains, operation of domestic terminals for freight and railroad telecommunications; and

x. Supply of fuel and lubricants for ships, airplanes, and railway equipment;

The limitations for foreign investment participation set forth in this article may not be exceeded directly, nor through trusts, agreements, corporate or shareholder pacts, pyramid schemes or any other mechanism which grants control or equity participation greater than that established, except pursuant to Title Fifth of this Law.

ARTICLE 8

Favorable resolution by the Commission is required for foreign investment participation in a percentage greater than 49% in the economic activities and companies referred to hereafter:

I. Port services for ships to effect their inland navigation operations, such as towing, mooring and lighterage;

II. Shipping companies engaged in exploitation of ships solely for high seas traffic;

III. Management of air terminals;

IV. Private education services at the pre-school, primary, secondary, upper middle, upper, and combined levels;

V. Legal services;

VI. Credit information companies;

VII. Securities classification institutions;

VIII. Insurance agents;

IX. Cellular telephone.

X. Construction of pipeline for the transportation of petroleum and products derived therefrom; and

XI. Drilling of petroleum and gas wells; and

XII. Construction, operation and exploitation of railroads that constitute a general communication route, and rendering of the public service railroad transportation.

ARTICLE 9

Favorable resolution from the Commission is required for foreign investment to acquire assets or shares in Mexican companies, regardless of the activity they engage in only whose total asset value at the time of acquisition exceeds the amount established annually by said Commission, and provided said acquisition implies that the direct or indirect participation of foreign investment in the capital of the companies in question exceeds 49% thereof.

* * *

TITLE THIRD

COMPANIES

Creation and Modification of Companies

ARTICLE 15

A permit from the Secretariat of Foreign Relations is required for the creation of companies. The Exclusion of Foreigners Clause or the agreement provided for in Constitutional Article 27, paragraph (1) must be included in the by-laws of companies that are created.

ARTICLE 16

A permit from the Secretariat of Foreign Relations is required for companies created to change their corporate name. Companies that replace the Exclusion of Foreigners Clause with a clause for admission of foreigners shall notify the Secretariat of Foreign Relations within the following thirty business days of the replacement.

TITLE FOURTH

INVESTMENT BY FOREIGN CORPORATIONS

ARTICLE 17

Without prejudice to that established in international treaties and conventions to which Mexico is a party, the following shall obtain authorization from the Secretariat:

I. The foreign companies that intend to habitually perform commerce acts in the Republic; and

II. The persons referred to in Article 2736 of the Civil Code for the Federal District in Common Matters and for the whole Republic in Federal Matters, that intend to settle in the Republic and that are not regulated by laws other than such Code.

ARTICLE 17A

The authorization referred to in the previous paragraph will be given when the following requirements are complied with:

a. That such persons prove that they are duly established according to the laws of their country;

b. That the by-laws and other incorporation documents of such persons are not contrary to the provisions of public order set forth under Mexican Laws; and

c. The persons referred to in Section I of the previous Article are settled in the Republic or have any agency or subsidiary in it; or, the person referred to in Section II of the previous Article have a representative domiciled in its place of operation authorized to comply with any acquired obligation.

All applications to obtain authorization to which the preceding paragraph refers to which meets the above mentioned requirements must be given within the 15 business days following the date of its filing. If after such period no resolution has been issued, such application will be deemed approved.

The Secretariat shall submit to the Secretariat of Foreign Relations a copy of its requests and authorizations given according to this Article.

TITLE FIFTH

NEUTRAL INVESTMENT

Chapter I
Neutral Investment Concept

ARTICLE 18

Neutral Investment is that investment made in Mexican companies, or trusts authorized pursuant to this Title and shall not be computed to determine the percentage of foreign investment in the capital of Mexican companies.

* * *

TITLE SIXTH

NATIONAL FOREIGN INVESTMENT COMMISSION

* * *

Chapter III
Operation of the Commission

ARTICLE 28

The Commission must decide on applications submitted for its consideration within a period not to exceed 45 business days counted from the date the relevant application is filed pursuant to the Regulations to this Law.

If the Commission does not enter a resolution within the aforesaid period, the application shall be deemed approved as filed. Upon request of interested party, the Secretariat must issue the corresponding authorization.

ARTICLE 29

To evaluate the applications submitted to its consideration, the Commission shall observe the following criteria:

I. The impact on jobs and training for employees;

II. The technological contribution;

III. Compliance of environmental requirements contained in the environmental statutes applicable; and

IV. Generally, the contribution toward increasing competitiveness in the Mexican production plant.

The Commission, in deciding whether an application is appropriate, may only impose requirements that do not distort international trade.

ARTICLE 30

The Commission may prevent acquisitions by foreign investment for reasons of national security.

TITLE SEVENTH

NATIONAL FOREIGN INVESTMENTS REGISTRY

* * *

ARTICLE 32

The following must register with the Registry:

I. Mexican companies in which foreign investors participate, including those in which foreign investors participate through a trust, and neutral investment;

II. Foreign individuals or corporations who habitually undertake commercial activity in Mexico, and branches of foreign investors established in Mexico; and

III. Trusts on shares or corporate equity interests, on real estate, and on neutral investment by which rights are derived for the foreign investment.

The obligation to register falls upon the individuals and corporations to which Paragraphs I and II refer, and in the case of Paragraph III, the obligation shall correspond upon the fiduciary institution. The registration must be done within 40 business days counted from the date of the creation of the corporation or the equity participation by foreign investors;

of formalization or protocolling of the documents relating to the foreign company; or of the creation of the relevant trust or granting of beneficial rights to foreign investors.

* * *

TRANSITIONAL ARTICLES

* * *

SECOND

The following are abrogated:

I. The Law to Promote Mexican Investment and to Regulate Foreign Investment, published in the Official Gazette (Diario Oficial) of the Federation, on March 9, 1973;

* * *

FOURTH

Until the Regulations to this Law are issued, the Regulations to the Law to Promote Mexican Investment and to Regulate Foreign Investment, published in the Official Gazette (Diario Oficial) of the Federation, on May 16, 1989 shall continue in force on all terms where its terms are not contrary hereto.[a]

* * *

TENTH

For purposes of the provisions of Article 9, and until the Commission establishes the amount of total value of the assets to which said article refers to, the amount set is of eighty-five million new pesos.

---

a. New regulations were adopted in 1998 which replace the 1989 regulations. They are not yet available in an English translation.

Document 34

The United Nations Convention Against Corruption 2003

Chapter V

Asset recovery

Article 51. General provision

The return of assets pursuant to this chapter is a fundamental principle of this Convention, and States Parties shall afford one another the widest measure of cooperation and assistance in this regard.

* * *

Article 53. Measures for direct recovery of property

Each State Party shall, in accordance with its domestic law:

(a) Take such measures as may be necessary to permit another State Party to initiate civil action in its courts to establish title to or ownership of property acquired through the commission of an offence established in accordance with this Convention;

(b) Take such measures as may be necessary to permit its courts to order those who have committed offences established in accordance with this Convention to pay compensation or damages to another State Party that has been harmed by such offences; and

(c) Take such measures as may be necessary to permit its courts or competent authorities, when having to decide on confiscation, to recognize another State Party's claim as a legitimate owner of property acquired through the commission of an offence established in accordance with this Convention.

Article 54. Mechanisms for recovery of property through international cooperation in confiscation

1. Each State Party, in order to provide mutual legal assistance pursuant to article 55 of this Convention with respect to property acquired through or involved in the commission of an offence established in accordance with this Convention, shall, in accordance with its domestic law:

(a) Take such measures as may be necessary to permit its competent authorities to give effect to an order of confiscation issued by a court of another State Party;

(b) Take such measures as may be necessary to permit its competent authorities, where they have jurisdiction, to order the confiscation of such property of foreign origin by adjudication of an offence of money-laundering or such other offence as may be within its jurisdiction or by other procedures authorized under its domestic law; and

(c) Consider taking such measures as may be necessary to allow confiscation of such property without a criminal conviction in cases in which the offender cannot be prosecuted by reason of death, flight or absence or in other appropriate cases.

2. Each State Party, in order to provide mutual legal assistance upon a request made pursuant to paragraph 2 of article 55 of this Convention, shall, in accordance with its domestic law:

(a) Take such measures as may be necessary to permit its competent authorities to freeze or seize property upon a freezing or seizure order issued by a court or competent authority of a requesting State Party that provides a reasonable basis for the requested State Party to believe that there are sufficient grounds for taking such actions and that the property would eventually be subject to an order of confiscation for purposes of paragraph 1 (a) of this article;

(b) Take such measures as may be necessary to permit its competent authorities to freeze or seize property upon a request that provides a reasonable basis for the requested State Party to believe that there are sufficient grounds for taking such actions and that the property would eventually be subject to an order of confiscation for purposes of paragraph 1 (a) of this article; and

(c) Consider taking additional measures to permit its competent authorities to preserve property for confiscation, such as on the basis of a foreign arrest or criminal charge related to the acquisition of such property.

Article 55. International cooperation for purposes of confiscation

1. A State Party that has received a request from another State Party having jurisdiction over an offence established in accordance with this Convention for confiscation of proceeds of crime, property, equipment or other instrumentalities referred to in article 31, paragraph 1, of this Convention situated in its territory shall, to the greatest extent possible within its domestic legal system:

(a) Submit the request to its competent authorities for the purpose of obtaining an order of confiscation and, if such an order is granted, give effect to it; or

(b) Submit to its competent authorities, with a view to giving effect to it to the extent requested, an order of confiscation issued by a court in the territory of the requesting State Party in accordance with articles 31, paragraph 1, and 54, paragraph 1 (a), of this Convention insofar as it relates to proceeds of crime, property, equipment or other instrumentalities referred to in article 31, paragraph 1, situated in the territory of the requested State Party.

2. Following a request made by another State Party having jurisdiction over an offence established in accordance with this Convention, the requested State Party shall take measures to identify, trace and freeze or seize proceeds of crime, property, equipment or other instrumentalities referred to in article 31, paragraph 1, of this Convention for the purpose of eventual confiscation to be ordered either by the requesting State Party or, pursuant to a request under paragraph 1 of this article, by the requested State Party.

3. The provisions of article 46 of this Convention are applicable, mutatis mutandis, to this article. In addition to the information specified in article 46, paragraph 15, requests made pursuant to this article shall contain:

(a) In the case of a request pertaining to paragraph 1 (a) of this article, a description of the property to be confiscated, including, to the extent possible, the location and, where relevant, the estimated value of the property and a statement of the facts relied upon by the requesting State Party sufficient to enable the requested State Party to seek the order under its domestic law;

(b) In the case of a request pertaining to paragraph I (b) of this article, a legally admissible copy of an order of confiscation upon which the request is based issued by the requesting State Party, a statement of the facts and information as to the extent to which execution of the order is requested, a statement specifying the measures taken by the requesting State Party to provide adequate notification to bona fide third parties and to ensure due process and a statement that the confiscation order is final;

(c) In the case of a request pertaining to paragraph 2 of this article, a statement of the facts relied upon by the requesting State Party and a description of the actions requested and, where available, a legally admissible copy of an order on which the request is based.

4. The decisions or actions provided for in paragraphs 1 and 2 of this article shall be taken by the requested State Party in accordance with and subject to the provisions of its domestic law and its procedural rules or any bilateral or multilateral agreement or arrangement to which it may be bound in relation to the requesting State Party.

5. Each State Party shall furnish copies of its laws and regulations that give effect to this article and of any subsequent changes to such laws and regulations or a description thereof to the Secretary–General of the United Nations.

6. If a State Party elects to make the taking of the measures referred to in paragraphs 1 and 2 of this article conditional on the existence of a relevant treaty, that State Party shall consider this Convention the necessary and sufficient treaty basis.

7. Cooperation under this article may also be refused or provisional measures lifted if the requested State Party does not receive sufficient and timely evidence or if the property is of a *de minimis* value.

8. Before lifting any provisional measure taken pursuant to this article, the requested State Party shall, wherever possible, give the requesting State Party an opportunity to present its reasons in favour of continuing the measure.

9. The provisions of this article shall not be construed as prejudicing the rights of bona fide third parties.

* * *

Article 57. Return and disposal of assets

1. Property confiscated by a State Party pursuant to article 31 or 55 of this Convention shall be disposed of, including by return to its prior legitimate owners, pursuant to paragraph 3 of this article, by that State Party in accordance with the provisions of this Convention and its domestic law.

2. Each State Party shall adopt such legislative and other measures, in accordance with the fundamental principles of its domestic law, as may be necessary to enable its competent authorities to return confiscated property, when acting on the request made by another State Party, in accordance with this Convention, taking into account the rights of bona fide third parties.

3. In accordance with articles 46 and 55 of this Convention and paragraphs 1 and 2 of this article, the requested State Party shall:

(a) In the case of embezzlement of public funds or of laundering of embezzled public funds as referred to in articles 17 and 23 of this Convention, when confiscation was executed in accordance with article 55 and on the basis of a final judgement in the requesting State Party, a requirement that can be waived by the requested State Party, return the confiscated property to the requesting State Party;

(b) In the case of proceeds of any other offence covered by this Convention, when the confiscation was executed in accordance with article 55 of this Convention and on the basis of a final judgement in the requesting State Party, a requirement that can be waived by the requested State Party, return the confiscated property to the requesting State Party, when the requesting State Party reasonably establishes its prior ownership of such confiscated property to the requested State Party or when the requested State Party recognizes damage to the requesting State Party as a basis for returning the confiscated property;

(c) In all other cases, give priority consideration to returning confiscated property to the requesting State Party, returning such property to its prior legitimate owners or compensating the victims of the crime.

4. Where appropriate, unless States Parties decide otherwise, the requested State Party may deduct reasonable expenses incurred in investigations, prosecutions or judicial proceedings leading to the return or disposition of confiscated property pursuant to this article.

5. Where appropriate, States Parties may also give special consideration to concluding agreements or mutually acceptable arrangements, on a case-by-case basis, for the final disposal of confiscated property.

* * *

DOCUMENT 35

CONVENTION ON COMBATING BRIBERY OF FOREIGN PUBLIC OFFICIALS IN INTERNATIONAL BUSINESS TRANSACTIONS (OECD 1997)

(Adopted by the U.S. and used as a basis to amend the Foreign Corrupt Practices Act)

Preamble

The Parties,

Considering that bribery is a widespread phenomenon in international business transactions, including trade and investment, which raises serious moral and political concerns, undermines good governance and economic development, and distorts international competitive conditions;

Considering that all countries share a responsibility to combat bribery in international business transactions;

Having regard to the Revised Recommendation on Combating Bribery in International Business Transactions, adopted by the Council of the Organisation for Economic Co-operation and Development (OECD) on 23 May 1997, C(97)123/FINAL, which, *inter alia,* called for effective measures to deter, prevent and combat the bribery of foreign public officials in connection with international business transactions, in particular, the prompt criminalisation of such bribery in an effective and coordinated manner and in conformity with the agreed common elements set out in that Recommendation and with the jurisdictional and other basic legal principles of each country;

Welcoming other recent developments which further advance international understanding and co-operation in combating bribery of public officials, including actions of the United Nations, the World Bank, the International Monetary Fund, the World Trade Organisation, the Organisation of American States, the Council of Europe and the European Union;

Welcoming the efforts of companies, business organisations, trade unions as well as other non-governmental organisations to combat bribery;

Recognising the role of governments in the prevention of solicitation of bribes from individuals and enterprises in international business transactions;

Recognising that achieving progress in this field requires not only efforts on a national level but also multilateral co-operation, monitoring and follow-up;

Recognising that achieving equivalence among the measures to be taken by the Parties is an essential object and purpose of the Convention, which requires that the Convention be ratified without derogations affecting this equivalence;

Have agreed as follows:

Article 1

The Offence of Bribery of Foreign Public Officials

1. Each Party shall take such measures as may be necessary to establish that it is a criminal offence under its law for any person intentionally to offer, promise or give any undue pecuniary or other advantage, whether directly or through intermediaries, to a foreign public official, for that official or for a third party, in order that the official act or refrain from acting in relation to the performance of official duties, in order to obtain or retain business or other improper advantage in the conduct of international business.

2. Each Party shall take any measures necessary to establish that complicity in, including incitement, aiding and abetting, or authorisation of an act of bribery of a foreign public official shall be a criminal offence. Attempt and conspiracy to bribe a foreign public official shall be criminal offences to the same extent as attempt and conspiracy to bribe a public official of that Party.

3. The offences set out in paragraphs 1 and 2 above are hereinafter referred to as "bribery of a foreign public official".

4. For the purpose of this Convention:

   "foreign public official" means any person holding a legislative, administrative or judicial office of a foreign country, whether appointed or elected; any person exercising a public function for a foreign country, including for a public agency or public enterprise; and any official or agent of a public international organisation;

   "foreign country" includes all levels and subdivisions of government, from national to local;

   "act or refrain from acting in relation to the performance of official duties" includes any use of the public official's position, whether or not within the official's authorised competence.

Article 2

Responsibility of Legal Persons

Each party shall take such measures as may be necessary, in accordance with its legal principles, to establish the liability of legal persons for the bribery of a foreign public official.

Article 3

Sanctions

1. The bribery of a foreign public official shall be punishable by effective, proportionate and dissuasive criminal penalties. The range of penalties shall be comparable to those applicable to the bribery of the Party's own public officials and shall, in the case of natural persons, include deprivation of liberty sufficient to enable effective mutual legal assistance and extradition.

2. In the event that, under the legal system of a Party, criminal responsibility is not applicable to legal persons, that Party shall ensure that legal persons shall be subject to effective, proportionate and dissuasive non-criminal sanctions, including monetary sanctions, for bribery of foreign public officials.

3. Each Party shall take such measures as may be necessary to provide that the bribe and the proceeds of the bribery of a foreign public official, or property the value of which corresponds to that of such proceeds, are subject to seizure and confiscation or that monetary sanctions of comparable effect are applicable.

4. Each Party shall consider the imposition of additional civil or administrative sanctions upon a person subject to sanctions for the bribery of a foreign public official.

Article 4

Jurisdiction

1. Each Party shall take such measures as may be necessary to establish its jurisdiction over the bribery of a foreign public official when the offence is committed in whole or in part in its territory.

2. Each Party which has jurisdiction to prosecute its nationals for offences committed abroad shall take such measures as may be necessary to establish its jurisdiction to do so in respect of the bribery of a foreign public official, according to the same principles.

3. When more than one Party has jurisdiction over an alleged offence described in this Convention, the Parties involved shall, at the request of one of them, consult with a view to determining the most appropriate jurisdiction for prosecution.

4. Each Party shall review whether its current basis for jurisdiction is effective in the fight against the bribery of foreign public officials and, if it is not, shall take remedial steps.

Article 5

Enforcement

Investigation and prosecution of the bribery of a foreign public official shall be subject to the applicable rules and principles of each Party. They shall not be influenced by considerations of national economic interest, the potential effect upon relations with another State or the identity of the natural persons or legal entities involved.

Article 6

Statute of Limitations

Any statute of limitations applicable to the offence of bribery of a foreign public official shall allow an adequate period of time for the investigation and prosecution of this offence.

Article 7

Money Laundering

Each Party which has made bribery of its own public official a predicate offence for the purpose of the application of its money laundering legislation shall do so on the same terms for the bribery of a foreign public official, without regard to the place where the bribery occurred.

Article 8

Accounting

1. In order to combat bribery of foreign public officials effectively, each Party shall take such measures as may be necessary, within the framework of its laws and regulations regarding the maintenance of books and records, financial statement disclosures, and accounting and auditing standards, to prohibit the establishment of off-the-books accounts, the making of off-the-books or inadequately identified transactions, the recording of non-existent expenditures, the entry of liabilities with incorrect identification of their object, as well as the use of false documents, by companies subject to those laws and regulations, for the purpose of bribing foreign public officials or of hiding such bribery.

2. Each Party shall provide effective, proportionate and dissuasive civil, administrative or criminal penalties for such omissions and falsifications in respect of the books, records, accounts and financial statements of such companies.

Article 9

Mutual Legal Assistance

1. Each Party shall, to the fullest extent possible under its laws and relevant treaties and arrangements, provide prompt and effective legal assistance to another Party for the purpose of criminal investigations and proceedings brought by a Party concerning offences within the scope of this Convention and for non-criminal proceedings within the scope of this Convention brought by a Party against a legal person. The requested Party shall inform the requesting Party, without delay, of any additional information or documents needed to support the request for assistance and, where requested, of the status and outcome of the request for assistance.

2. Where a Party makes mutual legal assistance conditional upon the existence of dual criminality, dual criminality shall be deemed to exist if the offence for which the assistance is sought is within the scope of this Convention.

3. A Party shall not decline to render mutual legal assistance for criminal matters within the scope of this Convention on the ground of bank secrecy.

Article 10

Extradition

1. Bribery of a foreign public official shall be deemed to be included as an extraditable offence under the laws of the Parties and the extradition treaties between them.

2. If a Party which makes extradition conditional on the existence of an extradition treaty receives a request for extradition from another Party with which it has no extradition treaty, it may consider this Convention to be the legal basis for extradition in respect of the offence of bribery of a foreign public official.

3. Each Party shall take any measures necessary to assure either that it can extradite its nationals or that it can prosecute its nationals for the offence of bribery of a foreign public official. A Party which declines a request to extradite a person for bribery of a foreign public official solely on the ground that the person is its national shall submit the case to its competent authorities for the purpose of prosecution.

4. Extradition for bribery of a foreign public official is subject to the conditions set out in the domestic law and applicable treaties and arrangements of each Party. Where a Party makes extradition conditional upon the existence of dual criminality, that condition shall be deemed to be fulfilled if the offence for which extradition is sought is within the scope of Article 1 of this Convention.

Article 11

Responsible Authorities

For the purposes of Article 4, paragraph 3, consultation, Article 9, mutual legal assistance and Article 10, extradition, each Party shall notify to the Secretary-General of the OECD an authority or authorities responsible for making and receiving requests, which shall serve as channel of communication for these matters for that Party, without prejudice to other arrangements between Parties.

Article 12

Monitoring and Follow-up

The Parties shall co-operate in carrying out a programme of systematic follow-up to monitor and promote the full implementation of this Convention. Unless otherwise decided by a consensus of the Parties, this shall be done in the framework of the OECD Working Group on Bribery in International Business Transactions and according to its terms of reference, or within the framework and terms of reference of any successor to its functions, and Parties shall bear the costs of the programme in accordance with the rules applicable to that body.

Article 13

Signature and Accession

1. Until its entry into force, this Convention shall be open for signature by OECD members and by non-members which have become or have been invited to become full participants in its Working Group on Bribery in International Business Transactions.

2. Subsequent to its entry into force, this Convention shall be open to accession by any non-signatory which is a member of or has become a full participant in the Working Group on Bribery in International Business Transactions or any successor to its functions.

Article 14

Ratification and Depositary

1. This Convention is subject to acceptance, approval or ratification by the Signatories, in accordance with their respective laws.

2. Instruments of acceptance, approval, ratification or accession shall be deposited with the Secretary–General of the OECD, who shall serve as Depositary of this Convention.

Article 15

Entry into Force

1. This convention shall enter into force on the sixtieth day following the date upon which five of the countries which have the ten largest export shares set out in document DAFFE/IME/BR(97)18, and which represent by themselves at least sixty percent of the combined total exports of those ten countries, have deposited their instruments of acceptance, approval, or ratification. For each state depositing its instrument after such entry into force, the Convention shall enter into force on the sixtieth day after deposit of its instrument.

2. If, by 31 December 1998, the Convention has not entered into force under paragraph 1 above, any state which has deposited its instrument of ratification may declare to the depositary its readiness to accept entry into force of this convention under this paragraph 2. The Convention shall enter into force for such a state on the sixtieth day following the date upon which such declarations have been deposited by at least two states. For each state depositing its declaration after such entry into force, the

Convention shall enter into force on the sixtieth day following the date of deposit.

Article 16

Amendment

Any Party may propose the amendment of this Convention. A proposed amendment shall be submitted to the Depositary which shall communicate it to the other Parties at least sixty days before convening a meeting of the Parties to consider the proposed amendment. An amendment adopted by consensus of the parties, or by such other means as the Parties may determine by consensus, shall enter into force sixty days after the deposit of an instrument of ratification, acceptance or approval by all of the Parties, or in such other circumstances as may be specified by the Parties at the time of adoption of the amendment.

Article 17

Withdrawal

A Party may withdraw from this Convention by submitting written notification to the Depositary. Such withdrawal shall be effective one year after the date of the receipt of the notification. After withdrawal, co-operation shall continue between the Parties and the State which has withdrawn on all requests for assistance and extradition made before the effective date of withdrawal which remain pending.

Document 36

Foreign Corrupt Practices Act of 1977 (Selected Provisions)

Public Law 95–213, 91 Stat. 1494, Dec. 19, 1977 (amending The Securities Exchange Act of 1934, 15 U.S.C.A. §§ 78q(b), 78dd, 78ff(a) (1976)); as amended by Public Law 100–418, 102 Stat. 1107, Aug. 23, 1988; as amended by Public Law 105-366, Nov. 10, 1998 (International Anti–Bribery & Fair Competition Act)

15 U.S.C. § 78m(b)

Accounting Standards

* * *

(2) Every issuer which has a class of securities registered pursuant to section 78*l* of this title and every issuer which is required to file reports pursuant to section 78*o*(d) of this title shall—

(A) make and keep books, records, and accounts, which, in reasonable detail, accurately and fairly reflect the transactions and dispositions of the assets of the issuer; and

(B) devise and maintain a system of internal accounting controls sufficient to provide reasonable assurances that—

(i) transactions are executed in accordance with management's general or specific authorization;

(ii) transactions are recorded as necessary (I) to permit preparation of financial statements in conformity with generally accepted accounting principles or any other criteria applicable to such statements, and (II) to maintain accountability for assets;

(iii) access to assets is permitted only in accordance with management's general or specific authorization; and

(iv) the recorded accountability for assets is compared with the existing assets at reasonable intervals and appropriate action is taken with respect to any differences.

* * *

15 U.S.C. § 78dd–1

Prohibited foreign trade practices by issuers

(a) Prohibition. It shall be unlawful for any issuer which has a class of securities registered pursuant to section 78*l* of this title or which is required to file reports under section 78*o*(d) of this title, or for any officer, director, employee, or agent of such issuer or any stockholder thereof acting on behalf of such issuer, to make use of the mails or any means or instrumentality of interstate commerce corruptly in furtherance of an offer, payment, promise to pay, or authorization of the payment of any money, or offer, gift, promise to give, or authorization of the giving of anything of value to—

(1) any foreign official for purposes of—

(A)(i) influencing any act or decision of such foreign official in his official capacity, (ii) inducing such foreign official to do or omit to do any act in violation of the lawful duty of such official, or (iii) securing any improper advantage; or

(B) inducing such foreign official to use his influence with a foreign government or instrumentality thereof to affect or influence any act or decision of such government or instrumentality,

in order to assist such issuer in obtaining or retaining business for or with, or directing business to, any person;

* * *

(3) any person, while knowing that all or a portion of such money or thing of value will be offered, given, or promised, directly or indirectly, to any foreign official, to any foreign political party or official thereof, or to any candidate for foreign political office, for purposes of—

(A)(i) influencing any act or decision of such foreign official, * * * in his or its official capacity, (ii) inducing such foreign official, * * * to do or omit to do any act in violation of the lawful duty of such foreign official, * * *, or (iii) securing any improper advantage; or

(B) inducing such foreign official * * * to use his or its influence with a foreign government or instrumentality thereof to affect or influence any act or decision of such government or instrumentality,

in order to assist such issuer in obtaining or retaining business for or with, or directing business to, any person.

(b) Exception for routine governmental action. Subsections (a) and (g) shall not apply to any facilitating or expediting payment to a foreign official, political party, or party official the purpose of which is to expedite or to secure the performance of a routine governmental action by a foreign official, political party, or party official.

(c) Affirmative defenses. It shall be an affirmative defense to actions under subsection (a) or (g) that—

(1) the payment, gift, offer, or promise of anything of value that was made, was lawful under the written laws and regulations of the foreign official's * * * country; or

(2) the payment, gift, offer, or promise of anything of value that was made, was a reasonable and bona fide expenditure, such as travel and lodging expenses, incurred by or on behalf of a foreign official * * * and was directly related to—

(A) the promotion, demonstration, or explanation of products or services; or

(B) the execution or performance of a contract with a foreign government or agency thereof.

(d) Guidelines by the Attorney General. Not later than one year after August 23, 1988, the Attorney General, after consultation with the Commission, the Secretary of Commerce, the United States Trade Representative, the Secretary of State, and the Secretary of the Treasury, and after obtaining the views of all interested persons through public notice and comment procedures, shall determine to what extent compliance with this section would be enhanced and the business community would be assisted by further clarification of the preceding provisions of this section and may, based on such determination and to the extent necessary and appropriate, issue—

(1) guidelines describing specific types of conduct, associated with common types of export sales arrangements and business contracts, which for purposes of the Department of Justice's present enforcement policy, the Attorney General determines would be in conformance with the preceding provisions of this section; and

(2) general precautionary procedures which issuers may use on a voluntary basis to conform their conduct to the Department of Justice's present enforcement policy regarding the preceding provisions of this section.

* * *

(e) Opinions of the Attorney General. (1) The Attorney General, after consultation with appropriate departments and agencies of the United States and after obtaining the views of all interested persons through public notice and comment procedures, shall establish a procedure to provide responses to specific inquiries by issuers concerning conformance of their conduct with the Department of Justice's present enforcement policy regarding the preceding provisions of this section. * * *

(f) Definitions. For purposes of this section:

(1)(A) The term "foreign official" means any officer or employee of a foreign government or any department, agency, or instrumentality thereof, or of a public international organization, or any person acting in an official capacity for or on behalf of any such government or department, agency, or instrumentality, or for or on behalf of any such public international organization.

(B) For purposes of subparagraph (A), the term "public international organization" means—

(i) an organization that is designated by Executive Order pursuant to section 1 of the International Organizations Immunities Act (22 U.S.C. § 288); or

(ii) any other international organization that is designated by the President by Executive order for the purposes of this section, effective as of the date of publication of such order in the Federal Register.

(2)(A) A person's state of mind is "knowing" with respect to conduct, a circumstance, or a result if—

(i) such person is aware that such person is engaging in such conduct, that such circumstance exists, or that such result is substantially certain to occur; or

(ii) such person has a firm belief that such circumstance exists or that such result is substantially certain to occur.

(B) When knowledge of the existence of a particular circumstance is required for an offense, such knowledge is established if a person is aware of a high probability of the existence of such circumstance, unless the person actually believes that such circumstance does not exist.

(3)(A) The term "routine governmental action" means only an action which is ordinarily and commonly performed by a foreign official in—

(i) obtaining permits, licenses, or other official documents to qualify a person to do business in a foreign country;

(ii) processing governmental papers, such as visas and work orders;

(iii) providing police protection, mail pick-up and delivery, or scheduling inspections associated with contract performance or inspections related to transit of goods across country;

(iv) providing phone service, power and water supply, loading and unloading cargo, or protecting perishable products or commodities from deterioration; or

(v) actions of a similar nature.

(B) The term "routine governmental action" does not include any decision by a foreign official whether, or on what terms, to award new business to or to continue business with a particular party, or any action taken by a foreign official involved in the decisionmaking process to encourage a decision to award new business to or continue business with a particular party.

(g) Alternative Jurisdiction

(1) It shall also be unlawful for any issuer organized under the laws of the United States, or a State, territory, possession, or commonwealth of

the United States or a political subdivision thereof and which has a class of securities registered pursuant to section 12 of this title or which is required to file reports under section 15(d) of this title, or for any United States person that is an officer, director, employee, or agent of such issuer or a stockholder thereof acting on behalf of such issuer, to corruptly do any act outside the United States in furtherance of an offer, payment, promise to pay, or authorization of the payment of any money, or offer, gift, promise to give, or authorization of the giving of anything of value to any of the persons or entities set forth in paragraphs (1), (2), and (3) of this subsection (a) of this section for the purposes set forth therein, irrespective of whether such issuer or such officer, director, employee, agent, or stockholder makes use of the mails or any means or instrumentality of interstate commerce in furtherance of such offer, gift, payment, promise, or authorization.

(2) As used in this subsection, the term "United States person" means a national of the United States (as defined in section 101 of the Immigration and Nationality Act (8 U.S.C. § 1101)) or any corporation, partnership, association, joint-stock company, business trust, unincorporated organization, or sole proprietorship organized under the laws of the United States or any State, territory, possession, or commonwealth of the United States, or any political subdivision thereof.

15 U.S.C. § 78dd–2

Prohibited foreign trade practices by domestic concerns

(a) Prohibition. It shall be unlawful for any domestic concern, other than an issuer which is subject to section 78dd–1 of this title. [At this point, the language for the most part follows that of section 77dd–1, except injunctive relief is specifically allowed. Domestic concerns include individuals who are citizens, nationals or residents of the United States, or essentially any form of business with a principal place of business in the United States, or organized in one of the United States, or a territory, possession or commonwealth of the United States.]

* * *

(g) Penalties

(1)(A) Any domestic concern that is not a natural person and that violates subsection (a) or (i) [alternative jurisdiction] of this section shall be fined not more than $2,000,000.

(B) Any domestic concern that is not a natural person and that violates subsection (a) or (i) of this section shall be subject to a civil penalty of not more than $10,000 imposed in an action brought by the Attorney General.

(2)(A) Any natural person that is an officer, director, employee, or agent of a domestic concern, or stockholder acting on behalf of such domestic concern, who willfully violates subsection (a) or (i) of this section shall be fined not more than $100,000 or imprisoned not more than 5 years, or both.

(B) Any natural person that is an officer, director, employee, or agent of a domestic concern, or stockholder acting on behalf of such domestic concern, who violates subsection (a) or (i) of this section shall be subject to a civil penalty of not more than $10,000 imposed in an action brought by the Attorney General.

(3) Whenever a fine is imposed under paragraph (2) upon any officer, director, employee, agent, or stockholder of a domestic concern, such fine may not be paid, directly or indirectly, by such domestic concern.

* * *

15 U.S.C. § 78dd-3

Prohibited foreign trade practices by persons other than issuers or domestic concerns

(a) Prohibition. It shall be unlawful for any person other than an issuer that is subject to section 30A of the Securities Exchange Act of 1934 or a domestic concern, (as defined in section 104 of this Act), or for any officer, director, employee, or agent of such person or any stockholder thereof acting on behalf of such person, while in the territory of the United States, corruptly to make use of the mails or any means or instrumentality of interstate commerce or to do any other act in furtherance of an offer, payment, promise to pay, or authorization of the payment of any money, or offer, gift, promise to give, or authorization of the giving of anything of value to—[At this point, the language follows that of active 78dd-1, except injunctive relief similar to that in section 78dd-2.]

* * *

(e) Penalties

(1)(A) Any juridical person that violates subsection (a) of this section shall be fined not more than $2,000,000.

(B) Any juridical person that violates subsection (a) of this section shall be subject to a civil penalty of not more than $10,000 imposed in an action brought by the Attorney General.

(2)(A) Any natural person who willfully violates subsection (a) of this section shall be fined not more than $100,000 or imprisoned not more than 5 years, or both.

(B) Any natural person who violates subsection (a) of this section shall be subject to a civil penalty of not more than $10,000 imposed in an action brought by the Attorney General.

(3) Whenever a fine is imposed under paragraph (2) upon any officer, director, employee, agent, or stockholder of a person, such fine may not be paid, directly or indirectly, by such person.

(f) Definitions. For purposes of this section:

(1) The term "person," when referring to an offender, means any natural person other than a. national of the United States (as defined in 8 U.S.C. § 1101) or any corporation, partnership, association, joint-stock company, business trust, unincorporated organization, or sole proprietorship organized under the law of a foreign nation or a political subdivision thereof.

* * *

15 U.S.C. § 78ff

Penalties

(a) Willful violations; false and misleading statements. Any person who willfully violates any provision of this chapter (other than section 78dd–1 of this title), or any rule or regulation thereunder the violation of which is made unlawful or the observance of which is required under the terms of this chapter, or any person who willfully and knowingly makes, or causes to be made, any statement in any application, report, or document required to be filed under this chapter or any rule or regulation thereunder or any undertaking contained in a registration statement as provided in subsection (d) of section 78*o* of this title, or by any self-regulatory organization in connection with an application for membership or participation therein or to become associated with a member thereof, which statement was false or misleading with respect to any material fact, shall upon conviction be fined not more than $1,000,000, or imprisoned not more than 10 years, or both, except that when such person is a person other than a natural person, a fine not exceeding $2,500,000 may be imposed; but no person shall be subject to imprisonment under this section for the violation of any rule or regulation if he proves that he had no knowledge of such rule or regulation.

* * *

(c) Violations by issuers, officers, directors, stockholders, employees, or agents of issuers

(1)(A) Any issuer that violates subsection (a) or (g) of Section 30A of this title shall be fined not more than $2,000,000.

(B) Any issuer that violates subsection (a) or (g) of Section 30A of this title shall be subject to a civil penalty of not more than $10,000 imposed in an action brought by the Commission.

(2)(A) Any officer, director, employee, or agent of an issuer, or stockholder acting on behalf of such issuer, who willfully violates subsection (a) or (g) of Section 30A of this title shall be fined not more than $10,000, or imprisoned not more than 5 years, or both.

(B) Any officer, director, employee, or agent of an issuer, or stockholder action on behalf of such issuer, who violates subsection (a) or (g) of Section 30A of this title shall be subject to a civil penalty of not more than $10,000 imposed in an action brought by the Commission.

(3) Whenever a fine is imposed under paragraph (2) upon any officer, director, employee, agent or stockholder of an issuer, such fine may not be paid, directly or indirectly, by such issuer.

†

